PREFACE to the second edition

In this edition, new material on the rise of the corporation and on Indian, women's, and black history has been included in Chapter 1. We have expanded the section on suburbia in the 1950s in Chapter 12, and have rewritten and enlarged the analysis of the 1970s in Chapter 16. New chapter insert essays have been included on the "Beat" poets of the 1950s and the Evangelicals of the 1970s, and other insert essays have been updated. A number of pages in the remainder of the book have been rewritten to take account of suggestions made by instructors who have used the book. All chapter bibliographies have been updated, of course, and many new illustrations as well as several new maps and tables are included. We appreciate the encouragement this edition has received from the John Wiley staff, especially editor Wayne Anderson, Stella Kupferberg, Marge Graham, Ron Nelson, Angie Lee, Janet Sessa, Malcolm Easterlin, Rosemary Wellner, Connie Rende, and Wiley's field representatives.

We are most grateful to the teachers and students who have found this text useful in understanding twentieth century America. A number of them took the time to review the first edition and offer helpful criticism that has been the basis for revising this edition. We are especially indebted to George Skau of Bergen State Community College and former Cornell graduate students Jim Hijiya, Ken Jones, and Joanne Volpe Florino.

March 1979   *Walter LaFeber   Richard Polenberg*

THE AMERICAN CENTURY

A History of the United States Since the 1890s

THE AMERICAN CENTURY

A History of the United States Since the 1890s

Walter La Feber
CORNELL UNIVERSITY

Richard Polenberg
CORNELL UNIVERSITY

second edition

John Wiley & Sons, Inc.
NEW YORK   CHICHESTER
BRISBANE   TORONTO

text design by
EDWARD A. BUTLER

cover photo by
FRANCISCO HIDALGO
cover designed by
ANGIE LEE

photo research by
MARJORIE GRAHAM

Library of Congress Cataloging in Publication Data:
LaFeber, Walter.

   The American century.
   Includes index.
   1. United States—History—20th century. 2. United
States—Foreign relations—20th century. I. Polenberg,
Richard, joint author. II. Title.
E741.L25 1979   973.9   79-12000
ISBN 0-471-05135-7

Printed in the United States of America

10 9 8 7 6 5 4 3 2 1

PREFACE to the first edition

For some years we have taught both the American introductory survey class as well as more specialized upperclass courses in twentieth-century America. After some experimenting, we concluded that these courses required a basic text that could be supplemented with readings and documents, preferably a moderately priced book that would present the post-1890 years in a style that would be concise and, at the appropriate places, not overly serious.

In considering what this book should contain, we began with one of the themes stressed in our own courses: the impact of war and foreign relations on twentieth-century America and, more particularly, their impact on economic and urban growth, civil liberties and civil rights, and social and political change. We have devoted approximately half the book to the post-1941 years, a period that is too often slighted and yet one in which college students have an intense interest. Since as much attention is paid to foreign as to domestic policies, developments in other parts of the world have been analyzed. We believe that in order to understand recent American history, for example, one must know something about Stalinist Russia in the 1940s, Latin America in the 1950s, and Vietnam in the 1960s, so sections on these topics have been included.

Paintings, architecture, the performing arts, and popular culture are crucial to an understanding of American development; consequently, we have inserted special sections describing particular artists and how their work reflects their era. Other special sections emphasize football, baseball, and boxing, not only because we follow these sports at least as closely as we follow the activities of the American Historical Association, but also because we discovered as teachers that Babe Ruth or Jack Johnson could provide crucial, as well as highly readable, insights into their America. And so can songs, the forgotten as well as the known, for they set the mood for their time.

Thus we have attempted to write a book that will serve as a basic reference yet at the same time be interpretive and interesting. The research for this book was supported, in part, by the Colonel Return Jonathan Meigs First (1740–1823) Fund, which was created with money left by Dorothy Mix Meigs and Fielding Pope Meigs, Jr. of Rosemont, Pennsylvania. We are greatly indebted to the fine staff at John Wiley and Sons, especially Wayne Anderson, Marge Graham, Arthur Vergara, Ron Nelson, and Carl Beers. We also thank scholars who read various drafts and were unsparing in their comments: Charles M. Dollar of Oklahoma State University, Richard S. Kirkendall of Indiana University, Fred R. Mabbutt of Santa Ana College, Otis L. Graham, Jr., of the University of California–Santa Barbara, Allen Yarnell of University of California at Los

Angeles, and David Trask of the State University of New York at Stony Brook. We learned that their knowledge of American history is matched only by their candor.

CORNELL UNIVERSITY   *Walter LaFeber   Richard Polenberg*

CONTENTS

Henry Ford in his first car, 1896.

CHAPTER ONE

1890s
The Beginnings
of Modern America

YOUR GOD COMES FIRST, YOUR COUNTRY NEXT, THEN MOTHER DEAR

Words and music by **Paul Dresser**

A lad was going to the war, 'twas on a summer's day,
The sun was slowly sinking in the west
As if to hide a mother's tears, unbidden tho' they fell,
As her head lay upon his youthful breast.
"Keep up your courage, lad, so much comfort I have had,
You never caused your mother's heart to ache.
From the hearthstone and the plough, war and duty call you now;
I bid you go, fight for your Country's sake."

The smoke of battle cleared away, and 'neath the moon's pale light
A gallant hero of the U.S.A.
Lay dying with a dear old mother's picture in his hand,
Just one more look ere life should pass away.

His heart had proven true to the old Red, White and Blue;
'Twas mother's wish and yet her heart will ache
When she hears her darling boy, on the battlefield alone,
Gave up his young life for his Country's sake.

Chorus:
"You're going to the war, my boy, and while you are away,
Remember that a mother's pray'rs are with you night and day.
In battle, lad, remember there is no such word as fear;
Your God comes first, your country next, then mother dear."

Copyright 1898 by Howley, Haviland & Co.

1

Modern America emerged during a forty-year crisis that began with the Civil War (1861–65) and ended with the war against Spain in 1898. The crisis, which recast every part of the nation's life, climaxed in the 1890s. At the Chicago Columbian Exposition of 1893, Americans celebrated their triumphs in industry and technology while, ironically, enduring the nation's worst economic depression. A young historian, Frederick Jackson Turner of the University of Wisconsin, delivered a speech at this world's fair that helped explain the irony. American social and political institutions, Turner asserted, had been shaped by the vast open lands of the West. According to the 1890 census, however, these lands had finally been settled. Turner concluded: "And now, four centuries from the discovery of America, at the end of a hundred years of life under the Constitution, the frontier has gone, and with its going has closed the first period of American history." Scholars later agreed that Turner overemphasized the importance of the frontier in the shaping of American character, but few, then or since, would deny that a different America was indeed born in the last years of the century. The birth pains were terrifying as well as promising.

THE SCULPTOR OF MODERN AMERICA: THE CORPORATION

Between 1860 and 1900 no birth was more notable than that of the modern industrial corporation. Barely conceived of before the Civil War, it quickly came to dominate Americans' lives by determining what they possessed, where they worked, and, in general, by producing everything they needed from their baby food to their tombstones.

Before the Civil War, state and national governments had created corporations largely to operate public highways and banks. But shrewd business executives soon realized that merely by obtaining a charter of incorporation from a state government, they suddenly had the right to acquire great sums of capital through sales of stock. At the same time, the liability of each investor was limited to the amount he or she invested. It was like magic. The new creature first appeared to build railroads during the 1850s boom. It was the Civil War, however, that shaped the industrial corporation.

The mammoth armies of the North and South created an immense market that demanded rapid production of goods. Through privately owned corporations, such men as Gustavus F. Swift (meat), Gail Borden (dairy and groceries), and Andrew Carnegie (railways and later steel) got their start by supplying the sinews of war. Equally important, when Southerners deserted Washington in 1861, unopposed Northern politicians were able to whip legislation through Congress to aid their section's factories. Between 1862 and 1865 members of Congress consequently built a tariff wall insulating American producers against foreign competition, passed bank laws to standardize and liberalize the monetary system, and allowed owners to import cheap labor from Europe. Most striking, Congress simply gave away tremendous amounts of land and mineral resources to corporations that were building the transcontinental railway (completed in 1869) and other transportation systems. By the early twentieth century, the government had given private railway builders free land equivalent to the areas of Maine, New Hampshire, Vermont, Massachusetts, Rhode Island, and much of New York. Some of this acreage held rich deposits of coal, lead, and iron ores.

This was hardly "private enterprise." Corporations obtained incalculable favors from government to develop the country's wealth. An intimate, sometimes questionable, relationship developed between business and government. One member of the House of Representatives observed in 1873 that Congress had become like an "auction room where more valuable considerations were disposed of under the speaker's hammer than in any other place on earth." More cynically, one presidential candidate advised another during the 1870s that businessmen wanted "men in office who will not steal but who will not interfere with those who do." By the 1890s, corporate and national interests were viewed as much the same thing. "After all," one business journal declared in 1895, "the government is the servant of the people." The result was historic: in 1850 the laws had shaped the corporation, but by 1900 the corporation shaped the laws.

As the nationwide infrastructure of railways and telegraph lines appeared, the pace of industrial revolution quickened. Except for Western Union and Montgomery Ward, companies that operated across the nation were nonexistent in the 1870s. By 1910, however, they dominated production and distribution. Using the new transportation network, a business could draw raw materials from the Midwest, transform them into processed goods in the East, and sell them nationwide. The isolated, rural, "island communities" of the 1870s became part of an integrated and more homogeneous America. Small local firms suddenly faced competition from giant producers and either copied the giant, merged with it, or were wiped out by it. Local business executives lost ground to distant managers who controlled vast flows of money and goods and so controlled the market.

Such a revolution not only hit the oil, steel, food, and camera industries, but even the making of soap. Before 1870 the soap market was divided among small firms and some European companies. In 1879, however, one small company—Procter and Gamble (P&G) of Cincinnati—accidentally discovered a soap that floated. The discovery, moreover, occurred just as inventors were devising new machinery to mass produce soap. Thus doubly blessed, P&G soon shaped 200,000 cakes of Ivory Soap each day. It then pioneered in developing a national advertising campaign and networks of offices to push sales. P&G built a more efficient factory, established a purchasing department to ensure supplies of animal and vegetable fats for the soap, and diversified into salad oils and other soaps. Competitors, such as Colgate, had to develop similar nationwide systems or go under.

In 1880 such firms as P&G, Colgate, Eastman Kodak, American Tobacco, Quaker Oats, Campbell Soup, Pillsbury Flour, and Borden were little known or nonexistent. Twenty years later they were household words and, indeed, some—such as Eastman Kodak and American Tobacco—ranked among the first American multinational corporations by selling their products in such exotic places as Central Europe and China. Little wonder that the President of Columbia University, Nicholas Murray Butler, announced, "In my judgment the limited liability corporation is the greatest single discovery of modern times. . . . Even steam and electricity are far less important," for "they would be reduced to comparative impotence without it."

Inheriting a chaotic and decentralized America, the corporation streamlined and centralized the nation's economic life. It also produced unimagined wealth that marked the beginning of an affluent America. In 1860, 31 million Americans turned out manufactures valued at $2 billion, traveled on 30,000 miles of railroads, and produced little iron or steel. Forty years later, 70 million people produced manufactures worth $11 billion, used 200,000 miles of rails, and overtook Great Britain and Germany to become the world's greatest iron and steel (and soap) producers. The corporation helped create such new cities as Chicago, Atlanta, Kansas City, Minneapolis, and Dallas.

The creators naturally believed this was the best of worlds. In 1886 Andrew Carnegie looked at his steel empire and observed, "If asked what important law I should change, I must perforce say none: the laws are perfect."

BOOM HIDDEN IN BUST

Not all Americans agreed with Carnegie. During the quarter-century following 1873, the country suffered from increasingly severe periods of economic depression. The 1873 panic was triggered by overexpansion and stock exchange corruption. The economic crisis worsened until labor violence erupted in 1877, 1886, 1892, and then sporadically between 1893 and 1895. Overproduction caused this twenty-five-year crisis. Industries and farms produced so much that markets were glutted, prices fell, and both farmers and laborers suffered. Pig-iron production, for example, doubled between 1873 and 1893, while its price dropped from $50 to $13 a ton. Production of cotton, traditionally the nation's leading export, increased more than 50 percent during these years; Americans eventually produced more than the entire world could consume. Some corporations, like some farmers, could not stand the competition and went bankrupt. But others prospered during depressions. Andrew Carnegie's foresight enabled him to build plants cheaply during economic panics and even to buy out competitors. "So many of my friends needed money," he recalled, "I bought out five or six of them. That was what gave me my leading interest in this steel business."

New York City in 1885: Broadway at Cortlandt Street and Maiden
Lane.

As men like Carnegie learned that efficiency and cost-cutting were
necessary for survival, they tended to drive others out of business until
such vital industries as sugar refining, oil, steel, and tobacco were dominated by only one or two companies. In these fields competition increasingly disappeared. Prices were then determined not by many sellers in an
open marketplace, but by a few corporations on the basis of their own
costs and whatever return they thought desirable on their investment.
Companies banded together to fix prices in "pools" or formed giant combinations known as "trusts," which destroyed competition. To form a trust
a number of corporations would join together, giving a group of trustees
the power to set prices for all of them; thus the corporations fixed prices,
cut out competition, and their profits skyrocketed. During the 1890s depression, companies rushed to join together for survival. In the early part
of the decade dozens of mergers occurred annually. But the figures
soared to nearly 3000 between 1897 and 1902. The lone American entrepreneur who made his fortune by competing in an open marketplace
would hereafter be an extremely rare phenomenon.

But at the very moment competition was vanishing and opportunity
narrowing, belief in the self-made man flourished. Business tycoons
helped popularize the idea that success came to those who worked hard
and saved their money. "Perseverance is the great thing," said John D.
Rockefeller, creator of Standard Oil. "The young man who sticks is the

one who succeeds." The view that there was room at the top for all who were virtuous received its most popular formulation in the novels of Horatio Alger. The typical Alger hero, such as "Ragged Dick" or "Mark the Match Boy," began life as a poor orphan. But he was "manly and self-reliant" and through honesty and hard work attained a position of solid respectability with the further assurance that he would "go far." The belief that success resulted from virtue sanctified corporate practices and led to the exaltation of entrepreneurial liberty as the highest social value.

When state or national legislatures tried to control corporations, they were often stopped by the courts. Carnegie might have believed the laws were perfect, but the Supreme Court tried to improve on perfection. It did this by radically changing the idea of "due process," a basic tenet of American law. Before the 1880s due process referred to procedure. For example, the Constitution's Fifth Amendment provided that no person could "be deprived of life, liberty, or property, without due process of law," that is, be subjected to arbitrary arrest, unlawful forfeiture of property, and the like. In 1868 the Fourteenth Amendment strengthened this guarantee by providing that no state government could take away individual rights without due process. This amendment was aimed especially at preventing Southern states from depriving black citizens of voting and other rights. The Supreme Court, however, interpreted it in quite another way.

Between 1886 and 1898 the Court ruled on whether the Minnesota and Nebraska legislatures could regulate railroads in those states. The judges held the state laws invalid, not because the legislatures had violated *procedural* due process in passing the regulations, but because in the Court's opinion the laws were unfair *in substance* to the railroads. The Court asserted the right to decide whether the railway rates were reasonable, instead of deciding, as it had in the past, whether the procedures used in passing the laws were constitutional. Judges thus declared that their own views, rather than those of elected officials, should determine the substance of these particular state laws.

This was potentially an explosive situation, for the Court had put itself above elected officials in order to protect private corporations. Its view was often shaped by Justice Stephen J. Field, who served on the Supreme Court from 1863 to 1897. His beliefs, in turn, had been molded by his experience as an ambitious businessman on the California frontier (where in self-defense he learned the art of shooting to kill without taking the pistol out of his pocket), and from his reading of classical economists who believed an open marketplace existed in which everyone competed equally.

In the *Wabash* case of 1886 the Court struck down an Illinois law regulating railroads that went into other states. The Court declared that since the railway was in interstate commerce, only Congress could deal with it. This decision forced Congress in 1887 to establish the Interstate Commerce Commission to stop such unfair practices as rebates to favored customers. At first the railroads fought the ICC, but shrewd railway lawyers, such as Richard Olney of Boston, adopted different tactics. Olney argued that the ICC was inevitable because public opinion demanded it; therefore the railroads should only ensure that their spokesmen controlled the agency. This was one reason why the ICC proved ineffectual; the other was a series of Supreme Court decisions that stripped it of any powers to set fair rates. The same fate paralyzed the Sherman Antitrust Act, passed by Congress in 1890 to outlaw business combinations that tried to monopolize markets or engaged in "restraint of trade" in interstate commerce. The impact of the Sherman Act was so pitiful that it was followed by the spectacular merger and trust movement between 1897 and 1902.

Americans, who have always professed reverence for both efficiency and competition, found by the 1890s that they could not always have both. With the aid of the Supreme Court they chose efficiency. Some critics might tab the corporate leaders of the cut-and-thrust post–Civil War era "Robber Barons." Most Americans, however, were willing to overlook the brutal, often illegal, practices if Rockefeller could deliver cheap, dependable oil for home lamps, or if Cornelius Vanderbilt's New York Central Railroad could reduce the price of bread by cutting transportation costs for flour from $3.45 a barrel in 1865 to only 68 cents in 1885. When writers debated whether Shakespeare or Vanderbilt had contributed more to the human race, Shakespeare inevitably lost.

The Robber Barons helped corrupt politics, undercut laws, and stifle competition, but many people nevertheless agreed with Carnegie's assessment: "It will be a great mistake for the community to shoot the millionaires, for they are the bees that make the most honey, and contribute most to the hive even after they have gorged themselves full." For those Americans who questioned whether they should serve as drones to such queen bees as Carnegie, alternatives seemed quite limited. The crucial question became: what kind of checks could the society produce to limit the corporation's spreading power? Queen bees, after all, are quite brutal.

THE COLLAPSE OF THE FIRST BARRIER: THE SOUTH, WHITE AND BLACK

Five forces in American society might have made the corporation more responsible: the South, labor unions, organized religion, protest movements, and the political parties. During the 1880s and 1890s each of these either finally accommodated itself to the new industrial America or else was swept aside.

Historically the South had led opposition to the corporation's dominance, for that section had fought for low tariffs, agrarian values, and easy credit. However, Southern resistance halted after the Civil War as Northern capitalists followed Union soldiers into the defeated South, making the area a virtual colony of the North. Spurred by new wealth, cheap labor, and nonexistent taxes, the South doubled the number of its industrial laborers and tripled its investment in manufacturing between 1880 and 1900. By 1900 the region contained half the nation's textile mills. In 1870 one house stood at a rail intersection in Alabama; thirty years later this site, named Birmingham, produced $12 million of manufactures annually and competed with Pittsburgh as leader in world steel production. Yet the South industrialized only as rapidly as the rest of the country. Its spectacular development simply allowed it to keep pace with the North.

Much of the new Southern industry, moreover, depended on Northern capital. Many southerners, known as "redeemers," rushed to make their own fortunes by cooperating with the entrepreneurs from above the Mason-Dixon line. The redeemers sacrificed tax income, thereby sacrificing schools and community facilities, in order to induce industry to build in their towns. One redeemer believed that "it were better for the state to burn the schools" than levy heavier taxes on corporations to pay the state debt. The thirteen Southern states together had less taxable property than the single state of New York and spent $3 million less each year on education than did New Yorkers. In 1900 illiteracy afflicted nearly half of all southerners and more than three-quarters of the section's blacks. State universities in the South were nearly bankrupt. In 1900 Harvard alone received more income than all Southern colleges combined. The institutions that did thrive, such as Vanderbilt in Tennessee and Johns Hopkins in Maryland, depended on Northern funds. Even in higher education, the South was colonized by the North.

The agrarian South did not disappear, but its character greatly changed. The average farm, approximately 350 acres before the Civil War, shrunk to less than half that acreage afterwards. Meanwhile the number of farms doubled to over a million, one-third of them operated by tenants or sharecroppers for absentee owners. This was hardly an economic base from which the South could challenge the mighty corporation.

Blacks particularly depended on tenant farming or sharecropping. White farm owners preferred former slaves to white workers, for as one owner remarked, "No other laborer [than the Negro] . . . would be as cheerful or so contented on four pounds of meat and a peck of meal a week, in a little cabin 14 by 16 feet with cracks in it large enough to afford free passage to a large-sized cat." During the 1890s, however, race relations underwent a transformation. On the farms blacks saw that tenant farming renewed their slave ties to the land, now without even the relative security that slaves had possessed. When blacks tried to gain employment in the new factories, bloody clashes with whites resulted.

During the late 1880s radical whites attempted to weld together the poor of both races into a class movement that became the Populist party. But redeemers broke up this coalition with racist attacks that first split apart the whites and then turned them violently against blacks. Racism proved stronger than common economic interests shared by both blacks and whites. Lynchings multiplied until they averaged 188 a year during the 1890s. So-called "Jim Crow" laws were rushed through state legislatures, segregating schools and transportation into supposed "separate but equal" facilities. In 1896 the Supreme Court upheld such laws in *Plessy* v. *Ferguson*. The Court brusquely overrode the lone protest of Justice John Marshall Harlan, who argued that "our Constitution is color-blind." By 1900 black illiteracy was six times as great as that of whites.

When the United States declared war against Spain in 1898, many blacks insisted they be allowed to fight for the liberation of Cubans and Filipinos from Spanish control. After overcoming considerable white opposition, McKinley finally allowed the creation of four black regular regiments and a volunteer force that reached about 10,000 men. The regulars distinguished themselves in Cuba, but when black soldiers returned home they found conditions worse than before. The President would do nothing. The New York *World* published a cartoon showing McKinley studying a map of the Philippines. In the background a figure pulled back a curtain to reveal murders and lynchings of blacks. The caption read: "Civilization Begins at Home."

Most black leaders responded to this crisis by accepting the policies of Booker T. Washington, a black educator. Washington advised acceptance of segregation, stressed the need for nonviolent accommodation to white society, and urged blacks to achieve equality ultimately by means of economic gains, particularly through vocational training. "The opportunity to earn a dollar in a factory just now is worth infinitely more than the opportunity to spend a dollar in an opera house," he observed. Washington hoped that self-help measures would eventually tear down most racial barriers: "In all things purely social we can be as separate as the fingers, yet one as the hand in all things essential to mutual progress." In effect Washington promised that blacks would constitute a docile labor force. "The Negro is not given to strikes," he noted.

Some black leaders dissented. T. Thomas Fortune, a New York editor, founded the Afro-American League in 1890. It protested strenuously against the spread of Jim Crow institutions, but died out within a short time. W. E. B. DuBois, who began teaching at Atlanta University in 1897, also criticized the accommodationist doctrine. He asserted that Washington's emphasis on vocational training cheated blacks of the cultural advantages of a liberal education and deprived them of leaders. But the great majority of black clergymen, professionals, and politicians flocked to Washington's side. His popularity grew when such corporate leaders as Carnegie applauded his policies and when President Theodore Roosevelt asked him to dine at the White House—the first black ever invited as a guest to the mansion. The ensuing anti-black uproar ensured that he was also the last of his race invited to the White House by Roosevelt. By the turn of the century it was impossible for either a black movement led by Washington or a South whose industry and culture were largely dependent on Northern capital to check the new corporation.

THE COLLAPSE OF
THE SECOND BARRIER:
LABORERS AND UNIONS

Like the South, the labor movement initially fought the corporation, then accommodated to it. Between 1860 and 1900 the number of industrial workers increased from 2.7 million (or 40 percent of all workers in farms and factories) to 13 million (65 percent). Several union movements attempted to organize laborers after the Civil War but fell victim to racism, the economic depression, and internal political divisions. The continual economic crises after 1873 drove workers to the breaking point, and some organized in small local groups. Nearly 24,000 strikes occurred during the last quarter of the century. Several were especially dangerous.

The general railroad strike of 1877 nearly paralyzed the nation, frightening some Americans into urging a third presidential term for General Ulysses S. Grant because he was the best hope to head off "another French Revolution." Nine years later the Haymarket Riot began when six laborers were killed during a clash with police during a strike in Chicago. At a protest meeting the next night in Haymarket Square a bomb was thrown. Eight policemen were killed. The bomb-thrower was never caught, but amidst the hysteria the anarchist movement, which preached individual freedom by abolishing all state controls, was conveniently blamed. Four anarchists were hanged. Haymarket became a symbol to critics of the new corporate system. The riot helped inspire a number of works that fundamentally criticized industrialism, among them Mark Twain's *A Connecticut Yankee in King Arthur's Court* (1889). Twain ends his novel with the free-wheeling Yankee entrepreneur using his industrial ingenuity to kill 25,000 people. The image of capitalism did not improve in 1892 when strikers at Carnegie's Homestead works in Pittsburgh were fired upon by hired Pinkerton detectives.

The new corporate America was born amidst bloodshed and violence. The terrible depression of 1893–96 worsened matters, as labor uprisings threatened to paralyze many cities. The most serious was a strike against the Pullman Company in Chicago. The trouble began when management sliced wages by 25 percent and fired many workers but refused to reduce costs in the model town of "Pullman," where most employees lived. The American Railway Union, led by Eugene V. Debs, refused to move Pullman coaches. The railroad owners then declared that they would not run trains without those cars, and blamed the union for disrupting transportation. On the advice of Attorney General Richard Olney, President Grover Cleveland obtained an injunction against the strikers and then, over the protest of Illinois Governor John P. Altgeld, sent federal troops into the city. The ostensible reason was to keep United States mail moving, but the effect was to break the strike for the benefit of a private corporation. In 1894 the Supreme Court upheld this use of a sweeping injunction, and Debs went to jail.

Labor's only major success occurred when **Samuel Gompers** organized the American Federation of Labor in 1886. **This union survived the**

Eugene V. Debs, ca. 1910.

horrors of the 1890s largely because Gompers reached an accommodation with the new corporation. One leader of an earlier, short-lived union had urged his members to become politically active in order to "strangle monopoly." But Gompers refused to identify labor's interests with those of any one political party, choosing instead to work for whichever candidates seemed most friendly at the time. Gompers, moreover, had little desire to "fight monopoly." Instead he tried to counter big corporations with big labor, using union techniques such as strikes and boycotts directly against a particular corporation in order to obtain recognition and benefits. He concentrated on organizing skilled workers along craft lines because he believed that only they could exert much leverage on employers. By 1900 the AFL had organized only 3 percent of the nation's nonfarm employees, but it had established the roots for its twentieth-century triumphs. Gompers survived by accepting the corporation and by accepting as well the antianarchist, antisocialist, and, to some extent, the nativist fears of most Americans.

The immigration question proved especially important. Through the mid-nineteenth century the country received over 2 million newcomers each decade, but this number doubled in the 1880s and 1890s. The source of the migration changed from Western Europe to Eastern and Southern Europe, which in turn meant accepting increased numbers of Roman Catholics and Jews. Both old-stock Protestant Americans, who considered the newcomers racially inferior, and segments of organized labor, which disliked the added competition for jobs, favored attempts to restrict immigration. The long-cherished notion that the country could transform immigrants into acceptable citizens through the so-called melting pot of schools and churches began to fade. In 1882 the first exclusion law in American history was passed; it was limited to keeping out Chinese. The nativist sentiment that would prove so powerful was foreseen in 1886 at the dedication in New York harbor of the Statue of Liberty. On the statue's pedestal are inscribed the words, "Give me your tired, your poor, your huddled masses yearning to breathe free." During the ceremonies not one speaker alluded to the inscription but instead emphasized how Americans must go forth to spread liberty to the rest of the world. The speeches symbolized a major change in the nation's history, for the speakers, like Frederick Jackson Turner seven years later, were serving notice that the frontier had closed. Americans were being urged to find new frontiers in other lands.

THE COLLAPSE OF THE THIRD BARRIER: PROTEST MOVEMENTS

Farmers already knew about the closed frontier. Following the 1873 depression, the great American West changed for them from being a promise to a hell. During the next quarter-century wheat and corn sometimes cost considerably more to grow than the price the crops brought on the market. With new machinery and vast lands, farm output soared. From 1860 to 1890 wheat production grew from 173 million to 449 million bushels. In the process, farmers produced so much that they had to rely on exports to other nations to absorb surpluses. But on the world market Americans had to compete with cheap grains from newly opened fields in Argentina and Russia. Terrible winter storms followed by intense heat and drought during the 1880s left many farmers with no crops at all. On particularly brutal frontiers, as in the Dakotas, the isolation and barrenness of rural life took a toll in the form of suicide and mental breakdown. Other agrarians tried to escape to the growing cities.

Some farmers, however, tried to fight. They organized such political movements as the Grange, the Greenback party, and the Populist party. The Populists hoped to improve the farmer's condition by gaining control of the federal government and then using it to regulate the railroads and trusts, provide more credit, impose graduated income taxes, and clean up corrupt politics. Corporate leaders attacked the Populists, and so did many urban laborers who feared that "farm power" might mean higher bread prices. The Populists' demand for government help led to their being labeled "radical" and "socialist." Such terms were beside the point, for corporations had been growing rich from government legislation since the Civil War. The real struggle was over who would use the government.

In 1892 the Populist presidential candidate, James B. Weaver, received more than a million popular, and 22 electoral, votes. The party also elected governors in Kansas, North Dakota, and Colorado. Two years later, in the congressional elections, Populist candidates received nearly 1.5 million votes. That was the peak of the party's power. The last hope for a racially tolerant party that could make important changes in industrial America disappeared when William Jennings Bryan and the Democratic party absorbed most Populists in the 1896 presidential campaign.

Another reform movement also challenged the social values of the new corporation. The women's-rights organization began in 1848 at Seneca Falls, New York, when a group of feminists resolved that since "all men and women are created equal," and since men refused them suffrage and thus made them "civilly dead," any law that made women inferior to men would have "no force or authority." In 1869 Wyoming territory gave women the vote. Such a success, however, made slight impact, in part because most women apparently cared little about voting. In Massachusetts, where 600,000 women could vote in state elections, only 20,000 chose to do so. By the 1870s, moreover, feminist leaders attempted to build on the Seneca Falls declaration by urging massive social change that would go far beyond the vote ("that crumb," as one leader termed it): reform of divorce laws, ending of job discrimination, legal equality (in many states married women could not testify in court against husbands or hold title to property), establishment of community kitchens and public nurseries, and a de-emphasis of the family.

Every feminist reform ran counter to the existing order and therefore seemed to threaten social stability. Business leaders, even as they utterly transformed the nation, tried to retain the image of a tranquil, stable society that rested on the family and on a clear division of labor within the family. When in the 1870s feminist leader Victoria Woodhull urged free love and licensed prostitution, she provided an excuse for all-out attacks on the women's movement, attacks that frequently linked the feminists to the anarchists and strikers as threats to social order.

The movement split into conservative and liberal factions, then reunited into an organization led by Susan B. Anthony, and later by Carrie Chapman Catt, that dropped demands for drastic reforms in order to gain the vote. To accomplish this, suffragists shrewdly used the arguments of their male opponents: women were concerned primarily with taking care of the family and consequently should have the vote since their concern for spiritual and traditional values, as opposed to men's money-grubbing, would raise the moral level of politics. But women were also capable of appealing to men's prejudices. Suffragists in the South exploited racial fears by asserting that the enfranchisement of white women would ensure white supremacy in the voting booths. Elsewhere, native, white, Protestant women, indignant because they could not vote—

whereas male immigrants ultimately could—spoke with disdain of "the ignorant vote." The drive for the franchise thus gained momentum. But in narrowing their program, feminists—like the South, the AFL, and Populists-turned-Democrats—had gone far in accommodating themselves to the America of the industrial corporation. In the end, conflicts in the post-Civil War era revolved not around the question of whether conservatives could carry out a class solution, but around the question of which class would succeed in carrying out a conservative solution.

American socialists never capitulated in quite the same fashion. Neither, however, did they gain many followers. Socialists like Daniel De-Leon, who espoused a straightforward brand of Marxism, had little influence. In the United States, unlike England and Germany, no close bonds ever developed between the socialist movement and organized labor. The socialists who achieved the widest recognition sought to modify Marxist ideology by smoothing its rough and jagged edges. The Christian Socialists, for example, sharply attacked the new corporate order and the suffering it caused, but called for the creation of a cooperative society in the name of traditional Christian morality. They rejected Marx's materialism and his belief in the inevitability of class struggle.

No one carried the attempt to reconcile socialism with American values further than Edward Bellamy, whose best-selling *Looking Backward* (1888) led to the creation of "Nationalist Clubs" across the country. Bellamy's novel described a society in the year 2000 that was organized according to socialist principles, one in which cooperation had replaced competition. But his utopia differed substantially from Marx's. Bellamy did not condone class conflict or assume that the working class was a repository of special virtue. He emphasized change in the United States rather than around the world; he found a place for religious worship in his new order; and he saw the new society developing in a gradual, peaceful way. One character explains: "Evolution, not revolution, orderly and progressive development, not precipitate and hazardous experiment is our true policy . . . prudence and conservatism are called for." This explains why Abner Doubleday, the father of baseball, could join a Nationalist Club, and why Bellamy found an honored place as an example of the best in American life in the popular *Sweet Home Family Soap Album.*

Frank Lloyd Wright: Architecture for the Old Frontier and the New City

"American architecture," a critic acidly observed in 1891, "was the art of covering one thing with another thing to imitate a third thing, which, if genuine, would not be desirable." Houses and of-fice buildings were mere boxes, banks resembled Greek temples, government buildings looked like Ancient Rome. There was little that could be called an American architecture. Then Frank

Frank Lloyd Wright.

Frank Lloyd Wright: Ward W. Willitts House (1902); Highland Park, Illinois.

Lloyd Wright burst upon the scene.

Born in Wisconsin in 1869, Wright's work by century's turn exemplified key American characteristics. Like the Frontier Thesis of Frederick Jackson Turner, Wright's genius emphasized the importance of space and the natural frontier environment in American life. "Intimacy with Nature is the great friendship," he insisted, then built structures that followed the land's contours and harmonized with the environment. His houses were not mere boxes ("more of a coffin for the human spirit than an inspiration," he sniffed), but a "prairie architecture" that would not be "on a hill," but "*of* the hill." Inside, room flowed into room, space into space, like the prairies outside, instead of being ar-

tificially separated by walls. These were the first ranch houses. In Wright's plans, they were to be wholly American and also functional for Americans, much as Greek temples were useful for Greeks, but less so for American business executives.

During the 1890s many became frightened that machines would soon strangle the natural environment. Wright, however, saw no conflict between machines and nature. In building his prairie architecture he was the first designer to use products of the industrial revolution that transformed the nation between 1870 and 1900. He innovated with such new building materials as steel, reinforced concrete and, later, plastics. Like Carnegie and

Frank Lloyd Wright: "Fallingwater" (1936); Bear Run, Pennsylvania.

18 Rockefeller, moreover, Wright was an ambitious American entrepreneur, and he hated any governmental interference in either his art or his business. "I believe in the capitalist system," he declared. "I only wish I could see it tried some time."

Yet he was too much of an individualist and nonconformist to be accepted by his countrymen. Scandal plagued him, particularly after he left his wife and children to travel in Europe with the wife of one of his clients. For his new love, he built the ultimate prairie-style house, Taliesen, in Wisconsin. In 1914 a crazed servant killed the woman and six others, then burned Taliesen. Wright rebuilt it, but after the scandal had difficulty obtaining work. Nearly bankrupt in 1929, he was saved by a commission to build the Johnson Wax Company's administration building in Racine, Wisconsin. He then entered his last, greatest period, creating magnificent homes, the entire campus of Florida Southern College, and a radical tubular structure for the Guggenheim Museum in New York City. He rightly considered himself the world's greatest architect, condemning cities that would not take his advice (on Dallas: "Seems to be made of rubber bath-mats"; on Pittsburgh: "Abandon it.") He died at ninety years of age, having completed 700 buildings and while working on plans for a mile-high, 528-floor skyscraper that would reach upwards like the great trees of his American West. His epitaph was written by a French newspaper editor: "Nothing was ever more deliberately and more profoundly American than the personality and career of Frank Lloyd Wright."

Frank Lloyd Wright: Sketch of the Guggenheim Museum; New York City.

THE COLLAPSE OF
THE FOURTH
BARRIER: CHURCHES

In an earlier America the church had been an outspoken critic of men who sought profit rather than godliness. By the post-Civil War era, however, both Protestant and Roman Catholic leaders in the United States had largely lost their capacity to make fundamental economic or political analyses. "Our churches are largely for the mutual insurance of prosperous families, and not for the upbuilding of the great under-class of humanity," a leading New York City clergyman commented in 1874. American Protestantism's last great theologian, Jonathan Edwards, had lived nearly 150 years before. Church leaders, moreover, confronted not only the complexities of the new industrialism, but an intellectual revolution that transformed every branch of knowledge.

Discovery of the quantum theory in physics demonstrated that energy is not emitted in predictable, continuous steps, but in unpredictable and interrupted stages. This discovery threatened to replace the ordered seventeenth-century world of Isaac Newton with an uncertain, rapidly changing universe that apparently had few if any absolutes. Sigmund Freud's investigations in Austria revealed new, treacherous depths in the unconscious. Such findings initiated the dilemmas that would characterize twentieth-century thought. American novelists, particularly the "naturalist" school led by Frank Norris, Stephen Crane, and Theodore Dreiser, pointed to the brutal side of human nature, stressed that social morality was shaped by industrialism instead of the reverse, and proclaimed that such formerly forbidden topics as sex were too important to be treated with silence.

Some church leaders worked to reconcile the new science and literature with their religious beliefs. The most popular response, however, was the new revivalism led by Dwight L. Moody, who condemned outright Charles Darwin's discoveries that species evolved over the ages and were not created in a particular moment, as the biblical version seemed to indicate. Moody handled such problems by proclaiming that reason was less useful in religion then emotion. His message was particularly well received in college communities. Between 1886 and 1888 Moody and John R. Mott of Cornell organized the Student Volunteer Movement; its modest slogan was "The Evangelization of the World in this Generation." Mott also spearheaded the spectacular growth of the Young Men's Christian Association. Churchgoers tended to solve their intellectual confusion through sheer activity.

Indeed the entire country seemed to seek activity as an escape from the cataclysms of the 1890s. Bicycling became the rage. Olympic sports grew so popular that Americans won nine of fourteen gold medals in the 1896 games and fourteen of twenty in 1900. Americans also grew so adept at boxing that the national champion automatically became the world's champion. It was the era of John Philip Sousa, his United States Marine Band, and rousing marches (like "Stars and Stripes Forever"), which comforted depression-ridden Americans with rambunctious nationalism. When such emotions eased the nation's entry into war against Spain in 1898, the churches rushed to join. As the *California Christian Advocate* exclaimed, "This war is The Kingdom of God coming!" That news must have surprised Roman Catholic Spain.

By 1900 the church had failed utterly to lessen the oppressiveness or the power of the rampaging industrialism. Its failure was so marked that new organizations, such as the Salvation Army, had developed to aid the human casualties in the urban slums. By 1902 coal-mine-owner George F. Baer could oppose strikers with the remark: "The rights and interests of the laboring man will be protected and cared for—not by the labor agitators, but by the Christian men to whom God in his infinite wisdom has given the control of the property interests in this country." Few church leaders disputed Baer.

THE COLLAPSE OF THE FIFTH BARRIER: THE POLITICAL PARTY SYSTEM

Some scholars believe that the last, best hope to check the corporation's rising power was the political system and particularly the choice it provided voters in the 1896 presidential election. This is doubtful. Given the experiences of the social groups and sections discussed above, the issue had been decided before 1896. The triumph of William McKinley over William Jennings Bryan in that year did no more than confirm a prevailing trend. It also established a political pattern that would govern the United States for nearly forty years. In perspective, McKinley and the Republicans won not only a victory but virtual unconditional surrender.

The roaring depression of 1893 was the destroyer, striking while a Democratic President, Grover Cleveland, and a Democratic Congress held power. The 1894 elections consequently brought about the largest turnover of congressional strength in the nation's history. The Democrats lost 113 House seats, their Capitol Hill leadership was virtually wiped out, in New England only a lone Democratic congressman survived (John F. Kennedy's grandfather, John "Honey Fitz" Fitzgerald), and even such southern states as Texas and Virginia elected Republicans.

Until this point, voters had been able to separate Democrats from Republicans rather neatly. Democrats preached limited government and noninterference in the affairs of individuals, states, and corporations. The marketplace, not the government, was supposed to encourage or regulate the society. As one Democratic leader proclaimed, "We are never doing as well as when we are doing nothing." The Republicans, on the other hand, urged a more active government and greater centralization of power. They used government to erect protective tariffs, give land to railroads, and make the monetary system more efficient for business. Republicans, however, did not plan to use power to reform or regulate. Thomas B. Reed, the 300-pound Republican from Maine who dominated the House

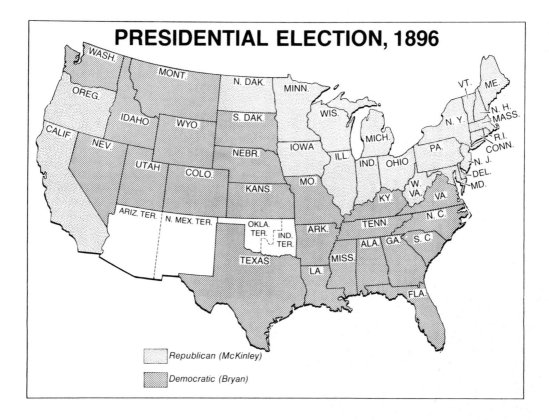

PRESIDENTIAL ELECTION, 1896

Republican (McKinley)

Democratic (Bryan)

of Representatives, dismissed reformers with sarcasm: "One, with God, is always a majority, but many a martyr has been burned at the stake while the votes were being counted." The corporations, therefore, had nothing to fear from Democrats and much to expect from Republicans.

But after the 1894 disaster, Democrats searched desperately for new blood. They found it when Bryan, a former Nebraska congressman, electrified the party's 1896 convention with his "Cross of Gold" speech. He urged increased coining of silver (which was cheaper than gold) to create more money and thereby enable farmers and other depression victims to pay their debts. The proposal found no support from leading businessmen. They feared mixing silver with gold as Bryan proposed would so cheapen the nation's currency that the banking and credit system would sink. They also feared the proposal would be condemned in European money markets that provided large amounts of capital for the building of American railroads, mines, and factories. Nor did urban wage laborers like Bryan's plan, for it could mean they would be paid in cheaper silver dollars and have to pay higher grocery prices.

The Nebraskan also had another major problem. Since the 1840s and 1850s American politics had been increasingly influenced by close-knit, well-organized ethnic and cultural groups (such as the German and Irish) that concentrated in the cities. These ethnic groups sought to preserve such traditions as beer fests and nonreligious activities on Sunday afternoons. The Democratic party, with its more tolerant view of pluralism and ethnic traditions, offered little interference and these groups had consequently become highly important in the party organization. Bryan was a Democrat, but he represented a largely rural view and constituency, was a "dry" on the burning question of whether alcoholic beverages should be prohibited, and practiced a religious fundamentalism abhorrent to many Roman Catholics and liberal Protestants in the Democratic party. He argued for an activist government that would move decisively in both society and the economy.

McKinley, meanwhile, transformed the Republican party. Republicans had long been friends of business, but since the anti-slavery crusade of the 1850s they had also become identified with attempts to impose their own moral and political standards on ethnic groups and newly arrived immigrants. When Republicans preached the evils of alcoholic drink, or the need to reserve Sunday for nothing but quiet meditation, Irish, German, and Jewish immigrants tended to vote Democratic. As a rising star in the political jungles of Ohio, however, McKinley had learned how to moderate such zeal so that he could win votes from ethnic settlements and "wets" in Cleveland and Cincinnati, as well as from traditional Republican rural areas. During the 1896 campaign he blurred the lines between the parties, welcoming the ethnic Democrats, whom Bryan was driving out, while keeping most traditional Republicans. McKinley vowed to end the depression through high tariffs to protect the home market and an unequivocal gold policy to restore confidence in the nation's credit.

The confrontation was perhaps the most dramatic in the country's political history. An unprecedented number of voters turned out to give McKinley a triumph. His administration raised the tariff and then, with the help of rising prices in 1897–98 caused by new discoveries of gold and increased agricultural exports to Europe, the President killed any hope for modifying the currency by having Congress pass the Gold Standard Act. With these issues decided, Americans began staying away from the polls on election day. One-party states became fixtures. Democrats owned the South (especially when blacks were kept from voting after the 1890s), and Republicans controlled much of the Northeast and Midwest. A new era of American politics began, characterized by a diminished concern for elections, little party competition in many states, and Republican power. The new industrialism had little to fear from Washington.

THE UNITED STATES BECOMES A GREAT WORLD POWER

Not coincidentally, the United States saw its economy mature at the same time that it became a world power. It joined England, France, Germany, and Russia in the great-power class at the moment the Europeans were most imperialistic: between 1870 and 1900 they conquered more than 10 million square miles (one-fifth of the earth's land) and 150 million people. (Imperialism may be defined as one sovereign people subjugating and controlling an alien and formerly sovereign people.) The United States, however, did not join the rush for land, thereby differentiating its empire from that of the Europeans, who sought colonial areas—that is, territory that they could formally control and populate. After the Civil War Americans sought empire primarily for trade, not territory, and preferred to allow native inhabitants to rule themselves under informal United States protection. This was the Americans' "new empire," as it was termed in the late 1890s.

The old empire had developed between the seventeenth century and the 1850s, and had been based on the land conquered by Americans in their march across the continent. This old empire ended with the settlement of the Pacific Coast, the frontier's close, and consolidation of the continent by the corporation. The last act had been a series of vicious Indian wars that climaxed white determination to drive red men from lands in the Dakotas, Oklahoma, and Wyoming that had been given the Indians earlier in the century. These lands had been thought barren, but settlers rapidly encroached upon them after the Civil War, whereupon the federal government concocted devices to expel the Indians. Between 1887 and 1934 they lost to whites about 86 million of their 138 million acres. One Sioux chief asked the obvious: "Why does not the Great Father put his red children on wheels, so he can move them as he will?" When some tribes refused to budge, the U.S. Army appeared. "We must act with vindictive earnestness against the Sioux, even to extermination, men, women and children," General William Tecumseh Sherman proclaimed in the late 1860s. The next quarter-century proved the General not guilty of overstatement. Sherman was especially ruthless, destroying buffalo herds, then attacking Indian camps in midwinter so that he could burn all provisions and thus cause mass starvation. The tribes were exterminated or reduced to begging, and their great chiefs—Geronimo, Big Foot, and Chief Joseph—died or fled, while Sitting Bull, the famous conqueror of General George Custer's cavalry, ended as an exhibit in a circus.

Perhaps the ultimate horror occurred at Wounded Knee, South Dakota, in 1890. After troops disarmed cooperative Sioux, someone fired a rifle. The cavalry opened full fire, then unloaded large cannon, which exploded nearly a shell a second in the defenseless camp. "We tried to run," one Sioux woman recalled, "but they shot us like we were buffalo." At least 150 and perhaps 250 of the original 350 men, women, and children were murdered. This occurred only eight years before the United States sent the cavalry against Spaniards; later it would be used against Filipinos and Chinese. The Indian campaigns sharpened the military's effectiveness. More important, they gave many Americans a rationale for warring against peoples of other colors.

Racism, however, did not trigger American imperialism in 1898. Its taproot lay in the post-1873 depressions and the need to find overseas

William McKinley in the White House, 1898.

markets for the overly productive factories and farms. That need became imperative during the strike-ridden days of the mid-1890s, when, in the words of Secretary of State Walter Quintin Gresham, "symptoms of revolution" appeared among unemployed laborers and farmers. Riots and strikes from Brooklyn to Chicago to California were capped by a march of thousands of unemployed (the so-called Coxey's Army) on Washington, D. C., in 1894. The "symptoms" would disappear only with employment, and that required expanded markets. "The prosperity of our people," the Secretary of the Treasury announced in 1894, "depends largely upon their ability to sell their surplus products in foreign markets at remunerative prices."

The United States exported less than 10 percent of its manufactures and about 18 percent of its farm products, but these figures were misleading. Products that formed the economy's backbone heavily depended on external markets: 70 percent of the cotton crop had to be sold abroad, 40 percent of the wheat, 50 percent of the copper, 15 percent of the iron and steel, and even 16 percent of the agricultural equipment. These figures were impressive, but they had also been inadequate, for they had not prevented a quarter-century of depressions. Even greater overseas markets were required. There was, of course, an alternative. Americans could reorient their system, making more equal the distribution of wealth. That alternative was never seriously considered by business and political leaders, who instead preferred greater production and expanded markets. The needed world outlets, however, were coming under the control of the aggressive Europeans. If Americans were to find overseas buyers, they needed the aid of the State Department and perhaps the army and navy. As one prominent Republican observed in 1897, "Diplomacy is the management of international business."

Two business possibilities dramatically opened, one in Asia, the other in Latin America. In 1895 a surging Japan humiliated China in a brief conflict that revealed the loser to be a paper dragon. The humiliation ultimately led to the outbreak of the Chinese Revolution. More immediately, the European powers rushed to carve out areas of China exclusively for their own trade and investment. This flew directly in the face of a half-century American policy, known as the "open door," whose objective was to trade with a whole, sovereign China. United States trade with the Chinese had spiraled upward during the mid-1890s, but the European encroachments threatened to shut off what many Americans believed to be their greatest potential market. McKinley knew that major American interests were deeply endangered, particularly after iron and textile exporters implored him to check the European moves. The President's hands were tied, however, by another crisis 90 miles off the Florida coast.

Since 1868 Cubans had revolted against the domination, corruption, and inefficiency of their Spanish rulers. The United States had barely avoided involvement during the 1870s. The conflict simmered down during the next decade but burst into flames once again in 1895. Under the leadership of José Martí, the Cubans announced the establishment of their own independent government. Several restraints initially kept Americans out of the struggle. For one thing, they feared that intervention might result in their having to annex Cuba, which they wished to avoid because of the racial, constitutional, and political problems that would inevitably arise. As it was, they were experiencing enough difficulty just keeping their own nation together during the 1890s. Moreover, the business community, with which McKinley was in close contact, did not at first want war. The depression finally seemed to be lifting in 1897. Seeing the light at the end of a long tunnel, businessmen feared that the demands of a war economy would threaten the growing prosperity.

In early 1898, however, both restraints disappeared. The first problem evaporated when Americans began to understand that they did not have to govern a free Cuba. They needed only a veto over certain Cuban actions so that, for example, the island could not fall under British power. The inhabitants could otherwise be allowed to govern themselves. McKinley and Congress devised a classic solution in which the United States would enjoy power over, but have little daily responsibility for, the Cubans.

The second restraint disappeared in March 1898, when the business community and McKinley began to fear that a continuation of the Cuban struggle endangered $50 million worth of American investments on the island and, more important, caused uncertainty and unrest in the United States, particularly as Spanish brutality brought outcries among some Americans to free Cuba. A political threat also existed. If McKinley let Cuba fester and uncertainty continue, Bryan might oust the Republicans in 1900 with the cry of "Free Cuba and Free Silver." "Look out for Mr. Bryan," remarked McKinley's top political advisor, Mark Hanna, in February 1898. But, he was asked, would not the Democrats hesitate before offering the nomination again to Bryan? "Hesitate?" Hanna replied, "Does a dog hesitate for a marriage license?"

In late January 1898 McKinley sent the warship *Maine* to Havana to protect United States property. Two weeks later it blew up, killing more than 250 Americans. The causes have never been determined, but the nation (although not the President) quickly blamed Spain. War sentiment grew, fueled by an increasing fear that the United States would not be able to protect its vital interests in China until the Cuban problem was solved. On March 25 a close political advisor in New York City cabled McKinley: "Big corporations here now believe we will have war. Believe all would welcome it as relief to suspense." Two days later the President presented an ultimatum to Spain. The Spanish surrendered to two of the demands by promising to stop their brutalities and to declare an armistice. But they refused a third request to promise eventual independence to Cuba and allow McKinley to act as a mediator in the negotiations. Any Spanish government that accepted that demand would have immediately fallen from power. On April 11 McKinley asked Congress to declare war. Not for the first or last time, Americans concluded they would have to fight abroad in order to have peace and prosperity at home.

"THE SPLENDID LITTLE WAR"

It would be one of the weirdest and most significant of wars. The first action occurred not in Cuba, but thousands of miles away in the Spanish-controlled Philippines. Six weeks before declaring war, McKinley ordered Admiral George Dewey, the American commander in the Pacific, to take the Philippines should war erupt. Dewey's force was not overly imposing. When it left Hong Kong to fight the Spanish fleet, British naval officials remarked that the Americans were "a fine set of fellows, but unhappily we shall never see them again." Dewey, however, easily blockaded, then smashed a decrepit Spanish flotilla, killing or wounding 400, while only several Americans suffered scratches. The United States had suddenly become a major military power in the Far East as the result of Dewey's victory at Manila Bay.

The campaigns in Cuba were not as spectacular. The American Army numbered only 28,000 regulars before the war, and when augmented with 200,000 volunteers it was short of modern rifles, had inadequate medical supplies, ate food that was unfit for human consumption, and wore uniforms designed for duty in Alaska. The War Department proved so ineffectual that McKinley had to fire his Secretary of War amidst a national scandal. America's only salvation lay in the fact that Spain was even more inefficient and corrupt. A broken-down Spanish navy struggled across the Atlantic only to be blockaded in Santiago. American troops overcame the heat and malaria long enough to win the heights overlooking that city. Theodore Roosevelt, who had the good taste to have his uniform custom-tailored by Brooks Brothers in New York City, led one charge up the heights, leading the troops directly into the enemy fire. They were saved only by the inability of the Spanish garrison to hit slowly moving targets. Americans held their precarious position for two days, in part because of the heroism of black units. Spain's navy was thus forced out into the harbor and then destroyed easily by the American fleet. Madrid asked for peace.

A war that lasted only three months made the United States a great world power. Americans held a commanding position in Asia and the dominant role in the Western Hemisphere. At home they felt only the exhilaration, for they never had to consider curtailment of their individual liberties or rationing of foodstuffs in order to fight the war. Only 500 Americans died in battle, but four times that number fell victim to diseases. It was an unreal war. One reporter noted that as an American warship shelled a Spanish fort in Cuba, the sailors "whispered and chuckled. . . . Meanwhile from below came the strains of the string band playing from the officers' mess. . . . War as it is conducted at this end of the century is civilized." The horrors of 1873–97 were over, with the new corporate system preserved by what Secretary of State John Hay called "that splendid little war." The conflict that made the nation a great power also, unfortunately, gave war a good name.

THE PEACE: CLOSING
CUBA, OPENING CHINA

McKinley had limited diplomatic objectives. He did not want to copy the Europeans by obtaining a large, expensive, unmanageable colonial empire. After obtaining Cuba, therefore, he allowed the Cubans to write their own constitution but forced them to accept the Platt Amendment passed by the United States Congress. This legislation gave the United States the right to land troops in Cuba to maintain law and order, limited the amount of debt the island could accumulate, and made Guantanamo an American naval base. When Cuba balked at these demands, the McKinley administration summoned Cuban leaders to Washington, courted them with an economic agreement that opened the American sugar market to them on favorable terms, and then threatened that if

U.S. soldiers guarding Filipino prisoners, 1899.

they would not agree to the amendment the administration would put it into effect by force. By a narrow vote the Cuban Constitutional Convention accepted the amendment. "There is, of course, little or no independence left Cuba under the Platt Amendment," the United States Army commander in Cuba accurately observed. Supposedly independent, the island would actually be controlled and exploited by the United States for 60 years. The President in addition took Puerto Rico from Spain, making that area an unorganized territory of the United States.

He also acquired the Philippines, but the Filipinos reacted quite unexpectedly. McKinley had decided that they were unprepared for self-government and that if left to themselves they would be victimized by some European power. He did not want all of the islands, only the magnificent port of Manila from which American merchants and warships could develop and protect interests in China. Manila, however, would be threatened if the remainder of the islands fell into European hands. McKinley therefore decided reluctantly that he had no alternative to taking all of the Philippines. As he later explained to missionaries who visited the White House, he had constantly prayed about the problem; then one night a voice told him to annex the Philippines for, among other reasons, "we could not turn them over to France or Germany—our commercial rivals in the Orient—that would be bad business and discreditable." Apparently everyone who had endured the post-1873 depressions knew the horrors of "bad business," even voices. The Filipinos, however, were not impressed. Led by Emilio Aguinaldo, they declared themselves independent and fought 120,000 American troops in a three-year struggle. Two thousand Americans and perhaps as many as 200,000 Filipinos died. The United States used increasingly brutal methods to end the insurrection. After some American troops were massacred, one general ordered the killing of every Filipino male over the age of ten. This order never took effect, but lesser barbarities continued until 1902, when Aguinaldo had been captured and resistance broken.

At home, anti-imperialist groups, led by conservative businessmen, intellectuals, and some Democrats, organized to blast McKinley's Philippine policy. "G is for guns/ That McKinley has sent/ To teach Filipinos/ What Jesus Christ meant," went one anti-imperialist poem. But despite financing from Andrew Carnegie and literature written by such figures as Mark Twain, these groups received very little support. Their only victory, if that is the proper word, was preventing Harvard from giving McKinley an honorary degree. In the election of 1900 Bryan tried briefly to gain the support of the anti-imperialists, but he decided to soft-pedal their cause in order to emphasize again the free-silver issue. Nothing could save either the anti-imperialists or Bryan. McKinley and his vice-presidential running-mate, Governor Theodore Roosevelt of New York, won a landslide victory larger than the Republican triumph of 1896.

Despite the Philippine bloodshed, the President had scored notable victories including an end to the depression, solution of the Cuban problem, and establishment of the United States as a great power in Asia. The last was particularly important. Using Dewey's victory as leverage, McKinley moved to stop the carving up of China by the Europeans; viewed another way, he sought to keep all of China open to American exporters and missionaries. In 1899 and 1900, Secretary of State John Hay issued two "open-door" notes asking the other powers to promise that they would keep China open on an equal basis to all outsiders; meanwhile Chinese sovereignty would be recognized in all parts of the empire. The other powers, particularly Russia, grumbled, but Hay publicly announced that everyone had accepted the American position. This was not accurate, for the Russians, and later the Japanese, would not agree that China should become a marketplace open to all. They believed that their proximity to the China market gave them—indeed, required that they have—favored position for their own economic and political interests. Hay and McKinley nevertheless insisted that American businessmen and missionaries enjoy an open door to compete for Chinese customers and souls on the same terms as anyone else, even Russians and Japanese. American statesmen would hold to that insistence until the 1940s.

The Civil War and the ensuing economic crisis marks the most threatening forty-year era in United States history, but McKinley's triumph at the end of the dark years gave Americans new optimism and reaffirmed their traditional belief that the nation had a special mission to perform in the world. For the country had not simply survived the terrors of the post-1860 years, but had done great works. It had spawned the corporation, an almost magical instrument for ordering and expanding wealth. With the conquest of Spain and the issuance of the open-door notes, the nation stood on the world stage as one of the great global empires. Frederick Jackson Turner had been proven correct: a new period was indeed opening in American history. With the continental frontier apparently closed, Americans were seeking new frontiers.

In September 1901, McKinley explained why to the Pan-American Exposition in Buffalo, New York. The United States possessed "almost appalling" wealth, the President announced, and must therefore move into the world market to trade: "Isolation is no longer possible or desirable." The next day McKinley was shot by an anarchist. Theodore Roosevelt, a most outspoken expansionist and a student of Turner's theories, moved into the White House.

Suggested Reading

The best overviews of the 1865 to 1900 years remain Robert Wiebe, *The Search for Order* (1968); and Samuel Hays, *The Response to Industrialism* (1957). Leading economic histories include Edward C. Kirkland's *Industry Comes of Age* (1961); Alfred D. Chandler's *The Visible Hand: The Managerial Revolution in American Business* (1977), a prize-winning account that is excellent on the nineteenth century; David F. Noble, *America by Design: Science, Technology and the Rise of Corporate Capitalism* (1977); Irwin Unger, *The Greenback Era . . . 1865–1879* (1964); and Mira Wilkins's pioneering *The Emergence of Multinational Enterprise: American Business Abroad from the Colonial Era to 1914* (1970). A new social history, making important contributions to understanding this pivotal era, includes Herbert C. Gutman, *Work, Culture, and Society in Industrializing America* (1976); John F. Kasson, *Civilizing the Machine: Technology and Republican Values in America, 1776–1900* (1976); Paul Boyer, *Urban Masses and Moral Order in America, 1820–1920* (1978); Zane L. Miller, *The Urbanization of Modern America* (1973); Stephan Thernstrom's ground-breaking *Poverty and Progress* (1964); Rowland Berthoff, *An Unsettled People* (1971); and two key works by James B. Gilbert, *Designing the Industrial State . . . 1880–1940* (1972), and *Work Without Salvation: America's Intellectuals and Industrial Alienation, 1880–1910* (1977).

Important volumes on intellectual and social history include Gilman M. Ostrander, *American Civilization in the First Machine Age, 1890–1940* (1970); David W. Noble, *The Progressive Mind, 1890–1917* (1971); Kevin Starr's provocative *Americans and the California Dream, 1850–1915* (1971); Cynthia E. Russett, *Darwin in America: The Intellectual Response, 1865–1912* (1976). Standard is Sidney E. Ahlstrom's magisterial *A Religious History of the American People* (1972). Legal-constitutional studies begin with Loren P. Beth, *The Development of the American Constitution, 1877–1917* (1971); and several works by J. W. Hurst, including *Law and the Conditions of Freedom in the 19th Century* (1956).

For analyses of the less-privileged groups, see Fred Shannon, *The Farmer's Last Frontier* (1945); Walter Prescott Webb's magnificent volumes *The Great Frontier* (1964) and *The Great Plains* (1931); and Ray Allen Billington, *Frederick Jackson Turner* (1973), for the frontier crisis. The black experience is described in John Hope Franklin, *From Slavery to Freedom* (1974); C. Vann Woodward, *The Strange Career of Jim Crow* (1974); David Gordon Nielson, *Black Ethos: Northern Urban Life and Thought, 1890–1930* (1977); and Louis R. Harlan's excellent biography *Booker T. Washington* (1973). On nineteenth-century women's history, the place to begin is Barbara Welter, *Dimity Convictions* (1976); Lois Banner's overview in *Women in*

Modern America (1974); Sheila M. Rothman, *Woman's Proper Place; A History of Changing Ideals and Practices, 1870 to the Present* (1978); and Aileen Kraditor, *The Ideas of the Woman Suffrage Movement, 1890–1920* (1965). The South's history is in C. Vann Woodward, *Origins of the New South, 1877–1913* (1951). The Indian tragedies are surveyed in Wilcomb E. Washburn, *The Indian in America* (1975); William T. Hagan, *American Indians* (1978); Angie Debo, *A History of the Indians of the United States* (1971); and Dee Brown's best-selling, *Bury My Heart at Wounded Knee, An Indian History of the American West* (1971). Immigration is well covered in Maldwyn A. Jones, *American Immigration* (1960); Oscar Handlin, *The Uprooted* (1951); and John Higham, *Strangers in the Land* (1955).

Political histories include R. Hal Williams, *Years of Decision: American Politics in the 1890s* (1978), which also has a good bibliography; Margaret Leech, *In the Days of McKinley* (1959); Allan Nevins, *Grover Cleveland* (1933); and on the dissenting side, Ray Ginger, *Eugene V. Debs* (1962); Harold C. Livesay, *Samuel Gompers* (1978); Norman Pollack, *The Populist Response to Industrial America* (1962); Lawrence Goodwyn, *The Populist Moment* (1978), the standard account; C. Vann Woodward's brilliant *Tom Watson* (1938); and John G. Sproat, *"The Best Men": Liberal Reformers in the Gilded Age* (1968). See also Richard Jensen, *The Winning of the Midwest, 1888–1896* (1971); Samuel T. McSeveney, *The Politics of Depression, 1893–1896* (1972); David P. Thelen, *The New Citizenship* (1972) on Progressivism in Wisconsin until 1900; Morton Keller, *Affairs of State* (1977).

The place to start on foreign policies is Thomas McCormick, *China Market* (1967), especially on the depression's impact; William Appleman Williams's pioneering *Tragedy of American Diplomacy* (1972); Ernest May, *Imperial Democracy* (1961); Peter Karsten's stimulating *The Naval Aristocracy* (1972) that can be compared with Robert Seager's definitive biography of *Mahan . . .* (1977); David Pletcher, *The Awkward Years* (1963); Milton Plesur, *America's Outward Thrust, 1865–1890;* and Charles Campbell's exhaustive *Transformation of American Foreign Relations, 1865–1900* (1976), with a splendid bibliography. An important biography is Howard Kushner and Anne H. Sherrill, *John Hay* (1977). The 1898 war and its aftermath can be traced through Philip S. Foner's two-volume *The Spanish-Cuban-American War* (1972); David Healy's excellent *The U.S. in Cuba, 1898–1902* (1963); Marilyn B. Young, *The Rhetoric of Empire* (1968); Paul A. Varg, *The Making of a Myth* (1969); Warren I. Cohen's overview, *America's Response to China* (1971); and Robert L. Beisner, *Twelve Against Empire* (1968).

Robert C. Twombly's biography, *Frank Lloyd Wright,* is the most recent (1973), but also consult Wayne Andrews, *Architecture, Ambition and Americans: A Social History of American Architecture* (1978).

Suffragist Parade: Mrs. C. Blaney, Mrs. H. M. Wilmarth, and Jane
Addams.

CHAPTER TWO
1900-1917
The Progressive Era

DON'T BITE THE HAND THAT'S
FEEDING YOU

Words by Thomas Hoier, *music by* Jimmie Morgan

Last night, as I lay a-sleeping,
A wonderful dream came to me.
I saw Uncle Sammy weeping
For his children from over the sea;
They had come to him friendless and
  starving,
When from tyrant's oppression they fled,
But now they abuse and revile him,
Till at last in just anger he said:

Chorus:
"If you don't like your Uncle Sammy,
Then go back to your home o'er the sea,
To the land from where you came,
Whatever be its name,
But don't be ungrateful to me!

If you don't like the Stars in Old Glory,
If you don't like the Red, White, and Blue,
Then don't act like the cur in the story,
Don't bite the hand that's feeding you!"

You recall the day you landed,
How I welcomed you to my shore?
When you came here emptyhanded,
And allegiance forever you swore?
I gathered you close to my bosom,
Of food and of clothes you got both,
So, when in trouble, I need you,
You will have to remember your oath.

An interest in reform has always characterized American history. There have been relatively few periods when at least some people did not want to change society for the better. What has varied over time have been the things people identified as evils, the intellectual justifications and political techniques used to eradicate those evils, the obstacles reformers encountered, and the degree of support they received. Seldom has a larger proportion of the population favored social improvement than during the opening years of the twentieth century, when Americans first tried in a systematic way to control the forces of industrialization and urbanization. Because the United States was becoming a major world power, the successes and failures of the Progressive movement affected not only Americans but people around the world.

THE REFORM IMPULSE

Although progressivism followed on the heels of the Populist revolt and sometimes echoed certain Populist demands, the two movements differed in important respects. Populism had drawn support primarily from farmers and had always remained a sectional force; progressivism won backing from city dwellers, including the middle classes, and had as wide a following in New York and California as in Kansas and South Carolina. Populists had sought for the most part to improve conditions in the countryside; Progressives devoted considerably more attention to political and social problems in the cities. Precisely because Progressives drew on a wider constituency and exhibited broader concerns, they achieved a measure of influence at the city, state, and national level that had eluded the Populists.

Progressives did, however, pay a price for this success. So many different people wanting so many disparate things styled themselves "Progressives" that the movement often seemed to lack a clearly defined program. Progressivism attracted surprisingly diverse groups: small businessmen who favored a curb on monopolies, and big businessmen who sought to extend their economic influence and eliminate their competitors; native Americans who feared the influx of Eastern European immigrants, and settlement-house workers who appreciated the newcomers' contributions to American culture; Southern whites dedicated to the preservation of Jim Crow, and Northern blacks just as fully committed to its eradication; social scientists who believed that planning held all the answers to human progress, and prohibitionists who imagined that closing the saloons would usher in a new world.

Yet for all its diversity, there was a distinctly Progressive approach to social problems. Progressives saw industrialization and urbanization as potentially disruptive forces. The burgeoning cities and corporations seemed to endanger social stability and to undermine older ideals of individual initiative and equal opportunity. To restore a sense of order, to impose a reasonable measure of control on the forces transforming American life, Progressives used the power of government in an unprecedented fashion. In some respects the concern with democratizing government through direct election of senators, the initiative and referendum, and woman suffrage followed logically from this recognition that government had to play an expanded role. Progressives were optimists, activists, and rationalists. They assumed that society was malleable and they devoted their energies to molding it in the proper way.

BIG BUSINESS

One major impetus to progressivism was an awareness of the social problems resulting from explosive economic growth. Between 1880 and 1900 the United States took over world leadership in industrial output. Not only did production increase, but it became concentrated in the hands of relatively few corporations and trusts, which often found it both possible and profitable to control market conditions. The creation of the United States Steel Corporation in 1901 symbolized the growth of industry, its consolidation, and its domination of the market. By purchasing Andrew Carnegie's steel interests, J. P. Morgan established the first billion-dollar corporation and controlled 60 percent of steel output. Yet this was only the most spectacular in a series of mergers that took place at the time. By 1904, one percent of American companies produced 38 percent of all manufactured goods.

Agreeing that the existence of mammoth trusts called for a measure of public control, reformers were divided over what course to pursue. Some wished to restore competition by dismantling the trusts, outlawing monopolies, and encouraging small enterprise. Others believed that big business was highly efficient. They saw nothing wrong with trusts so long as the government ensured that the benefits of efficiency were passed on to the public in the form of low prices, and that profits were kept within reasonable bounds. Despite sharp differences of opinion on this matter, Progressives agreed on the desirability of bringing private economic power under a larger measure of public control. Most reformers thought that government should regulate railroad rates, lower the protective tariff, and protect consumers from impure or unsafe products. What distinguished Progressives was less their unanimity on a solution to economic problems than their agreement that unruly economic forces required some form of discipline.

Those most directly affected by the growth of industry were factory workers themselves. The attempt to improve their conditions centered, in practice, on three issues: compensating workers injured on the job, regulating the hours and wages of working women, and restricting child labor (or what Progressives called "child slavery"). Reformers channeled most of their energies into activities at the state level. Not until relatively late in the Progressive era did they attempt to enact federal legislation, and then they met with only partial success. In 1908 a major obstacle to state regulation crumbled when the Supreme Court, reversing an earlier ruling, held in *Muller* v. *Oregon* that fixing a ten-hour day for women did not violate the Fourteenth Amendment's guarantee against deprivation of property without due process. Equally important, the Court based its decision on documentary evidence concerning the harmful social effects of long working hours, thereby accepting a key argument of reformers.

CITIES AND SLUMS

The United States became more highly urbanized as it became more highly industrialized. Progressivism represented as much a response to one as to the other. Between 1890 and 1920 the number of people living in cities increased by 300 percent, the number of rural dwellers by only 30 percent. Urban population grew by 11.8 million in the decade after 1900, so that by 1910 more than 44 million Americans—45.7 percent of the total population—lived in areas defined as urban by the Census Bureau. The largest cities grew at a spectacular rate: by 1910, 1.5 million people lived in Philadelphia, 2.1 million in Chicago, and 5 million in New York. Not only did big cities grow bigger, but there were also more of them. In 1860 there were nine cities with a population over 100,000; in 1910 there were 50. This urban expansion reflected a natural increase in population as well as the effect of both migration from rural areas and immigration from Europe.

Because cities grew so swiftly, contained such a diverse population, and furnished some with a chance to acquire fabulous wealth, they were plagued by mismanagement. Investigations into municipal government unearthed officials who took bribes or who, for the right price, granted lucrative gas and street-car franchises to private corporations. Many Americans assumed that for every corrupt official who was exposed, a dozen others continued to operate in darkness. Where city government was not corrupt it often seemed archaic, administratively unable to cope with the needs of modern urban life. Above all, there was what Jacob Riis termed "the blight of the tenement": dimly lit, badly ventilated slums, jammed with more people than it seemed they could possibly hold. To Progressives the slum was "the great destroyer of individuality" and as such posed a threat not only to the health of its residents but also to the health of the state. "Democracy was not predicated upon a country made up of tenement dwellers," said one reformer, "nor can it so survive."

Progressive solutions for these problems were as varied as the problems themselves. Some reformers concentrated on modernizing and de-politicizing urban government. They favored extending the merit system, streamlining municipal administration, freeing cities from state control, and transferring powers traditionally exercised by mayors to impartial city managers or commissions. Other Progressives, including Samuel "Golden Rule" Jones of Toledo and Tom Johnson of Cleveland, emphasized the benefits of municipal ownership of public utilities. Many reformers sought to tear down slums by enacting building codes that imposed structural and sanitary safeguards. New York City adopted such a tenement-

planning. One observer, with the confidence typical of progressivism,
predicted that Americans would not always be satisfied "to live in those
abominations of desolation which we call our great cities" but would insist
on a planned urban landscape, "every part of which shall be in perfect
harmony with every other part."

THE LIMITS OF REFORM

Some Progressives wanted to protect Americans not only from the perils
of urban and industrial life, but from their own impulses as well. Moral
uplift was an important element in reform, and perhaps nothing revealed
this relation more clearly than the link between progressivism and prohibition. Not everyone who supported prohibition was a Progressive in politics, but a large number of reformers favored a ban on alcohol and, what
is more significant, justified their stance on thoroughly Progressive
grounds. Starting with the premise that the saloon functioned as the
home of the political boss and a breeding-ground for corruption, reformers concluded that if they ended the sale of liquor they would take a
long step on the road to urban reform. Moreover, many believed that
liquor caused workers to squander hard-earned wages and neglect their
families. A Boston social worker thought that ignoring prohibition was
like "bailing water out of a tub with the tap turned on; letting the drink
custom and the liquor traffic run full blast while we limply stood around
and picked up the wreckage." In this view, prohibition seemed an indispensable weapon in the effort to stamp out poverty.

To achieve any of these goals—business regulation, urban reform,
social justice, moral uplift—required, in the view of Progressives, the extension of political democracy. Reformers favored the election of senators
directly by the people rather than by state legislatures, and in 1913, after
several states had made this change, it was incorporated into the Seventeenth Amendment. Similarly, Progressives endorsed the preferential primary, which gave voters a larger voice in the selection of candidates; most
states adopted some variant of this system. Progressives also favored
woman suffrage, in part because they expected women to vote in behalf
of social reform. Between 1909 and 1914 seven states extended the franchise to women. Finally, reformers supported the initiative and referendum. By 1915, twenty-one states had accepted such plans, under which
voters could introduce a measure into the state legislature and pass it at a
general election. A litmus-paper test for progressivism might well have involved attitudes toward popular rule.

The First World War would shake this confidence in the ability of the
people, once informed, to choose wisely and well. Many of the limitations
of progressivism would then become apparent. In retrospect, Progressive
optimism would seem hopelessly naïve. Assertions about serving the general interest would seem rationalizations for preserving narrower class in-

terests. Laws enforcing moral codes would seem self-righteous attempts to impose conformity. The Progressive effort to throw the weight of government on the side of the less fortunate would, to a later generation, appear inadequate or paternalistic. Even the struggle for political democracy might be construed as emphasizing form over content. But during the Progressive era only a handful of critics voiced such doubts. In the years before the war the Progressive faith burned brightly.

SIN AND SOCIETY: THE MUCKRAKERS

In 1907 the sociologist Edward A. Ross published *Sin and Society,* in which he asserted that modern society required a new definition of wrongdoing. The old personal categories of sin, such as theft or murder, failed to take account of new social crime. To Ross, the man who granted railroad rebates was no better than a pickpocket, the man who adulterated food no different from a murderer, the man who employed children on much the same level as a slaveholder. Yet although a new "criminaloid" type had emerged, a suitable moral code had not evolved along with it. "Our social organization has developed to a stage where the old righteousness is not enough," Ross concluded. "We need an annual supplement to the Decalogue." Ross's book never became a best-seller, but a group of journalists known as muckrakers popularized a similar message. By documenting the social costs of urbanization and industrialization, the muckrakers helped provide an audience for Progressive reform.

The development of this literature of exposure—Theodore Roosevelt first applied the label "muckraker" and meant it as a term of scorn—reflected technological changes in magazine publishing. In the decade of the 1890s new developments in printing and photoengraving made the publication of inexpensive magazines feasible. As the price dropped from 25 or 35 cents to 10 cents, the magazine-reading public tripled and advertising revenue soared. Not only could writers reach a wide audience, but that audience apparently wanted to read about what was wrong with America. Articles of a muckraking nature began to appear in the 1890s. As early as 1901 *McClure's* published "In the World of Graft," which exposed the alliance between police and criminals in various cities. The author defined certain underworld terms for his readers' benefit—"pinch" (arrest), "pull" (influence), "fix" (bribe)—and even thought it necessary to define "graft." A few years later, it is safe to say, Americans would not have needed a definition.

From 1903 to 1912 nearly 2000 articles in this genre appeared. Virtually no area of American life escaped the muckrakers' attention. They exposed corrupt city officials and United States senators who never cast a vote without consulting business interests. They zeroed in on fraudulent business deals. They described what it was like to live in a slum or work in a sweatshop. The muckrakers told of vermin scurrying around the floors of meat-packing plants: "The rats were nuisances; the packers would put poisoned bread out for them; they would die, and then rats, bread and meat would go into the hoppers together." They depicted workers horribly maimed when factories failed to install safety devices. They threw a harsh light on those who made a living from gambling, liquor, or, worst of all, the white-slave trade—"the recruiting and sale of young girls of the poorer classes by procurers." The muckrakers taught consumers about food adulteration, and about such innocent-sounding patent medicines as "Mrs. Winslow's Soothing Syrup," "Faith Whitcomb's Nerve Bitters," and "Lydia Pinkham's Vegetable Compound," many of which contained habit-forming drugs.

Behind these journalistic assaults rested characteristically Progressive assumptions. Muckrakers went after the inside scoop. They believed that the truth lay beneath the surface, that things were not what they seemed, that, as Richard Hofstadter has observed, "reality was the inside story. It was rough and sordid, hidden and neglected." In trying to get to the bottom of things, journalists often sought vicarious experiences. Jack London served time in a county penitentiary before he described the brutalizing effects of the prison system. Upton Sinclair worked in the Chicago stock-yards before he wrote *The Jungle*. John Spargo explained his attempt to do a child's work in a coal mine: "I tried to pick out the pieces of slate from the hurrying stream of coal, often missing them; my hands were bruised and cut in a few minutes; I was covered from head to foot with coal dust, and for many hours afterwards I was expectorating some of the small particles of anthracite I had swallowed." Muckrakers usually wrote fact, not fiction; they were concrete; they named names. They spent more time criticizing specific evils than proposing broad solutions.

THE REFORM IDEOLOGY

The muckrakers, by calling attention to social evils helped create a climate conducive to reform. Similarly, a generation of intellectuals, by developing a new approach to economics, law, and history, lowered another barrier to change. This barrier had taken the form of an ideology that rejected state aid for the victims of industrialization and urbanization. Conservatives, following what they believed to be Charles Darwin's path, reasoned that society, like nature, evolved through a struggle that assured the survival of the fittest. In economics conservatives stressed laissez-faire; in law they worshipped precedent; in history they dwelt on the sanctions for private property written into the Constitution. In each instance society was a captive—of natural law, of precedent, of the past. William Graham Sumner, perhaps the most prominent American Social Darwinist, summed all of this up in the title of an essay: "The Absurd Attempt to Make the World Over."

Unlike Sumner, a group of reform-minded sociologists and economists reasoned that the attempt to make the world over was anything but absurd. Rather, it seemed to them the height of common sense. Lester Frank Ward, for example, insisted on drawing a distinction between nature and society: human beings, unlike other species, could control their environment through intelligent planning. In *The Psychic Factors of Civilization* (1893) Ward tried to demonstrate that human progress often resulted from cooperation rather than from competition. A number of economists drew similar conclusions. Richard T. Ely of the University of Wisconsin denied that natural laws governed the workings of the economic system or that laissez-faire was an adequate guide to public policy. Thorstein Veblen, in *The Theory of the Leisure Class* (1899) and other works, pointed to the inefficient and unproductive consequences of the profit system as well as to the waste involved in conspicuous consumption and conspicuous leisure.

During the Progressive era the legal profession often acted as a stumbling-block to reform. "The right of property is of divine origin derived by title-deed from the universal creator of all things and attested by universal intuition," intoned a widely used legal text on which a generation of jurists was reared. But at the same time men like Oliver Wendell Holmes, Jr., who was appointed to the Supreme Court in 1903, Louis D. Brandeis, appointed in 1916, and Roscoe Pound of the Harvard Law School, began to transform the law from a bulwark of the status quo into a vehicle for change. Although they would not always be found on the same side of an issue, Holmes and Brandeis shared a similar conception of the relationship of law to society. Holmes believed that "the life of the law has not been logic: it has been experience." If the law was rooted in human history rather than in abstract principles, if men made laws to fulfill their needs, then the law must change as new needs arose. Pound, in "The Need for a Sociological Jurisprudence" (1907), held that law must conform to "the general moral sense" of the community. It could do so by placing a higher value on social justice than on individual property rights. Judges did not, and should not, hand down decisions in a vacuum.

Once legal scholars had reached this point it remained only for Progressives to interpret the Constitution itself as the product of particular social interests. A number of historians did so, but none captured more attention than Charles Beard in *An Economic Interpretation of the Constitution* (1913). Beard shared the Progressive concern with unmasking the "real" forces in history. He attempted to demonstrate that the upper classes, who had not been making out well under the Articles of Confederation, had organized the movement for adoption of the Constitution; that the document lacked widespread popular support; and that "the Constitution was essentially an economic document based upon the concept that the fundamental private rights of property are anterior to government and morally beyond the reach of popular majorities." Precisely the same issue was debated in the Progressive era and, not surprisingly, both conservatives and reformers regarded the book as a tract for the times. William Howard Taft wondered whether Beard would have been happier had the Constitution been drafted by "out-at-the-elbows demagogues, and cranks who never had any money." Conversely, a reformer believed that once

Americans realized that the Constitution was "a human document" they would not allow it to stand in the way of necessary change.

Muckrakers and intellectuals played the complementary roles of popularizing and rationalizing reform. Both showed less interest in how society was supposed to function than in how it really did. Both sometimes regarded ideology as nothing more than a cloak for economic interest. When Richard T. Ely said that imaginary natural laws of economics were "used as a tool in the hands of the greedy" he sounded rather like a muckraker dissecting the behavior of unscrupulous businessmen. Journalists and scholars assumed that just as a bad environment made bad citizens, so a good environment could work wonders, for "to upbuild human character in men you must establish for them the right social relations." While they ranged over the political spectrum—from the socialist Upton Sinclair to the rather conservative Oliver Wendell Holmes—their work resulted in a diagnosis of social problems and a theory of state action that provided the underpinning for progressivism.

NATIVISM VS. THE MELTING POT

In their search for social harmony, reformers discovered no greater source of dissonance than the twin issues of ethnicity and race. Progressivism coincided with a massive wave of immigration. In the 25 years before World War I, 18 million immigrants came to the United States, nearly four-fifths of them from Italy, Russia, Poland, Greece, and other countries in Southern and Eastern Europe. By 1917 one of every three Americans was an immigrant or the child of one. With the nation becoming more urban and industrial, these immigrants, to a greater extent than those who had arrived earlier, settled in big cities and took jobs in manufacturing. Some left Europe to escape political or religious persecution, some to avoid military service, but most were drawn by the magnet of economic opportunity. Industrialists who needed a supply of cheap labor often encouraged migration. Immigrants themselves wrote home urging their friends to join them. One Polish immigrant reported, "Let nobody listen to anybody but only to his relatives whom he has here, in this golden America."

Many Americans, Progressives among them, believed that the new immigrants were racially inferior and therefore genetically incapable of becoming good citizens. In 1910 this view drew support from the report of a commission headed by Senator William T. Dillingham. The commission, which had spent three years collecting data and expert testimony, concluded that ethnicity provided a reliable guide to one's capacity for Americanization. People from Southern and Eastern Europe, the commission tried to prove, did not assimilate as well as older immigrant groups, but rather committed more crimes and had a higher incidence of alcoholism and disease. A few Progressives, such as Edward A. Ross, rested

Immigrants aboard the S.S. Westernland.

their nativism squarely on racial grounds. Ross saw new immigrants as "beaten members of beaten breeds" with "sugar loaf heads, moon faces, and goose-bill noses," who "lack the ancestral foundations of American character." He described them in this way: "In every face there was something wrong—lips thick, mouth coarse, upper lip too long, cheek bones too high, chin poorly formed, the bridge of the nose hollowed, the base of the nose tilted, or else the whole face prognathous."

Most Progressives who wished to restrict immigration, however, wanted to do so for reasons of reform rather than of race. A number of reformers believed that immigration injured American workers. Not only did the immigrants depress wages by working for next to nothing, but they retarded the growth of trade unions. Employers understood all too well that a labor force in constant flux, composed of men and women of different nationalities speaking different languages, could not very easily be organized. Progressives often located the source of poverty in the boatloads of immigrants who, with few skills and little prospect of employment, became public charges. Immigrants, said Robert Hunter in *Poverty*

(1904), placed an intolerable strain on existing charities and social services. Finally, reformers realized that the immigrants provided the main prop for boss rule in the cities and believed that without immigrant votes political machines would die a natural death.

In truth, the reformers' ideal of good government contrasted sharply with that of the city boss. Reformers favored economy in public expenditures; bosses spent money hand over fist, building court houses and schools, paving streets, digging subways and in the process creating jobs for their constituents. Reformers believed in extension of the merit system; bosses made nepotism a fine art. Progressives emphasized the impartial administration of justice; machines, which often served as informal mediators between the courts and the immigrant, adopted the adage that it was "more important to know the judge than to know the law." Reformers stressed honesty; bosses took ballot-box stuffing for granted. The Progressive—whom one boss termed "the sweet-smelling geranium of reform"—thought of himself as applying the golden rule to politics, whereas boss Michael James Curley of Boston reputedly advised his followers, "Do others before they do you."

Although most Progressives appear to have viewed immigrants as their racial inferiors or as impediments to reform, there were some who took a considerably more tolerant position. Either they expressed confidence in America's capacity to absorb the immigrant, or they invoked the concept of a vast melting pot in which all peoples contributed something to a novel American type. In addition, the doctrine of cultural pluralism—that each immigrant group should preserve its own heritage—gained a number of converts. Norman Hapgood, Randolph Bourne, and Horace Kallen, among others, envisioned the United States as a world federation in miniature. "Our dream of the United States ought not to be a dream of monotony," said Hapgood. "We ought not to think of it as a place where all people are alike." Asserting that diversity enriched American culture, Kallen held that each immigrant group could preserve its own language, religion, and culture yet share equally in American life. He favored "a democracy of nationalities, cooperating voluntarily and autonomously . . . an orchestration of mankind."

The settlement-house movement provided the chief means of aiding urban immigrants. In 1889 Jane Addams founded Hull House in Chicago. By 1900, 100 settlements existed; by 1905, 200; by 1910, 400. The settlement house, once it overcame community suspicion, became the center of civic and social life in the neighborhood. Classes in arts and crafts, playgrounds for children of working mothers, meeting places for labor unions, instruction in homemaking, child care, and English—all could be found at settlement houses. Settlement workers—mostly young, college educated, and middle class—investigated housing and working conditions and fought for the enactment of reform legislation. Jane Addams hoped that by inculcating respect for Old World culture she could effect a reconciliation between immigrants who clung to tradition and their children who often rejected the past in their haste to adopt

American ways. The settlements were archetypically Progressive in their middle-class origins and in their emphasis on urban problems, yet they were unusual in their close involvement with the life of the working poor and their respect for immigrant culture.

RACISM AND REFORM

Black Americans occupied a more precarious political and economic position than did immigrants, yet attracted even less support from Progressives. Reformers belonged to a generation of white Americans that, for the most part, believed that blacks were by nature lazy, improvident, and incapable of mental discipline. Whatever difficulties the Negro faced, therefore, derived from hereditary shortcomings. Few Progressives saw any conflict between racial discrimination and social reform. In the South, woman suffragists promised that they would use the vote to maintain white supremacy. In the North, black women sometimes marched in a separate column at the rear of suffrage parades. Settlement houses often set aside segregated facilities, if they provided them at all, for blacks. One settlement worker described the Negroes in Boston as "low and coarse, revealing much more of the animal qualities than the spiritual." Most Progressives would surely have agreed with Theodore Roosevelt who, although he opposed the disfranchisement of Negroes, held that "as a race and in the mass they are altogether inferior to the whites."

During the Progressive era most Southern blacks lost the right to vote. In the 1890s three states disfranchised the Negro. After the Supreme Court ruled in favor of the literacy test in *Williams* v. *Mississippi* (1898), ten Southern states deprived blacks of the franchise. Some set literacy and property qualifications for voting, but added "understanding" and "grandfather" clauses that in effect exempted whites. Propertyless persons and illiterates could vote if they demonstrated an understanding of the Constitution or if they were the lineal descendants of someone who had voted in 1867. Most Southern states enacted poll taxes, which, although not very high, deterred poor blacks and whites from voting. Poll taxes had to be paid well in advance (usually during the spring when farmers had little spare cash) and were cumulative, so each additional year that a voter fell into arrears it became more difficult to catch up. Finally, the South adopted the white primary. Given the Democratic control of Southern politics, exclusion from the primaries amounted to virtual exclusion from the political process. These measures had an awesome effect. From 1896 to 1904 the number of black voters in Alabama plunged from 180,000 to 3000; the number in Louisiana from 130,000 to 5000. Southern Progressives defended these measures in part on reform grounds: removing Negro voters, they said, would end political corruption and produce good government. Indeed, one way to stop the stealing of ballots, historian C. Vann Woodward has remarked, was to stop people from casting them.

Nothing better illustrated the connection between racism and reform

W. E. B. DuBois.

than the career of James K. Vardaman as Governor of Mississippi (1903–07). Much of Vardaman's program was firmly in the Progressive tradition. He ended the system of convict leasing under which planters brutally exploited prison labor; he increased spending for education and brought about more effective regulation of railroads, banks, and insurance companies; he sought without success to enact child labor legislation. At the same time, however, Vardaman was a vicious race-baiter. He called for the repeal of the Fourteenth and Fifteenth Amendments, cut expenditures for black schools, and declared that the Negro was "a lazy, lying, lustful animal which no conceivable amount of training can transform into a tolerable citizen." He even offered a thinly veiled excuse for lynch law: "We would be justified in slaughtering every Ethiop on the earth to preserve unsullied the honor of one Caucasian home."

If progressivism could serve as the basis for white supremacy, in the hands of W. E. B. DuBois and other black leaders it provided a model for new strategies of protest. DuBois, who had studied at Berlin and received a doctorate from Harvard, taught at Atlanta University from 1897 to 1910. He served as a spokesman for Negro intellectuals who rejected Booker T. Washington's program of racial accommodation. DuBois also exhibited a characteristically Progressive faith in the redemptive powers of reason. He assumed that by presenting empirical data on the Negro's condition he could help persuade white Americans to eliminate racial injustice. In *The Philadelphia Negro* (1899) and other books, DuBois offered a microscopic examination of the conditions under which blacks lived in the hope that his readers would recognize the need to end discrimination. For DuBois, as for other Progressive intellectuals, research was the first step on the road to reform.

But it was no more than a first step. As early as 1905 DuBois attempted to found an organization devoted to the defense of civil rights. Five years later he succeeded in creating the National Association for the Advancement of Colored People, with the goals of abolishing segregation, restoring voting rights to blacks, achieving equal educational facilities, and enforcing the Fourteenth and Fifteenth Amendments. The NAACP had the support of such white reformers as Oswald Garrison Villard, Jane Addams, Lincoln Steffens, John Dewey, and Moorfield Storey, who became its first president. In 1915 the Association filed an *amicus curiae* brief in a Supreme Court test of Oklahoma's "grandfather" clause, which the Court found unconstitutional. With its emphasis on political and legal rights, its belief in educating the public, and its assumption that segregation hindered the free development of the individual, the NAACP accurately reflected the Progressive movement, of which it was part. Perhaps it did so in another way as well: during its first seven years, DuBois was the only black to serve in a policymaking position.

Boxing: Black Champions and White Hopes

Boxing in its modern form originated in England in the nineteenth century. Efforts were made to civilize the sport ("All attempts to inflict injury by gouging or tearing the flesh with the fingers or nails, and biting shall be deemed foul") that culminated in 1867 when John Sholto Douglas, the Marquis of Queensberry, proposed new rules. They eliminated "wrestling or hugging," provided for three-minute rounds (rather than rounds lasting until a knockdown), established a 60-second rest period between rounds, substituted padded gloves for bare fists, barred hitting a man who was down, and warned: "A man hanging on the ropes in a helpless state, with his toes off the ground, shall be considered down." For years, boxing in America was dominated by Irish immigrants, the most famous of whom was John L. Sullivan. But the era

Johnson and Jeffries at Reno, 1910.

48

of Irish supremacy was interrupted in 1908 when Jack Johnson, a black fighter, won the title.

During the seven years he held the championship, Johnson elicited a response from white America that reflected broader currents of racial tension in the Progressive era. Johnson flouted social conventions, most importantly the injunction against interracial sex. He lived openly with white mistresses and three of his four wives were white. One Negro newspaper speculated that his affairs had led directly to the introduction of bills banning interracial marriage in several state legislatures. In any event, a search rapidly began for a "white hope" who might defeat Johnson. It soon narrowed to Jim Jeffries who had retired unbeaten in 1905. Socialist Jack London joined the cry: "Jeffries must emerge from his alfalfa farm and remove the golden smile from Johnson's face. Jeff, it's up to

you!" The fight was scheduled for July 1912. Jeffries's supporters were confident, believing him superior "in both breeding and education." But Johnson won easily and collected $120,000. An outcry then arose against showing films of the fight, for many believed that youth would be "tainted, corrupted, and brutalized by such scenes." Reformers claimed a victory when Congress made it a federal offense to transport motion pictures of prize fights across state lines.

It was another act of Congress, however, that proved Johnson's undoing. The Mann Act (1910) was aimed at the "white slave trade," that is, at those who transported girls across state lines for purposes of prostitution. Given the existing prejudice, Johnson was a natural target. "In Chicago," thundered a Southern congressman, "white girls are made the slaves of an African brute." Johnson was unfairly convicted of violating the law and in 1913, rather than

Joe Louis and trainer Jack Blackburn in 1936.

serve a jail sentence, he fled to Canada and then to Europe. In 1915 he lost the title to Jess Willard in a match fought in Havana, Cuba. Johnson later claimed he threw the fight in a vain effort to appease his enemies in the United States. In July 1920 Johnson returned home, surrendered, and was sentenced to a year in the penitentiary. After his release he fought exhibition matches, worked in nightclubs, and perfected a vaudeville routine. He died in an automobile crash in 1946.

The next black heavyweight champion, Joe Louis, aroused no such bitter antagonism. Louis held the title from 1937 until his retirement in 1949, and his victories became occasions for celebration in black communities. "Everywhere Negroes marched through the streets, slapping backs, shaking hands, and congratulating each other." Novelist Richard Wright believed that Louis tapped the deepest springs of rebellion in the black community: "Joe was the concentrated essence of black triumph over white." Yet Louis was at the same time exceedingly popular among whites. He violated no racial taboos and he epitomized good sportsmanship in the ring. In 1938 his crushing first-round defeat of the German fighter, Max Schmeling, who supposedly believed in Aryan supremacy, was hailed as a vindication of democracy. When the United States entered World War II Louis enlisted and was frequently cited as a model of patriotism.

Attitudes toward military service affected the career of another black

50 fighter in a much different way. In 1964 Cassius Clay won the heavyweight championship. He then announced his conversion to the religion of Islam and changed his name to Muhammad Ali. His commitment to black nationalism provoked great hatred among those who favored integration. Former champion Floyd Patterson challenged Ali ("just so I can bring the championship back to America"), thereby becoming what one critic termed "the first black 'white hope' in boxing history." In 1967 Ali refused induction into the army on the grounds of religious objection. He told newsmen,

"I ain't got no quarrel with them Viet Cong." Indicted for draft evasion, Ali was stripped of his title and denied a chance to fight until March 1971 when he lost a decision to Joe Frazier. Ali later regained his title, but his most significant victory came in June 1971 when the Supreme Court found that his religious convictions entitled him to a draft exemption.

In Ali's case, as in that of Jack Johnson and Joe Louis, the heavyweight championship had itself become an arena for contending social issues.

Muhammad Ali at Black Muslim Convention, Chicago, 1966.

THEODORE ROOSEVELT

Theodore Roosevelt's standing with historians has undergone mercurial changes. For a decade after his death in 1919 biographers presented his life as an inspiring example of moral rectitude. One author entitled his concluding chapters: "Roosevelt—Not Impulsive," "Roosevelt—Broad-Minded," "Roosevelt—Wonderful Brain." A harsher appraisal emerged in the 1930s and 1940s. Historians began to notice that, beneath all the grand rhetoric, Roosevelt at bottom was a conservative, an opportunist, a militarist, someone who had never grown up. The index of Henry Pringle's Pulitzer Prize-winning biography (1931) contained six entries under the heading "adolescence in manhood." Since the 1950s Roosevelt's reputation has been somewhat refurbished. Conceding all the unlovely traits, scholars have nevertheless concluded that Roosevelt developed presidential powers, acted as "a skillful broker of the possible," and embodied his generation's search for "a pragmatic sanction that would validate the activism of a modern state."

No disagreement exists over the broad outline of Roosevelt's career. Born in New York of a well-to-do family in 1858, Roosevelt was graduated from Harvard in 1880 and then elected a Republican state assemblyman. A profound personal tragedy struck in 1884 when his first wife died of Bright's disease shortly after giving birth to a child. Roosevelt sought refuge for a time in the Dakota Badlands but returned to New York and began his ascent up the political ladder. In 1889 he became a member of the Civil Service Commission, in 1895 President of the New York City Police Board, and in 1897 Assistant Secretary of the Navy. In 1898, after his service with the Rough Riders in Cuba, he was elected Governor of New York. Two years later the Republican leaders decided to exile Roosevelt to the vice-presidency. Boss Thomas C. Platt said, "Roosevelt might as well stand under Niagara Falls and try to spit water back as to stop his nomination." Roosevelt complained that he would "a great deal rather be anything, say professor of history, than Vice-President," but, like the good party man he was, he went along. In September 1901, with the assassination of William McKinley, Theodore Roosevelt stepped into the presidency.

Roosevelt shared a good deal in common with the conservatives of his day. He believed in the essential goodness of American institutions and he hated those who wanted to tear down what had taken so long to construct. He always considered the muckrakers overly concerned with the seamy side of life, and throughout his career he denounced Populists, trade unionists, and socialists who threatened the existing order of things. In the 1890s he had noted that "the sentiment now animating a large proportion of our people can only be suppressed as the Commune in Paris was suppressed, by taking ten or a dozen of their leaders out, standing . . . them against a wall, and shooting them dead." The realities of political life in 1901 nourished his conservative instincts. In the White House only by accident, Roosevelt faced a Republican party and a Congress dominated by conservatives. Mark Hanna, a powerful party leader and Senator from Ohio, warned the new President to "go slow."

What set Roosevelt apart from the stand-patters and validated his Progressive credentials was his belief in orderly change. Reform, by perfecting the system, would help to preserve it. "The only true conservative," Roosevelt remarked, "is the man who resolutely sets his face toward the future." Not only did he welcome moderate change, but Roosevelt also thought that the national interest transcended the claims of any particular class, and he assumed that the President had an obligation to act as spokesman for that interest. These beliefs helped shape the response of his administration in four important areas: business, labor, reform legislation, and conservation.

THE SQUARE DEAL

Despite his reputation, Roosevelt never believed in trust-busting. Combination seemed to him a natural process, but one that required federal supervision to protect consumers. Eventually Roosevelt came to a tacit understanding with some of the biggest businessmen: he would not enforce the antitrust law if they would open their books for inspection and keep their dealings aboveboard. But in some cases Roosevelt considered government intervention necessary. During his presidency the Justice Department instituted 44 antitrust suits, the most famous of which involved the Northern Securities Company. J. P. Morgan had created this $400,000,000 holding company through a merger of important northern railroad lines. In 1902 the Justice Department invoked the Sherman Antitrust Act, claiming that the Morgan firm unfairly restrained trade, and two years later the Supreme Court narrowly upheld the government. (Of one dissenter Roosevelt said, "I could carve out of a banana a judge with more backbone than that.") The significance of Roosevelt's move lay less in its impact on the railroad—the ruling merely banned one particular holding company—than in its clear assertion of his willingness to act in behalf of the public interest.

Roosevelt's action in the anthracite coal strike showed him serving as mediator between rival power blocs. In 1902, 50,000 Pennsylvania miners struck for higher wages, an eight-hour day, and union recognition. Management refused point-blank to negotiate. By October, when the fuel shortage threatened homes, hospitals, and schools, Roosevelt called both sides to the White House. Even then the owners refused to talk to the union leaders, whom they considered "outlaws" responsible for "anarchy" in the coal fields. Furious at what he termed their "arrogant stupidity," Roosevelt, without any clear constitutional authority, declared that he would send 10,000 soldiers to the mines, not to break the strike, but to dispossess the operators. If this was a bluff, the owners did not call it. They quickly agreed to the creation of an arbitration commission which, in March 1903, proposed a 10 percent increase in wages (and the price of coal) and establishment of an eight- or nine-hour day, but did not recommend union recognition. Roosevelt did not consider himself a champion of labor—on other occasions he used troops against strikers in Colorado,

Arizona, and Nevada—but a steward of the national interest. In his successful campaign against the Democrat Alton B. Parker in 1904, TR said that his behavior in the coal strike provided all sides with a "square deal."

The Square Deal reached a culmination in Roosevelt's second term with the enactment of three major pieces of legislation. The Pure Food and Drug Act of 1905 made it a crime to sell adulterated foods or medicines and provided for correct labeling of ingredients. The Meat Inspection Act of 1906 led to more effective supervision of slaughterhouses, provided for the dating of canned meat, and prohibited the use of dangerous chemicals as preservatives. The Hepburn Act of 1906 authorized the Interstate Commerce Commission to set aside railroad rates on the complaint of a shipper and to establish lower rates. The courts would then pass on the "reasonableness" of commission rulings. This legislation, much of which had attracted public backing as a result of muckraking exposures, broke new ground in regulating business practices.

Yet some businessmen strongly supported these measures. In the case of meat inspection, for example, large packers believed that government supervision would drive out smaller competitors who could not meet the costs of inspection, and would also open the European market to the export of American meat by vouching for its good quality. But those who agreed on the need for regulation could not always agree on the kind of regulation needed. Reformers favored broad supervision and substantial administrative discretion in enforcement. Businessmen favored a narrower kind of regulation and judicial review of administrative rulings. Most of the legislation passed under TR fell somewhere between the two positions, and indeed resulted from his willingness to compromise.

Perhaps no cause was more closely linked to Roosevelt's name than that of conservation. Unlike aesthetic conservationists who wished to save the forests from commercial exploitation, Roosevelt preferred a utilitarian approach to natural-resource development. Roosevelt favored the commercial use of such resources in a controlled and scientific manner. He popularized conservation through several White House conferences and broadened its definition to include coal fields, mineral lands, and oil reserves as well as forests. And he supported the Newlands Reclamation Act (1902), which enabled the proceeds from the sale of western lands to be used for federal irrigation projects. Under Frederick H. Newell, the Bureau of Reclamation undertook work on 25 major projects within a few years. Roosevelt created the Forest Service in the Department of Agriculture and made Gifford Pinchot its chief. He appointed an Inland Waterways Commission, which in 1908 submitted a plan for multipurpose river development. Through the use of executive authority, TR created five new national parks, established 51 wildlife refuges, restricted the uncontrolled development of coal fields and water power sites, and added 43 million acres to the national forests.

TR and Gifford Pinchot on the river steamer *Mississippi,* 1907.

THE NEW NATIONALISM

By the end of his second term Roosevelt did not stand just where he had at the start of his first. Historians have pointed out that Roosevelt, in his last two years in office, called for increased federal controls, taxes on income and inheritances, stricter regulation of railroad rates, extension of the eight-hour day and workmen's compensation, and limitations on the use of injunctions in labor disputes. Roosevelt spoke indignantly about "certain malefactors of great wealth" and condemned the conservatism of the courts. This posture may have reflected Roosevelt's concern over the strength shown at the polls by socialists, his resentment at the effort of businessmen to attribute the economic slump of 1907 to his policies, or his willingness to speak out more boldly since he did not expect to seek renomination. Whatever the reason, Roosevelt had gone far toward embracing the doctrine that came to be known as the New Nationalism.

That doctrine received its fullest statement in Herbert Croly's *The Promise of American Life* (1909). A prominent Progressive who later helped

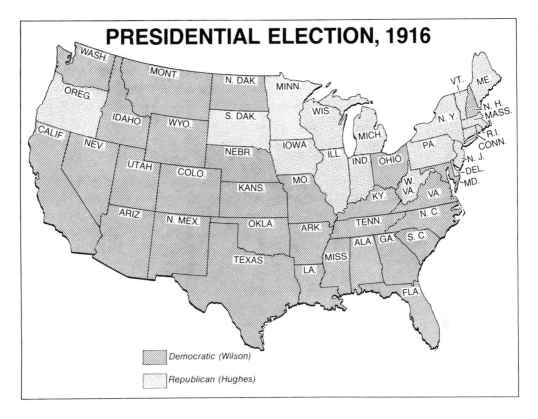

PRESIDENTIAL ELECTION, 1916

Democratic (Wilson)

Republican (Hughes)

found the *New Republic,* Croly believed that a "morally and socially desirable distribution of wealth" must replace the "indiscriminate individual scramble for wealth." A Jeffersonian fear of positive government, Croly said, had kept American reformers in a strait jacket. To achieve order and rationality they must reject laissez-faire in favor of positive action, competition in favor of concentration, and equal rights in favor of aid to the underprivileged. Croly, who regarded labor as another selfish interest group and opposed the common ownership of property, was not a socialist. But he went as far toward accepting the welfare state as any Progressive when he said: "Every popular government should have, after deliberation, the power of taking any action which, in the opinion of a decisive majority of the people is demanded by the public welfare."

TAFT AND THE INSURGENTS

Theodore Roosevelt handpicked William Howard Taft as his successor, but two men could hardly have been temperamentally more unalike. Roosevelt was an athlete; Taft was a ponderous man who in 1904 weighed 326 pounds. Roosevelt was never happier than when stalking a wild animal in the jungle; Taft never wanted to kill anything. Roosevelt had a flair for the dramatic; Taft did nothing to cultivate his public image.

Roosevelt loved the rough-and-tumble of politics; Taft hated it. Unlike his predecessor, Taft had made his career in the law and in public administration. He had served as a superior court judge in Ohio, United States Solicitor-General, federal circuit court judge, Governor-General of the Philippines, and Secretary of War. Roosevelt inspired strong feelings, but Taft had a natural instinct for accommodation. One Republican noted that "the trouble with Taft is that if he were Pope he would think it necessary to appoint a few Protestant Cardinals."

As President, Taft helped win important victories for progressivism. He proved to be a vigorous trust-buster. His Attorney General brought 22 civil suits, and the courts returned 45 criminal indictments, for violations of the Sherman Act. Taft continued Roosevelt's conservation program by withdrawing additional forest lands and oil reserves. Taft favored the Mann-Elkins Act (1910) which placed telephone and telegraph companies under the jurisdiction of the ICC and authorized the commission to examine railroad rates on its own initiative. He reformed government administration by creating the Department of Labor, establishing a Children's Bureau, and introducing the eight-hour day for federal employees. Two constitutional amendments ratified in 1913—the Sixteenth authorizing an income tax and the Seventeenth providing for direct election of senators—obtained congressional approval during Taft's years in office.

Despite this record, however, Taft gradually lost the confidence of Progressives. Even at the start of his administration, Republicans were divided between reformers like Senator Robert M. La Follette of Wisconsin and conservatives like Senator Nelson Aldrich of Rhode Island, men who, although nominally members of the same party, held virtually opposite political and economic views. Between 1909 and 1912 the division became irreconcilable and the party ultimately split in two. Taft's position on three major issues—legislative reform, trade, and conservation—helped that process along. In each case Taft sympathized with the Progressive position but his political technique, or lack of one, brought him inexorably into the conservative camp.

For many years the Speaker of the House of Representatives had dominated that body. He served as Chairman of the Rules Committee, made all committee assignments, and granted or withheld recognition during debate. Progressive Republicans disliked this arrangement because they considered the power itself inordinate and believed that the Republican Speaker, "Uncle Joe" Cannon of Illinois (whose favorite saying was "this country is a hell of a success"), used his position to subvert reform. Taft was no admirer of Cannon's either, but conservatives threatened to block other legislation if he sided with the insurgents. Taft backed away from the fight and in 1909, when the challenge to Cannon failed, Progressives attributed their defeat in part to Taft's desertion. The revolt later succeeded: in 1910 the Rules Committee was enlarged and the Speaker removed from it, and in 1911 the Speaker lost the right to make committee assignments. But Taft took none of the credit; instead, insurgents regarded him as an ally of the old guard.

Controversies over the tariff drove yet another wedge between Taft and the reformers, both of whom, ironically, favored downward revision. Their differences first emerged over the Payne-Aldrich Tariff of 1909. The bill, to which protectionist Nelson Aldrich had attached 847 amendments in the Senate, effected a modest reduction in the tariff. But it did not go as far as some Progressives would have liked, and they strongly resented Taft's claiming credit for the measure and heralding it as a major reform. Again, in 1911 Taft urged Congress to adopt a reciprocal trade agreement with Canada which would remove tariffs between the two nations. Many midwestern Progressives, who came from dairy and lumber states, feared competition from Canadian imports and opposed this particular form of tariff revision. It passed over their objections but Canada refused to cooperate and the plan died. Republican insurgents and Democrats then enacted three low tariff bills. Taft, claiming that they were politically motivated attempts to embarrass him, vetoed the measures.

A bitter dispute over the activities of Secretary of the Interior Richard Ballinger completed the rupture between Taft and the insurgents. In the summer of 1909 Louis Glavis, an investigator for the Interior Department, informed Gifford Pinchot that Ballinger had, shortly before taking office, apparently profited from aiding a Seattle group in its effort to deliver rich Alaskan coal fields to a large business syndicate. Pinchot brought the accusation to Taft who, after listening to both sides and asking Attorney General George W. Wickersham to investigate, exonerated Ballinger and fired Glavis. Pinchot leaked his side of the story to the press and in January 1910 publicly condemned Ballinger. Taft then dismissed Pinchot, the idol of conservationists, from his post as chief of the Forest Service. From January to June 1910 a joint congressional committee conducted an investigation. It found no proof that Ballinger was corrupt, but it turned up a damaging fact: Taft had asked Wickersham to predate his report so it would appear that the decision to fire Glavis resulted from it rather than from a preliminary verbal report. Those who lived through the Ballinger-Pinchot controversy never forgot it. An entire generation of reformers convinced itself that Ballinger and Taft had betrayed the conservation movement.

Dissatisfaction with Taft led Pinchot, La Follette, Governor Hiram Johnson of California, and others to create the National Progressive Republican League in January 1911. Designed to push La Follette's candidacy within the Republican party, the League ended by endorsing Theodore Roosevelt's candidacy on a third-party ticket. At first it seemed doubtful that Roosevelt would make the race. He had returned from a hunting expedition to Africa in June 1910 with no thought of seeking renomination and with some hope that Taft could heal the wounds in the Republican party. But in 1911, as his disenchantment with the President grew, Roosevelt changed his mind. Taft's attempt to negotiate arbitration treaties as a means of resolving international disputes peacefully, and his remark that the War of 1812, the Mexican War, and the Spanish-

American War "might have been settled without a fight and ought to have been," offended Roosevelt. Taft's decision to bring an antitrust suit against U.S. Steel for its acquisition of the Tennessee Coal and Iron Company in 1907, a merger to which TR had tacitly assented, infuriated the former President.

By the time the Republican convention met in June 1912 the two men, once good political friends, had become bitter personal enemies. If Roosevelt, who had done well in the primaries, was the people's choice, Taft was the convention's. His control of the Republican National Committee and of the party machinery in the South assured Taft's renomination on the first ballot. Reformers walked out in disgust, and in August Roosevelt agreed to run as the candidate of a new Progressive party. His assertion that "every man holds his property subject to the general right of the community to regulate its use to whatever degree the public welfare may require it" summarized the party's platform. His cry to the convention—"We stand at Armageddon and we battle for the Lord"—captured the movement's religious fervor.

WOODROW WILSON

Republican disunity, however, permitted the Democrats to capture the White House for the first time in 20 years. Their candidate, Thomas Woodrow Wilson, was born in Virginia in 1856, the son of a Presbyterian minister. After being graduated from Princeton (1879), Wilson studied law at the University of Virginia but gave up his practice for graduate work in political science at the Johns Hopkins University. His doctoral dissertation, *Congressional Government,* appeared in 1885. In it Wilson held that American politics, characterized by a powerful but irresponsible Congress and a weak President, was inferior to the Cabinet system that linked the interests of the executive and legislative branches. He then taught at Bryn Mawr, Wesleyan, and finally at Princeton, which named him its president in 1902. There, Wilson encouraged the introduction of small seminars and tried unsuccessfully to abolish the exclusive "eating clubs," which he regarded as anti-intellectual. In 1910 the New Jersey Democratic leaders, considering Wilson a safe but attractive figure, invited him to run for the governorship. He did, and to the bosses' dismay, presided over a reform administration, enacting a direct primaries law, a corrupt practices act, and workmen's compensation. In 1912 Wilson won the Democratic presidential nomination on the forty-sixth ballot. That November, with Roosevelt and Taft dividing the normal Republican vote, Wilson, although he received only 41.8 percent of the popular vote, carried 40 states and won an overwhelming electoral victory.

His Calvinist training and Southern upbringing helped mold Wilson's political outlook. A devoutly religious man, Wilson believed that God had given the universe a moral structure and had placed men on earth to do His work. Once he cast an issue in moral terms or defined a conflict as one between good and evil, Wilson would no more think of compromising than he would of endorsing only five of the Commandments. One politician noted that Wilson "said something to me, and I didn't know whether God or him was talking." Some thought that Wilson also had trouble telling the difference. His boyhood in the South influenced the President as much as his religious upbringing. Wilson, whose father had owned slaves and served as a chaplain in the Confederate Army, remarked, "The only place in the country, the only place in the world, where nothing has to be explained to me is the South." He later demonstrated his loyalties to section and party by rigidly segregating Negro and white officeholders in government agencies, and by removing Southern blacks from federal jobs. Like most white Americans, Wilson saw no contradiction between his religious convictions and his racial practices.

In 1912 Wilson campaigned on the slogan of the "New Freedom," which he presented as an alternative to Roosevelt's New Nationalism. The New Freedom, which Wilson worked out in discussions with the prominent Boston attorney Louis D. Brandeis, held that government should intervene in the economy to the extent necessary to restore competition. Unlike Roosevelt, who now viewed antitrust actions as a throwback to the past, Wilson asserted that trusts were inefficient, the product of financial manipulation, and the cause of artificially inflated prices. He would not go on a rampage against trusts, but believed that by stripping them of special privileges they would fall of their own weight. Unlike Roosevelt, who favored child-labor legislation and a minimum wage for women, Wilson denounced paternalism. He told a group of workers: "The old adage that God takes care of those who take care of themselves is not gone out of date. No federal legislation can change that thing. The minute you are taken care of by the government you are wards, not independent men." Whereas Roosevelt, in advocating welfare measures, implied that the condition of the poor did not necessarily reflect a failure on their part, Wilson placed the issue squarely on moral grounds: under the rules of free competition an individual's character—as measured by thrift, hard work, ingenuity—would determine the individual's reward.

ENACTING THE NEW FREEDOM

Once elected, Wilson met with remarkable success in enacting his program. This resulted from a receptive legislative climate as well as from his inventive use of presidential authority. In 1913 the Democrats controlled both houses of Congress. With Wilson only the second Democrat to occupy the White House since the Civil War, the party was determined to demonstrate its capacity for national leadership. Moreover, presidents have ususally received wide support from newly elected congressmen, and of the 290 House Democrats, no fewer than 114 were first-termers. Wilson used every device at his disposal to corral supporters. He conferred regularly with legislative leaders, enforced party discipline through patronage, stressed loyalty to caucus decisions and, when he thought it necessary, appealed directly to the people. All of this reflected Wilson's admiration for English government and his belief that the President "must be prime minister, as much concerned with the guidance of legislation as with the just and orderly execution of law." Indeed, it was during Wilson's tenure that, for the first time since Jefferson abandoned the practice, a President delivered his messages to Congress in person.

Within a year and a half of Wilson's inauguration, Congress placed the New Freedom on the statute books. The Underwood Tariff (1913) substantially reduced import duties. During the debate Wilson had publicly denounced the lobbyists who were swarming into Washington to look after their clients' interests. He aroused such a furor that, before voting, senators felt obliged to reveal how the tariff affected their own financial holdings. The act also included the first income tax passed under the Sixteenth Amendment. The tax rose from 1 percent on personal and corporate income over $4000 to 4 percent on incomes over $100,000. The Federal Reserve Act (1913), which reformed the banking and currency system, resulted in part from a congressional inquiry into the "money trust." The investigation revealed that Morgan and Rockefeller interests held a tight grip on credit institutions. The act provided for a more flexible currency and established a measure of public control over private bankers. It created twelve Federal Reserve Banks that, although privately controlled, also were responsible to a Federal Reserve Board. Finally, the Clayton Anti-Trust Act (1914) bolstered the attack on monopoly by prohibiting interlocking directorships and other devices that lessened competition. The Clayton Act made a gesture toward exempting labor unions, but the wording remained ambiguous enough so that the Supreme Court could later rule certain kinds of strikes and boycotts illegal.

With the passage of this legislation Wilson considered his work largely done. Ten or twelve years ago, he mused in November 1914, "deep perplexities and dangerous ill humours" had marked American life. "The country was torn and excited by an agitation which shook the very foundations" of its political and economic system. Those in power were regarded with suspicion, and they in turn mistrusted the people. "There was ominous antagonism between classes," Wilson admitted. But the New Freedom promised to turn everything around: it would replace class conflict with harmony, and mutual distrust with confidence. Wilson predicted that "suspicion and illwill" would fade away and that Americans would march together toward "a new cordiality of spirit and cooperation." The New Freedom, he believed, had performed its mission of reconciliation.

Convinced that reform had gone far enough, Wilson wanted to go no further. The only important Progressive measure he endorsed in 1915, and grudgingly at that, was the La Follette Seamen's Act. It freed sailors on merchant ships from a contract system that, in practice, amounted to forced labor. In other areas Wilson drew the line. He opposed establishing federally financed credit institutions to provide long-term loans to farmers on the grounds that this would unduly favor one interest group. He continued to regard federal child-labor legislation as unconsti-

Campaigning for Wilson, 1916.

tutional, and he refused to support woman suffrage. In February 1915 he nominated five men to serve on a newly created Federal Trade Commission. But Wilson, in the words of a Cabinet member, regarded the FTC as "a counsellor and friend to the business world" rather than as "a policeman to wield a club over the head of the business community." For the most part his appointees interpreted their task in the same way.

Yet by early 1916 Wilson began to modify his position, and he did so largely because he reassessed the political situation. The Democrats had done poorly in the 1914 elections, losing two dozen seats in the House and giving up the governorship of New York, New Jersey, Illinois, and Pennsylvania. Moreover, the Bull Moose party had begun to disintegrate after Roosevelt's defeat. Lacking a formal grass-roots organization, beset by financial problems, torn by dissension over its policy toward business, the party met with disaster in 1914, losing virtually every contest it entered. Ironically, the demise of the Progressive party, by raising the spectre of a unified Republican opposition, helped move Wilson toward an accommodation with the Progressive platform. To win reelection, Wilson knew he must make inroads into Roosevelt's old constituency.

This he attempted to do in a number of ways. In January 1916 Wilson nominated Louis D. Brandeis to the Supreme Court, a move that infuriated conservatives and touched off a bitter four-month struggle for Senate confirmation. Wilson also reversed his position on several issues. He supported the Federal Farm Loan Act (1916) which created 12 regional banks to provide long-term, low-interest loans to farmers. Similarly, in July he asked the Senate to approve a child-labor bill that had already cleared the House. His efforts helped pass the Keating-Owen Act (1916), which barred the products of firms employing child labor from interstate commerce. (In 1918 Wilson's earlier fears proved correct when the Supreme Court, in *Hammer* v. *Dagenhart,* found the measure unconstitutional.) Having made overtures to agrarians and social reformers, Wilson turned his attention to labor. He backed the Kern-McGillicuddy Act (1916), which provided workmen's compensation for federal employees. In September, to head off a railroad strike, Wilson urged Congress to pass a law giving the union essentially what it wanted: an eight-hour day for railroad workers in interstate commerce. Congress obliged by passing the Adamson Act (1916). Finally, Wilson moved still closer to the ground Roosevelt had once occupied by supporting the Webb-Pomerene bill (which did not pass until 1918), that exempted the overseas operations of business firms from the antitrust laws.

Wilson's strategy succeeded against a Republican opponent, Charles Evans Hughes, who had himself compiled a reform record as Governor of New York and as a member of the Supreme Court. Campaigning not only on his record of Progressive achievement but also on a pledge to keep America out of the European war, the President won a narrow victory. Wilson received 9.1 million votes to 8.5 million for Hughes, and managed a 23-vote margin in the electoral college. Nearly 3 million more people voted for Wilson than in 1912, including many farmers, workers, and New Nationalist Progressives who approved of the direction his administration had taken in 1916. Also, the peace issue apparently helped Wilson among German-Americans and socialists, and among women in the 11 states—particularly California, Washington, and Kansas—which granted them the vote.

Early in 1917, therefore, most Americans expected Wilson's victory to keep the nation at peace and permit completion of the Progressive agenda. Few had any reason to suppose that, within a few months, Wilson would lead the nation into war. Reformers had achieved a measure of success in applying Progressive principles within the American context, but they would find it considerably more difficult to implement those principles throughout the world. Even at home they never attained what they termed "a justice that is as unerring as any rule in arithmetic." Abroad they were forced to deal with a considerably different set of variables.

Suggested Reading

Important, but conflicting, interpretations of progressivism are presented in Richard Hofstadter, *The Age of Reform* (1955); Gabriel Kolko, *The Triumph of Conservatism* (1963); Robert Wiebe, *The Search for Order* (1967); James Weinstein, *The Cor-*

Progressivism in America (1974).

The social consequences of industrialization and urbanization are considered in Robert Bremner, *From the Depths: The Discovery of Poverty in the United States* (1956); Blake McKelvey, *The Urbanization of America, 1860–1915* (1963); and Charles N. Glaab and A. Theodore Brown, *A History of Urban America* (1967). For the response of social workers, reformers, and religious leaders, see two works by Allen Davis—*Spearheads for Reform: The Social Settlements and the Progressive Movement, 1890–1917* (1968) and *Jane Addams* (1973); Roy Lubove, *The Progressives and the Slums: Tenement House Reform in New York City, 1890–1917* (1962); and Henry May, *Protestant Churches and Industrial America* (1949).

The theoretical foundations of progressivism are explored in Morton White, *Social Thought in America: The Revolt against Formalism* (1957); Eric Goldman, *Rendezvous With Destiny* (1952); Charles Forcey, *The Crossroads of Liberalism* (1961). Richard Hofstadter, *The Progressive Historians* (1968), evaluates Charles Beard and other academics; Christopher Lasch, *The New Radicalism in America, 1889–1963* (1965), offers insight into Jane Addams, Lincoln Steffens, and other Progressives. For the literature of exposure, see David Chalmers, *The Social and Political Ideas of the Muckrakers* (1964).

Progressive attitudes toward racial and ethnic minorities are considered in Rayford Logan, *The Negro in American Life and Thought: The Nadir, 1877–1901* (1954); David Southern, *The Malignant Heritage: Yankee Progressives and the Negro, 1901–1914* (1968); George Frederickson, *The Black Image in the White Mind, 1817–1914* (1968); John Higham, *Strangers in the Land: Patterns of American Nativism* (1955); and Roger Daniels, *The Politics of Prejudice: The Anti-Japanese Movement in California* (1962). For the relationship of Negro protest to progressivism, see Elliott Rudwick, *W. E. B. DuBois, Propagandist of the Negro Protest* (1969); and Charles F. Kellogg, *NAACP, 1909–1920* (1967). The disfranchisement of blacks is discussed in J. Morgan Kousser, *The Shaping of Southern Politics* (1974).

Social and intellectual currents in the Progressive era are considered in Henry F. May, *The End of American Innocence, 1912–1917* (1959); Barbara Rose, *American Art Since 1900: A Critical History* (1967); and Nathan G. Hale, Jr., *Freud and the Americans: The Beginnings of Psychoanalysis in America, 1876–1917* (1971). Important monographs on the period include Samuel Hays, *Conservation and the Gospel of Efficiency, 1890–1920* (1959); Sheldon Hackney, *Populism to Progressivism in Alabama* (1969); James Timberlake, *Prohibition and the Progressive Movement, 1900–1920* (1963); Thomas Kessner, *The Golden Door: Italian and Jewish Mobility in New York City, 1880–1915* (1977); and Martin J. Schiesl, *The Politics of Efficiency* (1977), a study of municipal reform from 1880 to 1920.

For the presidency of Theodore Roosevelt, see two studies by George Mowry: *Theodore Roosevelt and the Progressive Movement* (1947), and *The Era of Theodore Roosevelt, 1900–1912* (1958). Also useful are John M. Blum, *The Republican Roosevelt* (1954), and William H. Harbaugh, *The Life and Times of Theodore Roosevelt* (1961). The standard work on Roosevelt's successor is Henry Pringle, *The Life and Times of William Howard Taft* (1939), but see also Norman Wilensky, *Conservatives in the Progressive Era: The Taft Republicans of 1912* (1965), and Donald E. Anderson, *William Howard Taft* (1973). Five volumes of Arthur Link's *Wilson* (1947–1965), taking the account to 1917, have appeared. A briefer analysis appears in Link, *Woodrow Wilson and the Progressive Era, 1900–1917* (1954).

On boxing, begin with Jack Johnson, *Jack Johnson Is a Dandy: An Autobiography* (reissued 1969); Barney Nagler's story of Joe Louis, *Brown Bomber* (1972); and Jose Torres, *Sting Like a Bee* (1971), the biography of Muhammed Ali.

TR at the Panama Canal, 1906.

CHAPTER THREE

1900-1917

A Progressive Foreign Policy: From Peace to War

DON'T TAKE MY DARLING BOY AWAY
Words by William Dillon, music by Albert Von Tilzer

A mother kneeling to pray
For loved ones at war far away
And there by her side,
Her one joy and pride,
Knelt down with her that day.
Then came a knock on the door,
Your boy is commanded to war,
No, Captain please,
Here on my knees,
I plead for one I adore.

Chorus:
Don't take my darling boy away from me,
Don't send him off to war,
You took his father and brothers three,
Now you come back for more;
Who are the heroes that fight your wars,

Mothers who have no say,
But my duty's done, so for God's sake leave
  one,
And don't take my darling boy away.

A hero is now laid to rest,
A hero and one of the best
She fought with each son,
The battles he'd won,
And the battles that proved a test;
Tho' she never went to the war,
She was the hero by far,
They gave the guns,
But who gave the sons,
M-O-T-H-E-R.

65

The ideals and policies that Americans adhere to at home determine their ideals and policies around the globe. Between 1900 and 1917 the Progressives exemplified this rule of American history. Dedicated to cleansing the cesspools of the new industrialism in the United States, the Progressives also developed foreign policies to help solve the problems raised by the corporations. And as Progressives searched desperately for order and stability at home amidst the industrial revolution, so overseas they used the newly developed American economic and military power in an attempt to impose order and stability in such areas as China, Mexico, and Western Europe.

Many Progressives believed that only in orderly societies could the United States hope to find political cooperation and the long-term markets for the glut of goods and capital its corporations produced. Without such help from foreign friends, unemployment and radical movements could threaten Progressive programs at home. Thus the era began with Theodore Roosevelt trying to make the Caribbean safe from revolution and ended with Woodrow Wilson taking the nation into World War I in order to make the world safe for democracy. These two men hated one another by 1917 (in one of his quieter moments Roosevelt called Wilson a "Byzantine logothete" whose soul was "rotten through and through," largely because Wilson did not lead Americans into war as quickly as Roosevelt wished). Their general foreign policies, however, were quite similar. The most important of the similarities was the determination by each man to create conditions for the overseas expansion of what one observer very accurately called in 1908, this "great economic corporation known as the United States of America."

TR

Theodore Roosevelt once remarked that a man's mission in life could be summed up with the admonition to "work, fight, and breed." He did all three rather well. TR achieved particular success as a fighter in 1898 when his exploits at the victory of San Juan Hill associated his name with militant American expansionism and helped catapult him into the vice-presidency in 1900. After McKinley's assassination in September 1901, Roosevelt assumed personal control of American foreign policy.

The new President's alternatives were analyzed in an article published by his close friend Brooks Adams in the *Atlantic Monthly* in 1901. Adams observed that since 1860 the Republicans had helped create the nation's great industrial complex by passing high tariffs which protected American producers from cheap foreign competition. That complex had become developed, and now the need was to find world markets for its products. The President would have to chose one of two paths. He could try to lower the tariff as part of a deal in which other nations would reduce their tariffs on American goods. This policy, however, could result in a violent struggle within the Republican party between high- and low-tariff advocates, and might not ensure that other high-tariff nations, such as Germany, would reciprocate by lowering their tariffs to benefit U.S. products. The second alternative was to retain the high tariff, but then (1) to use the powers of the federal government to make American production and transportation so efficient that United States products could compete globally regardless of tariff policy, and (2) to develop a great military force, which would assure American producers that their government could protect their interests in such vital potential markets as China, Latin America, and Africa. Not one to rock his own political boat, and deeply committed to the idea that military force ultimately decided world affairs, Roosevelt enthusiastically chose the second alternative. In this way he hoped to have both political peace at home and expansion overseas.

Roosevelt was clear about the tactics for achieving these goals. To make American producers yet more competitive, he espoused such Progressive measures as the Hepburn Act, which aimed at making the nation's transportation and production more efficient. He wrote Brooks Adams in 1903:

As you so admirably put it, it is necessary for us to keep the road of trade to the east open. In order to insure our having terminals, we must do our best to prevent the shutting to us of the Asian markets. In order to keep the roads to these terminals open we must see that they are managed primarily in the interest of the country.

Roosevelt also extolled the "strenuous life" of the military, continued the rapid building of the battleship fleet, and built an isthmian canal in Panama so that the fleet could more easily shift from the Atlantic to the Pacific theater. To ensure rapid decision-making, and to protect his foreign policy from what he believed to be the provincialism of American domestic politics, he concentrated the power to make decisions in the White House. This drained the power from Congress, a body he believed was "not well fitted for the shaping of foreign policy." And, as did most Progressives, he praised the nation-state as the ultimate arbiter in world affairs. Roosevelt refused to allow any international agencies to infringe on the nation-state's power.

In formulating his foreign policy strategies, TR distinguished sharply between friendly and potentially threatening nations. Although he had mistrusted the British during the 1890s, Roosevelt now understood that they no longer threatened the United States in Latin America and that the two nations had similar interests in Asia. Anglo-American cooperation, moreover, fitted in with Roosevelt's views of the superiority of the Anglo-Saxon people, who were, in his eyes, destined to "civilize" the non-industrialized areas of the world. Another partner would be Japan, which Roosevelt believed shared American open-door policies in Asia. Japan was certainly not Anglo-Saxon, but it had become industrialized and efficient, and thus, in the words of Captain Alfred Thayer Mahan (one of TR's close friends and a leading naval strategist), Japan had become "Teutonic by adoption." On the other hand, Roosevelt feared Germany and Russia, the former because its rapidly growing navy threatened British dominion in Europe and Africa, the latter because the Slavs seemed to be the people that endangered Anglo-Japanese-American interests in Asia.

Roosevelt possessed the personality and political power needed to carry out these policies. Above all, he was willing to use the mushrooming American industrial and military power to expand the nation's interest. Roosevelt agreed not with Shakespeare's "Twice is he armed that has his quarrel just," but rather with the version of American humorist Josh Billings: "And four times he who gets his fist in fust."

"I TOOK THE CANAL"

TR followed Billings's admonition in Latin America. Throughout the late nineteenth century the United States had tried to escape from an 1850 treaty made with England that pledged each nation to construct an isthmian canal only in cooperation with the other. Beset by problems in Africa and Europe, the British finally agreed to negotiate the point. In the Hay-Pauncefote Treaty of November 1901, England gave the United States the power to build and to fortify a canal.

As late as 1902 it seemed that the least expensive passageway could be built in Nicaragua. But a group of lobbyists who had interests in Panama used political pressure and bribes to win congressional support for the Panamanian site then ruled by Colombia. A treaty of January 1903 (the Hay-Herrán pact) gave the United States rights over a six-mile strip in Panama in return for $10 million and a $250,000 annual payment to Colombia. But the Colombian Senate then demanded $25 million. Roosevelt angrily—and ingeniously—announced that if the Panamanians revolted against Colombia, he would keep Colombian troops out of Panama by invoking an 1846 treaty in which the United States had promised Colombia to keep Panama "free and open." The lobbyists gratefully helped arrange the revolution in November 1903, and TR sent a warship to make sure that Colombia would not interfere. He then recognized the new government, gave it the $10 million, and made the new country an American protectorate by guaranteeing its independence. Later Roosevelt bragged, "I took the Canal Zone and let Congress debate." That remark showed little appreciation for Latin American feelings, and even less for the American constitutional system.

—AND ALSO
SANTO DOMINGO

Fomenting revolutions was quite out of character for one as strongly anti-revolutionary as TR. More characteristic was his policy in the Caribbean nation of Santo Domingo. The stage was set in 1903 when Great Britain and Germany temporarily landed troops in Venezuela in order to protect the property of their citizens. The resulting uproar in the United States, and the threat that in the future such temporary landings might become a permanent occupation, led Roosevelt to conclude that he could not allow an open door for European force in Latin America. The Europeans informed TR that they did not like sending their military to Latin America, but that they would have to do so unless the United States policed the area so that the revolutionary disturbances, and resulting dangers to foreign investors, would not occur.

Roosevelt's opportunity soon appeared in Santo Domingo, a country wracked by dictatorial governments as well as by struggles between German and American business interests. The President initially moved into Santo Domingo, however, not to check European threats to American security, but to fight the inroads that German shipping lines were making on American shippers. State Department officials on the scene told TR that the immediate threat was a revolution that the Germans might use as an excuse to land troops for the enforcement of their business claims.

The President responded by announcing a formula in December 1904 that has become known as the Roosevelt Corollary to the Monroe Doctrine. Any "chronic wrongdoing" might "require intervention by some civilized power," he warned. In the Western Hemisphere the United States would act as this "civilized power," exercising "international police power" to correct "flagrant cases of such wrong-doing or impotence." In early 1905 Roosevelt displayed American strength by sending warships to Santo Domingo. He then made a pact with that country giving the United States control of the customs houses through which the Dominicans collected most of their revenue. In return Roosevelt promised to use the receipts from the customs to pay off the Dominican debts and the foreigners' claims. Although the American Senate refused to consent to this agreement, Roosevelt enforced it by calling it an Executive agreement (that is, an agreement that would last at least through his presidency, but not necessarily be binding on the next president). He had again circumvented the constitutional restraints on his actions, and in 1907 the Senate reluctantly ratified the treaty. The President meanwhile kept warships in control of the waters around Santo Domingo, instructing the naval commander "to stop any revolution." TR hardly solved the Dominican problem. In order to stop recurring revolutions, U.S. troops were periodically stationed in that country through the administrations of the next five American presidents.

The Roosevelt Corollary is important primarily because it committed American power to maintain stability in the Caribbean area. With that commitment, TR once and for all destroyed the ideal of the Monroe Doctrine of 1823, which had aimed at preventing outside forces from controlling sovereign nations in Latin America. Contrary to the principles of 1823—and 1776—New World revolutionaries were no longer necessarily allowed to work out their own nation's destiny. Roosevelt best summarized the results when he claimed that the American intervention would free the people of Santo Domingo "from the curse of interminable revolutionary disturbance" and give them "the same chance to move onward and upward which we have already given the people of Cuba."

Cuba, however, was hardly a good example. In 1906 infighting between the two major political parties threatened to paralyze the island's government. Anti-American factions again surfaced in Havana. Roosevelt thereupon ordered United States troops to land and restore an acceptable government.

ROOSEVELT LOSES HIS BALANCE

Outside the Caribbean, the President faced a tougher job. In Europe and Asia he had to expand American interests not by unilateral military power, but by the delicate game of balance-of-power politics.

During 1905, for instance, Germany challenged France's protectorate over Morocco, and the German Kaiser asked his good friend Theodore Roosevelt to mediate the crisis. Although he had gotten along well personally with the Kaiser, Roosevelt was alarmed by the rapid rise of German naval power, and he was not anxious to help Germany gain an important foothold in northern Africa. After TR finally arranged a conference at Algeciras, Spain in January 1906, France's claims were upheld by nearly every European power attending. The President meanwhile worked through the two American delegates at the conference to ensure that the United States did not come away empty-handed. He gained a pledge from the powers for an open door in Morocco for American and other interests. After World Wars I and II the State Department would use this 1906 pledge as an entering wedge to gain oil and trade concessions in northern Africa for American entrepreneurs.

Roosevelt did not, however, display such surefootedness in the Far East. The focus in that area was on the struggle between Japan and Russia over the Chinese province of Manchuria. In that confrontation, TR much preferred the Japanese. As for China, which was the victim in the struggle, he observed that it was able neither to industrialize nor to militarize; when he wished to condemn an incompetent person, Roosevelt would call him "a Chinese." His racism, combined with his Progressive enchantment with efficiency, led him to view the Chinese less as actors on the world scene than as a people to be acted upon.

American missionaries and exporters viewed China from the same perspective. Businessmen particularly were watching the development of China. In 1900 they sent $15 million worth of products to the area, in 1902 $25 million, and by 1905 $53 million. The China market was apparently being realized at last. Most of these goods went into Manchuria and North China, that is, to precisely the area over which the Japanese and Russians were struggling. When Japan suddenly struck the Russians with a devastating sneak attack on February 8, 1904, Roosevelt exultantly wrote his son that the Japanese were "playing our game."

But as Japan destroyed the Russian fleet, consolidated its control over Korea and Manchuria, then threatened to invade Siberia, the President had second thoughts. Fearing that a precarious Russian-Japanese balance

Japanese immigrant children, California.

was being replaced by an aggressive Japanese empire, Roosevelt moved to
stop the war by calling on the two belligerents to meet at Portsmouth,
New Hampshire in mid-1905. TR was delighted with the conference's
work. Japan received control over Korea and in return promised an open
door in Manchuria for the United States and the other powers. The Japanese also obtained key Russian bases in Manchuria, vital parts of the
Chinese Eastern Railway running through Manchuria, and the southern
half of the strategic island of Sakhalin.

The promise of the open door, however, soon proved empty. Such
major American exporters as Standard Oil, Swift and Company, and the
British-American Tobacco Company found themselves increasingly
driven out of Manchuria by Japan. Tokyo's policy was capped in 1907
when Japan and Russia, bloody enemies just 24 months before, agreed on
a de facto division of Manchuria, with the Japanese exploiting the south
and the Russians the north. Roosevelt's first attempt to form a profitable
partnership with the Japanese had ended badly.

In 1907 another threat arose to endanger TR's dream of Japanese-
American cooperation in developing Asia. Since the 1890s the number of
Japanese living in California had leaped from 2000 to nearly 30,000.
Many of them were laborers who were willing to work more cheaply than
Americans. Threatened by what the governor called a "Japanese men-
ace," the California legislature tried to pass an exclusion bill. Anti-Asian

riots erupted. Having just defeated a major white power, the Japanese were in no mood to back down before laws that restricted the rights of their citizens to travel, either to Manchuria or to California. Roosevelt temporarily quieted the tumult by working out a deal: California dropped the impending exclusion act and the Japanese promised that in their own way they would voluntarily restrict passports issued to laborers wishing to move to the United States.

THE FAILURE OF BIG STICK DIPLOMACY

Roosevelt's hope that Japan would manhandle Russia in 1904 had produced not an open door but a one-way street for the movement of the Japanese empire. "I am more concerned over this Japanese situation than almost any other," TR admitted privately. So the man who gave his countrymen the phrase "Speak softly and carry a big stick," decided to send 16 American battleships on a goodwill cruise to the western Pacific. Congress blanched when it heard of the plan, for it feared that Japan would destroy the fleet with a sneak attack like that launched against the Russians in 1904. Some congressional leaders announced that they would not appropriate money to send the fleet. Roosevelt thereupon bellowed that he had enough money to send the ships to Japan; if Congress wished to leave them there it was Congress's responsibility. Again outmaneuvered by the President—even humiliated—Congress approved the funds. The visit of the Great White Fleet to Japan in 1907 produced effusions of friendship on both sides, but it failed resoundingly to persuade Tokyo officials to retreat in Manchuria.

On the eve of his departure from the presidency, TR made one last attempt to bring the Japanese into line. In the Root-Takahira agreement of November 1908 (negotiated for Roosevelt by his Secretary of State, Elihu Root), the United States and Japan reaffirmed their meaningless pledge to maintain the open door, but in the wording of the agreement, Root accepted Japan's control of South Manchuria. Roosevelt had apparently surrendered to Japan's predominant power.

Apparently, but not quite. While negotiating with the Japanese, Secretary of State Root quietly told the Chinese that the United States would return nearly $12 million of the indemnity that they had paid the United States after American property had been destroyed in China's Boxer Rebellion eight years before. Root said that he was returning the money "unconditionally," which meant that the Chinese could use the money in any way they chose. Root knew, however, that American officials in Asia had already worked out a scheme with the Chinese for a China-owned bank in Manchuria that would have as its objective the undermining of Japanese economic influence. Root was now, in reality, offering to help fund that bank. Because of a political crisis in China, nothing resulted from the American offer, but clearly Roosevelt had decided not to withdraw from Manchuria. He intended to fight it out with Japan.

His gentle encouragement to Japan in 1904 had resulted in cruel policy dilemmas for Roosevelt. But perhaps the greatest irony of the Russo-Japanese war was that, although American Progressives wanted to avoid revolution at all costs, the conflict ignited the Russian Revolution in 1905. The victory of yellow over white also set off unrest in the French empire in Indochina, helped trigger revolutions in Persia and Turkey, and fueled the Chinese revolutionary outbreak of 1911.

Roosevelt never understood that force does not determine who is right, but who is strong. He therefore had been initially pleased with the Russo-Japanese war. TR failed to understand how the chaos and disruption of such a conflict as the Russo-Japanese struggle could produce the revolutionary outbreaks that he and all Americans so dreaded.

REPLACING BULLETS
WITH DOLLARS

Roosevelt's successor, William Howard Taft, was too conservative for most Progressives, but his experiences as Governor-General in the Philippines and as TR's diplomatic troubleshooter in Cuba and Asia had made Taft a practitioner of the Progressives' ardent search for order and stability. He had learned from these experiences that military force had only a limited capacity for solving problems. Taft consequently hoped to use the burgeoning American financial power, instead of the army, as his main foreign policy instrument. He could point to the expansion of American overseas investments from about $800 million at the time of the 1898 war to more than $2½ billion in 1909 as proof that his countrymen were obtaining the power for the economic reordering of the world.

Taft advocated Dollar Diplomacy not because of any special ties to American bankers. He appointed such leading New York corporation lawyers as Philander C. Knox to be Secretary of State and Henry Stimson to serve as Secretary of War, but Taft also thought that "Wall Street, as an aggregation, is the biggest ass that I have ever run across." For this reason, Taft believed that private interests often needed direction from Washington. As State Department officials understood, however, Dollar Diplomacy was not new, but only the financial side of John Hay's open-door policies: Taft would attempt to do with money what Hay had failed to do with diplomacy. The dangers of changing the tactics but not the objectives of policy soon became evident in both Asia and the Western Hemisphere.

REPLACING DOLLARS
WITH BULLETS

Roosevelt's actions in the Caribbean had spread ill will and fear throughout Latin America. Taft wanted a quieter policy, but the full force of Dollar Diplomacy was quickly made apparent in Nicaragua. That nation was the alternate site for an isthmian canal, and a country particularly watched by Secretary of State Knox because of his past associations with extensive American mining interests there. Events began to unfold in 1909 when a long-term dictatorship was overthrown by revolutionaries, including numerous Americans. Knox immediately sided with the revolution. He moved in to control the situation by seizing the customs houses, which were the country's main source of revenue. The Secretary of State urged the new government to pay off long-standing claims to Great Britain by borrowing large sums from American bankers. When Nicaraguans balked at Knox's demands, he dispatched a warship. The agreement was then quickly signed. But the fires of Nicaraguan nationalism had been lit, and the American-controlled government could not maintain order. In 1912 Taft took the logical step required by his Dollar Diplomacy. More than 2000 Marines landed to protect American lives and property and to prevent European powers from intervening to shield the interests of their own citizens.

While the President dispatched troops to Central America, the United States Senate also tried to protect American interests in the area. In 1912 the Senate added the so-called Lodge Corollary to the Monroe Doctrine in reaction to the threat of a private Japanese company obtaining land on Magdalena Bay in Lower California. The Lodge resolution stated that no "corporation or association which has such a relation to another government, not American," could obtain strategic areas in the hemisphere. This greatly extended the compass of the Monroe Doctrine, which had previously applied only to foreign governments, not companies. The State Department used the resolution during the next quarter-century to stop the transfer of lands, particularly in Mexico, to Japanese concerns.

CANADA

The giant neighbor to the north could not be dealt with in such summary fashion. Americans and Canadians had last warred against one another in 1814, but during the 1830s, 1860s, and 1870s conflict had threatened over border incidents. Canada was extremely sensitive to growing American power, particularly since it had discovered that, although it was a member of the British Empire, London officials were anxious to please the United States even when the matter involved conflicting Canadian-American claims. In 1903, for example, Canada had protested Roosevelt's demand that a disputed part of the Alaskan-Canadian boundary be settled in favor of the United States. When both parties agreed to submit the dispute to a jury of "six impartial jurists of repute," TR loaded the jury with his own type of expansionists and threatened to deploy the army if he did not have his way. The British jurist, casting the deciding vote, ruled in favor of Roosevelt and against the Canadians.

The Canadian government had scarcely recovered from this humiliation when in 1911 it signed a long-sought reciprocity trade agreement with the Taft administration. Canadian officials were intially pleased, believing that the pact opened the mammoth American market to their country's raw material producers. But the agreement also made these producers an integral part of the United States industrial complex, a fact noted publicly when a congressional report in Washington likened the treaty to "another Louisiana Purchase." When the Speaker of the House of Representatives added that it would not be long before the American flag would be flying over all the territory to the North Pole, the ensuing uproar forced the Canadian government to call a national election. A new administration came to power, repudiated the reciprocity pact, and passed higher tariffs against United States goods. The annexationist movement was dead, but even the bungling in 1911 could not stop the successful American exploitation of Canada as virtually an economic colony over the next half-century. Taft, of course, would not live to see that result. During his own presidency Dollar Diplomacy had worked no better in the north than in the south.

CHINA ONCE AGAIN

The results were even worse in China, although in this labyrinth of revolution, power politics, and diplomatic double-dealing, Taft and Knox were not wholly to blame. But they certainly made a bad situation worse.

In late 1909 Knox feared that the Chinese would be unable to prevent Manchuria from being carved once and for all into Japanese and Russian protectorates which would exclude American products. Waving the open-door principle, and insisting that the United States must share in the investment opportunities, the Secretary of State proposed a "neutralization" scheme whereby Americans and Europeans would pool their money to help China buy back the key railroads in Manchuria from the Russians and Japanese. This would effectively "neutralize" the area, reopening it to American traders and investors. But Knox had made a blunder of the first magnitude, for when he tried to push his way into Manchuria, he only further united Russia and Japan against all outsiders. The neutralization plan was stillborn.

Apparently learning nothing from the experience, Knox made a second attempt to retain China as a frontier for Americans. In 1910 he insisted that the United States be allowed to participate in an international banking consortium organized by the British, French, and Germans to build railroads in the province of Hukuang. After Washington exerted great pressure, these nations finally allowed American financiers into the scheme, but the Europeans did so reluctantly, for they knew that once outsiders like the Americans entered, Russia and Japan would also demand entrance. This indeed occurred, and the Russians and Japanese proceeded to paralyze the Chinese Consortium so that it could not endanger their own private spheres of interest.

Faced with the utter failure of Dollar Diplomacy in the Far East, the only remaining tactic left to Taft seemed to be the use of American military force to prop open the gates to Manchuria. But the President knew the United States did not have the military power to scare either Russia or Japan. Theodore Roosevelt had finally seen the light on this score when he wrote privately to Taft in 1910: "Our vital interest is to keep the Japanese out of [the United States] and at the same time to preserve the good will of Japan." The Japanese, TR continued, must therefore be allowed to exploit Manchuria and Korea unless Taft was prepared to go to war. "I utterly disbelieve in the policy of bluff, . . ." Roosevelt railed, "or in any violation of the old frontier maxim, 'Never draw unless you mean to shoot!'" Unfortunately Roosevelt had not followed such a course while he was President, nor did Taft ever consider leaving Manchuria. The mess was left for Woodrow Wilson.

THE ULTIMATE PROGRESSIVE DIPLOMAT

Woodrow Wilson has exerted a greater influence on modern American foreign policy than any other person in the twentieth century. Richard Nixon, for example, privately remarked in 1968 that "Wilson was our greatest President of this century. . . . Wilson had the greatest vision of America's role." Much like Nixon, Wilson was highly complex, insecure, and driven by ambition. He once recalled that a classmate asked him, "'Why, man, can't you let anything alone?' I said, 'I let everything alone that you can show me is not itself moving in the wrong direction, but I am not going to let those things alone that I see are going downhill.'"

He wanted to move the world uphill—uphill, that is, to the political and economic system of the United States. The touchstone of Wilson's dealings with other nations was whether these countries were moving rapidly enough in the direction of a democratic, capitalist system. Although he and Roosevelt disliked each other, they did not differ in their conviction that American nationalism was the proper mold for other peoples, especially the nonindustrialized peoples. "When properly directed," Wilson observed, "there is no people not fitted for self-government." He determined to provide the direction, not merely with self-righteousness, but within a framework in which morality, politics, and economics were closely integrated.

Since his objectives were so exalted, Wilson, like Roosevelt, did not worry often enough about the means he used to achieve them. He even told his closest friend and advisor, Colonel Edward House, that lying was perhaps justified if it involved a woman's honor or a matter of public policy. Those categories gave Wilson ample room for maneuver. Politically, his beliefs exemplified the Progressive faith that effective government could best come from an educated elite; to Wilson, this elite sometimes numbered only one man. Even as a young professor of political science he had advocated strong presidential rule that would subordinate the often messy pluralistic politics of the American congressional system. During an explosive crisis with Germany in 1915, he refused to see not only congressmen but even his closest advisors, and communed only with himself for several days. Given the opportunity to exert wide power in foreign policy during the First World War, Wilson set the pattern of the strong, self-sufficient President, largely free of Congress, that has been followed by Franklin D. Roosevelt, Lyndon Johnson, and Richard Nixon. Wilson also exemplified how such powers so often end in disaster.

His policies rested on a crucial belief: the world must look to the United States for its example and, in turn, Americans depended on the rest of the world for their survival. Wilson had been deeply affected by the depression and threats of revolution within the United States during the 1890s. He was therefore open to the influence of Frederick Jackson Turner's Frontier Thesis, which argued that the 1890s crisis could be understood as the terrible result of the closing of America's landed frontier. After 400 years, Turner had warned in 1893, the United States had lost that frontier. Wilson, who knew Turner personally, paraphrased the Frontier Thesis several years later: "The westward march has stopped upon the final slopes of the Pacific; and now the plot thickens." The world market must act as the new frontier for the American system, Wilson warned during the 1912 presidential campaign, or disaster impended: "Our industries have expanded to such a point that they will burst their jackets if they cannot find free outlets in the markets of the world."

His genius was an ability to reconcile this need for overseas expansion with his political and moral views. He believed that open markets and capitalism were absolutely necessary for democratic political systems. His famous remark, "Without freedom of enterprise there can be no freedom whatsoever," applied, in his mind, home and overseas. In terms of foreign policy, this view meant that he felt justified in intervening in revolutions in Mexico and Russia because such upheavals threatened to become both antidemocratic and anticapitalist. These revolutions thus gravely endangered what he believed were American needs in the world arena. The meshing of his economic, political, and moral beliefs was perhaps most strikingly phrased by Wilson during his first presidential term:

Lift your eyes to the horizons of business . . . let your thoughts and your imagination run abroad throughout the whole world, and with the inspiration of the thought that you are Americans and are meant to carry liberty and justice and the principles of humanity wherever you go, go out and sell goods that will make the world more comfortable and more happy, and convert them to the principles of America.

Wilson tied the American need to export its goods, its political system, and its morality in a single package of red, white, and blue.

In encouraging such expansion, he went beyond the acts of previous presidents in two respects. First, he not only used military force to a greater degree, but also utilized it in an attempt to reform entire societies (see below). Second, he employed the powers of the federal government to a greater extent in capturing markets. The Federal Reserve Banking Act of 1913, for example, created new powers that American bankers and industrialists could use in competing for credit and money in foreign money markets. In 1914 Wilson sponsored the creation of a Bureau of Foreign and Domestic Commerce within the Department of Commerce. This bureau sent government agents abroad to be, in the President's words, the "eyes for the whole business community." The Webb-Pomerene Act of 1918 allowed exporters to organize associations for development of overseas trade, associations that previously had been outlawed by antitrust laws. The act ran counter to the supposed Progressive ideal of breaking up trusts, but to the Wilsonians, exploiting overseas markets assumed a higher importance. These markets, after all, could be opened only by American groups large enough to compete with the powerful industrial combines of Europe. The Edge Act of 1919 provided similar privileges for American bankers, and for the same reasons.

In all, it was a beautifully integrated program. The key was restoring vitality and competition at home by exporting goods, political ideals, and morality abroad. The government was to play a central role, creating new agencies and laws for the benefit of various exporters. This was hardly traditional "free-enterprise" capitalism but, as the Progressives understood, the rules of that game had become dangerously old-fashioned with the appearance of the Robber Barons, Populists, and the 1890s crisis. And if Progressive agencies did not do the job, there was always the Marine Corps.

The New York City Armory art show of 1913 was perhaps the greatest shock American culture felt in the twentieth century. The shock occurred because like all great art, the show, in the words of one observer, was "not only about art but about everything," including "politics, industry . . . and human values." For nearly a century American artists had painted photograph-like scenes of canyons, rivers, or people. The canyons and rivers had become polluted, and the people changed by industrialism, but the painters nevertheless had continued to draw the old, assuring scenes.

In 1900 a few men determined to change this. They shared a Progressive faith that by stripping away corruption and hypocrisy, Americans would see clearly and then save their republic. Some, like John Sloan and George Luks, worked as illustrators or cartoonists for newspapers, and so were outside the dominant art traditions but in positions to witness the social problems. When art organizations refused to show their pictures, eight artists presented their own exhibition in 1908. As the titles demonstrated, these pictures depicted striking new subjects: Sloan's "Sunday, Women

Inside the Armory.

Duchamp: *Nude Descending a Staircase.*

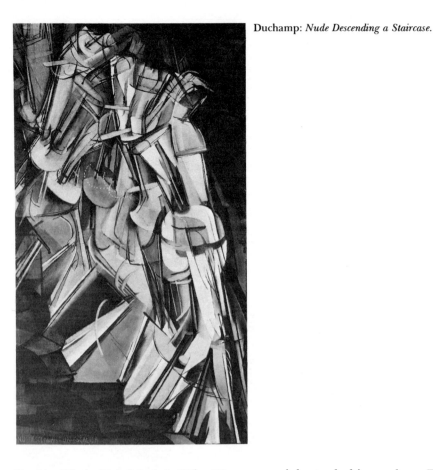

Drying Their Hair," Luks's "The Wrestlers," Everett Shinn's "Sixth Avenue Elevated [Train] after Midnight." Some critics condemned them for "exhibiting our sores," denounced them as "The Ash Can School," and excluded them from polite art exhibitions.

In 1912 members of the "Ash Can School" and others excluded by art associations decided to hold an exhibition at the New York City Armory. This time they accompanied their work with recent European painting by Cubists, Expressionists, and Neo-impressionists. These new artists included Van Gogh, Cezanne, and Picasso, the fathers of twentieth-century art, whose pictures often showed unrecognizable or weirdly distorted forms, and were composed of violent, clashing colors. They differed as much from earlier painting as the New York City tenements differed from seventeenth-century English countrysides. Duchamp's "Nude Descending a Staircase" symbolized the show, for the figure was unrecognizable (newspapers ran "Find the Nude" contests), while being dynamic and flowing. One critic called it: "Explosion in a Shingle Factory."

Theodore Roosevelt stormed through the exhibition, according to a witness, "waving his arms . . . pointing at pictures and saying 'That's not art! That's not art!' " But he wrote a moderate review, praising the more traditional American works. That was a misjudgment, for the Europeans overpowered

John Sloan: *Sunday, Women Drying Their Hair.*

American art. Even the "Ash Can School" called the European paintings too radical. Americans were particularly frightened by the European claim that art was not decoration, but a judgment on Western society and especially the fragmentation of the human spirit resulting from the industrial revolution. The artist now claimed total freedom to show this world, refusing to be bound by photograph-like art. If the machine created a new environment, and if psychiatrists were discovering darker worlds inside man's unconscious, then artists had to be free to show these new worlds in new ways. The Progressive "Ash Can School," European art proclaimed, might be too extreme for Americans, but it, like Progressivism it-self, was too conservative to understand the twentieth century.

Such radical art has never been welcome in traditional societies. Nearly 300,000 Americans saw the 1300 paintings in New York, Chicago, and Boston, but in Chicago art students burned in effigy the show's organizer as well as a copy of Matisse's "Blue Nude." The exhibition, however, was applauded by others, especially women whose own drive for equality made them more sensitive to the new art's demands for freedom. The Armory Show shocked the United States into twentieth-century culture, while warning of a breakdown in Western culture itself, a breakdown made real in the horrors of World War I.

82

Robert Henri: *Portrait of John Sloan.*

George Luks: *The Wrestler.*

THE FAR EASTERN
MERRY-GO-ROUND

Shortly after entering the White House, Wilson destroyed the China Consortium, which had been established by Taft and Knox, by allowing American bankers to leave the group. This did not signify an American retreat from Asia, however. Realizing that the Consortium was useless in maintaining the open door, Wilson attempted to devise an independent, go-it-alone approach to China that would provide American financial support unfettered by any European or Japanese controls. The President believed that this unilateral approach would build China to the point where Japan and Russia could no longer exploit it at will.

Wilson's first attempt at making his Progressivism work abroad never had a chance to succeed. The Chinese Revolution, which erupted in 1911, made a shamble of his policies, and the approach collapsed when World War I began in August 1914. Japan took advantage of the European struggle to seize German possessions (including the strategic Shantung Peninsula), then tried to impose the so-called "Twenty-one Demands" upon the Chinese. If China had acquiesced, these demands would not only have consolidated the Japanese hold on Manchuria, but also have given them economic and political concessions in China proper. Wilson strongly protested the demands, but it was British pressure and Chinese resistance that finally forced the Japanese to retreat. By 1917, as he prepared to go to war in Europe, Wilson had been ineffective in trying to roll back the Japanese.

During the summer of 1917 he had to come to terms with Japan. In the Lansing-Ishii agreement, Wilson agreed to observe Japan's "special" interests in China, a recognition that actually undercut the open-door principle in Manchuria. In return, the Japanese secretly promised that they would not take advantage of the world war to seek privileges in China that would abridge the rights or property of Americans and the Allied powers. That gave Wilson breathing space, but the lines had been drawn for a showdown with the Japanese after the war.

MARINE CORPS
PROGRESSIVISM

The open door was also closing in the Caribbean area, but here the United States played the role Japan assumed in Asia. Wilson and Secretary of State William Jennings Bryan (who served from 1913 until June 1915) vigorously excluded European powers from the area, supporting American traders and bankers, who proved highly successful in seizing the markets, banks, and customs houses. In the Progressive foreign policy tradition, Wilson sought stability and control in the Caribbean, especially after the Panama Canal opened in 1914 and war broke out in Europe.

In 1914, for instance, Bryan signed a treaty with Nicaragua giving the United States rights to a future isthmian canal, bases on the Pacific, and the right to intervene in Nicaragua to protect these new interests. In

U.S. marines with wounded Haitian prisoner, 1915.

Santo Domingo, Wilson mistakenly thought he had averted a revolution by holding an election in 1914. When the new government failed to show its friendship by extending financial favors to Americans, however, chaos developed, and Wilson finally sent the Marines in 1916 to control the country. The following year U.S. troops entered Cuba once again, remaining until 1921 in order to protect American-controlled sugar plantations, particularly from attacks by armed Cubans.

But it is Haiti that provides a case study of the tragedy of Wilsonian Progressive diplomacy. Black slaves had successfully revolted against France in 1801, making Haiti the oldest independent nation in the hemisphere except for the United States. In a population of two million the vast majority were small independent farmers, and more than 95 percent were illiterate. Politics were controlled by and for an elite, and presidential political life was about as violent as in American politics—between 1862 and 1914 three presidents were assassinated in each nation. Until 1910 the United States had displayed relatively little interest in Haiti. But then the harbor of Môle-Saint-Nicolas became attractive to the growing American Navy, and the Banque Nationale (the key financial institution in the country, controlled by French-German interests), fell into the hands of New York City bankers after a slight push had been given by the State Department.

The American bankers next sought to control the customs houses. Since these provided the government's main source of income, however, Haiti refused. The bankers went to Bryan, giving him false information about the impending dangers of revolution and European control if they did not have their way. The Secretary of State was hardly capable of making his own estimate. Both he and Wilson were largely ignorant of Latin American affairs, and both shared the racism that had influenced Roosevelt's diplomacy; when a New York banker tried to inform the Secretary of State about the language and culture of Haiti, Bryan could only utter with amazement, "Dear me, think of it! Niggers speaking French."

In 1915 the Haitian President was killed by a mob because of his supposed involvement with a mass murder of political opponents. Wilson seized on this disruption as an excuse for landing over 300 Marines and sailors in July. The Haitian treasury was given to the bankers, while the United States gained control of the customs houses. The State Department succeeded in finding an acceptable president only after promising to use the Marines to protect him from his own countrymen. But still the Haitians fought back with guerrilla warfare in 1915 and again more massively in 1918–19. After Wilson imposed martial law, the American military killed over 2000 Haitians while losing 16 Marines. In several major actions, Americans slaughtered their opponents rather than take prisoners.

Progressive diplomacy succeeded in tearing up Haiti's society by the roots. A 1918 constitution (written largely by Assistant Secretary of the Navy Franklin D. Roosevelt) legalized American economic interests and the military occupation. The principle of that occupation, which lasted until 1934, was stated by a United States officer in Haiti: "You can never trust a nigger with a gun." Years later Americans had difficulty understanding why Haitians were impoverished and endured repressive dictators who received support from Washington.

THE FIRST TWENTIETH-CENTURY REVOLUTION: MEXICO

Wilson's attempts to apply some of these methods to Mexico ended in failure. In that nation the President encountered his first twentieth-century revolution, one of those upheavals that, because of their turmoil and radical redistribution of power, gravely endangered the American hope for orderly change. United States interests in Mexico were large. With the help of dictator Porfirio Díaz, Americans had amassed holdings amounting to between 1 and 2 billion dollars. Most of this investment was in railroads, oil, and mines. During 1910–11 the aged Díaz surrendered to the superior force of Francisco Madero, but when Madero threatened foreign economic holdings, opposing forces under the control of General Victoriano Huerta overthrew Madero. Huerta was strongly supported by the American ambassador in Mexico City. Then, to the horror of the ambassador and the world, Madero was murdered by Huerta's forces.

Entering the White House at this point, Wilson refused to accept Huerta's methods, and his refusal became adamant as it appeared that British oil interests were supporting the Mexican General. In fact, Wilson would not recognize Huerta's government, thereby marking a historic shift in American recognition policy. Before 1913 the United States had recognized any government that controlled its country and agreed to meet its international obligations. Wilson now insisted that the government also be politically acceptable, that is, that it be elected through democratic procedures. The President threw his support to Venustiano Carranza, a military leader enjoying successes in northern Mexico. But when Huerta did hold elections in late 1913, he himself won the presidency.

Deeply angry, Wilson redoubled his efforts to support Carranza and cut off British aid to Huerta. Great Britain finally gave in to Wilson amid the growing shadows of a European war, but only after the President guaranteed that he would try to preserve British oil holdings in Mexico. In mid-April 1914, on learning that a German ship was bringing supplies to Huerta at Vera Cruz, Wilson landed troops to occupy the port. Mexican cadets opened fire, and over 300 Mexicans and 19 Americans were killed. Wilson's display of force, and Carranza's steadily successful campaigns, finally forced Huerta to flee to Europe in August 1914. When Carranza assumed power in Mexico City, however, Wilson discovered that, like his predecessors, the new ruler would make no deals with the United States.

The President now searched for an alternative to Carranza and thought that he had found his man in the notorious bandit Pancho Villa. But Carranza succeeded in isolating Villa, then began preparations for a convention that would issue a revolutionary constitution promising agrarian reform and the placing of all subsoil mineral rights (such as oil and mines) in Mexican hands. Outmaneuvered by Carranza and spurned by Wilson, Villa retaliated with attacks against American citizens, including a mass killing of 17 Americans in Columbus, New Mexico. In March 1916 Wilson insisted that U.S. troops be allowed into Mexico to capture Villa. Carranza agreed most reluctantly, and was then horrified to discover that an army of 6000 men under the command of General John J. ("Blackjack") Pershing was marching into his country. As the American troops penetrated farther south, Carranza finally tried to stop them with force. Forty Mexicans and 12 Americans lost their lives. Carranza continued to refuse to listen to Wilson's demands for new elections and pro-

Pershing leads troops across the Rio Grande, 1917; to his left, Lt.
George S. Patton.

tection of foreign holdings. The President, moreover, now faced the
much greater problem of American involvement in Europe.

In early 1917 the last American troops left Mexico. Carranza issued
his constitution several months later. Wilson had utterly failed to control
the Mexican revolution. In a larger sense, he had also provided a preview
of how the United States would be unable to cope with later revolutions in
Russia, China, and Cuba.

AMERICAN ENTRY INTO
WORLD WAR I—
FIRST PHASE

Wilson's immersion in the revolutions of China and Mexico was unfortunate, particularly since he had little experience in foreign policy before
becoming President. His policies tended to emerge from an understanding of the marketplace requirements of the American industrial
complex and his personal preferences for the order, stability, and gentle-
manly processes that he associated with Anglo-Saxon institutions. As a
young professor, he had venerated the British political system. When
World War I exploded in August 1914, therefore, Wilson asked the im-

possible even of himself when he pleaded that the American people be "neutral in fact as well as in name" and "impartial in thought as well as in action." Within a year Wilson told Colonel House he "had never been sure that we ought not to take part in the conflict," especially if Germany appeared to be growing stronger. By that time, the United States was well down the road to war. The American approach to the conflict evolved through three phases.

The first occurred in 1914 and early 1915 when the Allies (Great Britain, France, and Russia) seriously discriminated against American and other neutral shipping by blockading the Central Powers (Germany and Austro-Hungary). The Allies mined shipping routes through the North Sea and forbade neutrals even from trading with other neutrals if the goods traded appeared to be heading ultimately for Germany. After extended negotiations the United States accepted these Allied policies.

Several factors shaped the American surrender. Since 1900 Germany, not England, had been viewed by American officials as the gravest military threat to United States interests in the Western Hemisphere. Once war broke out, moreover, England played on such fears by flooding the American press with stories of supposed German atrocities. The effect of this propaganda has probably been overestimated, but it intensified the sympathy most Americans already felt for England. On the official level, Washington's responses to London were written not by Wilson (who was grieving over the death of his first wife), but by Robert Lansing, Counselor to Bryan in the State Department. A former member of the New York City mercantile community that had strong economic and social ties with England, Lansing did not even pretend to be neutral. He later bragged that he weighted down the American protests with complex legal language that would prolong the dispute until Americans perceived that "German absolutism was a menace to their liberties and to democratic institutions everywhere. Fortunately this hope and effort were not in vain." But Lansing did not wholly have to fabricate a case for England. Judged by traditional international law, most of the British actions were not illegal.

Most important, however, the ultimate recourse against the British acts, short of war, would have been an American embargo on exports to England. This alternative was never seriously considered because, Wilson admitted, an embargo would be "a foolish one as it would restrict our plants." During the summer of 1914 the economy was already depressed. An embargo on exports, even on ammunition and other articles related to war, could gravely affect the American system. When Wilson made this assumption—that is, that the United States had to be able to carry on its large international trade with all the markets the British Navy would allow—he had ceased being neutral. The *Literary Digest* phrased this perfectly: "The idea generally held is that we are not our brother's keeper. We can make and sell what any nation wishes to order. . . . If it happens that only certain nations control the Atlantic, . . . that is not our fault or concern."

By early 1915 Great Britain and France were running short of money to pay for these American goods. During the early days of the war Wilson and Bryan had determined that no loans or credits could be issued by American bankers to either side, for "money was the worst of all contraband" in that it determined all other trade. That policy was completely undercut by the President's determination to keep overseas markets open. By late autumn of 1914 the administration agreed to turn its head away while bankers gave both Germany and the Allies credits, that is, money tagged for specific purchases in the United States. A year later, in August 1915, an intense debate within the Wilson Cabinet ended in permission for American bankers to float a half-billion-dollar loan to the Allies. The lid was completely off. By early 1917 Americans had provided $2½ billion in credits or loans to the Allies, and less than $300 million to the Central Powers. Wilson explained the necessity for this policy in 1916: "There is a moral obligation laid upon us to keep out of this war if possible. But by the same token there is a moral obligation laid upon us to keep free the courses of our commerce and of our finance."

SECOND PHASE: SUBMARINES

Once Wilson accepted the British blockade, another major obstacle to American trade—German submarine warfare—arose. Unable to compete with British surface naval power by February 1915, the Germans launched a submarine campaign that hardly distinguished among armed ships of war, unarmed merchant ships, and transports carrying civilians. Americans found this relatively new mode of warfare full of horrors. They sharply distinguished between British blockades, in which the English could leisurely search suspected merchant ships, and German submarines, which (because their thin plates and light arms rendered them an easy target), could not surface to ask a ship to identify itself or evacuate civilians before sinking the ship. Nor did the British make Wilson's situation easier when they illegally flew American flags from some of their vessels.

Although the President warned that he would hold Germany to "strict accountability" for any underwater attacks on American shipping, he did little when an American was killed in the sinking of a U.S. tanker ship in March 1915. But on May 15 the British liner *Lusitania* went down with the loss of 1198 lives, including 128 Americans. Historians later discovered that the ship was carrying a large amount of ammunition from New York to London. Even had that been known at the time (and there is evidence the President did indeed know the *Lusitania* was carrying war materiels), Wilson doubtless would have sent the same strong protest to Berlin. When Germany seemed to snub this note, he sent one that threatened war. Secretary of State Bryan resigned over the dispatching of this second note, insisting that if Wilson protested so strongly against submarines, the President should also wage a stronger fight against the British blockade, which threatened the Central Powers with starvation. Wilson refused to take that position, nor did the ensuing anti-German sentiment over the *Lusitania* make Americans more neutral. A leading Democratic newspaper editor wrote of Byran's resignation, "Men have been shot and beheaded, even hanged, drawn and quartered, for treason less heinous." Bryan's departure removed the only relatively neutral member of Wilson's Cabinet. Lansing became Secretary of State.

Although the Germans finally promised not to attack passenger liners, they stepped up their attacks on merchant vessels. In February 1916 many Americans feared that the sinkings would soon pull the United States into war. Congress threatened to pass the McLemore Resolution warning Americans not to travel on belligerent ships, but Wilson waged an all-out effort to kill the measure, vowing that he would never "consent to any abridgement of the rights of American citizens in any respect." It was a brave statement, but his reaction further limited his alternatives. Refusing to restrict the rights of Americans to trade or travel in wartime, he would have to protect those rights.

Germany interpreted the wide support for the McLemore Resolution as proof of the American reluctance to go to war. Berlin did not change this view even after the uproar in the United States over the sensational discovery of German spies in 1915 and 1916 and the continuation of the submarine attacks. Then on March 24, 1916 an unarmed French passenger liner, the *Sussex,* was torpedoed and several Americans suffered injuries. This sinking marked a turning-point in Wilson's diplomacy. He demanded that underwater attacks on both passenger and unarmed merchant vessels cease or the United States would have to go to war. Germany responded with the so-called *Sussex* pledge: it would sink no more such vessels until adequate search and safety procedures were carried out, but Germany asked that Wilson also issue a strong protest against the British blockade of Central Europe. The President ignored the German request. In obtaining the pledge, Wilson believed he had scored a significant diplomatic victory.

THIRD PHASE: MAKING THE WORLD SAFE FOR DEMOCRACY

After receiving the *Sussex* pledge, Wilson pushed the submarine problem to the background and concentrated on devising a method of intervening in the war; he hoped to act as a mediator trusted by both sides. As early as 1915, he saw himself as the central figure in reconstructing a postwar world in accord with Progressive principles.

During the early months of the war, Colonel House journeyed twice to Europe in attempts to prepare the ground. House got nowhere with the Germans, who clearly perceived the American's pro-Allied bias; the British and French refused to cooperate because they believed they could win a military victory. In any event, Allied and Central Power peace terms were irreconcilable by late 1915. So much blood had already been shed that a compromise peace was not possible. The President's situation worsened in 1916. The British not only refused to ask for his mediation, but raised American anger by further restricting United States mail, goods, and passengers that had to travel through the war zones. Even House and Lansing became bitter at the British refusal to cooperate with Wilson.

In 1916 the President started out on a course more independent of the Allies. He had carefully laid the groundwork the year before with his "Preparedness" program that started the construction of new warships and armed additional men. In July 1916 he supported legislation for more warships and submarines. As he told House, "Let us build a navy bigger [than Great Britain's] and do what we please." This remark was not in the same spirit as the slogan "He kept us out of war," which Democrats were then spreading across the country to urge Wilson's reelection. But the President did not care for that slogan. During the presidential campaign he warned that Americans must help in the search for peace, for they could not "any longer remain neutral as against any wilful disturbance of the peace of the world." Throughout the year he elaborated on his idea, first revealed in May 1916, when he called for a "universal association of nations" that would carry out worldwide progressivism by creating global free trade, freedom of the seas, and stability through territorial guarantees.

Wilson's hopes for the postwar world became more urgent in June 1916 when the French, British, and Russians met secretly at the Paris Economic Conference to make plans for economic warfare against the United States. The Allies agreed on schemes for government-subsidized industries that would be able to compete against such American giants as U.S. Steel and Standard Oil, and they urged common higher tariffs to choke off American trade. When Wilson and Lansing learned of these agreements they drew up their own economic plans, but equally important, the President increasingly feared what might happen to American interests if the Allies won an overwhelming victory and then dictated a peace without his mediation. Such a victory could produce an overwhelmingly dominant power (such as Great Britain or Germany), which could dictate a peace that threatened both specific American global interests and, more generally, Wilson's hope for worldwide progressivism.

But the President was given little choice. A month after his reelection, Germany decided to wage all-out submarine warfare, even if such a policy brought the United States into the war. German war aims had grown with the length and bloodshed of war until only a quick military victory could obtain those prizes—neutralization of Belgium, annexation of French territory, naval bases in the Atlantic and Pacific, perhaps even economic reparations from the Allies. The German Navy confidently told the Kaiser, "England will lie on the ground in six months, before a single American has set foot on the continent."

Learning of this decision, Wilson went before Congress on January 22, 1917, in a last dramatic attempt to preserve his role as a neutral broker in the postwar peace. Urging a "peace without victory," the President again urged "not a balance of power" (by which he meant a world comprised of exclusive, closed blocs of nations), but "a community of power" that would be open to all. The Allies responded with cynicism, and on January 31 the German underwater warfare began.

But Wilson continued to stall, and would not move to declare war for two months. He feared above all that taking the United States into the conflict would guarantee an overwhelming Allied victory, ruin his own hopes of acting as a mediator, and help ensure the carrying out of the Paris Economic Conference's plans. Wilson worried, moreover, that American entry would decimate the "white civilization" needed to rebuild the postwar world, while allowing the "yellow race—Japan, for instance, in alliance with Russia," to exclude the United States from China. That was an exclusion Wilson swore he would never allow.

The President also encountered determined antiwar opposition led by Republican Progressive Senators Robert La Follette of Wisconsin and William Borah of Idaho. Since 1900 a small band of Progressives had vigorously opposed the use of military intervention by Roosevelt, Taft, and Wilson, particularly since foreign involvements could take the nation's attention off domestic reforms. They now also feared that entry into war could tie Americans into a power structure that would force the United States to support European empires and to fight wars for European, not American, interests. On March 1st the antiwar group suffered a severe defeat with the publication of the Zimmermann telegram. British agents had intercepted and given to Wilson a note written by the German Foreign Minister, Arthur Zimmermann, which proposed to Mexico a Mexican-German alliance. If Mexico cooperated, Germany would help it retrieve the "lost provinces" of Texas, New Mexico, and Arizona, taken from Mexico in the 1840s. Newspapers headlined the telegram, and prowar sentiment flashed to new highs—especially in the Southwest. But despite this sensation, antiwar voices were not stilled in Congress. Having no illusions that wars necessarily produce peace, 6 Senators and 50 Representatives voted against entering the conflict, while 82 Senators and 373 Congressmen supported Wilson's request for war.

As his nation finally entered the struggle, Wilson tried to preserve part of his status as a neutral by designating the United States an "Associated" power rather than as a full-fledged Allied nation, but this was equivalent to a hope of losing only part of one's virginity. The President went to war because Germany declared submarine warfare against the United States, but equally important, because American economic requirements, which had developed since 1914, left no alternative but to work with the Allies. Wilson rationalized that only by becoming a belligerent could he force Britain and France to open the world to the stabilizing influences of American Progressivism. As he explained privately, he had to participate in the war if he hoped to have a seat at the peace table rather than "shout through a crack in the door." So in April (appropriately, on Good Friday) he asked Americans to go to war to

Senator Robert LaFollete at opening of Congress, 1917.

"make the world safe for democracy." Progressive diplomacy had once again ended in the use of military force, this time on a level never before seen in world history. Given the record of 1900 to 1917, too few Americans were asking whether Progressivism was safe for the world.

Suggested Reading

Stimulating views of Progressive diplomacy include John Milton Cooper, Jr., "Progressivism and American Foreign Policy: A Reconsideration," *Mid-America* (1969), pp. 260–277; Richard D. Challener, *Admirals, Generals and American Foreign Policy, 1898–1914* (1973); Lloyd Gardner's essay in Barton Bernstein, ed., *Towards a New Past* (1968); Jerome Israel, ed., *Building the Organizational Society* (1972); and Robert E. Osgood, *Ideals and Self-Interest in America's Foreign Relations* (1953). The two standard works are Howard K. Beale's sweeping *Theodore Roosevelt and the Rise of America to World Power* (1956); and Walter and Marie Scholes, *The Foreign Policies of* the *Taft Administration* (1970). Conflicting interpretations can be found in Raymond A. Esthus, *Theodore Roosevelt and the International Rivalries* (1970); Charles E. Neu, *An Uncertain Friendship: Theodore Roosevelt and Japan* (1966); Charles Vevier, *U.S. and China, 1906–1913* (1955); Michael H. Hunt, *Manchuria in Chinese-American Relations, 1895–1911* (1973); Jerome Israel, *Progressivism and the Open Door* (1971); and William A. Williams, *American-Russian Relations, 1781–1947* (1952). Caribbean affairs are analyzed in Dana G. Munro, *Intervention and Dollar Diplomacy in the Caribbean, 1900–1914* (1964).

The standard biography is Arthur S. Link's magnificent multivolume study of Wilson; see especially *The New Freedom* (1956) on Mexico and China; and *The Struggle for Neutrality* (1960) and *Campaigns for Progressivism and Peace* (1965) for the entry into war. The best short analysis is Martin J. Sklar, "Woodrow Wilson and the Political Economy of Modern United States Liberalism," *Studies on the Left* (1960), pp. 17–47. The Mexican Revolution is well analyzed in Peter Calvert, *The Mexican Revolution, 1910–1914* (1968); and Robert Freeman Smith, *The U.S. and Revolutionary Nationalism in Mexico, 1916–1932* (1972). For a stimulating overview, see Lloyd Gardner, ed., *Wilson and Revolutions, 1913–1921* (1976), especially for Wilson's background and his Mexican policy. Besides Link and Munro, Caribbean policy is noted in Hans Schmidt, *The U.S. Occupation of Haiti, 1915–1934* (1971); David Healy, *Gunboat Diplomacy in the Wilson Era: The U.S. Navy in Haiti, 1915–1916* (1976), with fresh perspectives on both the Haitian and U.S. sides; and Charles C. Tansill, *The U.S. and Santo Domingo* (1938). Standard accounts of entry into war include Link's work; Ernest May's excellent *The World War and American Isolation* (1959); and Daniel Smith, *Robert Lansing and American Neutrality* (1958); while Ross Gregory, *The Origins of American Intervention . . .* (1971) is a good synthesis.

On art and the Armory show, see: Meyer Shapiro, "Rebellion in Art," in Daniel Aaron, ed., *America in Crisis* (1952); and Milton W. Brown, *American Painting from the Armory Show to the Depression* (1955).

World War I poster.

CHAPTER FOUR
1917–1920
The Failure
of World War I

OVER THERE

Words and music by George M. Cohan

Johnny get your gun, get your gun, get your
  gun,
Take it on the run, on the run, on the run;
Hear them calling you and me;
Ev'ry son of liberty.
Hurry right away, no delay, go today.
Make your daddy glad, to have had such a
  lad,
Tell your sweetheart not to pine,
To be proud her boy's in line.

Chorus:
Over there, over there,
Send the word, send the word over there,
That the Yanks are coming, the Yanks are
  coming,
The drums rum-tumming ev'ry where.
So prepare, say a pray'r,
Send the word, send the word to beware,

We'll be over, we're coming over,
And we won't come back till it's over over
  there.

Johnny get your gun, get your gun, get your
  gun,
Johnny show the Hun, you're a son-of-a-
  gun,
Hoist the flag and let her fly,
Like true heroes do or die.
Pack your little kit, show your grit, do your
  bit,
Soldiers to the ranks from the towns and the
  tanks,
Make your mother proud of you,
And to liberty be true.

When Woodrow Wilson addressed Congress in April 1917 he proclaimed that World War I would be fought for the cause of humanity, not for mere conquest. The President and his supporters justified intervention on the grounds that while Germany stood for reaction, the United States and its allies fought for liberalism. Confident that an American victory would make the world safe for their brand of democracy, Progressives also assumed that at home the war could be conducted in accord with their principles. Progressives had always valued efficiency, harmony, and the search for a "constructive social ideal." Now, many reasoned, wartime mobilization would be entrusted to the very experts in whom they had such confidence, and nagging social conflicts would be swept away in a wave of patriotic unity. The terrible realities of war soon shattered these expectations. Far from making the world safe for anything at all, the war undermined progressivism and unleashed revolutionary forces on an unparalleled scale.

MOBILIZATION AND REFORM

A month after Wilson's war message, Walter Lippmann (an influential Progressive journalist) remarked that the nation stood "at the threshold of a collectivism which is greater than any as yet planned by the Socialist party." Few Progressives wanted to go quite that far, but most assumed that war would bring with it a substantial amount of economic regulation. Surely, they thought, the need to equip America's troops and provision her allies would allow the government no alternative. Wasteful economic competition would be ended and order would emerge from chaos. In fact, the war did enable Progressives to push through much of their program, not only in the field of economic policy but also with regard to moral uplift and political reform. For a brief, euphoric moment Progressives imagined that the war served their own purposes. "Into a year has been packed the progress of a decade," one reformer exulted in 1918. Only gradually did it become apparent that, whatever the immediate accomplishments, World War I had exacted a frightful toll.

The War Industries Board served as the chief vehicle for directing the production and distribution of war materials. Created in July 1917 and headed after March 1918 by financier Bernard Baruch, the Board embodied several features of the business-government partnership envisioned by New Nationalist Progressives. One wartime administrator even termed Baruch the "supreme interpreter of the national good." Under his guidance the Board performed a variety of functions: it allocated scarce materials, coordinated purchasing, determined priorities, encouraged the development of new facilities, and fixed prices. It also standardized production lines to effect savings, and it occasionally granted exemption from the antitrust laws to promote efficiency. All of this usually gained the voluntary consent of businessmen. Indeed, the Board's central idea was later described as "industrial self-control for patriotic purposes." Patriotism, however, was not all that the Board had going for it. Businessmen cooperated because they respected Baruch (himself a highly successful Wall Street operator), were given a large role in deciding Board policy, and could almost always count on making a handsome profit from war orders.

The Progressive crusade, moreover, included the attempt to increase wartime food production. Because European nations relied heavily on American wheat and sugar exports, Food Administrator Herbert Hoover got farmers to bring additional land under cultivation by offering to purchase agricultural commodities at high prices. At the same time Hoover urged consumers to observe "wheatless," "meatless," and "porkless" days, and he also asked grocers to restrict each person's sugar ration to two pounds per month. Hoover ruled that restaurants could not serve bread until after the first course, and insisted that they put out small cubes of sugar rather than sugar bowls. Posters and billboards appeared everywhere with such slogans as "Food Will Win the War," "Serve Just Enough," and "Use All Left-Overs." Conserving food itself came to be known as "Hooverizing." Meanwhile, food exports nearly tripled during the war.

In two additional areas—fuel and transportation—the Wilson administration assumed far-reaching power. The Fuel Administration under Harry A. Garfield helped bring about a substantial increase in coal and oil production, in part by increasing the mechanization of mines. When a coal shortage threatened, Garfield ordered many factories producing civilian goods to close down for a few days and to observe subsequent "heatless" days as a conservation measure. In December 1917, faced with a massive transportation tie-up, the administration took over the railroads. William G. McAdoo, who headed the Railroad Administration, proceeded to integrate rail schedules, limit passenger traffic, modernize equipment, and increase the amount of uniform track gauge. Private owners continued to direct the trains, but as government functionaries they took directions from the Railroad Administration. The owners received a rental fee that guaranteed them a substantial return on their investment.

Besides encouraging these new techniques of industrial control, the war also paved the way for other reforms that Progressives had been demanding for years. For the first time the government interceded on behalf of trade unions. The War Labor Board supported the right of workers to unionize and bargain collectively, and it succeeded in obtaining the eight-hour day in many places. Even the steel industry, in which the twelve-hour day was traditional, adopted a plan under which men continued to work twelve hours but received time-and-a-half for the extra four hours. A newly created U.S. Employment Service helped workers find war jobs. The government, in addition, took pioneering steps in the fields of social insurance and public housing. The Military and Naval Insurance Act (1917) provided for the retraining of disabled veterans and established a voluntary insurance system under which families of servicemen received federal aid. Finally, a dream of reformers seemed to come true with the initiation of a public housing program for workers who had gone to cities in search of defense jobs in shipyards and munitions plants.

PROHIBITION AND WOMAN SUFFRAGE

Progressives had always exhibited a keen concern with moral questions, and World War I gave the uplift forces a golden opportunity. Starting with the premise that men in uniform must not be led into temptation or exposed to venereal disease, social hygienists, with the support of the War Department, launched a successful campaign to shut down brothels in the vicinity of military bases. They adopted the motto "Men must live straight if they would shoot straight." Lecturers from the YWCA travelled across the country, warning young women against the hazards of illicit love, attempting to foster "a higher standard of personal conduct and civil cleanliness," and exhorting their listeners to "Do Your Bit to Keep Him Fit." The obsession with cleanliness was sometimes carried quite far. One crusader noted that a boy who joined the army was "swept into a machine that requires cleanliness first, last, and all the time," and consequently became a person with "clean motives and higher desires."

The forces of moral uplift won by far their most important victory with the enactment of prohibition. Although prohibitionists had always put forth a variety of medical, moral, and social arguments, the war provided them with just the ammunition they needed. Since the manufacture of beer required barley, temperance seemed a means of food conservation. Since many brewers were German-Americans, temperance could be equated with Americanism. Since drunkenness lowered the efficiency of defense workers and the potential fighting ability of soldiers, temperance achieved the status of a patriotic necessity. Liquor manufacturers, said William Jennings Bryan, "would, if they could, make drunkards of the entire army and leave us defenseless before a foreign foe." The year 1917 saw a form of creeping prohibitionism. In May the sale of liquor around military camps was forbidden. In December the alcoholic content of beer was reduced, and Congress passed the Eighteenth Amendment. Even before the Amendment was ratified in January 1919, a Prohibition Act (1918) outlawed the sale of all intoxicating beverages. Elated by their success, some reformers believed that World War I might yet make the world safe for teetotallers. A speaker at an Anti-Saloon League Convention proclaimed, "With America leading the way, with faith in Omnipotent God, and bearing with patriotic hands our stainless flag, . . . we will soon . . . bestow upon mankind the priceless gift of World Prohibition."

Finally the war helped Progressives win the battle for woman suffrage. By the time the United States entered the war women had gained the vote in 11 states. In 1917, however, the House had defeated a constitutional amendment that would have given the women the vote, and the suffrage movement seemed stalled. But then the incongruity of fighting a war for democracy while denying the vote to half the population—at the very time that women were playing an increasingly essential part in industry—suddenly became too painful. Besides, many claimed that women possessed nurturing qualities of tenderness and mercy that a war-ravaged world desperately required. Even Charlotte Perkins Gilman, a suffragist who always stressed the "human qualities" men and women shared, believed that "the basic feminine impulse is to gather, to put together, to construct; the basic masculine impulse to scatter, to disseminate, to destroy." In 1917 six states—including New York, Ohio, Indiana, and Michigan—gave the vote to women; in January 1918 the House adopted the suffrage amendment. By then Woodrow Wilson had finally come over to the side of suffrage. He began to define it as a war measure, "an essential psychological element in the conduct of the war for democracy." For a time Southern Democrats, who apparently feared that enfranchising women might set a precedent for protecting the right of Negroes to vote, helped block action by the Senate. But in 1919 the Nineteenth Amendment obtained the needed congressional majority and a year later became law when ratified by three-fourths of the states.

PROPAGANDA AND POLITICS

Although the war smoothed the passage of political, moral, and economic reforms long sought by Progressives, it also led to government actions that conflicted sharply with Progressive values. Perhaps the best example of this was wartime propaganda. More than anything else progressivism meant faith in an informed citizenry and a conviction that government should assist in the educative process. In its search for wartime unity, however, the Wilson administration conducted a massive propaganda campaign, one designed to inspire rather than to instruct. The Committee on Public Information under George Creel published millions of pamphlets, all hammering home the same message: the forces of a peace-loving democracy were pitted against those of a war-crazed autocracy. The Creel Committee recruited 75,000 "Four Minute Men" who, in some 7.5 million speeches at theaters, clubs, and churches, described German atrocities and urged people to buy Liberty Bonds. One pamphlet, written for the CPI by a professor at Stanford University, predicted the consequences of a hypothetical enemy invasion: German soldiers would "pillage and burn," demand huge sums of money, execute anyone who refused to cooperate, and then "look on and laugh" while a priest and minister were "thrown into a pig-sty." "This is not just a snappy story," the author concluded. "Every horrible detail is just what the German troops have done in Belgium and France."

The war injected new issues into politics that badly shook Wilson's electoral coalition. Economic and manpower policies, for example, gave rise to sharp sectional rivalry. Because the administration imposed controls on wheat but not on cotton prices, Democrats representing midwestern wheat growers charged that Wilson unfairly favored the South. Democrats from the South and West called for stiffer corporation taxes and complained that the administration, under the influence of the party's Eastern wing, was coddling war profiteers. Many Southern Democrats opposed Wilson on the issue of conscription. They asserted that volunteers would make better soldiers and that a draft would "saturate the country with undemocratic and illiberal influences, with the overbearing spirit of West Point and Annapolis." Although conscription bills passed in 1917 and 1918, with the result that 24 million men registered and 3 million were drafted (along with 1.8 million volunteers), Democrats in Congress were sharply divided.

Not only did the war distort certain Progressive principles and disrupt Wilson's coalition, but it gradually eroded the reformers' confidence in progress, rationality, and order. With the western world in flames, with senseless slaughter occurring daily and national passions aroused beyond all reason, it became increasingly difficult to sustain the old faith in the perfectability of either people or institutions. If this were not serious enough, Progressives' confidence in Wilson's policies and in their own ability to control events was badly shaken by the administration's response to war-time dissent and to the Russian Revolution.

CURBING DISSENT: WHY

In November 1917 the motion picture *The Spirit of '76*, which depicted various atrocities committed by British soldiers during the American Revolution, played in Los Angeles. The film was seized and the producer indicted under the Espionage Act, for in 1917 England was an ally. The judge conceded that "history is history and fact is fact," but added that the film tended to "question the good faith of our ally, Great Britain." In the case, known as *U.S.* v. *The Spirit of '76*, he sentenced the producer to a $10,000 fine and a ten-year prison term (later commuted to three years). Although extreme, this was not an atypical case. During World War I the government imposed harsh restrictions on the expression of antiwar opinion; and when official action was not swift enough to suit the public, vigilante groups took matters into their own hands. The targets of repression were radicals who opposed the war, pacifists who opposed all wars, and German-Americans and other immigrant groups who were suspected of having a divided allegiance.

The amount of dissent a nation tolerates in wartime is usually proportional to the internal threat it perceives. In 1917 many Americans felt a keen sense of peril from within because of the nation's very heterogeneity. In the preceding 25 years nearly 18 million immigrants had come to the United States, most of them from countries involved in the war. One of every three Americans at the time was either an immigrant or the child of an immigrant. Many people, who imagined that the newcomers retained Old World loyalties, feared that entering the war with a divided populace would destroy the bonds of social cohesion. Wilson himself had once warned of the danger that Americans might be divided into "camps of hostile opinion, hot against each other." For those plagued by fears of disunity, war created a grave threat.

Such fears led to different sorts of defensive reactions. Some attacked German culture: several state legislatures eliminated the "Kaiser's tongue" from school curricula, a few universities revoked honorary degrees bestowed in the past on noted Germans, and a town in Oklahoma even burned German-language books as part of a Fourth of July celebration. These actions went along with a virulent attack on "the German mind" for its "reversions to grossness, coarseness, and bestiality." Others revealed their fears by insisting on a formal observance of patriotic ritual. Mobs often forced people who had criticized the war to buy large amounts of Liberty Bonds, to sing the national anthem in public, or even to kiss the American flag, presumably with the proper ardor.

For those who were not satisfied with symbolic acts of conformity there remained yet another possibility—joining a patriotic organization. The war led to a blossoming of groups such as the Home Defense League, the Knights of Liberty, the Sedition Slammers, and the Terrible Threateners. By far the largest and most energetic, however, was the American Protective League. With a membership that eventually climbed to 250,000, the League pried into people's opinions and checked on who was buying war bonds. To uncover "slackers," the League stopped men on the street and demanded that they produce their draft cards. Emerson Hough's *The Web* (1919), the League's official history, perfectly conveyed its sense of alarm: "No loyal American was safe. We did not know who were the disloyal Americans. We faced an army of masked men. They outnumbered us . . ." The League received something approximating official status. Its stationery read "Organized With the Approval and Operating Under the Department of Justice of the U.S."; its members received cards identifying them as federal agents; and in May 1918 the Attorney General named it an "Auxiliary to the Justice Department."

In addition to this widespread feeling of insecurity, the behavior of government officials fanned the flames of repression. Woodrow Wilson considered dissent dangerously disruptive, and he regarded the Socialist leader Eugene V. Debs and other antiwar spokesmen as little better than traitors. George Creel, admittedly not the most impartial witness, quoted Wilson to the effect that free speech in wartime was "insanity." Unable to give personal attention to each civil liberties case, Wilson delegated broad responsibility to members of his Cabinet and usually stood by their decisions. Postmaster General Albert Burleson wanted to bar from the mails any publication that criticized the reasons for American entry into the conflict or said anything "to hamper and obstruct the Government in the prosecution of the war." Attorney General Thomas Gregory advised opponents of the war to seek mercy from God "for they need expect none from an outraged people and an avenging government." Gregory boasted that members of the American Protective League were "keeping an eye on disloyal individuals and making reports of disloyal utterances." On oc-

casion Wilson would overrule his subordinates, as when Burleson barred
an issue of the liberal journal *The Nation* from the mails. Also, such officials as Secretary of Labor William Wilson and Secretary of War Newton
D. Baker held more libertarian views. But usually the Wilson administration cracked down on dissenters with little hesitation.

SOCIALISTS AND PACIFISTS

It could do so in part because of the nature of the opposition to war. Not
only were there relatively few war critics, but most were Socialists, anarchists, or members of the Industrial Workers of the World, people on the
margins of society who had little political or economic weight and who
made convenient targets. The war, in fact, proved disastrous for the Socialist party, which had until then achieved a modest degree of success. In
1912 Debs had polled 900,000 votes—six percent of the total—in the
presidential election. Even in 1916 the party received 600,000 votes,
elected candidates to office in scores of cities and towns, and reached a
wide audience through its press. But when the United States entered the
war the Socialists, unlike their European counterparts, kept faith with the
ideal of international proletarian solidarity. In April 1917 the party declared that the war benefited the ruling, not the exploited, classes and
called on American workers to repudiate the government. It branded the
declaration of war "a crime against the people of the United States and
against the nations of the world. In all modern history there has been no
war more unjustifiable."

This posture weakened the socialist movement for several reasons.
Although most Socialists opposed the war, not all party leaders did. A
small but influential segment, including Upton Sinclair, Charles Edward
Russell, and Jack London supported Wilson. Some went quite far: Algie
M. Simons became Director of the Bureau of Literature of the Wisconsin
Loyalty Legion, and John Spargo denounced the antiwar faction for
"upholding the impudent claims of the guilty Hohenzollern dynasty." Not
only did the war split Socialists into warring camps, but it linked the party
in the public mind with treason and thereby robbed it of a good deal of its
respectability. Finally, suppression broke the back of the party in some
areas. Socialists found their literature barred from the mails, their headquarters wrecked, and their leaders indicted for sedition. Other developments at the time contributed to the party's decline. The Russian Revolution, for example, caused a bitter division between those who wanted to
apply Lenin's tactics to the United States and those who, while friendly to
the Bolsheviks, denied that it was possible to "transfer Russia to America."
But the war itself was crucially important in weakening the Socialists.

Unlike radicals who rejected World War I as an imperialistic venture
but fully intended to fight some day for working class liberation, those
whose pacifism derived from their religious precepts opposed all wars.
The historic peace churches—the Quakers, the Mennonites, and the
Church of the Brethren—adhered to their traditional stand, but the war

produced a crisis in the pacifist conscience. In an atmosphere in which an ordinarily tolerant man like attorney Clarence Darrow could remark that "the pacifist speaks with the German accent," and in which conscientious objectors were labeled parasites whose liberties were being preserved by others on the battlefield, it is not surprising that many pacifists recanted. In 1916 the American Peace Society declared that Jesus Christ was a pacifist; in 1917 it backed the war. More than 100 prominent Quakers announced their "loyalty to the Cause of Civilization, and to the President of the United States."

For those conscientious objectors who stood by their convictions the government made provisions of a sort. The Selective Service Act of 1917 exempted from combat service members of recognized religious sects whose teachings forbade participation in war. These men had to register for the draft and accept induction as noncombatants in the medical, engineering, or quartermaster corps. Of the 24 million registrants, 65,000 requested this classification. Only 21,000 were actually inducted, but fewer than 4000 of them made use of their noncombatant status. The rest apparently took up arms. Approximately 500 men who refused to cooperate in any way, or whose opposition to the war rested on political grounds and did not qualify them for consideration, were sent to jail; the last was not freed until 1933. In all, the number of conscientious objectors never approached the number of draft dodgers, which the War Department estimated at 171,000.

CURBING DISSENT: HOW

The Wilson administration launched a three-pronged assault on dissenters. First, it attempted to deport radical aliens. Existing laws already excluded immigrants who favored the forcible overthrow of the government. Immigration acts of 1917 and 1918 tightened these provisions and gave the government additional power to deport aliens who advocated the destruction of private property or who belonged to organizations that worked for revolution. No trial was needed. Deportation could be accomplished through an administrative proceeding. Second, the government dispatched troops to break strikes led by the Industrial Workers of the World in lumber camps in Washington and in copper mines in Montana. The IWW, which had since its creation in 1905 rejected bread-and-butter unionism and called for revolution, made no secret of its opposition to the war. One of its songs, a parody of "Onward Christian Soldiers," included the lines, "Onward Christian soldiers, rip and tear and smite/Let the gentle Jesus bless your dynamite." Claiming that the IWW engaged in sabotage and that it instigated strikes, not to improve working conditions, but to cripple war production, the government threw union leaders into jail and held them for months on the flimsiest of evidence or on no charge at all.

The third and most widely used weapon to curb dissent was prosecution under the Espionage Act (1917) and the Sedition Act (1918). The Espionage Act made it a crime to obstruct military recruitment, and it authorized the Postmaster General to deny mailing privileges to any material he considered treasonous. Under its terms Burleson barred dozens of periodicals, including an issue of *The Masses,* which had a cartoon captioned "Making the World Safe for Capitalism," and an issue of *The Freeman's Journal and Catholic Register,* which cited Thomas Jefferson's opinion that England should grant Ireland independence. The Sedition Act went still further, making it illegal to "utter, print, write, or publish any disloyal, profane, scurrilous, or abusive language" about the government, the Constitution, the flag, the armed forces, or even the "uniform of the Army or Navy." The House passed the measure by a vote of 293–1. One congressman regretted only that it did not carry the death penalty. More than 1000 persons were convicted under these laws. One case involved leaders of the IWW who, President Wilson noted privately, "certainly are worthy of being suppressed." The trial dragged on for five months but the jury needed less than an hour to find 101 men guilty.

The Supreme Court ultimately approved these wartime prosecutions. In *Schenck* v. *United States* (1919) a unanimous Court found that a Socialist who had mailed circulars to men eligible for the draft, circulars stating that conscription was unconstitutional and should be resisted, had violated the Espionage Act by interfering with the legitimate power of the government to raise an army. Oliver Wendell Holmes, who delivered the opinion, tried to define the boundaries of permissible speech. The question, Holmes said, "is whether the words used are used in such circumstances and are of such a nature as to create a clear and present danger that they will bring about the substantive evils that Congress has a right to prevent. It is a question of proximity and degree." The Court also upheld the conviction of Eugene Debs for making an antiwar speech. In *Abrams* v. *United States* (1919) the Court found the Sedition Act constitutional. Jacob Abrams and several friends had dropped leaflets out of a window. The leaflets condemned American intervention in the Soviet Union, but the government contended that they adversely affected the war against Germany, for if workers went on strike to protest the steps taken against Bolsheviks, their action would also hamper the war effort. The Court, with Holmes and Brandeis dissenting, accepted the prosecution's reasoning. Abrams received a 20-year sentence but was later released on condition that he emigrate to the Soviet Union.

The suppression of free speech had both predictable and unforeseen consequences. It seriously weakened the radical movement. Indeed, groups were sometimes singled out not only for their antiwar stand but precisely because of their radicalism. For example, the war furnished employers who had always hated the IWW with a patriotic pretext for attacking it. But restrictions on civil liberties also dismayed many Progressives who, though they supported the war, believed that the Wilson administration had gone overboard in curbing individual rights. The crusade for conformity also substantiated the argument of intellectuals, like Randolph Bourne, who rejected all along the notion that war could be directed

Oliver Wendell Holmes, Jr.

toward humane ends. War was an inexorable situation, Bourne reasoned, in which the government would do anything it thought necessary to achieve victory. Intellectuals who believed that war could be "moulded toward liberal purposes" were therefore deceiving themselves. The attack on civil liberties, as much as anything else, proved Bourne correct.

ANOTHER REVOLUTION

If the war profoundly affected Americans, it was because, as Bourne observed, they expected too much from the conflict, not because—as compared with the other belligerents—they sacrificed too much for it. The growing American disillusionment with Russia was an excellent example. In March the Russian people, bankrupt and bled to the breaking point, overthrew the hollow, corrupt regime of Czar Nicholas II, replacing it with a liberal republic headed by Prince G. E. Lvov. President Wilson welcomed the new government, particularly after Lvov promised to keep Russia in the war whatever the cost. The change of government confirmed Wilson's faith that democracy, not authoritarianism, would shape the future. By summer 1917, however, the war continued to take its murderous toll of the dispirited, inefficient Russian army. The slow collapse of Lvov's regime allowed a corresponding rise in the power of V. I. Lenin, a Communist leader who had recently returned to Russia from Switzerland. Disillusionment with Lvov's inept policies resulted in July in a new, more conservative regime headed by Alexander Kerensky. The Kerensky government refused to listen to Lenin's demands for withdrawing Russia from the war.

Wilson closely followed these events, even appointing a special commission to visit Russia during the summer. The commission's report was optimistic, a mood shared by neither Wilson, nor, particularly, by Secretary of State Lansing, who was convinced the Russians were not merely replaying the moderate American upheaval of 1776 but sailing straight into another bloody French Revolution. This view was confirmed on November 8, 1917, when Lenin's Bolsheviks overthrew the Kerensky regime. Wilson's and Lansing's pessimism turned to hatred as Lenin began confiscating private property, radically redistributing political power, proclaiming the need for worldwide revolution, and in March 1918 making peace with Germany. The Bolsheviks "are avowedly opposed to every government on earth," Lansing privately exclaimed. He hoped they would "go to pieces," but doubted this would occur, for "their cry of 'Peace and Land' is popular with the ignorant Russians who have suffered grievously in the past." Wilson's and Lansing's fear of Lenin, however, did not get in the way of their understanding that the Bolsheviks fundamentally challenged Western "political institutions as they now exist and [are] based on nationality and private property," in Lansing's words. Lenin threatened Wilson's entire postwar program, and the President did not dismiss this threat by accepting the popular belief that the Soviet leader was an agent installed by Germany to take Russia out of the war. Wilson realized that for the first time he faced a fundamental danger from the left.

His Fourteen Points speech of January 1918 was Wilson's first response to Lenin. The President's program was to be both a cure and a preventive for Bolshevism—a cure in that he hoped to offer an alternative program that would win over left-wing parties in Europe, and a preventive in that he planned to create a new world system that would provide immunity against another world war. The key was Wilson's attempt to replace the old balance-of-power diplomacy (that is, a diplomacy dominated by several great powers) with a concert of many nations that he hoped would keep the world system fluid and open to all who could compete. Since the United States was becoming rich and powerful militarily as a result of the war, Wilson also knew that his countrymen would be able to compete wonderfully well in the world system he was proposing. These two motives, the fear of Bolshevism and the desire for American postwar economic expansion, explained why the Fourteen Points speech demanded open covenants openly arrived at; freedom of the seas in peace and for neutrals in war; the removal of tariffs, trade preferences, and other economic barriers; reduction of armaments; self-determination as a political principle; recognition of a Russia that would be a reasonable neighbor (to Wilson this obviously meant a non-Communist neighbor); and, finally, "a general Association of Nations" that would uphold all of these principles.

Not even Wilson's allies would accept the entire program. At the Paris Economic Conference of 1916, for example, they planned for closed economic blocs that would keep ambitious Americans out of British, French, and Italian markets. Great Britain, France, and Czarist Russia, moreover, had signed secret agreements with Japan and Italy that promised territorial and economic booty from the war if they maintained a common front against Germany. Wilson knew about these treaties since Lenin had gleefully published them, and the President understood that they ran directly against his self-determination principle. In order to keep Japan away from China while American attention was on Europe, Wilson had even neglected several of his own points by negotiating a secret deal with Japan, secretly arrived at, in which the United States agreed to recognize Japan's "special" interests in China. Tokyo officials in turn promised not to use the war as a cover for seizing "special rights or privileges in China." The President knew that this pact (the Lansing-Ishii agreement of November 1917) might later be used by Japan to claim special interests in Manchuria, but Wilson believed that at a postwar conference his own moral stature and his nation's mushrooming economic power would overcome the Allied and Japanese plans. The Bolsheviks, however, were another matter.

INTERVENING IN THE SOVIET REVOLUTION

Lenin's government seemed to be beyond Wilson's control. As the American humorist Peter Finley Dunne once observed, a revolution cannot be bound by the rules of the game, for it is rebelling against those rules. The President was therefore open to demands by the British and French that he join them in intervening militarily in Russia to overthrow the Bolsheviks and reopen the Eastern war front. At first Wilson refused, in part because of opposition from young liberals in the State Department who were led by William Bullitt. A handsome, ambitious, aristocratic Philadelphian, Bullitt argued that Leninism could be destroyed only if Wilson moved farther to the left politically and undercut the Bolshevik program.

The President rejected such advice, refused to go beyond the Fourteen Points, and in June 1918 agreed to land Americans at Murmansk in northern Russia. The landing was made in cooperation with the French and British troops. The Japanese then moved into Siberia, threatening to control the vital Trans-Siberian railway system while disguising their takeover as "anti-Bolshevism." In July Wilson sent 10,000 troops to Vladivostok in Siberia, then established an American-controlled group to run the

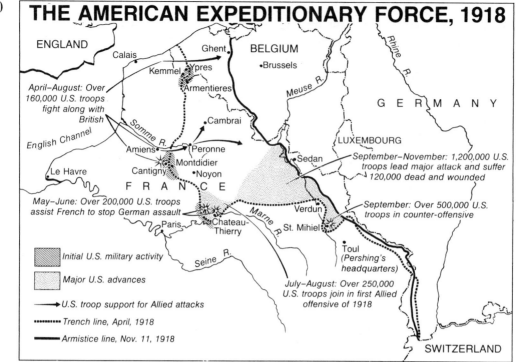

THE AMERICAN EXPEDITIONARY FORCE, 1918

ENGLAND

Calais

Ghent

BELGIUM

•Brussels

Kemmel Ypres

Armentieres

Meuse R.

Rhine R.

GERMANY

April–August: Over 160,000 U.S. troops fight along with British

English Channel

Somme R.

•Cambrai

LUXEMBOURG

Amiens •Peronne

Le Havre

Cantigny Montdidier

•Noyon

F R A N C E

•Sedan

September–November: 1,200,000 U.S. troops lead major attack and suffer 120,000 dead and wounded

May–June: Over 200,000 U.S. troops assist French to stop German assault

Marne R.

Verdun

St. Mihiel

September: Over 500,000 U.S. troops in counter-offensive

•Paris Chateau-Thierry

Seine R.

Toul (Pershing's headquarters)

Initial U.S. military activity

Major U.S. advances

July–August: Over 250,000 U.S. troops join in first Allied offensive of 1918

U.S. troop support for Allied attacks

Trench line, April, 1918

Armistice line, Nov. 11, 1918

SWITZERLAND

railways. He thus assumed responsibility in that far-off part of the world to stand guard against both Japanese and Bolsheviks. Making the world safe for democracy obviously was becoming a big job.

Wilson publicly justified the intervention in Murmansk on military-strategic grounds, but within days the Allied forces were fighting Bolsheviks, not Germans. The American force remained there, moreover, until June 1919, nearly eight months after the war ended. The President excused the Vladivostok operation by arguing that he hoped to help some 60,000 Czech soldiers, who had been fighting Germany and now apparently wanted to escape through Vladivostok to fight on the Western front. When the Americans landed, however, the Czechs were fighting Bolsheviks. The United States protected the rear of the Czech forces as they waged their battle, and also supported White Russian troops that were trying to overthrow Lenin. The American soldiers remained in Siberia until April 1920.

The interventions made little sense in the overall war effort. They were crucial, however, if Wilson hoped to extinguish the Communist regime and keep Siberia out of Japanese hands. As Secretary of War Newton D. Baker candidly remarked in September 1919, American troops remained in Siberia because withdrawal would leave the area "open to anarchy, bloodshed and Bolshevism." But Wilson failed to overthrow Lenin, only making worse an already poisonous relationship between Russia and the West. The President fully realized the dilemma. In 1919 he declared that using troops to stop a revolution was "like using a broom to hold back a great ocean." He nonetheless tried the broom, for as a Progressive dealing with revolution he could see no better alternative.

THE YANKS IN EUROPE

A central problem for Wilson was that he had to watch closely not only Germans, Bolsheviks, and Japanese but also his European allies. The political relationship with London and Paris, already strained by the Fourteen Points speech, was not improved by the timing and nature of the American military effort.

No major United States force landed in France until eight months after Wilson's war message of April 1917, and not until the spring of 1918 did Americans decisively affect the fighting. But they were then pivotal in turning back a major German offensive just 40 miles from Paris. The Americans won a major victory at Chateau Thierry, a triumph that Wilson mistakenly thought would put the French in his debt at the postwar peace conference, and then drove the Germans back along the southern front until Berlin asked for peace in November 1918.

The Yanks had arrived none too early, for throughout 1917 and early 1918 the Allies nearly bled themselves to death. In one offensive alone they expended more than a half million lives to move the battle line several miles. An entire generation of Europeans was being exterminated. Nearly 3 million Allied soldiers lost their lives, probably 10 million people were slaughtered in all, but of this number only 52,000 were Americans. These figures help explain why British and French leaders were so driven by hatred for Germany at the peace conference in 1919, and why they scorned Wilson's pleas for moderation. Such feelings, combined with the President's great reluctance to place American troops under European commanders and his refusal to participate fully in several war-time planning conferences, did not augur well for the peace conference. But then the problems Wilson was enduring at home were similarly ominous for his postwar plans.

1919: RED SCARE

In 1919, as peace came to Europe, industrial warfare flared in the United States. That year more than 4 million workers took part in 3600 strikes. Most of the walkouts had similar causes. Workers who had won union recognition and improved their conditions during the war now attempted to solidify or extend those gains. It seemed essential to do so because wages were lagging behind rising prices, and many workers feared that they could lose their jobs as factories converted back to civilian production. Employers, however, wanted to withdraw many of the concessions made during the war; consequently, they often refused even to negotiate. All of this took place in the wake of the widespread anxiety aroused by the Russian Revolution. Although only a few strikes were led by radicals and none had radical objectives, employers, hoping to capture public opinion, claimed that labor turmoil posed a revolutionary threat.

Two of these disturbances—the Seattle general strike and the Boston police strike—seemed in particular to endanger law and order. In January 1919, when Seattle shipyard workers struck for higher wages, unions throughout the city voted to walk out in support. Although the unions set up a committee that attempted to provide essential health services, many viewed the general strike as, in the words of one presidential advisor, "the first appearance of the Soviet in this country." The government dispatched the Marines, the AFL leadership insisted that Seattle locals return to work, the mayor beefed up the police and issued an ultimatum. Under fierce pressure from all sides the strikers capitulated. Then, in September, policemen in Boston demanded the right to join a union, a right denied them by the police commissioner. A strike followed during which some theft and looting occurred. The reaction was intense. One newspaper declared that "Bolshevism in the U.S. is no longer a spectre"; the President branded the strike "a crime against civilization"; and Governor Calvin Coolidge of Massachusetts proclaimed that there was "no right to strike against the public safety by anybody, anywhere, anytime." The city dismissed everyone involved and recruited an entirely new police force.

In September 1919 the United States also faced the most massive industrial dispute in its history when 350,000 steel workers left the mills. The men, many of whom still worked twelve hours a day, seven days a week, wanted an AFL union recognized as bargaining agent. Indeed, pressure from the rank-and-file apparently forced the AFL to authorize a strike before it felt strong enough to sustain one. The owners, for their part, welcomed a showdown over the principle of the open shop. Judge Elbert Gary, the President of United States Steel, accurately reflected the opinion of management when he claimed that most workers were satisfied with their conditions, wanted nothing to do with the union, and were being misled by the "coercion, threats, insults or wild promises" of outside agitators. As in Boston and Seattle, charges of radicalism were hurled at the union leaders, particularly at William Z. Foster. A former syndicalist, Foster believed that unions, in achieving one small gain after another, would slowly erode the foundations of capitalism. In this case the union gained nothing at all. By January 1920, its resources exhausted by a long and costly struggle, the AFL called off the strike.

Baseball has been America's National Pastime. It combines raw individual effort with precise team play, compiles masses of figures that excite statistic-loving Americans, has a long tradition that allows fans to link past heroes to the present, and is played during the school-free halcyon days of summer. It appeals to boys ("Every boy likes base-ball," novelist Zane Gray wrote, "and if he doesn't he's not a boy"), while its complexity makes it a favorite of intellectuals ("Baseball is a religion," a distinguished philosopher proclaimed in 1919).

The game's roots go back to Ancient Egypt. Modern American teams appeared in the 1840s, organized—as has

The Sultan of Swat—Babe Ruth.

been every popular American sport except basketball—by wealthy gentlemen in the Northeast. Nationally popular by the Civil War, the first professional team, the Cincinnati Red Stockings, formed in 1869. The National League appeared in 1876, the American League in 1901, and World Series competition between the two leagues began two years later. Baseball grew quickly at century's turn because of rapid urbanization, new street railways, and, particularly, increased leisure time created by the mechanization of farm and industry.

Equally important, the game was developed by men who viewed it as business, not sport. They organized it along the lines of such corporations as U.S. Steel. A division of labor existed between management and players, with owners monopolizing the athletes through a "reserve clause" that made players the property of a single club.

Owners controlled their market by giving each team absolute rights over its own urban area. Supreme Court rulings meanwhile exempted baseball from antitrust laws (a benefit not even U.S. Steel received from the courts). Attendance rose dramatically, the value of some clubs multiplying ten times between 1900 and 1918. Then in 1919 members of the Chicago White Sox (soon tabbed the "Black Sox") were accused of accepting bribes to lose the 1919 World Series.

The sport was severely shaken. But three people managed to resurrect baseball so that it became the rage of the sportsminded 1920s. Kenesaw Mountain Landis, a tough U.S. District Court Judge, was brought in by the frightened owners to clean up the game. He did so brutally, even trying to ban players and owners from attending racetracks (where, Landis believed, lurked shadowy figures who "would sell out the Virgin Mary and their mother.") He

Opening the season in New York, 1886.

Judge Landis at opening of World Series, 1923.

ruled baseball until his death in 1944. The second savior was Babe Ruth of the Boston Red Sox and New York Yankees. His 29 home runs in 1919 broke an 1884 record, revolutionizing baseball by making it a game of exciting power. Son of a Baltimore barkeeper and a drunk at age eight, Ruth glamorously flouted Prohibition in the 1920s, and ordered the clubhouse boy to discard all letters except "those with checks or from broads." Landis was the puritanical Calvin Coolidge of baseball while Ruth was Babylonian America having an illegal and immoral—but wonderful—time.

The third figure was Branch Rickey, a religious, Ohio-born, sharpeyed lawyer who developed the "farm system" whereby Major League clubs developed their own players in minor leagues. This resembled Standard Oil's system of controlling its profitable product from the oil well to the filling station. The devout Rickey would not play ball on Sunday,

but liked the player who "will break both your legs if you happen to be standing in his path to second base." His corporate techniques won championships at St. Louis, Brooklyn, and Pittsburgh. In 1947 he forced reluctant owners to allow the first black, Jackie Robinson, to play in the Majors.

Robinson's appearance marked the first of many changes. He was followed by such other black superstars as Willie Mays, Hank Aaron (who broke Ruth's all-time home run record), and Bob Gibson (who struck out more hitters than any other National League pitcher). In 1958 the fabled Brooklyn Dodgers deserted "Flatbush" and became the Los Angeles Dodgers as they made big league baseball a continental sport for the first time. And in the mid-1970s, the law courts finally broke the owners' monopoly over their employees.

Players with a specific number of years of experience, the courts decided, could test their worth in the open market. Wealthy clubs, such as the Yankees, were accused of "buying championships" when they won pennants after paying millions for several such stars. Average players soon earned $90,000 and more, while Dave Parker of the Pittsburgh Pirates became the highest paid player in all sports with an annual salary of nearly $1 million (or four times the U.S. President's salary). These huge sums were made possible by steadily increasing attendance and especially television contracts that paid $94 million to owners in 1978. The sport prospered, but it had been a close call, for in the 1920s baseball had nearly struck out before Landis, Ruth, and Rickey stepped in to save it.

Branch Rickey and Jackie Robinson at Dodgers' Florida camp.

Belief in the imminence of revolution was shared by radicals who often talked and acted as if the United States were about to follow the Russian example. Communists in Chicago, for example, asserted that mass strikes would lead to a "proletarian dictatorship, which will crush the capitalist as the capitalist state now crushes the workers." Moreover, a series of bombings and attempted bombings in the spring of 1919 badly frightened the American people. In April a bomb was sent to the mayor of Seattle. Another, mailed to a Georgia politician, exploded, and the maid who opened the package lost both her hands. When the Post Office intercepted 34 identical parcels addressed to J. P. Morgan, John D. Rockefeller, and other prominent businessmen, and all were found to contain bombs, headlines blared: "REDS PLANNED MAY DAY MURDERS". In June bombs went off at approximately the same time in eight cities, adding to the fear that these acts were the work not of an individual but of a conspiracy. One of the bombs shattered windows in the home of Attorney General A. Mitchell Palmer.

As Americans felt increasingly threatened by the prospect of violent revolution, they hunted for preventive measures. No fewer than 28 states passed peacetime sedition acts of some sort, under which 1400 people were arrested and 300 convicted. Legislatures sometimes refused to accept men who held unorthodox views. In November 1919 the House of Representatives refused to seat Milwaukee Socialist Victor Berger. When he won reelection the House again balked at accepting him. In January 1920 the New York State legislature expelled five Socialists, although most of them had held office during the war. States tried to uproot subversive influences by investigating public school teachers and requiring them to sign loyalty oaths. Congress further tightened the immigration laws in 1920 by providing for the deportation of aliens who possessed revolutionary literature or contributed to radical causes. Violence also marked the Red Scare. In November 1919 IWW member Wesley Everest was taken from prison in Centralia, Washington by an angry mob. He was beaten, castrated, hung from the girders of a railroad bridge, and shot to death.

The Red Scare reached its crescendo with the Palmer raids. Shaken by the bombing attempt on his home, Attorney General Palmer came to believe that "the blaze of revolution [is] sweeping over every American institution of law and order . . . burning up the foundations of society." Under intense public pressure to take strong action, Palmer, with the aid of other officials, worked out policies that effectively deprived radical aliens of due process. The Department of Justice launched surprise raids on the headquarters of radical organizations, seized correspondence and membership lists, detained suspects under astronomical bail, and cross-examined witnesses before they could obtain legal advice. To permit a radical alien to see an attorney before interrogation, J. Edgar Hoover of the Justice Department explained, "defeats the ends of justice." In the first week of January 1920 federal agents, employing these tactics, arrested 3000 alleged Communists in 33 cities. Many were imprisoned, although no charges were brought against them; 550 were later deported. Palmer's action violated every civil libertarian principle, but momentarily made him a national hero.

The wartime suppression of civil liberties differed in several respects from the postwar Red Scare. In the former Americans feared subversion, in the latter revolution. The target in 1917 was frequently the German-American; the target in 1919 was often organized labor. But in important ways the two episodes resembled each other. Both occurred because society felt threatened from within, both involved legal and extra-legal forms of repression, both exploited antiimigrant and antiradical sentiments. Each had a crippling effect on the American radical movement which by 1920 was weak, fragmented, and in disarray. The Palmer raids, no less than wartime intolerance, angered many Progressives who condemned Wilson for permitting, if not actually encouraging, these excesses. By mid-1920 the Red Scare had run its course. With communism clearly confined to Russia, with labor turmoil and bomb scares at an end, fears began to evaporate. The Wilson administration had won praise for its antiradical stance early in 1920, but had a more difficult time defending its record by the end of the year.

1919: BLACK SCARE

The postwar years were marked not only by labor turmoil but also by intense racial discord. In 1919 lynch mobs murdered 78 blacks, at least 10 of whom were veterans. From April to October race riots erupted in 25 cities—including Washington, D.C.; Omaha, Nebraska; and Longview, Texas—and claimed the lives of 120 people. The worst riot, during what came to be known as the "Red Summer," took place in Chicago; it left 38 dead and 537 injured. In truth, race riot was a less accurate term than race war. Marauding bands of whites and blacks, armed with guns and clubs, roamed the streets and hunted each other down. Racial turbulence, like the Red Scare, had its roots in postwar social and economic dislocations. The war had dramatically altered the position of black Americans and raised their expectations. When those expectations clashed with the ingrained prejudices of whites, the stage was set for the Red Summer.

World War I spurred a mass exodus of blacks from Southern farms to Northern cities. In 1915 and 1916 floods and boll weevils ravaged crops in the cotton-belt and forced many tenant farmers off the land. At about the same time, the war opened magnificent opportunities in the North. The demand for industrial labor seemed insatiable as factories were swamped with military orders, workers left their jobs for the army, and the flow of immigration from Europe came to a virtual halt. Black newspapers, particularly the Chicago *Defender*, encouraged migration by playing up the opportunities available to Negroes in the North. Labor agents swept through the Southern states attempting to recruit black workers. Some companies even issued free railroad passes to anyone who promised to work for them. From 1916 to 1918, hundreds of thousands of Negroes moved North. The black population of Chicago doubled in just four years.

For most, migration had a racial as well as an economic dimension. The letters written by migrants, and their behavior as well, reveal their sense of embarking on a pilgrimage out of bondage and into a promised land. "I am in the darkness of the south," said an Alabama Negro in explaining his request for train fare to Chicago; ". . . please help me to get out of this low down country [where] i am counted no more thin a dog." A group of blacks from Hattiesburg, Mississippi, on crossing the Ohio River, knelt, prayed, kissed the ground, and sang hymns of deliverance. The North, with its absence of legal segregation, surely afforded some an exhilarating sense of freedom. A black carpenter, who had moved to Chicago, wrote to his brother in Mississippi, "I should have been here 20 years ago. I just begun to feel like a man."

Most blacks genuinely believed that the war would usher in an era of social justice. The NAACP urged Negroes to support the war by enlisting and buying bonds, for if they did, whites could no longer ignore their appeals for equality. A similar conviction led W. E. B. DuBois to advise blacks to "close our ranks shoulder to shoulder with our own white fellow citizens and the allied nations that are fighting for democracy." Several concessions made by the Wilson administration bolstered the prevailing optimism. Although the army remained rigidly segregated, the War Department established an officers' training camp for blacks, created a black combat division, and accepted blacks into medical units. The Railroad Administration, while preserving separate facilities for passengers, paid the same wages to white and black workers, and agreed to bargain with a Negro Pullman union. All this, in the context of 1918, represented progress.

The end of the war, however, disappointed the hopes of DuBois and the others. With the return of millions of veterans, competition for jobs and housing grew fierce. In 1919 blacks discovered that many of their wartime gains were vanishing into thin air. They were again the last hired and the first fired. They still paid the highest rents for the most squalid dwellings. The Wilson administration no longer showed the slightest interest in them. Disillusionment was profound. Nearly 400,000 blacks had served in the military, half of them in France where racial distinctions were less important. Then too, Negroes who had left farms in Mississippi to work in iron foundries in Chicago were often free to express the bitterness they had formerly concealed. For the first time, a number of black spokesmen openly advocated the use of violence for purposes of self-defense. This heightened race consciousness coincided with heightened fears among whites—fears that blacks would drive down property values or, more generally, forget their "proper place."

The race riots should be viewed against this background of blacks and whites thrown together in cities, of competition for places to live and work, of increased black militancy and corresponding white anxiety. Though no two riots followed exactly the same pattern, there were some

Escorted by a policeman, blacks move their belongings to a safety
zone during the race riots, Chicago, 1919.

similarities. The riots, which usually broke out during a heat wave when
tempers were on edge, were often triggered by rumors of an interracial
rape or other assault. Once the rioting began, the police seldom acted im-
partially; rather, they treated Negroes more brutally than whites. Both
sides committed acts of violence. Usually whites were the aggressors, and
Negroes defended themselves by trading rifle fire with their foes and
making sorties into white neighborhoods. A few riots lasted a long time. It
took 13 days to restore order to Chicago. Invariably the riots left a legacy
of bitterness and led not to mutual understanding but to a hardening of
racial animosities.

Some Americans, seeking an explanation for the race riots, alleged
that radicals stirred up the black community, and thereby linked the labor
and racial turmoil of 1919. *The New York Times* thought it more than coin-
cidental that the race riots in Chicago followed so shortly after those in
Washington, and guessed "that the bolshevist agitation has been extended
among the Negroes." Attorney General Palmer submitted a report that
made the point more sharply. Palmer criticized black leaders for
their "ill-governed reaction toward race rioting," their "threat of retal-
iatory measures in connection with lynching," their "more openly expressed demand for social equality, in which the sex problem is not in-
frequently included," and their "identification of the Negro with such
radical organizations as the IWW and an outspoken advocacy of the Bol-

shevik or Soviet doctrines." The race riots, though, had even less to do with communism than did the strikes. Racial violence, in fact, reflected deep hostility between black and white workers. Yet Palmer's response was understandable. He, like many Americans, was puzzled by the eruption of bitter class and racial antagonism in the aftermath of a war fought, supposedly, in accord with Progressive principles.

THE ROAD TO PARIS

The class and racial antagonisms in the United States mirrored those of the world community. If Americans had difficulty handling these problems at home, there was absolutely no hope that they could make the entire world, or even Europe, safe for Progressive democracy. Yet Wilson set out to try.

He immediately ran into a string of disasters. Throughout the war the President had refused to discuss peace terms with the Allies. He feared that such talks could lead to splits that would retard the war effort, and believed that as the war continued, American economic and military power would give him an increasingly stronger hand. But when he did approach the Allies to discuss the Fourteen Points in late 1918, Wilson discovered that the British adamantly refused to negotiate freedom of the seas (a principle that would protect neutrals against the powerful British fleet). The French insisted on destroying German power regardless of Wilsonian principles. The President's cases were weak, for he had refused to recognize neutral rights on the high seas in 1917–18 and had singled out Germany as primarily responsible for starting the war. After all, such policies had been necessary to sustain the American commitment at home.

On the way to Paris Wilson told his advisors that "the United States was the only nation which was absolutely disinterested" in peace-making. Allied leaders knew better, and they comprehended how history had shaped the American position as well as their own. Harold Nicolson, a member of the British delegation to Paris and later a distinguished historian, observed that Americans, like Europeans, had used brutal force to conquer territory in the nineteenth century. Then he asked, "Can we wonder that [Europeans] preferred the precisions of their old system to the vague idealism of a new system which America might refuse to apply even to her own continent?" As Europeans like Nicolson understood, Wilsonian principles were designed to protect American interests.

The President also informed his advisors that, whereas he embodied the hopes of all progressive peoples, "the leaders of the allies did not really represent their peoples." This was a colossally mistaken belief. David Lloyd George and Georges Clemenceau, the prime ministers of Great Britain and France respectively, received thumping votes of support at home before the peace conference convened, and both ran on platforms pledging to squeeze every possible *pfennig* and acre out of Germany. Wilson, however, in one of the great American political fumbles, had proclaimed in late October 1918 that patriotism required the election of a

Democratic Congress. In a congressional election year the Republicans would probably have gained some seats, but they won a major victory by blasting Wilson for impugning their wholehearted support of the war. Republicans even captured the Senate (49–47), the body that would have to ratify Wilson's work at Paris.

Nor did the President ease the situation by naming a peace commission that contained not a single important Republican or senator. This colorless group was designed so that it would raise few problems for the plans of the delegation's leader, Wilson himself. The President decided that no other person could be entrusted with the mission, not even his Secretary of State, whom Wilson once unfairly dismissed as "so stupid" that the President "was constantly afraid he would commit some serious blunder." In heading the commission, Wilson would have to sacrifice a more detached view of the essentials in order to immerse himself in the time-consuming details of diplomacy. He also gave his political opponents and those who disliked the Fourteen Points a very visible figure to attack.

All of these political errors, however, are less important in understanding Wilson's failure than are his substantive policies. The Fourteen Points had aimed at two objectives: (1) replacing the European balance of power with a world that was open and free economically and largely self-determined politically, and (2) replacing Lenin's revolutionary program with Wilsonian liberal alternatives. But the President soon learned he could not gain both objectives at once.

AT PARIS

In the wake of the war's devastation, Communist uprisings appeared in Germany. A Communist government actually controlled Hungary for several months. Threatened left-wing riots in Austria were in part averted by an American warning that food supplies would be shut off if trouble occurred. "We are sitting upon an open powder magazine," Colonel House worried, "and some day a spark may ignite it." By early 1919 Wilson's fear of Bolshevism overshadowed his mistrust of the Western Europeans. He increasingly found himself on their side in a common effort to contain Leninism. He did reject their suggestions that a larger military force be sent to topple the Bolsheviks, but agreed that Lenin should not be invited to Paris. The President allowed William Bullitt to sound out the Soviet leaders, and Bullitt believed he had worked out an agreement with Lenin that the Allies could accept. By the time Bullitt returned from Russia, however, the President refused even to talk with him. Wilson had decided to use pressure, not negotiation, in handling Lenin.

Wilson continued to have faith that Leninism could be conquered through a "slow process of reform." Since it was his League of Nations that would carry out the reform, Wilson, over the vigorous objections of the French and British (who wanted to settle first the precise, strangulating terms for Germany), forced the peace conference to begin in January 1919 with discussions on the League. Within a month the organiza-

The Big Four of 1919: Lloyd George, Orlando, Clemenceau, Wilson.

tion was formed. It would consist of an Assembly, containing nearly 40 nations (but not revolutionary Mexico, Russia, and Germany); a Council, comprised of nine nations with the five permanent seats given to the United States, Great Britain, Japan, France, and Italy; and a Secretariat. Except for procedural matters, most decisions would require unanimous consent in the Council.

Article XIV established the Permanent Court of International Justice, which could decide international cases taken to the Court by both parties involved. Article XVI pledged all members to penalize aggressors by cutting off trade and economic aid. It was Article X, however, that Wilson termed "the heart of the covenant."

The members of the League undertake to respect and preserve as against external aggression the territorial integrity and existing political independence of all Members of the League. In case of any such aggression or in case of any threat or danger of such aggression the Council shall advise upon the means by which this obligation shall be fulfilled.

This wording deserves close study, for in the end Article X contributed to Wilson's doom.

Returning to the United States for a short time in February 1919, Wilson encountered strong opposition to the Covenant from Republicans in the Senate led by Henry Cabot Lodge of Massachusetts. Lodge made public a petition signed by 39 senators condemning the League, six more than the one-third necessary to defeat the pact. This opposition was partly personal. Some Republicans, Lodge and Theodore Roosevelt in particular, hated Wilson, a feeling not lessened by the President's partisan attack on Republicans and his often condescending manner. But the opponents primarily attacked several aspects of the treaty. Article X, they feared, committed Americans to uphold the status quo around the world, pledged the United States to preserve British and French imperial interests, and weakened Congress's power to declare war by providing a nearly automatic American commitment to intervene. The anti-League forces also attacked the lack of a provision protecting America's use of the Monroe Doctrine in the Western Hemisphere, and the failure to exclude domestic questions (such as tariffs) from League authority.

The President was furious with the Senate. "I am going to resume my study of the dictionary to find adequate terms in which to describe the fatuity of these gentlemen with their poor little minds that never get anywhere," he remarked privately. "I cannot express my contempt for their intelligence." Wilson then made a critical mistake. Returning to Paris, he demanded changes in the Covenant—although not in Article X—that would meet some of the Senate's objections. Time that was to have been devoted to drawing up carefully the German Peace Treaty was, at the President's insistence, spent on rewriting the Covenant. Lloyd George, Clemenceau, and Vittorio Orlando, the Italian leader, knew that they had Wilson over a barrel, and consequently gave in to some of his requests only after he gave them much of what they wanted on the German treaty. The President was forced to surrender key parts of his Fourteen Points, particularly those on self-determination and territorial settlements.

As one American official later commented, "One came to Paris when hope was riding high, and each day you could see these hopes just—well, you soon detected that it was a great enormous balloon and gradually all the air was coming out of it. . . . Then there was Russia, a vast black cloud that overhung the whole thing." As the conference wore on and revolution threatened Germany, Hungary, and Austria, the key problem was, indeed, how the Soviet Union could be isolated and Central Europe, particularly a weakened Germany, protected from the virus of communism. Wilson and Lansing hoped to rebuild Germany so that it would be strong enough to provide its own immunity. Clemenceau, however, and to a lesser extent Lloyd George, determined that Germany must be stripped so that it could never again launch war. Territory taken from Germany was given to France, Poland, and the new independent state of Czechoslovakia. Millions of Germans were therefore wrenched from their native government and placed within the boundaries of other, weaker nations.

Equally important, Germany was saddled with $33 billion of war reparations that had to be paid out of a decimated economy. The French had actually asked $200 billion, but Wilson fought Clemenceau and scaled

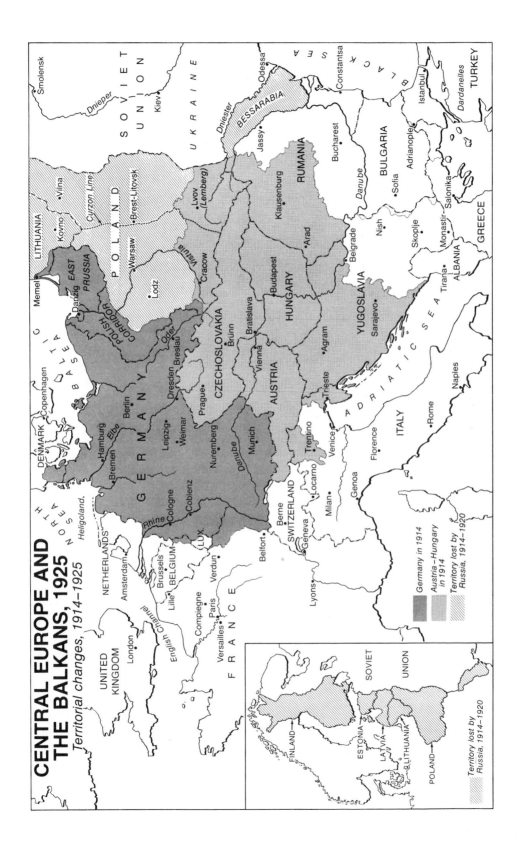

CENTRAL EUROPE AND
THE BALKANS, 1925
Territorial changes, 1914–1925

Germany in 1914

Austria–Hungary in 1914

Territory lost by Russia, 1914–1920

Territory lost by Russia, 1914–1920

down the French demands. In return, however, the President and Lloyd George signed a security treaty promising France aid if it were attacked by Germany. The plan thus became clear: to assist a weakened Germany to withstand the onslaughts of communism sweeping in from the east, the peace conference essentially threw out the principle of self-determination, particularly for Germans, in order to build the newly independent states of Poland, Hungary, and Czechoslovakia, which were to act as buffers, or a *cordon sanitaire*, between Russia and Germany. In reality, of course, these states were too weak to stand between two potential giants, so France gave territorial guarantees to the Eastern Europeans by pledging to assist if they were attacked by a third party.

Self-determination was also sacrificed in the Pacific, where the Chinese province of Shantung, formerly controlled by Germany, was claimed by Japan. Wilson initially fought this transfer, but surrendered when the Japanese threatened to leave the League unless they received Shantung. The President did prevent Italy from claiming non-Italian territory along the Adriatic Sea, even though Orlando dramatically walked out of the conference in protest. Finally, Wilson accepted a compromise on the question of Germany's former colonies in Africa and the Pacific that, in actuality, gave France, England, and Japan the complete control they demanded in these areas. He had wanted the League to be responsible for these colonies under a mandate principle. Instead the three Allies divided up the colonies among themselves, pledging only to submit annual reports to the League. Germany was never consulted on these terms, but simply given the hurriedly written treaty in May to sign—or else. The "or else" probably would have been an economic blockade designed to starve the Germans until they did sign. Wilson fought plans for such a blockade, fearing that this would be the quickest way of transforming Germans into Bolsheviks. Berlin officials finally accepted the treaty only after bitterly protesting its terms. One war had ended.

REJECTION

As Wilson returned to do battle with the Senate, he found three groups preparing to fight the Covenant and the peace treaty. One, centering around Lodge and other conservative Republicans, determined to defeat anything Wilson recommended, but focused its objection particularly on the automatic commitment implied in Article X. A second was comprised of such Progressives as Herbert Hoover and Charles Evans Hughes. This group did not personally dislike Wilson (Hoover, indeed, had been one of the President's important advisors at Paris), but attacked Articles X and XVI and was afraid that the Covenant would endanger Congress's constitutional control over domestic affairs. A third group, led by Progressive Republicans William Borah of Idaho and Hiram Johnson of California, formed the "Irreconcilables," for they refused to agree to American participation in any international organization resembling the League. They moreover blasted Wilson's refusal to deal with Russia, a policy described

Henry Cabot Lodge, 1921.

by Johnson as "an exhibition of the crassest stupidity." One common thread united the three groups: all wanted to maintain maximum U.S. freedom of action in the world, particularly so that Americans could freely exploit their new economic power without having to worry about political restraints.

Wilson's opponents enjoyed a strong position. With the Republicans in control of the Senate, Lodge became chairman of the Foreign Relations Committee, which would first have to act on the Covenant and treaty. As it became clear that Lodge was mustering support, the President attempted to pressure the Senate by embarking on an exhausting speaking tour. After 36 formal speeches in three weeks, the 63-year-old Wilson suffered the beginnings of a paralytic stroke on September 26 in Colorado. Desperately ill, he nevertheless angrily stuck to his refusal to compromise with the Senate. When that body added reservations that modified Article X and withdrew approval of Japan's hold on Shantung, Wilson ordered Democratic senators not to vote for the amended Covenant. In November 1919 the League charter, with reservations, was rejected 39–55. Four months later it again fell short of the necessary two-thirds needed for ratification, 49–35. Twenty-three Democrats, obeying Wilson's orders, ironically joined Irreconcilables in defeating American entry into the League.

The President made one final effort during the 1920 presidential campaign. At first Wilson apparently decided to try for an unprecedented third term, but his illness and realistic Democratic political advisors ended that dream. He then declared the election a "solemn referendum" on the League, urging the Democratic ticket of Governor James Cox of Ohio and young Franklin D. Roosevelt of New York to support the Covenant strongly. The Democratic ticket equivocated, however, while the Republicans, led by Senator Warren G. Harding of Ohio and Governor Calvin Coolidge of Massachusetts, talked on both sides of the League issue. Harding won overwhelmingly, obtaining 60.3 percent of the popular vote and carrying 37 of the 48 states. Foreign policy issues, however, were peripheral, as indeed they have been in nearly every presidential election in the twentieth century. Once elected, Harding clearly stated that he would not push for American association with the League.

Wilson must bear primary responsibility for the American failure to join the League of Nations. His refusal to appoint an important Republican or senator to the delegation, his procedures at Paris, and his unwillingness to compromise with the Senate doomed the Covenant. But in the long run, American participation might have made little difference anyway. The fundamental problem was not the League but the ill-constructed peace, which no organization of mere mortals could have saved. Its treatment of Germany territorially and economically sowed the seeds for the terrible depression and the Nazism of the 1930s. The exclusion of Russia, and then Wilson's announcement in March 1920 that the United States would not even recognize the existence of the Soviet government, piled unreality upon unreality. The failure to handle the problems posed by Germany and Russia set off a right-wing reaction not only in the United States, but in Italy, France, Germany, and Eastern and Southern Europe, where the stage rapidly filled with Fascists and National Socialists.

"What gave rise to the Russian Revolution?" Wilson finally queried in 1923, one year before his death. "The answer can only be that it was the product of a whole social system. It was not in fact a sudden thing." The same explanation can also be applied to the appearance of the right-wing forces in the 1920s and 1930s. For the Paris Peace Conference in the end decided not on peace but on vengeance; not on a sanitary Europe but on a *cordon sanitaire;* not on economic justice—for there was little discussion of such issues at Paris—but on a political settlement that would allow economic exploitation; not on an inclusion of all peoples but on an exclusion of many, particularly revolutionary regimes.

The result was best summarized by William Bullitt in Paris after he resigned from the American delegation. He declared that the peace treaty could result only in "a new century of wars." As he left his hotel, Bullitt was asked by reporters where he would go. "I am going to lie in the sands

of the French Riviera," he replied, "and watch the world go to hell." He
went. And it did.

Suggested Reading

The most important work on wartime mobilization is Robert D. Cuff, *The War Industries Board: Business-Government Relations During World War I* (1973). Propaganda and public opinion are analyzed in J. R. Mock and C. Larsen, *Words That Won the War* (1939); George T. Blakey, *Historians on the Homefront* (1970); and Carol S. Gruber, *Mars and Minerva: World War I and the Uses of the Higher Learning in America* (1975). On woman suffrage see William L. O'Neill, *Everyone Was Brave* (1969); and Andrew Sinclair, *The Emancipation of the American Woman* (1965).

For the war's impact on civil liberties, consult William Preston, Jr., *Aliens and Dissenters: Federal Suppression of Radicals, 1903–1933* (1963); H. C. Peterson and Gilbert C. Fite, *Opponents of War, 1917–1918* (1957); and Paul L. Murphy, *The Meaning of Freedom of Speech . . . Wilson to FDR* (1972). The effect of the war on radicalism is discussed in James Weinstein, *The Decline of Socialism in America, 1912–1923* (1967). The Red Scare is well covered in Stanley Coben, *A. Mitchell Palmer* (1963), and Robert K. Murray, *The Red Scare* (1955); the labor turmoil in David Brody, *Labor in Crisis: The Steel Strike of 1919* (1965); and racial conflict in William M. Tuttle, Jr., *Race Riot: Chicago in the Red Summer of 1919* (1970), and Arthur Waskow, *From Race Riot to Sit-in* (1966). See Burl Noggle, *Into the Twenties* (1974) for an account of reconversion.

An excellent overview of military strategy is Russell F. Weigley's, *The American Way of War* (1973); and a comprehensive analysis of Wilsonian diplomacy is found in G. Gordon Levin, *Woodrow Wilson and World Politics* (1969). For the peace conference, the following are valuable: Carl Parrini, *Heir to Empire . . . 1916–1923* (1969); Jeffrey J. Safford, *Wilsonian Maritime Diplomacy, 1913–1921* (1978), Lawrence E. Gelfand, *The Inquiry, 1917–1919* (1963); two landmark works by Arno J. Mayer, *Wilson vs. Lenin* (1959), and *Politics and Diplomacy of Peacemaking* (1965); Thomas A. Bailey's highly readable *Woodrow Wilson and the Lost Peace* (1944), and *Woodrow Wilson and the Great Betrayal* (1945). For the Russian problem, different perspectives are provided in Lloyd Gardner, ed., *Wilson and Revolutions, 1913–1921* (1976); George Kennan, *Russia Leaves the War* (1956), and *Decision to Intervene* (1958); William Appleman Williams, *Russian-American Relations* (1952); and John Lewis Gaddis, *Russia, the Soviet Union and the United States* (1978). Wilson's opponents are discussed in John Garraty, *Henry Cabot Lodge* (1953); Ralph A. Stone, *The Irreconcilables* (1970); and Robert Maddox, *William E. Borah* (1969). Wesley Bagby's *The Road to Normalcy* (1962) analyzes the 1920 election.

The following are "don't miss" books on baseball: Harold Seymour's scholarly *Baseball* (1960), now in two volumes; Lawrence S. Ritter, *The Glory of Their Times* (1965); Robert W. Creamer, *Babe* (1974); and Marshall Smelser, *The Life That Ruth Built* (1975).

Flagpole sitter: Shipwreck Kelly.

CHAPTER FIVE
1920–1929
The New Era

WALL STREET BLUES

Words by Margaret Gregory *&* W. C. Handy, *music by* W.
C. Handy

I can sing the blues from the bottom of my
heart,
I can sing the blues from the bottom of my
heart,
All my profits gone 'fore I even got a start.
Never had the blues like the blues I'm blue
with now,
Never had the blues like the blues I'm blue
with now,
Oh! what I recall of the street called Wall
and how!
Wailing Wall, Oh Jerusalem!
There's one in New York too,
Where I got a-whalin'
Now I'm ailin'
Wailin' 'cause I'm blue.

Patter:
Margin callin' brokers, miles of ticker tape,
Got a many poor old sap-head wearin' crepe,
Wailin' Wall Street, I just can't enthuse,

Boo-hoo-hoo-in', I've got the Wall Street
Blues.

Blues:
More margin, that's the broker's call,
More margin, I can't meet this call,
No more margin, now he's got it all.

Oh Wall Street you've got me depressed,
Down-hearted, you can guess the rest,
River's East end, graveyard's at the west.

Progressivism had appealed to many Americans because it promised stability to a nation experiencing rapid change. By 1920, however, the Wilsonian years had linked reform not with orderly change but with war and revolution. Consequently, Americans in the 1920s turned toward other leaders who invoked traditional values and played on the widespread nostalgia for a simpler, happier past. But Progressivism did not die. If anything, the decade was characterized by a quickening of those forces that were transforming American life—urban and corporate growth, racial and ethnic heterogeneity, concern for social morality, active government, and international involvement. The sharpest conflicts arose not over economic policy or foreign affairs, where something close to a consensus emerged, but over such issues as religion, ethnicity, and morality. Then, in 1929, Americans suddenly entered a chamber of economic horrors that transformed them, their world, and their Progressivism.

REPUBLICAN POLITICS: HARDING AND COOLIDGE

In 1925 a book entitled *The Man Nobody Knows* climbed to the top of the best-seller list, not because it had great literary merit but because it accurately reflected the prevailing ethos. It was written by advertising executive Bruce Barton, who wanted to dispel the myths surrounding the figure of Jesus Christ. In the gospel according to Madison Avenue, Jesus was the prototype of the modern businessman, indeed the "founder of modern business." A good executive and a regular fellow, He was also an aggressive go-getter. Barton noted that there was no demand for a new religion 2000 years ago. Jesus created one by applying the "principles of modern salesmanship." In deifying businessmen and their values, Barton also preached an ethic of consumption that placed satisfaction above self-denial, luxury above hardship, and spending above thrift. Presumably one served God not only by following a calling, but also by taking advantage of the installment plan. But then He was, in Barton's view, "a great Companion, a wonderful Friend, a kindly, indulgent, joy-loving Father."

This, ironically, might well have served as a description of Warren G. Harding, who won a landslide victory in the 1920 election. A senator from Ohio since 1914 (and the first man ever to move directly from the Senate to the White House), Harding was jovial and expansive, a backslapper who joined as many fraternal lodges as possible. He loved to meet people, had a remarkable memory for faces, and played tennis or golf whenever he could. Harding's chief virtue was that he usually recognized his own limitations, his chief defect that he believed in rewarding old friends with federal jobs. Many of them abused his trust by swindling the government, and when Harding died in August 1923, scandals were erupting on every side. The director of the Veterans' Bureau was convicted of stealing hundreds of millions of dollars; the Attorney General resigned when charged with authorizing the sale of alcohol from government warehouses to bootleggers; and the head of the Alien Property Custodian's Office was found guilty of accepting bribes. The most famous scandal centered around allegations that Harding's Secretary of the Interior, Albert Fall, had leased government oil reserves in Teapot Dome, Wyoming, to private owners in order to line his own pocket. Fall resigned in disgrace and later served a one-year prison sentence.

These revelations, however, did not harm the Republican party, partly because Harding had not been personally involved in the scandals and partly because his successor, Calvin Coolidge, had built his political career on a reputation for honesty and frugality. A former Governor of Massachusetts, Coolidge was a cold, austere individual whose childhood, according to an admiring biographer, was "simple, wholesome and unfurtive." He observed proper protocol, and engaged in no sport more arduous than riding a mechanical horse. His low-key behavior led critics to remark that Coolidge's "ideal day is one on which nothing whatever happens" or to claim that, during his administration, there was "grim, determined, alert inactivity in the White House." But Coolidge's outlook may well have been conditioned by the tragic death of his sixteen-year-old son in the summer of 1924. When Calvin Jr. died, Coolidge recalled, "the power and the glory of the Presidency went with him."

Miles apart in temperament, Harding and Coolidge nevertheless shared similar social and economic views. Both believed that government should foster business enterprise. This meant a hands-off policy in areas where businessmen wanted freedom of action and intervention in areas where they wanted help. "This is a business country," Coolidge remarked, "and it wants a business government." On the other hand, both presidents regarded intervention on behalf of other interest groups as socially undesirable, financially irresponsible, and morally wrong. Such paternalism, Harding warned, "would stifle ambition, impair efficiency . . . and make us a nation of dependent incompetents." This outlook governed Republican policies toward business, labor, agriculture, and public power. It won sanction too from the Supreme Court.

Big business benefited handsomely from Republican rule. Indeed, the *Wall Street Journal* considered Coolidge "sound from every angle." In 1922 Congress enacted the Fordney-McCumber Tariff, which raised import duties to their highest level ever. Harding and Coolidge filled federal regulatory agencies with men who considered it their task to assist the business community. One of them was William E. Humphrey. Appointed to the Federal Trade Commission in 1925, he decided not to prosecute companies that had violated the law so long as they promised to behave in the future. Republicans placed tax policy in the hands of Andrew Mellon, who served as Secretary of the Treasury from 1921 to 1932. Mellon, who resigned from the boards of directors of 51 corporations on assuming office, feared that if high taxes deprived the businessman of a fair share of his earnings, then "he will no longer exert himself and the country will be deprived of the energy on which its continued greatness depends." Mellon fought long, hard, and successfully to reduce taxes on inheritances,

Grace Coolidge, Andrew Mellon, and Calvin Coolidge, 1926.

corporate profits, and the well-to-do. By 1926 Congress had cut the tax
rate on an income of $1 million from 66 percent to 20 percent. Mellon
received honorary degrees from Pittsburgh, Dartmouth, Rutgers, Columbia, Kenyon, Amherst, Harvard, Yale, and Princeton, the latter noting
that "his name bids fair to stand with the greatest masters of finance in
modern times."

While business received all kinds of support, organized labor went
into eclipse. Union membership fell from 5 million in 1920 to 3.4 million
in 1930. This occurred for several reasons: unions had no foothold in industries undergoing the most rapid expansion such as automobiles, rubber, and chemicals; the American Federation of Labor clung to an increasingly obsolete craft structure; employers conducted a vigorous
open-shop drive, which included the use of spies and blacklists to block
organizers; and several large companies introduced welfare measures—
pension, insurance, and stocksharing plans—which stifled union growth.
When walkouts occurred, however, the White House occasionally intervened on the side of management. This happened during the railroad
strike of 1922, when Attorney General Harry Daugherty persuaded

Harding that the nation faced imminent peril. In Daugherty's view, the workers' support for government control of the railroads "was a conspiracy worthy of Lenin" and raised the possibility that "our time-tables and freight-rates would be made out in Moscow." Daugherty obtained a sweeping court injunction that barred virtually all union activities and proved instrumental in breaking the strike.

Harding and Coolidge rejected any government role either in supporting farm prices or in developing power facilities. At the time agricultural interests supported the McNary-Haugen plan, which authorized the government to purchase farm products at prices above those offered in the world market. The government would export the goods at the world market price, and therefore take a loss. Farmers would reimburse the government from the profits they realized on sales to American consumers at inflated domestic prices. Congress defeated this proposal in 1924 and 1926. It passed the plan in 1927 and 1928, only to have Coolidge veto it as "vicious" and "preposterous" special-interest legislation. Republicans also did their best to extract the government from its involvement in the construction of power facilities in the Tennessee Valley. During World War I the government had built power plants at Muscle Shoals. Harding and Coolidge wished to sell these facilities to private entrepreneurs, but Congress blocked their plans. In 1928 when Congress approved completion of the Wilson Dam and the sale of surplus power, Coolidge killed the measure with a pocket veto.

During the 1920s the Supreme Court mirrored the social philosophy that reigned in the White House. This was hardly surprising since Harding appointed four judges to the bench, including William Howard Taft who served as chief justice from 1922 to 1930. In a series of decisions concerning organized labor, the Court ruled that unions engaged in certain types of strikes (such as secondary boycotts) were liable to antitrust prosecution, that strict limits could be placed on picketing outside factory gates, and that court injunctions could be used to enforce contracts in labor disputes. The Supreme Court also struck down key welfare legislation. In *Bailey* v. *Drexel Furniture Co.* (1922) the justices ruled against a child labor act passed in 1919 that imposed a 10 percent tax on the profits of firms employing child labor. A majority found that the tax was levied to regulate business practices rather than to produce revenue and therefore was inappropriate. The Court decided in *Adkins* v. *Children's Hospital* (1923) that states could not establish minimum wages for women workers. Since women could now vote, they no longer merited special protection. Chief Justice Taft, although generally content with the Court's performance, nevertheless feared for the future. "The only hope we have of keeping a consistent declaration of Constitutional law," he noted, "is for us to live as long as we can."

A NEW ORDER: REPUBLICAN ALTERNATIVES TO WILSON'S LEAGUE

In foreign policy as at home, the Harding-Coolidge administrations knew that they could not retreat into isolationism or nostalgia for a pre-1914 world. "There never again will be precisely the old order," Harding declared in 1922. "Indeed, I know of no one who thinks it to be desirable. For out of the old order came the war itself." A new order, constructed and dominated by U.S. economic power, would avert future world wars and revolutions. That power was immense. In 1914 Americans owed the world about $3.5 billion; after they financed the Allies in war, the world suddenly owed the United States $13 billion. Fueled by the new radio, airplane, and especially automobile industries, the booming domestic economy doubled its industrial production between 1921 and 1929. Never had a nation become so rich so fast. That success seemed to confirm superiority in other areas. As *The Ladies Home Journal* trumpeted, "There is only one first-class civilization in the world today. It is right here in the United States." Americans seemed to have the right as well as the power to reconstruct the world.

The new world order was to rest on certain principles. First, military force was to be reduced everywhere. Money spent on rifles was better invested in automobiles so standards of living could rise. The military power required to maintain world stability was to be replaced by a more benign, effective, and profitable economic power. Second, money and trade would be the dynamics of the new order. Amerians naturally wanted to set ground rules that complemented their own greatest strength in international affairs. Third, economic activities were to be undertaken primarily by private individuals, not governments. If government directed investment and trade, individual rights could disappear and fascism or socialism result. "Constantly I insisted [in the 1920s] that spiritual and intellectual freedom could not continue to exist without economic freedom," Herbert Hoover recalled. "If one died, all would die."

Government's primary responsibility was to ensure that private investment and trade could flow freely into any market. Unfair monopolies were therefore to be broken up, state-controlled enterprises (as in Russia) undermined, and, above all, freedom of enterprise was not to be shackled by such political alliances as Article X of the League Covenant. In 1928, for example, the French again pressed Washington for a political alliance against a revived Germany. Secretary of State Frank Kellogg quickly transformed the request into a meaningless 15-nation agreement in which each signatory renounced war, except, of course, for self-defense. The Kellogg-Briand Pact was later laughed at as nothing more than an "international kiss," but most important for Americans it retained their complete freedom of action.

These principles carried on many of the international policies of Roosevelt and Wilson. The most powerful decision-makers in foreign affairs were Secretary of State Charles Evans Hughes and Secretary of

Secretary of Commerce Herbert Hoover at home with his radio set.

Commerce Herbert Hoover. Both had long been identified with Progressive programs. They used to the utmost such Wilsonian instruments as the Edge Act and Webb-Pomerene Act, which allowed bankers and industrialists to combine for the exploitation of foreign markets without regard to American antitrust laws.

Hoover emphasized that the key to happiness and prosperity was an "American Individualism," which he defined as "an equality of opportunity." To ensure such opportunity, Hoover, like Wilson, stressed the need for an expanding overseas economy. To exploit global opportunities Hoover also believed that American entrepreneurs should combine in global associations so that they could both compete with foreign cartels and end cut-throat competition at home. One leading American banker caught this policy exactly: businessmen must stop "scrambling amongst each other for the plums which fall," learning instead "by cooperative effort to plant more plum trees that we might share the larger yield." Since Hoover defined the national interest as the interest of business, his Commerce Department blazed the way. Particularly active was its Bureau of Foreign and Domestic Commerce, which during the 1920's quadrupled its budget as it established 50 offices around the world to help businessmen plant new "plum trees" in foreign markets.

The Republicans had helped block U.S. entry into the League of Nations not out of spite or narrow political motives, but because they disliked the restraints imposed by the League on American power. They believed that they had a better idea. Economic individualism and political freedom would join to make a new, just, and lasting order. If they failed, it was because these assumptions were wrong, not because they attempted to retreat into a supposed isolationism.

THE WASHINGTON CONFERENCE

The first bold stroke of Republican diplomacy appeared when President Harding asked nine major nations to attend the Washington Naval Conference in November 1921. In a brilliantly conceived scheme, Hughes planned to reduce drastically expenditures on warships, dissolve political alliances dangerous to the United States (particularly the Anglo-Japanese alliance in existence since 1902), and work out an international agreement to maintain the open door to the fabled China market. The last point was crucial, for since 1914 the Japanese, bolstered by their pact with England, had been trying to close the door.

In February 1922 the conference produced three interrelated documents. In the Five-Power pact, the United States, Great Britain, Japan, France, and Italy received respective ratios of 5:5:3:1.7:1.7 for the size of their battleship fleets. Cruisers, destroyers, and submarines were excluded from the agreement. The Japanese demanded equality with the Americans and British, but retreated after the other powers promised not to fortify further their naval bases in the Pacific. In reality, the ratios gave Japan naval superiority in East Asia. American naval officers strongly protested the arrangement, arguing that if the Japanese decided to attack in the Far East, no one could stop them. Hughes overruled the Navy with the argument that the ratios also gave the United States dominance in the Western Hemisphere, and England and France control in European waters. Such a realistic division of world power satisfied the Secretary of State.

Bessie Smith and the Blues

Thomas A. Edison invented the phonograph in 1877. It did not come into general use, however, until the 1890s, when grooved records replaced cylinders and an inexpensive "gramophone" was developed. Some, expecting that recorded music would discourage spontaneity, asked fearfully whether children put to bed by recorded lullabies would not become "simply human phonographs—without soul or expression?" Despite the skeptics, the popular demand for recordings proved overwhelming. In 1919 more than 2.25 million phonographs were manufactured; two years later, over 100 million records were produced. The first blues recording by a black singer—Mamie Smith's "Crazy Blues"—was released in 1920. It sold extremely well and encouraged

"The world in a jug, the stopper in my hand": Bessie Smith, 1923.

Gertrude "Ma" Rainey, 1924.

record companies to sign other Negro artists. A large "race market" seemed to exist, particularly among blacks who had migrated to Northern cities during the World War.

Of all the blues singers in the 1920s, none was more popular than Bessie Smith. Born in Tennessee in 1894, she began working with traveling road shows when she was a teenager. For a time she worked with another famous entertainer, Gertrude "Ma" Rainey. In 1923 Bessie Smith made her first recording, "Down Hearted Blues." Columbia Records paid her $125 a side for the record which sold 780,000 copies within six months. (Throughout her association with Columbia, which lasted until 1931, she never received royalties based on sales but instead was paid a flat recording fee.) In 1925 Bessie Smith

organized a traveling tent show, the "Harlem Frolics," which toured in a custom-made 78-foot-long railroad car complete with seven staterooms, kitchen, and bath. Audiences acclaimed her performances and her records sold remarkably well.

The blues idiom had several characteristics. The music was intensely personal. Songs dealt with the singers' own experiences—broken love affairs, natural disasters, tragedy, sorrow. Bessie Smith's own life, while often marked by lavishness and extravagance, had its full share of such misfortune. Songs overtly concerned with racial injustice are hard to find, although, it should be added, studios would surely have been reluctant to record them. The blues appealed mainly to the lower classes, for middle-class Negroes, and whites, were often offended by the emphasis on gambling, drugs, and, above all, sex. When Bessie Smith sang "Empty Bed Blues" ("Bought me a coffee-grinder, got the best one I could find/ So he could grind my coffee, 'cause he has a brand new grind") few doubted her meaning. The blues, finally, was race music. "Race" records were advertised in separate catalogues and sold in stores in black communities. The first Negro-owned record company, Black Swan, advertised: "The

Cab Calloway.

Only Genuine Colored Record—Others Are Only Passing for Colored." Bessie Smith almost always sang before black audiences and was booked in black theaters. Only on rare occasions did she perform for whites.

With the stock market crash of 1929 Bessie Smith's career, and that of many other Negro performers, went into decline. Record sales nosedived and theater attendance dropped. Increasingly, the radio replaced the phonograph as the chief source of home entertainment. The blues, rough and raw-edged, gave way to the softer sound of "swing." Bessie Smith continued to sing, but she never matched her earlier success. On September 26, 1937, she was fatally injured in an automobile accident outside Memphis, Tennessee. A legend quickly arose that she died after being refused admittance to a white hospital. Although unfounded, the legend provided the basis for Edward Albee's play, "The Death of Bessie Smith." The singer was buried in Philadelphia. Her grave remained unmarked for over 30 years until in 1970 a plaque was placed on the site. Half the cost was donated by Janis Joplin, the rock singer, as a tribute to a woman who had exerted so important an influence.

"Cold sober and in a quiet reflective mood": Bessie Smith in 1936.

More important, in return for naval superiority in the Far Pacific Hughes extracted from Japan an agreement to a Nine-Power treaty pledging the maintenance of the open door in China. Clearly the United States was trusting that the Japanese would use their superior power to maintain an open marketplace in China for all nations. Hughes' successes were finally capped by a Four-Power pact that destroyed the Anglo-Japanese alliance, replacing it with an agreement among the United States, Japan, England, and France in which each pledged to respect the others' possessions in the Pacific, and to consult with other powers in the event of aggression in that area.

These three agreements provided the framework for American diplomacy between 1921 and 1941. They marked a triumph for Hughes, for although Japan enjoyed a strong military position, it had pledged itself to the open door. Moreover, after American pressure was applied, the Japanese also agreed to withdraw their troops from Siberia and to surrender Shantung to China. The pressure took the form of a financial arrangement, which had been completed before the Washington Conference convened, between the J. P. Morgan banking house in New York and the Tokyo government. Without that economic leverage on the Japanese, it is doubtful whether Hughes would have wanted to call the conference at all. The deal marked the beginning of a close Tokyo–New York economic relationship. By 1925 American bankers had more than $200 million outstanding to the Japanese.

China attended the conference, complained bitterly about being treated like a bone between dogs, and was ignored. To Western eyes the Chinese were doubly troublesome, for not only were they weak, but also unstable. In May 1919 the revolution led by Sun Yat-sen's Kuomintang party had accelerated. The major powers refused to recognize the revolutionaries. Americans tried to go on with business as usual, but in 1924 the revolution veered leftward as the Kuomintang cooperated with Soviet Russian agents. Effective economic boycotts and bloody personal attacks were launched against foreign missionaries and businessmen. One Chinese leader warned, "The time has come to speak to foreign imperialism in the language it understands." But with Sun's death in 1925, his mantle fell on Chiang Kai-shek. Chiang completed the Kuomintang triumph in 1927, broke with the Soviets, and greatly moderated the revolutionary program. In 1928 he worked out agreements with the United States and Western Europe that restored China's control over her own tariffs. Beyond this, however, Washington would not go. American Marines remained stationed in three Chinese cities to protect property, and six new U.S. gunboats moved to the Yangtze. A stable, wealthy, cooperative Japan, tied to American interests through the strong bonds of money, was a much preferred partner to a revolutionary, erratic, and poverty-ridden China.

THE NEW ORDER
RECONSTRUCTS
THE OLD

The Washington Conference also aided American policy in Europe, that most crucial of all diplomatic priorities. Before the war Europeans had taken half of all American exports. Equally important, Latin America and Asia were so interlinked with Europe's economy that until that area was rebuilt the United States could not count on finding steady customers in the less industrialized countries. Some European nations had recovered quickly. Italy was a model after 1922 when Benito Mussolini assumed power. Despite his Fascism, many Americans admired the dictator for embodying their own supposed traits of efficiency, stability, and masculinity; in the words of former Progressive journalist Ida Tarbell, he was the "despot with a dimple." Germany, France, and Great Britain, however, recovered more slowly, and Americans became concerned. "The prosperity of the United States largely depends upon the economic settlements which may be made in Europe," Hughes observed in 1921, "and the key to the future is with those who make those settlements."

Again American economic leverage allowed Hughes to shape such settlements. His fulcrums were the flush New York money market and the $11 billion loaned to Europe during and immediately after the war. The Republicans insisted this money be repaid on American terms, not because their puritan conscience required it, but because these war debts and the European need for capital provided the United States with great power. Washington's attention centered on Germany, for European (and therefore American) prosperity was impossible without a healthy Germany. That nation had been the industrial hub of the continent before 1914, and promised to be so again if properly reconstructed. Moreover, only a stable Germany could protect Europe against the spread of Bolshevism.

Disagreeing strongly with this moderate American approach, France pressed the Germans for high reparations payments until in 1923 they defaulted. When the French Army retaliated by trying to separate the Rhineland from Germany, the German economy went completely out of control. All of Europe was threatened with catastrophe. Hughes coolly stepped into the chaos, convincing J. P. Morgan to join with British bankers in injecting a $200 million loan into the moribund German system. In return, Hughes demanded that Germany be given easier reparation terms. Despite some French objections, the deal was completed at a 1924 conference headed by Chicago banker Charles G. Dawes. The Dawes Plan became the key to rebuilding Europe.

But the results were rather different from what Hughes and Dawes anticipated. When Morgan sold $100 million of securities for the German loan in the United States, the offer was oversubscribed in hours. Americans, rushing to invest in a stabilized Germany, snapped up some 180 bond and stock issues amounting to nearly $2 billion. When some U.S. investors discovered a Bavarian hamlet needing $125,000 for a small municipal project, they talked the village fathers into taking instead a $3 million loan. Dollars were not only flowing into increasingly questionable projects, but were merely moving in a circular fashion: the United States sent money to Germany, which used it to pay reparations to England and France, which in turn sent it back to New York for payment of war debts and interest on loans. One broken link could make the western economies appear to be a row of collapsing dominoes.

Between 1925 and 1929, however, those economies looked less like dominoes than a game of monopoly. During those four years Americans loaned more than $5 billion abroad. By 1928 such giant corporations as Standard Oil of New Jersey, DuPont, Ford, General Motors, and Singer Sewing Machine had invested $3 billion in their own overseas subsidiaries. Americans put another $8 billion into overseas portfolio investments, that is, into stocks and bonds of foreign-owned companies. The State Department welcomed most of these ventures. The rebuilding of Germany, of course, was a primary diplomatic goal. In the Middle East American capitalists bitterly struggled with the British and French for control over the world's greatest oil reserves. The competition ended in 1928 with the "Red Line agreement," in which the giant oil companies divided a large Middle Eastern area, marked on a map with a red pencil, among themselves. Even Russia welcomed capital for developmental projects. Despite its refusal to recognize the Bolsheviks, Washington determined to encourage American businessmen to rush into what Hoover called "an economic vacuum" in order to beat out European entrepreneurs. Hoping that even Soviets could be transformed into capitalists, such American corporations as Ford, Westinghouse, and W. Averell Harriman's ventures invested millions of dollars in Lenin's country. In this area, however, Germany had become a foe, not a friend. Not only did it dominate foreign investments in Russia, but in 1922 the two outcasts publicly agreed to cooperate economically. Secretly they helped rebuild each other's military machine.

Despite the successes in rebuilding Germany, the Middle East, and Russia, Hoover watched the outflow of capital with growing concern. He knew that much of it was going into doubtful enteprises and that other American money, such as that helping Japan develop Manchuria, injured American export interests. United States bankers were following selfish policies that badly hurt other American businessmen. Manufacturers, for example, not only hated the bankers for helping Japanese industry take over former American markets in Manchuria, but also for investing money in bond issues abroad rather than in industrial export enterprises at home. As early as 1922 Hoover had tried to control the bankers by giving the government power informally to approve or disapprove each loan made overseas. The bankers' violent objections, as well as Hoover's own fear of such governmental involvement in private business, ruined the plan. Virtually uncontrolled, the bankers blithely went on, investing in dubious projects until, like lemmings, they nearly self-destructed in 1929.

THE NEW ORDER
IN LATIN AMERICA

American capital was also the key to relations with Latin America. In this area, however, Washington officials were not reluctant to use military force as well to maintain stability. Latin America had so long been counted a United States preserve that when new recruits entered the State Department's Foreign Service School in the mid-1920s, they were told not to expect too much from South Americans; their "Latin temperament" and "racial quality" were weaknesses—although Latin Americans could become "very easy people to deal with if properly managed." A 1924 survey revealed that of the 20 Latin American nations, only 6 were free of some kind of United States "management." The remainder were either under the Marine Corps or had their finances controlled by New York bankers. With stability assured, United States investments in Latin America more than doubled to $5.4 billion between 1924 and 1929, or at a rate more than twice as great as that in any other part of the world. Much of this went into oil exploration and development. The southern part of the hemisphere was to provide the raw materials for the industrial progress of the northern part.

United States officials tried to make Latin America the showcase of American foreign policy. They believed that through cooperation between government and business, the area could produce prosperity and democracy for its peoples and profits for its developers. Hoover's Commerce Department helped investors by coming up with new approaches for building the infrastructure (the highways, communications, and utilities) needed to attract private capital. Such ideas anticipated the Alliance for Progress of the 1960s, and both programs fully understood that undercutting potential Latin American revolutions had to be a paramount objective. "The number of rebellions per capita is highest in those republics where the per capita mileage of highways is lowest," a Commerce Department official announced in 1929. "Romance may have been driven out by the concrete mixer, but the mixer has paved the way for law and order and for better understanding, as well as better business among the far-flung provinces of these sparsely populated commonwealths."

Hoover also tried to help by announcing new political policies. He changed the Wilsonian principle that the only acceptable government was a properly elected regime. Control of the country, a promise to meet international obligations, and the intent to hold elections in the future would now be sufficient to merit American recognition. After becoming President in 1929, Hoover also repudiated the Roosevelt Corollary of 1904–05 and began pulling Marines out of Caribbean nations. Problems did exist, particularly with revolutionary Mexico. The United States had finally recognized the Mexican government in 1923 but continued to object to the Mexican Constitution's Article 27, which provided for national ownership of such subsurface minerals as oil. A heated dispute developed in 1926–27, and it was not helped when the American ambassador accused Mexico of exporting Bolshevism to Central American countries. Wilson's former Secretary of the Interior, Franklin K. Lane, now an attorney for American oil companies, perfectly captured the prevailing view: "When I say that Russia may go her own way and Mexico hers, I say so with a sense that I have a right in [both countries] and also a right to see that they do not go their own way to the extent of blocking my way to what of good they hold." In 1927 a temporary compromise was finally reached on the oil controversy.

By 1928 hemispheric relationships were becoming badly skewed. The United States had loaned $2.5 billion and increased exports to Latin Americans, but when they tried to pay their debts they ran into American tariff walls that prevented many of their products from entering the United States. As in Europe, United States investors swamped South America with dollars; in 1928 Peru received twice as much in loans as it could legitimately use. Anti-Yankeeism flourished in such conditions. At the 1928 Inter-American conference, the Latin Americans proposed that no state had the right to intervene in the internal affairs of another. When the United States objected, it was joined by only four countries, three of which were under American control. A year later depression struck. Seven revolutions erupted in Latin America between 1929 and 1931. Given its own assumption that a foreign policy's success was measured by the stability it produced, the Pan American policies of the United States lay in shambles.

THE POLITICS OF CULTURAL CONFLICT

Social reformers found that the most pressing domestic issues of the decade were precisely those, such as immigration restriction and prohibition, on which they were most bitterly divided. Cultural issues—those relating to ethnicity, morality, and religion—dominated political discourse for several reasons. First, prosperity led to a decline in the relative importance of economic concerns. Indeed, there was a wide area of agreement on these matters between Democrats and Republicans. Second, large numbers of second-generation immigrants became more assertive and demanded a greater share of political power at the national level. The groups that felt themselves being elbowed aside counterattacked. Third, the spread of cosmopolitan mores and values troubled many small town Americans who associated big cities with vice, crime, and immorality. Fourth, the most controversial of the issues, prohibition, assumed new importance simply because it had become the law of the land and could no longer be ignored. Where one stood on such an issue had little to do with one's position on child labor or railroad regulation. It had everything to do with where one's parents had been born, which church one attended (or did not attend), and whether one lived in a village or large city.

Proposals to curb immigration clearly exposed some of these cultural tensions. In 1921, after the arrival of 1.2 million immigrants in just one year, President Harding approved a measure drastically limiting further admission. But this was merely a prelude. In 1924 the National Origins Act sailed through Congress with a huge majority. The Act provided for the annual entry until 1927 of only 164,000 European immigrants under a quota system determined by the composition of the U.S. population in 1890. Under this arrangement the combined quotas for Russia and Italy were less than that for Norway; the combined quotas for Poland and Greece less than that for Sweden. Beginning in 1927 the United States would admit 150,000 European immigrants each year under quotas based on the national origins of the white population in 1920. The measure also barred all Japanese, but set no limits on immigration from Canada, Mexico, or South America. The National Origins Act won broad support from Progressives, including Senators Hiram Johnson of California and George Norris of Nebraska. But urban reformers, whose constituencies included the ethnic and religious groups under assault, expressed dismay at the bigotry of those who had "a fixed obsession on Anglo-Saxon superiority."

If immigration restriction illustrated the divisions among reformers, the experience of the Progressive party in 1924 demonstrated their essential weakness. The party was formed by diverse groups uniting out of weakness rather than strength: former Bull Moose Progressives, leaderless since the death of Theodore Roosevelt; socialists, whose movement lay in ruins as a result of the war and the Red Scare; midwestern farmers, resentful over a sharp decline in agricultural prices; and railroad workers, embittered by the Harding administration's role in breaking their 1922 strike. In some respects the Progressive platform of 1924 was a throwback to 1912. It called for public ownership of railroads, the breaking up of monopolies, direct election of the president, and a constitutional amendment barring child labor. The party also favored prohibiting the use of injunctions in labor disputes, promoting public works in time of depression, and imposing high taxes on business profits. To the Progressives and their 69-year-old presidential candidate, Robert M. La Follette of Wisconsin, "that government is deemed best which offers to the many the highest level of average happiness and well-being."

La Follette faced an uphill struggle in his race against Calvin Coolidge and John W. Davis, the conservative lawyer nominated by the Democrats. His opponents, assailing La Follette for having opposed American entry into World War I, branded him a dangerous radical, the candidate of "the Reds, the Pinks, the Blues, and the Yellows." The Progressives, moreover, faced many of the same obstacles that traditionally hamper third parties: lack of funds, absence of grass-roots organization, inability to get on the ballot in every state. Although the American Federation of Labor formally endorsed La Follette's candidacy, labor gave the ticket less support than expected. Similarly, as agricultural prices improved in 1924, farmers' enthusiasm for La Follette waned. In November La Follette obtained 4.8 million votes—under 17 percent of the total—and captured only Wisconsin's 13 electoral votes. Davis received 8.3 million votes, and Coolidge a whopping 15.7 million. Apparently the Republican slogan—"I

Governor Al Smith and family.

like silence and success better than socialism and sovietism"—hastened the downfall of the reform-minded third party.

During the 1920s a new style of urban reformer began to emerge, best symbolized, perhaps, by Democrat Alfred E. Smith and Republican Fiorello H. La Guardia. Smith, the son of Irish Catholic immigrants, epitomized New York City in his manner, accent, and very person. He had worked as a boy in the Fulton Fish Market, honeymooned at Coney Island, served an apprenticeship in Tammany Hall, and then became Governor of New York. He was only being candid when he said, "I'd rather be a lamppost on Park Row than Governor of California." La Guardia, who represented East Harlem in Congress from 1922 to 1933, was an Italian-Jewish-American Episcopalian, who spoke seven languages, and whose wife was a German Lutheran. La Guardia, his biographer has commented, "was a balanced ticket all by himself." Smith and La Guardia supported a broad range of social welfare proposals, but what set them apart was precisely their stand on cultural issues. Both championed the cause of immigrants. Both openly flouted prohibition. Both served as spokesmen for urban cosmopolitanism in a bitter struggle with rural fundamentalism.

This struggle reached a climax when the Democrats selected Smith as their presidential candidate in 1928. Smith favored such reforms as public power and McNary-Haugenism, but his contest with Republican Herbert Hoover did not center on economic issues. Smith in fact chose as his campaign manager John J. Raskob, a former Republican and General Motors

PRESIDENTIAL ELECTION, 1928

Republican (Hoover)

Democratic (Smith)

executive who listed his occupation in *Who's Who in America* as "capitalist." The election turned on the issues of religion, immigration, prohibition, and the city. One New England Protestant reformer expressed the sense of cultural cleavage when she wrote in her diary: "My America against Tammany's. Prairie, Plantation and Everlasting Hills against the Sidewalks of New York!" Given the prevailing prosperity, Hoover was probably unbeatable, but his margin of victory demonstrated the pervasiveness of cultural tensions. Smith received only 87 electoral votes, and 15 million votes to Hoover's 21.4 million. For the first time since Reconstruction, the Republicans broke the Solid South, capturing Virginia, North Carolina, Texas, Florida, and Tennessee. The only consolation for the Democrats was that Smith did extremely well in the nation's largest cities.

PROHIBITION AND CRIME

Many Americans greeted the advent of prohibition in January 1920 with unwarranted optimism. Prohibitionists had long promised that, given a chance, they would eradicate pauperism and improve the condition of the working class. They had also predicted a sudden reduction in crime since "90 percent of the adult criminals are whisky-made." Closing the saloons, many believed, would improve the nation's physical health and strengthen its moral fiber as well, for drys were always saying that liquor "influences the passions" and "decreases the power of control, thus making the resisting of temptation especially difficult." On the day the Eighteenth Amendment took effect, the evangelist Billy Sunday conducted a mock funeral service for John Barleycorn in Norfolk, Virginia. He prophesied: "The slums will soon be only a memory. We will turn our prisons into factories and our jails into storehouses. . . . Men will walk upright now, women will smile, and the children will laugh. Hell will be forever for rent."

Prohibition, however, proved more attractive to some than to others, and the distinction often followed religious, ethnic, and geographic lines. Typically, the prohibitionist was likely to be a Baptist or Methodist rather than a Catholic, Jew, Lutheran, or Episcopalian; an old-stock American rather than a first- or second-generation immigrant. He was more likely to live in a small town, and in the South or Midwest, than in New York, Boston, or Chicago. Undaunted by accusations that they were narrow-minded fanatics striving to enforce conformity to their moral code, prohibitionists saw themselves allowing the "pure stream of country sentiment and township morals to flush out the cesspools of cities and so save civilization from pollution." At the heart of the struggle between wets and drys were contrasting cultural styles.

The Eighteenth Amendment, ratified in January 1919 and ultimately approved by every state except Connecticut, Rhode Island, and New Jersey, contained several glaring loopholes. It did not forbid the consumption of intoxicating beverages but only their sale or manufacture. As a result, those who could afford to store up an adequate supply were not terribly inconvenienced. Out of deference to property rights, liquor dealers were permitted a full year's grace in which to wind up their business affairs. The amendment also failed to define the word "intoxicating" or to provide any means of enforcement. The Volstead Act (1920) attempted to remedy these deficiencies: it arbitrarily defined as "intoxicating" any beverage with one-half of 1 percent alcoholic content, and it provided rudimentary enforcement machinery.

Yet the task of enforcement proved truly Herculean, particularly in those communities where a majority saw no moral virtue in temperance. There seemed an endless number of ways to evade the law. People smuggled whiskey across the Canadian and Mexican borders, made denatured industrial alcohol palatable by adding chemical ingredients, prepared their own "moonshine" at home in one-gallon stills, falsified druggists' prescriptions, stole liquor reserved for legitimate medicinal and religious purposes in government warehouses, and pumped alcohol back into "near-beer" to give it more of a kick. Those administering the law encountered many difficulties. The Prohibition Bureau, understaffed and underpaid, was the target of a series of attempted briberies. Some evidently succeeded, for one of every twelve agents was dismissed for corrupt behavior and presumably others were never caught.

For all its inadequacies, the law almost certainly cut down on alcoholic consumption. But people who wanted to continue drinking, and those for whom liquor filled an important psychological need, managed to get around the law. Moreover, the attempt to enforce a moral code to which many did not adhere led to widespread hypocrisy and disrespect for the law. This received formal recognition when the Supreme Court ruled that the government could request income-tax returns from bootleggers. The Court found no reason "why the fact that a business is unlawful should exempt it from paying the tax that if lawful it would have to pay." The memoirs of a leading prohibition agent also testified to the laxity of enforcement. He related how long it took to buy a drink on arriving in different cities: Chicago—21 minutes; Atlanta—17 minutes; Pittsburgh—11 minutes. In New Orleans it took but 35 seconds. The agent asked a cab driver where he could find a drink; the driver, offering him a bottle, replied "right here."

Prohibition was associated not only with a cavalier attitude toward the law but also with a more sinister phenomenon: the rise of organized crime. Criminal gangs had existed in the past, but in the 1920s they evidently became larger, wealthier, and more ostentatious. Gangland weddings—and funerals—became occasions for lavish displays of wealth and influence. The 1924 funeral of the Chicago gunman Dion O'Banion included 26 truckloads of flowers, an 8-foot heart of American beauty roses, and 10,000 mourners among whom were several prominent politicians. Gangs also became increasingly efficient and mobile as a result of the availability of submachine guns and automobiles. And they grew somewhat more highly centralized, dividing territory in an effort to reduce internecine warfare. Although criminals made money through control of prostitution, gambling, and racketeering, bootleg liquor provided a chief source of revenue.

As organized crime blossomed, new theories arose to account for it. Sociologists at the University of Chicago, for example, argued that criminal behavior did not result from mental or biological inferiority, but represented a logical response to the environment. The gangster, growing up in a climate of lawlessness and graft, was simply a product of his surroundings. In his study of crime in Chicago, John Landesco noted that the gangster developed a self-image that legitimized his behavior. He viewed himself as doing what everyone else in America was doing—seeking wealth and power—but being more open about it. He thought of himself as satisfying a public demand for liquor and other illicit, but essentially harmless, pleasures. He perceived himself as a community benefactor who lent a helping hand to the poor. Indeed, Frank Uale was known as "the Robin Hood of Brooklyn," and "the godfather of 1000 children." A remark attributed to Al Capone summed up much of this rationale: "They call Capone a bootlegger. Yes. It's bootleg while it's on the trucks, but when your host at the club, in the locker room, or on the Gold Coast hands it to you on a silver platter, it's hospitality."

By the end of the decade, opponents of prohibition had successfully turned the tables on its advocates. Once the drys had promised that prohibition would reduce crime; now the wets held prohibition responsible for organized crime and pledged that with repeal, "the immorality of the country, racketeering and bootlegging, will be a thing of the past." Formerly the drys had claimed that prohibition would eliminate poverty; now the wets asserted that the liquor industry could provide needed jobs and revenue to a nation beginning to experience mass poverty in the Great Depression. Prohibition was repealed in 1933. Yet it failed less because it triggered a crime wave or weakened the economy than because it attempted the impossible: to regulate moral behavior in the absence of a genuine consensus that the proscribed behavior was, in any real sense, immoral.

THE KU KLUX KLAN

In the years following the Civil War, white southerners had organized the Ku Klux Klan to terrorize Negroes and prevent them from voting. This early organization passed away with the end of Reconstruction, but in 1915 a new Klan was founded by William J. Simmons. In the early 1920s millions of Americans joined the hooded order, although membership probably never exceeded 1.5 million at any time. Yet the new Klan was not simply a reincarnation of the old. The Klan of the 1920s, although strong in the South, was stronger still in Indiana, Illinois, and Ohio. Perhaps three of every five members did not live in the South or Southwest. The new Klan also was not as heavily rural, but enlisted members in Chicago, Detroit, Atlanta, Denver, and other cities. One of every three Klansmen lived in a city with a population of over 100,000. Finally, the Klan was no longer primarily a white supremacist group. Its chief targets in the 1920s were immigrants and Catholics.

The Klan began its rapid ascent in 1920 when two public-relations experts, Edward Y. Clarke and Elizabeth Tyler, made an arrangement with Simmons that turned the Klan into a highly profitable business venture. To sell Klan memberships they recruited a legion of high-powered salesmen, known as "Kleagles," and adopted the latest sales techniques. More than 1000 organizers set forth in search of recruits, and since each membership cost $10, of which the Kleagle kept $4, the incentive was rather high. Simmons and the other Klan leaders eventually grew wealthy by taking a rake-off on everything from membership fees to the sale of official robes and hoods. With so much at stake, power struggles inevitably occurred. In 1922 the Klan changed hands. Hiram Wesley Evans, a Dallas dentist, ousted Clarke and Tyler and agreed to buy out Simmons who held the copyright on Klan regalia. Simmons retained his title but no authority. He later recalled, "Not long after Evans got in I noticed a coldness among all the office help. I didn't have any office to go to. I just sort of had to hang around the place even though my title was Emperor."

The Klan created a world of make-believe by carrying ritual, pageantry, and secrecy to the furthest extreme. Klansmen met in a Klavern, held Klonklaves, carried on Klonversations, and even sang Klodes. They aspired to such high offices as that of "Grand Goblin," "Grand Dragon," and "Exalted Cyclops." They followed a Kalendar in which 1867 was the year 1, and in which awe-inspiring names were assigned to days (dark, deadly, dismal, doleful, desolate, dreadful, desperate), weeks (woeful, weeping, wailing, wonderful, weird), and months (bloody, gloomy, hideous, fearful, furious, alarming, terrible, horrible, mournful, sorrowful, frightful, appalling). Klan members spoke a secret language by forming strange, new words from the first letter of each word in a sentence. Thus "sanbog" meant "strangers are near, be on guard." The symbol "KKK" was exploited to the fullest. An advertisement in a Klan journal offered members a "Kluxer's Knifty Knife," a "real 100% knife for 100% Americans."

Clever organization and secret ritual did not alone account for the Klan's success. It also preached an ideology that appealed to Americans who feared that alien groups were threatening a traditional way of life. Hiram Wesley Evans asserted that blacks could never "attain the Anglo-Saxon level. . . . The low mentality of savage ancestors, of jungle environment, is inherent in the blood-stream of the colored race in America." He regarded Jews as "alien and unassimilable." The Klan was hysterically anti-Catholic. It believed in a Papal conspiracy to subvert American liberties and blamed Catholics for the deaths of Presidents Lincoln, McKinley, and Harding. Klansmen even suggested that the two antique cannons on the lawn of Georgetown University were pointing at the Capitol for a reason. Racism, anti-Semitism, and anti-Catholicism were all subsumed under a broader fear of the "mongrelization" of America through immigration. As Simmons put it, "The dangers were in the tremendous influx of foreign immigration, tutored in alien dogmas and alien creeds, slowly pushing the native-born white American population into the center of the country, there to be ultimately overwhelmed and smothered."

Klan activities were a strange mixture of benevolence and terrorism. In some cases the Klan functioned primarily as a fraternal organization. Members patronized each other's businesses, helped out in case of sickness or accident, and contributed to various churches and charities. Klansmen attended picnics together and held beauty contests, on one occasion choosing a "Queen of the Golden Mask." But the Klan also set itself up as a watchdog of community morals. It spied on people, reported acts of marital infidelity, attacked "indecent" shows and publications, and promised "to drive the bootleggers forever out of this land and place whiskey-making on a parity with counter-feiting." To uncover every possible scandal, the Klan sometimes tapped telephone wires and intercepted mail at post offices. It punished transgressors by burning crosses outside their homes, ostracizing them, or brutally beating and torturing them. Some victims were immigrants or Negroes, others native white Protestants who failed to measure up to Klan standards.

The Klan acquired formidable political power. It helped elect senators in Oregon, Ohio, Tennessee, and several other states. In Texas it elected a senator, held a majority in the state legislature for a time, and controlled Dallas, Fort Worth, and Wichita Falls. The Indiana Klan, under David Stephenson, built a machine that dominated state politics and placed a functionary in the governor's mansion. In Denver a Klansman was named manager of public safety. The Klan's political goals, aside from power for its own sake, were to prohibit immigration, prevent United States entry into the World Court, enforce prohibition, and weaken parochial schools. The Klan put up its own candidates, endorsed others whom it considered friendly, and, above all, sought to prevent the nomination of, or else defeat, candidates like Al Smith who stood for everything it abhorred.

Despite Smith's defeat, the Klan by 1928 had passed its peak. Torn by internal conflicts between Evans and state leaders, placed on the defensive by politicians who considered it a disruptive force, appeased by enactment of the National Origins Act, the Klan after 1924 began losing members and influence. Then Stephenson was arrested for abducting a young woman, sexually molesting her, and refusing to let her visit a doctor after she poisoned herself. Convicted and sentenced to the penitentiary, Stephenson opened his private files, which exposed Klan lawlessness. Supposedly created to enforce strict moral codes, the Klan could not survive this scandal or the ensuing revelations. By 1930 the organization was everywhere in shambles. Eventually the Klan sold its national offices in Atlanta to a purchaser who, in turn, sold the building to the Catholic Church. Appropriately, it thereafter served as an archbishop's official residence.

FUNDAMENTALISM AND THE SCHOOLS

In the summer of 1925 the town of Dayton, Tennessee, witnessed an event that symbolized the decade's cultural conflicts. John Thomas Scopes was put on trial for having violated state law by teaching the theory of evolution in the public schools, but the nation's attention was focused on the lawyers for the two sides. Prosecutor William Jennings Bryan was the most prominent spokesman for the traditional values of rural, Protestant America. Defense attorney Clarence Darrow, by contrast, was a skeptic, a relativist, and an agnostic. There seemed no common ground between them. To fundamentalists the theory of evolution was a scientific sham the acceptance of which would erode the moral underpinnings of society. Evolutionists, on the other hand, placed fundamentalists on a par with those who had once refused to believe that the earth revolved about the sun.

Religious fundamentalists believed in the literal truth of the Bible. The story of Adam and Eve was, in their view, a matter of historical fact. Darwin's theory of evolution, which contradicted the biblical account of Creation, was incompatible with divine revelation and therefore wrong. Many fundamentalists, however, misunderstood Darwin's theory and became easy targets for ridicule. The editor of the *Bible Champion,* for example, discounted the theory of evolution because while visiting a zoo he noted that "the monkeys and apes conducted themselves precisely as he had seen others behave many years ago in his boyhood days. He could see no signs of growing intelligence." Fundamentalists sometimes assumed an overt posture of antiintellectualism, as when Bryan declared it more important to know the Rock of Ages than to know the age of rocks. Yet if fundamentalists oversimplified Darwin, the theory of natural selection—that evolution occurred through a gradual accretion of useful variations that fit an organism to survive—had by no means been proven. Bryan noted sarcastically that Darwin, in two major books, resorted to the phrase "We may suppose" more than 800 times.

Fundamentalists were disturbed by what they considered a breakdown in moral values, and by this they meant everything from "vile and suggestive" motion pictures and dance styles to "unchaperoned automobile riding at night." They attributed this, at least in part, to the popularity of the theory of evolution. By calling the Scriptures into question, Darwin was undermining Christian faith. By emphasizing man's animal nature, he was excusing immoral conduct. In addition, reformers understood that conservatives had taken Darwin's theory, applied it to human society, and concluded that government assistance to the needy violated the natural law of survival of the fittest. Bryan believed that the Darwinian model held that man evolved "by the operation of the law of hate—the merciless law by which the strong crowd out and kill off the weak." If Darwin was not responsible for the uses to which his theory had been put, Bryan nevertheless realized that the application had pernicious results.

Fundamentalist opinion was strongest in the South and Southwest but hardly dominated those regions. During the 1920s, bills designed to prohibit the teaching of evolution were introduced in 20 state legislatures. The measures always encountered stiff opposition and were usually defeated. Only five states—Oklahoma, Florida, Tennessee, Mississippi, and Arkansas—enacted such bills, and even there they were regarded less as weapons of repression than as symbolic expressions of legislative concern. The Butler bill in Tennessee, which led to the Scopes trial, barred the teaching of "any theory that denies the Story of the Divine Creation of Man as taught in the Bible, and [holds] instead that man has descended from a lower order of animals." It passed easily since educators feared that opposing a popular measure might jeopardize state university appropriations. No one took it very seriously. "Probably the law will never be applied," said the Governor on signing it.

It was applied only when some acquaintances persuaded Scopes to test the law, and the American Civil Liberties Union agreed to provide legal counsel. No one had interfered with the way Scopes conducted his high school biology class, but he agreed to the trial as a matter of principle. The chief courtroom drama occurred when Bryan took the witness stand and engaged Darrow in a verbal duel over the literal interpretation of the Bible that revealed Bryan's limited knowledge of science. The outcome, however, was a foregone conclusion, for Scopes admitted breaking the law and the judge ruled that evidence supporting the theory of evolution was inadmissible. The jury took nine minutes to find Scopes guilty, and he was fined $100. Offered his old job back, Scopes turned it down to pursue graduate study in geology at the University of Chicago. William Jennings Bryan died five days after the trial ended. Forty-two years later, Tennessee repealed the Butler act.

The furor surrounding the evolution controversy concealed the more subtle pressures exerted on teachers nearly everywhere in the United States. Most Americans believed that the public schools should instill certain values in the young, but typically the sensitive areas involved politics or economics rather than religion. In 1927 Nebraska provided that its teachers emphasize "honesty, morality, courtesy, obedience to law, respect for the national flag, the constitution, . . . respect for parents and the home, the dignity and necessity of honest labor and other lessons of a steadying influence, which tend to promote and develop an upright and desirable citizenry." As Howard K. Beale's investigation *Are American Teachers Free?* revealed, school boards commonly established curricula, selected textbooks, and hired teachers—all with an eye toward excluding unpopular ideas. In this sense the antievolution crusade did not represent an entirely atypical effort to restrict what teachers might tell their students. But because it attempted to reassert the validity of an older system of values through legislation, it expressed the cultural tensions that characterized the 1920s.

THE GHETTO
AND GARVEYISM

As cities in America got larger, so too did their black ghettoes. The northward migration of Negroes, stimulated by the war, continued into the 1920s. During the decade New York City's black population climbed from 152,000 to 328,000, Chicago's from 109,000 to 233,000. People left the rural South to improve their lives and some undoubtedly succeeded, but large numbers did not. In Harlem and Chicago's South Side they crowded into grimy tenements for which they paid exorbitant rents. In 1927 an investigator said of Harlem that "the State would not allow cows to live in some of these apartments." Most Negroes could find jobs only as menial or unskilled workers, and even then took home less pay than their white counterparts. As always, poverty produced chronic ill-health: in the mid-1920s the death rate in Harlem was 42 percent higher, and the infant mortality rate 70 percent higher, than elsewhere in the city. Even those who did reasonably well often seem to have found adjustment to urban life a disorienting and alienating experience.

These conditions made possible the spectacular success of Marcus Garvey and his nationalist doctrine. A Jamaican who came to the United States in 1917, Garvey dreamed of "uniting all the Negro peoples of the world into one great body to establish a country and Government absolutely their own." His Universal Negro Improvement Association claimed hundreds of thousands of followers in the early 1920s, most of them uprooted blacks who had left the rural South for the urban North. Garvey appealed to race pride by glorifying blackness. His paper, unlike other Negro journals, did not ordinarily accept advertisements for skin-lightening lotions or hair-straightening formulas. Whites, he claimed, had distorted the black past: "When Europe was inhabited by a race of cannibals, a race of savages, naked men, heathens and pagans, Africa was peopled with a race of cultured black men, who were masters in art, science and literature." Garvey also employed pomp and pageantry. His followers wore the resplendent uniforms of the "Knights of the Nile," the "Dukes of the Niger," or the "Black Eagle Flying Corps."

The coin of black pride had a reverse side: distrust of whites. In Garvey's view, "potentially every white man is a Klansman." As population growth increased the competition for jobs and resources, whites would become ever less tolerant of black success. The goal of integration, therefore, was a delusion, for the white majority would never accord justice to the black minority. "All true Negroes are against social equality," Garvey wrote, "believing that all races should develop on their own social lines." This could happen if blacks were free to build their own nation in Africa. Garvey did not expect the emigration of all black Americans but rather of a dedicated cadre of trained people. When whites saw that Negroes were capable of constructing an advanced civilization of their own, they would show blacks more respect. If not, a powerful African state would drape a protective mantle around blacks wherever they might live.

Garvey's approach to economics was wholly in keeping with the business ethos of the 1920s. Deeply influenced by Booker T. Washington's self-help program, Garvey asserted that the Negro worker's only ally was the white capitalist who needed his labor. Blacks should steer clear of white trade unions and, indeed, work for just under union wages because employers would always prefer to hire a white unless there was some incentive to hire a black. In the long run, though, Negroes could become autonomous only by developing their own business and commerical establishments. Garvey sponsored several such undertakings, but by far the most important was the Black Star Line, a steamship company designed to link the colored peoples of the world commercially and to transport repatriates to Africa. It thus united the twin themes of African redemption and black entrepreneurship.

But the Black Star Line was also the immediate cause of Garvey's downfall. The company sold thousands of shares at $5 each to black investors, but it quickly went bankrupt. Lacking managerial experience, Garvey fell victim to unscrupulous dealers who sold him run-down ships at inflated prices. The vessels constantly broke down and failed to pass inspection. The fiasco led to charges in 1922 that Garvey had used the mails to defraud investors. The government was only too happy to prosecute, for it had long regarded Garvey, in the words of the State Department, as "an undesirable, and indeed a very dangerous, alien" who was organizing "all of the negroes in the world against the white people." The trial began in May 1923 with Garvey, who believed himself the victim of persecution, conducting his own defense. He was found guilty and sentenced to five years in prison. In February 1925, when the courts rejected his appeal, Garvey entered the penitentiary. Late in 1927 President Coolidge commuted his sentence and the government deported him as an undesirable alien.

Most other black leaders, who always considered Garvey's ideology dangerous and his movement a threat, seemed relieved by the outcome. The NAACP opposed Garvey because he rejected integration and challenged its authority as spokesman for American Negroes. A. Philip Randolph and other socialists placed their hopes in an alliance of black and white workers. They resented Garvey's enmity toward unions, emphasis on black enterprise, and insistence that race was more important than class. Randolph bitterly attacked Garvey as "A Supreme Negro Jamaican Jackass" and launched a "Garvey Must Go" campaign. Even W. E. B. DuBois, while sympathetic to the Pan-African ideal, regarded Garvey as a demagogue. Garvey in turn assailed his opponents as "Good Old Darkies" and "Uncle Tom Negroes," but the hostility of the black establishment undoubtedly hurt his movement.

Even had Garvey possessed greater business acumen and received a more sympathetic hearing, his plan still would have foundered. It was easier to talk about black unity than to achieve it, for people in Africa were themselves sharply divided along tribal and cultural lines. Even Liberia, seeking to placate France and England which held adjacent colonies, decided in 1924 not to admit any of Garvey's followers, whom it considered politically unreliable. What had lasting import was less Garvey's plan for a return to Africa than his emphasis on race pride. In 1927 the *Amsterdam News* assessed Garvey's influence on Negroes in this way: "In a world where black is despised, he taught them that black is beautiful. He taught them to admire and praise black things and black people." Garvey's appeal was, characteristically for the 1920s, along cultural, racial, and ethnic lines.

THE DISCONTENT OF THE INTELLECTUALS

Before the war, intellectuals had been outraged by economic injustice and political corruption. Intellectuals in the 1920s, however, while by no means apologists for Harding and Coolidge, were more often incensed by the materialism and conformity they found at all levels of society. Where the target had once been the crooked politician, now it was more likely to be the bluenosed puritan who, unable to enjoy life himself, wanted to make sure that no one else did either. Formerly, intellectuals had drawn up manifestos for social betterment; in the 1920s they were more acutely conscious of the barriers to change, and some lost interest in politics altogether. Three books, all published in 1922, illustrate these themes: Harold Stearns's *Civilization in the United States,* Sinclair Lewis's *Babbitt,* and Walter Lippmann's *Public Opinion.*

The thirty intellectuals who contributed to the volume edited by Stearns examined different aspects of American society and found them uniformly stilted, oppressive, and dull. Stearns himself discovered proof of America's "emotional and aesthetic starvation" in "the mania for petty regulation, the driving, regimenting, and drilling, the secret society and its grotesque regalia." Lives devoted to acquiring material possessions, the contributors believed, were essentially barren and, even worse, marked by hypocrisy. The contradictions between what people said and what they did were so sharp that in practice the moral code "resolves itself into the one cardinal heresy of being found out, with the chief sanction enforcing it, the fear of what people will say." Given this diagnosis, it is not surprising that the book proposed no programmatic solutions. On completing the manuscript Stearns left Greenwich Village for France; other exiles would look down on him sleeping in a Paris café and say, "there lies civilization in the United States."

Of the writers who satirized the values of the business culture, perhaps none did so more effectively than Sinclair Lewis. In George F. Babbitt, Lewis created a figure who personifies boosterism, complacency, and conformity. A small-town real-estate agent, Babbitt is a thoroughgoing materialist whose "symbols of truth and beauty" are mechanical contraptions, who advises his son that "there's a whole lot of valuable time lost even at the U., studying poetry and French and subjects that never brought in anybody a cent." In a speech to his fellow realtors Babbitt defines "the ideal of American manhood and culture" as "a God-fearing, hustling, successful, two-fisted Regular Guy, who belongs to some church with pep and piety to it, who belongs to the Boosters or the Rotarians or the Kiwanis, to the Elks or Moose or Red Men or Knights of Columbus." Vaguely discontented with these values Babbitt finally rebels against them. But finding "nonconformity" hardly more satisfying, Babbitt is disillusioned, and when he is subjected to terrific personal and financial pressure from the community, he gratefully reenters the fold. Lewis's target, therefore, was not Babbitt himself so much as the society that produced him and prevented him from becoming anything else.

Walter Lippmann, meanwhile, expressed profound disillusionment with traditional American political beliefs. Lippmann believed that people thought in stereotypes—"for the most part we do not first see, and then define; we define first and then see"—and therefore irrationally. Democratic theory, he held, had "never seriously faced the problem which arises because the pictures inside people's heads do not automatically correspond with the world outside." Since public affairs were too complex for most people to grasp even if they wanted to, and since most people lacked the time and interest to try, it was not reasonable to suppose that voters would instinctively or intuitively make the right choices. Instead, Lippmann called for "an independent, expert organization for making the unseen facts intelligible to those who have to make the decisions." Social scientists, organized in a network of intelligence bureaus, might perform such a function. Social progress, Lippmann argued, depended

Bartolomeo Vanzetti and Nicola Sacco, 1921.

not on the old Progressive faith in an enlightened citizenry, but rather on the scientific organization of intelligence.

Many intellectuals in the 1920s assumed a coolly detached stance toward public affairs. "It was characteristic of the Jazz Age," said F. Scott Fitzgerald, "that it had no interest in politics at all." But even those who held themselves most aloof were caught up in the Sacco-Vanzetti case. Nicola Sacco and Bartolomeo Vanzetti, two Italian anarchists, had been charged with murder and robbery in 1920, convicted the following year, and sentenced to die. Legal appeals dragged on for six years until, in August 1927, both men were electrocuted. The case stirred immense moral outrage because elementary rules of due process were ignored, the judge was viciously biased, and the Commonwealth of Massachusetts seemed determined to carry out an unjust sentence rather than concede the possibility of error. For a generation of intellectuals, Sacco and Vanzetti came to symbolize all that America was not. In a nation of conformists they were rebels; in a nation of materialists they were "the good shoemaker and poor fishpeddler." They were, it seemed, martyrs crucified by an unfeeling society. If the great majority of Americans followed Bruce Barton in apotheosizing businessmen, most intellectuals followed Malcolm Cowley, who wrote: "March on, O dago Christs, while we/ march on to spread your name abroad/ like ashes in the winds of God."

THE END OF THE
NEW ORDER: 1929

Other Americans had a quite different view of what they had to contribute to the world. "The work that religion, government, and war have failed in must be done by business," an *Atlantic Monthly* correspondent declared in 1928. "That eternal job of administering the planet must be turned over to the despised business man." One of the great businessmen, not at all despised, was the newly elected President. A multimillionaire mining engineer, Herbert Hoover embodied the success stories of the 1920s. His efficiency, realism, and faith in technology were exemplified when he installed the first telephone on the President's desk. (Before that the Chief Executive had to use a booth in an adjoining room.) He turned to social scientists for programs that would make the society run yet more efficiently and profitably. The roots of the system needed no examination. As Hoover told a crowded Stanford stadium in 1928, "We in America today are nearer to the final triumph over poverty than ever before in the history of any land. The poorhouse is vanishing from among us."

Such economic triumphs of American individualism, moreover, had eradicated the causes of world wars. "It seems to me," Hoover wrote his Secretary of State, Henry Stimson, in 1929, "that there is the most profound outlook for peace today that we have had at any time in the last half century." Most Democrats were forced to agree. When the influential periodical *Foreign Affairs* asked a Republican and a Democratic spokesman to discuss their differences on foreign policy in 1928, the Democrat, Franklin D. Roosevelt, could find little of substance for which to criticize the Republicans.

Hoover and many others fully realized that international stability depended on the strength of the American economy. Since becoming the world's leading creditor during the World War, the United States had dominated the international economy as England had before 1914. That power increased during the 1920s, as the efficient American system exported ever larger amounts of goods. When foreign customers tried to repay with their own goods, however, they encountered walls erected by the 1922 Fordney-McCumber Tariff, which raised average rates on imports to 33 percent. In 1923, United States merchandise exports exceeded imports by $375 million, but by 1928 by $1.1 billion. Profiting handsomely, Americans covered the difference by loaning their dollars to foreigners for the purchase of United States goods, and by investing directly in overseas stocks and bonds. The dollar made the world economy go around.

By 1929, however, the dollar had begun staying at home. New overseas investment opportunities did not appear, and a glamorous alternative, the New York Stock Exchange, quickly seduced big and small spenders. In 1924 *The New York Times* industrial average of stocks was 106; by 1928, 331; and during the summer of 1929, it shot up another 110 points. This wild speculation was fueled by "buying on margin," in which an investor bought stocks for a small downpayment while borrowing the remainder at interest rates as high as 10 to 20 percent. The government and the banking community watched this with happy hearts, even encouraging the speculation since they believed the stock exchange rested on a sound American economy.

But that economy was being eaten away by a rash of illnesses. Three became obvious in 1929–30. First, the mass of Americans were too poor to buy the glut of goods being produced. Productivity shot up nearly 50 percent between 1919 and 1929 until the gross national product (the sum of all goods and services produced in the country) reached $104 billion in 1929. But wages did not keep pace. By 1929, 5 percent of the people received one-third of all personal income. As the gap between rich and poor widened, the economy became increasingly unstable. The government refused to consider measures, such as higher income taxes, to make income more equal. Farmers, miners, and textile workers especially suffered. Between 1919 and 1929 farm debt more than doubled. Farmers were further hurt in 1928 and 1929, when their foreign markets, now lacking American dollars, were no longer able to buy large amounts of wheat and cotton. Throughout the decade the rate of bank failures had also been high. In truth, stock prices rested not on a strong economy, but on bankers' loans and on holding companies that had gained control of smaller firms through complex stock manipulations and business hocus-pocus. In October 1929 the stock market suddenly stalled. Excited bankers demanded repayment of their loans, forcing borrowers to declare bankruptcy, disappear, or jump from high buildings. A run on stocks began, and within a month after "Black Thursday" of October 24, stock prices plummeted 50 percent. The holding companies proved to be merely paper, for when one of their firms went bankrupt, the rest of the company's properties were also dragged down.

A second illness, the inability of the government to control the economy, next became obvious. Throughout 1927 and 1928 the Federal Reserve System had helped stock speculation with a low interest-easy money policy. When the System tried finally to slow the wild lending, large private banks refused to cooperate. As the stock decline accelerated, 800 banks closed in 1930. The government did little to save the banking system. Unemployment of 1.5 million in 1929 shot up to 4.2 million in 1930, further cutting purchasing power. The Federal Reserve System then set lending rates at historically low levels so money would be very cheap. But there were no takers, for there appeared to be nowhere to invest the money. As American capitalism crumbled, the government passed the Hawley-Smoot Tariff in 1930, raising average rates on imports to 40 percent in order to keep out cheap foreign goods.

But the tariff starkly revealed the third illness. The world economy could survive only with the aid of either dollars or American markets. Now both disappeared. Without dollars foreigners could neither buy American goods nor repay earlier loans. As their own economies began to collapse, they too sought protection behind tariff walls which would exclude American goods. From 1929 to 1933 world trade dropped 40 per-

Wall Street, 1929.

cent in value, with the leading exporters—England, Germany, Japan, and the United States—especially hard hit. A domino effect occurred: the American depression caused foreign economies to decline, and the disappearance of these traditional markets for American products in turn worsened conditions in the United States. In trying to cure their own maladies, Americans had instead infected the rest of the world. Meanwhile, President Hoover announced that the economy was basically sound, and a group of Harvard economists declared, "a serious depression . . . is outside the range of possibility."

Actually the world tottered on the edge of catastrophe. The great British economist, John Maynard Keynes, held out little hope: "A general breakdown is inevitable," he privately commented. "America will revert to a Texas type of civilization, France and Germany will go to war." Keynes's conclusions were appropriate, for without a healthy international economy the treaty system, so painfully constructed at Washington in 1922 and in Europe between 1924 and 1929, could not survive. The problem was not that Americans had become isolationist during the 1920s. Indeed, the internationalization of the American system had been so successfully accomplished that as the domestic economy slowly sank, it dragged the rest of the world down with it.

Useful accounts of American society in the 1920s are William E. Leuchtenburg, *The Perils of Prosperity* (1958); Paul A. Carter, *Another Part of the Twenties* (1977); and Robert Elias, *Entangling Alliances with None: An Essay on the Individual in the American Twenties* (1973). See in addition the essays in John Braeman, ed., *Change and Continuity in Twentieth-Century America: The 1920s* (1968). Republican politics is analyzed in Robert K. Murray, *The Harding Era* (1969); Eugene P. Trani and David L. Wilson, *The Presidency of Warren G. Harding* (1977); and Donald McCoy, *Calvin Coolidge* (1967). For a discussion of labor unions, consult Irving Bernstein, *The Lean Years* (1960); and Robert Zieger, *Republicans and Labor, 1919–1929* (1969).

A general discussion of foreign affairs is in L. Ethan Ellis, *Republican Foreign Policy, 1921–1933* (1968). Useful studies of foreign economic policy are Joan Hoff Wilson's two important works, *American Business and Foreign Policy, 1920–1933* (1971), and *Ideology and Economics: U.S. Relations with the Soviet Union, 1918–1933* (1974); and Herbert Feis, *The Diplomacy of the Dollar* (1966). The American role in international conferences is analyzed in Roger Dingman's important *Power in the Pacific: The Origins of Naval Arms Limitation, 1914–1922* (1976); and Robert H. Ferrell, *Peace in Their Time* (1952), a study of the Kellogg-Briand pact. For relations with Asia and Latin America, see Akira Iriye, *After Imperialism: The Search for a New Order in the Far East, 1921–1931* (1965); and Joseph Tulchin, *The Aftermath of War: World War I and U.S. Policy Toward Latin America* (1971). Charles Chatfield, *For Peace and Justice . . . 1914–1941* (1971) analyzes pacifism in this era. And see the important insights in *The Making of the Diplomatic Mind: The Training, Outlook, and Style of United States Foreign Service Officers, 1908–1931* (1975) by Robert D. Schulzinger.

Some of the problems confronting reformers are considered in biographies, particularly Lawrence W. Levine, *Defender of the Faith: William J. Bryan, 1915–1925* (1965); Matthew and Hanna Josephson, *Al Smith* (1970); Howard Zinn, *La Guardia in Congress* (1958); and David P. Thelen, *Robert M. La Follette and the Insurgent Spirit* (1978). Additional information may be found in Clark Chambers, *Seedtime of Reform, 1918–1933* (1963); and David Burner, *The Politics of Provincialism* (1968), a study of the Democratic party.

Cultural conflicts during the 1920s are considered in Don Kirschner, *City and Country: Rural Responses to Urbanization in the 1920s* (1970). On prohibition, see Andrew Sinclair, *Prohibition: The Era of Excess* (1962), and Norman H. Clark, *Deliver Us From Evil* (1976); on the Klan, Kenneth T. Jackson, *The Ku Klux Klan in the City, 1915–1930* (1967), and Charles C. Alexander, *The Ku Klux Klan in the Southwest* (1965). Norman F. Furniss, *The Fundamentalist Controversy, 1918–1931* (1954) discusses Protestant fundamentalism; Ray Ginger, *Six Days or Forever?* (1958), describes the Scopes trial.

The development of black ghettoes is explained in Gilbert Osofsky, *Harlem: The Making of a Ghetto* (1966); Alan H. Spear, *Black Chicago* (1967); Kenneth L. Kusmer, *A Ghetto Takes Shape: Black Cleveland, 1870–1930* (1976); and David G. Nielsen, *Black Ethos, 1890–1930* (1977). See also Florette Henri, *Black Migration, 1900–1920* (1975). Contrasting evaluations of the Garvey movement are provided by David Cronon, *Black Moses* (1962); and Theodore Vincent, *Black Power and the Garvey Movement* (1970). For aspects of Negro culture in the 1920s, see Nathan Huggins, *Harlem Renaissance* (1971).

The intellectuals' critique of the business culture is recorded in Malcolm Cowley, *Exile's Return* (1934), and evaluated in Frederick J. Hoffman, *The Twenties* (1955). The most famous trial of the decade is assessed in Roberta Strauss Feuerlicht, *Justice Crucified: The Story of Sacco and Vanzetti* (1977). Herbert Hoover's view of the depression is set forth in his *Memoirs,* 3 vols. (1932). Other accounts are John K. Galbraith, *The Great Crash* (1955); Robert Sobel, *The Great Bull Market* (1968); and the relevant portions of William A. Williams, *The Contours of American History* (1961).

On Bessie Smith, see Chris Albertson, *Bessie* (1971); on the blues, Paul Oliver, *Blues Fell This Morning* (1960), and *The Story of the Blues* (1969).

Apple seller, 1932.

CHAPTER SIX
1929–1936
Depression
and New Deal

BROTHER, CAN YOU SPARE A DIME?

Words by E. Y. Harburg, *music by* Jay Gorney

They used to tell me I was building a dream,
And so I followed the mob;
When there was earth to plow or guns to
  bear
I was always there, right there on the job.

They used to tell me I was building a dream
With peace and glory ahead;
Why should I be standing in line
—just waiting for bread?

Chorus:
Once I built a railroad, made it run,
Made it race against time.
Once I built a railroad, now it's done—
Brother, can you spare a dime?

Once I built a tower, to the sun,
Brick and rivet and lime;
Once I built a tower, now it's done—
Brother, can you spare a dime?

Once in khaki suits—gee, we looked swell,
Full of the Yankee Doodle-de-dum.
Half a million boots went sloggin' thru Hell,
I was the kid with the drum.

Say, don't you remember, they called me Al,
It was Al all the time;
Say, don't you remember, I'm your pal!
Buddy, can you spare a dime?

169

The Great Depression had a cataclysmic effect on all areas of American life. It produced an unprecedented amount of human anguish and, consequently, severely tested the dominant theory of government's social responsibilities. Within a few brief years that theory, which rigidly restricted federal intervention in the economy, had failed dismally. Yet the fear that disillusioned Americans would turn to revolution on the left, or to dictatorship on the right, proved without foundation. Most people favored more moderate change, and that is exactly what the New Deal provided. Franklin D. Roosevelt's first administration erected the foundations of a welfare state. New Deal policies concerning business, agriculture, conservation, labor, and welfare, while benefiting certain interest groups considerably more than others, nevertheless enabled the Democrats to fashion a new political coalition that dominated American politics for several decades.

HERBERT HOOVER AND THE DEPRESSION

Perhaps no one had ever assumed the office of president with more prestige, or left it so utterly discredited as did Herbert Hoover. Entering the White House in 1929 as a renowned humanitarian, one who would lead the nation "to the previously impossible state in which poverty in this country can be put on a purely voluntary basis," Hoover exited four years later with his name a synonym for suffering and hard times. People who spent the night on park benches covered by newspapers said they were sleeping under "Hoover blankets." Those who hitched broken-down cars to mules or horses said they were riding in "Hoover wagons." Men who turned their trouser packets inside out to show that they were empty claimed they were waving "Hoover flags." Hoover had once symbolized the application of scientific intelligence to social problems. By 1932 many considered his refusal to face facts squarely a national scandal.

During the 1920s Hoover had expressed boundless confidence in the potential of American capitalism. In *American Individualism* (1922) he asserted that the American system, by promoting equality of opportunity, permitted the "free rise of ability, character, and intelligence." Yet individualism, he added, by no means required the government to pursue a laissez-faire policy. As Secretary of Commerce under Harding and Coolidge (a position for which he turned down a $500,000-a-year offer as a mining and metallurgical engineer), Hoover endorsed government intervention in the domestic economy. He favored increased spending for public works to create jobs in periods of distress. He supported a constitutional amendment prohibiting child labor. He also advocated the creation of trade associations. By promulgating voluntary codes of business ethics, approved by the government, these associations would allow businessmen to avoid wasteful competition and to pool technical knowledge without violating the antitrust laws. In 1927, when floods ravaged the Mississippi

Valley, Hoover brilliantly mobilized state, local, and private resources to aid the victims. Hoover's supporters in 1928 dubbed him "The Master of Emergencies."

As President, Hoover adhered to the same doctrine of limited intervention in battling the depression. Unlike some of his advisors, who recommended a hands-off policy, Hoover believed that government could cushion the impact of the slump. But if he was willing to intervene, he would do so only within clearly defined limits. Hoover never considered legislation a cure-all, for "economic wounds must be healed by the action of the cells of the economic body—the producers and consumers themselves." The government must not unbalance the budget, for that would destroy business confidence; nor should it centralize power in a Washington bureaucracy, for that would erode individual initiative. Instead, the government should encourage voluntary, cooperative action on the part of private citizens and local officials. "Each industry should assist its own employees," the President said. "Each community and each State should assume its full responsibilities for organization of employment and relief of distress." Hoover conceived his task to be largely one of exhortation and coordination, almost as if the depression were a gigantic natural catastrophe, like a flood or an earthquake.

In practice, this program consisted of five parts. First, Hoover summoned business and labor leaders to the White House in an effort to persuade them to maintain wages, keep up production, and proceed with plant expansion. Second, the President stepped up expenditures for the construction of roads, bridges, and public buildings. Federal aid for highway construction jumped from $105 million to $260 million annually, and the number of workers on such projects increased from 110,000 to 280,000. Third, Hoover signed the Hawley-Smoot Act (1930) which substantially raised tariff rates in the hope of protecting American manufacturers and farmers. Fourth, Hoover declared a moratorium on war debts in June 1931. Convinced that economic collapse abroad was prolonging the depression in the United States, Hoover sought to improve the ability of European nations to purchase American goods and thereby stimulate domestic output. Fifth, the President somewhat grudgingly accepted direct aid to big business. Early in 1932 Congress created the Reconstruction Finance Corporation (RFC) in order to assist businesses in financial trouble. In Hoover's last year in office, the RFC loaned $1.78 billion to 7400 banks, insurance companies, railroads, and other institutions.

Some of these initiatives helped, but none succeeded in reversing the downturn. The "conferences for continued industrial progress," as they were called, produced little more than empty promises. Most businessmen simply could not afford to maintain wages or prices while the economy continued to slide downward. The public works program did some good, but even as the federal government was expanding its program, bankrupt states and municipalities were trimming back theirs. Consequently, the total amount spent on such improvements and the total number of men employed declined. The Hawley-Smoot Tariff was an unqualified disaster. As European countries sold less to the United States, they retaliated by erecting high tariff walls of their own. The debt moratorium had little domestic impact. Eventually it led to what its critics had feared—a decision by France, England, and most other nations to default on further payments. The Reconstruction Finance Corporation, whose activities were confined largely to bailing out large concerns, was said to dispense a "millionaire's dole."

By the end of 1932 Hoover's policy lay in ruins. Every statistic revealed a startling degree of deterioration. From 1929 to 1933, gross national product fell from $104 billion to $74 billion and national income from $88 billion to $40 billion. Almost every day there were more bank failures: 1350 closed their doors in 1930, followed by 2293 and 1453 in the next two years. Stock prices tumbled precipitously. General Motors had sold for a high of 91 in 1929; in January 1933 it sold for 13. In the same period Standard Oil declined from 83 to 30 and U.S. Steel from 261 to 27. Farmers watched in dismay as their income plummeted by 61 percent. A pound of cotton, which had sold for 16 cents in 1929, brought 6 cents in 1932; a bushel of corn, which had sold for 79 cents, brought 31 cents. Only the number of unemployed workers rose steadily. In 1929, 1.5 million workers—3 percent of the labor force—were jobless. By 1933, at least 13 million workers—25 percent of the total—were idle. An average of 75,000 workers lost their jobs every week for three years.

THE BREAKDOWN OF RELIEF

Hoover's unwillingness to provide federal relief for the unemployed revealed more clearly than anything else the inadequacy of his approach. The United States in the early 1930s had an unwieldy and anachronistic system of administering relief. Existing agencies were equipped to deal on a temporary basis with individual victims of accident or illness, but not over a period of years with millions of jobless workers. Private charities had small staffs and limited funds; even municipalities often lacked the revenue to make sufficient money available. Only families that had become destitute, that had spent every dime of savings and sold every possession of value, could ordinarily qualify for assistance. Even then, those lucky enough to get on the relief rolls received barely enough for food. Rent, clothing, medical care—all were considered luxuries.

Despite all this, the President vigorously opposed direct federal relief in any form. To his mind it would open a Pandora's box, for it would cause a sizeable increase in taxes, thereby discouraging private investment; lead to an unbalanced budget, thereby sabotaging confidence in the nation's credit; and require a gargantuan bureaucracy, thereby jeopardizing states' rights. Above all, the fearful "dole" would undermine its recipients' moral character, which Hoover took to mean "self-reliance," "sturdiness," and "independence." Yet as the situation went from bad to worse the President was forced to take notice. The agencies he created to deal with the problem, however, illustrated perfectly Hoover's commitment to voluntary, cooperative action and his conviction that government could more properly dispense advice than funds.

In September 1930 Hoover set up the President's Emergency Committee for Employment under Colonel Arthur H. Woods. The Committee at first subscribed to the view that relief was a local function, but by April 1931 even Woods recognized the need for federal involvement. When Hoover refused to concur, Woods resigned. In August Hoover created the President's Organization on Unemployment Relief, headed by Walter S. Gifford of American Telephone and Telegraph. Gifford arranged for a series of advertisements designed to stimulate charitable donations. But his group confined itself largely to a cheerleading function, considering that, as one member put it, "our job is not to raise funds ourselves." By November Gifford was assuring Hoover that "there is every indication that each state will take care of its own this winter." Two months later, testifying before a Senate committee, Gifford confessed that he did not know how many people were unemployed, how many were receiving relief, or how much money the states had available to assist the needy.

While Hoover held to the fiction that no one was starving, pressure for federal action mounted in Congress. In June 1932 Congress appropriated $2.1 billion in loans for public works and relief. Hoover vetoed the measure, but in July he accepted a watered-down version that met some of his requirements. The Emergency Relief and Construction Act (1932) provided for loans, not outright grants, to the states of up to $300 million. To qualify, states had to provide conclusive proof of need, and to receive further assistance they had to repay the loans within 30 days. The states themselves, rather than a federal bureaucracy, administered the program. Finally, loans were made by the Reconstruction Finance Corporation, whose chairman remarked, "I have a very high regard for social workers, but God forbid they should have the purse-strings." The RFC guarded the purse-strings very closely: by the end of 1932 it had allotted less than half the money at its disposal.

Hoover had edged away from his original opposition to any federal relief whatsoever, but he had moved inches when the situation demanded he move miles. By late 1932 the rickety relief system was collapsing in many places. Reports from cities across the country told of funds dried up and resources exhausted. Toledo: "There is only a commissary available for most families which is distributing the cheapest grades of food at a cost of six cents per person per day." Chicago: "Some families are being separated, husbands being sent to the men's shelter and wives to the women's shelter." Houston: "Applications are not taken from unemployed Mexican or colored families. They are being asked to shift for themselves." In Philadelphia, families on relief received $4.23 a week; in New York City, $2.39. Tragically, the special precautions taken to aid children revealed how bad things were. The American Friends Service Committee provided free lunches to children in the coal towns of Pennsylvania, West Virginia, and Kentucky. Funds were so limited that the Quakers could distribute meals only to children who were 10 percent underweight. In Oklahoma City, veterans collected discarded food from produce houses and scraps from butcher shops to feed the hungry. "All delicacies (such as figs that had spoiled and canned fruit that had gone a bit sour) were saved for the children."

THE BONUS ARMY

The long years of hardship apparently left many Americans psychologically numb. No matter how bad conditions were throughout the country, people often regarded their inability to find work or support their families as a sign of personal inadequacy. Yet sporadic acts of protest, sometimes accompanied by violence and lawlessness, eventually occurred. In Minneapolis, several hundred people stormed a produce market, smashed windows, and helped themselves to meat, fruit, and canned groceries. In Dearborn, Michigan, a demonstration by unemployed Ford workers led to a skirmish with the police and four deaths. Unemployment councils in New York City tried forcibly to prevent the eviction of jobless workers from their homes. The Midwest saw the invention of "penny auctions": when banks foreclosed a farmer's mortgage and attempted to auction off his possessions, neighbors appeared, armed with rifles, and no one bid more than a penny. The two most important movements of organized protest occurred in the summer of 1932—the Bonus Army and the Farm Holiday Association.

The career of the Bonus Expeditionary Force demonstrated that even the most disillusioned Americans continued to seek improvement within the system rather than outside it. The bonus issue originated in 1924 when Congress, over Coolidge's veto, promised a bonus of several hundred dollars (depending on length of military service) to World War veterans but deferred payment until 1945. By 1932, however, many unemployed veterans wanted to be paid immediately, since they considered the money rightfully theirs and they desperately needed it. When Congress took up a bill providing immediate payment, veterans converged on Washington to lobby for passage. The veterans aroused considerable sympathy, but the Hoover administration believed the case against them to be overwhelming: payment of the bonus would wreck hopes for a balanced budget, give preferential treatment to veterans over other needy citizens, and entitle those veterans who were financially well-off to payment at a time of declining tax revenues.

In June 1932 some 22,000 veterans, led by Walter W. Waters of Oregon, streamed into Washington. They set up camp across the Anacostia River by building shanties furnished from garbage dumps. Many were joined by their wives and children. The Chief of Police of Washington, Pelham D. Glassford, himself a former army officer, provided some funds and provisions. In a sense, the veterans attempted to recreate the life they had known in the army, with its roll calls, discipline, and sense of purpose. One reporter described the march as a "supreme escape gesture . . . a flight from reality—a flight from hunger, from the cries of the

Bonus Army encamped by the Capitol, July, 1932.

starving children, . . . from the harsh rebuffs of prospective employers."
Although the House passed the bonus bill, the Senate rejected the measure on June 17 by a large margin. Congress adjourned in July after making available $100,000 to provide loans for marchers who needed carfare
to return home. Only 5160 men took advantage of the offer. The rest,
presumably having no homes or jobs to return to, remained.

The presence of the Bonus Army embarrassed and frightened the Hoover administration. The veterans, with their silent, ominous "dead marches" around federal buildings, provided visible proof of hardship in a city where, because so many people worked for the government, the worst effects of the depression had been muted. Hoover refused to meet with a delegation of veterans, assuming that an interview would only dignify their cause, raise false hopes, and bring even more demonstrators to Washington. In addition, the President came to accept the view that communist agitators had infiltrated the ranks of the Bonus Army. Ultimately the government increased its pressure on the veterans, demanding that they leave an abandoned Treasury Department building in downtown Washington in which some were living. The evacuation led to a scuffle with the police in which two veterans were killed and which provided a pretext for dispersing the Bonus Army itself. On July 28, 1932, General Douglas MacArthur led cavalry and infantry troops, as well as a mounted machine-gun squadron, down Pennsylvania Avenue. With bayonets and tear gas the soldiers drove the veterans out of the business district and across the bridge to Anacostia, and there set fire to the encampment.

The decision to drive the veterans out of downtown Washington was made by Hoover, Secretary of War Patrick J. Hurley, and the District Commissioners, but the decision to pursue them to Anacostia and break up their encampment was MacArthur's alone. Convinced that the Bonus Army was "a bad-looking mob animated by the essence of revolution," MacArthur ignored explicit instructions not to follow the veterans across the Anacostia River. But if Hoover had not ordered this pursuit, he accepted MacArthur's estimate of the revolutionary threat, believed that public opinion would support MacArthur's action, and therefore accepted responsibility for it. To have done otherwise would have required the President to repudiate his Chief of Staff and side with forces he considered subversive. The President thus not only misunderstood what the Bonus Army represented, but also misjudged the public reaction to the government's panicky response. The veterans themselves conveyed something of the bitter public reaction in a ballad entitled "The Prisoner in the White House": "In a cage that is fit for a lion/He moves with the soul of a mouse."

AGRARIAN PROTEST

Even as the government was driving out the Bonus Army, corn and dairy farmers in Iowa and surrounding states, who could no longer make ends meet, were organizing the Farm Holiday Association. Like the veterans who went to Washington, the farmers wanted Congress to enact special-interest legislation. This took the form of the cost-of-production plan, under which the government would support food prices at a level that would guarantee farmers their operating cost, a 5 percent return on their investment, and a living wage for their operators. The plan would have raised the price of a bushel of oats from 11 to 45 cents, of a bushel of corn from 10 to 92 cents. The farmers, however, attempted to generate pressure on Congress not by camping on the Capitol doorstep but by withholding their products from market, hoping thereby to force prices upwards.

This movement received its greatest support not among tenant farmers or the very poor, but among those who had owned their own land and had done reasonably well before the crash. It was a protest not by the most deprived, but by landowning farmers, those most affected by a spiraling foreclosure rate. In some respects the movement testified to the lasting impact of Populist ideology, although the cost-of-production plan surely went far beyond anything farmers had demanded in the 1890s. Farm Holiday spokesmen characteristically blamed the farmer's difficulties on an international banking conspiracy. They regarded the countryside as productive, the cities parasitic. The Association's most prominent leader, Milo Reno, who had voted for William Jennings Bryan in 1896, continued in the 1930s to affirm the need to "break the grip of Wall Street and international bankers on our government."

The Farm Holiday Association began implementing its direct-action plan in August 1932. Despite its wide support, the plan proved unworkable. Blockading a few markets could not significantly affect overall supply or price levels. Even if prices temporarily rose, they would drop as soon as farmers resumed normal operations. Nor did all farmers wish to cooperate with the strike. As Farm Holiday supporters set up patrols and picket lines, they clashed with farmers seeking to transport their goods to market and with sheriffs' deputies attempting to keep the roads open. The resulting violence dismayed the movement's leaders, who called off the strike in September. By then attention was shifting to the presidential campaign and the opportunity of electing men who might relieve the distress. In November 1932 Herbert Hoover failed to carry a single rural county in his home state of Iowa.

FRANKLIN D. ROOSEVELT

To face Hoover in that election the Democrats nominated Franklin Delano Roosevelt. Born at Hyde Park, New York in 1882, the only child of wealthy parents, Roosevelt had entered Groton in 1896, Harvard in 1900, and then attended Columbia Law School. In 1910, having practiced law for a time, he entered politics, winning election to the New York State Senate. He strongly backed Woodrow Wilson, whom he later served as Assistant Secretary of the Navy, and in 1920 he ran for vice-president on the Democratic ticket with James M. Cox. In August 1921 Roosevelt, until then a vigorous and athletic man, was struck by poliomyelitis. Years of physical therapy helped somewhat, but his legs remained paralyzed. For the rest of his life FDR wore steel braces, could walk only with assistance, and had to be lifted into and out of automobiles. In 1928 he had recuperated sufficiently to run for Governor of New York. He won by a narrow margin, although Democratic presidential candidate Al Smith lost the

FDR campaigning in Sea Girt, New Jersey, August, 1932.

state, and he easily gained reelection two years later. In 1932, recognizing that Hoover's policies had alienated millions, and that the name Roosevelt was "still almost as much a Republican name as a Democratic one," he purposely conducted a vague campaign, promising to end hard times without ever explaining how.

Roosevelt entered the White House in March 1933 with several advantages. With 22.8 million votes to Hoover's 15.8 million, he could claim an undisputed popular mandate. He also had comfortable majorities with which to work in Congress. Democrats outnumbered Republicans 59–36 in the Senate, and 313–117 in the House. For economic advice Roosevelt could turn to members of his "brains trust," which included Columbia University professors Adolf A. Berle, Rexford G. Tugwell, and Raymond Moley. For political advice the President could rely on Louis Howe—an old friend and supporter—and James A. Farley, whom he made Postmaster General. Roosevelt's Cabinet contained talented administrators, among them Secretary of the Interior Harold L. Ickes, Secretary of Agriculture Henry A. Wallace, and Secretary of Labor Frances C. Perkins. Above all, FDR took office in the midst of a severe national crisis, one he likened to a war. He could depend, therefore, on an extraordinary degree of cooperation from Congress and the public.

New Deal policies were hardly monolithic. People who backed the Roosevelt administration held disparate views: some favored collectivism, others competition; some preferred deficit spending, others a balanced budget. Nor were New Deal programs in different areas always compatible, for they usually reflected pressures exerted by contending social groups. The New Deal also underwent an evolutionary process. Important changes took place between 1933 and 1935, and others occurred between 1935 and 1938. Yet to recognize the complexity of the New Deal is not to deny its unity. Most New Dealers accepted a few broad propositions: that the economy had reached a stage of maturity requiring an unprecedented degree of government intervention; that this must nevertheless be kept within strict confines; and that the test of any policy was how it worked in actual practice.

In a speech to the Commonwealth Club of San Francisco in September 1932 Roosevelt set forth his reasons for believing that the age of economic expansion had ended. In the past, he said, when growth and westward expansion had ensured equality of opportunity, "the business of government was not to interfere but to assist in the development of industry." But all that had changed. Now America's industrial plant was already built if not overbuilt, its last frontier long since closed, and its free land virtually gone. In words that echoed Frederick Jackson Turner's famous speech of 1893, FDR announced: "There is no safety valve in the form of a Western prairie." Under these circumstances, the task of government was no longer the encouragement of productivity but rather "the soberer, less dramatic business of administering resources and plants already in hand, of seeking to reestablish foreign markets for our surplus production, of adjusting production to consumption, of distributing wealth more equitably."

At the same time Roosevelt affirmed that the government owed each person the "right to make a comfortable living." This as well as anything else marked the distance between his approach and Hoover's. For New Dealers, the depression had exposed the bankruptcy of the existing order, characterized by what Tugwell termed its "violent contrasts of well-being, its irrational allotments of individual liberty, its unconsidered exploitation of human and natural resources." The New Deal, Berle noted, brought "a tremendous expansion of the area in which . . . government is prepared to accept responsibility." Roosevelt indeed saw no practical alternative. To rehabilitate the system of private enterprise, government must rescue its victims. Roosevelt feared that a revolution "could hardly be avoided if another president should fail as Hoover has failed."

Of course New Dealers never provided each individual with the right to make a comfortable living, in part because they believed too much intervention to be as dangerous as too little. Conservative critics of the New Deal never tired of pointing out what many reformers admitted from the start: that government intervention posed dangers of its own. Government might easily confuse the demands of highly organized minorities with the general interest of the community and might still more easily discourage individual initiative and enterprise. The task, as the Roosevelt administration saw it, was to strike a proper balance, not swing from one extreme to another. As late as 1939, Thurman Arnold, the head of the Anti-Trust Division of the Justice Department, reasserted the need to follow a middle course: "We do not wish to extend the area of government regulation any further than necessary."

When Arnold declared, "I am not an inspirational preacher," he also conveyed the pragmatic quality of New Deal thought. Roosevelt's followers said they wanted "hard facts," declared it "unwise to lay down too specifically the structure of new things," and even announced that " 'truth' is irrelevant as a test of an economic philosophy." They believed in trying something to see if it worked, discarding it if it did not, and then trying something else. This willingness to improvise, surely a source of strength, nevertheless raised certain problems. For one thing, it was not always clear how long a period was needed to judge whether a program was working or what criteria would be used in making that judgment. For another, new programs attracted support from political interests and developed bureaucratic structures that resisted change. Policies, once instituted, proved less adaptable in practice than they seemed in theory.

THE BLUE EAGLE

The keystone of the early New Deal was the National Recovery Administration (NRA), created in June 1933. The NRA rejected the theory of competition in favor of business cooperation in partnership with government. Businessmen were permitted to draft codes, subject to presidential approval, that regulated prices and wages and that forbade a broad range of competitive practices. Those participating in such agreements were exempted from the antitrust laws. In addition, the NRA supposedly guaranteed labor the right to organize, and it inaugurated a public-works program to pump money into the economy. This latter function was performed through the Public Works Administration, which FDR placed under Harold Ickes. To head the NRA, however, Roosevelt chose General Hugh Johnson, who had played an instrumental role in the World War mobilization.

Although Congress clothed the NRA with licensing powers, Johnson, fearing that they might not withstand the scrutiny of the courts, attempted to gain voluntary compliance from businessmen. He marshaled public opinion through parades and publicity, and all who took part displayed the NRA symbol—a blue eagle with the slogan We Do Our Part. Just as soldiers used certain insignia to distinguish friend from foe, Roosevelt said, so those fighting the depression "must know each other at a glance." "May God have mercy on the man or group of men who attempt to trifle with that bird," proclaimed Johnson. The codes, he explained, resembled the Marquis of Queensberry rules in boxing. "They eliminate eye-gouging and knee-groining and ear-chewing in business. Above the belt any man can be just as rugged and just as individual as he pleases." By the fall of 1933 every major industry had pledged its cooperation.

But in economics, as in the ring, heavyweights enjoyed a distinct advantage. Many corporate leaders had always disliked what they regarded as excessive competition. They saw nothing wrong with fixing prices, so long as they did the fixing. The antitrust laws had presumably blocked such concerted action, but their suspension provided business leaders with a long-awaited opportunity. As things worked out, big businessmen played the dominant role in drawing up the codes. The NRA, in consequence, generally kept production down and prices up. The codes restricted output by limiting factory hours and banning new plant construction. Similarly, they set minimum prices, prohibited sales below cost, and restricted combination sales, trade-in allowances, credit terms, and other competitive practices.

These policies caused a good deal of dissatisfaction. Consumers resented an arrangement that hurt their pocketbooks, and many small businessmen believed that the codes discriminated in favor of large concerns. At the same time, labor was becoming increasingly dissatisfied because Section 7(a), which was intended to protect the right to organize, was proving insufficient. While it prohibited employers from interfering with their workers' right to join unions and choose bargaining officials, it did not create adequate enforcement machinery or require employers to bargain in good faith. In 1934 Roosevelt appointed a commission, under Clarence Darrow, that investigated the NRA and submitted a highly critical report. The agency's initials, said the disaffected, stood for No Recovery Allowed, or National Run-Around.

The experiment in industrial planning had mixed results. The NRA apparently brought about a measure of economic improvement and, perhaps as important, established the principle of federal responsibility for working conditions. Yet the agency did not live up to expectations, in part because different groups—consumers and workers, large- and small-businessmen—expected different things of it. There was, in truth, little chance that the NRA could have satisfied all the competing demands made upon it. Having relied so heavily on public support at the outset, the NRA found itself in difficulty when enthusiasm waned. In early 1935 the Senate agreed to extend the NRA for one, not two, years. That May, the Supreme Court brought the troubled flight of the blue eagle to an end.

It did so in the "sick chicken" case. The Schechter brothers, who owned a poultry market in Brooklyn, purchased chickens raised in surrounding states, slaughtered them, and sold them to retailers. In October 1934 the firm was found guilty of violating NRA wage and hour provisions and of selling unfit poultry. The case eventually reached the Supreme Court, which handed down a unanimous opinion. Chief Justice Charles Evans Hughes ruled that the depression did not confer upon the government powers it might not otherwise exercise, that an excessive delegation of legislative powers occurred in the code-drafting process, and that the Schechter brothers were involved in intrastate commerce and therefore outside the scope of federal regulation. Hughes admitted that the chickens had crossed state lines but reasoned that they had come to a "permanent rest"—that is, were killed and eaten—within New York. They therefore were no longer part of a flow of interstate commerce. Through an extremely narrow reading of the Constitution, therefore, the Court declared the NRA illegal.

TRIPLE A

The New Deal program to aid agriculture consisted of four elements: helping farmers pay off their mortgages, encouraging a measure of inflation to facilitate debt payments, acquiring foreign markets through reciprocal trade agreements, and reducing acreage to limit supply. The last, known as the domestic allotment plan, served as the foundation of the Agricultural Adjustment Administration (AAA), which was established in May 1933. Under this plan—which affected wheat, cotton, hogs, tobacco, corn, rice, and milk—farmers signed acreage reduction contracts. In return for curbing output, they received government subsidies. In some respects the AAA was a counterpart of the NRA, for each involved a structural overhaul of the economy and a planned limitation of production under government auspices.

To obtain congressional approval for the AAA, the Roosevelt administration had to beat back proposals of a more extreme sort. The Senate, for example, attached the cost-of-production plan, favored by the Farm Holiday Association, to the measure creating the AAA. But the House, in which party discipline was stronger and White House influence correspondingly greater, rejected the amendment. The Senate also favored massive inflation through remonetizing silver, altering the gold content of the dollar, and issuing greenbacks. The administration finally settled for a compromise which gave Roosevelt discretionary authority, but did not obligate him to devalue the currency. The New Deal began experimenting with currency inflation in the fall of 1933 and continued to do so thereafter, but it never went as far as some congressmen wanted.

The AAA encountered two problems at the outset. George Peek, whom FDR chose to head the agency because of his long association with farm problems, never fully endorsed the idea of production controls. After repeated clashes with others in the administration, he was finally replaced by Chester Davis. A second difficulty concerned the destruction of existing crops. Making agreements to curb future output was relatively simple but did not affect the current harvest. The AAA therefore paid farmers $160 million to destroy one-fourth of their cotton. They plowed up 10 million acres, reducing the crop from 17 to 13 million bales. The administration also induced farmers to slaughter 6 million baby pigs and 200,000 sows. Although farmers received $30 million, and relief agencies distributed the pork to needy families, the extermination led to howls of anguish. "To hear them talk," Secretary of Agriculture Wallace said disgustedly, "you would have thought that pigs were raised for pets!" Roosevelt apparently regarded the matter less seriously than did his critics. He inquired jokingly, "Wouldn't birth control be more effective in the long run?"

The AAA helped farmers who owned their own land, but it often hurt those who did not. Of the 2.86 million tenant farmers and sharecroppers, 1.6 million, many of them black, labored in Southern cotton fields. The AAA policy of reducing farm acreage obviously reduced the need for farm laborers and consequently led to evictions and unemployment. Those tenants and croppers who remained received little under the policy of providing benefits to landowners, who, in turn, were supposed to apportion the money fairly among their tenants. This seldom happened. More often landlords would keep the money or apply it to debts, real or imaginary. The Roosevelt administration, believing that the AAA's success hinged on the cooperation of big farmers, would do nothing to jeopardize that support. As Chester Davis noted in February 1936, the elevation of sharecroppers "cannot be forced by the Federal Government to proceed much faster than the rate that the Southern opinion and Southern leadership will heartily support. To try to force a faster pace would merely be to insure violent controversy, lack of local cooperation in administration, evasion and ineffectiveness for the plan."

Not everyone shared this outlook. A number of AAA officials, led by General Counsel Jerome Frank, wished to protect the sharecroppers' position by requiring that planters continue to employ the same workers. Frank's dispute with Davis reached the point at which Wallace had to choose between them. Early in 1935 he "purged" the AAA of Frank and those who wanted to make agricultural policy into a vehicle of reform. In July 1935, however, the administration partially appeased Frank's group by supporting the creation of the Resettlement Administration, which took the first, tentative steps toward helping landless farmers acquire their own land and tools. In some cases dissatisfied tenant farmers took independent action. In mid-1934, Negro and white sharecroppers in Arkansas organized the Southern Tenant Farmers Union. Too frequently, they complained, Roosevelt "talked like a cropper and acted like a planter." When they sang "We Shall Not Be Moved," they were protesting against a New Deal policy that was driving them from the land they worked but did not own.

Despite all this, by 1936 the AAA had succeeded in raising gross farm income by 50 percent, commodity prices by 66 percent, and scaling down farm indebtedness by $1 billion. Then the agency met the same fate as had befallen the NRA. In January 1936, in *U.S.* v. *Butler,* the Supreme Court struck down the AAA by a 6–3 margin. Justice Owen Roberts, delivering the majority opinion, held that benefits paid to farmers for reducing acreage actually imposed a system of agricultural regulation under the guise of appropriations for the general welfare. In effect, Roberts said, Congress could not stipulate how its appropriations were to be used. In a stinging dissent, Justice Harlan Fiske Stone termed this "a tortured construction of the Constitution." He added that "the power to tax and spend includes the power to relieve a nationwide economic maladjustment by conditional gifts of money." This view New Dealers considered axiomatic for the continued functioning of the welfare state.

CONSERVATION AND PUBLIC POWER

Few causes meant more to Roosevelt than conservation. The existing pool of unemployed young men provided an opportunity to unite the functions of forestry and relief, and this the President proceeded to do in the Civilian Conservation Corps (CCC). Within three months after its creation in April 1933, the CCC had enrolled 250,000 young men in their teens and twenties. The volunteers fought forest fires, built water-storage basins, and reseeded grazing lands. They constructed roads, bridges, and camping facilities. They tried to protect trees against blister rust, bark beetles, and gypsy moths. In three years the CCC planted 570 million trees in the national forests. It also showed farmers how to prevent soil erosion. To conserve wildlife, the agency built refuges, fish-rearing ponds, and animal shelters. In September 1935 the CCC reached a high point with 500,000 volunteers in more than 2500 camps. The men received $30 per month, of which $25 went directly to their families as part of a relief program.

New Dealers proposed a still more ambitious plan to transform social and economic conditions in the 40,000-square-mile Tennessee River Valley. There, Roosevelt said shortly before his inauguration, "we have an opportunity of setting an example of planning . . . tying in industry and agriculture and forestry and flood prevention, tying them all into a unified whole." In May 1933 Congress established the Tennessee Valley Authority (TVA) thereby fulfilling—indeed, exceeding—the hopes of such public-power advocates as Senator George Norris of Nebraska. The TVA promised coordinated, multipurpose development. It not only provided electric power but also prevented soil erosion, helped control floods, allowed for navigation, and experimented with new fertilizers. It meant, FDR said, "national planning for a complete river watershed."

James Cagney and the Gangster Film

In the early 1930s many Americans were troubled by the existence of organized crime, and troubled even more by what they considered its source: the widespread disrespect for the law bred by prohibition, and by the closing of traditional paths to success as a result of the depression. The release of *Little Caesar* in 1931 marked the appearance of a new film genre, the gangster film, that reflected these concerns. The picture's box-office success led to the production of 50 other such films within a year.

The most revealing of these was *Public Enemy,* in which James Cagney played the gangster Tommy Powers. Even as a youngster Tommy was tripping little girls on roller skates. As a teenager he fell in with the wrong crowd and became a thief and bootlegger (although in Cagney's portrayal a rather jaunty, loveable one). As the archetypal gangster, Tommy Powers scorns traditional values, most of which are embodied in his brother, Mike. Tommy Powers cuts through social convention with a scalpel.

Mae Clark and James Cagney, 1931.

Bogart, Cagney, and Jeffrey Lynn in "The Roaring Twenties."

He sneers at education. When an accomplice asks him to involve Mike in a gangland operation, Tommy replies, "He's too busy going to school. He's learning to be poor." Similarly, Tommy exposes the hypocrisy of war. When Mike returns from military service a hero and accuses his brother of murdering rival bootleggers, Tommy snaps: "You didn't get those medals holding hands with Germans!" Tommy refuses to be domesticated. When his mistress, played by Mae Clarke, gently scolds him and says she wishes he wouldn't drink so early in the morning, Tommy mimics her savagely: "I wish, I wish, I wish you was a wishing well. Then maybe you'd dry up!" Mashing a grapefruit in her face, he walks out.

In deference to the Hollywood production code—which provided that "the technique of murder must be presented in a way that will not inspire imitation," and that "the use of firearms should be restricted to essentials"—*Public Enemy* opened by stating that it did not intend to glorify the criminal but rather to "depict an environment." There was also a mandatory unhappy ending, in which a rival gang abducts Tommy Powers from a hospital and deposits his corpse on his mother's doorstep. But despite all this, the film's message was plain. Its hero, after all, was a man who thumbed his nose at conventional virtues, and who followed the one career he found open to his talents. The film was reassuring in another sense. For while Tommy Powers disregarded the laws everyone else supposedly observed, his world had laws of its own. The underworld operated according to a clearly defined code, and gangsters dispensed an informal brand of justice by annihilating one another. Moreover, the world of the criminal was encapsulated. The gangster did not injure law-abiding citizens because he moved in a world separate and distinct from theirs.

The image of the police officer in the gangster film was that of a dumb flatfoot, either incompetent, corrupt, or both. Yet with the advent of the welfare state under FDR, crime films changed to reflect the new national mood. As the federal government extended its influence, the image of federal law enforcement was refurbished. Partly as a result of a massive public relations campaign by FBI Director J. Edgar Hoover, Americans came to regard federal agents as fearless, intrepid, and incorruptible. The circle was not complete, however, until the release of *G-Men* in 1935, starring none other than James Cagney. In the film Cagney joins the FBI to avenge the gangland slaying of a friend. " 'Public Enemy' Becomes Soldier of the Law," read advertisements; "Uncle Sam always gets his man." Now Cagney did his shooting from behind a badge, and, what was even more significant, a federal badge.

J. Edgar Hoover at the Justice Department, 1935.

John Dillinger, "Public Enemy No. 1," a few months before he was killed by FBI agents.

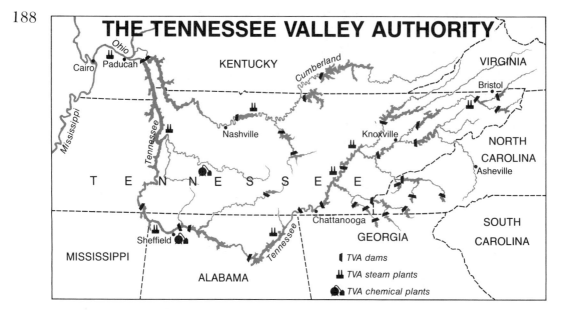

During the 1930s the TVA erected more than 20 dams with a generating capacity of 1 million kilowatts. Consumption of electricity in the region more than doubled. The TVA also cleared a 650-mile channel from Paducah to Knoxville, which greatly stimulated traffic on the river. Inevitably, though, the agency provoked sharp opposition from private electric companies, which took a dim view of government competition. These concerns similarly resented the concept of a federal "yardstick" against which their rates would be measured, arguing, with considerable justice, that TVA costs were not comparable with their own. Wendell Willkie of the Commonwealth and Southern Corporation, a chief spokesman for this opposition, branded the TVA "the most useless and unnecessary of all the alphabetical joyrides." Private utilities engaged the TVA in a long series of legal tussles. In February 1936 the agency won breathing room when the Supreme Court, in *Ashwander* v. *TVA,* upheld the government's right to sell the excess energy generated by Wilson Dam. The Court did not finally resolve the broader constitutional question in favor of the TVA until early 1939.

The TVA accomplished a great deal—as much as, if not more than, any other New Deal program—but it never brought about the "designed and planned social and economic order" for which some had hoped. Spokesmen for the agency advocated what David E. Lilienthal, one of its directors, termed "grass-roots democracy." Lilienthal believed that in assuming broad powers, the federal government must not lose touch with local mores and institutions. This required the "decentralized administration of centralized authority." The policy of encouraging local involvement, while helping to secure support, in effect made the TVA responsive to the largest and most influential interest groups. Its agricultural program, for example, was geared to wealthy farmers rather than to sharecroppers. Those who had the most extravagant expectations were must unhappy at what they viewed as the TVA's capitulation. Rexford Tugwell said, ruefully, that after 1936 the agency resembled nothing more than a "Tennessee Valley Power Production and Flood Control Corporation." No less than the NRA and AAA, the TVA often catered to the already powerful.

SOLIDARITY FOREVER?

When Franklin Roosevelt took office, 3 million workers belonged to trade unions, compared to 5 million in 1920. Only one in ten nonfarm workers carried a union card, about the same percentage as in 1910. In the steel, rubber, and automobile industries, unions played virtually no role at all. Thrown on the defensive in the 1920s by the open-shop drive and adverse Supreme Court rulings, labor suffered further losses in the early depression years. Unions found it impossible to keep old members, much less attract new ones, in a shrinking job market. Many workers shied away from union activities for fear of antagonizing employers. After 1933, although the economy slowly revived, the policies adopted by employers and American Federation of Labor officials continued to retard unionization.

The techniques employers used to block organizing drives included hiring spies and private policemen, stockpiling small arsenals for use in case of strikes, and recruiting professional strikebreakers. But in the years 1933 to 1935 employers relied chiefly on the company union, which had the advantage of appearing to comply with Section 7(a) of the NRA without actually doing so. These unions, set up and controlled by employers, lacked any semblance of autonomy. Management expected great things of them. A vice-president in charge of industrial relations at U.S. Steel declared that the union he had just organized would lead to "sound and harmonious relationships between men and management," similar to those prevailing "between a man and his wife." Mr. Dooley had once said that an employer's ideal union was one with "no strikes, no rules, no contracts, . . . hardly iny wages, an' dam' few mimbers." Except for the last point, company unions nicely fitted the definition. By 1935 nearly 600 of them existed, with well over 2 million members.

The AFL meanwhile was proving itself unequal to—indeed uninterested in—the task of organizing the unorganized, particularly unskilled workers in mass-production industries. With few exceptions, AFL unions followed craft rather than industrial lines. The Federation adhered to the principle of exclusive jurisdiction under which, for example, its metalworkers affiliate had a claim on all metal workers, no matter where they worked or what their own preferences. The creation of industrial unions in steel plants or automobile factories could easily demolish these jurisdictional rights. To justify their position, AFL leaders insisted that unskilled workers lacked the leverage to bargain successfully, for if they went on strike, employers could easily replace them. The eventual collapse of such old AFL rivals as the American Railway Union and the Industrial Workers of the World supposedly provided iron-clad proof that industrial unionism led up a blind alley.

The Roosevelt administration, unwilling to abandon the NRA concept of a business-government partnership, did little at first to spur union growth. "This is a time for mutual confidence and help," the President said in creating the NRA, but during 1934 capital and labor exhibited little of either. Not only were employers setting up company unions to avoid bargaining in good faith, but labor militancy rose sharply. In 1934, 1.5 million workers went on strike, and industrial violence reached its highest level since 1919. San Francisco longshoremen, Minneapolis truck drivers, Alabama cotton-mill workers—all struck for union recognition and improved conditions, and all clashed with the police or the national guard. Simultaneously, pressure began to mount in Congress, where Senator Robert F. Wagner of New York drew up a measure to make collective bargaining guarantees meaningful. Roosevelt, claiming that the bill needed more study, succeeded in having it shelved.

With the various strands of his labor policy unraveling, FDR finally accepted Wagner's position in the spring of 1935. At the last minute, when the Senate had passed the Wagner Act and the House was about to do so, Roosevelt endorsed it. The Wagner Act (1935) upheld the right of workers to join unions, and created the National Labor Relations Board to conduct shop elections. Most important, the measure substituted the principle of majority rule for that of proportional representation, ensuring that the union winning a majority of votes would represent all the employees. The act prohibited employers from blacklisting workers, refusing to reinstate strikers, engaging in industrial espionage, or setting up company unions. The bill passed by huge margins, in part because many assumed—mistakenly as it turned out—that the Supreme Court would nullify it.

Enactment of this legislation was like a shot of adrenalin to advocates of industrial unionism. A sizeable group within the AFL, led by John L. Lewis of the United Mine Workers, now demanded more strongly than ever that the Federation reverse its historic antagonism to industrial unions. Craft unions, Lewis asserted, may have served adequately in the past but were not suited to modern factories, in which technology had erased old craft distinctions. At the AFL convention in September 1935 Lewis presented a plan to allow the chartering of industrial unions. When the delegates rejected his motion by nearly a 2–1 margin, Lewis led a walkout. The depth of the disagreement, as well as the hatreds it evoked, was shown when William L. Hutcheson of the carpenters' union called Lewis a "bastard" and Lewis punched him in the jaw. In November Lewis, Sidney Hillman of the Amalgamated Clothing Workers of America, David Dubinsky of the International Ladies Garment Workers Union, and leaders of fledgling unions in the automobile, rubber, and steel industries created what became the Congress of Industrial Organizations. The AFL

Labor leaders: Philip Murray and John L. Lewis.

demanded the CIO's dissolution and, when it refused, suspended and later expelled the unions composing it. Yet in the long run, the split proved a prelude to success, for it enabled labor to take advantage of the spectacular opportunities for organizing unskilled workers provided by the Wagner Act.

RELIEF AND SECURITY

New Deal policies concerning relief, like those affecting labor, evolved in a halting fashion. This was no fault of Harry Hopkins who, before Roosevelt brought him to Washington to direct relief efforts, had performed a similar function in New York State. Hopkins's approach diverged sharply from prevailing practice. He believed that all needy persons, the unemployed as well as the chronically unemployable, were entitled to receive relief. He favored raising standards to furnish such necessities as clothing and medical care. He also believed that payments in cash rather than grocery slips helped preserve freedom of choice and self-respect. Finally, Hopkins preferred work relief to home relief. The former, while admittedly more expensive, enhanced the individual's feeling that he was a productive member of society; the latter was often degrading. Work relief should, where possible, utilize existing training and skills. Hopkins saw no

A Civil Works Administration project in New York City.

reason to insist that, as the price of obtaining relief, a teacher or engineer should have to dig ditches.

Hopkins's views regarding eligibility, standards, and programs went far beyond those of the Roosevelt administration and Congress. The first New Deal relief venture—the Federal Emergency Relief Administration (FERA)—showed this clearly. The FERA supervised relief activities from April 1933 to April 1935, except for a six-month period during the winter of 1934. At the outset Congress authorized expenditures of $500 million, half in direct grants to the states and half in matching grants on the basis of $1 for each $3 put up by the states. Administration of the program was left largely in state hands. The matching-grants provision had unfortunate consequences. States, hard-pressed to raise the money necessary to obtain such funds, had either to enact sales taxes, which imposed an unfair burden on the poor, or else cut other expenditures, such as those for education. If providing outright grants for relief broke sharply with existing practice, echoes of Herbert Hoover's policy lingered on in the decision to leave supervision to the states and in the attempt to squeeze yet more money out of them.

In November 1933, with the unemployed facing a long cold winter, the administration conceded the FERA's inadequacy and temporarily replaced it with the Civil Works Administration (CWA). The CWA differed from its predecessor in that the federal government administered it and met 90 percent of its cost. The agency also took on some workers who, although unemployed, had not qualified for relief. The CWA offered relatively high wages, paying unskilled workers 40 to 50 cents an hour, up to a maximum of 30 hours a week. Within two months the new agency had put 4.2 million men to work repairing streets, laying sewer pipe, building roads, improving schools and playgrounds, and, as critics always pointed out, raking leaves. Undoubtedly some projects were poorly conceived, but most accomplished useful purposes. Many people, particularly in the South, made more from the CWA than ever before in their lives. When employers bitterly complained about this, the CWA in January 1934 reduced working hours and wages. The average weekly wage declined from $15 to $11.50. Then, in April 1934, the administration, worried by the CWA's high cost and controversial nature, canceled the experiment and reverted to the FERA.

Not until April 1935, when it established the Works Progress Administration (WPA) did the New Deal fashion a workable relief program. The WPA only employed those certified as needing relief, but it was federally run, paid good wages, and made room for white-collar and professional workers. At its height, the WPA employed 3 million people a year, and, although starting with an initial appropriation of $4.8 billion, it ultimately spent $10.7 billion over seven years. The WPA included writers' and artists' projects, and also the Federal Theater Project. The latter in 1936 employed 12,500 actors who performed before audiences of 350,000 every week. The WPA never helped all the needy, and it was continually fighting off attempts to slice its budget. Yet it carried out many of the principles in which Hopkins believed: decent standards, work relief, and utilization of existing skills.

Roosevelt created the WPA in April, endorsed the Wagner Act in May, and in August 1935 signed a third measure—the Social Security Act—which further institutionalized government responsibility for the disadvantaged. The act set up an old-age pension system administered by the federal government and funded by a 1 percent payroll tax. Beginning in 1942 (the date was later advanced to 1940) retired workers over 65 would receive $10 to $85 a month, depending on the amount that they had contributed. Those who had already retired would receive pensions to which the government would contribute up to $15 a month. Second, the measure provided for a joint federal-state system of unemployment insurance based on employer contributions. Third, the act authorized federal aid for care of the blind, training of the physically handicapped, and aid to dependent children. Certainly, the Social Security Act had many imperfections: farm workers and domestic servants were excluded from its retirement provisions; state standards for unemployment compensation varied tremendously; and the payroll tax reduced mass purchasing power at the wrong time. The act may not even have amounted to what one Senator termed "a teeny-weeny bit of socialism." It did, however, place another brick in the arch of the welfare state.

THE NEW DEAL COALITION

Harry Hopkins was once quoted as saying, "We shall tax and tax, and spend and spend, and elect and elect." The remark may have been apocryphal, but it infuriated those who objected to New Deal relief and security policies. Many Republicans asserted, without justification, that social security would require federal prying into the private lives of citizens and would force millions of people to submit to fingerprinting or wear dogtags for identification purposes. Many of these same critics argued, with considerably better reason, that Democrats were attempting to extract partisan advantage from federal relief. Officials sometimes dispensed relief in ways calculated to bolster their political position and occasionally pressured WPA workers into voting a certain way. One Democratic leader privately requested the appointment of administrators who favored "using these Democratic projects to make votes for the Democratic Party."

In 1936, when Roosevelt defeated his opponent Alf M. Landon of Kansas, some Republicans blamed the magnitude of their loss on such unfair tactics. Certainly the dimensions of that defeat were stunning. Roosevelt received 27.5 million votes to Landon's 16.7 million and carried every state but Vermont and New Hampshire. The voters sent only 90 Republicans to the House of Representatives, and left only 16 in the Senate, giving the Democrats the largest congressional majorities since the mid-nineteenth century. The vote revealed a sharp split along class lines, with FDR in effect receiving most of his support from the lower classes and Landon most of his from more prosperous groups. Politics had moved full circle from the 1920s, when cultural tensions had overshadowed economic issues. The Roosevelt coalition embraced Southern whites and Northern blacks, rural dwellers and urban immigrants, middle-class intellectuals and blue-collar workers. In 1936 a person's income and occupation (or lack of one) provided the surest clues to party preference.

The Democratic triumph did not reflect illicit pressure exerted on relief recipients but rather public approval of the programs Roosevelt had instituted. At the time those policies were criticized as inadequate, and in retrospect they may appear even less adequate. In almost every field—business, agriculture, public power, labor, and relief—the New Deal moved cautiously and catered to more powerful groups at the expense of weaker ones. But this should not obscure the improvements in American life, or the changes in the role of government, that had occurred. In 1936 the clearest point of reference was 1932. The inadequacies of Roosevelt's policies, when compared with those of Hoover, did not seem so great after all.

Suggested Reading

The account most favorable to Hoover's handling of the depression is Eugene Lyons, *Herbert Hoover* (1964); perhaps the most critical is Arthur M. Schlesinger, Jr., *The Crisis of the Old Order, 1919–1933* (1957). Other useful works are Albert Romasco, *The Poverty of Abundance: Hoover, the Nation, the Depression* (1965); Joan Hoff Wilson, *Herbert Hoover: Forgotten Progressive* (1975); Martin L. Fausold and George T. Mazuzan, eds., *The Hoover Presidency: A Reappraisal* (1974); and Ellis W. Hawley *et al.*, *Herbert Hoover and the Crisis of American Capitalism* (1973). For the crisis of 1932, see Elliot A. Rosen, *Hoover, Roosevelt, and the Brain Trust: From Depression to New Deal* (1977); for the veterans' protest, Roger Daniels, *The Bonus March* (1971) and Donald J. Lisio, *The President and Protest* (1974); for the Farm Holiday movement, John Shover, *Cornbelt Rebellion* (1965).

Important books on Franklin Roosevelt and the New Deal are Frank Freidel, *Franklin D. Roosevelt,* 4 vols. (1952–1973), which covers the period through 1933; William E. Leuchtenburg, *Franklin D. Roosevelt and the New Deal* (1963); James M. Burns, *Roosevelt: The Lion and the Fox* (1956); and Arthur M. Schlesinger, Jr., *The Coming of the New Deal* (1959).

The literature on New Deal economic policy is extensive. Robert F. Himmelberg, *The Origins of the National Recovery Administration* (1976), and Ellis Hawley, *The New Deal and the Problem of Monopoly: A Study in Economic Ambivalence* (1966), are excellent accounts. New Deal agricultural programs are evaluated in David E. Conrad, *The Forgotten Farmers: The Story of Sharecroppers in the New Deal* (1965); Sidney Baldwin, *Poverty and Politics: The Rise and Decline of the Farm Security Administration* (1967); and Paul E. Mertz, *New Deal Policy and Southern Rural Poverty* (1978). On experiments in conservation and planning, consult Thomas McCraw, *TVA and the Power Fight, 1933–1939* (1970); and John Salmond, *The Civilian Conservation Corps, 1933–1942* (1967).

For a comprehensive account of workers during the depression, and of New Deal labor policy, see Irving Bernstein, *Turbulent Years* (1970). The sponsor of crucial labor legislation is treated in J. Joseph Huthmacher, *Senator Robert F. Wagner and the Rise of Urban Liberalism* (1968). The welfare programs of the Roosevelt administration are considered in Roy Lubove, *The Struggle for Social Security, 1900–1935* (1968); Searle F. Charles, *Minister of Relief: Harry Hopkins and the Depression* (1963); Jerre Mangione, *The Dream and the Deal: The Federal Writers' Project, 1935–1943* (1972); and Richard D. McKinzie, *The New Deal for Artists* (1973).

On the gangster film, see Robert Warshow's essay "The Gangster as Tragic Hero" in his *The Immediate Experience* (1962); and Andrew Bergman, *We're in the Money: Depression America and Its Films* (1971).

Texas Panhandle, 1938.

CHAPTER SEVEN

1933–1941

Hard Times:
Politics and Society

I AIN'T GOT NO HOME IN THIS WORLD ANY MORE

Words and music by Woody Guthrie

I ain't got no home, I'm just a ramblin' 'round,
I'm just a ramblin' workin' man, I go from town to town.
Police make it hard wherever I may go,
And I ain't got no home in this world any more.

My brothers and sisters are stranded on this road
It's a hot and dusty road where a million feet have trod.
Rich man took my home, and he drove me from my door,
And I ain't got no home in this world any more.

Was a farming on the shares and always I was down,

My debts was so many my pay wouldn't go around.
My wife took down and died upon the cabin floor,
And I ain't got no home in this world any more.

Now as I look around it's very plain to see
This wide and wicked world is a funny place to be,
The gambling man is rich and the working man is poor,
And I ain't got no home in this world any more.

Despite his efforts to combat the depression, and despite the vote of confidence he received in 1936, Franklin Roosevelt by no means succeeded in restoring prosperity during his first or, for that matter, his second administration. Millions of Americans who remained poor and insecure concluded that New Deal policies were inadequate. Some turned to socialism or communism, but more supported men like Dr. Francis E. Townsend, Huey Long, and Father Charles E. Coughlin, all of whom promised instant abundance without a radical alteration of the social order. If some complained that the New Deal was proceeding too slowly, conservatives believed it was traveling at breakneck speed. Limited at first to sniping at New Deal policies, Roosevelt's conservative critics launched a massive offensive after 1937. Faced with mounting hostility in Congress and declining public support, New Dealers went on the defensive. By the end of the decade the Roosevelt administration was devoting most of its attention to national defense and foreign policy, not to domestic reform.

THE OLD FOLKS' CRUSADE

In 1935 a California congressman arose in the House of Representatives to reflect on the passing of his mother. "She is the sweetest memory of my life," he said, "and the hands that used to feed me and cool my fevered brow now touch me only in my dreams. But if she were living today, . . . that little frail mother of mine . . . would say, 'Son, you be good to the old folks, and God will bless you.' " In the year 1935 being "good to the old folks" meant one thing: supporting the Townsend Old Age Revolving Pension Plan. Named for its originator, Dr. Francis E. Townsend, the plan gave birth to a movement whose widespread popularity pointed up the deficiencies of the New Deal and influenced the policies of the Roosevelt administration. Better than anything else, the appeal of the Townsend plan illustrated the devastating impact of the depression on the elderly.

For many elderly people the depression was in fact a nightmare. Many who wanted to continue working could not compete with younger workers. Unemployment among those over the age of 60 climbed to 40 percent. Many who had expected to retire on savings found themselves destitute when the banks failed. Others saw their incomes shrivel as the stock market fell or as private pension plans—often poorly conceived and badly financed—collapsed. Of the 7.5 million Americans over the age of 65, fully half could not support themselves. Some were forced to seek assistance from their children who, given the difficult times that everyone faced, were already experiencing hardship. Others had to apply for public charity even at the cost of sacrificing their self-respect. Only 28 states provided old-age pensions. For the most part they were sadly inadequate, with monthly payments ranging from $7 to $30. In 20 states no pensions of any kind existed.

All these problems were greatly magnified in California, which, as a haven for retirees, had seen its aged population climb from 200,000 to 366,000 during the 1920s. Five times as many people over the age of 65 lived in California as in any other state except Washington. In cities like Los Angeles and Long Beach, large numbers of retired men and women, separated from their relatives by hundreds or thousands of miles, had no one to fall back on when the depression hit. California's old-age pension plan was defective by every standard. No elderly person with a legally responsible relative able to provide support could receive aid. To qualify for assistance, an elderly person had to go on the relief rolls, sign a pauper's oath, submit to a "needs" test, and accept a lien on any property so that the state could recover part of the cost of the pension upon the person's death. Then, and only then, were the aged eligible for a sum of $22 a month. The system could hardly have been better calculated to deprive the aged of their dignity.

These conditions help explain the overwhelming response to the Townsend plan. Townsend, who had worked as a ranch hand and traveling salesman before becoming a doctor, had gone to Long Beach after the World War. In 1933, at the age of 66, he presented his "Cure for Depressions." Everyone in the country over the age of 60 would receive $200 a month, on two conditions: that they spend the full amount each month, and retire if still employed. This would pump money into the economy, open jobs for younger people, and permit a dignified retirement. The plan would be financed by a national sales tax, later called a transactions tax. Asked why he chose the figure of $200, Townsend explained, "the main reason was so that nobody would come along and offer more." In collaboration with Robert Earl Clements, Townsend set up Old Age Revolving Pensions, Ltd., in January 1934. Within two years 7000 Townsend clubs with perhaps 1.5 million members had sprung up across the country.

Townsend's appeal derived in part from his standing as a physician, a figure in whom the elderly placed a great deal of confidence. Moreover, Townsend clubs served important social and psychological functions. They sponsored dances, picnics, bazaars, and meetings, all of which tended to break down the loneliness and isolation that so many elderly people were experiencing. Membership cost only 25 cents, but "special Townsendites" who made larger contributions could join the Townsend National Legion of Honor. Townsend liberally sprinkled his talks with such phrases as "you dear old folks," "dang," and "by gum." The Townsend magazine carried a picture of the doctor alongside that of Lincoln with the caption: "We are Coming Father Townsend, Three Hundred Thousand Strong." The movement also had strong religious overtones. Its motto was "the Townsend plan is religion in action," and its followers were urged to "take up the cross of this crusade" for "God's plan."

The Townsend plan offered a married couple over 60 years of age $4800 a year, at a time when 87 percent of all American families had annual incomes below $2500. Yet the plan won support from many who believed in the values of thrift, hard work, and individualism precisely because it did not seem at all radical. For example, it did not call for deficit spending. The government would collect in sales taxes what it disbursed, and those taxes would not be levied on the rich but on all consumers. The plan required no bureaucracy other than the Treasury Department to make out the checks and the Post Office to deliver them. The plan in no way compromised private property rights. Nor did it imply a "dole." Rather, Townsend viewed the elderly as "Distributor Custodians," entrusted by society to spend $200 a month wisely. Critics, however, doubted the plan's feasibility, pointing out that it would cost $20 to $24 billion a year (or nearly half the total national income), that it would injure the poor through a regressive sales tax, and that it would require a far-flung bureaucracy to police spending by recipients.

The Townsend movement nevertheless crystallized popular sentiment for old-age pensions and helped move Congress and the administration to support the Social Security Act of 1935. Townsend condemned that measure because it excluded too many people from coverage and provided inadequate benefits. But, limited as it was, the act eroded Townsend's basis of support. His own plan lost on a voice vote in the House of Representatives. New Dealers responded to Townsend's challenge by attempting to discredit his movement. In the spring of 1936 a Senate committee began investigating the clubs in an effort to prove them a financial fraud. The investigators found that Robert Earl Clements had profited handsomely and that Townsend not only exercised absolute control over the clubs but privately referred to the members as "old fossils." (When Townsend refused to testify, he was cited for contempt and sentenced to a year in jail; Roosevelt later commuted the sentence because of Townsend's age.) By the summer of 1936 Townsend's estrangement from the New Deal was complete. Certain that "we shall be able to lick the stuffing" out of both major political parties, Townsend prepared to join forces with other foes of the administration.

"SHARE OUR WEALTH"

In 1933 Sinclair Lewis published a novel entitled *It Can't Happen Here*, in which a Senator named Buzz Windrip established a fascist regime in the United States. One character described Windrip as "a dictator seemingly so different from the fervent Hitler and the gesticulating Fascists . . . a dictator with something of the earthy American sense of humor of a Mark Twain." None doubted that this figure was patterned after Senator Huey Long of Louisiana or that Lewis was asserting that it could indeed happen here. In the highly charged political atmosphere of the 1930s perhaps no one aroused more intense feelings of love and hatred than did the Louisianan. To his supporters, Long had "changed Louisiana from a hellhole to a paradise. He was emancipator. He brought light." To his critics, Long was an unprincipled demagogue. In the summer of 1932 Franklin Roosevelt privately termed him one of the most dangerous men in America.

Huey Long after Senate filibuster, 1935.

Born in 1893, Long as a boy had done odd jobs—driving a bakery wagon, carrying water to construction crews, learning to set type— primarily, it seems, to avoid the drudgery of working on his father's farm. His favorite book was *The Count of Monte Cristo.* He later remembered, "That man in that book knew how to hate, and until you learn how to hate you'll never get anywhere in this world." He spent his teens as a traveling salesman and gambler, then borrowed money to attend Tulane Law School, where he crammed a three-year program into eight months and arranged to take a special bar examination. At age 24 Long was elected to the Louisiana Public Service Commission and over the next several years gained a reputation for his attacks on the oil and railroad companies that dominated state politics. Although Long cultivated a comical public image, adopting the name "Kingfish" and dubbing his opponents "Turkeyhead" or "Old Trashy Mouth," he was a keenly intelligent man and an astute politician.

In 1928 Long became Governor, and even after his election to the Senate two years later he continued to rule Louisiana very much as he pleased. He dominated the legislature, curbed the press, and built a disciplined political machine. When people protested that he was violating the state constitution, Long replied, "I'm the Constitution around here now." Yet for every one who resented Long's dictatorial manner, there were many who benefited from his reign. He improved the public schools, provided free textbooks, and initiated evening classes for adults; he built new roads, bridges, and highways; he eliminated the poll tax and property taxes on the poor. These reforms helped break down the isolation of the rural poor, provided voters with tangible evidence of his accomplishments, and created jobs for political supporters. Unlike most other Southern politicians, Long did not appeal to white supremacist sentiment. Once he harshly denounced the leader of the Ku Klux Klan: "When I call him a son of a bitch I am not using profanity, but am referring to the circumstances of his birth."

His advocacy of the "Share Our Wealth" program made Long a figure of national prominence in the 1930s. The government, he insisted, must "limit the size of the big men's fortune and guarantee some minimum to the fortune and comfort of the little man's family." To accomplish this, he proposed limiting individual wealth to $3 to $4 million, providing all citizens with a $5000 homestead and a guaranteed annual income of $2500, offering free education through the college level to all whose "mental ability and energy" qualified them, establishing a 30-hour work week, and financing generous old-age pensions through taxes on the rich. While this would not mean absolute equality, it would remove the most glaring inequalities. "So America would start again with millionaires, but with no multimillionaires or billionaires; we would start with some poor, but they wouldn't be so poor that they wouldn't have the comforts of life." In February 1934, Share Our Wealth clubs began forming; soon there were 27,000 claiming 4.7 million members. The movement's strength centered in Louisiana, Arkansas, and Mississippi.

The Share Our Wealth program went considerably beyond the Townsend plan. Long proposed a more sweeping change in economic relationships and assigned a more prominent role to the federal government than did Townsend. The Louisianan frankly advocated confiscating wealth in order to redistribute income. But in some respects the two resembled each other. Both Long and Townsend were charismatic leaders, both organized clubs that offered members a gratifying sense of personal involvement, and both promised a quick, certain path to good times. In addition, both appealed to those whom the New Deal had helped rather little. Long, who at first supported Roosevelt, broke with him decisively in 1935 on the grounds that the administration was proceeding too cautiously. Never one to hide his ambitions, Long then published *My First Days in the White House* (1935) to explain how he would transform America after his election. He even promised to find a place in his administration for Franklin Roosevelt—as Secretary of the Navy.

Roosevelt considered Long a veritable Pied Piper, leading people astray with spurious and impractical proposals. Nevertheless in June 1935 he moved several notches closer to Long's position by asking Congress to impose high taxes on inherited wealth, corporate profits, and "very great individual incomes." When the President's message was read, Long declared: "I just wish to say 'Amen.'" Roosevelt's recommendations brought anguished cries from the business community, and by the time Congress finished watering it down, the Wealth Tax Act (1935) barely resembled Roosevelt's original proposal, much less Long's. Even as he borrowed a plank from the Share Our Wealth platform, the President attacked Long by denying him federal patronage, by encouraging the Treasury Department to investigate alleged financial wrongdoing in Louisiana, and by permitting his aides to speak their minds. "The Senator from Louisiana has halitosis of the intellect," said Secretary of the Interior Harold Ickes; "that's presuming Emperor Long has an intellect."

None of this proved very effective. Then, in September 1935, a young doctor, Carl Austin Weiss, assassinated Long and was himself immediately killed by the Senator's bodyguards. With its leader gone, the Share Our Wealth movement came under the control of Gerald L. K. Smith, a minister originally hired to organize the clubs. Smith, who had idolized Long (even wearing suits of clothes his mentor had discarded), appealed to similar hopes and exploited similar grievances. Smith cried: "Let's pull down these huge piles of gold until there shall be a real job, not a little old sow-belly, black-eyed pea job, but a real spending-money, beefsteak and gravy, Chevrolet, Ford in the garage, new suit, Thomas Jefferson, Jesus Christ, red, white, and blue job for every man!" By 1936 Smith, like Townsend, was prepared for a head-on clash with the administration. It came with the blessing of the "radio priest," Father Charles E. Coughlin.

THE RADIO PRIEST
AND HIS FLOCK

Father Coughlin had been assigned to the parish of Royal Oak, Michigan, in 1926. There he conducted a Sunday-morning radio program, "The Golden Hour of the Little Flower," which at first consisted of inspirational readings and devotional messages. But in the early 1930s, with the depression worsening, Coughlin turned to economic and social issues. As he did, his audience grew by leaps and bounds. Each week more than 10 million listeners tuned in Coughlin's sermons. After every broadcast he received hundreds of thousands of letters, and thousands of dollars in contributions. Coughlin enjoyed an unusual latitude in his remarks because he had organized his own radio network after a CBS attempt to censor him in 1931, and because he had the solid support of his superior, Bishop Michael James Gallagher of Detroit.

His position in the Catholic Church goes far toward explaining Coughlin's popularity. Many regarded him, quite literally, as a father, one whose word could implicitly be trusted because it had religious sanction. "For those of us who haven't a material father," said one of his admirers, "he can be our father and we won't need to feel lonesome." Coughlin also set forth economic proposals that, if sometimes vague, proved highly attractive. He wanted to reform the monetary system by increasing the amount of currency in circulation, remonetizing silver, eliminating the

Doctor Townsend and Father Coughlin, 1936.

federal reserve banks, and replacing interest-bearing government notes with noninterest-bearing ones. He also favored nationalizing "those public necessities which by their very nature are too important to be held in the control of private individuals," providing a "just and living annual wage" for all workers, and imposing heavy taxes on the wealthy. "Modern capitalism as we know it is not worth saving," Coughlin said, but capitalism with its abuses eliminated would be very much worth saving.

In 1933 Coughlin, then a staunch Roosevelt supporter, asserted that "the New Deal is Christ's deal." Yet during the next two years he became disillusioned with the President. Coughlin particularly resented FDR's failure to accept monetary management as the key to recovery, his advocacy of United States membership in the World Court, and his opposition to refinancing farm mortgages by issuing millions of dollars in greenbacks. Late in 1934, following the example set by Long and Townsend, Coughlin created the National Union for Social Justice to lobby for his economic program. By mid-1936, having concluded somewhat inconsistently that the New Deal both "protects plutocrats and comforts Communists," Coughlin announced the formation of the Union party. It quickly gained the support of Townsend and Smith. Coughlin expected the party's nominee—William Lemke of North Dakota—to receive 9 million votes, enough to throw the presidential election into the House of Representatives.

During the campaign Coughlin accused "Franklin doublecrossing Roosevelt" of "flirting with Communistic tendencies" and predicted that FDR's reelection would mean "more bullet holes in the White House than you could count with an adding machine." Gerald L. K. Smith blasted New Dealers as "a slimy group of men culled from the pink campuses of America." This rhetoric, however, failed to save the Union party from a humiliating defeat. It received 892,000 votes, under 2 percent of the total. In part this resulted from the party's inability to get on the ballot in several important states or to run a full slate of candidates for local office. In addition, Lemke proved a singularly uninspiring figure. Nor could Coughlin, Smith, and Townsend agree on policy and procedure. Expediency had made them allies, but a good deal of rivalry and suspicion remained. Millions of people may have been attracted to economic panaceas, but they would not waste their votes on a hopeless third-party venture. The kind of support Coughlin and the others enjoyed could not be translated into votes on election day.

Dismayed by the outcome, Coughlin canceled future radio broadcasts but his retirement proved brief. By 1938 he was back on the air with sermons that had taken on a distinctly new tone. Coughlin had employed nativist themes in the past, but never so prominently. He insisted that a conspiracy of international Jewish bankers threatened America. His magazine, *Social Justice,* carried the "Protocols of Zion" (a forgery depicting an alleged Jewish conspiracy to take over the world), termed Hitler's Germany "an innocent victim of a sacred war declared against her nine years ago by the Jews," and honored Benito Mussolini as "Man of the Week." In July 1938 Coughlin founded the Christian Front to combat Communists and Jews. It prepared a Christian Index listing merchants who had pledged to patronize and employ other Christians as a means of curbing Jewish economic power. Coughlin, who had formerly denounced the anti-Catholic nativism of the Ku Klux Klan, ended by stirring up Catholic anti-Semitism.

THE POPULAR FRONT

During the 1930s the American Communist party gained a fairly wide influence, certainly wider than its membership (which hovered around 50,000) or its voting strength (which fell from 103,000 in 1932 to 80,000 in 1936) would indicate. Party members controlled several large CIO unions including the United Electrical Workers and the Mine, Mill, and Smelter Workers, held responsible positions in the National Labor Relations Board and other government agencies, and gained a firm footing in the American Labor Party in New York State and in other political organizations. Communist doctrines won a large audience among intellectuals. In 1932, for example, 53 prominent writers and artists—including Sherwood Anderson, Erskine Caldwell, John Dos Passos, Sidney Hook, Lincoln Steffens, and Edmund Wilson—endorsed the party's candidates, William Z. Foster and James Ford. They explained: "As responsible intellectual workers we have aligned ourselves with the frankly revolutionary Communist Party, the party of the workers."

Nevertheless, the 1930s hardly deserve to be called "the Red decade." The great majority of Americans remained hostile to communism, and most who joined the movement did so only briefly. The party consisted of a small cadre that remained loyal through thick and thin, and others who entered and left as through a revolving door. Surely one reason for this was the party's subservience to the Soviet Union. American Communist leaders consistently followed policies that conformed to Russian interests, not because they were hired Russian agents but because they believed that the needs of American workers were identical with those of the Soviet Union. They equated virtue with the Russian system and either rejected or discounted evidence of Stalinist terrorism. With every shift in party doctrine, those who could not adjust departed.

At first the party followed a line laid down in 1928 at the Sixth World Congress of Communist Parties. Stalin at the time was consolidating his authority and thought that Communist revolutions around the world would assist him by removing unfriendly capitalist regimes. Consequently, Communists in the United States repudiated halfway measures and called for a dictatorship of the proletariat. Communists refused to work through the American Federation of Labor, which they considered hopelessly reactionary, but tried to create their own militant unions. They claimed that Negroes in the black belt constituted a separate nation and therefore should exercise the right of self-determination. They branded Franklin Roosevelt "an abject tool of Wall Street" and condemned the New Deal for striving "to hold the workers in industrial slavery." As revolutionaries awaiting the day of revolution, Communists were equally critical of such reform gestures as the National Recovery Administration and the Wagner Act.

In the summer of 1935 the party dramatically modified its approach. By then Stalin had identified Nazi Germany as the greatest potential danger. Accordingly, he urged Communists to join liberals and socialists in an antifascist popular front. Communists in the United States worked diligently to soften their image. Their leader, Earl Browder, announced that "Communism is 20th-Century Americanism," and traced the party's lineage back to Tom Paine and Thomas Jefferson. The party sought to build bridges to the socialists, took an active role in union organizing, and deemphasized the idea of Negro nationality. Its view of the New Deal underwent a similar transformation. Communists praised Roosevelt as a progressive and backed almost every one of his proposals. This identification with American values may have reached its height when the *Daily Worker* informed members of the Young Communist League that by selling subscriptions they could "Win a Free Bicycle!" and obtain some "spending money." "Gradually you'll be able to build up a large profitable route," the journal promised.

These popular front tactics exacerbated divisions within the Socialist party. In 1935 Browder invited Socialist leader Norman Thomas to a debate in Madison Square Garden, with the proceeds going to the Socialists. When Thomas accepted, "old-guard" Socialists unjustifiably feared that he was ready to collaborate with the Communists. By 1936 thousands had deserted the Socialist party, whose membership dropped below 20,000. Thomas rejected other such overtures and, unlike Browder, kept up a steady attack on the New Deal. Roosevelt, he said, was trying to "cure tuberculosis with cough drops." The New Deal was ignoring the plight of tenant farmers and other dispossessed groups. Planning and capitalism, he added, simply did not mix. To those who urged him to support Roosevelt in 1936 Thomas replied: "The way to get Socialism is to proclaim the Socialist message not to declare a moratorium on it during an election campaign." But his vote—which fell from 903,000 in 1932 to 187,000 in 1936—indicated that the New Deal had neutralized Socialist appeal. Thomas confessed as much. "Roosevelt did not carry out the Socialist platform," he declared, "unless he carried it out on a stretcher."

Communist endorsement of the New Deal during the popular front years reinforced the convictions of those who considered Roosevelt a Red stooge. By 1936 antiadministration newspapers were printing doggerel about "The Red New Deal with a Soviet seal/ Endorsed by a Moscow hand,/ The strange result of an alien cult/ In a liberty-loving land." Generally, New Dealers discounted these attacks, asserting that Communist influence was, and would continue to be, negligible, so long as reform succeeded. Roosevelt also recognized that red-baiting was an old technique for discrediting social change. He was enough of a civil libertarian to want to judge people by how they behaved rather than by what they thought, which books they read, or which meetings they attended. The President evidently viewed Communists as well-intentioned but misguided people who often did the right things for the wrong reasons. Before the signing of the Nazi-Soviet pact, Roosevelt did not consider domestic communism a major threat.

Germany made that agreement with Russia on August 23, 1939, and went to war with England and France in September. While the pact remained in force—until June 1941, when Hitler invaded the Soviet Union—Communists in the United States completely reversed themselves, scrapping the idea of an antifascist popular front. They opposed American aid to the Allies, claiming that England and France were imperialist nations. They similarly opposed the buildup of defense industries, on occasion calling strikes to disrupt work in aircraft plants. Communists reverted to denouncing Roosevelt as "the leader and organizer of all reactionary forces in the country." The Communist party paid a heavy price for this turnabout. Thousands of members, attracted by the popular front ideology, deserted the party in disillusionment. Many liberals who had cooperated with Communists considered the party's justification of the Nazi-Soviet pact a symptom of its moral bankruptcy. Finally, the party's stance contributed to a Red scare that swept the country after 1939.

BLACK AMERICANS AND THE NEW DEAL

"People is hollerin' 'bout hard times, tell me what it all about," wailed a 1937 blues recording; "hard times don't worry me, I was broke when it first started out." In singing the blues, surely, people were laughing to keep from crying. The depression had a devastating impact on black Americans, even on those who had never shared in the prosperity of the 1920s. Southern black farmers in the early 1930s scraped by on $300 a year. Of those employed in agriculture, four of every five did not own their land but worked as sharecroppers, tenant farmers, or wage hands. Lacking any security, they often lost their homes as hard times settled over the countryside. In the cities conditions were worse. The unemployment rate for blacks was 30 to 60 percent higher than for whites, in part because of bias in hiring but also because the jobs blacks had held in service occupations were often eliminated. Industries employing large numbers of Negroes—such as building construction and bituminous coal—came to a virtual standstill. Desperate whites sometimes resorted to violence to displace blacks. On the Illinois Central Railroad white firemen terrorized Negroes, killing ten of them, to get their jobs. Whites also began taking jobs Negroes had formerly held as elevator operators, hospital attendants, cooks, waiters, bellhops, maids, and chauffeurs.

Hallie Flanagan and the Federal Theater

Drama in Washington: Hallie Flanagan before the Dies Committee.

In 1935, as part of its expanded relief program, the Roosevelt administration initiated various projects to aid unemployed writers, artists, and actors. To head the Federal Theater Project, Harry Hopkins called on Hallie Flanagan, whom he had first met while both were undergraduates at Grinnell College in Iowa. A person of great creative drive and intelligence, Flanagan had gone on to teach drama at Grinnell and win the first Guggenheim grant ever awarded a woman. In 1926 she made a comparative study of European drama and was particularly impressed by Constantine Stanislavsky's Moscow Art Theater. Then she became director of experimental theater at Vassar College

Federal Theater Project: *Macbeth.*

where she supervised some of the more imaginative productions of the early 1930s.

Under her guidance, the Federal Theater Project employed an average of 10,000 people a year for four years. Many of its plays had a frank social message. The "living newspaper" format, which vividly documented current issues, was well-suited for this purpose. *Triple A Plowed Under* (1936) called for a New Deal for farmers; *Power* (1937) advocated a greater measure of consumer control over public utilities; *One-Third of a Nation* (1938) exposed the poverty and filth of big-city slums. Some productions met with huge popular and critical acclaim. A dramatization of Sinclair Lewis's *It Can't Happen Here* played to 275,000 people in four months; it grossed $80,000 although the average

ticket was priced at 30 cents. The Federal Theater provided new opportunities for Negro performers who staged a jazz version of *Mikado,* and, under Orson Welles's direction, a version of *Macbeth* set in Haiti during the time of Napoleon (complete with witches and voodoo drums.) Members of the children's theater performed *Jack and the Beanstalk* in parks during the summer, and visited hospital wards to teach paralyzed children how to work marionettes.

Throughout its career the Federal Theater faced difficult problems. One concerned the competing demands of relief and art. Some unemployed people, who clearly deserved assistance, claimed to be "actors" even if they had little talent, and Flanagan sometimes felt obliged to give them jobs. In addition, disputes arose over the nature of

Federal Theater Project: *It Can't Happen Here.*

the productions. There was a built-in tension between the desire to appeal to a mass audience (particularly since public response was a means of justifying further appropriations) and the desire to stage avant-garde works that appealed to the actors' and directors' own aesthetic sensibilities. There was yet another hard question: as a government agency, funded by the taxpayers, how far could it safely go in advocating political views? Critics even complained about the production of *The Revolt of the Beavers,* a children's fairytale about exploited beavers who rose against a cruel chief. This, it was said, amounted to "Marxism á la Mother Goose."

The Federal Theater itself became a casualty of drooping New Deal fortunes. In 1939, with Congress anxious

212 to slash relief programs, Flanagan's agency seemed highly expendable. Since most of its employees lived in New York City, Chicago, or Los Angeles, the Federal Theater had a rather narrow political constituency. The agency also came under attack from the Dies Committee for being a "veritable hotbed of un-American activities." Some congressmen suspected that the performances were obscene. They snickered at such titles as *The Bishop Misbehaves* or *Old Captain Romeo's Four Wives*. Of *A New Kind of Love,* one Republican remarked, "I wonder what that can be. It smacks of the Soviets." In 1939 Congress killed the Federal Theater Project. Hallie Flanagan left to become a Dean at Smith College. Not until 1965 would the federal government again undertake a large-scale program of support for the performing arts.

Federal Theater Project: *Revolt of the Beavers.*

To people surviving at a subsistence level, the Roosevelt administration offered a ray of hope, primarily in the form of federal relief. Before 1933, localities administering relief often rejected black applicants, but the New Deal reversed this pattern. In 1935 nearly 30 percent of all Negro families were receiving some form of aid, and in certain cities the figure approached 50 percent. Proportionately, three times as many blacks were on relief as whites. New Deal programs sought to ensure fair treatment. The Works Progress Administration enabled hundreds of thousands of blacks to weather the depression. In Norfolk, where Negroes comprised less than one-third of the population, they accounted for more than two-thirds of the workers on WPA rolls. The Public Works Administration took a pioneering step by introducing nondiscrimination clauses, under which contractors had to pay black workers a fixed proportion of their payrolls, a proportion ultimately reflecting the number of Negroes in the labor force. This is not to say that other New Deal agencies never discriminated. On balance, however, blacks received a share of federal assistance in proportion to their numbers if not their need.

If the Roosevelt administration came to the rescue of jobless Negroes, it proved less responsive to demands for legal equality and social justice. Little in Roosevelt's background suggested any such concern. He had served under the segregationist Wilson administration in the archsegregationist Navy Department; he made his second home in Warm Springs, Georgia, and apparently never questioned local mores; he accepted "Cactus Jack" Garner, a conservative Texan, as his running mate in 1932 and 1936. As President, FDR maintained that economic recovery, not civil rights, would most effectively aid the largest number of Negroes. He believed that New Deal legislation would be lost without the support of Southern Democrats who headed important Congressional committees, and he recognized that civil rights was potentially a source of great friction within his party. As a gradualist and institutionalist, Roosevelt reasoned that only education would finally eradicate racial prejudice. "We must do this thing stride by stride," he said.

Roosevelt took few such strides, however, during his first or second term of office. Despite the angry protests of civil rights groups, New Deal programs in the South followed Jim Crow lines. The Tennessee Valley Authority segregated its work crews, hired only unskilled black laborers, and set up a "model village" that barred Negroes. The Civilian Conservation Corps maintained segregated work camps. The National Recovery Administration, which in theory prohibited wage differentials based on race, in practice left loopholes whereby blacks could be paid less. The Agricultural Adjustment Administration's acreage reduction program led to the eviction of thousands of black tenant farmers. The Justice Department refused to prosecute lynchers under a federal kidnapping statute on the grounds that the victims were not taken across state lines for financial gain. Roosevelt branded lynching a "vile form of collective murder" but refused to support an antilynching bill that provided for a federal trial if states failed to prosecute, specified prison terms for members of lynch

Mary McLeod Bethune and Eleanor Roosevelt, 1937.

mobs, and made counties responsible for damages. In 1937, after a mob in Mississippi had set two Negroes afire with a blow torch, the House passed the measure. It was filibustered to death in the Senate in 1938 without protest from the administration.

Given this record, the President won a truly astonishing amount of support from black Americans. In 1932 nearly three-fourths of them voted Republican; in 1936, more than three-fourths voted Democratic, and the percentage increased in the years that followed. New Deal relief programs—which primarily aided Northern and urban blacks, who could vote, rather than Southern and rural blacks, who could not—partially, but not fully, explain this shift. Certainly FDR benefited when compared with his predecessor. Having broken the Solid South in 1928, Hoover had hoped to convert white southerners to Republicanism. Unlike Roosevelt, he never even verbally condemned the lynchings that occurred during his presidency. In addition, Roosevelt offered important government positions to such prominent blacks as Mary McLeod Bethune and Robert Weaver. Eleanor Roosevelt and other New Dealers spoke up forcibly on behalf of racial justice. Partly as a result of his wife's prestige in the black community, Franklin Roosevelt received credit for what was good about the New Deal while escaping blame for much that was bad.

Developments during the 1930s subjected the National Association of Colored People, and the civil rights strategy it advocated, to a severe challenge. The NAACP had always held that Negroes could improve their economic position by obtaining the right training, working hard, and persuading white employers to give them an equal chance. It disparaged unified action by black and white workers, declaring it impossible to make an "advantageous alliance with white American labor because of its intense race hatred." In 1935 the organization opposed the Wagner Act, which did not contain a clause preventing discrimination, on the grounds that stronger unions would more effectively freeze out black workers. But the depression caused many members of the NAACP to place their hopes in some form of socialism, and their hand was strengthened when the newly formed Congress of Industrial Organizations proved receptive to Negroes. Dr. Ralph Bunche and other militants argued that the NAACP should adopt a radical economic platform. In their view, only an alliance of black and white workers could revamp the capitalist system and guarantee a decent living to all.

The NAACP also assumed that civil rights could be secured by lobbying in Congress and by arguing before the courts. Two events during the 1930s, however, weakened confidence in the possibility of ending Jim Crow through political and constitutional means. The first was the failure of the antilynching bill, which the NAACP had helped draft, and to which it devoted a considerable portion of its time, money, and energy from 1935 to 1940. A second event that eroded the gradualist approach was the Supreme Court's decision in *Grovey* v. *Townsend* (1935). The Court held that the Democratic party in Texas—and by extension elsewhere in the South—could exclude blacks from membership and thereby bar them from participating in primaries. The white primary did not violate the Fourteenth Amendment, the Court ruled, since the Democratic party was a voluntary political association whose actions did not involve discrimination by a state. The decision effectively disenfranchised Negroes since in one-party areas the only true contests occurred in primaries. The closed primary was an even more effective deterrent to voting than the poll tax or the literacy test.

The NAACP above all prized the goal of integration, yet during the 1930s this too came under fire. Led by W. E. B. DuBois, a number of black intellectuals advocated what one termed "the conscious development of nationalistic sentiment." DuBois, whose stand led to his resignation from the NAACP, continued to oppose forced segregation but saw distinct advantages in voluntary segregation. He asserted: "It is the race-conscious black man cooperating together in his own institutions and movements who will eventually emancipate the colored race." In his autobiography, *Dusk of Dawn* (1940), DuBois described his disenchantment with the view that education would wipe out prejudice. Convinced that racism was rooted in the subconscious and reinforced by economic self-interest, DuBois thought it pointless for a black minority to plead for justice from a white majority. Instead, Negroes should set up their own institutions—schools, churches, hospitals, theaters—and a largely autonomous economy founded on socialist principles. DuBois's doctrine, although in some respects reminiscent of Marcus Garvey's, appealed to intellectuals rather than the masses, did not contemplate a return to Africa, and combined economic radicalism with racial nationalism.

DuBois's vision of a cooperative commonwealth never approached realization, as indeed it could not, given the lack of economic resources in the black community. The nearest any sizeable group of Negroes came to attaining perfect security was in the religious "heavens" of Father Divine. In 1933 Divine, a preacher in Brooklyn and Long Island for more than a decade, moved to Harlem, where he attracted a huge following. Divine opened "heavens"—dormitory-like arrangements where his disciples lived and received adequate food and clothing as long as they worshiped their benefactor (and promised to abstain from sexual relations). His followers believed that Divine was God and that he and they were immortal. If someone died or became seriously ill he was said to have stopped believing. Divine, the vast majority of whose followers were black but among whom there were some whites, created a world in which racial conflict, indeed racial differentiation, no longer existed. He referred only to "people of the darker complexion" and "people of the lighter complexion." The names his disciples adopted similarly revealed their search for order and harmony: "Quiet Dove," "Perfect Love," "Sweet Music," and "Keep on Smiling." For thousands of Negroes beset by racial, economic, or family troubles, Divine provided a way out, and many remained steadfast in their faith until his death in 1965. During the depression years, when millions followed political messiahs, it was hardly surprising that some turned to a man who claimed he was the True Messiah.

THE CONSERVATIVE RESPONSE

Not all Americans sympathized with the New Deal or wished it to move further left. The conservative position—with its reverence for the past, recognition of man's innate limitations, distrust of the masses, emphasis on property rights, and quest for social harmony—also had its spokesmen and supporters. The New Deal had upset traditional ways of doing things, challenged older values, altered the relative power of social classes, and affected some groups adversely. For all these reasons, some people came to hate Roosevelt and everything he represented with a passion. Whereas criticism from the left made its strongest impression during FDR's first administration, thunder on the right was loudest after 1936.

Businessmen provided one important source of opposition, although sentiment in the business community was never monolithic. A handful of industrialists endorsed Roosevelt's policies, but organizations such as the

National Association of Manufacturers and the Chamber of Commerce consistently fought the New Deal, particularly after 1935. By then, speakers at NAM meetings were talking about the need to rid Washington of "economic crackpots, social reformers, labor demagogues and political racketeers." These critics charged that deficit spending undermined the nation's credit, that the tax on undistributed corporate profits curbed initiative, that the growth of executive power endangered individual liberties, and that the Wagner Act weighted the scales too heavily on labor's side. Roosevelt stirred up class antagonism, businessmen complained, by his unfair references to "economic royalists" who sought control of the government for selfish purposes.

The President believed that business critics failed to perceive the true intent, and effect, of his policies. He compared himself to one who jumped off a pier to save a rich gentleman from drowning; at first the gentleman was grateful, but he later complained bitterly that his silk hat was lost. Whether or not the New Deal rescued the capitalist system, it certainly enabled business to make higher profits than it had under Hoover. Despite all the fuss about fiscal irresponsibility, Roosevelt turned to deficit spending as a last resort, when nothing else seemed to work, and did so reluctantly. Nor did the New Deal redistribute wealth. The share of disposable income held by the rich did not change significantly from 1933 to 1939. Taxes, while higher than in the past, were hardly crushing. Late in the decade they ranged from 4 percent on incomes of $10,000 to 32 percent on incomes of $100,000. "It is the same old story of the failure of those who have property to realize that I am the best friend the profit system ever had, even though I add my denunciation of unconscionable profits," Roosevelt wrote.

In 1934 conservatives created the American Liberty League to mobilize public sentiment against the New Deal. Over the next two years the League enrolled 125,000 members, spent $1 million, and distributed 5 million pieces of literature. To achieve a nonpartisn appearance, it recruited several prominent Democrats, but it never quite managed to acquire that image. The Liberty League formulated the essential conservative indictment of the New Deal. It denounced Roosevelt as a dictator, although it had difficulty deciding whether he more nearly resembled a communist or a fascist. It affirmed that the welfare state aided the improvident and unfit at the expense of the hardworking and virtuous and was therefore immoral. It exploited popular reverence for the Constitution and the Supreme Court. Roosevelt's sweeping triumph in the 1936 election, however, discredited the Liberty League, which had found itself in the awkward position of insisting that the people break sharply with the practices of the past four years and dismantle the welfare state. Roosevelt, by contrast, could promise continuity and stability. Only the initiatives he took in 1937 altered this odd reversal of roles and, in so doing, gave conservatives another chance.

"COURT-PACKING"

At the time of his second inauguration Franklin Roosevelt seemed to stand at the pinnacle of his political career. Yet his second term witnessed a sharp decline in New Deal fortunes. In some ways, the very size of his congressional majorities—the House contained 331 Democrats and 90 Republicans, the Senate 76 Democrats and 16 Republicans—encouraged factionalism and discord. Also, relatively large numbers of Democrats were elected in 1936 from safe districts—that is, by a margin of more than 5 percent—and were therefore less responsive to the wishes of party leaders. But Roosevelt's problem stemmed less from the composition of Congress than from what he wanted it to do. This became apparent in February 1937, when he unveiled his plan to reform the Supreme Court. Asserting that the Court carried too heavy a work load, the President proposed to add an additional justice for each one who did not retire at the age of 70. A maximum of six new positions could be created, and the Court would revert to a smaller size upon the death or retirement of an elderly member.

Several considerations led the President to take this stand. He resented being rebuked by the Court in 1935 for dismissing William E. Humphrey, a reactionary member of the Federal Trade Commission, when in so doing he had followed earlier precedent. The Court, moreover, had struck down crucial reform legislation. It had ruled against the National Recovery Administration and the Agricultural Adjustment Administration, and in June 1936, by a narrow 5–4 margin, it agreed that a New York minimum-wage law violated the due process clause of the Fourteenth Amendment. Roosevelt believed that the same narrow reasoning would lead the Court to invalidate the Wagner Act and the Social Security Act, both of which were up for consideration. It also appeared that federal regulation of wages and hours, another item on the New Deal agenda, would not pass the judges' scrutiny even if Congress approved it. Roosevelt believed that the four conservatives on the Court—Willis Van Devanter, George Sutherland, James McReynolds, and Pierce Butler— were busily reading their own political prejudices into the Constitution under a cloak of judicial impartiality.

The President's decision to make an issue of the justices' age, when he really objected to their ideology, offended many, including the 80-year-old Justice Louis D. Brandeis. Yet in seeking to enlarge the Court, FDR chose the only course that seemed feasible. He rejected the alternatives—constitutional amendments requiring a two-thirds vote on the Court in order to declare an act unconstitutional, permitting Congress to override Court decisions, or broadening the legislative authority to regulate the economy. Roosevelt did not think for a moment that three-fourths of the state legislatures would approve any of these proposals, and certainly not soon enough to help. Besides, each proposed amendment might create more problems than it would solve. To demand a 6–3 vote on the Court would mean little, because five members could persuade another to join them so as to protect the Court's prestige; to permit Congress to overturn rulings would bring judicial review to an end; to broaden constitutional powers would be useless if justices with an Ice Age philosophy continued to interpret those powers. In FDR's view the Court, not the Constitution, needed changing.

The proposal triggered the most bitterly fought dispute of Roosevelt's presidency. Advocates said that the Supreme Court was already "packed" with reactionaries who were frustrating the popular desire for social reform as expressed in the election of 1936. There was nothing sacred about the number nine, they continued, for the Court's size had varied in the past. Legislation that affected millions of people should not stand or fall on the whim of a single judge. Opponents responded that the Court, far from obstructing the New Deal, had invalidated only a few measures, and badly drawn ones at that. Roosevelt had never received a mandate to pack the Court, since he had studiously avoided the subject during the campaign. Finally, they pointed out that Roosevelt's plan would set a dangerous precedent. If a liberal President could restructure the Court to suit his fancy today, what would stop a conservative President from doing the same thing tomorrow?

In the spring of 1937 the plan lost whatever momentum it had when the Court—largely because Justice Owen Roberts switched to the liberal side—upheld the Social Security Act and other vital reform measures. In *NLRB* v. *Jones and Laughlin* the Court sustained the Wagner Act by a 5–4 vote. The majority implicitly overturned earlier decisions by holding that the commerce clause was indeed broad enough to cover federal regulation of manufacturing. In *West Coast Hotel Co.* v. *Parrish,* again by a one-vote margin, the Court approved state minimum wage laws. Chief Justice Charles Evans Hughes asserted that "reasonable" regulation, adopted in the interests of the community, by definition fulfilled the Fourteenth Amendment's due-process requirements. In May 1937 Justice Van Devanter's resignation gave Roosevelt his first Court appointment. The administration continued to press a compromise permitting the appointment of one additional justice each year for every member who reached the age of 75. This seemed likely to pass because most senators assumed that Roosevelt would nominate their colleague, Majority Leader Joseph Robinson of Arkansas, to fill the first vacancy. In July Robinson died of a heart attack and the Senate quickly defeated the bill.

The Court debacle injured Roosevelt's standing with Congress and the public, although many who would have broken with him for other reasons merely used the episode as a convenient pretext. The struggle over the Court divided the Democratic party by alienating a number of liberals, aroused widespread distrust of FDR's leadership, and convinced Republicans that their best strategy was to maintain a discreet silence while Democrats battled among themselves. But Roosevelt did not come away empty-handed, for the Supreme Court in 1937 finally put its seal of approval on the New Deal. Roosevelt would make five appointments during his second term—including those of Hugo Black, William O. Douglas, and Felix Frankfurter—and after they took their seats, all judicial barriers to the welfare state came tumbling down.

THE WANING OF
THE NEW DEAL

From Roosevelt's vantage point, administrative reform was hardly less important than judicial reform. In 1936 he had appointed a committee to study administrative management. It reported in January 1937, urging Congress to furnish the President with six assistants, expand the civil service system, improve fiscal management, and establish the National Resources Planning Board as a central agency to coordinate government programs. The committee also suggested creating two new Cabinet positions (Welfare and Public Works), changing the name of the Department of the Interior to the Department of Conservation, and giving the President broad authority to transfer agencies, including certain functions of the independent regulatory commissions. In this fashion the committee hoped to find a permanent home for New Deal agencies and provide a suitable administrative apparatus for the welfare state.

But reorganization provoked a storm of opposition when it came before Congress in the spring of 1938. Roosevelt's critics charged that the measure would clamp "one-man rule" on the nation, and succeeded in frightening large numbers of people. After squeaking by the Senate, the bill went down to defeat in the House of Representatives when more than 100 Democrats deserted the President. Congressmen had various reasons for opposing the measure, including a desire to reassert legislative prerogatives, placate pressure groups, and protect their existing channels of access to administrative agencies. The conflict over reorganization resembled the earlier one over the Court in that both measures failed to elicit support from a sizeable constituency, opened Roosevelt to the charge of seeking dictatorial power, divided liberals, and led to stinging presidential defeats. In 1939 Congress passed a mild measure that enabled FDR to establish the Executive Office of the President and to streamline the bureaucracy. But the sweeping changes he favored were not made.

Democratic opposition to Court reform and reorganization crossed sectional lines. But three other measures—relating to housing, wages and hours, and civil rights—divided the Democratic party into rural and urban, Northern and Southern factions. The Wagner Housing Act (1937), which authorized expenditures of $500 million to aid the construction of low-cost units, passed only after Southerners had extracted concessions limiting the appropriation, the number of dwellings to be built, and the cost per family. The Fair Labor Standards Act (1938) similarly catered to the South, which wished to protect its competitive position as a cheap labor market. The measure regulated child labor and established a 40-cent per hour minimum wage and 40-hour work week, but it exempted domestic workers and farm laborers, and allowed regional wage differentials. The antilynching bill never had a chance against a Senate filibuster engineered by Southern Democrats. As the New Deal became more responsive to the claims of its Northern, urban constitutency, it sacrificed support from rural and Southern representatives.

The problems that the New Deal encountered after 1937 went beyond congressional reluctance to enact certain legislation in the form Roosevelt wanted. To a considerable extent Congress accurately reflected the popular mood. Every opinion poll between 1937 and 1939 indicated that between two-thirds and three-fourths of the American people wanted the Roosevelt administration to follow a more conservative course. Although the polls revealed class and party differences, even a majority of Democrats and the poor went along with the prevailing sentiment. In part the New Deal was a victim of the times. FDR's proposals for judicial and administrative reform promised few tangible benefits but seemed rather to demonstrate a lust for personal power just when dictatorships in Europe were arousing a deep suspicion of executive authority in any form. The New Deal declined after 1937 because most Americans did not want to extend it much further.

The administration's response to the recession of 1937–1938 increased this disenchantment with reform. In the fall of 1937 the economy went into a tailspin. Over the next ten months, millions of people lost their jobs, boosting total unemployment to 11.5 million. The slump occurred primarily because the administration, in attempting to balance the budget, had cut expenditures sharply. Yet Roosevelt resisted new deficit spending. Unlike the Keynesians, who favored unbalanced budgets in slack periods, FDR believed pump priming appropriate in 1933 "when the water had receded to the bottom of the well" but doubted its worth in 1938 "with the water within 25 or 30 percent of the top." Not until April, when it appeared that economic conditions would ruin the Democrats in the fall elections, did the President listen to advisers who favored additional spending. He then asked Congress to authorize a $3.75 billion relief appropriation. But the damage had already been done. Those who had lost their jobs or whose businesses had failed blamed the Democrats, not the Republicans, and concluded that the time for further innovation was past.

The President suffered yet another reversal in his attempt to purge the Democratic party in the 1938 primaries. Roosevelt fought unsuccessfully to unseat Senators Walter George of Georgia, Millard Tydings of Maryland, and "Cotton Ed" Smith of South Carolina. Many Southerners appeared to resent the President's intrusion into local affairs (what Walter George termed the "second march through Georgia"), while those benefiting most from New Deal relief programs and presumably most sympathetic to the President—Negroes and poor whites—hardly participated in Democratic primaries. Opinion polls indicated that even among the unemployed and those on relief a bare majority disliked the White House's intervention. The purge claimed only one victim. John O'Connor of New York City, Chairman of the House Rules Committee, was defeated by a local politician friendly to the New Deal. In the November elections Republicans went on to win a smashing victory: they gained 81 seats in the House and 8 in the Senate. Since all Democratic losses took place in the North and West, Southerners emerged in a much stronger position. For the first time, Roosevelt could not form a majority without the help of some Southern Democrats or Republicans.

Congress assembled in January 1939 and wasted little time in disposing of FDR's program. To demonstrate its resentment at what it judged the attempted politicization of relief, Congress passed the Hatch Act (1939), prohibiting all government employees except a few high-ranking executive branch officials from engaging in political campaigns. The House abruptly cut off funds for the Federal Theater Project, which, because most of its activities centered in a few large cities, was highly vulnerable. The tax on undistributed profits, which businessmen bitterly resented, was repealed outright. Congress also refused to increase expenditures for public housing. When the administration requested $3.86 billion for self-liquidating public works projects, the Senate trimmed the amount substantially, and the House voted not even to consider it. Recognizing how far the pendulum had swung, Roosevelt became more cautious. He opposed efforts to expand federal contributions to the social security program in order to equalize benefits, disapproved proposals for additional deficit spending, and withheld support from a national health bill that would have provided aid for maternity and child care, hospital construction, and "general programs of medical care."

NATIVISM AND THE APPROACH OF WAR

In the period from 1937 to 1941—years marked first by economic dislocation at home and then by international tension abroad—the United States experienced a sharp upsurge in nativist sentiment. This affected the New Deal because in the minds of some people the Roosevelt administration was playing into the hands of the very groups that seemed to pose the gravest danger—Communists, Jews, and labor agitators. Charges that the President had surrounded himself with dangerous advisors and had embraced an alien ideology were by no means new, but after 1937 they were voiced more frequently and accepted more widely. By 1940 the administration itself had grown concerned enough to crack down sharply on suspected subversives. But it did not succeed in quelling popular fears.

In 1937 workers in the Congress of Industrial Organizations adopted radical tactics to gain traditional goals of union recognition and improved conditions. Labor's new weapon, the sit-down strike, deeply frightened property-conscious Americans. No fewer than 477 such strikes, involving 400,000 workers, took place in 1937, the most notorious of which was the General Motors sit-down in Flint, Michigan in January. Most Americans assumed correctly that the union's occupation of a factory violated the law, but concluded erroneously that the automobile workers were inspired by

Sit-down strikers at Chevrolet plant, Flint, Michigan, December 1936.

revolutionary intent. Two out of every three people favored outlawing sit-down strikes and employing force against the union. "Armed insurrection—defiance of law, order and duly elected authority is spreading like wildfire," protested one group of citizens. Because Roosevelt refused to call out federal troops to evict the strikers he was accused of cringing before the forces of anarchy and disorder.

The popularity of the House Committee on Un-American Activities illustrated the administration's vulnerability to these charges. Created in the summer of 1938 and headed by Martin Dies of Texas, the Committee lashed out at New Deal programs and agencies. Dies insisted that leading New Deal officials hobnobbed with Communists, and during the 1938 campaign witnesses before the Committee attributed subversive leanings to administration candidates in Michigan, Minnesota, and California. Roosevelt publicly rebuked Dies on two occasions when the Committee behaved in an especially offensive manner. But the President attempted to avoid a direct clash, largely because he knew that the Committee had wide support. In December 1938 a Gallup poll showed that three out of four persons who knew of the Committee approved of its work. Dies came to believe that FDR's "left-wing followers in the government are the fountainhead of subversive activities."

With the outbreak of World War II in September 1939, Roosevelt, himself the target of anticommunist attack, became worried about the possibility of subversion by Fascist agents or by Communists (who were then celebrating the Nazi-Soviet pact). In 1940 Congress and the administration outdid each other in tracking down potentially disloyal groups. In February, after the Justice Department had decided to prosecute people who had recruited volunteers to fight in the Spanish Civil War (a conflict in which the U.S. was officially neutral), the FBI seized 12 former recruiters in early-morning raids and released them only when the arrests provoked a storm of criticism from civil libertarians. In March, Roosevelt approved the fingerprinting of all aliens applying for visas as temporary visitors, and two months later he authorized the use of wiretaps against anyone "suspected of subversive activities." Congress passed the Smith Act, which required aliens to register, and made it a crime to conspire to teach or advocate the violent overthrow of the government. Congress also required all political organizations subject to foreign control to register with the Attorney General. The government prosecuted Communist leader Earl Browder on the technicality of using a fraudulent passport; he received an unprecedented four-year jail sentence. Attorney General Frank Murphy caught the mood in September 1940. "Unless we are pudding-headed," he said, "we will drive from the land the hirelings here to undo the labors of our fathers."

At the same time, Roosevelt increasingly shifted his emphasis from domestic reform to foreign policy and national defense. By 1940 his chief legislative goal was to obtain approval for assisting England and France. This, given isolationist strength in Congress, required the backing of Southern Democrats. As one conservative Southerner put it, the President had begun "cultivating us in a very nice way." Similarly, FDR's interest in readying plans for economic mobilization in the event of war moved him to mend fences with the business community. In August 1939 he appointed a War Resources Board composed mainly of big businessmen and headed by Edward Stettinius of U.S. Steel. Roosevelt, however, came to fear that the Board's proposals might dilute his own authority in wartime and did not make them public. In May 1940, when he set up a National Defense Advisory Commission to expedite production, he again turned to

Stettinius and to William S. Knudsen of General Motors. By 1940 the process of repairing relations with businessmen and Southern Democrats alike was well under way.

New Dealers wasted little time in climbing aboard the defense bandwagon. As early as 1939 the Tennessee Valley Authority noted that it was "developing the power necessary for the large-scale operation of war industries in this well-protected strategic area." By 1940 New Deal bureaucrats commonly justified their programs on the grounds that they contributed to preparedness. The Works Progress Administration undertook projects of military value. The National Youth Administration stressed vocational training programs that were related to national defense. The Civilian Conservation Corps offered drills for its enrollees, provided instruction in reading blueprints, and performed tasks for army posts. All this reflected not only a belief in the worth of such projects but a recognition that they were most likely to receive funding from a stingy Congress.

By 1940 the agenda of American politics had been transformed, with foreign policy replacing reform as the central issue. The presidential campaign that year reflected this change. The international crisis persuaded Roosevelt to seek a third term and gave the Democrats an excuse to nominate him. The Republicans chose Wendell Willkie who, while a critic of many New Deal policies, accepted much of the welfare state. Moreover, as a spokesman for the internationalist wing of the Republican party, Willkie endorsed the main outlines of FDR's foreign policy, refusing, for example, to make issues of aid to England or the peacetime draft. The tense international situation undoubtedly worked to the President's advantage, although Willkie did surprisingly well with 22.3 million votes to Roosevelt's 27.2 million. But during the campaign, Roosevelt made his most famous and, given the events of the following year, his most unfortunate promise: "I shall say it again and again and again: Your boys are not going to be sent into any foreign wars."

Suggested Reading

There are several good studies of American thought and culture during the 1930s. See especially Richard H. Pells, *Radical Visions and American Dreams: Culture and Social Thought in the Depression Years* (1973); Edwin A. Purcell, Jr., *The Crisis of Democratic Theory* (1972); Arthur Ekirch, Jr., *Ideologies and Utopias* (1969); and Charles C. Alexander, *Nationalism in American Thought* (1969). Two more specialized accounts are William Stott, *Documentary Expression and Thirties America* (1973); and R. Alan Lawson, *The Failure of Independent Liberalism, 1930–1941* (1971).

Social ferment during the early New Deal is considered in Arthur M. Schlesinger, Jr., *The Politics of Upheaval* (1960). T. Harry Williams, *Huey Long* (1969) provides a wealth of information. On the old folks' crusade, consult Abraham Holtzman, *The Townsend Movement* (1963); and Jackson Putnam, *Old-Age Politics in California* (1970). For the career of the radio priest, see Charles Tull, *Father Coughlin and the New Deal* (1965); and Sheldon Marcus, *Father Coughlin* (1973). Two useful studies of the Union party and its background are David J. O'Brien, *American Catholics and Social Reform: The New Deal Years* (1968); and David H. Bennett, *Demagogues in the Depression: American Radicals and the Union Party, 1932–1936* (1969).

The standard accounts of American radicalism are Irving Howe and Lewis Coser, *The American Communist Party* (1957); and David Shannon, *The Socialist Party of America* (1955). The appeal of communism to intellectuals is explored in James B. Gilbert, *Writers and Partisans: A History of Literary Radicalism in America* (1968); Frank A. Warren, *Liberals and Communism* (1966); and Michel Fabre, *The Unfinished Quest of Richard Wright* (1973).

An excellent account of black ideology and New Deal economic policy is Raymond Wolters, *Negroes and the Great Depression* (1970). Other useful studies of Negroes during the depression include Dan T. Carter, *Scottsboro: A Tragedy of the Modern South* (1969); Sara Harris, *Father Divine* (1971); James O. Young, *Black Writers of the Thirties* (1973); and Nancy J. Weiss, *The National Urban League 1910–1940* (1974). Ralph J. Bunche, *The Political Status of the Negro in the Age of FDR* (1973) is a reissue of a report originally prepared during World War II that emphasizes Southern politics.

Conservative opposition to the New Deal is considered in George Wolfskill and John Hudson, *All But The People: FDR and His Critics* (1969); Frank Freidel, *FDR and the South* (1965); Donald McCoy, *Landon of Kansas* (1966); and James T. Patterson, *Congressional Conservatism and the New Deal* (1967). On the Supreme Court fight of 1937 see William E. Leuchtenburg, "The Origins of Franklin D. Roosevelt's 'Court-Packing' Plan," in Philip B. Kurland, ed., *The Supreme Court Review* (1966); Leonard Baker, *Back to Back: The Duel Between FDR and the Supreme Court* (1967); and Max Freedman, ed., *Roosevelt and Frankfurter: Their Correspondence, 1928–1945* (1967). The controversy over executive reorganization is discussed in Richard Polenberg, *Reorganizing Roosevelt's Government, 1936–1939* (1966). Sidney Fine, *Sit-Down: The General Motors Strike of 1936–1937* (1969) is an excellent account of labor turmoil. Information on nativism in the late 1930s may be found in J. Woodford Howard, *Mr. Justice Murphy* (1968); and in Geoffrey S. Smith, *To Save a Nation: American Countersubversives, the New Deal, and the Coming of World War II* (1973). The 1940 campaign is the subject of Herbert S. Parmet and Marie B. Hecht, *Never Again* (1968); see, in addition, Ellsworth Barnard, *Wendell Willkie* (1966).

On the Federal Theater Project, see Jane D. Mathews, *The Federal Theater, 1935–1939: Plays, Relief and Politics* (1967). More general accounts are Malcolm Goldstein, *The Political Stage: American Drama and Theater of the Great Depression* (1974); and John O'Connor and Lorraine Brown, eds., *Free, Adult, Uncensored* (1978).

Pearl Harbor, December 7, 1941.

CHAPTER EIGHT

1929-1941

The Big Breakdown:
The United States
and the World

WHITE CLIFFS OF DOVER
Words by Nat Burton, *music by* Walter Kent

I'll never forget the people I met
Braving those angry skies;
I remember well as the shadows fell
The light of hope in their eyes.
And tho' I'm far away, I can still hear them
  say
"Thumbs up!"; for when the dawn comes up

Chorus:

There'll be bluebirds over the white cliffs of
  Dover
Tomorrow, just you wait and see;
There'll be love and laughter and peace ever
  after,
Tomorrow, when the world is free.

The shepherd will tend his sheep,
The valley will bloom again,

And Jimmy will go to sleep
In his own little room again.

There'll be bluebirds over the white cliffs of
  Dover
Tomorrow, just you wait and see.

When night shadows fall, I always recall
Out there across the sea
Twilight falling down on a little town,
It's fresh in my memory.
I hear a mother pray, to her baby say,
"Don't cry"; this is her lullaby:

Chorus

229

The depression ripped apart the treaty agreements so carefully built during the 1920s to preserve world peace, for the pacts had utterly depended on a smoothly working economic system. The collapse of 1929 not only destroyed the political arrangements. It created such chaos and disillusionment that fascists and radical leftists replaced moderate governments in such nations as Germany, Spain, and Japan. Extremists did not grasp control in the United States, however, or even make noticeable political gains. In a remarkable performance Americans continued their allegiance to their traditional economic-political system, even though it was producing the most miserable and inhumane conditions in the nation's history. Franklin D. Roosevelt's foreign policy mirrored that moderation. The President even built his policies around the central belief of the 1920s, for he constantly tried to use international economic solutions, not political or military means, to stop Japanese and German aggression. That unfortunately worked no better for Roosevelt than it had for Hoover. The road to Pearl Harbor had been taken between 1929 and 1932. FDR was unable to find an exit from that road, and by 1938 Americans were tragically headed for the dead end of December 7, 1941.

"MAD DOGS" AND ENGLISHMEN: THE MANCHURIAN CRISIS OF 1931–1932

In June 1931 President Hoover tried to stabilize Western money markets by suggesting a one-year moratorium (or postponement) on the collection of reparations from Germany and war debts from France and England. "Perhaps the most daring statement I ever thought of issuing," as Hoover recalled, it was too daring for the French. They insisted on keeping the hatchet of reparations above German heads. When Paris stalled, the President's policy collapsed. In July the German banking system came apart, then Great Britain's economic system went into a tailspin, the French government fell, and panic struck Europe and the United States. In Asia Japan took its first step toward World War II by invading Manchuria.

The Japanese had been especially hard-hit by the depression. Their economy depended on overseas markets, which by 1931 had largely disappeared. Exports to the vital U.S. market, for example, dropped 30 percent in 1930. Japan's liberal government, like liberal regimes elsewhere, was undercut then destroyed by the collapse. By early 1931 dynamic political factions led by ambitious militarists demanded that Japan find its salvation not in the sick Western trading community, but in its own Asian empire. Since 1905 Tokyo had controlled and developed South Manchuria. North Manchuria, however, was coming under the domination of Chiang Kai-shek's new regime. Chiang and a rapidly multiplying Chinese population even endangered Japanese control of South Manchuria. In

September 1931 the Japanese militarists took affairs into their own hands. When a brief skirmish between Chinese and Japanese troops occurred along the South Manchurian railway, Japan's army launched a full-scale invasion of North Manchuria. Tokyo had bloodily repudiated its pledge at the Washington Conference to maintain the open door.

Hoover and Stimson were trapped. Throughout the 1920s American Far Eastern policy had depended on a cooperative Japan, particularly when the only alternatives as partners were a "revolutionary" China and the Soviet Union. Hoover privately remarked he had some sympathy for the Japanese, for they faced a "Bolshevist Russia to the north, and a possible Bolshevist China" to the west. Some officials wanted Japan handled gently because it was holding back the Chinese tide. "The Chinese are altogether too cocky," the American ambassador in London told the Japanese ambassador. "What you people need to do is to give them a thoroughly good licking to teach them their place and then they will be willing to talk sense." The Japanese army's political power also influenced Hoover and Stimson, for they feared that decisive American counteraction would be used by the army as an excuse to capture and mobilize the government for all-out war. In December 1931 the militarists overthrew the civilian regime and accelerated the Manchurian offensive, yet nearly a year later Stimson, who knew that "the situation [in Japan] is in the hands of virtually mad dogs," urged a moderate response so that "the little group of militarists" could not "make us a bogey in the whole matter." Fear of being made the villain would help paralyze Washington officials until Pearl Harbor.

During the next ten years the United States singlehandedly tried to protect its interests in the Far East. China was undependable, Russia too revolutionary, Great Britain hesitant and no longer a Pacific power. The only alternatives were stark: warring against Japan, working out something somehow with Tokyo, or else admitting that the United States had no vital interests in the area. No American President has ever opted for this third alternative. As the Japanese drove deeper into Manchuria in late 1931, Stimson discussed possible economic sanctions (for example, cutting off the considerable American oil and metal exports to Japan), but Hoover refused, fearing that sanctions would inevitably lead to war. The League of Nations investigated the outbreak, indirectly called Japan the aggressor, refused to recognize Japan's establishment of a "Manchukuo" puppet state in Manchuria, and then watched hopelessly as Tokyo responded by quitting the League. Stimson refused to work formally with the League. His main effort was to coordinate an Anglo-American reaffirmation of the Nine-Power pact backed by an increase of military strength in the Pacific. That policy collapsed when the British decided to work through the League while privately trying to appease Japan. From 1931 until Pearl Harbor, London officials, whose primary concerns lay in Europe, would support American actions against Japan only if they were certain the United States would accept the possible consequence of war and be willing to fight Japan virtually alone. Otherwise the British were prepared to make deals with the Japanese, and for that, the United States refused in turn to trust the British.

By early 1932 the United States could take only two steps to threaten the Japanese. Both were taken unilaterally. Stimson announced in January that Washington would not recognize any act (such as Japan's establishment of Manchukuo) that impaired American rights in China by violating the open-door principle. Then in a public letter to Senator William E. Borah (Republican of Idaho), Stimson warned that if Japan insisted on breaking the Nine-Power pact, the United States would not be bound by the Five-Power Treaty limiting navies. Such threats made little impact on the Japanese. They signed a temporary armistice with China in May 1932, digested their conquests, and prepared for further war.

NEW ORDER TO NEW DEAL

Hoover made one final attempt to put the pieces back together. Between 1930 and 1932 nearly every nation withdrew inside itself, erected tariff walls, and attempted to follow autarchic economic policies. In 1930 the United States passed the Hawley-Smoot bill, the highest protective tariff in its history. A more extreme example of autarchy was Britain's construction of the Imperial Preference system in 1932. Through a series of bilateral pacts, the British government and members of its Commonwealth promised to give one another favored trading privileges, thus largely excluding such third parties as the United States from traditional American markets in Canada, Australia, and South Africa. The United States bitterly fought such policies, not only because they gravely hurt trade, but also because they injected the government into the realm of private enterprise. In 1932 Hoover counterattacked by proposing an international conference in London that would negotiate war debts, reparations, and disarmament. The President hoped that settlement of the debts could be used to pressure England and France into accepting liberal trade policies.

Before the conference could convene, however, Franklin D. Roosevelt moved into the White House. When Hoover and Stimson asked Roosevelt to accept their policies in the Far East and the proposed London conference, FDR agreed not to recognize Manchukuo, but absolutely refused to commit himself on economic issues. During his first eight months in office he rejected Hoover's international approach, most dramatically when he destroyed the London conference by refusing to tie American tariff and monetary policy to any international agreement. Believing that the American economy might be able to resurrect itself if it was not tied to a disintegrating world economy, Roosevelt allowed the war-debt issue to die, took the country off the international gold standard, and began tinkering with the dollar to raise its purchasing power. None of these devices sufficiently spurred the economy. "Yes, it is the zero hour in Washington," critic Edmund Wilson observed in early 1934. "The first splendor of the New Deal has faded. . . . The emergency measures which revived our morale have not achieved all that they have promised."

By the spring of 1934 Roosevelt gave up his experiments and returned to Hoover's assumption that recovery required a booming American export trade. Quite clearly the domestic economy would not further improve without measures—such as some that smacked too much of socialism for FDR's taste—that would radically change the nature of the system. The President's only alternative therefore was to find help outside the system itself, that is, in the world marketplace. Also like Hoover, Roosevelt refused to tie his hands politically. He finally rejected political alliances and the League of Nations in favor of enjoying maximum freedom to trade with anyone, regardless of their political coloring.

Two major differences, however, separated FDR's foreign policy from Hoover's. Roosevelt was dealing with a world rapidly compartmentalizing into closed, government-controlled blocs. Japan's Manchukuo and the British Imperial Preference system, for example, were not open to American competition. More ominously, in January 1933 Adolf Hitler assumed power in Germany. Within three years he worked out exclusive and government-controlled trade arrangements in Europe and Latin America that made it difficult for private American traders to compete.

These developments led to the second distinguishing—if not revolutionary—characteristic of New Deal policy: the government had to involve itself directly, for example by giving subsidies to private businessmen who needed help in the marketplace. Hoover had avoided such direct involvement at all costs, fearing that it would change the nature of the system itself. Roosevelt believed that such danger could be averted. Moreover, he had little choice, for if Americans were to find economic salvation overseas, they could compete against Germans, Japanese, and British governmental policies only if the United States government provided similar aid. That, of course, raised the grave danger that if conflict arose in the marketplace, the governments themselves would be fully involved in the struggle.

The guiding genius behind this policy was Secretary of State Cordell Hull. An ardent Wilsonian, and former congressman from Tennessee who prided himself on complete command of the Tennessee mountaineer's earthy vocabulary, Hull was named Secretary of State because of his influence on Capitol Hill. He was driven by an obsession to reopen the clogged channels of trade. Only when high tariffs, currency manipulation, and the power of state trading enterprises were obliterated, he believed, could individual freedoms be restored and wars averted. For Hull was certain that friction between economic blocs inevitably led to political conflict. He therefore set out to replace such closed blocs with an open, multilateral trading system that had freely convertible currencies (instead of monies manipulated by the state), and which allowed private businessmen to buy and sell anywhere they chose. Hull used this standard of freer trade to judge nearly every diplomatic move he made between 1933 and his retirement in 1944, a standard that led him to condemn Germany in the 1930s, Japan in 1941, and the Soviet Union in 1944. This policy is central to an understanding of why he and FDR came to define these three nations as enemies politically as well as economically.

Between 1934 and 1939 more legislation was enacted in Washington

Secretary of State Cordell Hull, Undersecretary Sumner Welles, and Assistant Secretary Adolf Berle at the White House during the beginning of World War II, September, 1939.

to find markets abroad for American surpluses than in any similar period in the nation's history. Two measures stand out. The Reciprocity Act of 1934 was Hull's pet project. It sharply reversed post-1920 policy by giving the President power to reduce or raise tariffs by as much as 50 percent in bargaining with other nations for reciprocal reduction of tariff barriers. The policy also included the unconditional-most-favored-nation principle, that is, that trade favors given to one nation would be automatically given to all others that did not discriminate against American trade. That principle made it impossible for two nations to gang up economically against a third. If used successfully, the Reciprocity Act would be like a giant economic wrecking ball, swinging in all directions to batter down tariff and other state-created barriers that Hull and FDR so hated. Reciprocity pacts with 14 nations helped accelerate exports between 1934 and 1938 by over a half-billion dollars. Imports, however, lagged; this meant that other nations were not selling enough to Americans to obtain the dollars needed to buy expanded U.S. exports.

As in 1928–29, therefore, a dollar shortage threatened to stunt the growth of the world, and consequently the American, economy. In 1934 Roosevelt established a government-operated Export-Import Bank through which government credits would be made available to foreign customers so they could purchase U.S. exports. Funds to finance foreign trade would now be provided by the government, not just by the private bankers who had proven unequal to the job in the 1920s. American tax dollars were loaned overseas for the purchase of American goods. These acts creating the reciprocity policy and the Export-Import Bank proved so beneficial that both were renewed and expanded during the next 45 years.

AREAS OF SPECIAL INTEREST: LATIN AMERICA AND THE USSR

These economic initiatives were aimed at every corner of the world, but the New Deal selected several areas for special attention. Between 1933 and 1938, Roosevelt and Hull devoted great energy to making North and South America "good neighbors." During those years United States imports from Latin America leaped 114 percent to $705 million, while exports to the south rocketed 166 percent, over $640 million. In 1932 the United States accounted for 32 percent of Latin American trade, but after the reciprocity legislation took effect, Americans enjoyed 45 percent in 1938. Politically FDR continued Hoover's policy of noninterference militarily. A major step occurred at the Montevideo Conference in 1933 when Hull, somewhat against his will, pledged the United States to a clear declaration of nonintervention.

The increased economic leverage was providing Americans with an alternative diplomatic weapon. Cuba provided a classic example. Since 1903 the Platt Amendment had given officials in Washington the right to send troops to Cuba. Control became firmer between 1919 and 1921 when depressed sugar prices ruined plantations and Americans invested heavily, in the so-called "dance of the millions," in Cuban sugar. Throughout the 1920s a dictator protected these interests, but by 1933 the economy had collapsed and left-wing movements challenged the government. After 35 years as an American protectorate, Cuban trade with the United States had dropped 50 percent since 1929, its sugar sold for 1/10¢ per pound, and 500,000 of its 4 million people searched for work. In September 1933 junior army officers under Fulgencio Batista overthrew the government, putting a liberal politician into the presidency.

The regime was indeed too liberal for the State Department, which thought it saw Communists creeping into power. Hull and Under Secretary of State Sumner Welles, a close friend of Roosevelt's, asked FDR to make a show of force in Havana harbor. The President refused. He had a better alternative. In 1933–34 FDR and Batista—who desperately needed economic help—agreed to pump life into the Cuban economy by opening the American sugar market to Cuban cane at prices above the world level. Other foreign-produced sugar was effectively excluded from the United States. The American consumers thus paid extra for their sugar, but Batista lived up to his part of the deal by placing a more conservative president in power in Havana. The policy worked so well that in 1934 Roosevelt felt he could safely repeal all of the Platt Amendment except the section giving the United States the Guantanamo Naval Base. At the same time, Washington also promised to give the Philippines its independence in ten years, but again carefully made economic arrangements to protect American interests on the islands.

FDR pursued the same economic approach toward Russia, but with much less success. After frequent consultation with William Bullitt, who had returned from the French Riviera and Philadelphia to advise him, the President recognized the Soviets in November 1933. He had to overcome strong opposition from the American Legion, the Daughters of the American Revolution, Roman Catholic Church leaders, the American Federation of Labor, and, most important, his own State Department. Hull swore that no deals could be made with a state-controlled economy. He also argued that the Bolsheviks would try, as he believed they had in Cuba during the 1933 revolution, to interfere in American domestic affairs. Roosevelt did, however, receive strong support from businessmen, who argued that the potentially vast Russian market could help rescue Americans from the depression. Political recognition was a prerequisite, the businessmen emphasized, for Russia needed credit to buy goods, and without recognition no private or governmental institution would extend credit.

The Soviets welcomed FDR's initiative, but for very different reasons. They were less interested in trade than in working out a common policy to contain Japan. Since 1931 the Soviets, fearful that Tokyo's militarists would move from Manchuria into Siberia, had desperately searched for friends. One Moscow official remarked that Russia and the United States must join in "breaking [Japan] as between the two arms of a nutcracker."

Within two years after diplomatic relations were resumed, Moscow-Washington relations turned sour. Trade did not prosper because no agreement could be reached on proper credit arrangements. The Soviets became disillusioned when the State Department went out of its way to assure anxious Tokyo officials that recognition was not in any way directed against Japan. Roosevelt and Bullitt, who became the first American ambassador to the Soviet Union, plainly informed Russian leader Joseph Stalin they would make no anti-Japanese alliance. Washington preferred to consider a deal with its old friend Japan than to work with the mysterious, revolutionary Soviets. In 1934 Stalin gave up on the United States, began negotiating with Japan, joined the League, and—too late—reversed his attitude toward Hitler (whom Stalin had dismissed as a fool in 1932) in a last-ditch try at working out anti-Fascist alliances with Eastern and Western governments. Russia and the United States continued to go in opposite directions until they were startlingly thrown together by Hitler in 1941.

THE FAILURE OF
POLITICAL NEUTRALITY

Between 1933 and 1937 the Japanese carefully refrained from further aggression, but tightened their grip on Manchuria. When Roosevelt attempted to help China in late 1933 with wheat, cotton, and airplanes, Tokyo slammed back with the so-called Amau Statement of 1934, which warned that since foreign aid to China could "acquire political significance," Japan had the right to act unilaterally to maintain "peace and order in Eastern Asia." The State Department again reiterated the Nine-Power pact principles for an open door in China, but Japan threw that treaty on the scrapheap by excluding American oil and other interests from Manchuria. By late 1934 Tokyo demanded that the Five-Power principles be changed to allow Japan parity with the American and British fleets. When this was refused, the Japanese withdrew from the agreement, accelerating the building of their navy and fortifications in the Pacific.

In 1936 Tokyo found new friends. During the previous year Mussolini's Italy had suddenly ravaged the small African nation of Ethiopia. When the League and the major powers offered little response, Hitler embarked on his own campaign of aggression. The self-proclaimed Führer, determined to rectify the 1919 Peace Conference's dissection of Germany, marched unopposed to reclaim the Rhineland in 1936. During that summer civil war erupted in Spain between the five-year-old Republic and conservative army-church forces. Within a year Hitler and Mussolini funneled vast aid to help the advancing conservatives while the Republic obtained major help only from the Soviets. Great Britain and France remained on the sidelines of what they preferred to believe was only a civil war, and the United States followed suit. Germany was clearly on the move, and in November 1936 the Japanese climbed aboard by signing an Anti-Comintern Pact with Hitler, which secretly called for joint consultation if either party were attacked by the Soviets; both parties promised not to make treaties with Russia. Italy joined the Pact in 1937. The Japanese now had friends and security on their Russian flank if they wanted to move into China or areas to the south.

The United States responded to these developments with a series of neutrality laws. A Senate investigation headed by Gerald Nye, Republican of North Dakota, revealed in 1934–35 that private American bankers had become closely involved with the French and British war efforts during 1915–17. No evidence demonstrated that President Wilson's policies had been directly shaped by the bankers, but the conclusion was too easily drawn that the United States had been shoved into world war by the profit-lust of a few. Congress responded with the 1935 Neutrality Act: when the President declared that war existed, no arms, ammunition, or items of war were to be shipped to any belligerent, and American ships could not transport such supplies to a belligerent. In 1936 Congress passed a second Neutrality Act that prohibited loans to nations involved in war. A year later, in response to the Spanish conflict, other Neutrality

Japanese troops entering Peking, August 1937.

Acts forbade Americans from traveling on belligerent vessels and applied these various provisions to civil wars.

But one major change appeared in the 1937 legislation. In response to Roosevelt's anger that the acts tied his hands, and because the damming up of these items threatened vital parts of the country's economy, a "cash-and-carry" provision was added allowing nations to obtain nonmilitary supplies if they paid cash and transported them home in their own ships. Americans, in other words, hoped to avoid wars while making money from them. Obviously the cash-and-carry clause also helped Great Britain and France since in any European war their navies would control the Atlantic. As Japan soon demonstrated, however, the Neutrality Acts were written to prevent the previous war, not the next one.

In July 1937 the Japanese army attacked North China in an effort to build a buffer area around Japan's puppet state of Manchukuo. The Neutrality Acts were useless, for whereas Americans wanted to help China, the Japanese fleet controlled the western Pacific and hence could take advantage of the cash-and-carry provision. Roosevelt tried to escape from the dilemma by refusing to declare that a war existed in Asia. The neutrality provisions consequently did not take effect. He meanwhile desperately searched for ways to aid China.

On October 5, FDR delivered a "quarantine speech" in Chicago, the center of political isolationism. The President talked vaguely about quarantining aggressor nations, but offered no specific policies. Historians now believe that a majority of Americans probably supported Roosevelt's call, but the howls of opposition that arose drove Roosevelt and Hull to disclaim any intention of immediate action. The League of Nations, however, picked up the proposal, calling for an international conference to convene in Brussels in November.

Roosevelt was prepared to negotiate with Japan. He instructed the American officials at Brussels to work for the restoration of the Nine-Power pact principles. If Japan would agree to these the United States would discuss economic cooperation with Tokyo in North China but only, of course, within the framework of the open door. The British again dragged their feet, not at all sure that if Japan refused, the President would be prepared to fight. The Soviets offered the United States a security pact against Japan if the Americans and Western Europeans would in turn help fend off Germany. Washington flatly turned this proposal down. The Japanese finally refused even to attend the conference, insisting that the war concerned only themselves and the Chinese. A total failure, the Brussels Conference marked the last major American effort to work collectively to control the aggressors.

In December 1937 Japanese planes attacked an American gunboat, *The Panay,* as it stood guard over Standard Oil tankers in the Yangtze River. Two Americans were killed. FDR strongly protested, and Japan apologized, but the President then tried to take the offensive. In the House he waged a bitter and successful struggle against a constitutional amendment, proposed by Louis Ludlow (Democrat of Indiana), which if passed would have required a national referendum before a declaration of war unless the United States itself was attacked. The following month FDR proposed a 20 percent increase in the fleet and began rebuilding Guam and other Pacific bases.

THE FAILURE OF THE NEW DEAL

After these small successes the President had to turn from foreign policy to a crisis at home. In early 1937 he believed that the American economy had recovered sufficiently so that some New Deal measures could be cut back. FDR especially hoped to balance the budget, a move that would dry up vast federal monies that had been priming the economy. As Secretary of the Treasury Henry Morgenthau phrased it, "This was the moment, it seemed to me, to strip off the bandages, throw away the crutches, and see if American private enterprise could stand on its own feet." Roosevelt pulled governmental money out too rapidly, however, and like a patient drained of blood, the economy staggered, then collapsed into the most precipitous decline in American history. In nine months industrial production dropped 33 percent, payrolls 35 percent, industrial stock averages 50 percent, profits 78 percent. Only unemployment rose, spiraling upward 23 percent. The domestic New Deal had no other medicines to offer. Roosevelt, one of his Cabinet members noted, "did not know which way to turn." But something had to be done rapidly, for the crisis went beyond economics. Harry Hopkins, one of FDR's closest advisors, declared, "This country cannot continue as a democracy with 10 or 12 million people unemployed. It just can't be done."

Roosevelt's massive spending program on the navy, and later on a 5500-plane air force, provided one response to the crisis. By 1939 defense spending was putting Americans back to work again, although 10 million remained unemployed as late as January 1940. The full-scale war economy of post-1941 would finally solve the terrible economic problems that the New Deal could never remedy.

Another response to the crisis was the traditional hope of finding expanded foreign markets for the vast surplus of American goods. China provided the greatest potential market. "Probably never in its history has China offered greater promise for [U.S.] future trade, industry, and general economic progress," a Commerce Department official told a gathering of American businessmen in mid-1937. "We have built up in China organizations capable of those measures of expansion which are characteristic of American enterprise where very favorable trade conditions permit." The Japanese invasion threatened that dream and more: if the Japanese developed a large cotton industry in North China, then, Secretary of Commerce Daniel C. Roper warned FDR in late 1937, American exports would drop so low as to require "a recharting of the economy of the South and definite Federal production control procedures." Several years later a correspondent of *The New York Times* substituted rubber for cotton but came up with the same conclusion: "The future of China and the future of the United States in Asia may very well be determined by whether or not those rubber tires that roll on the Chinese roads are made in Akron or in Osaka [Japan]."

"Radio is a recent innovation that has introduced profound alterations in the outlook and social behavior of men," two noted psychologists concluded in 1935. This dramatic view was accurate, even though commercial radio was just 15 years old. The first national networks were formed in the mid-1920s by the National Broadcasting Company (NBC) and Columbia Broadcasting System (CBS), breakthroughs that led Secretary of Commerce Herbert Hoover to establish a governmental licensing and regulatory agency in 1927. He was concerned that radio be responsible: "It is inconceivable that we should allow so great a possibility for service, for news, for entertainment . . . to be drowned in advertising chatter."

That was a forlorn hope. Radio advertising grew in popularity even dur-

ing the depression. Albert Lasker, king of the advertising agents, tripled sales of Pepsodent by having the toothpaste sponsor the most popular 1930s program, "Amos n' Andy," in which two white men impersonated black minstrel-show types. Radio standardized habits of living, speech, and taste in a nation once famous for sectionalism and diversity.

Until the 1930s radio broadcast little news. NBC did not have a single daily news series, believing its job was to entertain the entire family while leaving current affairs to newspapers. Franklin D. Roosevelt changed this with his "Fireside Chats" in 1933. With a voice perfectly suited for the new medium, his broadcasts were so successful that, in the words of a columnist, "The President has only to look toward a radio to bring

Orson Welles directing the Mercury Theater of the Air.

242

Edward R. Murrow in London, 1941.

Congress to terms." As Europe moved toward war, news services increased until in 1937 CBS sent 28-year-old Edward R. Murrow to Europe to establish continent-wide broadcasts. Born in Polecat Creek, North Carolina, he had moved west to study at Washington State College where the nation's first courses on radio were being offered. As Murrow left for Europe, a CBS executive protested, "Broadcasting has no role in international politics," but should limit itself to radioing "the song of a nightingale from Kent, England," a program that had been voted the "most interesting broadcast" of 1932.

Murrow destroyed such illusions. CBS coverage of the 1938 Munich crises was followed hourly by millions. Its effect was noticeable a month later when the network produced Orson Welles's version of "War of the Worlds," a story of invaders from Mars landing in New Jersey. Welles utilized the news bulletin-spot interview techniques used at Munich. Within a half-hour after the program began, New Jersey residents were filling the highways heading out of the state, two Princeton professors had rushed out to study the invaders, and a

Pittsburgh woman, crying "I'd rather die this way than that," was stopped before she could take poison. News broadcasting had come of age.

Murrow built a continental staff headed by Eric Severeid and Howard K. Smith. His own most famous programs occurred during Hitler's air "blitz" of London in 1940–41. His rich, quiet, understated voice began each broadcast with "This—is London." He followed with graphic accounts that tried to "report suffering to people [Americans] who have not suffered," by providing eyewitness testimony of bombing ("that moan of stark terror and suspense cannot be encompassed by words"). Murrow pioneered new uses of the micro-

Queen Victoria Station, London, during the "blitz," May 1941.

244 phone, once simply putting it on a London sidewalk while sirens shrieked, antiaircraft guns fired, and people walked to shelters. As the foreign policy debate in Washington intensified, he shrewdly helped the pro-interventionist forces by reporting British belief that Americans were the last hope for democracy, while emphasizing Churchill's greatness and England's bravery. As American poet Archibald MacLeish wrote of Murrow: "You burned the city of London in our houses and we felt the flames that burned it. You laid the dead of London at our doors and we knew the dead were our dead." Murrow brought a new dimension to radio, for he used it to educate and improve society. Even after his death in 1965, his style and ideals shaped news broadcasting.

FDR giving a Fireside Chat, 1940.

Secretary of State Hull was caught in the middle of this maelstrom. In 1936 he had been impressed with advice from John A. Hobson, the great historian of imperialism, that the "last large possibility of maintaining capitalism lies in the Orient." It was doubtful, Hobson continued, that in exploiting this lush market "the Americans will care to play second fiddle to the Japanese, whose character and behavior are so baffling to the Occidental mind." That advice fitted perfectly with Hull's view that an open-door approach, rather than Japanese exclusiveness, was the only method to develop a healthy global trade, world peace, and the American economy. In November 1938, however, Hull suffered a severe setback when Japan proclaimed a Greater Asia Co-prosperity Sphere based on anti-Bolshevism and economic and cultural cooperation through the Far East. It was, Tokyo claimed, an Asian equivalent to the American Monroe Doctrine in the Western Hemisphere. Hull feared that all of Asia would go the way of Manchuria. "In our opinion," he sweepingly declared in late 1938, "an endeavor by any country in any part of the world to establish itself in favor of a preferred position in another country is incompatible with the maintenance of our own and the establishment of world prosperity." That statement requires close study, for it was the cornerstone of American foreign policy.

How to drive Japan from its "preferred position" was the central problem, one compounded by statistics in early 1939 showing Japan to be America's third-largest customer. During a severe depression such trade was not to be lightly discarded for the mere potential of the China market. Japan, moreover, had long been Washington's and London's most dependable ally in the Far East, a bastion against revolution. A war to protect the open door in China, on the other hand, could spawn new revolutions and be bloody as well as long lasting, particularly if the Japanese and Germans coordinated their efforts. "We would like to help China if we knew how, of course," Secretary of Interior Harold Ickes summed up the cruel dilemma in late 1938, ". . . without running the risk of our own involvement in war."

Two alternatives emerged. The first, championed by Hull and his State Department advisors, urged continued effort toward a cooperative policy with Japan. Only then, Hull believed, could traditional multilateral cooperation be maintained for the propping open of the door to Far Eastern markets. He believed that an international trade agreement based on his beloved reciprocity principle would restore economic cooperation and—as Hull's reasoning ran—therefore result in a political agreement. Once brought within such a trade-political network, Japan could find necessary markets peacefully, continue to receive strategic goods from a friendly United States, and quit its iniquitous partnership with Hitler.

A second answer came from Henry Morgenthau and the Treasury Department. He reasoned that Japan's militarists were uncontrollable and too ambitious to settle for a friendly division of the Asian market. Morgenthau urged direct bilateral aid to help China drive back the invader. He bitterly criticized Hull's complicated multilateral, cooperative approach ("while he was discussing it, one country after another goes under.") The Treasury's approach had an added attraction. Such aid could tightly link China to American trade and financial interests rather than allow it to be divided among a number of powers.

Roosevelt at first equivocated between the two alternatives but told Morgenthau in late 1938, "Henry, these trade treaties [of Hull's] are just too goddamned slow. The world is marching too fast." The Secretary of State's approach was also undercut as Japan insisted that only it and China could settle Chinese affairs; third parties were not wanted. Morgenthau won a victory in 1938 when FDR agreed to send a $25 million credit for China's war effort, then a major triumph in July 1939 when Hull finally agreed to terminate the 1911 Commercial Treaty, which governed trade with Japan. FDR was so happy with Hull's acquiescence that he blurted out, "Cordell, I feel like kissing you on both cheeks." Morgenthau next pushed for an embargo on oil, but Hull dug in his heels. No more would be done until Hitler had begun World War II.

THE GHOST OF 1919

As European peace disintegrated after 1935, Roosevelt offered only suggestions for disarmament or economic conferences. Not even the British would accept such proposals. The Conservative government of Prime Minister Neville Chamberlain embraced instead the policy of appeasement, a dirty word during the post-1945 era but not in the 1930s, for it meant adjusting the wrongs inflicted on Germany by the 1919 peace conference. In this sense Roosevelt and most Americans were also appeasers. Like Europeans, they were belatedly conscience-stricken by the harsh penalties pressed on Germany, and so stood paralyzed as Hitler's armies moved into adjoining territories during the mid-1930s. Also like Chamberlain, Roosevelt believed that issues could be compromised with Germany and Italy, especially if done through the personal, private, and manipulative diplomacy that each man preferred to more traditional methods.

When the Munich crisis flared in September 1938, Roosevelt encouraged Chamberlain to talk with Hitler. The President refused to take the side either of the German dictator, who demanded annexation of the Czechoslovak Sudetenland area containing several million Germans, or of the Czechs (supposedly supported by Britain and France), who did not want to surrender their only defensible frontier area. On September 9 Roosevelt angrily made clear to reporters that Americans had no moral commitment to European democracies. Chamberlain finally decided to make a dramatic flight to Munich for talks with Hitler, a decision that would result in Chamberlain's agreeing that Hitler should have his way. FDR wired the Prime Minister, "Good man." A month later Roosevelt told the Cabinet of his "shame" for supporting the Munich agreement and ordered the acceleration of plans for sending war goods to England and France.

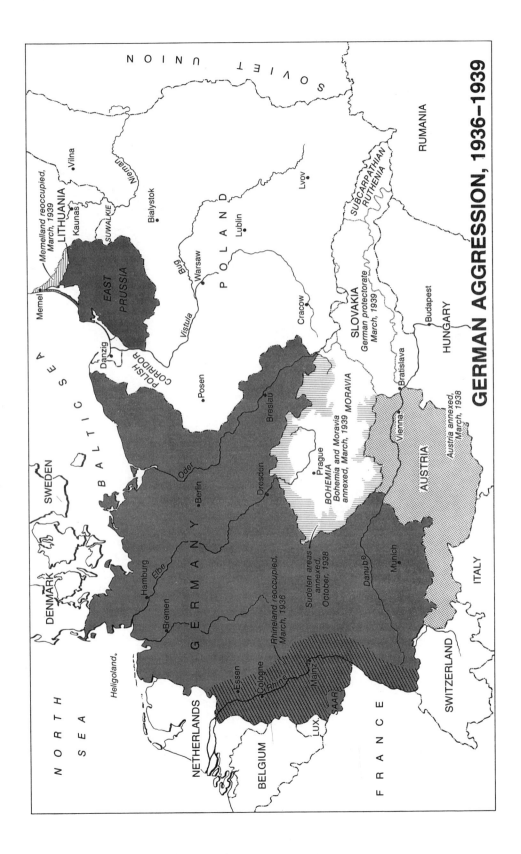

GERMAN AGGRESSION, 1936–1939

SOVIET UNION

NORTH SEA

BALTIC SEA

SWEDEN

DENMARK

Heligoland

NETHERLANDS

BELGIUM

LUX.

FRANCE

SWITZERLAND

ITALY

RUMANIA

HUNGARY

Budapest

Bratislava

SLOVAKIA
German protectorate
March, 1939

SUBCARPATHIAN RUTHENIA

Lvov

POLAND

Lublin

Bialystok

Warsaw

Cracow

Posen

Danzig

POLISH CORRIDOR

EAST PRUSSIA

LITHUANIA

Memel

Memelland reoccupied,
March, 1939

SUWALKIE

Kaunas

Vilna

Niemen

Bug

Vistula

Oder

BOHEMIA
Bohemia and Moravia
annexed, March, 1939 MORAVIA

Prague

Breslau

Dresden

Berlin

Vienna

AUSTRIA

Austria annexed,
March, 1938

Munich

Danube

GERMANY

Hamburg

Bremen

Elbe

Essen
Cologne

Rhine

Mainz

SAAR

Rhineland reoccupied,
March, 1936

Sudeten areas
annexed,
October, 1938

Nazi Party rally at Buckeberg, 1934.

The President's disillusionment with Hitler also resulted from Nazi activities in Latin America. German businessmen, including the powerful Lufthansa airline, scored repeated successes in South American markets. An Assistant Secretary of Commerce observed during 1938, "It used to be said that trade follows the flag. Observing world affairs today we might more appropriately say that political ideologies follow trade." As the Germans entered, moreover, traditional U.S. markets disappeared, a loss especially felt during the economic crisis of 1938. Roosevelt responded with increased governmental assistance to American businessmen and also pushed for a common anti-Axis front in the hemisphere. His success was marked in the 1938 Declaration of Lima when all the Inter-American nations agreed to cooperate fully against outside threats. A year later, after war began in Europe, the Americas agreed on a Declaration of Panama, which created a "safety belt" of nearly a thousand miles around the hemisphere in which there were to be no hostile acts by non-American belligerents.

By 1940 the only outstanding hemispheric problem was again the Mexican revolution. In March 1938 Mexico finally nationalized all foreign oil companies. Hull blew up, urging quick action against "those Communists down there." The previous U.S. pledges of nonintervention, however, and Roosevelt's fear that a tough policy would turn Mexico toward Japan and Germany, moderated Washington's response. A settlement was finally reached in November 1941 when Mexico agreed to pay $40 million in back claims and establish a committee of experts to settle compensation for the oil companies. In return, the United States helped finance Mexican currency and extended a $30 million Export-Import Bank loan to build a large section of the Pan American Highway from Mexico into Guatemala. Mexico was restored to the anti-Axis front that the United States was so anxious to forge. In this sense only, Roosevelt's appeasement policy toward the Axis had worked, for it helped forestall war until most of the hemisphere agreed to follow his lead against Germany and Japan.

Otherwise appeasement was a disaster. History catches and controls every decade, and never more tragically than when the 1919 treaty helped paralyze the anti-Hitlerian nations during the 1930s. One nation finally broke away. On August 23, 1939, Stalin signed a nonaggression treaty with Hitler in which they struck an agreement on the division of Poland and the Balkans. Since the Brussels Conference of 1937 Stalin had tried to negotiate a security agreement with France and England. This had foundered on French and British anti-Communist hatreds and the refusal of the Poles and Rumanians to entrust their existence to Russian hands. Stalin had also carried out a gigantic blood purge of his supposed political enemies, which probably exterminated several million Russians. This brutality turned many Westerners, even Communist party members, against the Soviets; a typical American account was entitled, "Stalin, Portrait of a Degenerate," in which he was compared—unfavorably—with "Scarface" Al Capone. Among the victims of the purge were leading Red Army officers. Western officials concluded that in any conflict the decimated Russian forces would be virtually useless. Hitler perceived Russia differently, for a treaty with Stalin would free Germany from the danger of a two-front war. Americans viewed all this incredulously, at first dismissing the Nazi-Soviet pact as a mere "grandstand play" designed by Stalin to frighten the West, then agreeing that there was no difference after all between communism and fascism. The latter fallacy would influence American policymakers during the post-1945 years.

Nine days after the Nazi-Soviet pact, Hitler invaded Poland. England and France, which had guaranteed Poland's boundaries, declared war on Germany. After an impassioned congressional debate, FDR won a modification of the Neutrality Acts. The arms embargo was changed to cash-and-carry in order to help the Allies, but loans remained illegal. Unlike Wilson, Roosevelt never asked Americans to be neutral in thought and deed. He did, unfortunately, insist that his policies would keep the United States out of war even as he was tying the country closer to the Allies.

In November, Russia invaded Finland to obtain strategic areas along the Finnish-Soviet boundary. Despite State Department urgings to do so, Roosevelt refused to break diplomatic relations with Russia, although he placed a voluntary, or "moral," embargo on airplanes and gas ticketed for the Soviets. An important side-effect soon appeared. Spurred by war orders, American employment jumped 10 percent in late 1939 as production rose sharply. The Second World War rescued the economy and between 1940 and 1945 would provide the greatest stimulus the system ever received. In sending that system's products to the Allies and to Finland, however, Roosevelt was giving hostages to the future.

THE TRIALS OF
UNNEUTRAL NEUTRALITY

The German blitzkrieg through Poland was followed by a lull, or "sitzkrieg" during winter and early spring of 1939–40. In May, Hitler suddenly occupied France and the low countries. By June, his forces stood triumphant on the English Channel. Only the British remained to face the Nazis. Winston Churchill, who throughout the 1930s had repeatedly condemned appeasement, replaced Chamberlain and mobilized England for a last-ditch fight. In the Pacific, Japan took advantage of the French and Dutch disasters to make demands on French Indochina and the Dutch East Indies. By September the struggle truly became global, for Japan, Germany, and Italy signed a tripartite mutual assistance pact clearly aimed at the United States. Americans now faced the prospect of a two-front war if they went to the rescue of Great Britain.

Roosevelt and his advisors concluded that Germany, not Japan, posed the gravest threat, and that England must have top priority for war supplies. That policy would continue to govern American actions between 1941 and 1945. Protecting Great Britain, however, also meant safeguarding the European colonial empires in South and Southeast Asia, which produced the vital rubber, oil, and metals for the Anglo-American war effort. Japan, therefore, could not be allowed to strike south. Roosevelt initially responded by proposing an unbelievable building program to construct 50,000 planes and over a million tons of shipping. In September 1940 he made an Executive Agreement with Churchill that sent 50 United States destroyers to England in return for 99-year leases to British naval bases in the Western Hemisphere. This act required considerable political courage, for Roosevelt had decided to run for an unprecedented third term and was confronting strong criticism for his earlier aid to England.

The opposition was led by the "America First" group comprised of anti-New Deal industrialists (Henry Ford, Sterling Morton of Morton Salt), old Progressives (Senator Burton K. Wheeler, journalist Oswald Garrison Villard), and public figures who warned of dire military and political consequences should the nation be sucked into the war (flying aces Eddie Rickenbacker and Charles A. Lindbergh, historian Charles Beard). The pro-Allied sentiment was mobilized by the Committee to Defend America by Aiding the Allies. The Committee vowed that it wanted to stay out of war, but argued that this uninvolvement required sending vast aid to nations resisting fascism. It was especially successful in creating public support for the destroyers-bases deal. FDR was also fortunate in that the 1940 Republican presidential nominee, Wendell Willkie, sympathized with the Committee to Defend America and so refused to criticize the President for helping England.

During the campaign FDR stressed that he did not intend to involve the country in war. After the election, however, he stepped up American involvement, often with the public assurance that further involvement would somehow lessen the need for Americans to fight. Roosevelt was trapped. He knew the American system could not long survive in a fascist-dominated world, but he feared making strong public statements because of his estimate of antiwar sentiment, especially on Capitol Hill. When one ardent interventionist urged more action, FDR replied, "Whether we like it or not, God and Congress still live." He consequently committed the United States to the Allies while issuing public explanations that fell short of the truth.

Such use of presidential power raised the classic question of whether the ends indeed justified the means. That question could be answered one way in 1941 and in a quite different fashion in the 1960s when Lyndon Johnson used FDR's actions as precedents for his own methods of committing Americans to Vietnam (see Chapter 14). Even in 1941, however, critics led by Charles Beard warned that the question of how Americans went to war was as important as whether they went, for, Beard argued, the misuse of presidential powers could destroy the delicate checks and balances built by the Founding Fathers to protect individual freedom and representative government.

Beard lost that argument. Roosevelt moved rapidly in 1941 against the Axis. In March he pushed Lend-Lease through Congress so that the country could be "the arsenal of democracy" and send vast amounts of goods to England regardless of its inability to pay for the supplies. The act was aimed, FDR said, at keeping "war away from our country and our people." Senator Burton K. Wheeler called Lend-Lease "the New Deal's triple-A foreign policy: it will plow under every fourth American boy." Roosevelt promptly shot back that this was "the rottenest thing that has been said in public life in my generation." But moving supplies to England through Nazi submarine-infested seas of the North Atlantic soon required Roosevelt to send American convoys to protect the supply ships. He ordered such convoying as far as Iceland despite telling a press conference in late May that he had no plans to permit the United States Navy to accompany British vessels. By late summer he ordered American ships to track and report the position of German submarines to British destroyers. When one submarine turned and fired a torpedo at the *Greer,* which had been following the German vessel for three hours, Roosevelt said that the attack was unprovoked and implied that henceforth American ships should feel free to shoot on sight. In November U.S. ships were armed and carrying goods to England. The nation was all but formally in war.

THE LAST STEP

The formal, constitutional declaration of war ironically resulted from an Asian, not a European, crisis. After Japan threatened Indochina in July

1940, FDR restricted exports of oil, aviation fuel, and scrap metals to Japan. This was a major step, for cutting off Tokyo's main source of these goods could force the Japanese to seize the oil and mineral wealth of South Asia. Yet Tokyo proceeded cautiously. In March 1941 Japan freed itself from the threat of a two-front war by signing a five-year nonaggression treaty with Russia. Hitler was stunned. England had been tougher than expected, and he had failed to reach agreement with Stalin on dividing booty in the Balkans, so Hitler had decided to invade Russia. Despite the Tokyo-Moscow pact, the German dictator struck on June 23 and by early winter had driven to within thirty miles of Moscow. Only the United States remained to keep Japan from taking what it wanted in the Far East.

In July 1941 the Japanese invaded Indochina and Thailand. Roosevelt froze Japanese assets in the United States, thus stopping nearly all trade. Hull had negotiated with Japan throughout mid-1941, but no agreement could be reached on three points: Tokyo's obligations under the Tripartite Pact (Hull wanted Japan to disavow the alliance); Japanese economic rights in Southeast Asia; and a settlement in China. The Secretary of State mumbled to friends that "everything is going hellward," but he refused to give up hope that Japan would be reasonable. Roosevelt supported Hull, restraining Cabinet members, such as Morgenthau, who wanted to have a showdown with the Japanese. The President desperately needed time to build American strength in both the Atlantic and Pacific.

Averting an immediate clash, Hull nevertheless stuck fast to his demands that Japan get out of China, Indochina, and the Tripartite Pact. The Tokyo government of Fuminaro Konoye was reaching the point of no return. American economic pressure was building. Konoye either had to meet Hull's demands and restore normal trade with the United States or remove all restraints and conquer the rich resources to the south. In August Konoye made a final attempt at conciliation by asking Roosevelt to meet him personally to thrash out the problem. FDR was initially attracted, but Hull convinced him the conference would be worthless unless Japan agreed before the meeting to acquiesce to Hull's earlier demands. Konoye naturally refused such preconditions and in early October the military regime of General Hideki Tojo assumed control in Tokyo.

There was one last effort to avert war. In November the Japanese offered to leave Indochina and implied that they did not feel bound by the Tripartite Pact. In return they demanded vast American economic aid. The United States had cracked the Japanese code, so Hull knew that this was the final offer. He rejected it, declaring on November 26 that Japan must in addition evacuate all troops from China and agree to an open-door policy in the Far East. This Japan would not do. The next day Tojo's regime agreed to attack the United States in a surprise raid on the Pearl Harbor naval base on December 7. At no time did the Japanese government harbor any hope of actually conquering the United States. Japan hoped that after destroying a large portion of the American fleet, Roosevelt would want to avert further conflict and be willing to talk more amicably about China and trade.

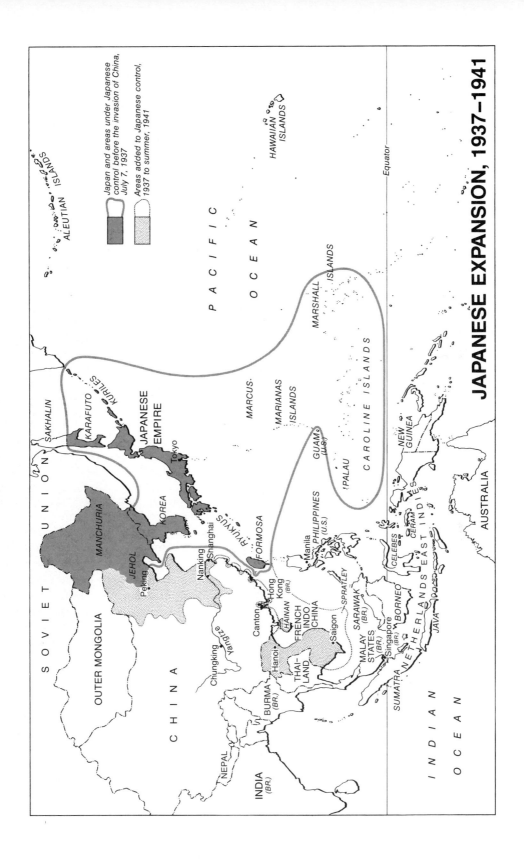

JAPANESE EXPANSION, 1937–1941

Japan and areas under Japanese control before the invasion of China, July 7, 1937

Areas added to Japanese control, 1937 to summer, 1941

ALEUTIAN ISLANDS

SOVIET UNION

OUTER MONGOLIA

CHINA

NEPAL

INDIA (BR.)

Chungking

Yangtze

BURMA (BR.)

THAI-LAND

Hanoi

FRENCH INDO-CHINA

Saigon

Canton

Hong Kong

HAINAN (BR.)

MALAY STATES (BR.)

Singapore

SUMATRA

NETHERLANDS EAST INDIES

JAVA

BORNEO (BR.)

SARAWAK (BR.)

SPRATLEY

CELEBES

CERAM

NEW GUINEA

AUSTRALIA

INDIAN OCEAN

SAKHALIN

KARAFUTO

KURILES

JAPANESE EMPIRE

Tokyo

KOREA

MANCHURIA

JEHOL

Peking

Nanking

Shanghai

RYUKYUS

FORMOSA

PHILIPPINES (U.S.)

Manila

PALAU

GUAM (U.S.)

MARIANAS ISLANDS

MARCUS

CAROLINE ISLANDS

MARSHALL ISLANDS

PACIFIC OCEAN

HAWAIIAN ISLANDS

Equator

Washington officials knew that Japan was preparing to attack, but they believed that the strike would be only against Southeast Asia. Some, such as Secretary of War Henry Stimson (whom FDR had named in 1940 in a bipartisan and pro-Allied gesture), even hoped that the Japanese would attack in the southern Pacific, for the United States would then be justified in declaring war to protect the Philippines. Japan instead struck in the mid-Pacific, crippling American naval forces in a matter of minutes with the worst losses they ever suffered in a single engagement. More than 3500 men lost their lives, and six large battleships and numerous auxiliary vessels settled to the bottom of the Hawaiian harbor.

Pearl Harbor was caught unprepared because of a massive breakdown in military intelligence and communication, not because FDR or Stimson conspired to use the navy as bait so that Japan would attack and thereby enable the administration to take a united country into war. No administration plans to begin a war by losing nearly half its navy. When FDR asked for war against Japan, moreover, he did not think it possible to declare war on Germany, and Hitler remained the primary objective of American policy. Many Americans wanted vengeance on Japan but were not yet ready to become embroiled in Europe. Hitler solved Roosevelt's dilemma on December 11 by declaring war on the United States. He did so in part because he had long promised the Japanese to honor their 1940 treaty, but more important because he felt that the United States was already fighting against him without a declaration of war. Hitler's unbounded ego apparently demanded that he, not Roosevelt, take the initiative in the life-and-death struggle. When and whether FDR would have been able to mobilize Americans to fight Hitler without the dictator's declaration of war remain "iffy" questions, as FDR himself liked to call them. That is no doubt fortunate.

The breakdown of intelligence at Pearl Harbor was remarkable. In Washington's last message to the base on December 7, the telegram said nothing about possible attack on Hawaii, went by slow commercial cable after a delay in transmission through military communications, and was finally delivered to authorities by a Japanese-American on a motorbike nearly seven hours after the strike. It was a symbolic end to the decade. The economic system had broken down by 1931, spawning fascism in Japan and Germany. The Washington Treaty system had consequently broken down, allowing Japan to destroy the open door in Asia. The 1919 peace arrangements had broken down, turning Hitler loose in Europe while Chamberlain and Roosevelt wrung their hands. The American economic system had broken down, leaving the New Deal a failure until it was rescued by war spending. American foreign policy had broken down, leaving Hull uttering platitudes about restoring peace by restoring an international marketplace that had not worked properly since before World War I. The Constitution's checks and balances had broken down, as Roosevelt sent Americans to kill and be killed on the high seas eight months before the formal declaration of war, and while he explained publicly that each step toward war was really a step away from war. After a decade like that, the intelligence breakdown at Pearl Harbor is easier to understand if, like the others, difficult to justify.

Suggested Reading

The depression's impact on diplomacy is well analyzed in Charles Kindleberger, *The World in Depression, 1929–1939* (1973); and Robert H. Ferrell, *American Diplomacy in the Great Depression* (1970). See also Akira Iriye's superb *Across the Pacific* (1967), actually covering the post-1840s era; Henry L. Stimson's autobiography, *On Active Service* (1948); Elting Morison's biography of Stimson, *Turmoil and Tradition* (1960); Raymond G. O'Connor, *Perilous Equilibrium* (1962), a fine study of naval policy through 1930; and for Latin America, Alexander DeConde, *Herbert Hoover's Latin American Policy* (1951).

New Deal foreign policy is well surveyed in Lloyd Gardner, *Economic Aspects of New Deal Diplomacy* (1964); Robert Divine, *The Reluctant Belligerent* (1965); Frederick Adams, *Economic Diplomacy: The Export-Import Bank* (1976); and Robert Dallek's detailed study of FDR in press. For specific topics, see Manfred Jonas, *Isolationism in America, 1935–1941* (1962); Wayne S. Cole's outstanding *Charles A. Lindbergh and the Battle Against American Intervention in World War II* (1974); Edward E. Bennett, *Recognition of Russia* (1970); two important studies of Latin American policy, Robert F. Smith, *U.S. and Cuba, 1917–1960* (1960) and Bryce Wood, *The Making of the Good Neighbor Policy* (1954). On the Far East see the splendid essays and bibliographies in Dorothy Borg and Shumpei Okamoto, eds., *Pearl Harbor As History* (1973); and Irvine H. Anderson, Jr.'s case study, *The Standard-Vacuum Oil Company and U.S. East Asian Policy, 1933–1941* (1975). Useful is Herbert Feis, *Road to Pearl Harbor* (1950), but the best recent work on the entry into war includes Robert Divine's two books, *Franklin D. Roosevelt and World War II* (1969), and *Foreign Policy and U.S. Presidential Elections, 1940–1960* (1974); James R. Leutze's prize-winning *Bargaining for Supremacy; Anglo-American Naval Collaboration, 1937–1941* (1977); Joseph P. Lash's important *Roosevelt and Churchill, 1939–1941* (1976); Warren T. Kimball's crucial study, *The Most Unsordid Act: Lend-Lease, 1939–1941* (1969); James MacGregor Burns, *Roosevelt, Soldier of Freedom* (1970); and Roberta Wohlstetter, *Pearl Harbor* (1962). On German relations, see Arnold Offner, *America's Appeasement of Germany* (1968), and the broad picture presented in William L. Langer and S. Everett Gleason's standard accounts, *The Challenge to Isolation* (1952), and *The Undeclared War, 1940–1941* (1953), to be used with Charles A. Beard's *President Roosevelt and the Coming of the War* (1948).

For the history of radio news, Erik Barnouw, *History of Broadcasting in the U.S.*, 3 vols. (1966–1970) is standard; and Alexander Kendrick's *Prime Time; The Life of Edward R. Murrow* (1969) is fascinating.

Women welders, New Britain, Connecticut, 1943.

CHAPTER NINE
1941-1947
War and Peace

THE HOUSE I LIVE IN
Words by Lewis Allen, music by Earl Robinson

What is America to Me?
A name, a map, a flag I see
A certain word Democracy
What is America to me?

The House I live in
A plot of earth, a street
The grocer and the butcher
And the people that I meet,
The children in the playground
The faces that I see
All races and religions
That's America to me.

The place I work in
The worker by my side
The little town or city
Where my people lived and died
The howdy and the handshake
The air of feeling free
And the right to speak my mind out
That's America to me.

The things I see about me
The big things and the small,
The little corner newsstand
And the house a mile tall
The wedding and the churchyard
The laughter and the tears
The dream that's been a-growin'
For a hundred and fifty years.

The town I live in
The streets, the house, the room
The pavement of the city
Or a garden all in bloom,
The church, the school, the clubhouse
The million lives I see,
But especially the people,
That's America to me.

World War II imposed severe strains on American political, economic, and social institutions. The Roosevelt administration had to devise a program that would release the nation's full productive energies and yet restrain rampaging inflationary forces. The government also had to impose restrictions on the daily lives of millions of people without alienating those who formed the basis of its political support. To a large extent Roosevelt found satisfactory solutions to these problems. Americans were united against a common enemy, one they regarded as the incarnation of evil, and were therefore willing to make certain sacrifices. The war, by producing a high level of prosperity, ensured that those sacrifices would not be too painful. Then, in April 1945, Harry S. Truman assumed the presidency, and four months later the war ended. The accumulated pressures of four years suddenly exploded, threatening to make a shambles of Truman's domestic program. Putting the pieces back together again proved an arduous task.

IMAGES OF WAR

In 1942 anthropologist Margaret Mead published *And Keep Your Powder Dry,* a study of the way in which American character and values might shape the future conduct of the war. Americans fought best, Mead observed, when they believed that the other side had wantonly provoked them and left them no alternative to war, and when they thought that the struggle was between antagonists of roughly equal strength. In addition, Americans needed to believe in the justice, indeed selflessness, of their cause. A steady succession of military advances, interrupted only temporarily by setbacks, would bolster these convictions. A protracted series of defeats, on the other hand, would call them into question. "To win this war," she said, "we must feel we are on the side of the Right."

Throughout the war years most people felt precisely that way. The attack on Pearl Harbor, widely viewed as proof of Japanese barbarity, enabled Americans to enter the war with more unity than had seemed possible during the bitter struggle between isolationists and interventionists. Most people believed that the war was being waged for "the right of all men to live in freedom, decency, and security," or, as Vice-President Henry A. Wallace put it, to usher in a "century of the common man," in which people around the world would gain political freedom and economic security. One congressman declared: "It is a war of purification in which the forces of Christian peace and freedom and justice and decency and morality are arrayed against the evil pagan forces of strife, injustice, treachery, immorality, and slavery." This was only an extreme statement of a commonly accepted view. "Never in our history," said one observer, "have issues been so clear."

The government did what it could to stimulate a sense of loyalty and unity by channeling civilian energies into war-related tasks. The Office of Civilian Defense (OCD) organized corps of air-raid wardens, fire fighters, auxiliary police, and nurses' aides. The agency maintained that people could, through discipline and self-denial, contribute to an American victory. The OCD gave a "V Home Award" as "a badge of honor for those families which have made themselves into a fighting unit on the home front" by conserving food, salvaging vital materials, buying war bonds, and planting victory gardens. Newspaper, magazine, and radio advertisements also attempted to persuade people to get by with less. B. F. Goodrich asked its customers to conserve rubber tires since "Hitler smiles when you waste miles." The government popularized the slogan, "Use it up, wear it out, make it do or do without." The daily use of certain symbols, particularly the ubiquitous "V" for victory, heightened the sense of shared purpose.

So, too, did the image of the enemy that emerged during the war. In the popular mind, Germany, at least since the time of Otto von Bismarck, had acted as an aggressor nation because of the influence of the Prussian military caste. *Life* magazine described those officers: "They despise the world of civilians. They wear monocles to train themselves to control their face muscles. They live and die for war." Adolf Hitler had seized power with an "insane desire to conquer and dominate the whole world," and had pursued a strategy of piecemeal conquest based on "treachery and surprise" with the ultimate goal of conquering the United States. The Japanese were portrayed as a fanatical people, addicted to the practice of Emperor-worship and unconcerned about the sanctity of human life. Racist stereotypes shaped perceptions of the Japanese. *Time* magazine referred to American soldiers at Iwo Jima as "Rodent Exterminators" and noted: "The ordinary unreasoning Jap is ignorant. Perhaps he is human. Nothing . . . indicates it." Similarly, a float in a patriotic parade "showed a big American eagle leading a flight of bombs down on a herd of yellow rats which were trying to escape in all directions."

If Americans viewed the enemy as power-mad, militaristic, and brutal, they saw themselves as just the reverse. Perhaps nothing illustrated this better than reporter Ernie Pyle's best-selling *Here Is Your War*. Ostensibly an account of U.S. forces in Africa, Pyle's book in reality assured civilians that, despite the rigors of war, their fighting men preserved fundamental American virtues. To Pyle, the army was a democratic one: enlisted men and officers addressed each other by their first names and observed an easy kind of battlefield informality. American soldiers were fierce in combat—"as indestructible as Popeye and as deadly as executioners"—yet they could not resist giving away candy to hungry children, adopting little puppies, or treating captives with consideration. Although the soldiers came from every section of the nation, the cauldron of war had dissolved all religious, ethnic, class, and racial enmities. Democratic, humane, Americans saw themselves as the polar opposites of the goose-stepping Nazis. Even when Americans retreated, Pyle concluded, they did so in an "unretreatlike" way, and then only because they lacked sufficient men and material to win. The lesson was plain: if factories turned out more tanks, more machine guns, more bullets, and more airplanes, victory would surely follow.

THE WAR ECONOMY

The economic problems posed by war differed from those associated with the depression. During the 1930s the Roosevelt administration had attempted to limit productive output, create jobs for the unemployed, and encourage a certain amount of inflation. During the 1940s, however, the government did a sudden turnabout. It endeavored to boost industrial and agricultural production, recruit a sufficient number of workers for defense plants, and hold down wages and prices. The administration sought, wherever possible, to obtain voluntary compliance from businessmen, workers, farmers, and consumers by offering them attractive incentives. But on occasion, when these groups refused to cooperate, it resorted to compulsion.

To supply the massive needs of the Allied forces the government not only induced businessmen to expand their facilities and convert them to war production, but also developed new sources of critical raw materials and doled those materials out in a systematic fashion. At the heart of this managerial effort was the War Production Board (WPB), which Roosevelt created in January 1942 to exercise general control over the economy. Donald Nelson, formerly an executive with Sears, Roebuck and Company, headed the agency. Nelson wanted "to establish a set of rules under which the game could be played the way industry said it had to play it." In this he echoed the sentiments of Secretary of War Henry L. Stimson, who believed that to carry on a war "you have got to let business make money out of the process or business won't work."

The WPB devised various procedures to allow businessmen to combine patriotism with high profits. The government underwrote much of the cost of plant expansion by permitting industry to amortize those costs over a short five-year period, thereby deflating taxable income while inflating earning capacity. The government also invented the cost-plus-a-fixed-fee contract, which guaranteed the military contractor a profit above his costs and removed almost all element of risk from the acceptance of war orders. Firms that entered into pooling arrangements were granted immunity from the antitrust laws provided they first obtained consent by demonstrating how their activities furthered war needs. These policies proved effective. By mid-1942 major producers had converted from civilian to military lines. Industry produced nearly twice as much in 1942 as in 1939. As much new industrial plant was built in three years of war as in the preceding fifteen years. Corporate profits after taxes climbed from $6.4 billion in 1940 to $10.8 billion in 1944.

In three other ways the government stimulated industrial output. To compensate for the loss of 90 percent of America's crude rubber supply when Japan seized the Dutch East Indies and Malaya, a new synthetic rubber industry was created. The government spent $700 million to construct 51 plants, which were leased to rubber companies and operated on a cost-plus-a-management-charge basis. By 1944 annual production of synthetic rubber exceeded 800,000 tons. To eliminate logjams in production caused by shortages of copper, steel, and aluminum (all widely used

Collecting scrap rubber, 1942.

in the manufacture of airplanes, tanks, and ships), the WPB introduced the Controlled Materials Plan. Under it, each agency awarding war contracts, such as the War or Navy Department, presented its material requirements to the WPB, which then allotted the agency a fixed quantity of scarce materials for distribution to its prime contractors. To prevent transportation bottlenecks from developing, the government coordinated rail transportation. Unlike World War I, when Washington had taken over the railroads, a system was devised under which the railroads submitted to central direction, pooled their resources, and streamlined their operations. By voluntarily complying, the railroads avoided nationalization.

The policies adopted in recruiting manpower resembled those applied in mobilizing industry. Again, Roosevelt relied heavily on what he termed "voluntary cooperation." At first the demand for labor was filled from the pool of unemployed workers, augmented by women and teenagers entering the job market. But by the end of 1942 high draft calls and 12-hour factory shifts had exhausted available reserves. The administration made only a feeble attempt to force workers into war-related jobs, however, and finally had to abandon even that. In January 1943 the War Manpower Commission (WMC) issued a "work or fight" order. It eliminated military deferments for everyone, including fathers with dependent children, who held unessential jobs. But this attempt to substitute occupational for familial responsibility as a criterion for deferment aroused a storm of disapproval in Congress, and in December the order was rescinded.

Not until midway through the war did the administration discover a partial solution to the manpower problem. Spurred to action by a dangerously high rate of turnover in aircraft plants and shipyards on the West Coast, the WMC adopted a plan to align production demands with labor supply. Local committees determined how many workers were available; firms in each area could then receive new war contracts only if a sufficient labor supply existed; and a central employment service had to approve new hiring. This plan went into effect in Seattle, Portland, San Francisco, Los Angeles, and San Diego in the fall of 1943 and rapidly spread to cities across the country. It represented a middle stage between voluntarism and compulsion. Workers could not change jobs at will, but were not forced to accept jobs against their will.

FIGHTING INFLATION

Booming industrial production and full employment, combined with a high level of federal spending and a scarcity of consumer goods, created huge inflationary pressures. Few economic problems proved more troublesome for Roosevelt. When someone suggested that "a little inflation would not hurt," the President replied that he was reminded of "a fellow who took a little cocaine and kept coming back for more until he was a drug addict." To curb inflation the administration employed several weapons: wage ceilings, price controls, rationing, taxation, and bond drives. Everyone agreed in principle on the need to check inflation, but no one wanted to come out on the losing end. The administration therefore had a choice: either freeze economic conditions as they stood at the outbreak of the war, and thereby perpetuate certain inequalities; or impose controls selectively, and thereby permit some groups to improve their relative position. The second approach, while perhaps less efficient, was politically more popular and was ultimately adopted.

This was well illustrated by the efforts of the National War Labor Board (NWLB) to halt spiraling wages. In July 1942 the NWLB adopted the "Little Steel" formula, which allowed a 15 percent wage increase to cover the rise in living costs since January 1, 1941. The formula, which applied to all workers, helped those who had not yet benefited from boom conditions. Even labor unions that had already obtained the permissible increase found the formula acceptable. The ruling permitted fatter weekly pay envelopes through overtime, allowed wage hikes that resulted from the upgrading of job classifications, and affected only cases involving labor-management disputes. Where employers were willing to grant increases—as was often the case, given the labor shortage—they were free to do so. In October 1942 the administration attempted to close this loophole by extending the NWLB's jurisdiction over voluntary wage boosts. When even this proved ineffective, FDR issued a "hold-the-line" order in April 1943. It prevented revision of the Little Steel formula but still allowed exceptions either in extraordinary cases affecting war production or where they were necessary to correct substandard conditions. By the summer of 1943 the government had largely removed wages from the realm of collective bargaining but had still not brought them under iron-clad rules.

Regulating the wages workers earned depended, of course, on controlling the prices they had to pay. In April 1942 the Office of Price Administration (OPA) required every merchant to accept as a ceiling the highest price he had charged that March. This general freeze was difficult to enforce and often unfair, for it failed to control the prices of products whose design or packaging had changed, and it penalized dealers who had not already raised their prices. The cost of living continued to creep upward until April 1943, when Roosevelt's hold-the-line order prevented further inflationary rises. Consumer prices advanced by less than 2 percent during the next two years. To a large extent the success of price control hinged on rationing. The OPA introduced ten major rationing programs in 1942, and others followed later. They served different purposes: gasoline was rationed to conserve automobile tires; coffee, to reduce the burden on ocean transport; and canned food, to save tin. The government could not entirely prevent black-market operations—in 1944 one racketeer was found with counterfeit coupons worth 38,000 gallons of gasoline and 437 pairs of shoes—but rationing ensured a reasonably fair distribution of hard-to-get items, and it protected consumers against inflation.

The Roosevelt administration also reduced inflationary pressure by siphoning off excess purchasing power. Wartime taxes imposed heavy duties on the wealthy. The introduction of the withholding system meant that for the first time in U.S. history virtually all wage earners paid federal income taxes and did so out of current earnings. In addition, FDR launched a campaign to sell war bonds, not through the compulsory plan favored by many of his advisors but instead through voluntary purchases. Secretary of the Treasury Henry Morgenthau believed that such an undertaking would "make the country war-minded." He recruited advertising men (who invented such slogans as "Back the Attack") and Hollywood entertainers (who put personal possessions up for auction) to aid in the drive. The voluntary program had mixed results as an anti-inflation measure. Seven bond drives netted $135 billion, but large investors bought most securities, and sales of low-denomination bonds were disappointing. Even so, 25 million workers signed up for payroll savings plans, and in 1944 bond sales absorbed more than 7 percent of personal income after taxes.

At various times both labor and business challenged the system of economic regulation and left Roosevelt no choice but to intervene. When Montgomery Ward, a huge mail-order concern, refused to grant privi-

leges to a union certified by the NWLB, the President authorized a takeover of the firm. Its head, Sewell L. Avery, shouting "to hell with the government," refused to leave the premises and had to be carried out bodily.
Yet on balance the administration succeeded in winning public approval
for its policies. This occurred in part because most Americans enjoyed
greater prosperity during World War II than ever before and therefore
did not find most regulatory measures oppressive. Equally important was
the manner in which the administration proceeded. It introduced a co-
herent system of controls but did so in piecemeal fashion and with a
heavy emphasis on inducing the consent of those affected. FDR never
used a stick when a carrot would do.

DR. NEW DEAL MEETS
DR. WIN-THE-WAR

World War II solved some of the most serious dilemmas facing social reformers. It brought about full employment and a higher standard of living. It strengthened trade unions, whose membership climbed from 10.5
to 14.75 million. It pushed farm income to new heights and reduced
tenancy as landless farmers found jobs in factories. The war also exerted
a modest leveling influence. Between 1939 and 1944 the share of national
income held by the wealthiest 5 percent of the American people declined
from 23.7 to 16.8 percent. In 1944 Congress passed the GI Bill of Rights,
a wide-ranging reform measure providing veterans with generous education benefits, readjustment allowances during the transition to civilian life,
and guarantees of mortgage loans. Finally, the war seemed to demonstrate once and for all the efficacy of Keynesian economics. Few doubted
that soaring government expenditures had produced the boom. In 1943
one reformer noted, "The honest-minded liberal will admit that the common man is getting a better break than ever he did under the New Deal."

Despite all this, the war in many respects weakened social reform and
led to profound disillusionment on the part of liberals. In part, this disillusionment derived from a mistaken reading of history. Many reformers,
looking back on World War I, remembered only that it had aided their
cause by permitting national planning and forgot how it had damaged
their movement. In 1943 and 1944, however, liberals detected signs of a
conservative resurgence everywhere they looked. Not only did Congress
jettison New Deal programs and the administration refuse to support new
reform measures, but in December 1943 Roosevelt declared that "Dr.
New Deal" had outlived his usefulness and should give way to "Dr. Win-
the-War." At that point liberal morale hit rock bottom.

The war obliged reformers to grant priority to military objectives.
This often required the setting aside of certain social reforms. Liberals either did not protest or did not protest very loudly when the working day
was lengthened to boost industrial output, rural electrification curtailed to
free copper for the military, and the antitrust law shelved to permit
greater business efficiency. States frequently diluted their child-labor laws

so that 14- and 15-year-olds could join the work force and work longer hours. From 1940 to 1944 the number of teen-age workers jumped from 1.0 to 2.9 million, and more than 1 million teen-agers dropped out of school. "Where a social service doesn't help to beat Hitler, it may have to be sacrificed," observed one reformer. "This may sound tough—but we have to be tough."

Just as the war shouldered aside reforms, so it provided an excuse to abolish various New Deal relief agencies. During 1942 and 1943 Congress—usually with the consent of the administration—snuffed out the Civilian Conservation Corps, the Works Progress Administration, and the National Youth Administration. As a result of job openings in national defense, these agencies' clientele had come increasingly to consist of those last to be hired—Negroes, women, and the elderly. Although the agencies tried to justify their continued existence by undertaking projects of military value, they could no longer count on strong backing from Roosevelt. Some reformers urged that the WPA be preserved in case it was needed after the war. But in December 1942, asserting that a national work relief program was no longer justified, the President gave the WPA an "honorable discharge."

As military costs escalated, so too did the federal deficit. Congress became more unwilling than ever to appropriate funds for domestic programs not directly related to the war, and Roosevelt, recognizing this, became reluctant to request such funds. When several Senate liberals introduced a plan to extend social security coverage, liberalize unemployment insurance benefits, and create a comprehensive health-care program, they failed to gain the backing of the administration and stood no chance of winning a legislative majority. Congress not only refused to broaden social security coverage but froze the rate of contributions at 1 percent, thereby postponing a small scheduled increase. The same desire to trim nondefense expenditures led Congress to slash the budget of the Farm Security Administration, an important New Deal agency that had helped marginal farmers purchase land and equipment.

If social welfare schemes stood little chance in wartime, proposals to help those on the lower rungs of the ladder stood even less. Although most Americans enjoyed higher incomes than ever before, not everyone was well-off. In 1944 a Senate committee reported that 20 million people "dwell constantly in a borderland between subsistence and privation." Ten million workers—one-fourth of those engaged in manufacturing—received less than 60 cents an hour. Yet the administration opposed granting them an across-the-board wage hike on the grounds that it would increase inflationary pressure. Raising the wages of the lowest-paid would send inflationary ripples through the economy, since to preserve wage differentials, adjustments would be made all along the line. The resulting higher prices would eventually rob the worker of any benefit. Roosevelt believed that in wartime the government could do no more than ensure that the poor were "not ground down below the margin of existence."

Changes in the composition of the federal bureaucracy also dismayed reformers. In the early 1940s the federal service underwent a major overhaul as men and women who had taken positions out of a commitment to New Deal principles left Washington in droves. Often their places were filled by business executives who possessed the skills needed to manage war production but who had little interest in social reform. Nothing infuriated liberals more than this steady movement of businessmen into positions of authority. "The New Dealers are a vanishing tribe," wrote one reformer, "and the money changers who were driven from the temple are now quietly established in government offices." The business community, of course, viewed this development with deep satisfaction. *Business Week*, noting that the war had placed a premium on "business talents" rather than on "braintrusters and theoreticians," observed that businessmen were "moving up in the New Deal administration, replacing New Dealers as they go."

The war weakened liberalism in one final respect: it raised issues that threatened to rupture the New Deal coalition. Roosevelt had built that coalition—consisting of blue-collar workers, Southern white farmers, ethnic and racial minority groups, and portions of the middle class—around economic concerns. So long as recovery remained the chief goal, those disparate groups had a good deal in common. But the war subjected this alliance to severe strain. Three sources of division were potentially most disruptive: heightened sensitivity to racial discrimination made it harder to retain the loyalty of both Northern blacks and Southern whites; issues concerning foreign policy and civil liberties affected the political sentiments of ethnic groups; and the need to curb strikes and regulate manpower ran the risk of alienating organized labor.

CIVIL RIGHTS AND THE SOUTH

If the Democratic party had an Achilles heel, it was the issue of racial justice. During Roosevelt's first two terms the depression had muted racial concerns. New Deal relief programs had proved as attractive to black voters in New York City, Chicago, and Detroit as to white voters in Mississippi, Georgia, and Alabama. But the war spurred blacks to insist more strongly on racial equality. Many believed that the policy of accommodation had backfired during World War I and that a militant posture would be most likely to win concessions from the Roosevelt administration. Claiming that only the end of racial oppression would ensure full Negro backing for the war, black leaders undertook a "Double V" campaign, one that stressed victory in the struggle for equality as well as victory on the battlefield. Yet throughout the war years white Southerners clung tenaciously to the doctrine of segregation. The President, inevitably, was caught in the middle.

The war inspired civil rights groups to develop new forms of protest. In the summer of 1941, A. Philip Randolph of the Brotherhood of Sleeping Car Porters called for a March on Washington to protest discrimination and "shake up white America." Randolph's movement differed from existing civil rights organizations in important respects: it attempted to mobilize the Negro masses rather than the middle class, it sought concessions through direct action rather than through court rulings, and it worked for reforms that would benefit northern urban blacks as much as those living in the South. Moreover, Randolph excluded white people from his organization on the grounds that "Negroes are the only people who are the victims of Jim Crow, and it is they who must take the initiative and assume the responsibility to abolish it."

Separatist in structure, the March on Washington Movement was wholly integrationist in objective. It demanded that the President withhold defense contracts from employers who practiced discrimination and abolish segregation in the armed forces and federal agencies. Anxious to have the march canceled, Roosevelt agreed to compromise. On June 25, 1941, he issued Executive Order 8802 providing that government agencies, job training programs, and defense contractors put an end to discrimination. He also created a Committee on Fair Employment Practices to investigate violations. The Executive Order, although it did not provide for integration of the armed forces, was nevertheless hailed by civil rights workers, who concluded "we get more when we yell than we do when we plead."

By 1943 Randolph was advocating disciplined acts of civil disobedience, and the newly created Congress of Racial Equality (CORE) took action along those lines. Founded by pacifists, CORE endeavored to apply the same tactics of nonviolent resistance to the cause of racial justice that Gandhi had used in the movement for India's independence. Unlike the March on Washington Movement, CORE was interracial, but it too stressed direct action and concentrated on the economic aspects of racial injustice. In 1943 CORE sit-ins helped eliminate segregation in movie theaters and restaurants in Detroit, Denver, and Chicago. Most civil rights activity during the war, however, was channeled through the National Association for the Advancement of Colored People. Relying on the traditional means of protest—exposure, propaganda, political pressure, and legal action—the NAACP greatly expanded its membership and influence.

Most Southern whites regarded these signs of increased militancy with mounting apprehension. Committed to the preservation of Jim Crow institutions, whites bitterly resented the charge that their racial beliefs resembled those of the Nazis. A former Governor of Alabama admitted privately in 1944 that the Germans had "wrecked the theories of the master race with which we were so contented so long," but added that the Germans had not dented his own belief in white superiority. Southerners attempted to explain away any evidence of black dissatisfaction as the product of outside agitation. A Memphis, Tennessee newspaper claimed in 1943 that the Southern Negro "has a care-free, child-like mentality, and looks to the white man to solve his problems and to take care of him.

To stir up sullen discontent and misguided hatreds is wrong." During the war a tidal wave of rumors swept the South, culminating in the widely held fear that black women would no longer work as domestic servants but were busily forming "Eleanor Clubs" (named after the President's wife) whose goal was "a white woman in every kitchen by 1943." Because Southerners played a pivotal role in the Democratic coalition, they warned the President to pay attention to their views or else "witness the annihilation of the Democratic party in this section."

In April 1944 a Supreme Court decision abolishing the white primary added to this unrest. The white primary, which effectively disenfranchised blacks in eight Southern states, had withstood several court challenges. But in 1941 the Supreme Court decided that primaries were an integral part of the election process, and in 1944, in *Smith* v. *Allwright,* it ruled that political parties were agents of the state and could not nullify the right to vote by practicing racial discrimination. In an effort to mollify Southerners, the Chief Justice assigned the majority opinion to Stanley Reed of Kentucky. But this did not prevent Democratic politicians or editorial writers in the deep South from construing the decision as part of a broad campaign "to ram social equality down the throats of the white people of the South." Actually, while the decision enfranchised a number of educated, middle-class blacks in large cities, other obstacles to Negro voting—such as literacy tests and poll taxes—remained as high as ever.

The career of the Committee on Fair Employment Practices (FEPC) illustrated Roosevelt's difficulties in mediating between the conflicting claims of white Southerners and civil rights activists. The FEPC represented an ambitious federal commitment to racial equality, and it succeeded in opening opportunities for some black workers. Yet the agency was hedged about with restrictions. Theoretically the FEPC had jurisdiction over firms holding defense contracts, but it could only act when a worker filed a formal complaint (many workers were unaware of their right to do so), and even then it could not require compliance with its orders but had to rely on moral suasion. The FEPC could, as a last resort, request the cancellation of a defense contract. But war production always took priority over fair employment practices. Nor could the FEPC always count on strong presidential backing. When the railroad unions flouted a directive to grant equal rights to blacks, the case went to Roosevelt, who swept it under the rug by appointing an investigating committee that never reported. Southerners in Congress bitterly denounced the FEPC. It lost half its budget in 1945 and dissolved within a year.

Black workers made sizeable economic gains during the war, usually as a result of manpower shortages. As the labor supply dwindled, many of the traditional barriers to Negro employment came tumbling down. Employers began to relax bars to hiring, and unions found it more difficult to maintain restrictive membership policies. Blacks, who accounted for just 3 percent of all war workers in the summer of 1942, comprised more than 8 percent three years later. The number of skilled Negro workers doubled, and even larger gains took place in semiskilled positions. Black people by the hundreds of thousands left the farm for the factory in search of opportunity. The government helped in various ways—by hiring more blacks for federal jobs and employing them in higher classifications, by outlawing wage differentials based on race, and by announcing in November 1943 that it would refuse to certify for collective-bargaining purposes unions that discriminated.

The armed forces offered as much resistance to racial equality as had industry, but once again the pressures of war forced a revision in policy. In 1940 military leaders expressed open disdain for black recruits. Negroes could not enlist in the Marines or Air Corps. They could join the Navy only as messmen. They were accepted in the Army but segregated rigidly. The Army maintained that "leadership is not yet imbedded in the negro race," that black soldiers were inferior fighters, and that the military should not serve as a laboratory for social experiments. Only when it became evident that the existing system involved an unacceptable waste of manpower was it modified. The Navy gradually integrated some of its ships, and the Army began the process of desegregating training camps. It also sent black combat units into battle more often but continued to resist integration in war zones except in extraordinary circumstances. By the fall of 1944 there were 700,000 Negroes in the armed services compared to 97,000 at the outbreak of war.

The wartime upheaval in race relations sometimes helped trigger deadly riots, especially in overcrowded cities and on Army bases. In June 1943 a violent racial clash engulfed Detroit, leaving 34 people dead and 700 injured. In such cases, civil rights workers and segregationists usually blamed each other for stirring up trouble. Roosevelt, recognizing that he could not satisfy both sides, generally allowed military needs to dictate his civil rights policy. He supported civil rights advances that contributed to the war and opposed those that seemed to interfere with it. The President summed up his own view in December 1943: "I don't think, quite frankly, that we can bring about the millennium at this time."

CULTURAL PLURALISM AND CIVIL LIBERTIES

Just as the issue of race affected Roosevelt's hold on blacks and Southerners, so issues concerning foreign policy and civil liberties affected his standing with key ethnic groups. The Democrats had always drawn heavy support from Irish-Catholics, Germans, Italians, Eastern Europeans, and Jews. New Deal economic programs solidified this support, for immigrants were heavily concentrated among the working classes. But in the 1940s the President faced a growing defection by German-Americans, who had grown increasingly isolationist, Italian-Americans, who feared that harsh terms would be imposed on their homeland, and Polish-Americans, who feared that Roosevelt would allow Russian postwar control over Eastern Europe. Even more serious, Irish-Americans objected to what they regarded as FDR's subservience to Great Britain and excessive collaboration with Russia. Reports to the White House spoke frequently of ethnic group dissatisfaction, of the "anti-Roosevelt sentiment of the Irish Catholics, Italians, and Germans."

To stem this drift away from the Democratic party, the President offered assurances that a vindictive peace would not be sought, praised the loyalty of German and Italian citizens, and took pains to build a good civil liberties record. "We know in our own land," he said in 1944, "how many good men and women of German ancestry have proved loyal, freedom-loving, and peace-loving citizens." During World War I, fearing the danger posed by hyphenated Americans, the nation had stressed assimilation and uniformity. But during the 1940s few were concerned about divided allegiances. Positive values were more often attached to pluralism and ethnic diversity. Patriotic rallies saw elaborate displays of these ideals. When the Illinois War Council staged a celebration in Chicago, 3000 people representing 24 different immigrant groups performed folk songs and dances of their native lands.

Tolerance toward persons of foreign descent was exhibited in several ways. The government placed relatively few restraints on enemy aliens: they could not travel without permission, were barred from areas near strategic installations, and could not possess arms, short-wave receivers, or maps. As the war progressed, however, restrictions were relaxed. Aliens could work in factories with defense contracts if they first obtained permission, and most applications were approved. Citizens of German and Italian extraction encountered little hostility. Spokesmen for the Italian community, testifying before a congressional committee, were treated with kid gloves. Congressmen asked about the nation's baseball idol, who was also an Italian-American: "Tell us about the Dimaggios. Tell us about Dimaggio's father." On Columbus Day in 1942, Attorney General Francis Biddle announced that Italian aliens would no longer be classified as aliens of enemy nationality. "For a long time," Biddle recalled, "I was not permitted to pay for a meal at an Italian restaurant."

Similarly, the Communist party supported the government during World War II and therefore did not find its liberties abridged. Under the leadership of Earl Browder, Communists opposed strikes that might impede production and benefit Hitler's forces. "We have to find out how to make the capitalist system work," Browder said, and this required a willingness to compromise and work for gradual, peaceful change. In 1944 Browder dissolved the party, replacing it with the more informal Communist Political Association. The contrast with the years 1917–18 was stark. During World War I the government had imprisoned Socialist leader Eugene Debs; but in 1942 Roosevelt commuted the sentence of Earl Browder, convicted earlier of passport fraud, in an effort to foster national unity. Under Woodrow Wilson the government had deported radical aliens; but in 1943 the Supreme Court restored the citizenship of a man who had been denaturalized for belonging to the Communist party at the time he swore allegiance to the Constitution.

During World War II the government was more interested in curbing the far right than the far left. The administration persuaded the Catholic Church to silence Father Charles Coughlin, whose magazine, in effect, was asserting that Jews and Communists had tricked America into entering the war. The Justice Department also indicted 26 "native fascists" for engaging "in a mass propaganda campaign spreading hatred against the Jews, prejudice against the Negroes, fear of the communists and distrust of our public officials." After courtroom turmoil marred several trials extending over two years, the case was dropped. In 1942 the FBI captured eight German saboteurs who were planning to dynamite railroad terminals and war plants. Roosevelt denied the saboteurs access to the civil courts and arranged a trial by military commission. The Supreme Court, meeting in special session, decided reluctantly that *Ex parte Milligan*—the case in which it had ruled unconstitutional Abraham Lincoln's use of military commissions to try civilians in areas remote from combat—did not apply. Six of the saboteurs were executed and two given long prison terms.

The government provided conscientious objectors with several alternatives to military service. The Selective Service Act (1940) provided that no one should serve as a combatant who "by reason of religious training and belief, is conscientiously opposed to war in any form." Conscientious objectors usually performed noncombatant duties. Perhaps 25,000 men, most of them Quakers and Mennonites, served in the medical corps and related branches of the military. Those who objected to military service in any form could do "work of national importance under civilian direction." Some 11,950 men worked in civilian public service camps, where they engaged mainly in forestry and conservation, building roads, clearing trails, fighting forest fires, and digging irrigation ditches. About 500 objectors volunteered to be subjects of medical experiments to find cures for typhus, malaria, and other illnesses. Alternatives to the draft, however, did not satisfy everyone. Those whose conscience did not permit them to register with Selective Service, and those whose objection to war rested on political rather than religious grounds, were imprisoned. About 5500 men went to jail, more than three-fourths of them Jehovah's Witnesses who were denied the ministerial exemptions they sought.

Significantly, the only group of immigrants to lose its rights—Japanese-Americans on the West Coast—was politically powerless. Foreign-born Japanese who had migrated before 1924 were barred from citizenship, and most of their children, although born in the United States and therefore citizens, were too young to vote. Japanese-Americans were vulnerable for other reasons as well. They formed a relatively small group, were concentrated in a few states, were largely confined to nonessential occupations (such as vegetable farming), and could be easily singled out. Powerless and poorly assimilated, Japanese-Americans were the victims of a collective judgment of racial guilt. During the spring of 1942 more than 110,000 people, two-thirds of them citizens, were herded into relocation centers. There most of them remained until 1945.

The decision to relocate Japanese-Americans reflected racial, mili-

Japanese Americans, California, 1942.

tary, and political considerations. General John DeWitt, who headed the Western Defense Command, expressed a widely held view when he claimed that racial attributes made all Japanese a menace. "Racial affinities are not severed by migration," he said. "The Japanese race is an enemy race." Military leaders believed the Japanese-Americans would commit sabotage at the first opportunity. The absence of any such overt acts was merely taken as proof that an "invisible deadline" was drawing near. Although some undoubtedly believed that military necessity justified relocation, others used the argument as a convenient pretext. Nativist groups had long agitated for Japanese exclusion, and some agricultural interests also expected to profit by the removal of Japanese competitors. West Coast congressmen badgered government agencies, urging drastic action. "There's a tremendous volume of public opinion now developing against the Japanese," DeWitt reported in January 1942. He added that this was the opinion of "the best people of California."

Throughout the war the Supreme Court often defended the rights of unpopular groups. It set aside the denaturalization of a German-born citizen charged with continued loyalty to the Third Reich; it protected a fascist sympathizer who savagely denounced Roosevelt; and it struck down a law compelling school children to salute the flag. Yet the Supreme Court did not challenge the government's policy toward Japanese-Americans. In June 1943 the Court unanimously held, in the Hirabayashi case, that military officials could impose a curfew that applied only to Japanese-American citizens. In time of war, the Court reasoned, "residents having ethnic affiliations with an invading enemy may be a greater source of danger than those of different ancestry." In December 1944, in *Korematsu v. U.S.*, the Court upheld the exclusion of Japanese-American citizens from the West Coast. One of the three dissenting justices branded the decision a "legalization of racism." At the same time, however, the Court ruled that the government could not hold citizens in relocation centers beyond a reasonable time without evidence of disloyal behavior. The decision, though, was handed down a day after the government had revoked the order banning Japanese-Americans from the coast.

LABOR AND POLITICS

Organized labor was the linchpin of the Democratic coalition. If proof were needed, it was furnished by the 1942 congressional elections. Democrats suffered a severe defeat primarily because war workers who had moved to new states often could not meet residency requirements. The Republicans captured 44 additional seats in the House of Representatives and 9 in the Senate. Roosevelt's policies took account of this dependence on labor. During the war, workers significantly improved their standard of living. Hourly wage rates rose by 24 percent, and weekly earnings (which included overtime) spurted by 70 percent. But as the war progressed, the President was confronted with two politically explosive problems: how to deal with strikes and tighten manpower controls without antagonizing labor.

Late in December 1941 spokesmen for labor and business had agreed to refrain from strikes and lockouts. But the pledge was not legally binding, and workers who suspected that they were being shortchanged ultimately proved willing to violate the agreement. During 1943, 3.1 million men took part in stoppages compared with fewer than 1 million the year before. The most serious was a strike by 400,000 members of the United Mine Workers under the leadership of John L. Lewis. Dissatisfied with federal wage controls, miners of bituminous coal refused to accept the decisions of the National War Labor Board. The strike caused severe public indignation. By mid-1943 John L. Lewis had apparently become the most hated figure in the United States. FDR remarked privately that he would be glad to resign as President if only Lewis would commit suicide.

Neither man resorted to such extreme measures. Even though Congress in June 1943 passed the War Labor Disputes Act, making it a crime to encourage strikes in plants taken over by the government, Roosevelt understood that a harsh response—such as an attempt to draft miners or send them to jail—might easily boomerang. Coal could not be mined without the UMW's cooperation, and besides, drastic measures would offend most of organizd labor. Roosevelt had to avoid taking any step that might cause labor to close ranks behind the coal miners yet not allow so attractive a settlement that other workers would follow them to the picket lines. The task, one official noted, was "to isolate Mr. Lewis and his assistants from other more responsible labor leaders."

Pulled in one direction by a desire to appease his labor constituency and pushed in the other by public opinion, the President charted a hazardous course between the two. He had the government take over the coal mines but placed them under Secretary of the Interior Harold Ickes, whose relationship with Lewis was reasonably cordial. He appealed to the miners to return to work but permitted bargaining to proceed even while they stayed off the job. He approved a settlement granting the miners a substantial raise, but which did so through a new system of computing working time that did not technically violate hourly wage ceilings. He vetoed the War Labor Disputes Act but requested authority to draft strikers (up to the age of 65) as noncombatants. Roosevelt managed to retain the good will of most labor leaders, who applauded his veto—which was promptly overridden by Congress—and paid little attention to his alternative proposal.

The need to adopt more stringent manpower controls also jeopardized FDR's alliance with labor. In January 1944, faced with a deepening manpower deficit, Roosevelt came out for national service. In its original form this proposal would have placed all citizens, men and women alike, at the government's disposal for assignment to whatever job seemed necessary. Roosevelt favored a less drastic version, but labor detested national service in any form. Union leaders termed the plan a disguised form of "involuntary servitude." It would, they said, serve as an effective anti-strike weapon and would threaten the closed shop. If the government ordered a worker to leave his job and report elsewhere, it could hardly require him to join a union as a condition of employment. The plan, therefore, seemed to imply a frontal assault on union security.

Martha Graham and Modern Dance

Martha Graham in *Chronicle*.

In the late 1930s and early 1940s a central theme in the work of writers, artists, photographers, composers, playwrights, filmmakers, and dancers was a fascination with America itself—with its history and geography, its folklore and heritage. This was nicely revealed in Pare Lorentz's documentary film, *The River* (1938), which dwelt lovingly on American place-names in describing the Mississippi's course: "Down the Rock, the Illinois, and the Kankakee/The Allegheny, the Monongahela, Kanawhy, and Muskingum." Appreciation of the val-

ues associated with the American past reached a culmination during World War II when those values seemed to offer a hopeful, decent, and humane alternative to totalitarian doctrine. The success of Frank Sinatra's *The House I Live In*—and, even more, that of the Broadway musical, *Oklahoma!*—attested to the depth of those sentiments. They were also reflected in modern dance, most notably in the work of Martha Graham.

Born in 1894, Martha Graham had spent her youth in California where, in 1916, she had begun to study dance with Ruth St. Denis and Ted Shawn. She eventually became dissatisfied with the "Denishawn" style, which stressed gossamer motion, oriental pageantry, and silken costumes. Graham was, however, equally dissatisfied with traditional ballet, with its graceful lifts, elegant postures, and classical themes. She sought to develop a new dance vocabulary in which movement was stark and down-to-earth, the costumes simple and severe. One critic noted: "Her idiom of motion has little of the aerial in it, but there's a lot of rolling on the floor."By 1926 she had moved to New York City, organized her own troupe, and given her first recital. Graham infused all she did with a fierce intensity. One student described her as "all tension—lightning. Her burning dedication gave her spare body the power of ten men."

Graham, who believed that dance should be relevant to contemporary concerns, was by the mid-1930s affirming American virtue and protesting fascist brutality. In *Chronicle* (1936) she sympathized with the Loyalist cause in the Spanish Civil War. *American Docu-ment* (1938) provided a capsule version of the nation's history—including sections on Puritanism, the Indian, and the Declaration of Independence—ending in what *The New York Times* described as "a final tableau in celebration of democracy." Graham's purpose, noted one critic, was to "bring to bear upon today's perplexities all that was sturdy and upright and liberating in the American dream." For the first time, Graham used a male dancer, Erick Hawkins, who created something of a sensation by performing bare-chested. For the first time, too, she employed a narrator who, by explaining events, made modern dance forms comprehensible to many who had previously found them mystifying.

Graham's celebration of American values reached a peak in the 1944 production of *Appalachian Spring*, which told the story of the marriage of a young couple in rural Pennsylvania in the mid-nineteenth century. The dance was set in a farmyard, the dancers employed portions of the Virginia Reel, and the music, by Aaron Copland, was based partly on the Shaker hymn, *Simple Gifts.*

American Document: "We hold these truths to be self-evident: That all men are created equal."

Appalachian Spring vibrated with a spirit of resilience and optimism.

After the war Graham gradually lost her place as the dominant figure in the world of modern dance, but those who replaced her—Merce Cunningham, Paul Taylor—had been her students. She performed for the last time in 1969 at the age of 75. Yet five years later *The New York Times* announced: "Gala Opening Night: The Theatre of Martha Graham. Miss Graham will lead her company as on-stage commentator in . . . excerpts from 'Appalachian Spring'." Still actively involved in choreography in her eighties, Martha Graham's extraordinary career epitomized one of her maxims: "The only freedom in life is that of the discipline one chooses."

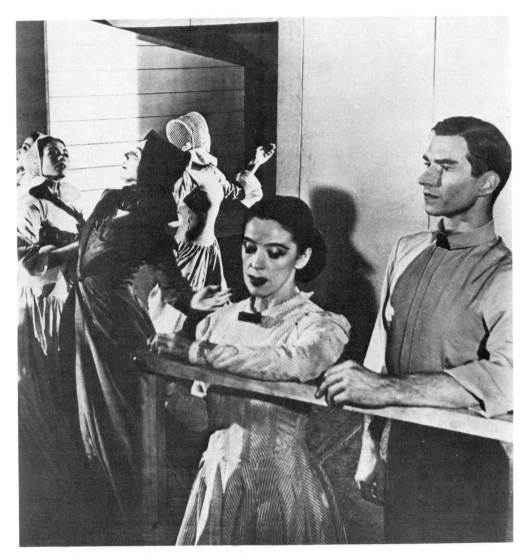

Martha Graham and Erick Hawkins in *Appalachian Spring*.

Merce Cunningham rehearsing, 1954.

PRESIDENTIAL ELECTION, 1944

Democratic (F.D. Roosevelt)

Republican (Dewey)

Opposition to national service united traditional enemies. Joining organized labor was organized business: just as union members did not want to be told where to work, businessmen did not want to be told whom to hire. Given the forces arrayed against it, even a badly watered-down national service bill made little headway in Congress during 1944. In coming out for the measure, Roosevelt had carefully protected his labor flank by insisting that Congress also impose higher taxes on corporations, scale down profits on defense contracts, and authorize effective consumer price ceilings. Congress showed little inclination to do any of these things. Consequently, FDR's advocacy of national service, although it annoyed labor, did not cause many workers to desert the Democratic party.

So successfully did Roosevelt cultivate labor that it provided massive assistance to his 1944 campaign. Inasmuch as two of every three union members considered themselves Democrats, labor knew that a light turnout, such as had occurred in 1942, would be a disaster. The CIO, therefore, set up a Political Action Committee (PAC) that undertook large-scale registration drives and distributed 85 million pieces of campaign literature. On election day, PAC volunteers made telephone calls reminding union members to vote, provided baby-sitters so that housewives could get to the polls, and arranged transportation for those who needed it. The CIO eventually spent $1.5 million, and labor's total contribution to the Democratic campaign—over $2 million—comprised 30 percent of the party's expenditures. Although unions had taken part in past campaigns, never had they done so much for any candidate.

Roosevelt nailed down the labor vote by stressing economic themes. He reminded audiences that the Republicans were the party of Hoovervilles and breadlines, the Democrats the party of collective bargaining and social security. Roosevelt endorsed an Economic Bill of Rights, which recognized each person's right to work at a job that would "provide adequate food and clothing and recreation," to live in a decent home, to receive adequate medical care, to obtain a good education, and to be protected against the hazards of sickness, accident, and unemployment. Ironically, Republican candidate Thomas E. Dewey of New York, although critical of FDR's management of the war, endorsed much of the reform program of the New Deal, at least that portion already on the statute books. He supported social security, unemployment insurance, relief for the needy, and collective bargaining. Some Democrats dubbed him "Little Sir Echo." The 1944 campaign helped place the welfare state beyond the range of partisan dispute.

Roosevelt, although carrying 36 states, won his most slender victory. The President obtained 53.4 percent of the popular vote, compared with 54.7 percent in 1940. He won by a margin of 3.6 million votes as against 5 million in 1940. The key to FDR's triumph was the labor vote in the big cities. In cities with a population over 100,000 Roosevelt garnered 60.7 percent of the vote. In seven states with enough combined electoral strength to have reversed the outcome—New York, Illinois, Pennsylvania, Michigan, Missouri, Maryland, and New Jersey—FDR's plurality in the largest city overcame a Republican majority in the rest of the state. The Democrats picked up 22 seats in the House and lost 1 in the Senate. Without the help of the CIO's Political Action Committee, Roosevelt would not have done so well. That help, in turn, reflected Roosevelt's ability to contend with the potentially disruptive issues posed by the war economy.

WAR AND SOCIAL CHANGE

World War II acted as a catalyst for social change. It increased the power of the federal government and of the presidency in an enduring way. During the war the government employed more people and spent more money than ever before. From 1940 to 1945 the number of civilian employees of the government climbed from 1 million to 3.8 million, and expenditures soared from $9 billion to $98.4 billion. When peace returned the government reduced its operations, but they remained well above prewar levels. The war also accelerated the growth of executive authority and a corresponding erosion of legislative influence. Congress delegated sweeping powers to the President, who in turn delegated them to administrators in war agencies. The big decisions during the war were usually made by men responsible to the President, not by congressional

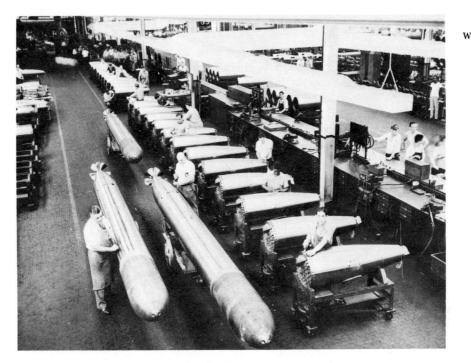

Manufacturing torpedoes, Forest Park, Illinois, 1944.

leaders. The Supreme Court, which had in the past scrutinized every del-egation of legislative authority, refused even to review such cases during the war.

War transformed the economic arrangements under which Ameri-cans lived. The huge outlay of funds for military purposes (which at the height of the war reached $250 million a day) enormously inflated indus-trial capacity. Manufacturing output doubled during the war, and gross national product rose from $88.6 billion in 1939 to $198.7 billion five years later. Wholly new industries, including synthetic rubber and syn-thetic fabrics, came into being. But the desire to obtain the greatest out-put in the shortest time resulted in awarding a predominant share of mili-tary contracts to large corporations and fostering the tendency toward business consolidation. Two-thirds of all military contracts went to 100 firms; nearly one-half went to three dozen corporate giants. From 1941 to 1943 half a million small businesses disappeared. In 1939 firms with more than 10,000 workers employed 13 percent of the manufacturing labor force, but in 1944 they accounted for fully 31 percent.

Since war contracts were awarded by Army and Navy procurement officers, close ties developed between business and the military. Corpora-tion executives and military officers found that they had much in com-mon, particularly in 1944, when they joined to oppose a plan providing for early reconversion to peacetime production. The military feared that reconversion would lull people into believing the war was already won and adversely affect war production. Large war contractors feared that reconversion would permit small competitors who were not committed to military orders to get a jump on them in manufacturing consumer goods. The mutuality of interest between the two groups was underscored by Charles E. Wilson, who had left General Electric for a top post in the War Production Board. In January 1944 Wilson spoke to the Army Ordnance Association and proposed a long-term arrangement under which business would maintain permanent liaison with the military. This would keep the nation prepared for any future emergency. The military-industrial complex reached maturity later, but it had its origins in World War II.

Just as the war modernized and consolidated industry, so it helped create big agriculture and big labor. Farm population declined by 17 percent from 1940 to 1945 as people left the countryside for jobs in factories and shipyards. But farmers' output and productivity climbed sharply as a result of good weather, increased use of fertilizers, greater mechanization, and the consolidation of small farms into large ones. A million more tractors were in use at the end than at the beginning of the war. Not only did the war hasten the appearance of large-scale, mechanized farming, but it also increased the strength of organized labor. Trade unions attracted millions of members, gained a foothold in new industries, and made collective bargaining accepted practice.

The United States emerged from the war a more highly urban and technological society. The government greatly expanded its role in supporting scientific research and training. Wartime advances in medicine, particularly in the production of penicillin, saved countless lives. Some 12 million men entered the armed services, and many later received a college education or technical training under the GI Bill of Rights. More than 15 million civilians moved to new homes. Cities with shipyards, aircraft plants, or munition factories grew at a staggering rate. Six large cities attracted 2 million migrants; California alone received 1.4 million people. As one observer noted, "the whole pattern of our economic and social life is undergoing kaleidoscopic changes, without so much as a bomb being dropped on our shores."

TRUMAN'S TROUBLES: THE POLITICS OF INFLATION

On April 12, 1945, a stunned nation heard that Franklin Roosevelt had suddenly died of a stroke at his retreat in Warm Springs, Georgia. Harry S. Truman, who succeeded to the presidency, was quite unlike his predecessor. Roosevelt had been born to wealth and status on a Hudson River estate; the Delano family traced its lineage back to William the Conqueror. Truman came from a family in modest circumstances; like FDR, he had a middle initial, but since his parents could not agree what the S stood for, he had no middle name. Roosevelt had attended Groton, Har-

vard, and Columbia Law School. Truman, upon graduation from high
school, worked as a railroad timekeeper, in a newspaper mailroom, as a
bank clerk, and on a farm. After a stint in the Army during World War I,
Truman entered the haberdashery business and then took evening courses
for two years at the Kansas City Law School. Later, Boss Tom Pendergast
of Kansas City chose him to run for county judge and in 1934 picked him
for the U.S. Senate. Roosevelt selected Truman as his running mate in
1944 because he was the second choice of each faction in the Democratic
party—labor, city bosses, the South—and the only candidate they all
found acceptable. Roosevelt seldom made a rash decision; Truman often
acted on impulse. Associates usually described FDR as "sphinx-like"; Truman told everyone just what he thought.

Truman, like Roosevelt, had to contend with the problem of inflation
but in a different and less favorable context. During the war Roosevelt
fought inflation with wage ceilings, price controls, rationing, and taxes.
This worked for several reasons: accepting sacrifices seemed the patriotic
thing to do; the system left room for improved living standards; the draft
removed millions of servicemen from the consumer-goods market; many
were content to save money and pay off old debts. Yet a day of reckoning
had to come, and it arrived in 1946, the first full year of peace. Truman
endeavored to keep a lid on wages and prices, but he found that people
who had postponed buying consumer goods for several years were no
longer willing to accept government controls. The longer those controls
lasted the more oppressive they seemed. Moreover, Truman faced a legislature that, having taken a back seat during the war, was anxious to reassert its prerogatives.

A battle soon developed over Truman's attempt to preserve the powerful wartime Office of Price Administration. The OPA faced criticism
from businessmen who wanted to raise prices and, ironically, from consumers who were tired of doing without certain items. In 1946, responding to these pressures, Congress extended the OPA but stripped it of
much authority. Truman recognizd that if he signed the measure he
would be expected to keep prices down even though the OPA would lack
the means of doing so. He vetoed the bill, controls expired on July 1,
1946, and prices skyrocketed. The cost of living index rose 6 percent in
just one month. The administration employed a few stopgap measures to
curb inflation but none was successful. The consumer price index rose
more than 24 points from July 1946 to July 1947, compared with less
than 4 points in the preceding year. Prices continued their upward spiral
through 1948.

Labor difficulties plagued the Truman administration no less than
rising prices. A rash of strikes broke out in 1946 as automobile, steel, electrical, and communications workers walked off their jobs in an effort to
win higher wages and consolidate wartime gains. In 1946, 4.6 million
workers went on strike, more than ever before in the nation's history.
Strikes by railroad workers and coal miners presented especially severe
challenges to the administration. In both cases, unions refused to accept

arbitrated settlements. Truman, believing that the walkouts jeopardized national security, intervened by taking over the railroads and mines. When the unions persisted the President was furious. He harshly denounced the railroad workers, called for legislation authorizing him to draft strikers, and spoke of the need to "hang a few traitors and make our own country safe for democracy." He sought and obtained an injunction against the United Mine Workers which, after the Supreme Court upheld the President, had to pay a stiff fine. Although both disputes were ultimately settled, Truman's proposal to draft strikers and willingness to use an injunction enraged organized labor.

By November 1946 the various strands in the old New Deal coalition were unraveling, and the Democrats suffered a sharp setback in the congressional elections. Running on the slogan "Had Enough?" the Republicans picked up 11 seats in the Senate and 56 in the House, thereby capturing control of Congress for the first time since 1928. Democrat J. William Fulbright of Arkansas even suggested that Truman provide the Republican administration the voters obviously wanted by appointing a Republican as Secretary of State (at that time the position next in order of presidential succession) and then resigning from office. Truman did nothing of the sort. Instead, by capitalizing on the behavior of the Republican Congress he began to reconstruct a viable political coalition.

First, Truman made a peace offering to organized labor by vetoing the Taft-Hartley Act in June 1947. Congress had passed the measure in response to postwar labor turmoil and opinion polls that showed two out of three people favoring tighter control of union activities. The bill outlawed the closed shop, banned such union activities as secondary boycotts, provided for an 80-day cooling-off period before calling a strike if the President thought it would cause a national emergency, barred union contributions to political parties, and required labor officials to sign affidavits attesting that they were not subversive. It also permitted states to pass "right to work" laws outlawing the union shop. (In a closed shop, only union members could be hired; in a union shop, anyone hired had to join the union.) Truman declared the act unworkable, unfair, and arbitrary, but a coalition of Republicans and Southern Democrats easily overrode his veto. Truman's message nevertheless went far toward mending fences with the labor movement.

Next, Truman appealed to religious and ethnic minorities by urging a liberal entrance policy toward refugees. More than 1.2 million "displaced persons," mainly Catholics and Jews from Eastern Europe, were living in camps in American-held zones. Many had been seized by the Germans during the war and used as forced laborers. Others had fled from areas that had fallen under Russian control. Truman admitted 42,000 displaced persons in 1945, and he then urged Congress to revise the immigration laws so as to admit 400,000 a year. The old restrictionist argument—that immigrants were dangerous radicals—hardly made sense when applied to people fleeing Communist rule. Yet Congress did nothing in 1947. The following year it passed a lukewarm measure admitting

200,000 displaced persons over a two-year period but excluding most Jews and many Catholics. Terming the bill "flagrantly discriminatory," Truman signed it reluctantly.

Finally, Truman attempted to allay any suspicion that his administration was "soft on communism," a theme successfully exploited by Republicans in the 1946 congressional elections. Public opinion polls that year revealed that most Americans considered communism an internal menace. Fear was reinforced when the Canadian government announced that it had broken a Soviet espionage ring and again when the House Committee on Un-American Activities began a new round of hearings into alleged subversion in government. In 1947 Truman responded. The Justice Department instituted deportation proceedings against aliens with communist affiliations and began drawing up a list of subversive organizations. The administration also introduced a comprehensive loyalty program under which all federal employees would undergo security checks. The program was couched in loose, and potentially dangerous, language. An employee could be fired if "reasonable grounds exist for belief that the person involved is disloyal." Those grounds included acts of treason or espionage, advocacy of violent revolution, or "membership in, affiliation with or sympathetic association with" any organization on the Attorney General's list.

These initiatives were closely related to the hardening of Cold War positions. By 1947, as relations with the Soviet Union deteriorated, Americans came increasingly to accept the view (which had earlier been held during the period of the Nazi-Soviet pact) that Russian communism closely resembled German fascism. Both were characterized by purges, concentration camps, secret police, and one-party rule. Both fomented subversion abroad. Both were aggressive and expansionist. Both understood only one thing: force. "A totalitarian state is no different whether you call it Nazi, Fascist, Communist," Truman told his daughter. "The oligarchy in Russia . . . is a Frankenstein dictatorship worse than any of the others, Hitler included." In 1941 the American people had developed an image of Germany that sustained them through four years of hot war. By 1947 they were developing an image of Russia that would prepare them for twenty years of cold war.

Suggested Reading

Wartime domestic policies are analyzed in Richard Polenberg, *War and Society: The United States, 1941–1945* (1972); James M. Burns, *Roosevelt: The Soldier of Freedom* (1970); Geoffrey Perrett, *Days of Sadness, Years of Triumph* (1973); and John M. Blum, *V Was For Victory: Politics and American Culture During World War II* (1976).

Useful studies of wartime economic regulation include George Flynn, *The Mess in Washington* (1979); David Novick et al., *Wartime Production Controls* (1949); and Herman Somers, *Presidential Agency: The Office of War Mobilization and*

Reconversion (1950). On taxation and finance, see John M. Blum, ed., *From the Morgenthau Diaries: Years of War* (1967); on price control, see Harvey C. Mansfield et al., *A Short History of the OPA* (1947). The impact of the war on agriculture is considered in Walter W. Wilcox, *The Farmer in the Second World War* (1947); and on labor in Joel Seidman, *American Labor from Defense to Reconversion* (1953). David Ross, *Preparing for Ulysses, 1940–1946* (1969) contains an excellent account of the GI Bill of Rights. Alan Winkler, *The Politics of Propaganda* (1978), evaluates the Office of War Information.

For the civil rights movement during the war, consult Neil A. Wynn, *The Afro-American and the Second World War* (1975); Herbert Garfinkel, *When Negroes March* (1959); Louis Ruchames, *Race, Jobs, and Politics* (1948); and August Meier and Elliott Rudwick, *CORE: A Study in the Civil Rights Movement, 1942–1968* (1973). Two important studies of black workers are Robert Weaver, *Negro Labor* (1946); and Herbert Northrup, *Organized Labor and the Negro* (1944). Racial policies of the military are analyzed in Richard M. Dalfiume, *Desegregation of the U.S. Armed Forces, 1939–1953* (1969); and racial tensions in Dominic J. Capeci, Jr., *The Harlem Riot of 1943* (1977).

General surveys of civil liberties include Edward S. Corwin, *Total War and the Constitution* (1947); C. Herman Pritchett. *The Roosevelt Court* (1948); Alpheus T. Mason, *Harlan Fiske Stone* (1956); and Francis Biddle, *In Brief Authority* (1962). Two excellent studies of conscientious objectors are Mulford Sibley and Philip Jacob, *Conscription of Conscience, 1940–1947* (1952); and Lawrence Witner, *Rebels Against War: The American Peace Movement, 1941–1960* (1969). Evacuation and relocation of Japanese-Americans have been explored most recently in Roger Daniels, *Concentration Camps: USA* (1971); Audrie Girdner and Anne Loftis, *The Great Betrayal* (1969); and Bill Hosokawa, *Nisei: The Quiet Americans* (1969). See, in addition, Jacobus ten Broek et al., *Prejudice, War and the Constitution* (1954).

Government policies concerning labor and manpower are considered in Melvyn Dubofsky and Warren VanTine, *John L. Lewis: A Biography* (1977); Byron Fairchild and Jonathan Grossman, *The Army and Industrial Manpower* (1959); and Albert A. Blum, *Drafted or Deferred* (1967). Labor's political role is discussed in Matthew Josephson, *Sidney Hillman* (1952). Useful studies of the social impact of war are Francis E. Merrill, *Social Problems on the Home Front* (1948); Robert Havighurst and H. G. Morgan, *The Social History of a War-Boom Community* (1951); Lowell Carr and James Stermer, *Willow Run* (1952); and Katherine Archibald, *Wartime Shipyard: A Study in Social Disunity* (1947).

For the problems confronting Harry Truman, see Alonzo Hamby, *Beyond the New Deal: Harry S. Truman and American Liberalism* (1973); Bert Cochran, *Harry S. Truman and the Crisis Presidency* (1973); and Cabell Phillips, *The Truman Presidency* (1966). Two more specialized studies are R. Alton Lee, *Truman and Taft-Hartley* (1966); and Susan Hartmann, *Truman and the 80th Congress* (1971).

Martha Graham's contribution to modern dance is explained in Don McDonagh, *Martha Graham* (1973).

GIs getting their first warm rations after fifteen days of fighting in the Hurtgen Forest, Germany.

CHAPTER TEN
1941–1947
One World into Two

PRAISE THE LORD AND PASS
THE AMMUNITION!
Words and music by Frank Loesser

Down with the gunner, a bullet was his fate;
Down went the gunner, and then the gun-
ner's mate;
Up jumped the sky pilot, gave the boys a
look,
And manned the gun himself as he laid
aside the Book, shouting:

Refrain:
"Praise the Lord, and pass the ammunition!
Praise the Lord, and pass the ammunition!
Praise the Lord, and pass the ammunition
And we'll all stay free!

Praise the Lord, and swing into position,
Can't afford to sit around a'wishin';
Praise the Lord, we're all between perdition
And the deep blue sea!"

Yes, the sky pilot said it,
You've got to give him credit,
For a son of a gun of a gunner was he,
shouting:

"Praise the Lord, we're on a mighty mission!
All aboard! We're not a-goin' fishin';
Praise the Lord, and pass the ammunition
And we'll all stay free."

On the home front Americans were single-minded in their pursuit of victory. On the battlefield they waged campaigns with the same determination. Diplomatically, however, United States policies were divided, even contradictory. On the one hand, the Roosevelt administration sought a united world, devoid of exclusive economic or political spheres, in which open access to all areas could be enjoyed by every nation that could compete. This vision was embodied in the Atlantic Charter of 1941. But on the other hand, Roosevelt had to come to an agreement with his two great allies, Great Britain and Russia, who feared that they had been so weakened by war that they could not compete peacefully against the gigantic American power. They therefore sought their own exclusive spheres of influence. Washington finally made England abandon its policies of spheres, but could never force Stalin to do so. In 1945 FDR, then Truman, finally opted for an open world and so opposed a Soviet sphere of influence in Eastern Europe. The confrontation thus began, slowly at first, then through a series of crises, until in 1947 the Truman Doctrine and the Marshall Plan publicly signaled the beginning of a quarter-century in which the two great powers divided, exploited, and nearly destroyed the world.

CHURCHILL AND STALIN VERSUS ROOSEVELT

Even before Pearl Harbor, the United States had begun preparing for the postwar peace. The planning took on new urgency on June 23, 1941, when Hitler suddenly invaded the Soviet Union. Except for a brief honeymoon period in late 1933, Russia and the United States had been opponents since the 1890s. The 1941–45 alliance provided only a brief interlude in this history of confrontation. Some Americans thought Hitler might quickly defeat the Soviets. Secretary of War Henry Stimson told FDR that Germany might need no longer than one to three months to conquer Russia. Senator Harry S. Truman, Democrat of Missouri, unfortunately made public his hope that Hitler's and Stalin's forces would bleed one another white on the plains of Russia. Roosevelt took a different course. He ordered immediate aid to Stalin and then began a Lend-Lease program, which by 1945 had pumped $11 billion worth of goods into Russia. He managed to do this despite strong anti-Soviet opposition in Congress. FDR and his top advisors hoped that Russia would stop the German armies, and as the summer passed, it seemed that Russia was succeeding. Churchill had stated the principle on which Roosevelt acted: he would make a pact with the devil himself, the Prime Minister declared, if this would help defeat Hitler.

Roosevelt then focused on another danger. After Hitler's invasion of Russia, Churchill and Stalin had exchanged messages that the State Department feared involved deals on postwar boundaries, possibly even a division of Europe into British and Russian spheres. To clarify this explosive problem, Roosevelt and Churchill secretly met off the coast of New-foundland in August. In the "Atlantic Charter" issued publicly after the meeting, two key provisions gave the President what he demanded. One clause pledged "respect [for] the right of all peoples to choose the form of government under which they will live." These words applied to victims of Germany and Japan, but they could relate to the Baltic states and to areas of Finland and Eastern Europe that the Soviets had claimed since 1939. The phrase could also mean that parts of the British Empire (such as India and Hong Kong) could leave the Empire—as Washington had long hoped they would.

Another provision of the Charter declared that Churchill and FDR "will endeavor with due respect for their existing obligations, to further the enjoyment of all States, great or small, victor or vanquished, of access, on equal terms, to the trade and to the raw materials of the world which are needed for their economic prosperity." Churchill strongly objected to this clause, for he knew that it aimed at destroying the exclusive British Commonwealth preferential trading system. The Prime Minister yielded only when "with due respect for their existing obligations" was added. But he finally had to lend his endorsement, owing to British dependence on American aid. In February 1942, the United States turned the screws tighter. In return for a long-term Lend-Lease pledge from FDR, the British had to promise to discuss the dismantling of their Imperial Preference system after the war.

Roosevelt and Hull were elated. The key to postwar planning lay in Anglo-American cooperation, for before the war these two powers accounted for half the world's trade. Postwar trade would now be done on American terms, not British. As Hull had long believed, moreover, economic success could be quickly translated into a political triumph. In mid-December, British Foreign Secretary Anthony Eden visited Stalin, who immediately demanded Anglo-American agreement to cutting up postwar Germany and giving Russia control of the Baltic states and a large slice of eastern Poland. Eden refused, arguing that he would have to clear the matter with Roosevelt. Stalin angrily replied, "I thought the Atlantic Charter was directed against [Hitler and Tojo]. It now looks as if the charter were directed against the U.S.S.R." Eden would not budge, but the following month when FDR asked Russia to agree to the Atlantic Charter, Stalin did so only after adding the formal reservation that "the practical application of these principles will necessarily adapt itself to the circumstances, needs, and historic peculiarities of particular countries. . . ." Behind these words lurked the causes of the Cold War: Soviet refusal to allow anyone to claim a right to interfere in Eastern Europe, an area which the Germans had twice used as an avenue to invade Russia during the past 25 years.

Roosevelt and Hull had brought the British to heel. Stalin, however, refused to accept the American vision of the postwar world when he added the reservation to the Atlantic Charter. He had given warning.

ONE WORLD—OR
GULLIBLE'S TRAVELS

The central issues of the Cold War were thus in plain view as early as 1942. The question was how FDR and Stalin would deal with them. Washington officials agreed that the most important priority must be a global economic program, resting on Atlantic Charter principles, that would remove the danger of another worldwide depression. Assistant Secretary of State William Clayton put it starkly: if Americans could not be assured of an orderly and secure postwar world, the United States itself would become an "armed camp," living "by ration books for the next century or so." Vice-President Henry Wallace warned that without comprehensive planning, "a series of economic storms will follow this war. These will take the form of inflation and temporary scarcities, followed by surpluses, crashing prices, unemployment, bankruptcy, and in some cases violent revolution." Wendell Willkie capsulized the solution to such dangers in the title of his best-selling book of 1943, *One World*. Willkie's blasts at exclusive spheres (particularly those in the British Empire) led Churchill sarcastically to suggest that Willkie's book be subtitled "Gullible's Travels." But the phrase "one world" said it all: haunted by the ghost of Depression Past, Americans determined to find markets for their inevitable postwar surpluses in a "one world" undivided and indivisible.

Of course this required, as Hull told FDR in early 1942, that the United States oppose any "arrangement which would make the Soviet Union the dominating power of Eastern Europe if not the whole continent." The last part of Hull's admonition was crucial. The Eastern European market itself was not of great importance to Americans, but Soviet control would present a grave danger as a precedent. If Stalin succeeded there, he might use it as a lever to gain influence in the remainder of Europe. If he did forge a private sphere, moreover, his success might encourage the British to repudiate the Atlantic Charter and reestablish their own spheres. Instead of "one world," there would again, as in the 1930s, be a world divided economically and politically. Roosevelt and his countrymen would be back in the dark days of 1938. As Wallace, Clayton, and many others warned, that simply could not be allowed to happen.

In early 1942 Roosevelt tried to bring the Russians around. In one sense his position was weak, for American military forces were inactive in the European theater and retreating in the Pacific. The Japanese mopped up the Philippines, humiliating captured Americans by driving them on a horrible "death march" on the Bataan Peninsula. General Douglas MacArthur, American commander in the Pacific, fled the Philippines to establish headquarters in Australia. The Japanese would not be stopped until mid-year at the gigantic naval battle of Midway, and then in hand-to-hand fighting at Guadalcanal. In Russia, Soviet troops only slowed Hitler's forces. This added to Roosevelt's problems, for Stalin pushed hard for Anglo-American armies to open a second front in Western Europe to relieve the German pressure.

Against this background, Soviet Foreign Minister V. M. Molotov arrived in Washington in May 1942. He wanted to discuss postwar boundaries, but FDR avoided embarrassing conversations by suggesting instead that after the war "four policemen" (the United States, the U.S.S.R., Great Britain, and China) should patrol the world. Molotov and later Stalin readily agreed, for they believed that as a "policeman," Russia would be able to take what it needed in Eastern Europe. This was not at all what Roosevelt had in mind, but the contradictions in the "four policemen" concept would not be faced for another three years. Despite the idea's problems, Roosevelt wanted to avoid discussing specific postwar settlements. Such a discussion could lead to Soviet-American arguments and disillusionment at home. Moreover, the longer he waited, the more financial and military power FDR thought he could bring to bear on Stalin.

A second remark to Molotov had immediate repercussions. Roosevelt promised a second front by late 1942. He probably did this to quiet Molotov on the boundary question. Whatever the reason, Molotov and Stalin were elated. They believed that the Russian people would shortly no longer be alone in engaging Hitler's main forces. But there was no second front in 1942. Churchill killed the plan by refusing to agree that such a campaign could be safely opened so soon.

The Prime Minister instead urged that Anglo-American forces invade North Africa, where the Nazis and their French collaborators, the Vichy French government, held strategic positions in the Mediterranean. Roosevelt realized that Churchill was advancing this plan in part because North Africa had long been vital to the British and French empires, but he finally acquiesced in order to get American soldiers engaged in the European theater. The operation also led Roosevelt into a closer working relationship with the Vichy French. If the Vichyites would cooperate, the invasion might be bloodless and a large part of the French fleet turned over intact to the Allies. This working with Nazi collaborators has since been roundly condemned, particularly after the invasion of November 1942 turned out to be not at all bloodless. FDR survived that mistake, but he could not overcome Stalin's bitterness that the second front had been promised—and then repudiated. It almost looked as if Churchill and Roosevelt preferred reclaiming the British and French empires while leaving Stalin alone to endure the full might of Hitler's armies.

1943—TURNING OF THE TIDE

The Grand Alliance was in trouble by early 1943. Roosevelt tried to repair the damage by asking Stalin and Churchill to meet him at Casablanca in January. Stalin refused, pleading that the climactic struggle at Stalingrad required his constant attention. He asked only that the second front be opened immediately. FDR replied that this certainly could be done in 1943. At Casablanca, however, Churchill once more refused, insisting that since the Allies were not yet militarily prepared, they instead should move from North Africa into Sicily and then Italy. FDR again reluctantly ac-

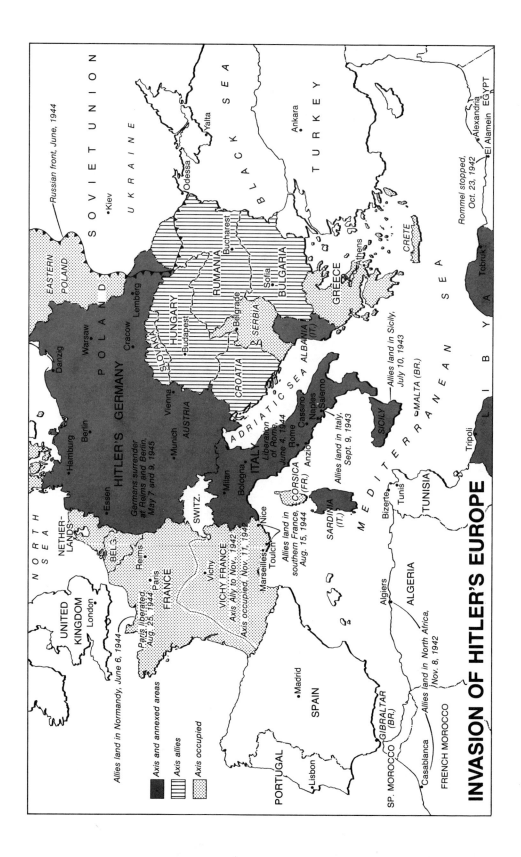

INVASION OF HITLER'S EUROPE

Legend:
- Axis and annexed areas
- Axis allies
- Axis occupied

Russian front, June, 1944

SOVIET UNION

UKRAINE

Kiev•

•Yalta

•Odessa

BLACK SEA

•Ankara

TURKEY

EASTERN POLAND

Danzig•

Warsaw•

POLAND

•Cracow

Lemberg•

SLOVAKIA

HUNGARY

•Budapest

CROATIA

SERBIA

•Belgrade

RUMANIA

•Bucharest

•Sofia

BULGARIA

ALBANIA (IT.)

Athens•

GREECE

CRETE

Germans surrender at Reims and Berlin, May 7 and 9, 1945

HITLER'S GERMANY

•Hamburg

Berlin•

•Vienna

AUSTRIA

•Munich

•Essen

SWITZ.

Milan•

Bologna•

ITALY

ADRIATIC SEA

Liberation of Rome, June 4, 1944

Cassino

Rome•

Anzio•

•Naples

•Salerno

SICILY

MALTA (BR.)

Allies land in Sicily, July 10, 1943

Allies land in Italy, Sept. 9, 1943

Tripoli•

MEDITERRANEAN SEA

LIBYA

•Tobruk

Rommel stopped, Oct. 23, 1942

Alexandria•

El Alamein•

EGYPT

NORTH SEA

NETHER-LANDS

BELG.

•Reims

Paris liberated, Aug. 25, 1944

Paris•

FRANCE

•Vichy

VICHY FRANCE
Axis Ally to Nov. 1942
Axis occupied Nov. 11, 1942

Marseilles•

Toulon•

•Nice

Allies land in southern France, Aug. 15, 1944

CORSICA (FR.)

SARDINIA (IT.)

Bizerte•

•Tunis

TUNISIA

Allies land in Normandy, June 6, 1944

UNITED KINGDOM

•London

SPAIN

•Madrid

PORTUGAL

•Lisbon

GIBRALTAR (BR.)

SP. MOROCCO

FRENCH MOROCCO

•Casablanca

Allies land in North Africa, Nov. 8, 1942

•Algiers

ALGERIA

quiesced, but tried to soften the blow for Stalin by announcing that unlike 1918, when the Germans were not thoroughly defeated, the Allies this time would only accept "unconditional surrender." This sudden announcement was risky, for it threatened to lengthen the war by driving the German people into a last-ditch resistance. Roosevelt and Churchill were willing to take that chance in order to placate Stalin. By insisting on unconditional surrender they assured Russia that although no second front was in sight, they would nevertheless continue the war until a defeated Germany would no longer threaten the Soviets.

It was interesting diplomacy, but also increasingly irrelevant. A week after FDR made his pledge, Russian armies stopped the Germans at Stalingrad, capturing hundreds of thousands of Hitler's finest troops. By mid-summer the Soviets had regained two-thirds of their lost territory. Russia had battled 80 percent of Hitler's total force, stopped it and was now driving it back, doing so without the often promised, but never delivered, second front. Stalin's need for his western allies was still great, but dropping markedly. Indeed FDR was becoming the supplicant, for he wanted the Soviets to promise they would fight Japan after the conclusion of the European struggle. The military campaigns of 1943 drastically changed the diplomatic relationships between Russia and her two allies.

And so did a political crisis in Italy. After invading that country, the Americans and British refused to allow the Soviets to have any influence in reconstructing the Italian government. Fearful that Stalin would help Italy's large Communist party gain power, Churchill argued, "We cannot be put in a position where our two armies [the American and British] are doing all the fighting but Russians have a veto and must be consulted." FDR agreed, observing that the Allied military commander, General Dwight D. Eisenhower, must have complete authority. The Russians were thus excluded, but at a tremendous cost. For Stalin would repeatedly use the Italian precedent to justify Russian control of postliberation policies in Eastern Europe. If the Russians were not to have "access" to Italy as the Atlantic Charter seemed to promise, then, Stalin could argue, the Charter might as well not apply to Eastern Europe either. He was indeed perfectly willing to accept such a division. Stalin believed that each ally had its own security interests. The question was whether the Americans would accept this splitting of Europe into political spheres or try to have it both ways: exclude the Soviets from Italy but insist that the United States have a voice in Eastern Europe. That key issue was becoming sharper.

Churchill, Roosevelt, and Stalin met for the first time at Teheran, Iran, in late November 1943 to bind together the splintering alliance. On the surface, discussions went smoothly. The three men established easy personal relationships, doubtlessly helped along by Churchill's and FDR's firm pledge that a second front would be opened in France within six months. Stalin in turn promised he would fight Japan after Hitler's defeat. FDR himself raised the crucial question of Russia's western boundary, telling Stalin that he "did not intend to go to war with the Soviet Union" over Russian absorption of the Baltic States. A quick agreement was also reached that the Polish-Russian boundary must be moved westward at the expense of Poland.

But the conference floundered on a pivotal question of the Polish postwar government. Since 1940 a pro-western Polish government-in-exile had operated in London, while a pro-Communist Polish regime worked out of Russia. When the London group refused to accept a new Polish-Russian boundary, Stalin would not recognize the group. The hatred burst into the open in mid-1943, when the bodies of 4200 Polish soldiers were discovered in Poland's Katyn Forest. The London Poles immediately—and probably correctly—charged Russia with having slaughtered the men during fighting in 1940. These charges added a tragic dimension to an already explosive problem. The Big Three could not reach agreement on either the composition of a postwar Polish government or a Polish-German boundary. Stalin wanted the boundary moved westward, but Churchill particularly resisted this move on two grounds: it would unduly weaken postwar Germany (a prospect that did not at all displease Stalin), and it would repeat the mistakes of 1919 by giving the Germans a cause for future aggression. For the next 18 months the sore of Poland festered, spreading a cancerous infection within the Grand Alliance.

Two acts of wartime diplomacy had now been played. The first had set the theme with the Atlantic Charter and the British and Russian opposition to its principles. The second act, played out in Italy and Teheran, had brought into the open the dilemmas that would wreck the postwar peace. The third act, which in traditional theater resolves the crises of Act II, would occur with the Yalta conference and its aftermath. Instead of resolving the crises, however, Act III would become a nerve-wracking, multibillion-dollar, thirty-five-year long serial.

ONE WORLD BECOMES TWO: YALTA AND AFTERWARDS

On June 6, 1944, Allied troops under the command of General Eisenhower swept ashore on the Normandy beaches in the largest amphibious operation in history. Led by General George Patton's Third Army, the forces broke through German resistance, liberating Paris in late August and crossing into Germany in mid-September. Devastating air raids hit German war industries, while an unsuccessful attempt to assassinate Hitler in July by some of his closest military advisors indicated the extent of the Nazis' internal weakness. Stalin meanwhile launched a major offensive that conquered much of Eastern Europe in 1944.

Churchill now faced a dilemma. The British had important economic and political interests in Hungary, Yugoslavia, and particularly Greece. The Greek situation was especially sensitive, for that nation bordered the Eastern Mediterranean (one of the so-called lifelines of the British Empire to Egypt and India). But Churchill's attempt to restore the Greek King's power had produced a civil war in which Greek Communists

D-Day: The Normandy Invasion, 1944.

helped the antimonarchical forces. The Prime Minister flew to Moscow and in a dramatic meeting with Stalin worked out, on a half-sheet of scrap paper, a deal that would give Russia control of Rumania and Bulgaria, give Churchill full power in Greece, and divide Yugoslavia and Hungary equally. Roosevelt warned that he would not be bound by this division, but Churchill went ahead, over violent American objections, to quell the Greek civil war with force. Stalin kept his part of the bargain by staying out of that situation and clamping firm control over Rumania.

As they made plans for the Big Three conference scheduled at the Soviet resort city of Yalta in February 1945, gloom was settling over Washington officials. It darkened when in December 1944 the Germans launched a last-ditch counteroffensive that drove a huge bulge into Eisenhower's lines. Only heroics by General Patton and a surrounded American force at Bastogne, Belgium, which delayed the German onslaught by refusing to surrender, finally ended the "Battle of the Bulge." The rapidly advancing Soviets were meanwhile only 50 miles from Berlin. As Roosevelt sat down at Yalta to reconstruct the world, he held few high cards. FDR nevertheless managed to work out agreements on four major problems.

First, the Big Three decided to flesh out a postwar United Nations organization. They had concluded in 1944 that the UN, like the League, would have a Security Council dominated by the four great powers, a General Assembly, a Secretariat, and an International Court of Justice. At Yalta FDR agreed to give Russia three votes in the General Assembly (in

Patton, Eisenhower, and U.S. servicemen, Germany, 1945.

order, so Stalin argued, to offset Great Britain's half-dozen votes of the Commonwealth nations), but only if the United States might, if it wished, also have three votes. Each of the Big Four (U.S., U.S.S.R., Great Britain, and China) would have a veto in the Security Council over substantive issues. Roosevelt had maneuvering room here, for both Stalin and the United States insisted on preserving maximum national power through possession of a veto. The UN, however, would be able at the most to *maintain* the peace. The question at Yalta was whether the Big Three would be able to *construct* a peace.

A second point of discussion offered some hope, for Roosevelt and Stalin quickly settled Far Eastern questions. In return for Russia's promise to fight Japan within three months after Hitler's surrender, FDR secretly agreed that Stalin could have influence in Manchuria, possession of southern Sakhalin and the Kurile Islands, and a lease on the base of Port Arthur. American military advisors, including General MacArthur, had warned FDR that Russian warfare against Japan was necessary if he were to avoid the 1 million Allied casualties that would probably result from an invasion of the Japanese home islands. Given such warnings, and the probability that, once in the Pacific war, Stalin would take by force what FDR had already promised, the Yalta agreements on the Pacific were justified.

A third discussion at Yalta did not end as amicably, for it involved Poland. The Teheran decision on a new Polish-Soviet border was quickly reaffirmed, but again no agreement could be reached on the Polish-German boundary. Stalin wanted the border moved to the Oder-Neisse Rivers, so that Poland would incorporate large areas of prewar Germany. Churchill objected: "It would be a pity to stuff the Polish goose so full of German food that it died of indigestion." (Stalin later provided the necessary medicine simply by removing hundreds of thousands of Germans from the area and giving it to Poland. The West would not recognize the boundary until the early 1970s.)

The major argument, however, centered on the composition of the Polish government. In late summer, 1944, a new controversy had further embittered this issue. When Russian troops drove to the outskirts of Warsaw, Polish underground fighters attacked the Nazis within the city. The Soviet attack then stalled, in part for military reasons, although Stalin was forthright in calling the anti-Soviet underground "a handful of power-seeking criminals." The Nazis then turned and exterminated the Poles. Stalin would not allow American planes to attempt dropping supplies to the underground fighters until it was too late. In January 1945, after the Soviets had finally captured Warsaw, Stalin moved in his own Polish regime as the legitimate government.

Churchill and FDR refused to go along, and finally obtained Stalin's agreement that the government was to be "more broadly based" and "reorganized with the inclusion of democratic leaders from Poland itself and from Poles abroad." The new government would hold "free and unfettered elections" as soon as possible on the basis of universal suffrage and a secret ballot. (Such an election would never be held.) Shortly after Yalta, FDR and Churchill exchanged angry notes with Stalin over the meaning of "reorganized." Stalin insisted this meant simply adding a few pro-western Poles to the Communist regime in Warsaw. FDR, however, demanded a complete restructuring of the government. He was on weak ground. At Yalta his Military Chief of Staff, Admiral William Leahy, had remarked that the Polish agreement was "so elastic that the Russians can stretch it all the way from Yalta to Washington without technically breaking it." FDR understood, but insisted that this was the best he could do. The President made only one other half-hearted effort to straighten out his policies when he asked Churchill and Stalin to sign a "Declaration on Liberated Europe," which pledged application of the Atlantic Charter principles to liberated countries. Stalin accepted only after inserting an amendment that made the Declaration meaningless.

The failure to reach an agreement on Poland made this issue the "symbol" of the Russian-American conflict. But that struggle increasingly focused on Germany, the fourth question discussed at Yalta. Roosevelt had been torn on this issue. He wavered between fixing the Germans once and for all ("they should be fed three times a day with soup from Army soup kitchens" he commented, and once even mentioned the possibility of mass castration), and rebuilding Germany under tight controls so it could be the core of a healthy Europe. He finally chose the second alternative under strong pressure from Hull and Stimson. They argued that American prosperity depended on a prosperous Europe, which in turn required a rebuilt Germany. That nation, after all, had been the industrial hub of the continent for nearly a century.

To Stalin, however, this policy looked suspiciously like 1919 all over again. "I will not tolerate a new *cordon sanitaire,*" he announced pointedly in the spring of 1945. Nor, above all, did he want a united, prosperous Germany as the cornerstone of such a *cordon.* When at Yalta Stalin tried to gain agreement on dismemberment of Germany, FDR and Churchill refused to agree. He then attempted to obtain $20 billion in German reparations (half for the Soviet Union), in order to limit Germany's industry and help rebuild Russia. FDR referred this to a study commission with instructions that the $20 billion figure be only a "basis for discussion."

The disagreement over reparations was a clue to the failure of the Yalta Conference. Stalin had two primary objectives: dismembering German power so that it never again could threaten Russia, and acquiring great quantities of industrial plant to reconstruct the Soviets' own war-devastated economy. Large German reparations would help Stalin gain both objectives. When Roosevelt and Churchill refused to agree on reparations, Stalin faced several alternatives: either obtain large loans and credits from the United States to rebuild Russia quickly, or else impose such absolute control over Eastern Europe (including East Germany) that it would serve as a Russian-dominated buffer zone between Germany and the Soviet Union and also be forced to surrender its industry for Russia's benefit.

Stalin tested the first alternative several times between 1943 and 1946. The critical moment came in January 1945, when Molotov asked Washington for a $6-billion credit. W. Averell Harriman, the American ambassador in Moscow, advised Roosevelt that the Russians "should be given to understand" that financial aid would "depend upon their behavior in international matters." Harriman's advice was accepted. The United States refused to discuss postwar aid to Russia unless the Soviets essentially opened Eastern Europe as the Atlantic Charter asked. This Stalin refused to do.

Within six weeks after Yalta, an iron curtain descended over parts of Eastern Europe. In Rumania, which had been an ally of Hitler, a Soviet official gave the King two hours to establish a government acceptable to the Communists, accentuating his demand by slamming the door so hard that the plaster cracked around the door frame. In Poland, Stalin refused to make radical changes in the pro-Russian government. Amidst this rapid deterioration, Roosevelt died on April 12, 1945. His legacy to Vice-President Harry S. Truman was not a Grand Alliance but the beginnings of the Cold War, caught perfectly by FDR in a comment made privately during his return from Yalta: "The Atlantic Charter is a beautiful idea." It was nothing more.

TRUMAN

A very different figure now entered the scene. Harry Truman had been a Missouri judge, politician, and United States senator, but he had no experience in foreign affairs. He entered the White House at precisely the time American policy was hardening against the Soviets. Truman was never confronted with the alternatives that Roosevelt had struggled with between 1942 and Yalta. FDR had tried to handle the dilemma—whether to try to enforce the Atlantic Charter or accept political-economic spheres—by delaying until, as in the Polish question, the problem had to be confronted. Truman's temperament was more impulsive and decisive. He disliked delays, preferring to decide on a policy and then make it work. This decisiveness was reinforced by a second influence: his jealousy of, and determination to protect, his presidential powers. This jealousy resulted in part from his realization that he was an accidental President following in the hallowed footsteps of FDR. Truman was adamant in not allowing these circumstances to weaken the presidential powers. This determination easily led him to be tougher than the toughest of his advisors.

Twenty-four hours after entering office, and before he was thoroughly briefed on incredibly complex foreign policies, he told his Secretary of State, "We must stand up to the Russians at this point and not be easy with them." This view was reinforced by advisors—Harriman, Leahy, Secretary of the Navy James Forrestal, Secretary of War Stimson—all of whom harbored deep suspicions about even negotiating with Russia. By late spring Truman was convinced that he might not get "100 percent of what we wanted; but that on important matters . . . we should be able to get 85 percent." He fully realized how American economic and military power, including the possibility of a newly developed atomic bomb, might obtain that 85 percent.

The restraints on Truman were few but significant. The Red Army controlled Eastern Europe and had been the first to reach Berlin. Eisenhower's troops might have raced the Soviets to the German capital, but the American commander wisely calculated that it would not be worth the lives lost. The political division of Germany and Berlin for occupation purposes, moreover, had been determined at earlier conferences. The mighty Russian force, astride the eastern half of Europe, was the most formidable barrier conceivable to Truman's hope for realizing "85 percent."

But the President also had problems at home. Between 1940 and 1944 American industrial production rose 90 percent, total production of goods and services 60 percent. Some place had to be found to sell the products of this system, or else Americans would relive the horrors of the 1930s. Many, particularly the business community, believed that the Soviets could become the great market. "Russia will be, if not our biggest, at least our most eager, consumer when the war ends," predicted the president of the United States Chamber of Commerce in 1944. Pro-Russian sentiment also had such other roots as the propaganda about the valor of "our Russian allies"; the movies sentimentalizing the Soviets (for example,

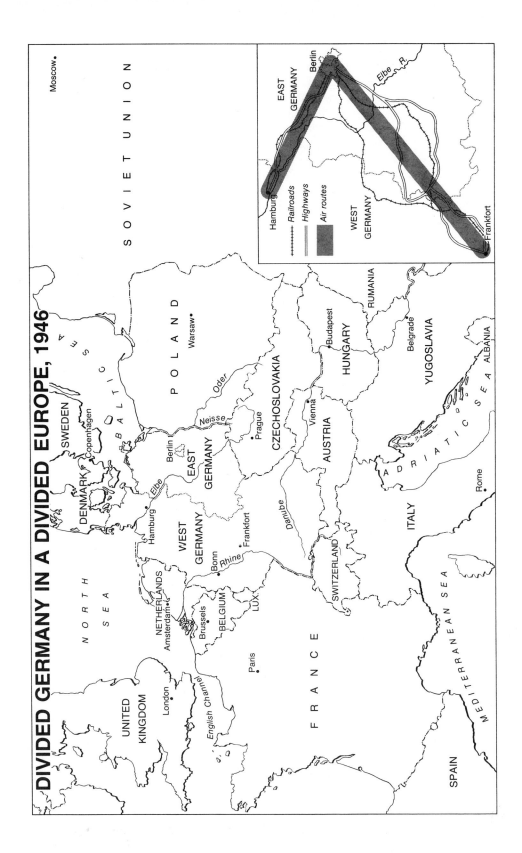

DIVIDED GERMANY IN A DIVIDED EUROPE, 1946

Moscow•

SOVIET UNION

SWEDEN

Copenhagen
DENMARK

BALTIC SEA

POLAND
Warsaw•
Oder
Neisse

Berlin
EAST
GERMANY
Elbe

Hamburg

NORTH
SEA

WEST
GERMANY
Bonn
Rhine
Frankfort

Prague
CZECHOSLOVAKIA

Vienna
AUSTRIA
Danube

Budapest•
HUNGARY

RUMANIA

Belgrade•
YUGOSLAVIA

ALBANIA

ADRIATIC SEA

NETHERLANDS
Amsterdam•
Brussels•
BELGIUM
LUX.

SWITZERLAND

ITALY

Rome•

UNITED
KINGDOM
London•

English Channel

Paris•

FRANCE

SPAIN

MEDITERRANEAN SEA

EAST
GERMANY
Berlin
Elbe R.

Hamburg

Railroads
Highways
Air routes

WEST
GERMANY
Frankfort

and the sanguine statements at the end of the conferences, which failed to mention the deep divisions separating the two nations. These Roosevelt also bequeathed along with an increasingly anti-Russian policy. Truman could not get "tough" with Stalin until Americans were ready to move straight from hot war against a common enemy to cold war against a former ally. Very few were ready to do that in 1945. The President therefore had to educate the country about the "85 percent." He received help from Stalin.

STALIN

The Soviet dictator, in the words of a fellow Communist who knew him well, combined "the senselessness of a Caligula with the refinement of a Borgia and the brutality of a Czar Ivan the Terrible." Nevertheless, this observer continued, "Viewed from the standpoint of success and political adroitness, Stalin is hardly surpassed by any statesman of his time." Seizing control after Lenin's death in 1924, Stalin became supreme through blood purges. He brutally collectivized Soviet agriculture, ruthlessly shaped Russia into a growing industrial power, and through luck and skill survived the hatreds of both the western powers and Germany between 1931 and 1945. The impact of World War II alone was incalculable: more than 15 million—perhaps 20 million—Russian dead (600,000 civilians starved to death in the battle of Leningrad alone), thousands of cities and villages decimated, agriculture and, to a lesser extent, industry destroyed. During the war, moreover, Stalin knew that his countrymen would fight harder for Mother Russia than for his Communist party, so he loosened some internal controls. But as the Nazi threat disappeared, he quickly reimposed an iron grip. He was Russian power in person.

In an attempt to explain why Stalin would not come to terms with the United States, a few historians have since blamed the dictator's paranoia, which made him increasingly deranged. This is slippery territory, but several facts are beyond dispute. No foreign diplomat—not even those dealing frequently with him—suggested at the time that Stalin showed any signs whatsoever of paranoia. More important, the substantive issues dividing Russia from the West were more than sufficient to start the Cold War. In the Soviet mind, East–West animosity was natural, for East was communist, West capitalist, and therefore, according to Leninist teachings, conflict was inevitable. Woodrow Wilson and other western leaders had earlier made Lenin appear to be a prophet when they sent troops into Russia. And during the 1930s the Soviets were convinced that the West, particularly at Munich, was trying to drive Hitler to war against Russia. These historical events were little emphasized by Americans after 1945, but they were stamped indelibly on the Soviet mind. Stalin determined that history would not repeat itself, and so he used the Red Army to dismember Germany and clamp his control over Eastern Europe. This was hardly classic communist revolution "from the bottom up." Instead, Stalin imposed control from the top down.

But he did so selectively at first. Hungary, Finland, Bulgaria, and Czechoslovakia remained independent to a considerable extent throughout 1946 and 1947. Eastern Europe did not fall behind the iron curtain with one loud clang but instead disappeared bit by bit as the victim of an escalating Soviet-American argument between 1945 and 1948. Nor did Stalin attempt to overthrow Western European governments during this time. The State Department told Truman in June 1945 that the Russians "are not too greatly concerned about developments in Western Europe so long as the Western European countries do not show signs of ganging up on them." Stalin had broken away decisively from the Marxist-Leninist ideal that world revolution be given top priority. He would settle for "socialism in one zone"—a zone of Eastern Europe, which would protect Russia strategically and help reconstruct it economically. In this zone Stalin would tolerate no intervention. After all, Churchill and FDR had tolerated none in their Italian zone. Consequently, when Truman vigorously urged democratic elections in Poland and Rumania, Stalin blandly replied, "If a government is not Fascist, a government is democratic." But on another occasion he was more candid with Truman: "A freely elected government in any of these countries would be anti-Soviet, and that we cannot allow." He would not complain if the West controlled Italy or Latin America, but, Stalin told the President bluntly, he expected Truman to show similar consideration for Russian interests.

Put simply, Russia's attention focused on Eastern and Central Europe, while America, as a worldwide, expansive economic power, took the entire globe as its province—including the Soviet sphere. For these reasons, the Cold War erupted not over questions in the Americas, Asia, or even Western Europe. It broke out because of American demands in Eastern and Central Europe, that is, in the areas that the Russians were determined to dominate.

Margaret Bourke-White and Photojournalism

If Edward R. Murrow's radio broadcasts brought the sound of war to Americans, then Margaret Bourke-White's photographs brought them its awful sight. Bourke-White's career had especially prepared her to document the terrible consequences of modern technology gone berserk. After graduating from Cornell University in 1927, Bourke-White, like many other artists at the time, became fascinated with the aesthetic of the machine. She photographed industrial plants and equipment for she thought them "sincere and unadorned in their beauty." In 1930, when Henry Luce began publishing *For-*

Margaret Bourke-White, 1943.

tune magazine—which believed that "any modern estheticism must embrace the machine"—he invited Bourke-White to serve as associate editor and photographer. Not only did she photograph examples of American technology, but she also documented military rearmament in Germany and the construction of huge dams and bridges in Russia.

By the mid-1930s Bourke-White had shifted her focus from the triumph of industry to the human anguish it produced. She began to photograph the depression's impact on America: the Dust Bowl, with its parched land and skeletons of dead animals; Southern prisons, with their pot-bellied guards and black chain-gangs; tenant farms, with their tar-paper shacks and ema-

Churchill sitting for Bourke-White, London, 1940.

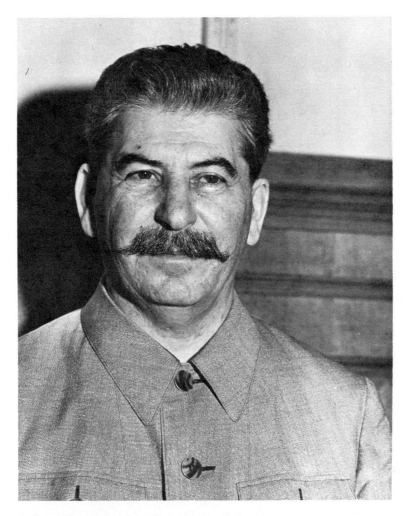

Stalin smiling for Bourke-White, Moscow, 1941.

ciated children. She published many of these photographs in *You Have Seen Their Faces* (1937), with commentary by Erskine Caldwell (to whom she was married for three years.) Bourke-White was not associated with the Farm Security Administration, which accumulated 200,000 photographs of rural America, but was, in the words of her biographer, "virtually a one-woman FSA photographic project." When Luce introduced *Life* magazine in 1936 Bourke-White became a major contributor. She

was instrumental in the development of photojournalism—structured photoessays that told a logically ordered story.

During World War II Bourke-White was at the height of her creative power. As an accredited Air Force photographer, she observed the assembling of airplane squadrons in England, flew with bombing missions over Africa, and documented American Army operations in Italy. She accompanied General George Patton in his final drive along the Rhine, and so was able to photograph the survivors of the concentration camp at Buchenwald and the charred corpses at the Leipzig-Mochau labor camp. When Patton ordered 2000 German civilians to walk through Buchenwald, Bourke-White photographed them attempting to avert their eyes from the piles of dead bodies. She also photographed Nazi officials who, fearing Allied retribution, had committed suicide along with their wives and children. Her account of all this appeared in *"Dear Fatherland, Rest Quietly"* (1946).

After the war Bourke-White photographed people and events in India and South Africa, and, when the Korean War began, she returned to the battlefield. She was one of the first to appreciate the possibilities for aerial photography provided by the newly developed helicopter. Then, during the 1950s, Bourke-White was stricken with Parkinson's disease, an illness that gradually deprived her of the ability to hold a camera steadily. She believed the disease had been triggered by the hardships she had experienced in Korea, but added: "If I had been in a position to make a choice between getting my photographs in the fog, rain and wild mountains of Korea set against the risks involved, I would still choose to get my story—Parkinson's or no Parkinson's." She battled the disease valiantly—a struggle she described in *Portrait of Myself* (1963)—until her death in 1971.

Nazi concentration camp, 1945.

POTSDAM: THE TURN
IN AMERICAN POLICY

The Soviets, so Washington officials thought, might not become capitalists overnight, but at least they might tolerate the economic plans that underlay the United States postwar program. "Nations which act as enemies in the marketplace cannot long be friends at the conference table," Assistant Secretary of State William Clayton announced in 1945. When this was applied to Communists and capitalists, Clayton was actually asking for oil and water to mix. Truman was meanwhile demanding at least an 85 percent dissolubility. But the President believed that there was no alternative.

In late April he had a stormy session with Molotov over the Polish issue, which produced only more mistrust. In June Stalin inserted several pro-Western Poles into a government that remained staunchly Communist. Making the best of a bad situation, Truman recognized the Warsaw regime, hoping that over time he could use American financial aid to change the government's policies. The Big Three then concentrated on the conference at Potsdam (on the outskirts of obliterated Berlin) where, it was hoped, German questions would be handled more satisfactorily than had those concerning Poland.

It was not to be. After acrimonious debates, the two central questions of the German-Polish boundary and reparations were lumped together and compromised. Stalin and the Poles received permission to govern part of East Germany de facto (although the area was not formally given to Poland), but Truman in turn required Stalin to accept a reparations package that gave Russia almost nothing out of the German industrial sectors controlled by British and American armies. The United States therefore retained the power to reindustrialize Western Germany (and in late 1945 and 1946 this was accomplished in rapid steps), but at the price of dividing the country. For if Stalin could not get reparations from the West, he would cordon off and exploit East Germany. The deal, therefore, helped ensure the permanent division of Germany.

It also marked a significant turn in American policy. A divided Germany meant a divided Europe. It meant giving up trying to apply the Atlantic Charter principles everywhere. Truman did not fall back immediately. Throughout 1945 and early 1946 his new Secretary of State, James F. Byrnes, worked on peace treaties that would open Eastern Europe, but the Soviets refused to agree. Potsdam was a portent. It demonstrated the abyss separating the Allies on the central issue of Germany, shook Truman with the realization that he would not get his "85 percent" after all, destroyed the hope for an immediately united and open Europe, and, therefore, forced American officials to return to the drawing board and devise new postwar plans.

CHINA: ANOTHER
REVOLUTION AMIDST
THE COLD WAR

At Potsdam, Truman and Stalin did extend earlier agreements on Asian affairs. The Asia that they discussed, however, was changing radically and rapidly. Japan, which had dominated the area for a half-century, reeled from military defeats. In 1944 American forces took Saipan and Guam in bloody fighting, providing bases from which the American air force devastated Japanese cities. Japan's industrial plants suffered (although not nearly as much as the Air Force claimed at the time), but the raids proved especially effective as a terror weapon. In one attack on Tokyo, windswept fires killed more than 80,000 Japanese.

As Japan tottered, American officials hoped that China might replace the Japanese as the balance-wheel of Asia. Roosevelt pursued this dream, for he clearly realized that if China became dominant in Asia, then it, in turn, would be dependent on American economic and military aid and, hopefully, advice. FDR's schemes even went beyond this. He believed that China and the United States in tandem could dismantle the British and French empires in Asia (including Hong Kong, India, Singapore, Burma, and French Indochina), allow China either to absorb or to police these areas, and then have China and the United States develop them. This vision explains why throughout 1943–44 Roosevelt refused to agree that after the war France should be allowed to re-enter Indochina. The President hoped that this area—comprising Vietnam, Cambodia, and Laos— would be a UN trusteeship area under the day-to-day control of China.

In mid-1944 FDR's dream collapsed when a crisis ripped apart Sino-American relations. The focal point was Chiang Kai-shek, China's leader and the pivot for FDR's plans. Harry Hopkins, Roosevelt's closest advisor, had commented that China could be one of the postwar Big Four, but only "if things go well with Chiang Kai-shek." During the spring of 1944 Chiang's government was gravely beset from two directions. The Japanese launched an attack on South China in an attempt to destroy airfields from which American planes (including the famed "Flying Tigers") were bombing Japan's bases. FDR pleaded with Chiang to throw his armies and American-supplied equipment fully into the battle, but Chiang stalled.

Roosevelt then urged him to name the American commander in China, General Joseph Stilwell, as head of the Chinese armies. Chiang and Stilwell had never gotten along; "Vinegar Joe" condescendingly called Chiang "Peanut" because of his bald head, but also because of his refusal to fight the Japanese. Chiang interpreted FDR's request as an insult, seizing the opportunity to throw Stilwell out of the country in September 1944. Roosevelt lost his illusions about China. At Yalta and Potsdam, Americans and Russians settled Asian problems without bothering to consult with the Chinese.

Chiang refused to fight the Japanese, since he was saving his troops for the more important struggle with the Chinese Communists. Since 1927 this battle had raged, primarily in the north where Mao Tse-tung's

Communist armies had taken refuge after their famous "long march" to escape Chiang's wrath in the mid-1930s. By 1944 Mao had consolidated and expanded his power, gaining support among the peasants (by 1945 he controlled one-quarter of China's population), and effectively fighting guerilla wars against both Chiang and the Japanese.

THE BOMB

In early 1945 the United States had decided to stick with Chiang and not deal seriously with Mao. By the time of the Potsdam conference in July, however, this policy was insufficient. Stalin's armies would be in the Pacific theater within a month, raising the unattractive prospect that his and Mao's forces might link up in Manchuria. At Potsdam Truman worked diligently to remove that threat, gaining from Stalin the promise that he would recognize Chiang as the official government of China. After a private lunch with Stalin, moreover, Truman told his advisors he had "clinched" the Russian acceptance of an open door in Manchuria. In return, the President reaffirmed the promises of Far Eastern territory made by FDR to Stalin at Yalta. Truman was elated, but not satisfied. By dropping an atomic bomb on Japan on August 6th and again on the 9th, he tried to end the war as soon as possible, before American troops had to die in an invasion of the home islands and preferably before Russian troops became too decisive in the fighting.

The terrible weapon that Truman now held before the world had resulted from a series of breakthroughs in physics during the interwar era. In 1939 Albert Einstein, the greatest and best-known of the physicists, wrote a simple one-page letter to Roosevelt urging him to begin development of the unknown weapon. Fearful that Hitler might obtain it first, FDR poured $2 billion into the secret Manhattan Project. (The fears were fortunately misplaced; German scientists ran into numerous dead ends and received little understanding from Hitler.) From the beginning, the bomb was built to be used under only American control. FDR evidently saw the bomb as giving him the military power he would need to police the postwar world without having to take the politically unpopular step of sending American armies overseas. At no time did he ever seriously consider sharing the bomb's secrets with Stalin. The President considered it a diplomatic as well as military weapon. Again, Truman fully accepted Roosevelt's policies. Scientists from the University of Chicago protested to Truman that a demonstration on an uninhabited area would be equally instructive to the Japanese and considerably more humane than laying it on a city. The President overruled the dissenters on grounds that the bomb might not work properly, or if it did, it should be used for maximum military effect. Besides, only two bombs could be built by August.

In mid-July 1945, the bomb was successfully tested for the first time. Truman was at Potsdam having difficulty with Stalin, but was greatly "pepped up" by news of the test. The President now began to assume an

Hiroshima, two hours after the atomic blast, two miles from the center of the explosion. The photographer later died of injuries from the explosion.

even tougher position with the Soviets. The Americans, as Churchill privately remarked at Potsdam, "do not at the present time desire Russian participation in the war against Japan." Truman no longer needed or wanted Stalin's help in the Far East. The Big Three urged Japan to surrender unconditionally, including abdication of the Emperor, or face "utter devastation." The Japanese government refused the ultimatum. Hiroshima was obliterated on August 6, killing, searing, and infecting with deadly radiation more than 100,000 people. Two days later Russia declared war and invaded Manchuria. On August 9 a second bomb destroyed Nagasaki. The militarists continued to hold out, but the Emperor took the virtually unprecedented step of overruling the government and accepting surrender if the terms did not destroy completely his role in Japanese society. Truman now accepted the condition. World War II was over. It might have ended days before, even before the two bombs were dropped, had Truman earlier accepted the Emperor's role.

The A-bomb had helped end one conflict, and throughout the summer of 1945 Truman, Stimson, and other top officials discussed how it might be used as a negotiating weapon against Russia to preclude a third world war. In June, according to Stimson's diary, he and the President had talked of possible concessions that the bomb might bring from

Russia, and Truman "mentioned the same things that I was thinking of, namely the settlement of the Polish, Rumanian, Yugoslavian, and Manchurian problems."

By September, however, Stimson had changed his mind. He warned the President that if the United States refused to cooperate with the Russians in controlling the bomb, but merely talked to them while "having this weapon ostentatiously on our hip, their suspicions and their distrust of our purposes and motives will increase." Truman refused either to negotiate the issue or to use the bomb as an explicit threat against the Soviets. Perhaps he felt that he did not have to, for Stalin well knew that the President had used it without qualms against the Japanese.

BACK TO THE 1920s

To drive home his concern over postwar Asia, Truman ordered American planes and troops to help Chiang's forces reach Manchuria ahead of Mao's Communist troops. By the end of 1945, 110,000 American soldiers were in China, many of them in the north. But all this was of no avail. Chiang was unable to consolidate his power, the Russians remained in Manchuria until they took out $2-billion worth of plant and equipment, and American officials failed to work out an agreement between Chiang and Mao.

Truman now turned to General George Marshall, the man primarily responsible for planning and coordinating the entire American military effort during the war. Marshall hoped to find a third faction in China that was "liberal" and middle-of-the-road, then construct a political solution embracing Mao's Communists, Chiang's Nationalists, and the third group. It was hoped that after a period of time Chiang would be able to absorb the third group and subordinate the Communists. During the spring of 1946 Marshall nearly pulled off the miracle, but by summer civil war had reopened.

China was too polarized between reactionaries and Communists to develop any third force. Chiang cared no more for Marshall's telling him—the leader of China—how to run the country than he had for Roosevelt's advice. Marshall reported home that he was confronted by "the incompetence, inefficiency, and stubbornness of the Central government—qualities which made it very difficult to help them." Chiang and Mao, moreover, hated each other. When skirmishes erupted between their forces Chiang decided that with his superiority in men (two-to-one over Mao's) and firepower (nearly three-to-one), he could destroy the Communists militarily. Chiang persisted despite Marshall's warning not to try to settle the problem on the battlefield. After initial defeats, the Communists inflicted a series of losses on the Nationalists in mid-1947. Truman privately berated Chiang, but stuck with him to the bitter end. As Admiral Leahy explained the cruel dilemma, "If we break with the Central Government the result will be that we will have no friends in either of the Chinese factions and no friends in China."

But Chiang was past help. In 1947 Washington officials seized the only alternative. They assumed that if Mao won, China would be too chaotic to govern and the Soviets too poor to provide major help. The United States decided to stay out of a situation it could not control. Truman instead turned to Japan to create once again the stability in Asia that Chiang could not provide. In 1947–48 Japanese industrial and political controls were lifted by the American occupation authorities. Stalin did not relish the idea of a revived Japan, but he had nothing to say about it, for the United States had frozen Russia completely out of the Japanese occupation. Japan was on the road back. Truman's approach to Asia smacked of the American policy at the Washington Conference of 1921–22, not of 1943. And it fit in perfectly with the new American approaches in Europe.

CRISES IN THE MEDITERRANEAN— AND AT HOME

There was no peace at the end of World War II. Instead of a world of the Atlantic Charter, Americans witnessed the failure of a settlement in Europe, the refusal of Russia to leave Austria (on the grounds that it was a conquered, not a liberated, state), and Soviet rejection of a plan to control atomic energy on American terms. In February 1946, Stalin warned the Russians that because of the outside threats they would have to revert to rigid state control and make additional sacrifices under new five-year plans. He was tightly closing off Russia and her sphere in Eastern Europe.

Washington buzzed with ominous rumors that Stalin's speech was the "declaration of World War III," since the world could not exist "half free and half slave" any more than it had in the 1930s. In March, former Prime Minister Churchill traveled to Truman's home state of Missouri to announce that "an iron curtain has descended across the continent." He pleaded for a joint Anglo-American atomic force to confront the Soviets, especially since "God has willed" that Anglo-Saxons, not Communists or Fascists, should first have the bomb. Stalin replied, comparing Churchill's "racial theory" with Hitler's and calling him a warmonger. For his part, Truman had no intention of tying American power to a declining England, but he believed, like Churchill, that the Soviets respected only superior strength.

The first test came in Iran during March 1946. During the war the United States, Great Britain, and Russia had occupied Iran to assure a route for the delivery of supplies to the Soviets. The Big Three agreed to leave six months after the war ended. But in February 1946, Russia refused to evacuate its troops, claiming that under western pressure the Iranians were not honoring earlier agreements with the Soviets on oil and security along the Iranian-Russian border. The security issue was of most importance; Stalin did not want to move his troops if the vacuum was filled by British oil and political interests. The United States swiftly reacted. It first took the issue to the United Nations. Then, as Stalin moved reinforcements toward the border, Secretary of State Byrnes issued a virtual ultimatum to stop the troop movement or the United States would take counter-measures. The Russians stopped, settled directly with Iran (on Iranian terms), and withdrew their forces.

Truman had won a significant victory. But the Russians continued to press for advantages and additional security around their southwestern borders, and especially pushed Turkey for a new treaty on the Dardenelles, the vital passage between the Black Sea and the Mediterranean. With American encouragement, including the beefing up of the United States fleet in the Mediterranean, Turkey refused to negotiate. In Greece, the civil war against the British-supported King picked up steam, with Yugoslavia's Communist regime funneling aid to the revolutionaries. The Cold War had expanded from Central Europe through the eastern Mediterranean.

In February 1947 the British suddenly informed the State Department that they could no longer afford to support the antirevolutionary forces in Greece. Decimated by two world wars, England's economy was suffering through one of the coldest and most destructive winters in history. The British Empire had reached the end of the line. The question became whether the United States would move into the British role. This question was actually academic, for in Iran and Turkey it had already taken the lead. The Truman administration had been waiting for this opportunity.

It was a chance not only to create a long-term anti-Soviet policy. Equally important, Washington officials needed to mobilize the United States for an all-out Cold War effort. This became urgent as they realized that such an effort would cost large sums of money, but that Congress was considerably more interested in budget-balancing and tax-cutting than in another expensive overseas commitment. Truman so judged the public temper that throughout 1946 he did not utter a single anti-Soviet statement publicly although privately, of course, he was willing to confront Stalin anywhere. Somehow, the American people's benign view of world affairs had to be transformed and brought into accord with the tough policies that Washington had actually been following since at least early 1945.

"SCARING HELL" OUT OF THE AMERICAN PEOPLE

In four stages, Truman encouraged the American people during late 1946 and early 1947 to commit themselves to an anti-Communist crusade. The first stage occurred in September 1946, when Secretary of Commerce Henry Wallace attacked American policies for alienating the Soviets. He urged a more conciliatory approach along economic lines that would open Russia to American goods. Wallace advocated much the same policy that Hull and others had pushed during the war. That approach, however, had not worked. Truman and Byrnes had moved to the next step: political and military confrontation. When Byrnes demanded Wallace's resignation, Truman fired his Secretary of Commerce. Some pro-Wallace support appeared, but of greater significance was the number of former New Dealers (led by a new organization called Americans for Democratic Action) who attacked Wallace as being naive and defended Truman's policies. The President purged the Cabinet of his leading critic and in the process discovered important political support.

The second stage of intensified anticommunism occurred during the 1946 congressional elections. The Republicans scored a stunning victory by capturing both houses of Congress for the first time since 1928. Truman was humiliated; one poll showed his support, which had stood at 87 percent of the electorate in 1945, sinking to only 32 percent. The President, however, turned the defeat to his own advantage. Many of the newly elected senators had advocated tax cuts but had also taken a tough line against subversives at home and abroad. Since Canada had just uncovered a spy ring that had apparently been sending atomic secrets to Russia, attacking subversives promised rich political rewards. Leading members of the Senate's new "Class of '46," including Joseph McCarthy of Wisconsin, John Bricker of Ohio, William Jenner of Indiana, and William Knowland of California, exemplified this Republican line.

Truman tried to undercut their position by proposing a government loyalty program under Executive control that would ferret out subversives in Washington. The President was taking the lead in the hunt for Communists. The loyalty program would not pry the needed monies from a tight-fisted Congress for a major foreign policy offensive. But it did enable Truman to play on Congress's fear of communism. The British retreat from Greece provided the opportunity for the President bluntly to inform Senate and House leaders that this was the moment to put up or shut up.

The third stage of Truman's program was magnificently handled by Undersecretary of State Dean Acheson when, in a private session, he told the congressional leadership that "like apples in a barrel infected by one rotten one, the corruption of Greece would infect Iran and all to the east." Asia Minor, Egypt, and then Europe would be next, as the dominoes would inevitably fall. Believing personally that "we were met at Armageddon," Acheson eloquently concluded that "The Soviet Union [is] playing one of the greatest gambles in history at minimal cost. . . . We and we alone [are] in a position to break up the play." After a stunned silence, the key Republican Senator on foreign policy issues, Arthur Vandenberg of Michigan, admitted that he had been persuaded. But he later warned Truman and Acheson that they would have to "scare hell" out of the American people if they hoped to get necessary public support for their new foreign policies.

Truman did just that with two speeches in the fourth stage of his program. The first address, at Baylor University in Texas on March 6, 1947, provided the classic explanation why Americans must embark on a new

crusade. "Peace, freedom, and world trade," Truman began, "are insepa-
rable." "Our foreign relations, political and economic, are indivisible," he
stressed. Then: "We must not go through the thirties again." Freedom of
worship and freedom of speech are related to freedom of enterprise, for
the first two "have been most frequently enjoyed in those societies" hospi-
table to free enterprise. And "least conducive to freedom of enterprise" is
governmental intervention. Yet, the President warned bluntly, unless the
world marketplace were quickly reconstructed and opened, even the
United States government would soon have to step in to control American
society in order to allocate goods and resources. Such governmental intervention "is not the way to peace," Truman concluded. The President's
meaning was clear: his administration defined the state-controlled Russian
economy as the deadly enemy of American prosperity, and he would do
everything possible to save the world on this side of the iron curtain for
the American form of "freedom of enterprise." If Americans did not join
him, they risked losing all their most precious freedoms.

Six days later he issued the call to action with the "Truman Doctrine"
speech. To make the case as forcefully as possible, Truman presented a
world divided simply between "free peoples" and areas where "the will of
a minority [is] forcibly imposed upon a majority." He included Greece
and Turkey in the first group, but unless Congress immediately appropriated $400 million for their aid, they would slide into the second. Only the
United States could now save the free world: "If we falter in our leadership, we may endanger the peace of the world—and we shall surely endanger the welfare of our own nation."

The speech "scared hell" out of many people. Senator Robert Taft
(Republican of Ohio and the Republican leader) disliked it because "I do
not want war with Russia." Doubts existed even within the State Department. Some officials had argued that Turkey, which had been pro-Hitler
and was not at all democratic, hardly ranked as a "free people." It shared,
moreover, a very sensitive boundary with Russia. But Truman nevertheless decided to use the opportunity in Greece to settle the Turkish crisis.
"Turkey was slipped into the oven with Greece because that seemed to be
the surest way to cook a tough bird," as one official observed. More generally, the speech was notable because it defined the Communist threat as
ideological, and therefore asked Americans to commit themselves against
that threat globally. This has been the most explosive part of the Truman
Doctrine, for once the threat was defined ideologically, Americans had to
be ready to intervene anywhere in the world where that threat was perceived, regardless of whether the area in question was in fact directly
threatened by Russia, or, later, China. Later presidents could use the Doctrine as a rationale for American military intervention in Southeast Asia
as well as in Europe.

It was "the most fundamental thing that has been presented to
Congress in my time," Vandenberg rightly observed, and so Congress
wanted to examine the proposal carefully. On March 21, Truman gave it
a major push when he issued the Executive Order that set in motion the

loyalty program to find Communists in the government. It was the first such program ever established by a President (Congress had earlier legislated the hunts), the first ever established in peacetime, and—most important—the first in which a person could be dismissed for political beliefs. Truman had defined the issue, created a growing consensus, and outflanked congressional opponents. One Truman supporter in Congress chuckled at the trap the President had sprung on Republicans who wanted to fight communism, but not spend money: "Course they don't want to be smoked out. . . . They don't like Communism, but still they don't want to do anything to stop it. But they are all put on the spot now and they all have to come clean." The $400 million was soon appropriated, allowing American military advisors and equipment to aid the Greek government. The revolution finally subsided, however, only after Yugoslavia defected from the Russian bloc in 1948 and quit sending aid to the Greek rebels.

AVOIDING THE 1930s: THE MARSHALL PLAN

Aid to Greece and Turkey was only a bandage on a large, festering wound that cut to the heart itself, the economy of Western Europe. Confronted with deteriorating economies, the Europeans were responding as Truman feared. A British Labor government, for example, nationalized leading industries, while in Italy and France large Communist and radical socialist factions gained strength. The American economy maintained its pace, but primarily because of a booming $15 billion in exports during 1946. If Europe could not continue to take its share of these exports, the United States would, in the President's words, "go through the thirties again."

The key to the problem was the lack of dollars that Europeans had to spend for American goods. Moreover, they could derive little from their war-ruined economies to sell to the United States in order to acquire dollars. Great Britain, France, Italy, and the Benelux countries needed about $5 billion if they hoped to buy goods from the United States to maintain a minimum standard of living.

In June 1947, the United States announced its plan to save itself and Western Europe. Newly appointed Secretary of State George Marshall offered massive economic aid but attached two conditions. First, the initiative in formulating a long-term program would have to come from the Europeans. They would have to commit themselves. Second, the program would have to be cooperative and open. This worked against Russian participation, for although the Soviets attended the first planning session in Paris, they quickly repudiated the Marshall Plan when they saw that they would have to accept American conditions, including the disclosure of Russian economic information. The Soviets claimed that the Truman Doctrine and Marshall Plan had irretrievably divided the world into "two camps." To solidify their own camp, they announced a "Molotov Plan."

Marshall and Molotov, 1947.

The Western Europeans finally asked for $29 billion, but the U.S. cut this to $17 billion for four years, with $5 billion the first year. The figures are revealing, for they show that the decision to give aid was not based merely on anticommunism. More immediately officials planned to provide the $5 billion they had long before calculated as the amount needed to keep American exports to Europe at necessary levels. When the aid was distributed, moreover, it went not primarily to Italy or France, where the Communist threat was most immediate, but to Great Britain and Germany, the potential industrial powerhouses for Europe. The Plan was publicly explained as part of the fight against communism, which it was to the extent that officials believed that poverty and unemployment in Europe would produce radicalism there and perhaps even in the United States. Most important, however, the Plan aimed at averting a repeat of the 1930s by rebuilding the great market for American products and moulding Western Europe into a long-term partner.

The United States had emerged from World War II as the greatest power in world history. Its incredible economic plant, monopoly of atomic energy, and success as the world's oldest republic seemed to indicate that

Americans were truly embarked on an "American Century," as *Life* magazine proclaimed in 1941. But by 1947 the American Century, like FDR's description of the Atlantic Charter, was only a "beautiful dream." By then the Truman administration had shifted from trying to create a free world (particularly in China and Eastern Europe) to rebuilding nations this side of the iron curtain. The Marshall Plan seemed an intelligent, manageable, and limited plan for maintaining "freedom of enterprise" in the West. On the other hand, the Truman Doctrine proposed world-wide ideological and even military warfare. Truman had beautifully built a public consensus around both.

It now remained to be seen which road Americans would choose: the path that was more modest and whose terminus could be clearly seen, or the one that required commitment without an apparent limit of dollars, energy, and perhaps even lives. As the ancient Greeks understood, the essence of human tragedy is choice. But then they too discovered this after it was too late.

Suggested Reading

Military strategy and decisions are well analyzed in Russell F. Weigley, *The American Way of War* (1973); Kent R. Greenfield, *American Strategy in World War II* (1963); and William Manchester's readable *American Caesar: Douglas MacArthur* (1978). Wartime diplomacy is detailed in William H. McNeill's superb *America, Britain and Russia, 1941–1946* (1953); Christopher Thorne's fine *Allies of a Kind: The United States, Britain and the War Against Japan 1941–1945* (1978); Herbert Feis, *Churchill, Roosevelt and Stalin* (1967); and Raymond G. O'Connor, *Diplomacy for Victory: FDR and Unconditional Surrender* (1971). More specific problems are well treated in Mark A. Stoler, *The Politics of the Second Front . . . 1941–1943* (1977); Robert Beitzell, *The Uneasy Alliance . . . 1941–1943* (1972); and Robert Divine's analysis of the domestic side, *Second Chance: The Triumph of Internationalism* (1967). Important interpretive studies include John L. Gaddis, *U.S. and Origins of the Cold War, 1941–1947* (1972); George C. Herring, Jr., *Aid to Russia, 1941–1946* (1973); Thomas Paterson, *Soviet-American Confrontation* (1974); Gabriel Kolko, *The Politics of War, 1943–1945* (1967); Joyce and Gabriel Kolko, *Limits of Power, 1945–1954* (1970); Diane Shaver Clemens, *Yalta* (1970); and Daniel Yergin, *Shattered Peace* (1977). The essays in Thomas Paterson, ed., *Cold War Critics* (1971); and Ronald Radosh, *Prophets on the Right* (1975) examine the dissenters. The best detailed analysis of the politics surrounding the atomic bomb is Martin J. Sherwin, *A World Destroyed* (1975).

For excellent overviews on Truman's policies to 1947, see Robert J. Donovan, *Conflict and Crisis . . . 1945–1948* (1977); Lloyd Gardner, *Architects of Illusion* (1970); Richard Freeland, *The Truman Doctrine and Origins of McCarthyism* (1971); Athan Theoharis, *The Yalta Myths, 1945–1955* (1970); Joseph M. Jones's inside account, *The Fifteen Weeks* (1955); George Kennan, *Memoirs, 1925–1950* (1967); and Dean Acheson's modestly entitled autobiography, *Present at the Creation* (1970). Important background is in Ralph B. Levering, *American Opinion and the Russian Alliance, 1939–1945* (1976).

For the era's economic policies, see Richard N. Gardner's splendid *Sterling-Dollar Diplomacy* (1956); for its Latin American affairs, David Green's *The Contain-*

ment of Latin America (1971); for its Asian affairs, Akira Iriye, *The Cold War in Asia* (1974); Michael Schaller, *The U.S. Crusade in China, 1938–1945* (1979); and Kenneth E. Shewmaker, *Americans and the Chinese Communists, 1927–1945* (1971).

Theodore Brown has done a definitive study in *Margaret Bourke-White, Photo Journalist* (1972).

General Douglas MacArthur.

CHAPTER ELEVEN

1947–1952

The America
of the Cold War

OLD SOLDIERS NEVER DIE
Words and music by **Tom Glazer**

There is an old Mess Hall not far away
Where we get pork and beans three times a
    day;
Ham and eggs we never see,
Even when we're on K.P.
And we're gradually fading away.

Privates they love their beer three times a
    day;
Corp'rals they love their stripes and that
    ain't hay;
Sergeants put you thru the mill,
They just drill and drill and drill
And they will drill until they fade away.

Young soldiers shine their shoes three times a
    day;
Young soldiers go on leave, they know the
    way;

Young soldiers say goodbye,
Kiss the girls and make them cry;
And the girls all wonder why they fade
    away.

Washington and Grant and Lee were all
    tried and true;
Eisenhower, Bradley and MacArthur too;
They will live forevermore
Till the world is done with war;
Then they'll close that final door, fading
    away.

Chorus:
Old soldiers never die; never die, never die.
Old soldiers never die. They just fade away.

Copyright 1951 by Warock Corp.

Two events in March 1947—the promulgation of the Truman Doctrine and the institution of a federal loyalty program—set the tone for American foreign and domestic affairs for at least a decade. Harry S. Truman's victory in the election of 1948 and his success in creating the North Atlantic Treaty Organization in 1949 marked the peak of his triumphs. With the outbreak of the Korean War in June 1950, however, the Democratic party became a victim of its own policies. In Truman's mind the North Korean attack closely resembled the fascist aggression of the 1930s, but the President found that waging a limited war imposed strains on the society quite unlike those associated with World War II. Those strains—political, economic, social, and military—nourished a mood of hysteria. The Truman administration was itself charged with being "soft on communism" at home and overseas. That mood was best expressed in the activities of Senator Joseph McCarthy, perhaps the only American political figure for whom an "ism" was named.

CRISIS DIPLOMACY
1947–1948

With the Truman Doctrine, the Marshall Plan, and the Molotov Plan, the world divided into what the Soviets called "two camps." Undersecretary of State Dean Acheson later observed that by 1948 the Truman administration had concluded that negotiations with Russia were useless, for "the world of the last half of the twentieth century was, and would continue to be, a divided world. The [decision] was to make the free—that is, the non-Communist-dominated—part of that divided world as secure and flourishing as possible." In 1947, Acheson wrote that since negotiations were not successful, "we must use to an increasing extent our second instrument of foreign policy, namely economic power," to protect the "free" world. The Marshall Plan indicated how the tremendous American economic strength would be used to create a postwar world on American terms. As Truman liked to put it, he was "tired of babying the Soviets."

The Republican-controlled Congress passed the $400,000,000 Truman Doctrine appropriations for Greece and Turkey but proved extremely reluctant to legislate the nearly $17 billion, four-year program that Truman was asking for the Marshall Plan. Secretary of State Marshall and other officials warned that without the Plan the American economy would lose its European markets, then shrivel. This, Marshall predicted, "would drive us to increased measures of government control." Such threats did not move Congress, for it believed that lowering taxes and encouraging private investment to go overseas would do the job. The administration vainly retorted that there was not enough time for such solutions and that private investors would not help until government monies rebuilt the infrastructure (roads, communications, banking facilities) of Western Europe. Congress refused to budge. Then came Czechoslovakia.

Although the Czechs survived as an independent people in 1945, their geographical position (bordering on both Russia and West Germany) forced them to be cautiously neutral in 1946. The Czech Communist party's power grew steadily, however, and by 1947 American diplomats had given up hope of bringing the nation into the West's camp. No one was prepared, though, for the sudden demand by Czech Communists in March 1948 for key government posts nor for the threat that this demand would be enforced by the Red Army, then camped on the border. The government surrendered. Foreign Minister Jan Masaryk, long a hero in the West because of his opposition to Nazism, fell to his death from an upper-story window. The Communists claimed that he committed suicide. Truman and many other Americans believed that the Czech leader had been murdered. Whatever the cause, Russia was tightening its grip in response to the challenge of the Truman Doctrine and Marshall Plan. Like Acheson and Truman, Stalin was also neglecting negotiations, relying instead on the Russian Army. Rumania fell under complete Communist control in February; Czechoslovakia followed; then non-Communist leaders in Bulgaria, Hungary, and Poland either disappeared or fled to the West.

Truman, comparing these events to those that had triggered world war in 1939, rapidly moved to a tougher military position which had long been urged by Secretary of Navy James Forrestal and other officials. Forrestal was the most fervent anti-Communist of the President's close advisors. He became especially powerful in mid-1947 when Truman named him the first Secretary of Defense. In the new position Forrestal was head of all the military services, now centralized in the Department of Defense. A former investment banker, Forrestal had entered government service early in World War II and soon issued scathing warnings about postwar cooperation with Stalin. As he wrote to a friend in 1944:

Whenever any American suggests that we act in accordance with the needs of our own security he is apt to be called a goddamned fascist or imperialist, while if Uncle Joe [Stalin] suggests that he needs the Baltic Provinces, half of Poland, all of Bessarabia and access to the Mediterranean, all hands agree that he is a fine, frank, candid and generally delightful fellow who is very easy to deal with because he is so explicit in what he wants.

Events after 1945 strengthened Forrestal's fears. He concluded that the United States and Russia would conflict politically, militarily, ideologically, and spiritually around the globe. To support this conclusion, he arranged that American diplomat George Kennan be brought back from the United States Embassy in Moscow so that Kennan could work out a long analysis of Soviet intentions that verified Forrestal's suspicions. Published in mid-1947 under the mysterious pseudonym of "Mr. X," Kennan's "The Sources of Soviet Conduct" concluded that two factors—Communist revolutionary beliefs and Stalin's need to create an external enemy as an excuse for tightening his dictatorship over the Russian people—made Russia like a "toy automobile" that, when wound up, would move inexorably onward until it struck a superior force. Some Americans disputed this view. Walter Lippmann, the nation's most respected journalist, argued that traditional national interests, not a vague revolutionary mentality or Stalin's personal needs, governed Soviet policy. Therefore, Lippmann concluded, sincere negotiations could end the Cold War by reconciling Russian and American national interests. Forrestal, however, found Kennan's analysis exactly suited to his own views and urged Truman to build the worldwide counterforce needed to stop the toy automobile. With the fall of Czechoslovakia, the President publicly advocated Forrestal's arguments.

On March 17, 1948, just seven days after Masaryk's death, Truman appeared before Congress to deliver a tough speech that urged restoration of selective service, universal military training for all young men (long a pet Forrestal project), and immediate passage of the Marshall Plan. A frightened Congress rushed the Plan through, although the legislators moved more slowly on the draft and rejected universal military training. But the President had gained a triumph, and, as in the case of the Truman Doctrine, had done so by frightening Congress, this time with claims that Stalin had monstrously subjugated another nation without any provocation from the United States. Americans were being conditioned to respond instantly whenever Truman rang out the Forrestal-Kennan version of Soviet policy. And Stalin was giving Truman ample opportunity to do so.

STALIN'S RESPONSE: THE BERLIN BLOCKADE

The Marshall Plan aimed at rapidly rebuilding Western Europe for two purposes: to make it a market for American farms and factories and to erect a bastion against Soviet expansion. To accomplish these objectives, the reconstruction of West Germany was necessary, for Germany had been the industrial core of Europe. Unless West Germany rebuilt there was little chance Western Europe could recover. The West Germans, however, suffered from inflation in early 1948, primarily because they had printed paper money in such volume that the currency had become almost worthless. In the weeks following the Czech crisis, the United States decided to cure West Germany's economic ills with drastic surgery. The Truman administration pushed for a currency reform program that would replace the bad money with new, better-supported bills. Despite Soviet objection that this had not been discussed with them, the program went ahead without their approval. Then in June 1948 the Western allies asked West Germany to form a Federal Republic, that is, an independent nation comprised of the American, British, and French occupation zones. The new nation, which would include West Berlin (located deep within the Soviet zone), would be rebuilt and closely tied to the West through the Marshall Plan.

These moves directly threatened Stalin's plans to keep Germany so weak that it could never again threaten Russia. At the same time, he was challenged from within the Soviet bloc itself. Yugoslavia's Communist

Berlin airlift, 1948.

leader, Josip Broz Tito, broke with Stalin, rooted out Russian attempts to
assassinate him, and declared Yugoslavia a Communist but independent
state. Tito had complete control of the nation, and his army was strong
enough to make Russian troops pay dearly if they attempted to invade.
"Titoism" became a new, hopeful sign to the West. The United States
soon sent aid to the Yugoslavs.

Confronted with these threats in Germany and Yugoslavia, Stalin
retaliated by trying to squeeze the West out of Berlin, thus removing that
listening post within the Russian zone and weakening the entire Western
position in Europe. In 1945 the Allies had made only oral agreements
about the right to use railroads and highways through the Soviet zone to
reach West Berlin. On June 24, 1948, the Russians stopped all surface
traffic into West Berlin. The city stood isolated.

Truman correctly viewed Stalin's action as a challenge to American
policy toward all of Germany. The President had three alternatives: pull
out; use force to open access to Berlin, perhaps starting World War III in
the process; or fly over the blockaded routes with supplies. Truman never
seriously considered the first point. When the question arose in a Cabinet
meeting, he interrupted to say "There [is] no discussion on that point, we

[are] going to stay, period." But he wanted no war and so followed the last alternative. The 2.5 million West Berliners required 4000 tons of food and fuel every day. With a massive airlift that landed a plane almost every minute of the day and night in the small West Berlin airport, the West soon delivered more than 12,000 tons each day. For more than 300 days pilots flew through impossible conditions, with some losing their lives in crashes during bad weather, in order to carry out "Operation Vittles." West Berlin held on, and in the early summer of 1949 Stalin agreed to lift some of the road blockades.

The President's tough responses to the Greek, Czech, and Berlin crises won support at home. So also did his foreign policy in the Middle East. Since 1945 hundreds of thousands of Jews, many of them survivors of Nazi concentration camps that had become slaughter-houses, flooded into Palestine. For many decades Palestine had been British-controlled, but since 1917, London officials had intimated that someday the territory could become the homeland that Jews had sought for centuries. As the Jews moved into Palestine, they met bitter resistance from Arabs already settled on the land. After a bloody conflict, the Jews proclaimed their new nation on May 14, 1948.

Fifteen minutes after the announcement, Truman recognized the new state of Israel. He did so over vigorous opposition from Cabinet advisors (particularly Forrestal) who feared recognition would turn the rich oil-producing Arab states against Washington. British Prime Minister Clement Attlee and other Western Europeans, who were utterly dependent on Arab oil, also opposed Truman's action. The President nevertheless listened to his political advisors. He acted because of his great admiration for what the Jews had accomplished in Palestine, but his recognition also assured Jewish political support in the 1948 presidential election. Attlee later observed, "There's no Arab vote in America, but there's a very heavy Jewish vote and the Americans are always having elections."

Whatever Truman's motivation, his handling of foreign crises during 1947–48 accelerated his triumphant run for the White House. In Europe Stalin had been especially helpful in this regard. Truman's closest political advisor told him that there was "considerable political advantage to the administration in the battle with the Kremlin."

COLD WAR POLITICS: THE 1948 ELECTION

In 1948 Truman's Fair Deal program combined two features: promises to bolster American defenses against the perceived Communist menace, and an expansion of New Deal benefits. On the domestic front, he appealed for civil rights legislation, federal aid to education, national medical insurance, power development in river valleys, increases in unemployment compensation and the minimum wage, higher taxes on corporations, and lower taxes on just about everyone else. Truman did not expect the Republican Congress to enact these measures, but he recognized that, in the words of one advisor, recommendations "must be tailored for the voter, not the Congressman." On the other hand, the Truman administration stepped up its attack on suspected subversives. Early in 1948 the Justice Department arrested a dozen aliens who belonged to the Communist party and instituted deportation proceedings against them. The Attorney General also drew up a list of subversive organizations. None of these groups had an opportunity to contest their listing, and most then experienced difficulty in renting meeting halls or recruiting members.

Yet despite Truman's brand of liberal anticommunism, Democratic prospects in 1948 appeared bleak. When the party convention met that summer newsmen reported that delegates looked like "mourners," that caucus rooms resembled "weeping chambers," and that the affair reminded them of a "wake." *The New York Times* observed: "The delegates drank bourbon, scotch, and rye as if it were so much embalming fluid—and with about the same effect." The reasons for such pessimism were apparent. The Republicans had captured Congress in 1946, and in the past when the party out of power had won control of Congress in an off-year election—Republicans in 1894, Democrats in 1910, Republicans in 1918, Democrats in 1930—it had gone on to victory in the next presidential election. Even worse, the Democratic party seemed to be coming apart at the seams. Henry Wallace was leading a defection on the left into the Progressive party, and Strom Thurmond a defection on the right into the States' Rights party.

Henry Wallace announced his willingness to run on an independent ticket in December 1947. In the year since he had left the Cabinet, Wallace's differences with Truman had sharpened. Wallace considered the President too cautious in defending the civil liberties of radicals and the civil rights of blacks. But the major source of disagreement concerned foreign policy. Where Truman regarded the Soviet Union as inherently aggressive, Wallace believed that Soviet moves often came in response to an American military buildup. Where Truman condemned Soviet control of Eastern Europe, Wallace held that Stalin had legitimate reasons for establishing a political sphere of influence in that area, provided that such a sphere remained open to American trade and investment. Wallace maintained that the American plan for controlling atomic energy was bound to be unacceptable to the Russians. He criticized the Marshall Plan for turning Western Europe into a "vast military camp," and believed that universal military training would persuade people of the inevitability of war. Fearing that "we are whipping up another holy war against Russia," Wallace accepted the Progressive party nomination in the summer of 1948.

"We're on the march. We're really rolling now," Wallace told a friend after a speech before 32,000 cheering admirers. But his candidacy, itself a product of the Cold War, soon became a casualty of that conflict. Wallace was widely denounced as a Communist dupe, in part because American Communists backed his candidacy, in part because he refused to repudiate their support, and in part because his views concerning the Soviet Union often coincided with the Communist party line. The Americans for

Henry A. Wallace campaigning, August 1948.

Democratic Action, a group of anti-Communist liberals, claimed that the Progressive party represented "a corruption of American liberalism" for it had "lined up unashamedly with the force of Soviet totalitarianism." Wallace drew his following, Democrat Lyndon B. Johnson of Texas chimed in, from "the sallow, deluded lunatic fringe that bores and scavenges like termites eating away at the foundations of a strong building." Wallace, a devout man who never subscribed to the Communist position, failed to repudiate Communist backing, although to have done so might well have helped his candidacy. He probably believed that the number of votes to be gained was not worth the price—that is, contributing to what he considered anti-Communist hysteria.

Even had a majority of Americans not come to believe that Communists ran the Progressive party, events in Europe—particularly the coup in

Czechoslovakia and the Berlin crisis—would surely have undercut Wallace's candidacy. As it was, the Progressives suffered a disastrous defeat. Wallace received only 1.1 million votes, or 2.4 percent of the total. The party received no electoral votes, and elected only one member, Vito Marcantonio of New York City, to the House of Representatives. Wallace made his best showing in New York, where he obtained 8 percent of the vote, and in California, where he received 5 percent. Nor did the Progressives have the murderous impact on the Democrats that had been predicted. Although Wallace garnered enough Democratic votes to cost Truman three states—New York, Michigan, and Maryland—his candidacy also acted as a lightning rod for anti-Communist sentiment. Wallace, not Truman, became the target, with the result that the Democrats could solidify their hold on voters, particularly Irish-Catholics, motivated by such sentiment.

Just as the Progressive party hurt Truman in some respects and helped him in others, so the States' Rights party cost Truman electoral support in the South but strengthened his position with black voters in the North. The States' Rights party (labeled "Dixiecrats" by some and "Dixiebrats" by others) was created when the Democratic convention narrowly adopted a civil rights plank calling on Congress to support the President in guaranteeing Negroes political and economic equality. A number of Southern delegates stormed out, called a convention in Birmingham, Alabama, and nominated J. Strom Thurmond, Governor of South Carolina, for the presidency. The Dixiecrats did not imagine that Thurmond could win. Rather they believed that his campaign would teach the Democrats not to take the South for granted and that it would possibly throw the election into the House of Representatives, where some sort of bargain might be struck with the Republicans.

The Dixiecrats bitterly criticized every attempt by the federal government to ensure racial justice. "We stand for the segregation of the races and the racial integrity of each race," they proclaimed. Proposals to outlaw the poll tax, to permit federal trials of lynch-mob members, to provide economic opportunity for blacks—all were said to violate states' rights. Attempting to turn Cold War rhetoric back on the Truman administration, Dixiecrats denounced the Fair Deal for its "totalitarian" features. The Fair Employment Practices Committee, Thurmond noted, was "patterned after a Russian law written by Joseph Stalin about 1920, referred to in Russia as Stalin's 'All-Races law.'" Although the party gained support chiefly for its stand on race, it also attracted other Southerners, particularly conservatives who had held a grudge against the welfare state since the late 1930s but had lacked a good political vehicle for expressing their displeasure.

Dixiecrats and Progressives stood at opposite poles on the issue of civil rights. Wallace was pelted by Southern whites for his vigorous advocacy of racial equality and his refusal to speak before segregated audiences. Nevertheless, the two parties faced problems that were in some respects analogous. Just as Wallace failed to win the backing of most liberals, so Thurmond found that many Southern politicians, even those who shared his outlook, would not risk forfeiting their patronage and seniority by abandoning the Democratic party. Both candidates found the electorate enormously reluctant to "waste" a vote on a third party. Progressives and Dixiecrats also faced a conflict between means and ends: each group wanted to bring the Democratic party around to its way of thinking, but their withdrawals proved only that the Democrats could win without them. Thurmond, like Wallace, polled 1.1 million votes, or 2.4 percent of the total. He carried four states (Mississippi, South Carolina, Louisiana, and Alabama), but by freeing the Democrats from the stigma of Southern racism he also simplified Truman's task of appealing to black voters. Negroes provided the Democrats' margin of victory in the crucial states of California, Illinois, and Ohio.

At the Republican convention, Congresswoman Clare Boothe Luce jibed that Truman presided over three Democratic factions: a "Jim Crow wing" led by "lynch-loving Bourbons"; a "Moscow wing," masterminded by Stalin's puppet, Henry Wallace; and a "Pendergast wing," run by the "wampum and boodle boys." In effect, the departure of the Progressives and Dixiecrats silenced two guns in the Republican arsenal. Republican candidate Thomas E. Dewey—who, according to one observer, sought the presidency "with the humorless calculation of a Certified Public Accountant in pursuit of the Holy Grail"—hardly made the most effective use of the weapons still at his disposal. Dewey often spoke in generalities, emphasizing national unity and avoiding harsh personal attacks. He did so for several reasons: his sharp criticism of Roosevelt in 1944 had not paid off; public-opinion polls all declared him an easy winner if he did not alienate voters already committed to the Republicans; and growing international tensions meant that voters might resent sharp attacks on Truman. Confident of victory, Dewey spent much time campaigning for other Republican candidates in states that were not central to his own contest.

The same polls that helped convince Dewey to pull his punches persuaded Truman to wage a bare-knuckled campaign. The Democrats emphasized welfare state liberalism but also exploited anticommunism. Truman endeavored to resurrect the Roosevelt coalition by promising to extend the Fair Deal and by charging that Dewey's election would usher in a depression as surely as did Herbert Hoover's. Truman peppered his speeches with references to "Republican gluttons of privilege," "bloodsuckers with offices on Wall Street," who had "stuck a pitch fork in the farmer's back" and had "begun to nail the American consumer to the wall with spikes of greed." Truman not only denounced the Progressive party as a Communist front. He also claimed that Communists supported the Republican party "because they think that its reactionary policies will lead to the confusion and strife on which communism thrives." The Republican party was, therefore, at the same time a spokesman for "powerful reactionary forces" and an "unwitting ally of the Communists in this country."

Truman's strategy paid rich dividends in November 1948. The poll-

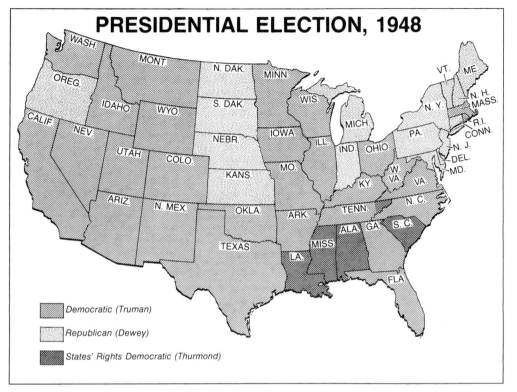

PRESIDENTIAL ELECTION, 1948

Democratic (Truman)

Republican (Dewey)

States' Rights Democratic (Thurmond)

sters made the dual mistake of ending their interviews a few weeks before election day and assuming that the "undecided" vote would divide evenly. But many voters changed their minds at the last moment, and Truman won a disproportionately large share of the undecided vote. "I talked about voting for Dewey all summer, but when the time came I just couldn't do it," said one farmer. "I remembered the depression and all the good things that had come to me under the Democrats." Truman received 24.1 million votes to Dewey's 22 million. The Democrats, by picking up 75 seats in the House of Representatives and 9 in the Senate, regained control of Congress. Having successfully navigated the shoals of Cold War electoral politics, it remained for Truman to guide his Fair Deal program through Congress.

THE FAIR DEAL: CIVIL RIGHTS

What Truman managed to do, however, was to extend and codify New Deal measures already on the statute books. Congress accepted his recommendations to expand three programs, all sorely in need of modernization: social security benefits, considerably increased, were extended to 10 million people; the minimum wage was raised from 40 to 75 cents an hour; and the federal housing program was further developed. The National Housing Act (1949), a modest measure calling for the construction of 810,000 low-cost units over a six-year period, won bipartisan support in the Senate. The bill was cosponsored by a Northern liberal Democrat (Robert Wagner of New York), a Southern conservative Democrat (Allan Ellender of Louisiana), and a conservative Republican (Robert Taft of Ohio). Where the New Deal had been innovative, the Fair Deal was more often imitative.

But Congress rebuffed Truman when he attempted to go beyond New Deal initiatives in agricultural policy, federal aid to education, health insurance, and civil rights. In 1949 Truman proposed the Brannan plan for agriculture, which would have substituted an "income support standard" for the concept of farm parity and would have limited the payments available to large, corporate farmers. When organized farm groups denounced the plan, Congress defeated it. The President's $300 million aid-to-education bill was strangled in the House Committee on Education and Labor, whose members were hopelessly divided on the issue of aid to parochial schools. Similarly, Truman's program for health insurance and medical care never got to the floor of Congress. Although the plan allowed patients to choose their own physician and hospital, leaving doctors free to participate or not, it was widely and inaccurately condemned as socialized medicine. The American Medical Association hired an advertising agency to manage its campaign against the measure. "Would socialized medicine lead to socialization of other phases of American life?" asked a leaflet distributed by the doctors. The answer: "Lenin thought so." Fair Deal programs stood no chance where they antagonized entrenched interest groups, offended influential congressmen, or could be labeled communistic.

Of all these Fair Deal setbacks, however, none was more revealing than the defeat of civil rights. That Harry Truman should have been the first President to support such legislation was surely ironic. Although Missouri was one of the slave states that did not secede from the Union in 1861, Confederate sentiment was strong, and Truman's family had favored the Southern cause. His uncle had fought in the Confederate army. Years later his grandmother had expressed dismay when she first saw young Harry in his National Guard uniform, remarking, Truman recalled, "that it was the first time a blue uniform had been in the house since the Civil War, and she said please not to come in it again." Truman described his mother as an "unreconstructed rebel" who, when visiting her son at the White House, warned that if he put her up in the room with Lincoln's bed, "I'll sleep on the floor." Truman observed "she was just the same Mama she had always been." Yet as Senator from Missouri, Truman supported civil rights measures, and as President, he did so even more strongly.

Dr. Kinsey and Sex Research

In 1938 Alfred C. Kinsey began offering a course on Marriage at Indiana University. Trained at Harvard as a zoologist, and a specialist in the behavior of the gall wasp, Kinsey had been teaching biology at Indiana for nearly two decades without causing a ripple. This abruptly changed when he introduced his new course. Dismayed at the lack of scientific evidence concerning human sexual behavior, Kinsey set out to compensate by taking the sexual case histories of anyone willing to cooperate. Kinsey assembled this data with the same compulsive care he had once devoted to collecting gall wasps, and soon found that people were volunteering information faster than he could transcribe it. By January 1948, when *Sexual Behavior in the Human Male* appeared, Kinsey's staff had accumulated more than 5000 case histories. Supported by a small grant from the Rockefeller Foundation, the Institute for Sex Research ultimately acquired 17,500 case histories, although it never reached Kinsey's goal of 100,000.

Viewing himself as a scientist, Kinsey attempted to exclude all moral judgments from his work. He trained interviewers to ask direct questions, telling them that "evasive terms invite dishonest answers." One of his associates recalled: "We also never asked *whether* a subject had ever engaged in a particular activity; we assumed that everyone had

Dr. Kinsey conducting an interview, 1948.

engaged in everything, and so we began by asking *when* he had first done it." Kinsey presented his findings in cold, clinical language: 86 percent of American males had engaged in premarital sexual intercourse, 37 percent had on some occasion engaged in homosexual activity to the point of orgasm, and 40 percent had carried on extramarital affairs. Kinsey concluded that existing laws were violently at odds with prevailing practices, that, indeed, better than nine of every ten American men at some time in their lives engaged in some form of sexual activity punishable as a crime. The book, in many respects, was a resounding plea to end this hypocrisy by bringing public moral codes into line with private behavior.

The report was hailed by most psychologists and sociologists. One writer even claimed that Kinsey had done for sex "what Columbus did for geography." But many criticized Kinsey's

"Well, I'm sure Dr. Kinsey never spoke to anyone in Upper Montclair."
Drawing by Peter Arno, © 1953 The New Yorker Magazine, Inc.

Drs. Masters and Johnson using dolls to illustrate their findings, 1970.

methodology, pointing out that his statistical sample was drawn too heavily from underworld characters (because it was easy to obtain their case histories), and that his interview technique did not allow for faulty recall. Others believed that Kinsey took an overly mechanistic approach. Lionel Trilling, professor of English at Columbia University, attacked the report for assuming that "the whole actuality of sex is anatomical and physiological" and thereby ignoring emotional and affective considerations. Yet the book proved amazingly popular. It went through six printings in ten days, sold 100,000 copies in three months, and remained on the bestseller list for 27 weeks.

In 1953 Kinsey published a sequel, *Sexual Behavior in the Human Female.* He claimed that since "the anatomic structures which are most essential to sexual response and orgasm are nearly iden-

tical in the human female and male," any dissimilarities in response reflected psychological and hormonal rather than physiological differences. Kinsey also reported "a marked, positive correlation between experience in orgasm obtained from premarital coitus, and the capacity to reach orgasm after marriage," and he found that women took part in premarital and extramarital affairs more often than was commonly supposed. The second report triggered an even sharper response than the first, partly because of the double standard concerning sexual behavior but also because of the growing conformity in the nation. One congressman denounced the book as "the insult of the century against our mothers, wives, daughters, and sisters," and a clergyman feared it "will in time contribute inevitably toward Communism."

In 1954, frightened by this public outcry, the Rockefeller Foundation (under

338 its new president, Dean Rusk) cut off further support for Kinsey's Institute. The man who had no difficulty probing the most intimate details of a person's behavior was virtually incapable of asking wealthy individuals for money. Bitter and disillusioned, Kinsey died in 1956 at the age of 60. His work, however, paved the way for many others, most notably William H. Masters and Virginia E. Johnson. Their books, *Human Sexual Response* (1966) and *Human Sexual Inadequacy* (1970), reported the results of laboratory experiments that measured the physiological changes—in heartbeat, pulse, skin coloration—the human body underwent during all phases of sexual stimulation. Yet their volumes, which also made the bestseller lists, caused less of a stir than had Kinsey's. Not only could their findings be more easily verified, but Kinsey's pioneering work had made sex research respectable.

Bookstore display, 1979.

This reflected not only his own convictions, but also his recognition of the importance of the Negro vote. Large numbers of blacks had migrated north and west during World War II. Strategically located in such states as Illinois and California, they exerted more political leverage than ever before. The more evenly balanced the Republicans and Democrats, the more influential the black vote. Truman's victory in 1948, when he received close to 70 percent of that vote in large cities, illustrated this. His pluralities in the black wards of Los Angeles, Chicago, and Cleveland enabled him to carry California, Illinois, and Ohio. In addition, Cold War requirements influenced Truman's policies. Since Soviet propagandists never failed to exploit racial discrimination in the United States, Truman argued that such discrimination alienated millions in Africa and Asia. The achievement of racial justice, therefore, could strengthen American diplomacy.

The administration took action on a number of fronts. First, the President appointed a Civil Rights Commission whose report, in October 1947, called for an end to segregation in every area of American life and recommended that steps be taken to implement political, economic, and social equality. Truman endorsed the report, although his own legislative proposals did not go nearly so far. Second, Truman issued executive orders in July 1948 designed to end discrimination in governmental hiring and to eliminate segregation in the armed forces. Third, the Department of Justice filed briefs in support of groups challenging the legality of segregated housing, education, and transportation. In October 1949 one such brief argued that " 'Separate but equal' is a constitutional anachronism which no longer deserves a place in our law." Finally, Truman asked Congress to pass legislation creating a Civil Rights Division in the Department of Justice with authority to protect the right to vote, providing harsh penalties for members of lynch mobs, abolishing the poll tax in federal elections, and setting up a Fair Employment Practices Committee with the power to prevent discriminatory hiring.

Southern Democrats made mincemeat of this legislative package. They threatened a perpetual filibuster that would bring the Senate to a standstill. Senate rules required approval by two-thirds of the total membership (64 votes) to close debate. Liberals attempted to amend the rules so as to permit cloture either by a simple majority or by two-thirds of those present and voting, but they met with no success. Southern Democrats also exploited the strategic committee posts they held by virtue of seniority. A subcommittee of the Senate Judiciary Committee had authority over the antilynching bill; it was headed by James Eastland of Mississippi (who believed that Truman's endorsement of the Civil Rights Commission report "proves that organized mongrel minorities control the Government"). A subcommittee of the Senate Rules Committee was responsible for poll tax legislation; it was headed by Mississippi's other Senator, John Stennis. Southerners ultimately offered a compromise: an FEPC with no enforcement powers, an antilynching bill giving jurisdiction to the states rather than the federal government, and a constitutional amendment

Grant Reynolds and A. Philip Randolph testifying before Senate
Armed Services Committee, 1948.

outlawing the poll tax that would require approval by three-fourths of the
states. Truman rejected the deal.

The Supreme Court proved more responsive to demands for racial
justice than did Congress. In *Shelley* v. *Kraemer* (1948) the Court held that
state courts could not enforce restrictive housing covenants. These covenants, under which a group of homeowners agreed not to sell or lease
property to non-Caucasians, played an important part in maintaining residential segregation. In St. Louis, 5.5 square miles were closed to blacks; in
Chicago, 11 square miles were off limits. If a non-Caucasian family—
black, Asian, or American Indian—moved into a home in a restricted
area, a state court would issue an injunction requiring it to leave. Those
who favored covenants reasoned that homeowners had the right to protect their neighborhood against "elements distasteful to them" and that
covenants, as private agreements, did not violate the 14th Amendment's
ban on discrimination. The NAACP, which argued the other side, held
that court enforcement of the covenants constituted state action within
the meaning of the 14th Amendment. In May 1948 the Supreme Court,
by a 6–0 vote, accepted the NAACP's reasoning. The decision allowed
homeowners to make covenants but not seek injunctions to enforce them.
The ruling by no means removed all the obstacles to integrated housing,
but it removed one of them.

If the restrictive covenant decision vindicated the NAACP, A. Philip Randolph's campaign against segregation in the armed forces proved the worth of a more militant approach. In the spring of 1948 Randolph demanded integration of the military, first through legislation and then, when that failed, through an executive order. Insisting that blacks would not fight for democracy abroad if they did not enjoy it at home, Randolph threatened a massive civil disobedience campaign. "I personally pledge myself to openly counsel, aid and abet youth, both white and Negro, to quarantine any Jim Crow conscription system." Asked if this did not border on treason, Randolph replied, "we are serving a higher law than the law which applies to the act of treason." On July 26, 1948, after protracted negotiations with Randolph, the President issued Executive Order 9981 asserting that equality of treatment and opportunity for all members of the armed services would be effected "as rapidly as possible." Randolph expressed satisfaction, and Truman later set up a committee to implement the new policy. The Navy and Air Force quickly agreed to integrate. The Army, however, raised one objection after another until in January 1950 it finally accepted a plan of gradual integration. The plan suddenly moved into high gear when American soldiers landed in South Korea.

NATO: MULTIPURPOSE MILITARISM

In early 1949, fresh from his triumphs over the Republicans at the ballot box and over the Russians in West Berlin, Harry Truman was at the peak of his powers. Some leading Senators even believed that the Cold War had been "won." But Truman determined to march on, using these victories to consolidate American power in Western Europe. In early 1949, after close consultation with Senate leaders, the President asked for a military alliance between the United States and Western Europe. Called the North Atlantic Treaty Organization (NATO), it became the first United States political tie with Europeans since 1778, when a treaty with France enabled the American revolutionaries to survive.

Truman urged this major break with the American past for several reasons. American officials worried that the Marshall Plan was not working as effectively as they had hoped because of widespread fear among Europeans, and among United States investors, that Russia could swarm over Western Europe at will. Truman's new Secretary of State, Dean Acheson, remarked that "economic measures alone are not enough," for their success depends "upon the people being inspired by a sense of security." One would not work without the other. Not for the first or last time in their history, Americans had to make a military commitment in order to gain economic benefits. But NATO also vastly increased American leverage in Western Europe. The European armies required American supplies, and the United States would be in a position to exact political and economic concessions in return for providing the supplies. The European armies, moreover, were ultimately dependent on the American

Harry S. Truman and Dean Acheson in 1955.

atomic bomb. As Truman's closest military advisor noted, in case of war with Russia, United States plans were "completely dependent upon full use of atomic bombs for success." Again, the United States held the high card and could ask Europeans to cooperate with its policies in return for atomic protection.

Secretary of State Acheson eloquently took the lead in urging the new policies. He became Truman's chief foreign policy spokesman. Acheson took that role from Forrestal, who had resigned from the Defense Department and then committed suicide after his fears and suspicions of communism deepened until he became mentally ill. The son of an Episcopal minister and a graduate of Yale, the elegant, mustachioed, subtle, and brilliant Acheson was a conservative who believed that the American future depended on close cooperation with Europe. To build this community, Acheson determined to deal with Russia only on American terms, which, given Stalin's views, meant not dealing with Russia at all. Acheson similarly dismissed public opinion at home: "If you truly had a democracy and did what the people wanted," he later declared, "you'd go wrong every time." As Secretary of State, he initially handled Congress as successfully as he had during the crises of 1947. His only allegiance was to Truman, a man completely different in appearance, background, and nearly every other respect except their common mistrust of Russia and their mutual desire to enhance presidential power. An associate of Acheson recalled that the Secretary once looked over a speech drafted for Truman, then "said with that magnificent manner of his: 'You can't ask the President of the United States to utter this crap.' " Demanding a typewriter, Acheson pecked out his own draft of the speech. It was clear who made foreign policy in Washington. When the bubble burst, Acheson would be a highly visible target for his enemies.

THE BURSTING OF THE BUBBLE: 1949–1950

Creating NATO marked the high point of American postwar policy. In April 1949 twelve nations (United States, Canada, Great Britain, France, Italy, the Netherlands, Belgium, Norway, Denmark, Iceland, Portugal, and Luxembourg), pledged that each would consider an attack on one as an attack on all and that each would respond as it deemed necessary, including the possible use of force. But within six months a series of events rocked the Truman administration.

Overseas the Soviets exploded an atomic bomb and China fell to the Communist forces of Mao Tse-tung. American officials knew that the Russians would have the bomb soon, but few expected it this early. Similarly, the fall of Nationalist leader Chiang Kai-shek in China had been expected, but the actual Communist proclamation of victory shocked Americans. Acheson correctly argued that the United States had no power to stop the Chinese Communists unless millions of American boys were sent to fight, and this not even the most vocal supporters of Chiang Kai-shek were willing to urge. The only hope had been Chiang himself, but despite American advice and $2 billion of aid between 1945 and 1949, his regime had become so corrupt and inefficient that it could not save itself. As Acheson phrased it, Chiang's armies "did not have to be defeated; they disintegrated." The fact remained that the world's two largest nations were Communist, and one of them had the atomic bomb. Senate Republican leader Arthur Vandenberg said it best: "This is now a different world."

Truman also faced dangerous conditions at home. The American postwar depression, which many prophesied and everyone feared, seemed to be approaching. Unemployment figures of 1.9 million in 1948 shot up to 4.7 million, or 7.6 percent of the labor force, by early 1950. The Marshall Plan helped keep the economy buoyant, for almost every dollar appropriated by Congress had to be spent by Europeans in the United States for American goods. (This would be the case with nearly every dollar of the $100 billion Congress appropriated for "foreign aid" during the next quarter-century.) The Plan, however, would last only several more years. When Congress stopped spending these monies—that is, when Americans had to return to a peacetime economy with more "free enterprise" and less government spending—the nation could find itself in conditions resembling the 1930s. Republican congressional leaders who had followed Truman in a bipartisan spirit began to have second thoughts. The administration became fair game for political attacks.

As the nation settled down into a winter of deep discontent, Truman and Acheson prepared to counterattack. The President ordered a complete review of American policy, a project completed in April 1950 and termed NSC-68 (National Security Council Paper No. 68). This document set American Cold War policy for the next twenty years. It assumed that only the United States could save Western Europe and Japan, which, along with North America, constituted the globe's great industrial centers. The United States would have to take the lead, letting its friends simply follow (much as satellites revolve around a primary planet, as NSC-68 phrased it), while Americans reorganized the "free world." According to NSC-68, reorganization meant militarization, and that, in turn, meant that the United States would soon have to accept a $50 billion defense expenditure instead of the $13 billion budgeted for 1950. Such spending would of course also pump up the deflating domestic economy.

Even while Truman planned a massive escalation of military strength, he and Acheson responded cautiously to developments in Asia. While refusing to recognize the Chinese Communists immediately, throughout early 1950 the Secretary of State maintained that the real danger to China came from Stalin's desire to control all Communists, including Mao, and not from Washington. United States trade with China continued into late 1950. In January 1950 the President's military advisors concluded that the island of Formosa (to which the Chiang regime had fled) would shortly fall to Mao's troops, and the United States should not lift a finger. Acheson clearly was flirting with the idea of recognizing the Chinese Communists. The flirtation cooled only after the Chinese seized United States property, mistreated American citizens, and signed a friendship pact with Stalin in February 1950.

At the same time, Acheson took steps to ensure that Japan would replace China as the American outpost in Asia. As early as 1947, when Washington officials saw the hollowness of Chiang's regime, they had encouraged Japan to rebuild more rapidly than the 1945 surrender terms allowed. Following this lead, United States businessmen trooped into the promising Japanese market, increasing their investment from $96 million in 1946 to nearly $500 million in 1949. With Japan recovering and an independent government at work in Tokyo in 1949, the question became how the United States could be assured that Japan would stay on Washington's side for the indefinite future. This question became pressing when China fell, for Japan had looked to China for decades as a market and source of raw materials. If something was not done, the Japanese might well fall into the Chinese Communist orbit.

Acheson's answer was a NATO-like device for Japan: the United States and Japan would sign a treaty ending American occupation but allowing United States military bases to remain. While the Japanese themselves would not possess a large military establishment, their islands would become an American outpost on Russia's Asian rim. Stalin did not care for this. As early as 1947 the Soviets had warned against any "intention to restore the economy of Germany and Japan on the old [pre-1939] basis provided it is subordinated to interests of American capital." Acheson had done much more, making Japan both an economic and military outpost. Faced with NATO to the west and long-term American military bases on his eastern flank, Stalin decided to act.

KOREA: JUNE 1950

His opportunity lay in Korea. That nation had been divided along its 38th parallel between American and Russian forces in 1945 in order to facilitate the surrender of Japanese troops. After the surrender, however, neither power would leave. Korea was too vital, for whoever controlled it also controlled strategic entrances to Japan, China, and the Soviet Union itself. Russian troops finally retreated in early 1949 but left behind a Communist North Korean government possessing a strong Soviet-equipped army. The United States exited from South Korea several months later; it left behind strongman Syngman Rhee and an army primarily useful for eliminating Rhee's political opponents.

Acheson believed that Rhee's troops and the American presence in Japan sufficed to protect South Korea. On January 12, 1950, the Secretary of State spoke at the National Press Club in Washington, defining the American defense perimeter in the Pacific as running from the Aleutians through Japan to the Philippines. That was the same defensive line that General MacArthur had agreed to in 1949. Acheson carefully added, however, that any aggression against Korea would be opposed by the United Nations. That statement alone would not serve to make Stalin quake in his boots. For his part, Stalin had little to lose and much to gain. His North Korean allies were eager to attack southward to reunite their country. A successful invasion could endanger Acheson's attempt to rebuild Japan. It would also show Mao, with whom Stalin was having difficulties over Sino-Russian border and economic problems, that Russia remained the dominant Communist power. Stalin could accomplish all this, moreover, without any direct Soviet involvement in the attack.

On June 25 North Korean troops moved across the 38th parallel. Truman quickly responded. On June 27 he sent in American air and naval forces. When these proved insufficient and South Korea faced certain defeat, he ordered United States combat troops into battle. Meanwhile Acheson obtained the support of the United Nations. On June 27 the UN resolved that its members should help repel the aggressors so that "peace and security" could return to the area. Angry over the American refusal to allow the Chinese Communists into the world organization, the Russians had been boycotting UN sessions and were not present when Acheson rushed the resolution through. The struggle against North Korea was to be fought by a UN army under General MacArthur.

But this was misleading. The United States actually controlled operations through MacArthur, and the UN simply followed Truman's lead. Americans contributed 86 percent of the naval power, more than 90 percent of the air support, and, along with the South Koreans, nearly all the combat troops. The President made these drastic decisions, moreover, without going before Congress to ask for a declaration of war as the Constitution required. He termed the struggle a "police action," not a war, hoping that this would limit the conflict before it expanded with atomic weapons and Russian participation. The President merely consulted and informed congressional leaders, of whom only Senator Robert Taft, the Ohio Republican, raised major objections. This procedure was clearly unconstitutional and later, when the war went badly, proved to be a political error as well, for it left Truman exposed to bitter partisan attack. The President's decision set a precedent for the later Kennedy–Johnson–Nixon commitment of American troops to Vietnam, a commitment again taken without a congressional declaration of war.

CHANGING "CONTAINMENT" TO "LIBERATION": THE U.S. ON THE OFFENSIVE

Truman and Acheson used the Korean War as an opportunity to take the initiative against communism not only in Asia but in Europe too. The remaining months of 1950 were the most active and crucial ones in the Cold War. During this time the President decided to change his policy of "containment," as defined in the 1947 Truman Doctrine, to the more active policy of actually trying to liberate a Communist-controlled area. Several motivations shaped the new approach. The war gave Acheson a perfect opportunity to build great military bastions in Asia and Europe as he had long desired. After all, he could argue, if the Communists struck in Korea, they might strike anywhere. In a larger sense, the war was the chance to put the global ideas of NSC-68 into effect. Driving back communism would also silence growing criticism at home. These critics, whom Acheson acidly called "primitives" and "animals," attacked the administration for merely containing, instead of eliminating, communism. Truman and Acheson used the Korean War as a springboard to launch a worldwide diplomatic offensive.

In Asia this offensive included the first full-fledged American support to Chiang Kai-shek's rump regime on Formosa. Truman sent the Seventh Fleet to protect Chiang and signed large-scale economic and military aid pacts. By August 1950, the United States had bedded down with Chiang to establish a new American military outpost on Formosa. In Southeast Asia, Acheson agreed to help France reimpose its control over the Indochinese peoples in May, a month before Korea erupted. By mid-summer the United States sent large military assistance and a military mission to aid the French. Here lay the beginning of the American in-

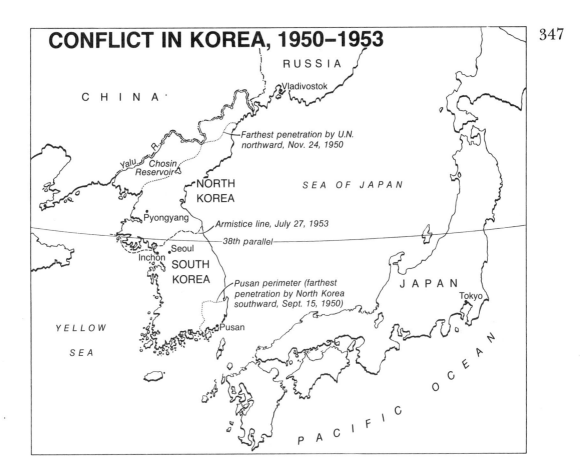

CONFLICT IN KOREA, 1950–1953

RUSSIA

CHINA·

Vladivostok

Farthest penetration by U.N.
northward, Nov. 24, 1950

Yalu R.

Chosin
Reservoir

NORTH
KOREA

SEA OF JAPAN

Pyongyang

Armistice line, July 27, 1953

38th parallel

Seoul

Inchon

SOUTH
KOREA

Pusan perimeter (farthest
penetration by North Korea
southward, Sept. 15, 1950)

JAPAN

Tokyo

Pusan

YELLOW

SEA

PACIFIC OCEAN

volvement in Vietnam. Acheson also hurried plans to sign the Japanese security treaty, doing so over strong objections from the Soviets and also from such friends as Australia and New Zealand, who feared the threat of a revived Japan.

The Secretary of State similarly took the diplomatic offensive in Europe. He used the Korean crisis as the opportunity to achieve goals that had been impossible to gain earlier because of opposition from allies and the Congress. Above all, Acheson determined to lock West Germany firmly to the West by rearming it and integrating the new German forces into NATO. France and England voiced strong opposition to any revival of German militarism, but Acheson refused to listen. Simultaneously, Truman, again without consulting Congress, tied the United States closer to Western Europe by stationing American troops on European soil. Both moves were completed despite strong congressional opposition. In 1949 Acheson had told Congress, "We are very clear that the disarmament and demilitarization of Germany must be complete and absolute." At the same time, he had guaranteed that there would be no Americans assigned to NATO duty without the assent of Congress. The shifting Cold War, especially the new Soviet atomic bomb, changed Acheson's mind. The United States commitment to Europe was fixed for at least the next quarter-century. Truman meanwhile increased defense spending until in 1952 it reached $50 billion, the figure envisioned by NSC-68.

Finally, Truman and Acheson decided not only to stop the North Koreans but to drive them back until all Korea was liberated. Such a triumph would teach Stalin a lesson, silence the critics at home, insure Japan's position, and put the United States on the border of Communist China itself. In July and August the tragic decision was taken to cross the 38th parallel. In September, General MacArthur made a brilliant landing at Inchon, trapping thousands of Communist troops. By late October, the UN forces were marching through North Korea towards the Yalu River, which separated Korea from China. At this point the Chinese issued blunt warnings that UN troops should not approach the Yalu. Acheson was not concerned. "Everything in the world" was done to assure China that its interests were not endangered, he later observed. "And I should suppose there is no country in the world which has been more outstanding in developing the theory of brotherly development of border waters [like the Yalu] than the United States."

This was an absurd statement. Such "brotherly development" of the Yalu was precisely what Mao determined to prevent. The Chinese wanted no help from the world's most powerful nation, particularly when that nation seemed intent on placing great military forces on China's border. In late November Mao's armies swarmed southward across the Yalu. Large units of American and South Korean troops were surrounded, killed, or left to freeze to death in a bitter winter. By late December the UN forces had fled south across the 38th parallel before MacArthur could counterattack. The war then turned into a bloody stalemate. More than 140,000 Americans were killed or wounded and more than a million South Koreans. Most of the casualties were suffered after Truman ordered UN forces to liberate North Korea.

The casualties were only part of the high price Americans paid for the administration's 1950 diplomatic offensive. The immense and rapidly mounting war expenditures skewed the nation's economy, infecting it with inflation and labor strikes. A renewed military-industrial alliance fattened on the defense budget, which, in turn, distorted the economy while wasting irreplaceable resources. Abroad, Americans discovered that their friends held serious doubts about U.S. stability. These allies found German rearmament so repugnant that it would be delayed for four years. Others feared a revived Japan. Some refused to follow Acheson's policy of aiding French colonialism in Southeast Asia. All were concerned how the United States might use its incredible power, particularly its atomic weapons.

The Truman administration was also on the defensive at home. Despite the President's assurance that communism could be contained and even driven back, communism had not only survived, but large numbers of American boys were being slaughtered in Korea. The administration and indeed the entire liberal tradition it claimed to represent were embattled. The struggle at home reached a peak in early 1951, when the President, in his words, reached "a parting of the way with the big man in Asia."

TRUMAN AND MacARTHUR

In April 1951, for the first time in twenty years, baseball fans booed the President of the United States when he threw out the ball to open the Washington Senators' season. For, a few days before, Truman had relieved General Douglas MacArthur of his command of United Nations forces in Korea. That action released a tidal wave of sympathy for the General who, on his return to the United States, received a hero's welcome. When MacArthur concluded a speech to Congress by quoting an old army ballad—"old soldiers never die, they just fade away"—and then added, "like the old soldier of that ballad, I now close my military career and just fade away, an old soldier who tried to do his duty as God gave him the light to see that duty," it seemed as if the applause would never end. The Truman administration, however, regarded MacArthur in a more sinister light. It saw him as an ambitious and dangerous man, one who wanted to subvert civilian control of policymaking and plunge the United States into nuclear war. Privately, members of the President's staff revealed their bitterness by composing an imaginary tour schedule for the General: "Burning of the Constitution. Lynching of Secretary Acheson. Twenty-one atomic-bomb salute. Three hundred nude D.A.R.'s leap from Washington Monument."

The basis of the conflict between Truman and MacArthur had existed in 1950 but was concealed because American forces had been successful until late in the year, and the administration, in deciding to cross the 38th parallel, in effect had endorsed MacArthur's goal of eliminating the Communist government in North Korea. Once Chinese forces intervened, however, the options available to the United States narrowed considerably: it could either accept a stalemate or risk nuclear war. Truman chose the first alternative and MacArthur the second. The two men, therefore, rapidly moved toward a showdown. In January 1951 MacArthur demanded permission to blockade China, bomb military and industrial targets across the Yalu River, use Chinese nationalist troops in Korea, and allow Chiang Kai-shek to attack the Chinese mainland. When Truman rejected all of this, MacArthur took matters into his own hands. In March he publicly threatened to destroy China if it did not concede defeat, and he stated that there was no substitute for victory. Truman then recalled him.

MacArthur not only repudiated the very concept of limited war but also disagreed with the administration's strategic priorities. As commander of United States forces in the Pacific during World War II, MacArthur had declared: "Europe is a dying system. It is worn out and run down. . . . The lands touching the Pacific with their billions of inhabitants will determine the course of history for the next 10,000 years." But the Truman administration regarded Europe, not Asia, as the key to containment. Provoking a war with China, as MacArthur seemed ready to do, would antagonize the nations of Western Europe and jeopardize the NATO alliance. By draining off the American forces and channeling them to the Pacific, such a conflict would weaken European defenses. When General Omar N. Bradley, speaking for the Joint Chiefs of Staff, asserted that an attack on China would involve the United States in "the wrong war, in the wrong place, at the wrong time, and with the wrong enemy," he left little doubt as to what he considered the right war, the right place, the right time, and the right enemy: a war waged to defend Western Europe against Soviet engulfment.

That General Bradley defended the Truman administration was of crucial significance. The conflict between Truman and MacArthur, often interpreted as one between civilian and military interests, actually involved sharp disagreement within the military. This, in turn, reflected the development of ties between the armed services and government that emerged during World War II and grew firmer during the Cold War. The Truman administration, indeed, often asked military men to fill policymaking posts in government; by 1948, 150 officers held such positions. The Joint Chiefs of Staff fully endorsed Truman's decision to recall MacArthur. So, too, did General George Marshall, who served as Secretary of State (1947–49) and Secretary of Defense (1950–51). "The S.O.B. should have been fired two years ago," Marshall commented. On the other hand, almost all the field commanders in Korea backed MacArthur. (The lone exception was General Matthew Ridgeway, and Truman selected him to replace MacArthur.) The military establishment's support of the President's Korean policy helped him ride out the storm created by MacArthur's dismissal.

LIMITED WAR AT HOME

The Korean War did not at all require the same level of economic regulation as World War II. Since military operations occurred on a limited scale, the armed forces absorbed a relatively small proportion of industrial output and consumer goods were plentiful. Inflationary pressures, strong during the first nine months of war, subsided in the spring of 1951. World War II had produced gargantuan deficits, but the government showed a budgetary surplus in 1951 and 1952. Even so, the administration took a number of steps to control inflation and encourage production: it limited credit purchases by requiring larger down payments, restricted new housing starts, and liberalized amortization for costs incurred in plant expansion. The President established an Office of Defense Mobilization, issued an order designated to hold the line on prices and wages, and took possession of the railroads when workers threatened to strike for higher wages. Truman bitterly assailed the union leaders for acting "like a bunch of Russians," but the workers eventually won most of their demands, and the government returned the lines to private owners.

The Supreme Court's response to the President's seizure of the steel mills illustrated the problems encountered in regulating the economy during a limited war. In March 1952 a federal wage panel concluded that steel workers deserved a raise, but the companies refused to grant the increase unless the administration approved a sizeable price increase. When the administration refused, the steel firms rejected a wage hike, and the union called a strike. Truman could have invoked the Taft-Hartley Act and ordered an 80-day cooling-off period, but he did not want to employ the law against workers with a legitimate grievance or risk alienating organized labor. Instead he seized the steel mills, citing as justification the existence of a national emergency, the importance of steel production in wartime, and his implied powers as Commander in Chief. The case rapidly moved to the Supreme Court, which, in *Youngstown Sheet and Tube Co.* v. *Sawyer* (1952), ruled against the President by a 6–3 margin. The majority held that the President had no constitutional authority to order the seizure and that in bypassing the Taft-Hartley Act he had ignored "the clear will of Congress." Chief Justice Fred M. Vinson, speaking for the minority, cited precedents under Abraham Lincoln, Woodrow Wilson, and Franklin Roosevelt for granting the President a broad range of discretionary authority in wartime. Obeying the Court, Truman then returned the steel mills to their owners and, when the union struck, refused to intervene. The strike lasted nearly two months and ended with the workers obtaining their raise and the administration reluctantly granting the steel companies their price increase.

Despite the limited nature of the mobilization, the Korean War greatly bolstered the American economy. Expenditures for purchasing armaments and other equipment, constructing bases, and meeting military payrolls rose sharply, from slightly more than $13 billion in the year ending June 1950 to slightly under $60 billion in the year ending June 1953. Although the percentage of gross national product devoted to national security never approached the World War II level (43.1 percent), it nevertheless rose from 6.4 percent in 1950 to 14.1 percent in 1953. As government spending created millions of new jobs, unemployment dropped to its lowest level in years. Federal expenditures, together with special tax incentives, encouraged industries to expand their productive facilities. From 1950 to 1954, steel capacity increased by 24 percent, electrical generating capacity by 50 percent, and aluminum capacity by 100 percent. Finally, the government began to stockpile petroleum, chemicals, and scarce metals to protect itself against shortages in the event of a long war. By 1954 it had acquired more than $4 billion worth of critical materials.

The Korean War also built up the nation's military strength by doubling the size of the armed forces and, more important, by hastening the construction of the hydrogen bomb. Truman had authorized development of the H-bomb in January 1950, but little progress was made in the next six months, and doubts about the bomb's feasibility persisted. The outbreak of the Korean War removed several obstacles to its completion. The national emergency convinced a number of scientists who had refused to work on thermonuclear weapons to put aside their moral qualms and also made it possible to justify testing within the continental United States for the first time since 1945. The war allowed Truman to pump billions of dollars into the bomb project; employment at the Atomic Energy Commission eventually reached 150,000 people. Tests in May 1951 proved the technical feasibility of a thermonuclear weapon. Finally, the first H-bomb was detonated over the Pacific on November 1, 1952, its 10.4 megaton explosion obliterating the uninhabited island of Elugelab. Russia, which had required four years to duplicate the American atomic bomb, obtained its hydrogen bomb only one year after the United States test.

If the Korean War had the effect of accelerating the development of bombs and weapons, it had a similar effect in desegregating the armed services. By mid-1950 the Navy and Air Force had taken long strides toward desegregation, but the Army, although it had yielded to administration pressure to abolish racial quotas on enlistments, still maintained separate black and white units. Yet segregation led to a wasteful duplication of facilities and an inefficient use of manpower. Moreover, the tendency to assign black units to noncombatant duties meant that whites suffered a disproportionate share of casualties. When white troops experienced heavy losses in the early days of the war, field commanders in Korea broke with existing policy and used black soldiers as replacements. In March 1951 the Pentagon announced the integration of all training facilities in the United States. A few months later the Army received a preliminary report from a team of social scientists emphasizing the advantage of integration and denying that it would damage morale. The Army then announced that it would integrate its forces in Korea and the Far East. Later it extended this policy to troops stationed in Europe. By the end of the Korean War, nearly all black soldiers were serving in integrated Army units.

CIVIL LIBERTIES UNDER SIEGE

The Korean conflict exacerbated the growing fear of Communist subversion, a fear that partly fed on the actions of the House Committee on Un-American Activities. In 1947 the Committee sought to prove that Communists had infiltrated the motion-picture industry. Several writers and producers who refused to answer questions concerning their political affiliations were jailed for contempt, and Hollywood adopted a blacklist barring the employment of anyone who failed to cooperate with congressional investigators. In 1948 the Committee stalked bigger game: Alger Hiss, president of the Carnegie Endowment for International Peace, who was charged with perjury for denying that, while working for the State Department in the late 1930s, he had given classified papers to a Communist party member for transmittal to the Soviet Union. After his first trial resulted in a hung jury, Hiss was convicted of perjury in January 1950. By

allegedly passed secret information about the atomic bomb to Russia. The
Korean War, coming on the heels of all this, had a chilling effect on civil
liberties. That effect could be measured by the behavior of Congress, the
President, and the courts.

Three months after American troops landed in Korea, Congress
passed sweeping legislation to curb subversive activities in the United
States. The Internal Security Act (1950) made it unlawful to conspire to
perform any act that would "substantially contribute" to establishing a totalitarian dictatorship in the United States. The measure required
members of Communist organizations to register with the Attorney General, barred them from employment in national defense, and denied
them the right to obtain passports. The act imposed stringent controls on
immigrants, aliens, and naturalized citizens. It blocked the entry of those
who had belonged to totalitarian organizations, provided for the deportation of suspected alien subversives, and permitted the government to re-
voke the naturalization of those who joined a subversive group within five
years of acquiring citizenship. Finally, the act authorized the President, in
the event of war or invasion, to detain persons if there were "reasonable
grounds" to believe that they might conspire to commit espionage or sabotage. This provision, first put forth by Senate liberals as a substitute
measure, was, ironically, added to all the other features. On September
22, 1950, Truman vetoed the bill, declaring that it would "strike blows at
our own liberties" by moving toward "suppressing opinion and belief."
Congress very easily overrode the veto.

The President's blistering veto of the Internal Security Act did not
prevent him from narrowing the rights of government employees under
the federal loyalty program. At its inception in March 1947 this program
provided for dismissal from federal employment in cases where "reasonable grounds exist for belief that the person involved is disloyal." But the
Loyalty Review Board, which supervised the program, found it difficult to
discover such grounds for belief. It therefore favored a procedure that
would take account of individuals "who are potentially disloyal or who are
bad security risks." In April 1951 Truman issued a new executive order
providing for dismissal from federal employment in cases where "there is
a reasonable doubt as to the loyalty of the person involved." In effect, the
burden of proof now fell on the employee who, to keep his job, had to
dispel all doubts. Since those doubts might rest on nothing more substantial than associating with persons considered to be Communists, attending
meetings to raise money for suspect causes, or even subscribing to radical
publications, the burden was a heavy one.

At the same time that the new loyalty program went into effect, a jury
in New York found Julius and Ethel Rosenberg guilty of conspiring to
commit espionage. The Rosenbergs were charged with having plotted to
arrange for the transfer of atomic secrets to the Soviet Union during
World War II. Ethel Rosenberg's brother, who had worked as a machinist
on the Manhattan Project, testified that he had transmitted such informa-

tion and received cash payments; the alleged courier supported this account. The defense denied everything, insisting that the entire story was a fabrication. On April 5, 1951, in handing down a death sentence, Judge Irving Kaufman attempted to tie the case to the Korean War. By helping Russia obtain the atomic bomb, he asserted, the couple had caused "the Communist aggression in Korea, with the resultant casualties exceeding fifty thousand. . . . We have evidence of your treachery all around us every day—for the civilian defense activities throughout the nation are aimed at preparing us for an atom bomb attack." Appeals dragged through the courts for two agonizing years, with the Rosenbergs protesting their innocence to the end, although their sentence would have been commuted to life imprisonment had they confessed. They were electrocuted on June 19, 1953. Even many who considered them guilty regarded the sentence as barbaric.

In June 1951 the Supreme Court moved with the prevailing tide by upholding the constitutionality of the Smith Act. Passed in 1940, the Act made it a crime to conspire to teach or advocate the forcible overthrow of the government. In 1949 Eugene Dennis and ten other Communist leaders had been found guilty of violating the Act, and the following year the Court of Appeals had sustained their convictions. In *Dennis* v. *U.S.* (1951) the Supreme Court approved the Smith Act by a 6–2 vote. Chief Justice Fred M. Vinson wrote the majority opinion. To prove the American Communists presented a clear and present danger to the United States, Vinson pointed to the formation of a "highly organized conspiracy" with "rigidly disciplined members," the "inflammable nature of world conditions," and the "touch-and-go nature of our relations" with Russia. Justices Robert Jackson and Felix Frankfurter, both of whom rejected this line of reasoning, nevertheless concurred with the majority on other grounds. Justices Hugo Black and William O. Douglas dissented. Affirming the value of free speech, Douglas denied that American Communists, whom he termed "miserable merchants of unwanted ideas," posed an immediate threat. He also expected that "in case of war with Russia they will be picked up overnight as were all prospective saboteurs at the commencement of World War II." The Dennis decision cleared the way for the prosecution of other Communist leaders. Nearly 100 of them were indicted in the early 1950s.

The Internal Security Act, the revamped loyalty program, the trials of alleged spies, the Smith Act prosecution—all trespassed to some extent on civil liberties. Of these measures, Truman's loyalty program undoubtedly affected the largest number of people. Yet of the 4.7 million jobholders and applicants who underwent rigid loyalty checks by 1952, only about 10,000 failed to gain clearance. Most of them quietly resigned or withdrew their applications; 560 people were actually fired or denied a job on the grounds of security. The Korean War's impact on civil liberties, however, would not stop at this point. With the rise to eminence of Senator Joseph McCarthy, open season was declared on liberals. The Truman administration itself became the quarry.

Joseph McCarthy, 1954.

McCARTHYISM

Joseph McCarthy, elected to the Senate as a Republican from Wisconsin in 1946, had a meteoric career in the early 1950s. Although he first achieved notoriety in a speech at Wheeling, West Virginia, a few months before the Korean War broke out, and although he remained a powerful political force for some time after the war ended, McCarthy's appeal derived largely from his success in exploiting the frustrations involved in waging a limited war. McCarthy declared at Wheeling that the United States, at the end of World War II, had been the most powerful nation in the world; but by 1950 it had "retreated from victory" and found itself in a "position of impotency." One thing alone, McCarthy said, was responsible: "the traitorous actions" of high government officials in the Roosevelt and Truman administrations. This explanation, as deceptive as it was simple, set the tone for all that McCarthy did and for much of what went by the name of McCarthyism.

There was nothing new in the charge that Communists had infiltrated government. What distinguished McCarthy was his assertion that the most eminent and reputable Democrats were serving the Communist cause by waging a "caricature of a war" in Korea. To McCarthy, Secretary of State Dean Acheson was the "Red Dean of the State Department," "the elegant and alien Acheson—Russian as to heart, British as to manner." Similarly, the Wisconsin Senator believed that General George Marshall had been hoodwinked into aiding "a great conspiracy, a conspiracy on a scale so immense as to dwarf any previous such venture in the history of man." Again, Democratic Governor Adlai E. Stevenson of Illinois "endorsed and could continue the suicidal Kremlin-directed policies of the nation." McCarthy even found a trace of grim humor in the situation. "I do not think we need fear too much about the Communists dropping atomic bombs on Washington," he remarked savagely. "They would kill too many of their friends that way."

McCarthyism meant more than wild attacks on the Truman administration. It also signified a climate of all-embracing conformity. Many people became afraid to voice unpopular views or even to express controversial opinions. The drive to conform was sometimes carried to ludicrous lengths. One state required professional boxers and wrestlers to take a non-Communist oath before entering the ring. Efforts were made in Indianapolis, Indiana, to remove such "controversial" works as *Robin Hood* (whose indiscretion was stealing from the rich and giving to the poor) from public-school libraries. Names themselves often took on great significance: the Cincinnati Reds were solemnly renamed the "Redlegs," and a face powder known as "Russian Sable" was marketed as "Dark Dark." Dearborn, Michigan, crowned a "Miss Loyalty" at a beauty pageant complete with loyalty oaths. Not everyone surrendered to this mood, but pressures for ideological conformity in America have seldom been stronger than during the early 1950s.

McCarthyism was also closely identified with the use of heavy-handed tactics. McCarthy presented himself as a rough-and-tumble fighter; his supporters affectionately termed him "Jolting Joe," "The Wisconsin Walloper." Never far from the surface was the suggestion that the Truman administration was infested with moral, as well as ideological, perverts. The Senator, wrote one admirer, "learned that the State Department was literally crawling with so-called 'men' who wore red neckties and sometimes women's clothes—who wanted other men for lovers instead of women." McCarthy's allusions to homosexuality among government employees were hardly more circumspect. He referred to "those Communists and queers" in the State Department who wrote "perfumed notes." McCarthy insisted that the war against communism must be fought with brass knuckles, not kid gloves. The tactics he employed—from the juggling of statistics concerning the number of alleged security risks in the State Department to the browbeating of witnesses—seemed entirely legitimate to his followers.

Different critics saw in McCarthy the embodiment of their own worst fears. Socialists, who feared the intrigues of reactionary capitalists, regarded McCarthy as an agent of Texas oil-men and other new million-aires who wanted to impose a fascist order on the United States. Liberals, who feared the introduction into politics of moral issues that could not be resolved through a pragmatic process of give-and-take, thought that Mc-Carthy represented just such an issue. They believed that the Senator played on status resentments of middle class ethnic groups, especially the Irish and Germans, who, having achieved a measure of economic security, were seeking to prove their Americanism by attacking a social elite. A few conservatives believed McCarthy expressed the masses' hatred of aristo-cratic privilege and excellence. One asserted: "McCarthyism is the re-venge of the noses that for twenty years of fancy parties were pressed against the outside window pane."

Support for McCarthy closely followed political, religious, and oc-cupational lines. The Senator won more backing from Republican than from Democratic voters, more from Catholics than from Jews, more from Baptists and Lutherans than from Congregationalists and Episcopalians, and more from blue-collar workers than from white-collar professionals. McCarthy also exploited his position in the Senate. Even though some Republican Senators found his methods abhorrent, few dared to criticize him openly, because they either feared antagonizing him or recognized his partisan value. Moreover, the Senate customarily permits its members broad latitude, relying on tradition or unwritten rules to ensure discre-tion. McCarthy also manipulated the mass media with great success. He developed techniques for monopolizing headlines that kept his name before the public even when his allegations had no substance.

That McCarthy could have charged the Democrats with treason, and that anyone could have taken those charges seriously, seems, in retro-spect, incredible. In the years 1947–52 the Truman administration had built up Western European economic and military strength through the Marshall Plan and NATO, faced down the Russians in Berlin, taken stern measures against radicals at home, developed the hydrogen bomb, and fought a war against Communists in Korea. Nevertheless, Truman erred in supposing that the American people would be willing to make the terri-ble sacrifices war required without being convinced that the government was doing everything in its power to win that war. In the past, although war had sometimes been used as an instrument of diplomacy, it had always been presented as a crusade: to free Cuba in 1898, to make the world safe for democracy in 1917, to establish the four freedoms in 1941. When McCarthy asserted that the United States was "engaged in a final, all-out battle between communistic atheism and Christianity," when MacArthur claimed that "there is no substitute for victory," they were speaking the kind of language Americans had customarily spoken when waging war. If Truman was correct in believing that in the nuclear age only limited war was feasible, then his opponents were surely correct in recognizing that limited war provided them an unequalled political op-portunity. They would make the most of that opportunity in the 1952 election.

Suggested Reading

Two studies of Henry Wallace and the Progressive party are Norman Markowitz, *The Rise and Fall of the People's Century* (1973); and Edward and Frederick Schapsmeier, *Prophet in Politics* (1970). In *Democrats and Progressives* (1974), Allen Yarnell discusses the election of 1948. The Truman administration's civil rights program is explored at length in William Berman, *The Politics of Civil Rights in the Truman Administration* (1970); and Donald McCoy and Richard Ruetten, *Quest and Response* (1973). For the Supreme Court's decision on restrictive covenants, see Clement Vose, *Caucasians Only* (1957). James Patterson's biography of Robert Taft, *Mr. Republican* (1972), assesses an important critic of the Fair Deal.

The political consequences of the Korean War are considered in John Spanier, *The Truman–MacArthur Controversy* (1959); Richard Rovere and Arthur M. Schlesinger, Jr., *The MacArthur Controversy and American Foreign Policy* (1965); and Maeva Marcus, *Truman and the Steel Seizure* (1977). Contrasting views of the Truman administration's position on civil liberties are presented in Alan D. Harper, *The Politics of Loyalty, 1946–1952* (1969); Athan Theoharis, *Seeds of Repression: Harry S. Truman and the Origins of McCarthyism* (1971); and David Caute, *The Great Fear: The Anti-Communist Purge under Truman and Eisenhower* (1978). The Supreme Court's decision upholding the conviction of Communist party leaders is analyzed in Michal R. Belknap, *Cold War Political Justice* (1977); the decision's impact is discussed in Joseph R. Starobin, *American Communism in Crisis, 1943–1957* (1972). On Alger Hiss, see Allen Weinstein, *The Hiss-Chambers Case* (1978); on the Rosenbergs, Robert and Michael Meeropol, *We Are Your Sons* (1975). Important studies of the junior Senator from Wisconsin are Richard Rovere, *Senator Joe McCarthy* (1959); Michael Rogin, *McCarthy and the Intellectuals* (1967); Earl Latham, *The Communist Controversy in Washington: From the New Deal to McCarthy* (1966); Richard M. Fried, *Men Against McCarthy* (1976); and Robert Griffith and Athan Theoharis, eds., *The Specter: Essays on the Cold War and the Origins of McCarthyism* (1974).

Foreign policy is well covered in Godfrey Hodgson's survey, *America In Our Time; From World War II to Nixon* (1976); Gaddis Smith, *Dean Acheson* (1972); David S. McLellan, *Dean Acheson* (1976); John L. Gaddis, *Russia, the Soviet Union and the United States* (1978); Akira Iriye, *The Cold War in Asia* (1974); Acheson's *Present at the Creation* (1970); and Truman's second volume of *Memoirs: Years of Trial and Hope* (1956); while Adam Ulam surveys Soviet views in *Containment and Coexistence* (1973). Two books by Ronald Radosh are important: *American Labor and U.S. Foreign Policy* (1969), and *Prophets on the Right* (1975).

On Korea, useful work includes Iriye's study mentioned above; David Rees, *Korea* (1964); Glenn D. Paige, *The Korean Decision* (1968); Allen Whiting's now-standard work, *China Crosses the Yalu* (1960); Francis H. Heller, ed., *The Korean War: A Twenty-Five Year Perspective* (1977); and David Detzer's readable, *Thunder . . . The Short Summer in 1950* (1977). MacArthur gives his side in his *Reminiscences* (1964); and William Manchester's biography of the General, *American Caesar* (1978), is helpful.

On the Kinsey Reports, see Wardell Pomeroy, *Dr. Kinsey and the Institute for Sex Research* (1972); and Paul Robinson, *The Modernization of Sex . . . Kinsey, Masters, Johnson* (1976).

Levittown, Long Island, 1958.

CHAPTER TWELVE

1952-1957

Eisenhower and the American Consensus

SCHOOL DAY (RING! RING! GOES THE BELL)

Words and music by **Chuck Berry**

Up in the mornin' and out to school,
The teacher is teachin' the Golden Rule;
American Hist'ry and Practical Math,
You study 'em hard and hopin' to pass.
Workin' your fingers right down to the bone,
An' the guy behind you won't leave you
   alone.

Ring! Ring! goes the bell,
The cook in the lunchroom's ready to sell;
You're lucky if you can find a seat,
You're fortunate if you have time to eat.
Back in the classroom, open your books,
Gee, but the teacher don't know how mean
   she looks.

Soon as three o'clock rolls aroun',
You finally lay your burden down;
Close up your books, get out-a your seat,
Down the hall an' into the street.

Up to the corner an' 'round the bend,
Right to the juke-joint you go in.

Drop the coin right into the slot,
You gotta hear somethin' that's really hot
With the one you love you're makin' ro-
   mance,
All day long you've been wantin' to dance.
Feelin' the music from head to toe,
'Round an' 'round an' 'round you go.

Hail! Hail! Rock 'n' roll,
Deliver me from the days of old;
Long live Rock 'n' Roll,
The beat of the drums loud an' bold.
Rock! Rock! Rock 'n' Roll,
The feelin' is there, body an' soul.

Dwight David Eisenhower, reared on the Kansas frontier and the plains of West Point Military Academy, became famous as the commander of Allied forces in Western Europe during World War II. In 1952, campaigning for the presidency as a spokesman for traditional American values, he offered reassurance and hope to a people soured by the trials of the Cold War. Within two years of his election, the Korean War had ended and Joseph McCarthy had fallen from power. Americans then settled down to enjoy the piping prosperity that they believed they so richly deserved. It was, one critic observed, a classic case of "the bland leading the bland." Yet appearances deceived, for beneath a placid surface society was in ferment. Americans were restless, mobile, and undergoing an amazing population boom. Pressures were building that later would produce the massive civil rights movement. Abroad, the United States approached the Suez crisis of 1956, the turning-point of the Cold War. Not even the smiling, waving golfer in the White House was always what he seemed. Privately he could burst into unbelievable anger. Eisenhower, in the words of his Vice-President, Richard Nixon, was the "coldest, most unemotional, analytical man in the world."

THE SUBURBAN SOCIETY

The most distinctive demographic development in the United States at mid-century was the expansion of the suburbs. During the 1950s, the population of "standard metropolitan statistical areas"—defined by the Census Bureau as places containing a city with at least 50,000 inhabitants—jumped from 95 to 120 million. That growth took place primarily in the suburbs. Central cities grew by 11 percent, from 54 to 60 million, while suburbs grew by 46 percent from 41 to 60 million. Much of the urban growth in the South and West, however, occurred through the extension of cities' political boundaries to incorporate suburban tracts instead of through an increase in the existing population. In the North and Midwest this peripheral expansion was uncommon. From 1950 to 1960, fourteen of the fifteen largest cities in the nation experienced a population decline even as their suburbs underwent a population explosion: New York City's suburbs grew by 58 percent, Chicago's by 101 percent, Detroit's by 131 percent, and Cleveland's by 94 percent.

Suburban development depended, in the first instance, on the expansion of the automobile industry and the construction of new highways. The postwar years were boom years for American car manufacturers. Passenger car output rocketed from 2 million in 1946 to 8 million in 1955, and registrations jumped from 25 million in 1945 to 51 million in 1955. For nearly all suburbanites, the automobile was a necessity; indeed, by 1960, nearly one-fifth of suburban families owned two cars. At the same time, states and municipalities built or improved many thousands of miles of new roads. The federal government made an essential contribution. The Interstate Highway Act of 1956 provided for the construction of 41,000 miles of express highways at a cost of more than $100 billion. The new roads made it easier to commute and made it more feasible to commute over much longer distances.

The government aided suburban growth in other ways as well. The Veterans Administration offered to insure the mortgages of former servicemen on highly advantageous terms. More than 3.75 million veterans bought homes under VA programs that, typically, required only a token down payment and provided long-term, low-interest mortgages. The Federal Housing Administration also insured millions of mortgages, giving preference, in all instances, to buyers of single-family, detached dwellings. Those who wanted to buy a home in the suburbs could therefore count on a much more favorable response from federal agencies than those who wished to purchase an older home. Insuring mortgages in the central cities, the VA and FHA believed, represented a much higher risk, and a risk not worth taking. Government programs tipped the balance in favor of middle-income buyers, those looking at homes in the $7,000 to $10,000 range, and those seeking a suburban location.

The burgeoning suburbs began to lure commerce and industry from the cities. As the trend toward plant relocation gathered steam, employment in trade and manufacturing declined in the nation's largest cities and rose dramatically in the suburbs. The appearance of giant shopping centers also heralded the economic transformation of suburbia. At the end of World War II there were only 8 shopping centers; by 1960 the number had risen to 3840. In a three-month period in 1957, no fewer than 17 regional shopping centers opened for business, leading one observer to note that "at times it seemed they must be coming off a hidden assembly line."

The migration from cities to suburbs was predominantly a migration of whites; black Americans characteristically moved from farms to cities. In the decade of the 1950s, the twelve largest central cities lost 3.6 million whites and gained 4.5 million nonwhites. By 1960 more than half the black population, but only one-third of the white, resided in central cities. In the suburbs, however, whites outnumbered blacks by a ratio of more than thirty-five to one. The number of blacks residing in the suburbs did increase, from 1 million in 1950 to 1.7 million in 1960, but most of that increase occurred in older, all-Negro communities. Few blacks bought homes in the new, postwar suburban tracts. Either they could not afford to do so, or they were excluded by real estate brokers who would not show them homes, bank officers who would not grant them mortgages, or suburban zoning ordinances that artificially boosted home construction costs in order to restrict entry.

The word "suburbia" brought to mind images of small children, and with good reason. The 1950s saw an unusually high marriage rate and a truly extraordinary increase in the birth rate. The postwar "baby boom" crested in 1957, when the fertility rate reached the highest level since the government first began to compile statistics in 1917. At the rate prevailing in 1957, a group of 1000 women could expect to give birth to 3767 children during their child-bearing years. At the same time, improvements in medical care led to a steady increase in life expectancy. In 1954, for the first time in American history, life expectancy for white men and women reached 70 years. (Black men and women could expect to live an average of 64 years.) The rapid increase in the over-65 age bracket led one enterprising publisher to market a magazine designed exclusively for those preparing to retire. During the 1950s the population of the United States increased from 152.3 to 180.6 million. That represented an annual growth of 1.7 percent, the highest rate of change in four decades. Far from worrying about scarcity or overpopulation, most Americans confidently assumed that growth would trigger further economic expansion. As one business periodical happily proclaimed: "More People: It Means New Trade, Good Times."

THE MOOD OF THE FIFTIES

During the 1950s, many social critics diagnosed American society as suffering from a terminal case of conformity. The suburbs, they claimed, best illustrated the symptoms. In *The Organization Man* (1956), William F. Whyte described an emerging group of Americans, primarily middle-class junior executives, who subscribed to a new social ethic that included "a belief in 'belongingness' as the ultimate need of the individual." Organization men and women, Whyte reasoned, found their natural habitat in the new suburbia, with its emphasis on participation in community affairs, sociability for its own sake, and conformity to group values. To residents of Park Forest, Illinois, for example, the lack of privacy was itself a virtue. "I never feel lonely, even when Jim's away," beamed one young woman. "You know friends are near by, because at night you hear the neighbors through the walls." Suburban public schools stressed life adjustment and relied on peer-group disapproval to maintain discipline. "The teacher strives not to discipline the child directly but to influence all the children's attitudes so that as a group they recognize correct behavior."

Whyte concluded that the organization man "is not only other-directed" but "is articulating a philosophy which tells him it is the right way to be." David Riesman had first discussed the concept of "other-direction" in *The Lonely Crowd* (1950), one of the most influential books ever written by an American sociologist. Riesman argued that Americans were in the process of moving from an inner-directed to an other-directed society, one in which the peer group replaced parents as the dominant source of authority and in which those who failed to conform experienced anxiety rather than guilt. If the typical nineteenth-century American had a system of values implanted early in life which thereafter acted as a psychological gyroscope, then twentieth-century Americans had built-in radar systems tuned to the sounds around them. Riesmen detected the emergence of this other-directed personality chiefly "in the upper middle class of our larger cities." The children's story *Tootle* epitomized the new view. Tootle was a little engine who was taught to "always stay on the track no matter what" and who, when he strayed off the track to frolic in the fields, was pressured into returning. "The children who read Tootle," Riesman said, "are manipulated away from rebellion and taught the lesson of obedience to signals."

As sociologists found evidence of conformity in the American present, historians discovered evidence of consensus in the nation's past. Many historians in the 1950s minimized conflict and emphasized continuity. David Potter's *People of Plenty* (1954) held that material abundance—the product of "human ingenuity, human initiative, human adaptability, and human enterprise"—had shaped American character. Potter admitted the existence of some inequality (although the word poverty did not appear in his index) but noted that social inequality violated the nation's most cherished ideals. He concluded that "in every aspect of material plenty America possesses unprecedented riches and . . . these are very widely distributed."

Unprecedented affluence and the broad acceptance of middle-class liberal values meant that American society had escaped the bitter class antagonism that had plagued Europe, or so argued Louis Hartz in *The Liberal Tradition in America* (1955). Daniel Boorstin asserted that Americans had always shown a lack of interest in ideology. They had been concerned, rather, with finding practical solutions to everyday problems. That, to Boorstin, constituted "the genius of American politics." In the view of these historians, the American past was as free of doctrinal clashes as of widespread suffering or sharp class rivalry.

Boorstin believed that this historical tradition fitted Americans "to understand the meaning of conservatism." During the 1950s a group of self-styled "new conservatives" attempted to clarify that meaning. For the most part they merely reiterated the importance of religion, tradition, hierarchy, property rights, and the organic conception of society. The conservatives pointed to their own "sense of human limitation and frailty, as opposed to the megalomaniac faith in limitless progress through mass-movements and material reforms." They continued in varying degrees to oppose the expansion of the welfare state, which they thought rested on the dangerous premise that "justice is identical with equality." If anything identified the new conservatives it was their assault on "relativism," that is, on the unwillingness of society to uphold correct moral values and stamp out evil ones. This idea was carried furthest, perhaps, in William F. Buckley's *God and Man at Yale* (1951). Buckley, a recent Yale graduate, condemned the University for hiring professors who caused students to doubt the existence of God and the virtues of free enterprise. Buckley claimed that a private university had the duty to inculcate the values held by its financial backers—in this case, belief in Christianity and economic individualism. Professors who did not wish to teach those values had, of course, the right to seek employment elsewhere. The book went through five printings in the first six months of publication.

REPUBLICANS ON
THE POTOMAC

In Dwight Eisenhower the American people found a figure who perfectly suited their mood. In the 1952 campaign Eisenhower exploited the issues identified by the formula "K_1C_2"—Korea, communism, and corruption. Of the three, Korea was the most critical. By the fall of 1952 slightly more than half the electorate regarded the war—or, more accurately, how it might be resolved—as the single most important issue. Democratic candidate Adlai E. Stevenson of Illinois fully endorsed Truman's war policies, even suggesting that the nation brace itself for years of additional sacrifice. "The ordeal of the twentieth century is far from over," Stevenson said in accepting the nomination. Eisenhower, who also had backed the decision to wage a limited war in Korea, nevertheless seemed to offer a way out of the quagmire. Two weeks before the election he said "I shall go to Korea," and though he did not say what he would do when he got there, his pledge, coming from a man identified with victory in World War II, was a masterful stroke. Popularly regarded as the man best able to end the war, Eisenhower was politically irresistible. It was appropriate that the last word of his last campaign address was "peace."

The two other issues also worked to Eisenhower's benefit. Republican charges that the Truman administration was infested with Communists and that Stevenson was himself dangerously "soft" came not only from Joseph McCarthy but also from Eisenhower's running mate. Richard Nixon spoke of "Adlai the Appeaser," who lacked "backbone training" because he was a "Ph.D. graduate of Dean Acheson's cowardly college of Communist containment." Stevenson was vulnerable because he had once given a deposition attesting to Alger Hiss's good reputation. As Governor of Illinois, moreover, he had courageously vetoed a bill requiring loyalty oaths of all state employees.

The issue of corruption hammered a last nail into the Democrats' coffin. In its last years the Truman administration was plagued by scandals, many of them involving money-making schemes or influence-peddling by the President's cronies. Promising to "drive the crooks and the Communists from their seats of power," Eisenhower embarked on a moral crusade for decent government. Electing a Democrat to replace Truman, an Indiana Republican suggested, would be equivalent to "putting a new pin on a soiled diaper." On the eve of the inauguration one supporter told Eisenhower that "for the first time in many years the country feels clean again."

What was striking about the election was not so much the magnitude of Eisenhower's victory—he received 55 percent of the vote and carried 39 states—as the high level of voter interest. In 1948 only 51.5 percent of those eligible had voted, but in 1952 the turnout was 62.7 percent. Eisenhower broke through traditional Democratic strongholds, winning nearly half the popular vote in the South (doing particularly well in the cities) and carrying Virginia, Florida, Texas, and Tennessee. Stevenson's reluctance to campaign on the old New Deal slogans, and Eisenhower's reputation as a liberal Republican, combined to mute economic issues. The Republicans, therefore, did better than they had expected in working-class wards. Whether as a result of his promise to end the war, his crusade for clean government, or his reputation as a family man (in contrast to the divorced Stevenson), Eisenhower was even more popular with female voters (58.5 percent) than with male (52.5 percent). Most significant of all was his showing among the middle class in the burgeoning suburbs. Stevenson captured New York City, Chicago, Cleveland, and Boston, but in each case Eisenhower won the surrounding suburbs by even larger pluralities, thereby offsetting the Democrats' advantage. These expanding areas also had exceedingly high turnout rates.

Critics of Eisenhower interpreted the 1952 election as a popularity contest involving no real issues beyond Ike's famous grin and twinkling blue eyes. They were mistaken. So, too, were those who saw him as a babe-in-the-woods who did not understand politics or the use of power. If Eisenhower seemed to remain above political battles it was because he recognized that his reputation for nonpartisanship was an important political asset. As one advisor explained to him, "The people want another George Washington. They really think of you as a modern George Washington." If Eisenhower urged his program on congressional Republicans cautiously, it was because he knew that his party was torn between a liberal and conservative wing. He wanted to heal rather than widen the rift. If Eisenhower adopted a more restrained view of presidential authority than his Democratic predecessors, it was because of his belief in the separation of powers and his distaste for emotionally charged disputes. None of this, however, prevented him from manipulating his powers to influence legislation or from using patronage to reward loyal followers. He also fashioned an orderly administrative system based on a clear chain of command.

To staff his Cabinet, Eisenhower relied primarily on successful businessmen, many of whom had some political experience. Secretary of the Treasury George M. Humphrey, a staunch fiscal conservative, had headed a successful steel company in Ohio. Immediately upon moving into his new office, Humphrey removed a portrait of Harry Truman from the wall and replaced it with one of Andrew Mellon. Three other Cabinet members—Secretary of the Interior Douglas McKay, Postmaster General Arthur Summerfield, and Secretary of Defense Charles E. Wilson—had made their fortunes in the automobile industry, giving some point to Adlai Stevenson's quip that the New Dealers were making way for the car dealers. Wilson, who had served as president of General Motors since 1940, once explained his reluctance to use defense contracts for the purpose of reducing unemployment in words that few workers appreciated: "I've always liked bird dogs better than kennel dogs myself. You know, one who will get out and hunt for food rather than sit on his fanny and yell." The rhetoric of the automobile industry even crept into Cabinet discussions. On one occasion, explaining why large cuts in defense spending were necessary, Humphrey said to Wilson: "Charley, . . .

you just got to get out the best damn *streamlined model* you ever did in your life. . . . This means a *brand new model*—we can't just patch up the old jalopy."

These appointments fairly reflected Eisenhower's own outlook. The new President was determined to reverse the direction taken by the New Deal and Fair Deal, or, in his words, to remove "the Left-Wingish, pinkish influence in our life." Referring to the Tennessee Valley Authority, which symbolized such intervention in the economy, Eisenhower once blurted out: "By God, if ever we could do it, before we leave here, I'd like to see us *sell* the whole thing, but I suppose we can't go that far." The President demonstrated his economic orthodoxy by removing the moderate wage and price controls Truman had instituted, and by closing down many small federally operated establishments that appeared to compete with private business. In addition, Eisenhower cut the government payroll by 200,000 workers and trimmed federal spending by 10 percent—or $6 billion—in his first year. In 1954 Congress enacted an administration measure lowering price supports for farm products.

His position on natural resource development clearly revealed Eisenhower's desire to limit federal involvement. The President consistently favored private rather than public development of hydroelectric power plants. He reversed Truman's decision to proceed with federal construction of such a plant in Hell's Canyon, Idaho, licensed a private firm to build the dams, and threatened to veto any legislation looking toward federal development. Eisenhower opposed the Tennessee Valley Authority's request to build a new plant to furnish power for the Atomic Energy Commission. The AEC instead awarded the contract to a private concern known as Dixon-Yates. When a 1955 congressional investigation revealed that the consultant who advised the AEC to accept this arrangement was connected with an investment firm that marketed Dixon-Yates securities, a scandal erupted and Eisenhower had to cancel the contract. Finally, the President favored granting the states control of offshore oil deposits within their historic boundaries (usually a distance of three miles). Truman had twice vetoed such legislation on the grounds that tidelands oil belonged to the federal government. In May 1953, much to the delight of Texas, California, and Louisiana, Eisenhower signed the Submerged Lands Act turning these rights over to the states.

But despite Eisenhower's inclination, he in fact presided over a further enlargement of the welfare state. The social security system was expanded to include more workers, to increase benefits, and to lower the age of eligibility for old-age pensions. In 1954 an additional 4 million workers were brought under the unemployment insurance program. In 1955 Congress raised the minimum wage from 75 cents to $1.00 an hour (although Eisenhower had favored a 90-cent limit). The administration supported, unsuccessfully, a modest program to provide $200 million over three years to assist school construction in impoverished districts. The President also won authorization for building an additional 35,000 public housing units. Finally, the Interstate Highway Act (1956) pro-

vided more than $25 billion over 13 years to construct a modern inter-
state highway system. In urging its enactment, Eisenhower pointed out
that new roads could reduce traffic accidents, relieve the massive conges-
tion sure to develop as automobile use increased, and provide for quick
evacuation "in case of an atomic attack on our key cities."

In expanding government benefits the Eisenhower administration
was responding, in part, to congressional pressure. Although the Republicans won a slim victory in Congress in 1952 (they controlled the Senate by
one vote and the House by ten), the Democrats recaptured control of
both houses in 1954 and retained it throughout the remainder of Eisenhower's presidency. The administration was also taking account of economic realities. Sharp recessions in 1954 and 1958 led the President to
abandon his budget-balancing efforts and to accelerate spending. The
government therefore ran a deficit in five of his eight years in office. The
people had not elected Eisenhower to dismantle the welfare state, the
President's brother observed. Conveying the results of a public-opinion
poll, Milton Eisenhower said: "Please note the 'new conservatism' really
means that we should keep what we have, catch our breath for a while,
and improve administration; it does not mean moving backward." In the
main, that was the prescription the Eisenhower administration followed.

THE WANING OF
MCCARTHYISM

The President was as determined to step up the campaign against internal
subversion as he was to curb the expansion of the welfare state. Events,
however, sometimes worked out differently than he intended. Eisenhower
succeeded in toughening the government loyalty program. He turned responsibility for loyalty investigations over to departmental security
officers who evaluated all employees and submitted reports to each department head for action. The administration also introduced stricter
standards for measuring loyalty. The old criteria—reasonable grounds for
believing an employee disloyal (1947), or reasonable doubt as to an employee's loyalty (1951)—no longer sufficed. As of 1953 the government
would dismiss any "security risk," which meant that it would seek information concerning "any behavior, activities, or associations which tend to
show that the individual is not reliable or trustworthy." Partly to appease
right-wing Republicans, the State Department appointed an ardent Mc-
Carthyite, Scott McLeod, as security officer. Within a year, McLeod had
ousted 484 persons, including several career officials whose only crime
had been to tell the truth about the relative strength of the Communist
and Nationalist forces in China. Even Joe McCarthy seemed satisfied,
commenting that the new loyalty program was "pretty darn good, if the
administration is sincere."

Perhaps the most famous alleged "security risk" was Dr. J. Robert
Oppenheimer, who had done more than anyone else to develop the
atomic bomb during World War II. A man of profound intellect who ex-

J. Robert Oppenheimer.

erted a charismatic hold on his fellow physicists, Oppenheimer had associated with left-wing causes and individuals during the late 1930s. The government compiled a massive dossier on him during the war but knew him to be loyal, considered him indispensable, and regarded his activities as merely indiscreet. Disturbed by the nuclear arms race, Oppenheimer unsuccessfully opposed the decision to proceed with a hydrogen bomb in 1949. By 1953 he was head of Princeton's Institute for Advanced Study, retaining only a consultant's contract with the Atomic Energy Commission. When his old dossier was dragged out, Eisenhower directed that a "blank wall" be erected between Oppenheimer and sensitive material. Oppenheimer demanded a hearing. It was held in the spring of 1954 and deteriorated into a judicial farce. A special panel found, by a vote of 2–1, that reinstating Oppenheimer's clearance would be inconsistent with national security. The AEC upheld the ruling because Oppenheimer's association with radicals had exceeded the "tolerable limits of prudence and self-restraint," because his attitude toward the hydrogen bomb was "disturbing," and because of fundamental defects in his "character." Not until nine years later were amends made when the government presented the Fermi award for distinguished contributions to American science to Oppenheimer at a White House ceremony.

Congress, too, joined the continuing hunt for domestic radicals in 1954. When a conservative Republican endeavored to amend the Internal Security Act (1950) by requiring Communist-infiltrated (as well as Communist, and Communist-dominated) organizations to register with the Attorney General, a liberal Democrat offered a counter proposal: that the Communist party itself be defined as an "agency of a hostile foreign power" and stripped of the privileges political groups usually enjoyed. Hubert Humphrey of Minnesota, who proposed the change, declared: "I do not intend to be a half-patriot." In the end, the Communist Control Act (1954) incorporated both provisions, and it passed the Senate with but one dissenting vote. The act asserted that the Communist party was "an instrumentality of a conspiracy to overthrow the Government" and declared that its existence constituted a "clear, present and continuing danger." The measure was seldom invoked, although it once served to deny a Communist candidate a place on the ballot in a New Jersey election.

The new security program, the Oppenheimer case, and the mood in Congress all revealed the persistence of anticommunism. But by 1954 the worst of the hysteria was beginning to fade, and with it ebbed the power of Joseph McCarthy. Eisenhower was not primarily responsible for this. Although he strongly disapproved of McCarthy's tactics, the President had been reluctant to challenge the junior Senator from Wisconsin. Campaigning in Wisconsin in 1952, Eisenhower had agreed not to make a speech defending General George Marshall, one of his great heroes, on the grounds that to do so would alienate McCarthy's followers and hurt the Republican ticket. As one worried politician informed an Eisenhower aide, "When a man calls on the Pope, he doesn't tell him what a fine fellow Martin Luther was." After the election Eisenhower refused to criticize McCarthy publicly. Privately he said he would not "get into the gutter with that guy," although he confessed that "at times one feels almost like hanging his head in shame when he reads some of the unreasoned, vicious outbursts of demagoguery that appear in our public prints." Then, in 1954, McCarthy crossed swords with two institutions—the Army and the Senate—and they proved too powerful for him.

The Army seemed a most unlikely target, but McCarthy accused it of promoting and giving an honorable discharge to a dentist who, in filling out loyalty forms, had refused to answer questions about his political affiliations. McCarthy criticized the man responsible, General Ralph Zwicker, as not having "the brains of a five-year-old." The Senator warned Secretary of the Army Robert Stevens: "I am going to kick the brains out of anyone who protects Communists!" The Army retorted that McCarthy had tried to pull strings to obtain preferential treatment for a recently inducted member of his staff. Stevens and McCarthy then lumbered toward a showdown that knowledgeable Republicans desperately wanted to avert. One Senator advised McCarthy: "Joe, you're not dealing with Dean Acheson any longer. Let's look to the future." But McCarthy would not be swayed. Congressional hearings into the controversy began before a nationwide television audience in April 1954 and continued for two months. Toward the end, enraged by the attempt of attorney Joseph Welch to poke fun at his allegations, McCarthy savagely attacked a lawyer employed by Welch's law firm for having once belonged to a left-wing organization. Welch then berated McCarthy, concluding, "Have you no sense of decency, sir, at long last? Have you left no sense of decency?" That the congressional committee found some of the Army's allegations well-founded was less important than that many Americans, offended by McCarthy's blunderbuss manner, had begun to ask the same question.

By hurling wild accusations, McCarthy managed to alienate almost all Senate Democrats and a considerable number of Republicans. "The hard fact is that those who wear the label—Democrat—wear with it the stain of an historic betrayal," he thundered in 1954. McCarthy called Democrat J. William Fulbright "halfbright" and termed Republican Senator Ralph Flanders "senile. I think they should get a man with a net and take him to a good quiet place." In June 1954 Flanders introduced a motion to censure McCarthy. It was referred to a special committee that in September recommended censure on two counts: showing contempt for the Senate by refusing to testify before a subcommittee investigating the use of campaign funds in 1952, and abusing General Zwicker. In December, with the midterm elections safely past, the Senate censured McCarthy on the first count only. The vote was 67–22, with Democrats voting unanimously for censure and Republicans dividing evenly. Terming the action a "lynch party," McCarthy apologized to the people for having supported Eisenhower two years before. McCarthy retained his committee assignments but suffered a great loss of prestige. His popularity continued to diminish until his death three years later.

Eisenhower made his most significant contribution to civil liberties through his Supreme Court appointments. His choice of Earl Warren to replace Fred Vinson as Chief Justice in September 1953 was especially important. In 1956 Warren delivered an opinion in which the Court ruled that the federal Smith Act preempted the field of sedition, thereby rendering state sedition laws invalid. The Court upheld a lower-court decision that overturned the conviction of a Communist sentenced to 20 years in prison for having violated a Pennsylvania ordinance. A year later the Court dealt a crippling blow to the Smith Act in *Yates* v. *U.S.* (1957). John Marshall Harlan, another Eisenhower appointee, ruled for the majority that the Smith Act's injunction against conspiring to advocate the forcible overthrow of the government applied to the advocacy of concrete actions but not abstract principles. If one did not incite direct revolutionary acts, one could lawfully urge the overthrow of the government. The *Yates* decision rendered further prosecutions under the Smith Act all but impossible.

DESEGREGATION AND THE SOUTH

If the Supreme Court took a leading role in defending civil liberties, it came close to revolutionizing patterns of race relations. On May 17, 1954, in *Brown* v. *Board of Education,* the Court unanimously overturned the "separate but equal" doctrine. That doctrine, first elaborated in *Plessy* v. *Ferguson* (1896), had allowed states to provide segregated facilities so long as they were of the same quality. It provided the legal foundation for the intricate Jim Crow system in the South, which included everything from separate schools, hospitals, and railroad cars, to separate football fields, drinking fountains, and restrooms. By 1950, the Court had supported the right of a black to attend white universities or law schools, but on the grounds that those facilities could not be duplicated. In the *Brown* decision, however, the Court met the issue squarely, holding that separate public schools were inherently unequal and therefore unconstitutional. Unanimity was possible only because of the influence of Chief Justice Earl Warren. One member of the Court admitted that had the decision come a year earlier, four justices would have dissented and the majority would have written separate opinions. That, he believed, "would have been catastrophic," for only a unanimous decision stood much chance of winning public approval.

To achieve unanimity, however, Warren avoided claiming that the framers of the Fourteenth Amendment had intended to bar segregated schools, for the evidence was at best "inconclusive." Instead, the Court relied on the work of sociologists and psychologists. Even though the buildings might be of similar quality, Warren asserted, racially segregated schools had a harmful effect on black children by creating "a feeling of inferiority as to their status in the community that may affect their hearts and minds in a way unlikely ever to be undone." In asserting that this conclusion was "amply supported by modern authority," the Court relied largely on studies that indicated black children often placed a higher value on white skin color than on black, thereby revealing what one psychologist termed "basic feelings of inferiority, conflict, confusion in the self-image, resentment, hostility toward himself, hostility toward whites." The Court's reliance on evidence of this kind led such critics as Senator Sam J. Ervin of North Carolina to claim that the justices had "substituted their personal political and social ideas for the established law of the land."

Recognizing that its decision required a monumental change in Southern life and was sure to provoke intense opposition, the Supreme Court decided to allow ample time for implementation. In May 1955, in a second school decision, it asked local federal courts to determine the pace of desegregation. Insisting only that a "prompt and reasonable start" be made and that desegregation proceed "with all deliberate speed," the Court acknowledged that it would take time to iron out problems relating to administration, school size, transportation, and personnel. A "declaration of unconstitutionality is not a wand by which these transformations can be accomplished," one justice noted privately. "Not even a Court can in a day change a deplorable situation into the ideal. It does its duty if it gets effectively under way the righting of a wrong." The Court, fearing that the inability to enforce a decision would discredit the judicial process, was as committed to gradualism as to integration.

Public-opinion polls indicated that most white Southerners—perhaps more than 80 percent—opposed the *Brown* ruling. In March 1956, 101 of the 128 Southern senators and congressmen echoed this sentiment by signing a "Southern manifesto," which blasted the Supreme Court. This much the Court may have anticipated, but no one was prepared for the wave of massive resistance that followed. In states of the deep South, "White Citizens' Councils" were formed that applied economic pressure on blacks (and white businessmen) who were known to favor integration. In addition, measures of "interposition" were adopted whereby the states placed their authority behind local schoolboard officials who defied federal court orders. Various states hounded the NAACP by demanding its membership lists, using such membership as a basis for dismissal from state employment, and making it a crime to incite a disturbance by attacking local segregation ordinances. In some cases, rock-throwing mobs prevented black children from attending class with whites.

Of all the techniques of evasion and defiance, none was more effective than the pupil placement laws. Enacted in many states after 1954, these laws provided for the assignment of students on an individual basis. The criteria established by Georgia were typical. They permitted school boards to consider "the psychological qualification of the pupil for the type of teaching and associations involved," "the psychological effect upon the pupil of attendance at a particular school," "the ability to accept or conform to new and different educational environments," "the morals, conduct, health, and personal standards of the pupil," and "mental energy and ability." The result was that black and white children were invariably assigned to different schools. In 1958 the Supreme Court accepted the constitutionality of such laws. Consequently, ten years after the *Brown* ruling, the vast majority of black children in the South still attended segregated schools.

Nevertheless, the forces unleashed by the Supreme Court helped inspire Southern blacks to adopt a more militant posture. In December 1955 Negroes in Montgomery, Alabama began a boycott of city buses to protest Jim Crow seating practices which required blacks to vacate seats and move to the rear to make room for whites who had boarded after them. The protesters demanded courteous treatment by bus drivers, employment of black drivers in black districts, and seating on a first-come,

Central High School, Little Rock, Arkansas, 1957.

first-served basis with "Negroes seated from the back of the bus toward the front [and], whites seated from the front toward the back."

The boycott's leader was 27-year-old Martin Luther King, Jr., who, after having received a divinity degree and a doctorate in theology from Boston University, had become pastor of the Dexter Avenue Baptist Church. King considered his task that of "combining the militant and the moderate." He preached a philosophy of nonviolent resistance, declaring: "We must meet the forces of hate with the power of love; we must meet physical force with soul force." By arranging car and taxi pools and sometimes walking long distances, Montgomery's blacks made the boycott effective. They also adhered to King's teachings even when whites retaliated with mass arrests and intimidation. The movement finally achieved victory in May 1956, when a district court ruled segregation on the city buses illegal, and when the Supreme Court affirmed the ruling six months later. After another flurry of violence, beatings, and bombings, desegregation was carried out. In 1957 King also established the Southern Christian Leadership Conference, which served thereafter as his organizational base.

Turmoil in the South ultimately had repercussions in Washington. Eisenhower personally regretted the 1954 desegregation ruling, believing that law could not alter age-old customs overnight and that, in his words, "we can't demand perfection in these moral questions." The President also opposed federal infringement on states' rights. Yet in the District of Columbia, where the states'-rights problem did not arise, Eisenhower moved swiftly to comply with court orders. His administration ended segregation in Washington's restaurants, hotels, theaters, and public schools. Although Eisenhower approached the matter of legislation gingerly, he eventually concurred with Attorney General Herbert Brownell, who favored legislative action. In 1957 Congress passed the first civil rights act in 82 years, empowering the Justice Department to seek injunctions against interference with the right to vote and creating a Commission on Civil Rights to investigate such occurrences. Although clothed only with fact-finding powers, the commission viewed its chief task as "restoring the franchise to all American citizens." In its report, which demonstrated beyond any doubt that a pattern of discrimination barred Negroes from voting in the South, the commission recommended the appointment of temporary federal registrars as a solution.

The Eisenhower administration faced its most explosive civil rights crisis in Little Rock, Arkansas. Desegregation of Central High School was scheduled to begin in September 1957. But many whites wished to obstruct the plan, and the state's ambitious Governor, Orville Faubus, believed that supporting desegregation would mean political suicide. To avert violence when school opened, Faubus sent the National Guard to Little Rock with instructions to prevent integration. The guardsmen, bayonets at the ready, turned back nine blacks who sought admission and maintained segregation for nearly three weeks until a federal judge ordered them to desist. When Faubus removed the troops, a howling mob overwhelmed the police who tried to protect the black students. With the level of tension rising by the hour, the mayor appealed to Eisenhower, informing him that the "situation is out of control and police cannot disperse the mob." Eisenhower responded by sending federal troops to uphold the court order. The President told one unhappy Southern senator that "failure to act in such a case would be tantamount to acquiescence in anarchy and the dissolution of the union." Troops patrolled the high school for months, but the controversy over desegregation convulsed the city for two more years.

Jack Kerouac's novel *On the Road* was published in 1957 and instantly became a best seller. It had taken Kerouac six years to find a publisher but that was hardly surprising since the manuscript, in its original form, violated all literary conventions. Typed as an unbroken, seldom-punctuated, single-spaced paragraph, on a 250-foot roll of shelf paper (the last six feet of which were rewritten when a pet cocker spaniel chewed them up), the novel appeared only after it had

William Burroughs, Peter Orlovsky, Gregory Corso, and Allen Ginsberg.

378 been heavily edited by the publisher. According to Kerouac's biographer, Ann Charters, *On the Road* "captured the spirit of his own generation, their restlessness and confusions in the years immediately following World War II." Centering on a series of cross-country automobile trips taken by Kerouac and his friends in the late 1940s, the novel popularized the life style associated with the major figures in the Beat Movement. The fictional characters—Sal Paradise, Dean Moriarty, Carlo Marx, and Old Bull Lee—had real-life counterparts in Kerouac, Neal Cassady, Allen Ginsberg, and William Burroughs.

To say, as one critic has, that *On the Road* depicted "an underground subculture that departed entirely from the dominant middle class mores of the fifties" is to understate the matter. Beat writers, rejecting socially prescribed roles and socially approved forms of behavior, exhibited more contempt than pity for the "square" world, for "the middleclass non-identity which usually finds its perfect expression . . . in rows of well-to-do houses with lawns and television sets in each living room with everybody looking at the same thing and thinking the same thing at the same time." The Beats most admired those who in their view were the least tied down by obligations to career or country—the poets, the hoodlums, the junkies, the hoboes, the jazz musicians,

Jack Kerouac, 1958.

City Lights Bookshop, San Francisco, 1959.

and the Negroes. Those groups, generally regarded as among the most deprived in the nation, were from the Beat perspective among the most fortunate: free to take life as it came, to act with abandon, to appreciate the intensity of each experience, to "dig everything."

Though Beat writings contained a critique of conformity, technology, and mechanization, Beat writers shared no single political outlook. Allen Ginsberg (whose poem *Howl* began "I saw the best minds of my generation destroyed by madness, starving hysterical naked/dragging themselves through the negro streets at dawn looking for an angry fix") offered a thoroughly radical indictment of American society, its anticommunist paranoia, and a reliance on nuclear weapons. Yet William Burroughs, the author of another Beat

classic, *Naked Lunch* (1959), believed that "increased government control leads to a totalitarian state." In 1956 Kerouac declared that if he were to vote it would be for Dwight Eisenhower. The key word was "if." What united the Beats was a conviction that politics held few answers to life's most crucial problems. Those problems required personal rather than social solutions. The characteristic Beat stance was one of political disengagement.

Beat authors received much acclaim in the 1950s (a reviewer in *The New York Times* hailed publication of *On the Road* as a "historic occasion"), but they more commonly encountered hostility. *Time* magazine, denouncing the Beats as "disorganization" men concerned only with self-gratification, labelled Ginsberg "the discount-house Whitman of the Beat

Ginsberg at Kerouac's gravesite, 1969.

Generation." Another reviewer, in a blistering assault on "the Know-Nothing Bohemians," remarked on Kerouac's "simple inability to say anything in words." The Customs Bureau seized copies of *Howl*, attempting to repress it on the grounds of obscenity. In 1957, however, a judge in San Francisco cleared the poem of those charges. William Burroughs spent years in self-imposed exile to avoid indictment for drug possession, and Neal Cassady went to jail in 1958 for marijuana possession. Kerouac, a victim of alcoholism, died at the age of 47 in 1969. He had been too ill in his final years to realize that the cultural rebellion then sweeping across the nation owed much to the Beat Generation.

As massive change began at home, so similar rumbles began to shake a world supposedly divided rigidly into only "two camps." Secretary of State John Foster Dulles had difficulty comprehending the rumbles partly because of his own unbending anti-Communist views. The deeply religious son of a Presbyterian minister, Dulles hated atheistic communism. As the senior partner of a great New York law firm, Dulles had formed ties during the interwar period with Western nations that were staunchly anti-Soviet. His diplomatic experience reached back to 1919, and this long background plus his religious beliefs led Eisenhower to remark, "To me he is like a patriarch out of the Old Testament."

Several other convictions were perhaps most important in shaping Dulles's policies. He had served under Dean Acheson, notably as the negotiator for the Japanese security treaty. As Secretary of State he carried on his predecessor's Cold War policies. If anything, Dulles believed Acheson had not been tough enough, certainly not anti-Communist enough publicly to quiet such critics as Joseph McCarthy. Dulles therefore proclaimed in 1952 that his policies would aim at "peaceful liberation" of Communist areas, not mere containment. This meant no negotiations with the Soviets. Even after Stalin's death in March 1953 and Winston Churchill's public plea for a summit conference to reduce Cold War tensions, Dulles assured Americans that he would continue to fight rather than negotiate. Churchill disgustedly remarked that Dulles was "the only bull I know who carried his china shop with him." The Secretary's belief that he had to appease McCarthy and other congressmen also resulted in a purge of Foreign Service Officers that crippled the American diplomatic corps for the next decade.

Finally, Dulles assumed that for economic and strategic reasons, the United States had to intensify Acheson's drive to integrate the "free world" within a system controlled by Americans. Dulles constantly worried that communists would gain control of such third-world areas as Southeast Asia and the Middle East, which contained rich raw materials, and thus be able slowly to strangle the United States economy.

Despite Dulles's fears, American policies were usually restrained because Eisenhower kept a firm leash on the State Department. The President once remarked, "There's only one man I know who has seen more of the world and talked with more people and knows more than [Dulles] does—and that's me." Eisenhower rejected Dulles's advice to end the Korean conflict "before all Asia . . . by giving the Chinese one hell of a licking." Instead, the President, knowing military victory impossible, obtained an armistice in mid-1953 by using a combination of diplomacy and military threat (including the deployment of atomic-tipped missiles in Korea when China and North Korea refused to make peace). Eisenhower's primary concern was to balance the budget and thereby, he believed, invigorate the economy. He cut Truman's military budget, especially the expensive ground combat forces. Informing his Cabinet that "peace rests squarely on, among other things, productivity," the President

Dulles and Eisenhower.

emphasized "that unless we can put things in the hands of people who are starving to death we can never lick communism." His concern heightened when in the mid-1950s Russia's economy grew at the rate of 7 percent annually while the American increased at about half that figure. Eisenhower nevertheless retained faith in the free market system, refused to inject massive governmental monies during his first term, and left office warning about the dangers of "a military-industrial complex."

Dulles's diplomacy therefore had to rely not upon conventional ground troops, but rather upon nuclear "massive retaliation," or, as he defined it, the ability "to retaliate instantly against open aggression by Red Armies . . . by means of our own choosing." Dulles and new military strategists, such as 30-year-old Henry Kissinger of Harvard, declared that atomic weapons could be refined so that they could be effectively used in conventional wars. Cheaper than troops, such weapons could give the country "more bang for a buck." Meanwhile, Dulles flew around the globe establishing new alliances with nations on the Communist borders. These countries, especially those in the Middle East (where the Central Treaty Organization, or CENTO, was formed), and in Southeast Asia (where the

Southeast Asia Treaty Organization, or SEATO, developed), would hopefully provide the manpower while Dulles gave atomic support if necessary. The Secretary might have proclaimed "peaceful liberation," but Eisenhower was in effect following Truman's "containment" idea.

EISENHOWER AND
THE AMERICAN
CONSENSUS

To establish these policies, Eisenhower worked with Congress far more than had Truman. Yet the new President fought back hard and successfully in 1954 when conservatives, led by Republican Senator John Bricker of Ohio, tried to pass the "Bricker Amendment" to the Constitution. This proposal gave Congress additional power over the President's constitutional right to make treaties and especially struck at Executive agreements (those made by the President with a foreign power which would be binding only for the President's term in office, but which usually remained in effect much longer—as had Roosevelt's Executive agreements at Yalta). Eisenhower refused to compromise his power. Overcoming strong Southern Democratic-Republican support for the amendment, he defeated it by a narrow margin.

CRISES IN A THIRD CAMP: IRAN, GUATEMALA, AND SOUTHEAST ASIA

Fate tricked Eisenhower and Dulles. They were prepared to deal with Stalinist Russia, but Stalin died in March 1953. New Soviet leadership, soon headed by Nikita Khrushchev, changed some policies, concentrated on internal development, and made overtures to Tito and Mao Tse-Tung—leaders whom Stalin had angered with his iron-fisted methods. Eisenhower and Dulles had also planned to concentrate on European affairs, the area they knew best. In 1954, the Secretary of State and British officials pressured France finally to agree to German rearmament and membership in NATO. The following year Dulles could claim a victory for "liberation" as Soviet troops finally left Austria after the Austrians promised they would not join any anti-Soviet alliance. Washington's European policies seemed firmly in place.

But American energies soon had to switch to the newly emerging nations. The focal point of the Cold War was changing. Dulles understood the importance of this "third camp." "To oppose nationalism is counterproductive," he declared. He worked to remove British and French colonialism from the Middle East and Asia before the foreign domination triggered further radical nationalism. But he also expected the new nations to be pro-American and anti-Communist, hence his famous remark that "neutrality . . . is an immoral and short-sighted conception." Fearing that Khrushchev's economic and ideological power might woo the third world to the Soviets, Dulles grimly warned NATO leaders of the possible consequences: "The world ratio as between Communist dominated peoples and free peoples would change from a ratio of two-to-one in favor of freedom to a ratio of one-to-three against freedom. That," the Secretary of State emphasized, "would be an almost intolerable ratio, given the industrialized nature of the Atlantic community and its dependence upon broad markets and access to raw materials."

Within 18 months after entering office, Dulles scored two triumphs in the third world. In Iran, a nationalist government under Mohammed Mossadegh had taken over the nation's rich oil wells in 1951 from British companies that had long exploited them. Mossadegh's action set a dangerous precedent, for the Middle East held nearly 90 percent of all non-Communist oil reserves, and his success could lead to similar seizures elsewhere. In 1953 the U. S. Central Intelligence Agency worked with Iranian army officers to overthrow Mossadegh, give full powers to the friendly Shah of Iran, and restore the oil wells to the companies. But this time British oil firms were to share the profits with American companies.

Dulles performed an encore in Latin America. Since 1947 the United States had kept its southern neighbors in line by military aid, channeled through the Rio Pact of 1947 (a hemispheric military alliance that was a preview of NATO), and the establishment of the Organization of American States in 1948. In the OAS Charter, each nation promised not to intervene in others' internal affairs, to consult frequently, and to resolve disputes peacefully. The United States, however, refused to give economic aid the Latin Americans desperately needed, particularly when their raw materials dropped steeply in price during the mid-1950s.

Guatemalan officials took matters into their own hands. In this desperately poor nation, roughly the size of Tennessee, a 1944 revolution had weakened the dictatorial rule of a few wealthy Guatemalans who had long dominated affairs. During 1953 Colonel Jacobo Arbenz Guzmán accelerated the reform, seizing vast properties held by the American-owned United Fruit Company. Dulles demanded prompt payment for the property. Guatemala was obviously unable to pay immediately. In May 1954, when the Arbenz government received a shipment of arms from the Communist bloc, Dulles responded swiftly. He obtained a general anti-Communist resolution from the OAS clearly aimed at Guatemala. Then he armed an anti-Arbenz force that had gathered in neighboring Honduras. In June 1954 this unit of Guatemalans marched into their country, overthrew Arbenz, and restored United Fruit's property. Dulles lied in publicly disclaiming any connection with the coup. He had little choice, for the United States had broken its own OAS pledge not to intervene in another nation's internal affairs. When Arbenz tried to obtain a hearing at the United Nations, Dulles blocked it. The United States had overthrown a constitutional government, and guerrilla warfare soon erupted again in Guatemala, but Dulles believed that he had saved the hemisphere from communism.

The administration's next crisis was different. It occurred in Southeast Asia and required the delicate operation of removing French colonialism from Indochina (Cambodia, Laos, and Vietnam), while preventing Ho Chi Minh, who was both nationalist and communist, from obtaining power in Vietnam. Since 1950 American aid to France had multiplied until by 1953 it accounted for 80 percent of the French war budget for Indochina. France nevertheless suffered defeat after defeat at the hands of Ho's troops. In early 1954 the French made a catastrophic blunder by committing main forces to the indefensible city of Dienbienphu. Paris appealed for help. Dulles wanted to intervene, as did Vice-President Richard Nixon, and apparently the use of atomic weapons was seriously considered. Eisenhower's military sense stopped what could have been a tragedy. He refused to intervene with conventional forces unless congressional leaders approved and Great Britain agreed to join the effort. Neither would go along. The opposition of the Senate Democratic leader, Lyndon Johnson of Texas, was especially strong.

The defeated French then met with Ho's government and other interested nations at Geneva, Switzerland. Two agreements emerged in July 1954. The first, signed only by France and Ho's regime, worked out a cease-fire arrangement. To carry out this agreement, a temporary dividing line was drawn across the country at the 17th parallel. The second document, the "Final Declaration," provided for reuniting the country under procedures which were to climax with elections in 1956. It further stated that the 17th parallel line "is provisional and should in no way be interpreted as a political or territorial boundary." Dulles would not directly endorse this agreement. Ho could obviously win the election (Eisenhower later estimated he would have received 80 percent of the vote), and Dulles did not want to be a party to a pact giving Vietnam to a Communist regime. Instead, Eisenhower brought in Ngo Dinh Diem to head a new South Vietnam government. Diem had been living in an American Roman Catholic seminary. Dulles and Diem readily agreed that no national elections should be held. American aid rapidly flowed to Diem, and the United States now replaced France as the key foreign power in Southeast Asia.

The American commitment was neither accidental nor abrupt. The State Department had concluded in 1951 that Indochina had to be controlled for its "much-needed rice, rubber, and tin," and because its fall "would be taken by many as a sign that the force of communism is irresistible." A secret National Security Council paper in 1952 reiterated these points, adding that the loss of Southeast Asia would "make it extremely difficult to prevent Japan's eventual accommodation to Communism." Japan, which was the centerpiece of American policies in Asia, required Southeast Asia's markets and raw materials. Eisenhower publicly warned in 1954 that if Vietnam fell, the rest of non-Communist Asia could follow like a "fallen domino."

In late 1954 Dulles tried to keep the dominoes in place by establishing the Southeast Asia Treaty Organization (SEATO). The signatories (United States, France, England, Australia, New Zealand, Philippines, Thailand, and Pakistan) promised to "consult immediately" if aggression occurred in the area. It was a weak alliance, made weaker by India's, Indonesia's, and Burma's refusal to join, but it would provide a major pretext for the American involvement in Vietnam during the 1960s. The Senate overwhelmingly ratified the SEATO pact. Meanwhile, when Communist China threatened small islands around Formosa which it claimed were rightfully its own, Eisenhower warned that any move would be countered by the United States fleet. The President was even prepared to use nuclear weapons against China if it attacked the offshore islands. Dulles and Chiang then worked out a military alliance that assured long-term American support. To show its enthusiasm for these measures, the Senate vastly increased presidential powers by passing the "Formosa Resolution," which gave Eisenhower the right to respond to any crisis around Formosa without consulting Congress. To fight the Cold War more effectively, the Senate was surrendering its constitutional powers to declare war.

THE TURN: SUEZ AND HUNGARY, 1956

Centralized power had dangerous implications, particularly if it could be used irresponsibly in a world comprised not simply of "two camps," but rather of "gray areas," as the nations that disavowed both camps came to be known. The rapid emergence of such gray areas caused two momentous crises in 1956.

The first occurred early in the year when Nikita Khrushchev launched an attack against the ghost of Josef Stalin by condemning him as a repressive ruler and military blunderer. Khrushchev hoped to consolidate his own power, remove Stalinists who opposed him, and gain room to carry out his own policies. The results, however, were quite different. Soviet-controlled nations of Eastern Europe seized on the speech as an opportunity for throwing off Stalinist policies and seeking their own nationalistic goals. Riots occurred in Hungary and Poland as crowds demanded removal of Stalinist leaders. In early autumn, a confused Khrushchev bent to some demands, but the dissolution of the Soviet bloc continued.

Meanwhile the United States was also clashing with several of its client states. In 1952 the British had been forced by Egyptian nationalism to surrender their long hold on that country. Two years later, the government of General Abdul Nasser demanded that Britain turn over the vital Suez Canal to Egypt. Nasser's plans also included building a great Aswan dam on the Nile River to provide badly needed electric power. Dulles offered to help fund the dam, hoping that this would pull Nasser closer to the West. But Egypt then made an arms agreement with the Soviet bloc and recognized Communist China. Dulles retracted his offer, punishing Nasser before the world for dallying with the Communists. The Egyptian leader retaliated by seizing the Suez Canal in July 1956 so he could use the canal tolls to build the dam himself.

Dulles rushed across the Atlantic to work out a compromise. Before he could succeed, the British and French made a final effort in late October to restore their old imperial dreams by sending a military force into the Suez. They were joined by Israel, who hoped to improve the

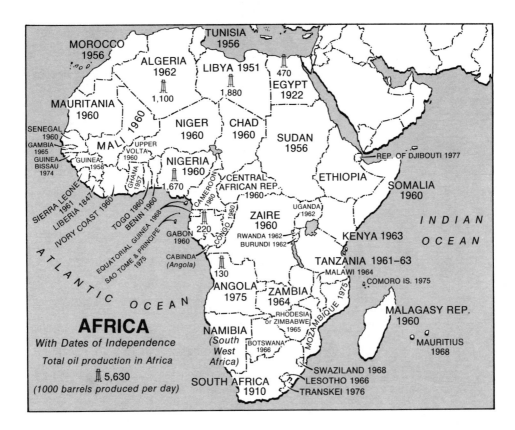

AFRICA

With Dates of Independence

Total oil production in Africa

⛏ 5,630

(1000 barrels produced per day)

dangerously insecure borders it had lived with since 1948. Dulles and Eisenhower were aghast. They feared that the conflict would turn the Arabs against the West, lead to seizure of the vast Western-controlled oil resources in the area, and give Khrushchev the chance to inject Russian power into the Mediterranean theater. The United States demanded an immediate withdrawal by the Anglo-French-Israeli forces, turning off large amounts of oil to England and France until they pulled back. Deserted by the Americans, the Europeans retreated, followed by the Israelis.

Khrushchev seized this opportunity to dispatch the Red Army and execution squads to end the anti-Stalinist uprisings in Hungary. Order was reimposed in Eastern Europe. The United States offered no aid to the Hungarian resistance—so ended Dulles's vaunted policy of "peaceful liberation." Russia then offered Nasser funds and experts to build the Aswan dam project. The Soviets were indeed a new presence in the Mediterranean. Equally important, Nasser had successfully defied one of the two superpowers, and the Poles, Hungarians, British, and French had vividly demonstrated that the world was no longer comprised of two monolithic camps. The second Eisenhower administration would begin in a radically altered world.

Suggested Reading

Useful accounts of the Eisenhower administration are Herbert Parmet, *Eisenhower and the American Crusades* (1972); Peter Lyon, *Eisenhower* (1974); Charles C. Alexander, *Holding the Line: The Eisenhower Era* (1975); and Douglas T. Miller and Marion Nowak, *The Fifties* (1977). Eisenhower's memoirs—*Mandate for Change* (1963) and *Waging Peace* (1965)—give his own side of the story. A somewhat more critical view is offered by Emmet John Hughes, who served as a presidential speechwriter, in *The Ordeal of Power* (1963). On the 1952 election, consult John Bartlow Martin, *Adlai Stevenson of Illinois* (1977). An important study of Republican conservation policies is Aaron Wildavsky, *Dixon-Yates* (1962); the best account of Eisenhower and Congress is Gary Reichard, *The Reaffirmation of Republicanism* (1975).

The sociological literature on the suburbs, while uneven, is indispensable. The more valuable studies include Herbert Gans, *The Levittowners* (1967); Scott Donaldson, *The Suburban Myth* (1969); William M. Dobriner, *Class in Suburbia* (1963); Bennett M. Berger, *Working-Class Suburb* (1969); and Barry Schwartz, ed., *The Changing Face of the Suburbs* (1976). Michael N. Danielson, *The Politics of Exclusion* (1976) discusses the exclusion of blacks. For conservatism, see William Newman, *The Futilitarian Society* (1961); and John P. Diggins, *Up From Communism: Conservative Odysseys in American Intellectual History* (1975).

Supreme Court decisions in the area of civil liberties are explored in Thomas Emerson, *The System of Freedom of Expression* (1970). For McCarthy's difficulties with the Army and the Senate, see Robert Griffith, *The Politics of Fear: Joseph R. McCarthy and the Senate* (1970); and Fred Cook, *The Nightmare Decade* (1971). Two fine studies of the most famous case involving science and national security are Philip Stern, *The Oppenheimer Case* (1969); and John Major, *The Oppenheimer Hearing* (1971).

For the 1954 desegregation ruling, its origins and consequences, see Richard Kluger, *Simple Justice* (1976); for a critique, see Lino A. Graglia, *Disaster by Decree* (1976). The Southern response is examined in Numan Bartley, *The Rise of Massive Resistance* (1969); and Francis M. Wilhoit, *The Politics of Massive Resistance* (1973). Martin Luther King describes the Montgomery bus boycott in *Stride Toward Freedom* (1958); see, also, David Lewis, *King: A Biography* (1978). The background of the 1957 Civil Rights Act is explored in J. W. Anderson, *Eisenhower, Brownell, and the Congress* (1964); its effect, in Foster R. Dulles, *The Civil Rights Commission* (1968).

A readable overview of the era's foreign policies is Townsend Hoopes, *The Devil and John Foster Dulles* (1973); while Louis Gerson, *John Foster Dulles* (1967), is more sympathetic. The Soviet view is in Nikita Khrushchev's remarkable two-volume memoir; see especially *Khrushchev Remembers* (1970). For specific crises, see Burton I. Kaufman, *The Oil Cartel Case* (1978) on Iranian affairs from a fresh perspective; Robert F. Randle, *Geneva, 1954* (1976); Chester L. Cooper's important books, *Lost Crusade, America in Vietnam* (1970), and *The Lion's Last Roar: Suez, 1956* (1978); Ronald M. Schneider, *Communism in Guatemala, 1944–1954* (1958); and Robert A. Divine's valuable studies, *Foreign Policy and U.S. Presidential Elections, 1940–1960,* 2 vols., (1974), and *Blowing on the Wind: The Nuclear Test Ban Debate, 1954–1960* (1978), crucial for its analysis of the American scientific community.

For analyses of the Beat generation, consult Ann Charters, *Kerouac: A Biography* (1973); and John Tytell, *Naked Angels: The Lives and Literature of the Beat Generation* (1976).

Kennedy, Pierre Salinger, and John Jr.

CHAPTER THIRTEEN

1957–1963

New Frontiers
at Home and Abroad

THE TIMES THEY ARE A-CHANGIN'
Words and music by **Bob Dylan**

*Come gather 'round people wherever you
  roam
And admit that the waters around you have
  grown
And accept it that soon you'll be drenched to
  the bone,
If your time to you is worth savin'—
Then you better start swimmin' or you'll sink
  like a stone,
For the times they are a-changin'!*

*Come writers and critics who prophecies with
  your pen
And keep your eyes wide, the chance won't
  come again.
And don't speak too soon for the wheel's still
  in spin
And there's no tellin' who that it's namin'
For the loser now will be later to win
For the times they are a-changin'.*

*Come senators, congressmen please heed the
  call
Don't stand in the doorway
Don't block up the hall
For he that gets hurt
Will be he who has stalled
There's a battle
Outside and it's ragin'*

*It'll soon shake your windows
And rattle your walls
For the times they are a-changin'.*

*Come mothers and fathers,
Throughout the land
And don't criticize
What you can't understand.
Your sons and your daughters
Are beyond your command
Your old road is
Rapidly agin'
Please get out of the new one
If you can't lend your hand
For the times they are a-changin'.*

*The line it is drawn
The curse it is cast
The slow one now will
Later be fast.
As the present now
Will later be past
The order is rapidly fadin'
And the first one now
Will later be last
For the times they are a-changin'*

The Suez and Hungarian crises transformed the Cold War. They demonstrated that the two great powers no longer monopolized global affairs and especially could no longer control the newly emerging areas. Confronted with this new world, American policymakers could respond in one of two ways: either continue to focus on Europe and relationships with Russia or begin to concentrate attention on such less industrialized areas as Vietnam and Latin America. The Eisenhower administration chose the first alternative, John F. Kennedy the second. Kennedy's fateful choice determined the nation's foreign policy for the next ten years. And like the 1956 crises in foreign affairs, so too would domestic decisions of the Eisenhower years shape American internal affairs into the distant future. The Supreme Court ruling of 1954 outlawing school segregation, for example, set in motion a chain of events that unleashed a massive civil rights movement in the early 1960s. Both abroad and at home Americans faced a transformed world. It remained only to be seen how they would respond to it.

AFTER SUEZ: EUROPE

Although the Suez and Hungarian crises reshaped world affairs, the transformation did not occur overnight. The most dramatic international event in the late 1950s was the Russian-American confrontation over Berlin, a city that had long symbolized the hostility between East and West. Situated inside Communist-controlled East Germany, Berlin had been divided into Russian and Western sectors since 1945. As Khrushchev bluntly remarked, West Berlin was a "bone in my throat," for it served as a display of Western wealth and power as well as a listening-post deep within the Soviet empire.

In 1958 Khrushchev decided to dislodge the bone. He believed that the launching of Sputnik in late 1957 gave him a military advantage, for projecting this earth satellite into the upper atmosphere demonstrated that Soviet missile capability was greater than the American. Moreover, in early 1958 Western Europe, with American encouragement, created a large common economic market (the European Economic Community, or EEC) by agreeing gradually to abolish tariffs and other restrictions on trade. The EEC included France, Italy, Belgium, Netherlands, Luxembourg, and—most crucial to Khrushchev—West Germany. With this decision, the Europeans had gone far to remove the nationalisms that had produced two world wars. But they had also tied West Germany more firmly within the Western camp. Faced with a rejuvenated, pro-West Germany—always a fearful sight to Russians—and believing that his new missile capacity gave him the necessary diplomatic leverage, Khrushchev struck at the Western Powers by demanding in November 1958 that they surrender control of West Berlin. Eisenhower and the European leaders rejected the demand and stood firm.

Khrushchev backed off, proposing that visits be exchanged with Eisenhower for personal discussions. The United States eagerly accepted, particularly since a visit would allow the President to see previously closed areas of Russia and spread the Eisenhower charm. "The name Eisenhower meant so much" to the Russians, one State Department official noted. "I mean, you could send [Vice-President] Nixon over, but the average Ivan wouldn't know who the hell he was. But Eisenhower meant something. It was victory. It was World War II and all that." Khrushchev arrived in the United States in mid-1959, visiting American farms and a movie set of "Can-Can" (whose uninhibited dancing girls appalled him), and discussing foreign policy with the President. Eisenhower, however, was never to see Moscow. He had planned to do so after a summit conference in early 1960 in Paris, but before world leaders could fly to the French capital, Khrushchev angrily announced that the Soviets had shot down an American spy plane, the U-2, which had been taking aerial photographs more than a thousand miles inside Russia.

At first Washington denied involvement. Khrushchev then produced evidence that the denials were lies, and Eisenhower hastily assumed full responsibility for sending the plane over Russia. The Soviet leader heatedly refused to talk with the President, and the summit was over before it had begun. The United States was embarrassed, but it is probable that neither Khrushchev nor Eisenhower had originally wanted to go to Paris, for neither side was willing to budge on the key Berlin question. Of equal significance, U-2 planes had been flying over Russia for four years, bringing back information that convinced Washington officials that despite Khrushchev's bragging about his missiles, he did not have missile superiority or even military equality with the United States. Khrushchev realized that he had been found out and therefore was not displeased to avoid talking with the President. Publicly, the Russian began softening his stand, downplaying the importance of missiles: "They are not like cucumbers, you know—you don't eat them, and more than a certain number are not required." The real loser was U-2 pilot Gary Powers. He was imprisoned in Russia for two years until exchanged for a captured Soviet spy.

AFTER SUEZ: NEWLY EMERGING AREAS

Berlin captured world attention, but the effects of the 1956 crises were already working profound changes elsewhere. For the Suez episode had demonstrated new and unexpected features of the Cold War. Despite its awesome power, the United States had been unable to control its junior partners, the British and French. The Soviets, meanwhile, had needed tanks and planes to keep its supposed ally, Hungary, within the Russian bloc. The old bipolar globe—the world divided and controlled by the two powers—was disappearing. This disappearance was hastened as China and Russia became enemies in 1960 because of differences over Communist ideology and their 1200-mile common boundary.

The effects of these changes were especially noticeable in the newly independent nations in Asia and Africa, which had recently freed themselves from European colonialism. The leaders of these countries often refused to join either the Soviet or American side. They instead tried to play Washington off against Moscow in order to acquire aid from both camps. This had been Nasser's policy in Egypt, and although he had suffered a military setback in 1956, he had retained control of the Suez Canal while receiving aid from both Americans and Russians. Nasser set an example that sparked nationalist revolutions in the Middle East.

Eisenhower and Dulles feared that the new nations would be unstable, anti-Western, and, therefore, pro-Communist. As Dulles had once blurted out, neutrality was "immoral." These changes in turn could threaten the supply of oil which Europe and the United States required from the Middle East. The results could be disastrous. "In my view," Dulles remarked in early 1957, "we are in a war situation right now." Consequently, in the spring of that year Congress passed a resolution proposed by Eisenhower that allowed him to commit American power to stop "overt armed aggression" by Communists in the Middle East if a nation in the area asked for such help. This "Eisenhower Doctrine" was unfortunate. It angered some Middle Eastern nations, divided others, and forced some to choose between East and West, something they did not want to do.

The Doctrine, moreover, was largely irrelevant. The area was not threatened by overt Communist invasion but by intense, internal nationalism, which the proclamation did not cover. Yet when the monarchy in Iraq was suddenly overthrown by an internal coup led by pro-Nasser nationalists in 1958, the government of neighboring Lebanon asked for American protection. No "overt" Communist threat was apparent; indeed, Eisenhower knew the Lebanese President needed help against *internal* opposition, not external. Eisenhower nevertheless immediately landed 14,000 American troops in Lebanon to display his muscle. The bikini-clad bathers on the shore scarcely moved as the Marines waded in, and the effect on Iraq was equally slight. Despite the Eisenhower Doctrine and the Lebanon landings, Middle Eastern nationalism continued to flourish and unsettle the area. As the Suez crisis had demonstrated, foreign troops only worsened the situation. The world could not be rolled back to the pre-1956 years.

THE GOOD NEIGHBOR AND A CHANGING NEIGHBORHOOD

Nationalism also threatened American policies in Latin America, where the United States had seemed to have sure control. By 1955 American companies produced 10 percent of Latin America's products, 30 percent of its export goods (and in such nations as Venezuela and Cuba two or three times that percentage), invested more than $3 billion directly, and dominated the continent's great oil and mineral resources. That domination, however, had brought no prosperity to most Latin Americans. With

CENTRAL AND SOUTH AMERICA IN THE 1954–1970 ERA

UNITED STATES

CUBA
Batista overthrown 1959
Attempted anti-Castro invasion 1961
Soviet military aid, U.S. quarantine 1962

Miami

BAHAMAS
(Br.)

DOMINICAN REP.
U.S. broke diplomatic ties 1960
Trujillo assassinated 1961
Diplomatic ties restored 1962
U.S. and O.A.S. intervention 1965

MEXICO

Havana

Mexico
City

BR.
HONDURAS

JAMAICA

HAITI

GUATEMALA
*Arbenz
overthrown 1954
Castillo Armas
assassinated
1957*

HONDURAS
Diaz overthrown 1956

BARBADOS
Pérez Jiménez overthrown 1958
Anti-Nixon riots 1958

NICARAGUA
Canal Zone

EL SALVADOR

COSTA RICA

TRINIDAD AND TOBAGO

Caracas

VENEZUELA

GUYANA

SURINAM (Neth.)

FR. GUIANA

PANAMA
Anti-U.S. riots 1959

Bogota

Rojas Pinilla forced out 1957

COLOMBIA

P A C I F I C

O C E A N

EQUADOR Quito

PERU

B R A Z I L

Anti-Nixon riots 1958
Military coup 1962
Military coup 1968

Lima

BOLIVIA
La Paz

Brasília

*Average annual per capita income
late 1960's*

Argentina	$800
Barbados	428
Bolivia	165
Brazil	350
Chile	465
Colombia	262
Costa Rica	380
Cuba	310
Dominican Rep.	212
Ecuador	183
El Salvador	245
Guatemala	264
Guyana	250
Haiti	75
Honduras	209
Jamaica	431
Mexico	600
Nicaragua	347
Panama	477
Paraguay	192
Peru	241
Trinidad & Tobago	515
Uruguay	537
Venezuela	902

PARAGUAY
Asuncion

Rio de Janeiro

*Salvador
Allende
elected 1970*

CHILE

Santiago

Buenos Aires

URUGUAY
Montevideo

ARGENTINA

*Punta del Este Conferences
1961, 1962*

A T L A N T I C

O C E A N

⫽⫽⫽	*Under $200*
▒▒▒	*$200-399*
▓▓▓	*$400-599*
∕∕∕	*Over $600*

little industrialization, the area depended on world market prices for its oil and other raw materials, but most of these prices declined in the late 1950s. Foreign investment worsened this drain of money, for Americans took more profits out of Latin America than they put back in. This economic trap was aggravated by the highest population growth in the world. In other words, the key sections of Latin America's economy were largely exploited by foreign capital, and that economy was scarcely growing fast enough to keep up with the population increase.

Washington officials understood this, but since 1947 had poured their resources into Europe while taking Latin America for granted. During these years Belgium and Luxembourg alone received three times more economic aid than the twenty Latin American nations combined. Over two-thirds of the aid that did go south was for military purposes, not economic growth. The political results were all too obvious: instability, frequent changes of government, repressive right-wing dictatorships, and a heightened anti-American nationalism among intellectuals and jailed politicians. Between 1930 and 1965, 106 illegal and often bloody changes of government occurred throughout the continent. Only Mexico of all twenty Latin American governments had peaceful presidential changes through this period. (Woodrow Wilson, who had bitterly opposed the Mexican Revolution between 1913 and 1916, would doubtless have been surprised but pleased.)

Latin America differed fundamentally from Africa or Southeast Asia, for it had been free of direct colonial control for more than a century, and was politically more experienced. Latin Americans knew that their problems could not be solved by throwing off foreign rulers as Egypt, Vietnam, and others were doing, for there was no such formal colonialism in the area. Instead, they had to control and develop their internal resources, that is, loosen the *neo-colonial* grip that the United States held on their economies. The question was whether Washington would help or hinder that aspiration. In 1954 Dulles had given his answer by helping overthrow a nationalistic left-wing government in Guatemala. The area had then quieted somewhat. In early 1958 a high State Department official was asked whether he thought there was much anti-Yankee feeling among Latin Americans. "No sir, I do not," he promptly replied.

Two months later Vice-President Nixon traveled south. From Uruguay to Venezuela crowds hurled eggs and stones at his car, nearly tipping it over in Caracas, Venezuela. Eisenhower ordered a thousand Marines to prepare to rescue Nixon, who escaped back to Washington before the troops were dispatched. The outburst shocked the United States. The President ordered a review of Latin American policies. He finally initiated economic-aid programs, which, after 1961, the Kennedy administration would enlarge and attempt to glamorize with the title "Alliance for Progress." But this was too little and too late to prevent anti-American nationalists from working fundamental, revolutionary changes.

It was, for example, too late to insulate Cuba from such a revolution. This was striking, for nowhere had United States control been so com-

Castro at the United Nations, 1960.

plete. Americans controlled 80 percent of the island's utilities, 90 percent of the mines, ranches, and oil, owned half the great sugar crop, and surrounded Cuba with military might. The island had one of the highest per-capita income figures in the southern hemisphere, but the wealth fell into the hands of foreign investors and a few Cubans, while the mass of the people suffered in poverty. In 1952, Fulgencio Batista overthrew a moderately liberal regime and created a military dictatorship. He received support from highly unlikely bedfellows, the United States military (which helped train and equip Batista's forces), and a well-behaved Communist party, which sought to survive by whipping up local support for the dictator. The United States Air Force pinned the Legion of Merit on Batista's breast, calling him "a great president."

That sentiment was not shared by most Cubans. In 1953 a young, middle-class lawyer (unemployed, as were most Cuban lawyers) started a revolt. Fidel Castro was captured and imprisoned, but by 1957 he was again free, and then collected a force of peasants and middle-class Cubans that successfully chopped up the police units sent out to destroy them. The

Communists refused to cooperate with Castro until late 1958, when Batista was preparing to escape with millions from the Cuban treasury for a luxurious exile in Spain. On January 1, 1959, Castro marched triumphantly into Havana. Washington officials, an authoritative journalist reported, generally agreed that "there was no dominant Communist influence. . . . One official went so far as to say that there was very little trace of Communism in the movement."

As Castro moved to change the distribution of wealth, and especially of land ownership, his relationships with the Communists and the United States altered. The Communists provided disciplined organization and an ideology, which Castro required. When the Cuban leader visited the United States, Eisenhower left Washington to go golfing. There was little to talk about. Castro insisted that American companies and land holdings be placed in Cuban hands. He could not pay for these without borrowing money from abroad and again becoming indebted to foreigners. As *The New York Times* editorialized in mid-1960, "So long as Cuba is in the throes of a social revolution directed by her present leaders, she is going to be in conflict with the United States. We think it is wrong, but it is a fact of life. The revolution harms American interests in Cuba and in Latin America generally." Castro turned to the Soviet Union for credits, machinery, and military equipment. Eisenhower first cut back Cuban sugar imports, then authorized the secret training of 1400 anti-Castro Cubans by the Central Intelligence Agency, although the President never did decide when—or even whether—they might be used. Assuming that Castro was "beyond redemption" as a State Department official commented, the United States and Cuba broke diplomatic relations in January 1961.

THE EISENHOWER LEGACY AND THE NEW FRONTIER

Eisenhower presided during a decade that many Americans would later recall with nostalgia. The generation that came of age during the 1950s seemed quiet, apolitical, and more concerned about personal security than international crises. It would later be tagged as "the generation that never showed up." This was how Eisenhower wanted it. Despite provocations in Korea, the Middle East, and Berlin greater than those that later faced Presidents Kennedy and Johnson, Eisenhower, unlike his successors, did not involve the country in war. His use of power was restrained. He frequently remarked that he had seen enough war. Moreover, Eisenhower cared more about balancing the budget and strengthening the American economy than he did about creating a great military force that might intervene at will in the post-1956 world.

He did not disavow anti-Communist policies, but neither did he think that those policies were worth undermining the American economic, political, and even educational systems. Between 1950 and 1960, for example, such leading universities as Harvard, Chicago, Columbia, Pennsylvania, California, and Johns Hopkins had obtained large amounts of money, both from such private foundations as Ford and Carnegie and from the federal government, to establish defense-policy centers. Instead of questioning governmental power, many American intellectuals were justifying that power. With this in mind, Eisenhower issued a warning in his Farewell Address of January 1961. He spoke of "the prospect of domination of the nation's scholars by Federal employment, project allocations, and the power of money," and noted that too often "a government contract becomes virtually a substitute for intellectual curiosity." Eisenhower believed that two "threats, new in kind or degree," had appeared:

This conjunction of an immense military establishment and a large arms industry is new in American experience. The total influence—economic, political, even spiritual—is felt in every city, every state house, every office of the federal government. We recognize the imperative need for this development. Yet we must not fail to comprehend its grave implications. . . . In the councils of government, we must guard against the acquisition of unwarranted influence, whether sought or unsought, by the military-industrial complex. The potential for the disastrous rise of misplaced power exists and will persist. . . . We should take nothing for granted.

In part this warning expressed Eisenhower's fear that the incoming Kennedy administration would try to control world affairs by spending even greater sums on arms. His fear was well-founded. In accepting the Democratic presidential nomination in 1960, John F. Kennedy called not for caution, but for "sacrifices" on "the New Frontier." He spoke in Los Angeles in late afternoon as the sun went down on what had been the last of the old American frontier territory. The New Frontier, Kennedy declared,

sums up not what I intend to offer the American people but what I intend to ask of them. It appeals to their pride, not to their pocketbook; it holds out the promise of more sacrifice instead of more security.

But I tell you the New Frontier is here whether we seek it or not . . . uncharted areas of science and space, unsolved problems of peace and war, unconquered pockets of ignorance and prejudice, unanswered questions of poverty and surplus.

This call to action was most eloquently stated in Kennedy's Inaugural of January 1961. His words sharply contrasted with Eisenhower's Farewell Address. Kennedy proclaimed:

Let every nation know, whether it wishes us well or ill, that we shall pay any price, bear any burden, meet any hardship, support any friend, oppose any foe to assure the survival and the success of liberty.

This much we pledge—and more. . . .

In the long history of the world, only a few generations have been granted the role of defending freedom in its hour of maximum danger. I do not shrink from this responsibility; I welcome it. . . .

And so, my fellow Americans, ask not what your country can do for you; ask what you can do for your country.

JOHN F. KENNEDY AND
THE PRESIDENCY

In April 1960 Richard E. Neustadt, a political scientist at Columbia University, published *Presidential Power*. Neustadt believed that a strong President "contributes to the energy of government and to the viability of public policy." He attempted, therefore, to show how a chief executive might surmount the obstacles to the effective exercise of power. "The Sixties, it appears, will be a fighting time," Neustadt concluded. "It follows that our need will be the greater for a Presidential expert in the Presidency." Shortly after the book appeared, John F. Kennedy, the Democratic nominee for President, recruited Neustadt as an advisor. In truth, the two men held quite similar views. Kennedy thought that the President "must serve as a catalyst, an energizer, the defender of the public good and the public interest." He must "place himself in the very thick of the fight," for he was "the vital center of action in our whole scheme of government."

"Energy," "fight," "vitality," "public interest"—the words conveyed not only Kennedy's view of the presidency but also the values that had molded much of his life. In the fall of 1941, a year after his graduation from Harvard, Kennedy had enlisted in the Navy. After Pearl Harbor he volunteered for duty in the South Pacific and was decorated for heroism when he helped rescue several crewmates. In 1946 he won a seat in the House of Representatives. Six years later he was elected to the Senate. Hospitalized with a severe back ailment, Kennedy wrote *Profiles in Courage* (1956), a study of politicians who had demonstrated the "most admirable of human virtues." The book won a Pulitzer Prize. In 1956 Kennedy failed to obtain the vice-presidential nomination, but in 1958 he won reelection to the Senate by the largest margin any candidate in Massachusetts had ever received for any office.

In December 1960 Kennedy wrote an article for *Sports Illustrated,* in which he urged Americans to toughen themselves physically, and as President he continued to preach the virtues of the strenuous life. At a 1962 press conference the President was called on to defend his Secretary of Agriculture, Orville H. Freeman, against charges of showing favoritism in a case involving cotton-planting allotments. Freeman, Kennedy noted, "worked his way through the University of Minnesota; he was a football player, graduated Phi Beta Kappa. He had most of his jaw shot off at Bougainville as a captain in the Marines; he was Governor of Minnesota for three terms." This had nothing to do with the specific allegations against Freeman, but everything to do with John F. Kennedy. The qualities he mentioned—hard work, athletic ability, intellectual achievement, physical courage, and public service—were those he most admired.

CONGRESS AND THE
NEW FRONTIER

Yet Kennedy found that the limitations of presidential authority were far greater than he had imagined and that they had several sources. Unlike

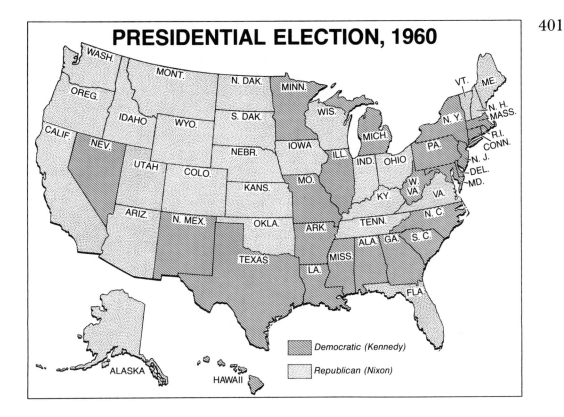

PRESIDENTIAL ELECTION, 1960

Democratic (Kennedy)

Republican (Nixon)

ALASKA

HAWAII

Roosevelt and Eisenhower, Kennedy did not take office with a resounding popular mandate. He barely edged out Richard Nixon, winning by the smallest margin of any President in the twentieth century. Kennedy, who received 49.7 percent of the popular vote to his opponent's 49.6 percent, actually carried fewer states than did Nixon. Although Kennedy secured a 303–219 majority in the electoral college, had 4500 people in Illinois and 28,000 people in Texas voted Republican instead of Democratic, Nixon would have emerged the victor in the electoral college. President by a razor-thin margin, Kennedy was not in a position to demand that Congress follow his lead.

Nor could Kennedy turn for support to first-term congressmen carried into office on his coattails. In 1960 Kennedy invariably trailed the Democratic ticket; worse still, his party lost 22 seats in the House and 2 in the Senate. Although the Democrats maintained comfortable majorities in both houses of Congress, those majorities were deceptive, consisting largely of Southerners who regarded many New Frontier programs with distaste. The seniority system gave Southern Democrats representing rural constituencies control of key committees: Wilbur Mills of Arkansas headed the House Ways and Means Committee, Harry Byrd of Virginia chaired the Senate Finance Committee, and Howard Smith of Virginia ran the House Rules Committee. Kennedy barely won a bitterly contested struggle to liberalize the Rules Committee by enlarging its membership, and then only because he had the backing of Speaker Sam Rayburn of Texas. Even the Kennedy style appeared to offend some congressmen. "All that Mozart string music and ballet dancing down there," said one; "he's too elegant for me, I can't talk to him."

In some respects religion acted as another constraint on the President. Kennedy's Catholicism had played an important role in the 1960 election. Many Protestants bolted the Democratic party, but Kennedy received 80 percent of the Catholic vote (rather than the 63 percent a Democrat could ordinarily expect). On the whole, the religious issue appears to have cost Kennedy votes. However his loss of support occurred primarily in the South, where the Democrats could afford it; meanwhile he gained support in such critical states as Illinois and Michigan. As the first Catholic President, Kennedy leaned over backwards to dispel any suspicion that he was under Church influence. He did not favor sending an American ambassador to the Vatican, and he similarly opposed "unconstitutional aid to parochial schools." It was easier to prove that a Catholic could be elected President than to convince skeptics that a Catholic President could be scrupulously fair.

The conflict over federal aid to education illustrated Kennedy's difficulties with Congress. Early in 1961 Kennedy proposed spending $2.3 billion over three years to build new schools and to raise teachers' salaries. The wealthiest states would receive $15 per child, the poorest nearly twice that amount. A separate program to aid college students would bring the package to $5.6 billion. But federal aid to education raised divisive issues. In a vain effort to appease Southern Democrats, the administration agreed not to withhold aid from segregated school districts. The religious issue proved more difficult to resolve. Kennedy declared that the Constitution prohibited aid to parochial schools, but the Catholic Church replied that the Constitution did not prohibit long-term, low-interest loans to help such schools improve their facilities. An arrangement was seemingly worked out restricting the federal aid bill to public schools, but attaching an amendment to the National Defense and Education Act authorizing loans to parochial schools for expanding their mathematics, science, and language facilities. At the last minute, a Northern Catholic Democrat on the Rules Committee, fearing that Congress would renege on aid to religious schools, joined Republicans and Southern Democrats to oppose the education bill. In July 1961 the President watched helplessly as the Rules Committee, by a one-vote margin, buried the measure.

A second New Frontier proposal—Medicare—met a similar fate. In February 1961 Kennedy asked Congress to extend social security benefits to people over the age of 65 to cover hospital and nursing home costs. This would be financed by a small increase in the social security tax. The President pointed out that the elderly had, on the average, half the income of people under 65 but medical expenses that were twice as high. Kennedy insisted that his plan, which would not cover surgical expenses or physicians' fees, ensured "absolute freedom" in the choice of a doctor and hospital. The American Medical Association, however, viewed Medicare as a giant step toward socialized medicine. Doctors foresaw a "bureaucratic task force" invading "the privacy of the examination room." The 25-member House Ways and Means Committee was the real hurdle. Its chairman, Wilbur Mills, opposed the plan, as did 10 Republicans and 6 Southern Democrats. They easily bottled up the bill. In July 1962 the Senate defeated the measure by a vote of 52 to 48, with 21 Democrats opposing the administration. The limitation of presidential leadership in domestic affairs was rapidly becoming clearer.

THE NEW ECONOMICS

Yet the picture of a stodgy, conservative Congress frustrating the hopes of an energetic, liberal President is accurate only in part. Kennedy understood the need to establish domestic priorities, and in the process he often sacrificed reform programs. This was true even in the case of Medicare, for Kennedy, recognizing that he needed Wilbur Mills's support for tax reform and trade expansion, did not press the Ways and Means Committee too hard. Moreover, to attract Southern Democratic support for economic proposals Kennedy postponed introducing civil rights legislation for as long as possible. He always put first things first, and in his view what came first was the economy. In January 1961 the nation was in the throes of a recession: unemployment stood at 5.4 million, more than 6 percent of the labor force. Kennedy's goal was to stimulate economic growth and reduce unemployment while at the same time balancing the budget and preventing inflation.

The administration applied a number of remedies to the sluggish economy. To aid jobless workers, Kennedy extracted from Congress, though usually in a diluted form, legislation that increased unemployment compensation, created manpower retraining programs, and provided for public works in depressed areas. Congress also raised the minimum wage from $1.00 to $1.25 an hour and brought an additional 3.6 million workers under the law's protection. To stimulate business expansion, Congress granted a 7 percent tax credit to firms investing in new equipment. Kennedy attached the greatest significance to the Trade Expansion Act (1962). This facilitated the export of American goods to the European Common Market by authorizing the President to arrange mutual tariff reductions of 50 percent on certain categories of goods and, in other cases, to eliminate tariffs completely. To assist industries threatened by foreign competition, the government would help businessmen change or diversify their products and retrain workers who lost their jobs.

The keys to curbing inflation were labor's willingness to limit wage demands to an amount justified by gains in productivity and industry's corresponding readiness to keep prices down. Early in 1962 Kennedy helped persuade the steelworkers to accept a noninflationary wage settlement. Then in April, U.S. Steel announced a price hike of $6 a ton, and other steel companies immediately followed suit. Furious at what he termed this "utter contempt for the public interest," Kennedy mustered every ounce of executive authority to salvage his economic program. He pressured smaller steel companies into holding the price line, threatened to take government contracts away from the offending concerns, and hinted that the Justice Department would determine whether the price increases violated the antitrust laws. Faced with massive presidential and public pressure, U.S. Steel backed down and rescinded the increase.

Kennedy's stance earned him the lasting resentment of the business community. The remark attributed to him at the time—"My father always told me that all businessmen were sons-of-bitches, but I never believed it till now"—did nothing to allay suspicion. When, in May 1962, the stock market hit the skids, dropping 35 points in a day and 100 points in two weeks, Wall Street attributed the disaster to a lack of confidence in the administration. Whatever businessmen may have thought, their fears were illogical. Not only did Kennedy's tax and trade policies favor business interests, but the administration also sponsored a plan, bitterly resented by Senate liberals, that conceded a dominant interest in the newly developed communications satellite to the American Telephone and Telegraph Company. (The satellite, launched into outer space, relayed television and radio signals around the world.) In addition to this, during his first 18 months in office Kennedy worked hard to achieve a balanced budget. So orthodox did the New Frontier's fiscal program appear that journalist Walter Lippmann commented, "It's like the Eisenhower administration 30 years younger."

Not until late in 1962 did Kennedy endorse the planned use of budget deficits as the only certain means of spurring further economic growth. In January 1963 the President called for a $13.5 billion reduction in corporate and personal taxes over three years. With the closing of loopholes, this would inject $10 billion into the economy, but it would also produce a $12 billion deficit in a total budget of $98.8 billion. Kennedy's plan, while thoroughly Keynesian in its assumptions, did not satisfy all liberals. John Kenneth Galbraith, the Harvard economist whom Kennedy had appointed Ambassador to India, believed that "money from tax reduction goes into the pockets of those who need it least; lower tax revenues will become a ceiling on spending." Galbraith wished to create a deficit by expanding programs to aid the needy rather than by cutting taxes. On the other hand, Kennedy's proposal shocked conservatives. Dwight Eisenhower offered a homely bit of economic wisdom: "Spending for spending's sake is patently a false theory. No family, no business, no nation can spend itself into prosperity."

Unfortunately for Kennedy, more congressmen, and particularly more members of the House Ways and Means Committee, preferred Eisenhower's brand of economics to Galbraith's. Once again, as in the case of Medicare and federal aid to education, a House committee blocked consideration of a key New Frontier proposal. But by 1963 Kennedy had somewhat lowered his sights, at least with respect to domestic matters. The exercise of power proved a sobering experience. Although he never repudiated his activist view of the presidency, Kennedy came to see the office in terms of its limitations as well as its opportunities. "The problems are more difficult than I had imagined they were," he conceded. "Every President must endure a gap between what he would like and what is possible."

KENNEDY AND CIVIL RIGHTS

The same practical considerations that modified Kennedy's view of presidential authority also affected his stand on civil rights. In 1960 Kennedy declared that the President should throw the full moral weight of his office behind the effort to end racial discrimination. "If the President does not himself wage the struggle for equal rights—if he stands above the battle—then the battle will inevitably be lost." Once in office, however, Kennedy found himself torn between the claims of white Southerners, whose support he needed, and the pressure applied by an increasingly militant civil rights movement. Not until 1963 did Kennedy cease standing above the battle, and he then acted only after segregationist resistance to demands for racial equality provoked massive turmoil.

Unlike Eisenhower, Kennedy relied heavily on the black vote. In the 1960 campaign he expressed agreement with the Supreme Court ruling on desegregation, but perhaps nothing did more to solidify his support among blacks than his intervention on behalf of Dr. Martin Luther King. Late in October a Georgia judge jailed King for taking part in a protest demonstration. In a well-publicized move, Kennedy telephoned King's wife, both to express his concern and to offer assurances regarding her husband's safety. The next day, Robert F. Kennedy, the candidate's brother, helped arrange King's release on bail. Kennedy's phone call, a symbolic act at best, nevertheless had the right personal touch. When Nixon remained silent, the Democrats printed two million copies of a pamphlet entitled *No-Comment Nixon versus a Candidate with a Heart, Senator Kennedy.* In 1960 black voters provided Kennedy's margin of victory in Texas, Illinois, New Jersey, and Michigan. Had only white people voted, Nixon would have received 52 percent of the vote and gone to the White House.

Kennedy understood this, yet he placed civil rights lower on his legislative agenda than other New Frontier measures. To introduce a civil rights bill, Kennedy believed, would alienate Southerners, split the Democratic party, snarl Congress in a filibuster, and dissipate administration energies. He considered the chance of passage too slim to justify these risks. So the President turned instead to other techniques. He issued an Executive Order designed to pressure federal agencies and government contractors into hiring more black workers. In addition, Kennedy sought to achieve through litigation what he doubted was possible through legislation. Under Attorney General Robert F. Kennedy, the Justice Department attempted to speed the pace of school desegregation by entering court cases on the side of those challenging separate facilities. The policy had some success. In Eisenhower's last three years, 49 school districts had begun the process of desegregation. In Kennedy's three years, 183 did so.

In the eyes of New Frontiersmen, the franchise held the key to racial equality. Litigation to win the vote seemed crucial, for if blacks attained political strength commensurate with their members, politicians would accord them justice and the Jim Crow system would topple. Many states in the deep South systematically excluded blacks from the polls. In Mississippi, where Negroes constituted over 40 percent of the population, they made up less than 4 percent of the eligible voters. To attack this system, the Justice Department utilized the Civil Rights Act of 1957, which authorized it to seek injunctions against interference with the right to vote. The Eisenhower administration had brought only 10 suits under the act. The Kennedy administration filed 45 such suits.

Yet the reliance on litigation had three fatal defects. First, it assumed that the law sanctioned racial equality, which, in much of the South, it did not. Second, it assumed a degree of judicial impartiality that did not exist. A number of judges in Southern district courts held harshly segregationist views and stymied moves toward integration. Judge Harold Cox, a Kennedy appointee, informed a Justice Department official: "I spend most of my time in fooling with lousy cases brought before me by your Department in the Civil Rights field." Cox could find no pattern of discrimination in Clarke County, Mississippi, although only one black, a high-school principal, had succeeded in registering to vote in 30 years. Another judge branded the 1954 Supreme Court ruling "one of the truly regrettable decisions of all time." Even where successful, litigation was a glacial process, and this proved to be a third source of weakness. Many blacks were no longer willing to let the law run its course. They insisted that equality was a moral as well as a legal issue. By taking direct action to end segregation, they forced Kennedy to choose sides.

The first such case involved the "freedom rides," which were themselves an offshoot of the sit-in movement. In February 1960 a group of black college students in Greensboro, North Carolina sat down at a Woolworth's lunch counter and refused to leave until served. Within a year, 50,000 people had participated in similar demonstrations in over 100 cities and had succeeded in desegregating many hotels, stores, theaters, and parks. The freedom ride seemed a logical extension of this tactic. In May 1961 white and black students boarded buses in Washington with plans to travel through the deep South, desegregating depots as they went. Angry mobs met the buses, though, and attacked the riders with chains and rocks. The President finally sent 500 marshals to Montgomery, Alabama to prevent further violence. Kennedy then asked the Interstate Commerce Commission to ban segregation at all bus and train stations. In November 1961 such an edict took effect, although some Southern communities continued to evade it. The Justice Department also persuaded airlines to desegregate their terminals. The freedom riders had, in effect, created the conditions under which Kennedy was willing to employ executive authority on behalf of civil rights.

Kennedy's hand was forced a second time in September 1962 when James Meredith tried to integrate the University of Mississippi law school. The controversy originated when a U.S. Court of Appeals found that the university had rejected Meredith solely on the basis of race and ordered his admission. After a segregationist judge stayed the ruling, Supreme Court Justice Hugo Black ordered its enforcement. Meredith flew to Oxford, Mississippi in a federal plane and was escorted to the campus by federal marshals. Governor Ross Barnett tried to convince Robert Kennedy that Southern sentiment would never tolerate the integration of Ole Miss. Barnett thought Meredith was "being paid by some left-wing organization to do all this. He has two great big Cadillacs, no income, riding around here. . . . We never have trouble with our people, but the NAACP, they want to stir up trouble down here." The Attorney General responded that "if we don't follow the order of the federal court, we don't have anything in the United States." In the end, white students and outside troublemakers, massed behind Confederate battle flags, attacked the federal marshals. A 15-hour riot ensued in which two men were killed and the campus was shrouded in tear gas. The President dispatched thousands of federal troops to restore order, to protect Meredith's right to attend class, and to demonstrate that, in Robert Kennedy's words, only the rule of law permitted a nation "to avoid anarchy and disorder and tremendous distress."

The nine months following the Mississippi crisis saw the administration move haltingly toward an affirmative civil rights posture. In November 1962 the President issued a long-awaited Executive Order banning segregation in all new housing subsidized by the federal government. In February 1963 Kennedy introduced a civil rights bill designed to prevent biased registrars from using spurious tests to deprive blacks of the vote. The bill provided that the completion of six grades of public school would automatically constitute proof of literacy. Yet civil rights activists now considered these steps inadequate. They pointed out that the Executive Order did not affect housing that was already built or that would be privately financed. They noted that Kennedy, while favoring a civil rights bill, refused to support an effort to amend the Senate rules to make easier the termination of debate. Without such a change, a Southern filibuster seemed certain to block passage of any civil rights measure. Assessing Kennedy's record in March 1963, Martin Luther King found that the administration had settled for "tokenism." Nearly a decade after the Supreme Court decision, only 7 percent of black children in the South attended class with white children, and 2000 districts remained segregated. King concluded: "The administration sought to demonstrate to Negroes that it has concern for them, while at the same time it has striven to avoid inflaming the opposition."

In the spring of 1963 civil rights demonstrations in Birmingham,

Birmingham, Alabama, 1963.

Alabama, made further fence-straddling impossible. Black leaders in the city—where Negroes constituted 40 percent of the population—launched a drive to end segregation in stores and to pressure businessmen to hire black sales and clerical help. Adhering to King's philosophy that "you can struggle without hating; you can fight war without violence," blacks engaged in protest marches, sit-ins, and even kneel-ins at white churches on Good Friday. The city government reacted savagely. Police Commissioner Eugene "Bull" Connor met the marchers, many of them school children, with fire hoses and snarling police dogs and threw thousands into jail. The Mayor, who had lost the previous election but was contesting the result in court, called white businessmen who favored some form of accommodation "a bunch of quisling, gutless traitors." He said of Robert Kennedy: "I hope that every drop of blood that's spilled he tastes in his throat, and I hope he chokes on it." In May, riots and bombings rocked the city. The following month, with the crisis in Birmingham still unresolved, Governor George C. Wallace challenged an attempt by two black students to integrate the University of Alabama. To safeguard their entrance, the President federalized the national guard.

In June 1963, responding directly to these events in Alabama, Kennedy endorsed a sweeping civil rights bill. It would prevent segregation in hotels, restaurants, theaters, and other public places; permit the Justice Department to file suits for school desegregation; prohibit discrimination in state programs receiving federal aid; and remove racial barriers to employment and trade-union membership. "We are confronted primarily with a moral issue," the President asserted. The demand for racial justice had grown so loud, the "fires of frustration and discord" had begun to burn so brightly, that government could no longer stand aside. Indeed, the government must prove that revolutionary changes in race relations could occur in a "peaceful and constructive" way.

In three years Kennedy had traveled a considerable distance. Yet one element remained constant: his effort to link New Frontier programs at home with initiatives abroad. In justifying his attempt to place federal authority squarely behind the movement for racial equality, Kennedy noted: "Today we are committed to a worldwide struggle to promote and protect the rights of all who wish to be free. And when Americans are sent to Vietnam or West Berlin we do not ask for whites only."

THE WORLDWIDE NEW FRONTIER

The problems afflicting Americans at home could deeply affect Kennedy's foreign policies. His diplomacy assumed a united homefront that would unquestioningly support the President in Asia as it had in Europe, and that would see racism and poverty at home as less important than using national resources to fight communism overseas. For Kennedy, like most of his generation, was the product of World War II and the Cold War. As a young congressman in 1949, he attacked Truman for "losing" China, refused as a senator to take a public position on Senator Joseph McCarthy's vicious attacks, and in 1956 justified American support to Ngo Dinh Diem's autocratic regime in South Vietnam. By 1960, Kennedy had focused on the newly emerging areas as the key to victory in the Cold War. The new President believed that Americans must confront communism everywhere. "What is at stake in the election of 1960 is the preservation of freedom all around the globe," he proclaimed during the campaign, and he made this the central theme of his administration's foreign policy.

That remark seemed to make little-known countries in Southeast Asia, for example, as important to American interests as Western Europe. But as Kennedy saw it, the global battle would be to the finish. "Freedom and communism are locked in a deadly embrace," he believed in 1960, and later declared, "The world cannot exist half slave and half free." In a speech in May 1961 he was specific: "The great battleground for the defense and expansion of freedom today is the whole southern half of the globe—Asia, Latin America, Africa, and the Middle East—the lands of the rising peoples." His famous Inaugural was a trumpet call to that battle. It was also a speech that never mentioned domestic problems, Those could be assumed as secondary to the "historic mission" of America abroad. Nor did Kennedy set any limits on that mission. "I don't believe that there is anything this country cannot do," he declared during his television debates with Vice-President Nixon in 1960.

A strong presidency was required to carry out the mission, one even stronger than that developed by Roosevelt, Truman, and Eisenhower. The President "must be prepared to exercise the fullest powers of his office—all that are specified and some that are not." He even believed that the office not only spoke for all Americans, but represented "all of the people around the world who want to live in freedom." Kennedy established a separate foreign-affairs group in the White House under his National Security Advisor, McGeorge Bundy, former Dean of Harvard College. Bundy would be followed by Walt W. Rostow and then in 1969 by Henry Kissinger. All three would use their location to drain power from the Department of State and congressional foreign-affairs committees. In diplomacy, the President had become a virtual king—only more so, for he was an elected king, complete with advisors who did not have to be responsible to Congress or to anyone but the President.

ICBMs AND GREEN BERETS

As Commander in Chief Kennedy had at his disposal the most powerful military force in history. During the campaign he had charged Eisenhower with allowing a "missile gap" to develop in favor of the Soviets. Having seen the U-2 and other intelligence reports, Eisenhower knew that there was no gap. Kennedy also soon learned this, but refused to believe that American power was sufficient. Without evidence of Russian intentions, the new President assumed that Khrushchev would try to build new missiles as rapidly as possible. The Soviets had in fact decided to move slowly in this area, but Kennedy nevertheless accelerated American missile building. Khrushchev interpreted this to mean the Americans wanted a first-strike capability (that is, forces sufficient to wipe out Russia in one strike without fear of a return salvo), and so he ordered a step-up of Russian production and began nuclear testing at an increased rate. The most expensive arms race in history had begun, with China and France rushing to build their own nuclear weapons. Secretary of Defense Robert McNamara later believed that the Kennedy decision was "not justified" but was "necessitated by a lack of accurate information." By 1964 the United States force of 750 ICBMs (intercontinental ballistic missiles) was four times greater than that of the Soviets.

David Smith: the Machine Shop and Sculpture

As had Frank Lloyd Wright in architecture, David Smith transformed twentieth-century sculpture by combining the American machine shop with the radical versions of modern art. Reaching the peak of his powers between 1958 and 1965, Smith's work exemplified the new American leadership in world art at precisely the same time John F. Kennedy proclaimed in his Inaugural Address that his "new generation" of Americans would assume world political leadership.

Smith learned about machines in Decatur, Indiana, where he was born in 1906. One of his ancestors had been a frontier blacksmith. Leaving home at 16, he enrolled briefly at Ohio State and Notre Dame before learning to weld in the Studebaker automotive works in South Bend. Smith then traveled to New York City, encountering modern art just as leading European artists were fleeing Nazism to live in the United States. As these emigrés helped make New York City the center of the art world, Smith lived among them, beginning as a painter, then moving into "Constructivism," whereby objects other than paint (for example, bits of newspaper, glass, or metal) were placed on the picture, changing it from a painting to a construction. At that point, Smith recalled, "I was then a sculptor." To develop his craft he believed he needed nothing "outside of factory knowledge," which he had as a welder.

David Smith welding.

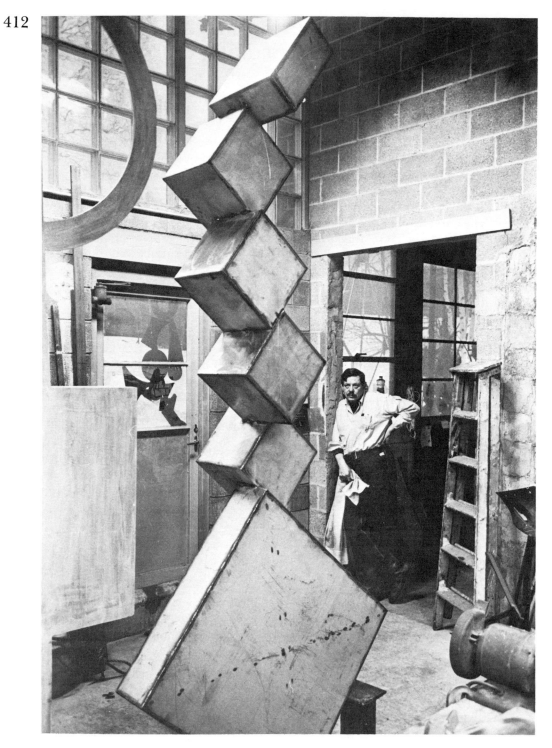

David Smith with Cubi I, 1963.

During the late 1930s, as many artists protested the drift toward war, Smith became politically involved. He expressed his vision in fifteen horror-filled, yet magnificently designed "Medals for Dishonor." These depicted scenes of such "dishonors" as "War-Exempt Sons of the Rich," "Munitions-Makers," and "Elements Which Cause Prostitution." In the 1940s his work became increasingly abstract, and for the first time he combined painting with sculpture so that the colors seemed to change the form of his pieces. One critic noted that Smith was among the first to practice "drawing in space," calling some of his work "a graceful abstract drawing that has leaped off the page into three-dimensional life."

Smith was soon exploring all forms, from overpowering monoliths to light, lyrical creations that, although made from heavy steel, seemed to float in air. His greatest work was done at his studio on the shore of Lake George in upper New York State, where he could display his works outdoors, the only place he thought large enough for them. Here

Medal for Dishonor No. 9: Bombing Civilian Populations, 1939.

he extended and transformed European art styles, particularly Cubism, which drew natural subjects in simplified lines and basic geometric shapes, usually to show the subject simultaneously from several points of view. In 1958 he began his spectacular "Cubi" series, shaping great slabs of stainless steel in pure geometrical construction and then polishing and arranging them so their three dimensions reflected changing sunlight—sometimes with dazzling intensity, sometimes with a delicateness that one critic called "purely optical poetry." In these new forms, Smith expressed the essence of Cubism. He indeed worked with steel, he declared, because it was at once "so beautiful" while "also brutal: the rapist, the murderer, and the death-dealing giants are also its offspring." In "Cubi" he brought the beauty and brutality into one.

A burly man who lived life to the full, Smith had by the 1960s not only created an American sculpture, but shaped world art as well. Yet in 1965 he could declare, "I'm 20 years behind my vision." In the spring of that year he perished in an automobile crash.

David Smith in his sculpture garden.

Green Berets training.

Kennedy, however, determined that since nuclear weapons would be of little use in the jungles and hamlets of the newly emerging areas, he would need conventional forces. Eisenhower, the foremost American military figure of the post-1950 era, believed that such power would be too expensive and ineffective, but Kennedy assumed that it was crucial if the new nations were to be saved from communism. He increased the number of conventional Army troops, created the Special Forces (and suggested the "Green Beret," by which they would be known) to fight guerrilla wars, and spent billions increasing the nation's helicopter and weapon capacity for fighting in the Third World. The Kennedy administration indeed tended to define the world primarily in military terms. Rostow told Special Forces troops in mid-1961: "I salute you, as I would a group of doctors, teachers, economic planners, agricultural experts, civil servants, or others who are now leading the way in fashioning the new nations."

THE NEW FRONTIER
CONTAINED: 1961–1962

Kennedy had determined on these policies before entering office, but in early January 1961 Khrushchev delivered a speech that spurred on the new President. The Soviet leader declared that revolutions, such as the "national liberation war" in Vietnam, were "not only admissible but inevitable." He asserted that the Communists did not have to start such wars, for nationalists within each country would fight to drive out imperialism. Communists would, however, "fully support" such conflicts. Khrushchev then focused, perhaps unfortunately, on Cuba, saying Castro's victory was a herald of what was to come.

Kennedy interpreted this speech as a direct challenge. One reaction was to announce with great publicity the Alliance for Progress. Over a ten-year period the Alliance was to use $100 billion of United States and Latin American funds to develop and stabilize the southern continent, that is, to prevent any more Castros from appearing. The Alliance quickly encountered innumerable problems. In Washington these included bureaucratic mix-ups, lack of funds, and the growing involvement in Vietnam, which absorbed money and attention. In South America there were few funds, mistrust of Yankees, entrenched interests refusing to budge, and disputes between nations. Washington too often forgot that Latin America consisted of twenty very different countries.

But a serious blow struck the Alliance dream at the beginning when Kennedy agreed to allow the Cuban exile force, with American air cover, to invade Cuba at the Bay of Pigs in an attempt to overthrow Castro. It was a disaster from the start. Afraid that the aircraft would too deeply involve the United States, Kennedy recalled them at the last minute, leaving the small exile army at the mercy of Castro's planes and tanks. The invaders were either killed or captured. Washington had assumed that the invasion would trigger a massive uprising against Castro, but Cubans instead rallied to his side. Contrary to the expectations of the Central Intelligence Agency and the White House, there would not be a successful replay of the 1954 invasion of Guatemala. By supporting the exiles, Kennedy had broken numerous American pledges not to use force in inter-American affairs. It marked a terrible start for the Alliance and Kennedy's struggle to win the newly emerging peoples. But it redoubled his determination. He secretly ordered an immediate review of policy in other areas and soon sent 500 more special "advisors" to Vietnam. Publicly, he tried to rebuild American prestige by announcing that the country would develop the missile and technological power to land a man on the moon within the decade. (Eight years and $24 billion later, Neil Armstrong touched down on the moon, but by 1969 riots at home and interventions in newly emerging areas had nearly destroyed that prestige.)

In June 1961 Kennedy and Khrushchev met in Vienna. They worked out a ceasefire for one part of Indochina (Laos) but engaged in a heated debate on "wars of liberation." Khrushchev's next move, however, was not to support such wars, but to resolve the Berlin question. Russia had become deeply embarrassed as thousands of East Germans fled the Communist zone to find new homes in the West. Announcing that this outward flow of talent would have to stop, Khrushchev demanded an immediate Berlin settlement. Kennedy responded by adding $3 billion more to the defense budget, calling up some national reserve units to prepare for battle, and warning Americans to begin building civil-defense shelters. This last idea was questionable; there was no way to protect even half the population from being killed in a nuclear war, but Kennedy had at least replied to Khrushchev. As Russian and American tanks faced one another in Berlin, the Russians brutally solved the problem by building high concrete walls along the East German borders and ordering guards to shoot anyone who tried to escape.

ON THE BRINK OF NUCLEAR WAR

The Berlin confrontation paled in comparison with the Cuban missile crisis of October 1962. On October 14, a U-2 plane took pictures of Soviet medium- and long-range ground-to-ground missiles being emplaced in Cuba. Why Khrushchev decided to take this step will probably never be known, but good evidence suggests several reasons. The Russian missiles in Cuba changed the military balance of power very little since the Soviets already had the capacity to destroy American targets from Russian bases. Knowing that he was behind in the missile race, Khrushchev probably thought that placing weapons 90 miles from American soil would be a political and psychological triumph. Such a success might be used to squeeze Kennedy on such international problems as Berlin. Pressures from the ruling elite in Moscow and from the Chinese Communists might also have convinced Khrushchev that he should demonstrate how tough he could be with the Americans. He could meanwhile claim publicly that the missiles protected Castro from another Washington-sponsored invasion.

Kennedy reacted with a dramatic television speech on October 22. He demanded that the ground-to-ground missiles be immediately removed, announced an American naval blockade around Cuba to search and prevent Soviet ships with missiles from reaching Havana, and warned that if any missile was fired from Cuba, the United States would fully respond— by attacking Russia. The American and Soviet forces went on full alert, with airborne bombers full of fuel and nuclear weapons. For the next six days the world was closer to nuclear obliteration than it had ever been before. Soviet ships finally turned around in mid-ocean to return to Russia, but Khrushchev refused to remove the missiles already emplaced. The fourteen-man committee advising Kennedy split, with some arguing for only a blockade, others for a "surgical strike" on the missile bases (which would probably kill Russian advisors), and a few for a full-scale attack on the sites and the Castro regime. Attorney General Robert Kennedy, the President's brother, later recalled that this was "probably the brightest kind of group that you could get together," but "if six of them had been President . . . I think that the world might have been blown up."

Just hours before an American attack was planned, a deal emerged: in return for removal of the missiles, Kennedy publicly pledged not to invade Cuba, and his brother privately informed the Soviets that outdated American missiles in Turkey, on the border of Russia, would be removed. Actually, the President had ordered the removal of the missiles in Turkey months earlier. The crisis was over. As Secretary of State Dean Rusk remarked to another committee member, "We have won a considerable victory. You and I are still alive."

The reverberations of the crisis were felt long after. Kennedy emerged as a hero for facing down Khrushchev, although some suggested that the President overreacted, and not because of a military threat but for political reasons. He could not suffer another Bay of Pigs or Berlin setback, this argument went, particularly since some Republicans had warned weeks before about the Russian missiles being emplaced in Cuba. Whatever their motivations, Khrushchev and Kennedy decided to install a "hotline" telephone between Washington and Moscow so that future crises could be handled more intelligently. They next negotiated a nuclear test-ban treaty in 1963 prohibiting above-ground testing. This stopped further creation of deadly radiation that was building in the earth's atmosphere from earlier tests, but it did not stop all testing. The bombs were taken underground, and more nuclear tests were conducted during the next ten years than had occurred during the previous ten. The United States military and some members of Congress demanded that Kennedy allow such expanded testing as a condition of their support of the treaty. The two great powers had nevertheless taken a first, if small, step toward arms control. One other by-product of the crisis, however, was not as constructive.

VIETNAM

The American involvement in Vietnam had begun between 1950 and 1954. Kennedy transformed that involvement. When he became President, 675 American military advisors helped the South Vietnam government of Ngo Dinh Diem, a number that had been determined by the 1954 Geneva agreements. When Kennedy was assassinated, 17,000 American troops were in South Vietnam.

Kennedy's commitment is easily understood. He had repeatedly declared that the Cold War would be determined in the newly emerging areas, and Washington officials saw Vietnam as the key to the Asian struggle. A worse place for such a commitment could hardly be imagined, for Americans and Vietnamese lived in worlds so totally different that each easily misunderstood the other. In *Fire in the Lake,* the best book on the Vietnam war, Frances Fitzgerald noted, "There was no more correspondence between the two worlds than that between the atmosphere of the earth and that of the sea."

Americans thought in terms of expansion, open spaces, limitless advance, and reliance on technology. They preferred to stress the future rather than think about their past, especially if that history showed their limitations, as it often did. They liked a society that was mobile, competitive, and individualistic. But Vietnamese life depended on self-contained villages that had remained unchanged for centuries. Vietnamese considered individualism destructive to the integrated, settled, and rural life that centered on the family and the memories of ancestors. Habits were carefully handed down through generations, and when old Vietnamese died they would often be buried in the rice field to help provide sustenance for their grandchildren. Vietnam's economy depended on rice, for the country shipped large amounts to other Asian nations besides using it for its own staple diet. The people developed sophisticated growing methods, but they did not depend on technology. Change was to occur over centuries, and order, not change, was most highly desired. Otherwise the village could be disrupted, ancestral ties neglected, society torn apart. More than 80 percent of the Vietnamese were Buddhists, and their religion was tightly integrated with their everyday life.

If society did fail to work properly, if its order did disintegrate, the Vietnamese expected their leaders to step down, committing suicide if necessary, so that new leaders could make necessary changes to restore order. These changes could be radical as long as the village life retained its wholeness. For this reason, the Vietnamese could accept the revolutionary doctrines of Communist leader Ho Chi Minh, for he carefully worked through the villages to drive out French colonialism between 1946 and 1954. The Communists later used the same tactic against the Americans. The United States, on the other hand, fought Communist successes in the villages by destroying the villages. In so doing, Americans destroyed the very foundation of the society they thought they were saving.

The people of Southeast Asia had long dealt with foreign invaders. For more than a thousand years China controlled much of the area, but in the eleventh century A.D. the Chinese were driven out. During the next 800 years vigorous societies developed in present-day Vietnam, Laos, Cambodia, and Thailand, while the peoples continued to repulse Chinese attempts to control the area. In the nineteenth century France established a colonial empire over Cambodia, Laos, and Vietnam, but its control was strongest in the present area of South Vietnam and weakest in the north. During the 1920s a strong nationalist movement under Ho Chi Minh developed. His great opportunity appeared when Japan defeated and humiliated the French in 1940–41. With American help, French power reappeared in 1946. Ho believed that a settlement could be worked out and preferred dealing with France than with closer, more threatening neighbors: "It is better to smell the French dung for awhile than eat China's all our lives." The settlement, however, broke down in late 1946, and war ensued until Ho's victory in 1954.

The Geneva Agreements of 1954 temporarily divided the country along the 17th parallel until elections could be held in 1956. Historically, South Vietnam had not been a separate nation. But with American support, South Vietnamese President Diem, who had been installed in Saigon during late 1954 with Washington's aid, refused to hold the elections. He knew that his own weakness in the south, Ho's reputation as a nationalist, and Ho's iron hand in the north would result in a lopsided victory for the Communists. Believing that American support made his own position secure, Diem cut back drastically on promised land reforms. He concentrated power within his own family. That family was Roman Catholic, a religion adopted by only 10 percent of the Vietnamese. Elections were rigged and the South Vietnamese constitution forgotten.

Civil war finally erupted against Diem in 1958. In March 1960 the Viet Cong was organized as the Communist-led political front of the rebellion. Guerrilla warfare accelerated. In the fall of 1960 Diem's own army tried to overthrow his government but failed. As Diem approached the brink, he called for help. Kennedy responded.

THE NEW FRONTIER IN VIETNAM, 1961–1963

The United States tried to build a nation where none had existed, by supporting a ruler who was under attack by his own people. Kennedy nevertheless thought the effort necessary. Secretary of State Dean Rusk fully supported the policy. Rusk had been an army officer in Asia in 1944–45 and Assistant Secretary of State for Far Eastern affairs during the Korean War. He fervently believed that the 1960s would test whether Americans could contain communism in Asia as they had in Europe. Utterly loyal to Kennedy and, later, to President Johnson, Rusk remained dedicated to winning in Vietnam even after Kennedy's policies had failed and White House officials tried to blame their own mistakes on Rusk.

In the Department of Defense, Secretary Robert McNamara quickly built the armed force needed by Kennedy and Rusk. A brilliant product of the Harvard Business School and former president of the Ford Motor Company, McNamara employed computer and other new quantitative techniques to build and demonstrate the superiority of American power. "Every quantitative measurement we have shows we're winning this war," he declared in 1962. But in Vietnam, numbers were not enough. They could even be misleading, for the war involved a struggle in the villages that required political and cultural judgments. McNamara's computers could not make such judgments.

As a consequence, Kennedy continued to try to prop up Diem even as Diem's support was dwindling. During 1961–62, 10,000 Americans departed for Vietnam. Kennedy made the commitment even though he fully realized it was nothing more than a start. He compared aiding Diem with being an alcoholic: "The effect [of one drink] wears off and you have to take another." But given his own call to action against communism, he believed that he had no alternative. Diem saw clearly what was happening. The weaker he became, the more he could expect Kennedy's help. Diem could consequently pay little attention to American advice. He could do as he pleased since Kennedy had no alternative but to support the South Vietnamese regime. Meanwhile Diem's generals dreamed up statistics to feed McNamara's computers, and the computers told McNamara and Kennedy what they wanted to hear.

After the Cuban missile crisis, Kennedy's determination increased. He believed that the crisis had forced Khrushchev to retreat in the world

McNamara, Gen. Maxwell D. Taylor, and Gen. Paul Harkins stroll by
barb-wire barricade near Saigon, South Vietnam, September 1963.

struggle but that Russia's place would be taken by Mao Tse-tung's China.
Mao, the President privately believed, was the true revolutionary, and
when China developed nuclear weapons, that country would be the great
threat to world stability. It was only a short step for Kennedy to conclude
that since Vietnam bordered on China, and since Mao aided Ho Chi
Minh, the Vietnamese struggle would decide whether Chinese communism would triumph in the newly emerging nations. All of Kennedy's assumptions were doubtful: Ho and the Vietnamese feared China and
would not cooperate politically with Mao; Chinese communism had little
to do with Vietnamese communism, which was highly nationalistic; and
above all, Vietnamese nationalism, not communism, was the main cause of
the war against Diem. As nationalists, Vietnamese were determined to be
free of all foreigners, whether French, American, or Chinese. But Kennedy, who too easily defined the world as simply "half slave and half
free," was unable to see these differences.

Despite Washington's help, Diem's forces lost ground in 1962. Kennedy was reluctant to admit this publicly, but Americans learned of
Diem's setbacks through American newspaper correspondents in Vietnam. Washington officials tried to silence these reports. The American
commander in the western Pacific shouted at one critical journalist, "Why
don't you get on the team?" Kennedy even privately suggested to the pub-

lisher of *The New York Times* that he give a "vacation" to one reporter who was telling the story accurately but not the way Kennedy wanted it reported. To the publisher's credit, he rejected the President's advice. American-Vietnamese relations worsened as Diem would not take United States suggestions concerning political and land reforms.

The turning point came in mid-1963. Buddhist leaders celebrated Buddha's 2587th birthday with flags and religious demonstrations. Diem had banned such displays. He ordered his troops to fire on the Buddhist leaders. Anti-Diem forces immediately rallied to the Buddhists, and civil war threatened within the principal cities. Several Buddhists responded by publicly burning themselves to death, an act that the government ridiculed as a "barbecue show." The deaths, however, dramatized the growing opposition. Kennedy decided to move.

In late August, American officials told South Vietnamese military leaders that there would be no objection if Diem were deposed. On November 1 the South Vietnamese President and his brother were captured and shot by army leaders. Although they had not known about, and indeed had disapproved of, the assassination, American officials had encouraged Diem's overthrow. In doing so, they had again demonstrated their deep involvement in the Vietnamese conflict and their determination to "save" the country even if this required helping overthrow the government. The Kennedy administration was now fully committed to the war and to a new government. What the President would have done next is unknown. On November 22, 1963, while on a political junket to Dallas, Texas, John F. Kennedy also fell victim to an assassin's bullet.

A later governmental investigation headed by Chief Justice Earl Warren concluded that the murderer was probably Lee Harvey Oswald, young, embittered, and, it seems, especially angered by Kennedy's anti-Castro policies. But Oswald never told his story, for shortly after his arrest he was shot—on national television and while surrounded by police guards—by a smalltime nightclub owner, Jack Ruby. In the following years many self-appointed investigators produced evidence suggesting that Oswald was innocent, or that he was only one of several killers, or that he was the front-man for a powerful secret group still at large. Loving mysteries of this kind, especially when it involved a glamorous President, Americans debated at length the circumstances of the tragedy. They would have been better advised to have followed the age-old adage, "Let the dead bury the dead," for while they focused on Dallas and the shattered dreams of the Kennedy promise, a new tragedy was growing 12,000 miles away that would destroy more than 50,000 American lives.

Suggested Reading

John F. Kennedy's career prior to the 1960 election is portrayed in James M. Burns, *John Kennedy* (1960). Two participants in the Kennedy administration have written full-length works defending the New Frontier: Arthur M. Schlesinger, Jr., *A Thousand Days* (1965); and Theodore Sorensen, *Kennedy* (1965). For more critical appraisals, see Henry Fairlie, *The Kennedy Promise* (1973); and Bruce Miroff, *Pragmatic Illusions: The Presidential Politics of John F. Kennedy* (1976).

Aspects of economic policy are considered in Seymour Harris, *The Economics of the Kennedy Years* (1964); Jim Heath, *John F. Kennedy and the Business Community* (1969); and Daniel Knapp and Kenneth Polk, *Scouting the War on Poverty: Social Reform Politics in the Kennedy Administration* (1971). Lawrence Fuchs, *John F. Kennedy and American Catholicism* (1967), is a useful work, as is David J. O'Brien, *The Renewal of American Catholicism* (1972). For a critique of the New Frontier's approach to civil rights, see Victor Navasky, *Kennedy Justice* (1971); for a more sympathetic view, Carl M. Brauer, *John F. Kennedy and the Second Reconstruction* (1977). The civil rights movement, and the response of southern whites, are considered in Howard Zinn, *SNCC: The New Abolitionists* (1964); Martin Luther King, *Why We Can't Wait* (1964); and James Silver, *Mississippi: The Closed Society* (1964).

For the era's foreign policy, see Seyom Brown, *The Faces of Power* (1968); Godfrey Hodgson, *America In Our Time* (1976); Robert Divine, *Foreign Policy and Presidential Elections, 1940–1960*, 2 vols., (1974); Roger Hilsman, *To Move a Nation* (1965); David Halberstam, *The Best and the Brightest* (1972); the Schlesinger and Sorensen books noted above, and a dissent from those accounts: Richard Walton, *Cold War and Counterrevolution* (1972). Good analyses of the festering Cuban crisis are Robert F. Smith, *The U.S. and Cuba, 1917–1960* (1961); Lester D. Langley's survey, *Cuban Policy of the U.S.* (1968); Herbert S. Dinerstein, *The Making of a Missile Crisis*, especially the 1978 edition containing newly-declassified documents; Elie Abel, *The Missile Crisis* (1966); and Robert F. Kennedy, *Thirteen Days* (1969). On Africa, the best work is Stephen Weissman, *U.S. and the Congo* (1973).

An excellent introduction to David Smith is anything on the sculptor written by Hilton Kramer; see especially his *The Age of Avant-Garde* (1973). Barbara Rose, *American Art Since 1900* (1967), is also helpful.

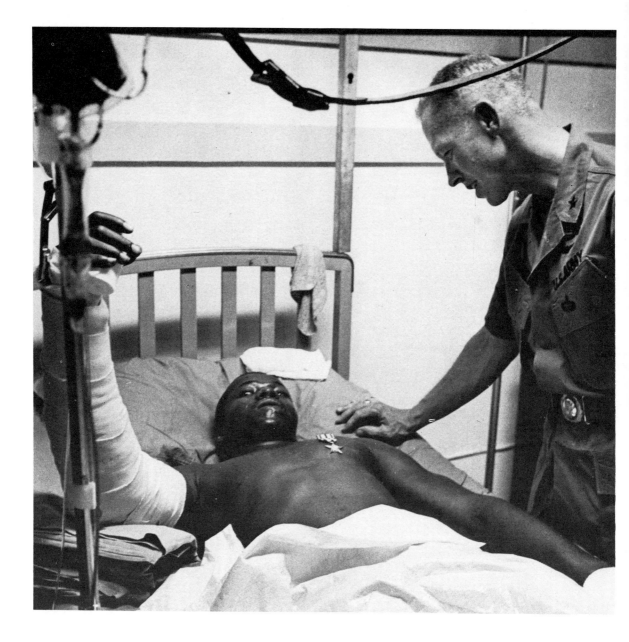

Wounded and decorated in Vietnam.

CHAPTER FOURTEEN

1963–1972

The
Imperial Presidency
and Vietnam

I FEEL LIKE I'M FIXIN' TO DIE RAG

Words and music by Joe McDonald

Well come on, all of you big strong men,
Uncle Sam needs your help again,
He's got himself in a terrible jam,
Way down yonder in Vietnam,
So put down your books and take up a gun,
We're gonna have a whole lot of fun.

Chorus:
And it's one, two, three, what are we fight-
ing for;
Don't ask me, I don't give a damn, next stop
is Vietnam.
And it's five, six, seven, open up the pearly
gates;
Well, there ain't no time to wonder why—
Whoopee, we're all gonna die.

Come on wall street don't be slow,
Why, Man, this is war a-Go-Go.
There's plenty good money to be made
By supplyin' the Army with the tools of its
trade.

But just hope and pray that if they drop the
bomb,
They drop it on the Viet Cong.

Come on Generals, let's move fast;
Your big chance has come at last.
Now you can go out and get those Reds—
Cause the only good Commie is one that's
dead.
And you know that peace can only be won,
When we've blown 'em all to kingdom come.

Come on Mothers through the land,
Pack your boys off to Vietnam.
Come on Fathers, don't hesitate,
Send your sons off before it's too late.
And you can be the first ones in your block
To have your boy come home in a box.

John Kennedy bequeathed to Lyndon Johnson a strong presidency, a disintegrating social consensus at home, and a policy of military interventionism in Vietnam. That was a highly combustible mixture. During his five years in the White House (November 1963 to January 1969) Johnson carried the Kennedy policies out to their explosive conclusions. Even the new President's broad social programs in civil rights, education, and welfare failed to alleviate the worsening tensions and divisions in America. Vietnam exemplified and aggravated all of the root problems, for the American intervention was directed by an increasingly unresponsible, isolated, yet unchecked presidential power. The results were so disastrous that riots, burning of major cities, closing of disrupted colleges, and political assassinations became tragically common in both Vietnam and the United States. Crucial diplomatic alliances became undone overseas. After five years of war, Johnson was replaced by Richard Nixon. The new President attempted to quiet the home front by emphasizing law and order, that is, by cutting back liberal reforms, tightening the economy, and increasing police activity. Nixon, however, could not control Vietnam. Between 1963 and 1972 domestic and foreign policies intermeshed, producing a massive tragedy.

LBJ AND THE 1964 ELECTION

Lyndon Johnson knew more about the exercise of political power than any American in the post-1945 era. He had grown up in central Texas, learning state and national politics during the New Deal era from such masters as fellow-Texan Sam Rayburn, Speaker of the House of Representatives. During the 1950s Johnson became leader of the Senate Democratic majority, where he wheeled and dealed, whipped and cajoled, flattered and intimidated until he became one of the strongest of all Senate leaders. Johnson often gathered votes by haranguing fellow-Senators in intense, private, person-to-person talks. Such encounters became known as the "treatment;" it was described by one victim as "a great overpowering thunderstorm that consumed you as it closed in around you." When he moved into the White House, Johnson was perfectly prepared to use the Executive's vast powers. Almost nothing could stop him from having his way, and he wanted his way on every issue. "When we made mistakes, I believe we erred because we tried to do too much too soon and never because we stayed away from challenge," he later wrote. "If the Presidency can be said to have been employed and to have been enjoyed, I had employed it to the utmost, and I had enjoyed it to the limit."

The Founding Fathers had tried to make the presidency responsible by subjecting it to checks from Congress and the voting public. Johnson effectively removed both checks during his first year in office. During the 1964 presidential campaign he ran against Republican nominee Barry Goldwater, a conservative Senator from Arizona. Under the best of cir-

cumstances, Goldwater had little chance. Johnson had been masterful in
quieting fears and assuring continuity of government after Kennedy's
murder. There seemed to be a political truce, during which nearly all
Americans supported the new President's efforts to pass a vast array of
domestic legislation. Goldwater worsened his chances by opposing Johnson's initiatives, thereby seeming to be cautious and negative while the
Texan was pushing the country forward. "I just want to tell you this,"
Johnson told a cheering crowd during the campaign, "we're in favor of a
lot of things and we're against mighty few." What those "things" were in
foreign policy was not clear, although he had vowed to carry on Kennedy's Vietnam policies.

Goldwater then made the mistake of appearing to be tougher than
Johnson by asserting that the Democrats had dallied in Southeast Asia instead of winning a total victory. He further suggested that such a triumph
would be hastened if military commanders in the field, rather than the
President, had the final word in using nuclear weapons. Conservative
Republicans had moved to the other extreme since their so-called "isolationist" views of the 1930s. Johnson effectively seized on these remarks to
score Goldwater for being irresponsible and bloodthirsty. As for Vietnam,
"We don't want our American boys to do the fighting for Asian boys,"
LBJ announced on September 25, 1964. "We don't want to get involved
in a nation with 700 million people [Red China] and get tied down in a
land war in Asia." The President preached peace.

But he was having it both ways, for Johnson also threatened wider
war. During the first week of August he announced that two American
destroyers were attacked in international waters (the Gulf of Tonkin) by
North Vietnamese torpedo boats. "The attacks were unprovoked," Johnson solemnly announced. He ordered air strikes against North Vietnam's
naval base, then urged Congress to pass a broad resolution giving him the
authority to "take all necessary measures to repel any armed attack
against the forces of the United States and to prevent further aggression."
(It was later discovered that this resolution and the list of bombing targets
had been drawn up by the White House two months before.) Several
Senators wanted more information. Democrats Wayne Morse of Oregon
and Ernest Gruening of Alaska opposed the resolution, arguing that the
circumstances of the attack were not clear. It seemed weird, they declared, that several small boats would challenge the strength of the United
States Navy. They also believed such broad powers should not be given to
the President. Senator Gaylord Nelson, Democrat of Wisconsin, urged an
amendment opposing "extension of the present conflict," but this was
dropped when he was assured that this was understood by Johnson. The
House passed the Gulf of Tonkin Resolution 416–0, the Senate 88–2.

Four years later Secretary of Defense Robert McNamara admitted
that the American people had been misled in 1964. He revealed that the
American destroyers had been accompanying South Vietnamese ships
and commandos that were attacking North Vietnamese bases. Shortly
after the engagement, moreover, the North Vietnamese had approached

the United States for peace discussions. Fearful that the South Vietnamese government was too weak even to negotiate with the North, Johnson had rejected the approach and again withheld the information from the American people.

The truth arrived much too late. Congress gave Johnson a blank check in 1964, then allowed him to cash it over and over again in the following years as he escalated the fighting into full-scale war without asking for a formal declaration of war from the legislative branch. That vital congressional restraint upon the wielding of incalculable power by a single man had disappeared. So too did the possible check from the electorate. Johnson humiliated Goldwater in the election, winning 61.1 percent of the popular vote, the largest margin in American history. The President used this mandate to draw decision-making increasingly into his own hands until finally the fundamental choices in Vietnam—choices that would ultimately lead to hundreds of thousands of deaths—were made by four men in a regularly scheduled Tuesday luncheon group: Johnson, McNamara, Rusk, and the President's National Security Advisor, McGeorge Bundy (replaced in 1966 by Walt Whitman Rostow). There would be few effective restraints on an imperial presidency during the next four years.

THE GLOBAL BACKGROUND TO VIETNAM

That presidential power was exercised in a rapidly changing world. In the Soviet Union Nikita Khrushchev fell from office in October 1964, victimized by his ineptness during the Cuban missile crisis and more importantly by his bungling of the Russian economy. He was replaced by two men, Aleksei Kosygin and Leonid Brezhnev, both of whom had risen to power under Stalin. They aimed at two objectives. First, they determined to mobilize Russian society for rapid economic advances. This determination and their apprenticeship under Stalin led the two leaders ruthlessly to squash any internal opposition. Dissident Soviet intellectuals, particularly Jews, were harassed, imprisoned, or declared insane. Second, the Soviets vowed to keep Chinese power contained. The two leading Communist nations were at each other's throat, deeply divided over ideology and, more important, over clashing national interests. By 1965 fighting between Chinese and Soviet troops had erupted along a 1200-mile frontier. When Kosygin visited Chinese leader Mao Tse-tung in 1965, Mao said that differences between the two nations were so profound that they would last for 10,000 years. When Kosygin protested, Mao agreed to make it only 9000 years.

These disagreements gave the Johnson administration an opportunity to reduce Cold War tensions by improving relations between the two superpowers. The Russians needed American economic aid and would welcome any easing of relations in Europe, for then they could concentrate on their more dangerous enemy in Peking. East-West trade did improve. Moscow and Washington, moreover, agreed in a Nonproliferation Treaty that they would work to prevent the spread of nuclear weapons. But no major initiative to end the Cold War occurred. American officials were too preoccupied with Vietnam. They insisted, moreover, that the Soviets were not truly mellowing. Secretary of State Rusk warned that while Americans had come to see Khrushchev as "an affable old grandfather, he was 68 and a half when he put missiles in Cuba." That perception seemed verified in August 1968, when Soviet troops suddenly marched into their satellite state of Czechoslovakia to terminate a new regime that, while remaining Communist, was nevertheless becoming more liberal and pro-Western.

As the two great powers struggled to keep the status quo, much of the rest of the world struggled to survive. In 1965 the North Atlantic nations (United States, Canada, and Western Europe) accounted for only 20 percent of the world's population but 70 percent of its income. The United States *added* as much to its income each year as Latin America had in total income, and twice as much as the total income received by Africans. Lyndon Johnson's childhood and his memories of the 1930s depression made him aware of this maldistribution of the world's wealth. When mass starvation threatened India in 1965–67, he mobilized 600 ships to dispatch one-fifth of the gigantic American grain crop. In one especially revealing remark the President warned Americans that "There are 3 billion people in the world and we have only 200 million of them. We are outnumbered 15–1. If might did make right they would sweep over the United States and take what we have. We have what they want."

In dealing with such immense problems, however, Johnson increasingly resorted to guns rather than food. He was not entirely free to choose. Foreign economic-aid programs had failed to work miracles in the newly emerging nations and were increasingly unpopular in Congress. Special commissions assigned to investigate the problem reported to Johnson that since government programs had failed, he should encourage private investment in Latin America, Asia, and Africa. That approach, however, was hollow. Private investors preferred to operate in secure, expanding Europe rather than in the chaotic third world. When they did go into the newly emerging nations, their primary investment went into oil, minerals, and other raw materials, thereby further unbalancing economies that were already overly dependent on a single product. Sometimes investors refused to move unless the American government assured their holdings. The Overseas Protection Insurance Corporation (OPIC) was thus created to insure investment against losses caused by confiscation or war. Investors who suffered such losses would be reimbursed by the United States government—that is, by the American taxpayers. Even this measure proved woefully insufficient to narrow the rapidly widening gap between the world's rich and poor. United Nations studies revealed in the mid-1960s that peoples in the newly emerging areas were closer to starvation than they were before World War II, and that their real income had shrunk so that it actually bought fewer goods than it had ten years earlier.

The Johnsons viewing Emanuel Leutze's *Heading West.*

LATIN AMERICA: A CASE STUDY—AND AFRICA

Latin America provided a case study of Johnson's response to these problems. United States businessmen had invested $15 billion directly into American-owned firms in these southern nations by 1965. They accounted for one-third of Latin America's industrial and mining output, one-third of its exports, and one-fifth of its taxes. These investors, however, were taking more out of Latin America than they were putting in. Between 1965 and 1970 the southern continent sent more money to Americans than it received in every year but 1967, and in 1969 the gap amounted to more than a half-billion dollars. In 1966 Latin Americans were receiving only enough development loans and grants to pay back the interest on the massive loans that they had needed during the 1955–65 period. While money for future development disappeared back into the United States, the population increased by 3 percent a year, one of the largest rates of increase in the world.

President Johnson had few remedies for these predicaments. Kennedy's Alliance for Progress was nearly dead, the victim of too little support in both North and South America. And while Johnson was devoting nearly all of his attention in foreign affairs to Vietnam, private interests lobbied in Congress to profit at Latin America's expense. For example, economic aid was given only when the recipient nation promised to spend it on American goods, regardless of the cost. Thus Bolivia had to spend American funds to buy ore carts for its vast mines from the United States even though the carts cost three times more than Belgian-made carts.

Increasing political tension resulted. The Alliance for Progress tried to build a new middle class, for such a class, in South as well as in North America, would be least likely to be revolutionary. But the middle classes were actually losing ground in Latin America by the 1960s, for their incomes were eaten by galloping inflation in the stagnant economies. "It is significant," a United Nations report observed, "that groups falling within the narrower definitions of the middle classes, such as bank employees and school teachers, have been among the most frequent and militant participants in strikes in recent years." As those middle classes grew bitter, societies polarized between very rich and very poor. Revolution grew more likely. Military governments rose to power in Brazil, Bolivia, Guatemala, and Ecuador. But leftist terrorism and guerrilla activities meanwhile increased in Venezuela, Columbia, Guatemala, and Bolivia. Latin America was being torn apart.

Lyndon Johnson responded forcefully to a rebellion in Santo Domingo. In 1961 the thirty-year dictatorship of Rafael Trujillo ended in assassination. Three years of confusion followed until the army took control. In April 1965, however, a strange combination of liberals, radicals, and low-ranking army officers tried to replace the military rulers with a more liberal government. As the military regime crumbled, it pleaded for help from President Johnson, using the bait that supporters of Fidel Castro were gaining power. Johnson immediately dispatched 22,800 American troops into the Caribbean nation to put down the rebellion. At first the President said he only wanted to assure the safety of American citizens. It soon became clear that he intended to use force to establish a stable, pro-American government. He did this even though the United States had signed the Charter of the Organization of American States (1948) which said in part, "No state or group of states has the right to intervene, directly or indirectly, for any reason whatever, in the internal or external affairs of any other state." The administration proclaimed that the troops had prevented "the Communists . . . from taking over."

This was proven a lie. No one has ever been able to demonstrate that either Communists or Castroites were important in any way in the uprising. But that did not prevent the President from announcing the "Johnson Doctrine": the United States would use force, if necessary, anywhere in the hemisphere to prevent Communist governments from coming to power. The Latin Americans did not appreciate this reappearance of Theodore Roosevelt's and Woodrow Wilson's gunboat diplomacy. "It is fall here," one reporter wrote from South America, "and U.S. flags as well as leaves are being burned." But Johnson had stabilized Santo Domingo, perhaps as Roosevelt and Wilson had ironically stabilized Cuba for the eventual coming to power of Fidel Castro.

American policies in Africa (especially in those nations south of the

Sahara) were not dissimilar. Between 1945 and 1970 more than 40 African nations gained independence as the old European empires fragmented. Few of the new governments had the economic or political experience to hold together national, freely-elected regimes. For its part, the United States provided little help. In 1965 American development aid amounted to $200 million spread among 33 nations. One country received $50,000. Such a program only worsened conditions internally and relations with the United States externally. Eight countries fell to army coups between 1964 and 1966 as parts of the continent seemed headed towards tribal warfare. American investment meanwhile centered on two white-dominated governments, South Africa and Southern Rhodesia. In addition, South Africa received military aid because of its strategic location at the tip of the continent. Both nations appeared prosperous and stable, but appearances were at the expense of the black population, which comprised the overwhelming majority in both countries. The blacks were victimized by *apartheid,* a white-controlled system that, through legislation and violence, brutally separated and exploited the blacks.

The Johnson administration intervened directly into the former Belgian Congo. That area of 17 million blacks had suddenly become free in 1960 despite the lack of any preparation by the former Belgian rulers. Civil war erupted, but the United Nations, with American and Russian support, stabilized the area. By 1964 the United States was the dominant foreign power in the Congo, and the vast copper and diamond mines again produced their riches. Then nationalist revolts began, with rebels massacring thousands of blacks and whites. Despite help from the Central Intelligence Agency, the Congolese government could not quell the rebellion. The United States staged a paratroop strike to free a number of hostages, including 16 Americans, whom the insurgents had threatened to kill, and by late 1965 the situation was quieted. When it flared again in 1967, President Johnson prepared large-scale military aid for the Congo, but Senate leaders, particularly conservative Democrats from the South, forced a scaling-down of the aid. The Senators argued that the administration had enough racial problems at home and enough military activity in Vietnam. The Congolese government then settled its own internal problems.

VIETNAM ABROAD

The President's responses in Santo Domingo and the Congo differed only in degree from those in Vietnam. In each case the United States chose armed might as a solution for the social ills that generated nationalist revolts. Johnson's preoccupation with force led humorist Art Buchwald to claim that the President wanted to alert two airborne divisions, four Marine brigades, and the Atlantic Fleet—before proclaiming Mother's Day. Americans would learn that military intervention not only failed to solve the root problems but often aggravated them.

The Gulf of Tonkin incidents in August 1964 were followed by five months of little fighting, but the Johnson administration was exceptionally busy. The murder of President Diem in 1963 had created political chaos. Vietnamese regimes changed so frequently that Johnson twice felt that he had to reject North Vietnamese peace overtures for fear that the American-supported regime in Saigon lacked the strength to negotiate an acceptable peace. These peace feelers were kept secret from the American people.

On February 5, 1965 (two days after the final American rejection of the second North Vietnamese peace approach), the Communists killed 7 Americans at a base in Pleiku. The President immediately ordered bombing of the north in carefully selected attacks aimed at cutting off supplies flowing south to the Communist National Liberation Front of South Vietnam (the NLF). The raids were also to be a warning that North Vietnam should not try to escalate the pressure on the rickety regime in Saigon. South Vietnamese governments, however, had fallen owing to lack of support within the country. As for supplies coming from the north, a careful study by the Department of State, written to justify the bombings, actually revealed that of 15,000 weapons taken from Communist soldiers, fewer than 200 were made in Communist factories. The remainder had been captured from South Vietnamese troops.

The United States escalation, therefore, was aimed less at stopping North Vietnamese intervention in the south (for in February 1965 that intervention was not significant) than at propping up Saigon regimes, which seemed incapable of defending themselves in the civil war. In March the escalation took a drastic turn. Johnson sent in Marine battalions, thus starting a buildup of American troops who were to participate directly in the combat rather than merely be "advisors" to South Vietnamese soldiers. During the summer, over 100,000 more Americans poured into the country. The President tried to cover these actions by declaring that the troops would only secure American and South Vietnamese bases. In a speech in April, he announced that he would enter "unconditional discussion" with North Vietnam but that the Communists would have to begin the discussions by accepting the fact of an independent South Vietnam, something that the North Vietnamese would never accept. The government of Ho Chi Minh responded with its own four-point offer, including a return to the 1954 Geneva Agreement (which stated that the boundary between north and south would only be temporary) and settlement of South Vietnam's affairs "by the South Vietnamese people themselves in accordance with the program of the [NLF] without any foreign interference." The United States replied with accelerated use of force.

With few pauses, American bombing continued for seven years. More bombs were dropped on Vietnam than on Germany, Japan, and their Axis allies during World War II. The bombing had little military effect. By 1966, eleven tough regiments of North Vietnamese troops were in the south to fight 200,000 Americans and 550,000 South Vietnamese. The Russians and Chinese supplied ever larger amounts of goods to the Communists. Most ominous of all, the North Vietnamese, who historically had fought and feared the Chinese, were necessarily moving closer to Peking in order to receive aid. The Kennedy-Johnson policy was aimed at blocking the influence of China, but the policy seemed to be producing the opposite result.

By April 1966, more Americans were being killed in action than South Vietnamese. In July, the number of American dead reached 4440, more than the number killed in the American Revolution and ten times the dead in the Spanish-American War. The results were discouraging. The South Vietnamese controlled less than 25 percent of their own 12,000 hamlets. But a stable government was finally established in Saigon by the army. Its leaders were Major-General Nguyen Van Thieu as head and, as Premier, Nguyen Cao Ky, a swashbuckling Air Force officer who had fought with the French against the Vietnamese nationalists and who had been overheard expressing admiration for Adolf Hitler.

The new regime failed to reverse the course of the war. Lieutenant Colonel John Vann, perhaps the most perceptive American advisor to serve in Vietnam, put his finger on one fundamental problem: "This is a political war and it calls for discrimination in killing. The best weapon for killing would be a knife, but I'm afraid we can't do it that way. The worst is an airplane. The next worse is artillery." Americans were not prepared either politically or militarily to fight such a war. They wanted to resort to their unimaginably powerful technology to blow up the enemy from the air or engage him in massive ground battles. The Communists actually had little to blow up (except their ports, where the presence of Russian ships made attacks dangerous), and they refused to stand still in large groups as targets for United States artillery. They fought more like George Washington's guerrilla forces of 1777 than like the Chinese in Korea during 1951. The war was confusing and frustrating in both Vietnam and, increasingly, at home. In 1966 Johnson blurted out the problem: "Most people wish we weren't there; most people wish we didn't have a war; most people don't want to escalate it, and most people don't want to get out."

Football [and Politics]

It began in eleventh-century England, when players representing towns pushed animal skulls, and later cow bladders, between towns that stood for "goals." King Henry II outlawed the sport in the twelfth century because its popularity interfered with archery practice needed to defend the kingdom. Reborn 400 years later on playing fields, it became the British sport of rugby and then caught on with the American East Coast, where British games were popular. The first college game of football was won by Rutgers' six goals to Princeton's four in 1869.

Within twenty years coaches were selecting the best players on "All-America" lists. Through the mid-1890s only one non-British name was on such lists, but Irish, Jewish, and finally Polish and Hungarian players were honored after 1900. These names exemplified the new immigration from Europe that created an increasingly pluralistic society. The social divisions led American players to make rules that all could understand. Thus instead of having wild scrambles (as in rugby), the game was controlled by having fixed scrimmage lines. The new rules also allowed growing numbers of spectators to learn and follow the sport. Football was nevertheless brutal. The bloody Stanford-California game of 1904 was followed by riots in San Francisco. Even Theodore Roosevelt, who prided himself on the "strenuous life," finally ordered that football be civilized or, he thundered, it would be ended by presidential proclamation.

The Four Horsemen of Notre Dame, 1924.

436 So the forward pass was legalized in 1906 to open and speed up the game. This weapon was used by an unknown Notre Dame team to upset mighty Army in 1913. Thus began the Notre Dame tradition, for the school soon attracted the athletic sons of Roman Catholic immigrants. Colleges began recruiting players in 1915, so some immigrants and other poor Americans suddenly found higher education available simply by playing football in the autumn. The sport entered glory days in the 1920s and professional teams appeared. The most renowned coach was Notre Dame's Knute Rockne, who believed that "After the Church, football is the best thing we have." His backfields moved in precise motion like the mass production techniques that Americans so admired. And like industry, football became a game for specialty teams of defense, offense, and even kicking. But Americans who preached the virtues of rugged individualism could proudly point to the exploits of Red Grange ("the Galloping Ghost") of 1920s Illinois teams, Charlie ("Choo-Choo") Justice of 1940s North Carolina squads, and, in the 1960s, Joe Willie ("Broadway Joe") Namath of Alabama and O. J. ("Orange-Juice") Simpson of Southern California.

Football popularity peaked in the 1970s. Its quick action and pageantry suited color television screens, and television in turn provided immense wealth ($13.5 million in 1973 for college games alone) for football teams and such $250,000-a-year quarterbacks as Namath. In the 1970s George Allen of the

Knute Rockne.

Red Grange, 1925.

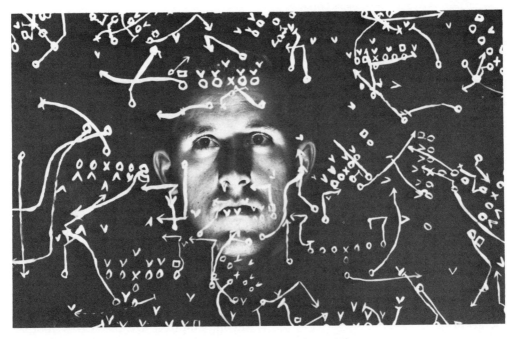

Fran Tarkenton of the Minnesota Vikings studies offensive plays, 1961.

October 1978: N.Y. Jets vs. St. Louis Cardinals.

professional Washington Redskins symbolized the tough, disciplined life with his 18-hour-a-day attention to detail and his remark, "Losing is like death. If you don't win you're dead and you don't know it." Allen's good friend, President Richard Nixon, was the nation's leading fan. "The President thinks football is a way of life," Allen observed. "He is a competitor." The game provided the language for politics and diplomacy. The American bombing of North Vietnam in late 1972 was code-named "Operation Linebacker," and Nixon's code-name was "Quarterback." Conversely, such metaphors of war as the "blitz" and the "bomb" were applied to the gridiron.

The University of Oklahoma Athletic Director declared, "We teach a philosophy, we teach a skill, and we danged sure also teach a little bit of religion. And we teach discipline. This is one of the last areas where true discipline is taught, where love for the American flag and respect for the American President is taught, through discipline." Others, however, deplored football's commercialism and its use as an example for fighting the Cold War. Former star Dave Meggysey quit the game, claiming that he had illegally received money for playing in college and had been treated as an animal by professional coaches and owners. "Politics and pro football," Meggysey declared, "are the most grotesque extremes in the theatric of a dying empire." By the 1970s football seemed to have replaced baseball as the so-called National Pastime.

VIETNAM IN THE
WHITE HOUSE

Yet the President insisted on remaining in the war. Escalating troop strength to 485,000 by 1968, he committed the country to the longest and most tragic of all its wars. He did so for several reasons.

First, he believed that South Vietnam was the test of whether the United States could prevent communism—particularly the Chinese brand, which resulted from peasant revolution—from controlling all of Asia. After a fact-finding journey to Vietnam in 1961, Johnson reported to President Kennedy that since "there is no alternative to United States leadership in Southeast Asia," Americans must make a "fundamental decision whether we are to attempt to meet the challenge of Communist expansion now in Southeast Asia by a major effort . . . or throw in the towel." He never changed that view. Nor did he ever doubt that the civil war was caused not by Vietnamese nationalism but by Vietnamese who were part of a worldwide Communist movement inspired by China. The Chinese were his primary concern: "Communist China apparently desires the war to continue whatever the cost to their Allies," the President remarked on May 13, 1965. "Their target is not merely South Vietnam. It is Asia."

Second, Johnson believed that he was carrying on an essential American policy, for he was stopping communism in Asia just as President Truman had contained the Russians in Europe. He did not wish to repeat the mistake made at Munich in 1938, when England and France allowed Hitler to take Czechoslovakia and open the way for World War II. Johnson and Secretary Rusk directly compared Munich and Vietnam, a comparison that would have resulted in an instant "failure" for any college student who tried to make it in a history class. But neither Johnson nor any of his close advisors suggested that Asian economic and political conditions differed fundamentally from those of Europe, or that the United States enjoyed strong allies in Europe (allies tied together by language, culture, and wealth) whereas no such friends existed in Asia. Instead, the President attacked critics who pointed out these vital differences by calling them "special pleaders who counsel retreat in Vietnam. . . . We cannot accept their logic . . . that subjugation by an armed minority in Asia is different from subjugation by an armed minority in Europe."

Third, he claimed that he was defending commitments in Vietnam made by Eisenhower and Kennedy. His relationship with Kennedy's ghost, however, involved both love and hate. He publicly pledged to carry out the late President's policies, but privately Johnson never forgave Kennedy for relegating him into the background between 1961 and 1963, and he especially grew bitter as many of Kennedy's former aides quit the foundering Johnson administration to protest against the war they had helped begin. When once reminded of a Kennedy policy, Johnson barked, "The touch football crowd isn't making decisions around here anymore." But the Texan was equally determined not to give up where Kennedy had taken the stand. He would maintain the hallowed commitment and also show the Kennedyites.

Fourth, the President believed that the commitment was consistent with American interests at home as well as abroad. He emphasized "one overriding rule: . . . that our foreign policy must always be an extension of this nation's domestic policy." This "rule" had an ironic ring in the 1960s, for the fire, rioting, and violence that ripped American cities between 1965 and 1968 mirrored the much greater destruction inflicted on Vietnam. Johnson was not, of course, referring to *that* mirror, but was pointing to the New Deal tradition, which shaped his political outlook. The New Deal had used government action in an attempt to improve living conditions for poor Americans. As President, Johnson announced a "Great Society" program to modernize and complete the New Deal. He believed that in a world made smaller by technology, Americans had to help others if they hoped to improve their own society. He proposed an Asian Development Bank and a vast plan to enrich the Mekong Valley in Southeast Asia, much as the New Deal had built the Tennessee Valley Authority. Only the Communists stood in the way. To eliminate them, however, became so costly that by 1966 Johnson was forced to cut back his Great Society at home. "Because of Vietnam," he finally admitted, "we cannot do all that we should, or all that we would like to do" in the United States.

Fifth, economic bonds between the United States and Vietnam developed, but quite differently than the Great Society had planned. The money pumped into the military buildup brought a rosy glow to the American economy. One economic expert concluded that American defense expenditures supported 95 percent of the employment in aircraft and missile industries, 60 percent in shipbuilding, and 40 percent in radio and communications. Including three million in the armed services, nearly seven million Americans were dependent on the Defense Department budget, and Vietnam expenditures constituted an increasingly larger proportion of that budget. When peace rumors circulated in 1965–66, the New York Stock Exchange was hit with heavy losses as investors rushed to cash in their securities before prices dropped. One broker believed that "a genuine peace offer" would "knock the market out of bed." After all, he observed, the government had scheduled a $60-billion defense budget on the assumption that the war would continue. In Vietnam itself, American oil companies and banks led the way, investing to benefit from the war and particularly from the gigantic reconstruction effort that would follow. The government encouraged such investment; its Agency for International Development (AID) provided a 100 percent guarantee against loss of money because of war or confiscation. This effort was well summarized by Senator Clair Engle, Democrat of California:

We must bring to bear upon the economic development of Asia all the manifold talents, skills and resources of American private enterprise, and we will get returns not only in expanded export markets, but also in the political and human benefits that will spring from progress in Asia.

The American business community did not turn against the war until after 1967, when the conflict began to erode rather than accelerate the economy.

Sixth, Johnson believed that he possessed the presidential power required to realize his objectives. By the mid-1960s the presidency dominated the nation in a manner undreamed of by the Founding Fathers. The Constitution's framers had feared unchecked power, and with Congress's abdication of responsibility in the Gulf of Tonkin Resolution, the President's power in foreign affairs had few limits. As journalist James Reston observed, "Something important has happened in America since Woodrow Wilson went to his grave" believing that a President's foreign policy could be paralyzed by Congress. Military efficiency as well as Congress's weakness had helped create that power. Johnson was the first President in the nation's history to enter war with a great army prepared to fight. Indeed, it was too easy to order this remarkable striking force halfway around the world.

Finally, the President had strong public support. In December 1965, as he rapidly escalated the conflict, public opinion polls indicated that 58 percent of the American people believed that increased bombing was the way to peace, and 82 percent said that United States troops would have to remain in Vietnam until the Communists agreed to terms. One-third of those having an opinion thought nuclear weapons should be used if they would shorten the war. (Such opinion allowed Johnson, who opposed using nuclear weapons, to appear as a moderate as he escalated the conventional war.) Support came from all sectors. Some 477,000 students in 322 colleges gave their written commitment to the President's policies in 1966. The American Federation of Labor's national convention pledged "unstinting support" for all measures necessary "to halt Communist aggression" and bring peace to Vietnam. When antiwar spectators got in a shouting match with AFL delegates, union leader George Meany ordered that "those kookies" be thrown out of the hall. The president of the 250,000-member U.S. Jaycees—formerly the Junior Chamber of Commerce—announced a program to expose "leftists" and "peace advocates," adding that the Jaycees would work closely with the FBI. A critical newspaper suggested that the Jaycees might better sponsor discussions of the Bill of Rights.

Both the public and Congress were supporting an anti-Communist, Cold War policy that had existed since 1947. Neither was capable of questioning that policy. Nor was Johnson. "The President is still confusing popularity with policy," James Reston noted in late 1965. "And this could easily lead us deeper into the bog."

VIETNAM AT HOME

By 1966 important segments of public opinion were beginning to change, and this change was partly inspired by a group of intellectuals. In the fields of History, Sociology, and Political Science, a number of scholars developed a "new left" position that raised fundamental questions about maldistribution of power and wealth at home and abroad. Indeed, the thread that ran through most of this literature was the fear of uncontrolled power, a fear that had earlier characterized such apparently dissimilar Americans as the Founding Fathers, the Populists, and the Liberty Leaguers.

In many ways the new-left critique could be traced to the work of sociologist C. Wright Mills, who, during the 1950s, had criticized the prevailing consensus by arguing that American society was governed by a power elite composed of businessmen, military officials, and political leaders. At the top of American society, Mills claimed, "there has emerged an elite whose power probably exceeds that of any small group of men in world history." Mills also defined the task of the new left: "structural criticism and reportage and theories of society, which at some point or another are focused politically as demands and programmes." Mills had also been a critic, though a lonely one, of American foreign policy. By 1966 Mills had died, but the war in Vietnam caused many to share his early doubts about America's anti-Communist crusade.

Neither the President nor Congress would debate the fundamental questions. Americans therefore created their own groups for discussion and political action. Universities organized "teach-ins" to replace the debate that should have been occurring in Congress. Teach-ins began at the University of Michigan in March 1965, then had spectacular success at the University of California-Berkeley, Columbia, the University of Wisconsin, Rutgers, and Cornell, among many others. The administration refused to participate until mid-1966, when McGeorge Bundy debated with scholars, including political scientist Hans Morgenthau, in a nationally televised teach-in. Bundy, however, neglected issues, instead smearing Morgenthau by alleging that the political scientist had made mistakes in his writings published during the 1950s. With little help from Congress or public opinion, a relatively few colleges and intellectuals were doing what intellectuals are supposed to do: study the national political and economic system and then as outside observers criticize it fundamentally so that it could correct and heal itself.

Johnson and Rusk refused to take these intellectuals seriously. The Secretary of State's remark, "That a man knows everything there is to know about enzymes doesn't mean that he knows very much about Vietnam," evaded the point that many leading critics were specialists in Asian and international affairs. The President found more agreeable intellectuals, particularly Walt Whitman Rostow of the Massachusetts Institute of Technology. A vocal advocate of "staying the course," Rostow replaced Bundy as Johnson's advisor. The President privately announced that Rostow was "going to be *my* goddamned intellectual." The louder the protest became, the more determined the President grew in surrounding himself with those who would not question his policies.

By 1967–68, the rhetoric escalated with the war until it seemed the society was on the edge of mental breakdown. The President implored American troops to "hang the coonskin on the wall." In Vietnam when Colonel George Patton III asked an army chaplain to pray for the killing of many North Vietnamese, the chaplain allegedly prayed, "Oh Lord, give us the wisdom to find the bastards and the strength to pile it on." After troops devastated a Communist-controlled village, an American officer blurted out, "It became necessary to destroy the town in order to save it." At home protesters chanted, "Hey, hey LBJ, how many kids have you killed today?" as they tried to invade army training camps and block troop trains. One person burned himself to death at the door of the Pentagon. Students publicly set fire to their draft cards even after Congress passed a law imposing a $10,000 fine or five years in jail for such an act.

Soon the disenchantment approached the White House itself. Senator J. William Fulbright, Democrat of Arkansas and Chairman of the powerful Senate Foreign Relations Committee, had long been a close friend of Johnson's, but turned after he discovered that the President had lied about the Gulf of Tonkin affair and the Santo Domingo intervention. Even more ominous, Secretary of Defense Robert McNamara began doubting. The President depended on him more than on any other man in the government. In August 1967, McNamara publicly called the bombing campaign a failure. Three months later Johnson sent him off to become president of the World Bank, a position that McNamara would hold with great distinction through the next decade as he multiplied the bank's resources for helping feed and develop newly emerging areas.

The closest American allies also fell away. Western Europeans enjoyed prosperity and new political cohesion from their European Economic Community (EEC). When it accepted Great Britain as a member in 1970, the EEC joined the United States, Russia, and Japan as the world's great economic powers and had the potential to move to the very top. The Europeans viewed the Vietnam war as a terrible mistake, for it forced Johnson to neglect vital ties with the Atlantic nations and severely weakened the American economy, the EEC's main overseas customer. Not even the British would help in Vietnam. Frustrated and angered, Secretary of State Dean Rusk exploded to a British journalist, "All we needed [from you in Vietnam] was one regiment. . . . But you wouldn't. Well, don't expect us to save you again. They can invade Sussex and we wouldn't do a damned thing about it." With few friends at home and even fewer overseas, Johnson observed that he was "in the position of a jackrabbit in a hailstorm, hunkered up and taking it."

THE 1968 ELECTION

The worst was yet to come. Throughout 1967, American military commanders confidently predicted victory, but the bombing had not prevented the North Vietnamese from doubling their army in the south to 475,000 between 1965 and 1967. The build-up on both sides had changed a civil war within South Vietnam to a war between the United States and

Tet, 1968: South Vietnamese national police chief shooting suspected
North Vietnamese terrorist.

North Vietnam. In early February 1968, during the Tet Lunar New Year
holiday, the Communists launched a devastating attack that resulted in
the seizure of vital portions of the country; in addition, they defeated
units of the American-South Vietnamese armies and even threatened the
supposedly impregnable U.S. Embassy in Saigon. Because large numbers
of Communists were killed in the offensive, the Johnson administration
claimed victory, but the truth slipped out when American generals reported that they needed 206,000 more men to continue the war.

The President ordered an in-depth analysis of the war by experts in
and out of government. They bluntly informed Johnson that he was
"being led down the garden path" by the American military in Vietnam.
This news was coupled with returns from the first Democratic presidential
primary in New Hampshire, where Johnson barely defeated antiwar critic
Senator Eugene McCarthy of Minnesota who received a surprising 42
percent of the vote. In late March, the President dramatically announced
on television that he was cutting back bombing in order to get North Vietnam to the peace table, and, so that he could concentrate on obtaining
peace, he would not run for reelection in 1968.

Lyndon Johnson had become a casualty of the war. Not only had the
fighting gone badly, but because the administration had underestimated
war expenses in 1966–67, the economy entered a sharp inflationary spiral.
It was the beginning of the worst sustained inflationary period in 20th-
century America. In April Martin Luther King's assassination set off riots

in many cities, including Washington D.C., where smoke from burning buildings floated over the White House. Two months later, presidential candidate Robert Kennedy, Democratic Senator from New York, was murdered in Los Angeles. Driven by a hatred for the war, and especially the draft, students staged destructive riots. A climax to the violence occurred with the Democratic Convention in Chicago during August, when Police and U.S. Army troops used tear gas to control antiwar demonstrators. Johnson could send a half-million men to Vietnam, but could not attend his own party's nominating convention. Through the smoke and the suffocatingly sweet smell of tear gas, Vice-President Hubert Humphrey was named as the Democratic nominee, and Senator Edmund Muskie of Maine the vice-presidential candidate.

The Republican ticket was Richard Nixon and Spiro Agnew, governor of Maryland. Nixon had risen from the political dead after his loss in 1960 and then another defeat in the California governor's race in 1962. In the next six years he traveled widely to cement his ties with grass roots Republicans and was in the forefront of those who attacked Johnson for not ending the Vietnam war on American terms. Nixon, however, emphasized law-and-order themes during the campaign while de-emphasizing the war by saying only that he had "a plan" for stopping it. Agnew was more direct, blasting Humphrey for being "soft on inflation, soft on communism, and soft on law and order."

In September the Republicans had a lead of 15 percent in the public opinion polls, but after Johnson began talks with the North Vietnamese and Humphrey improved the effectiveness of his campaign, the final margin of Nixon's victory was only 1 percent. Voting analyses indicated, however, that Vietnam itself was not the central issue in the election. Crime, riots, and other law-and-order issues (which sometimes covered strong racial feelings) were more important. A large percentage of Americans continued to support Johnson's war policies while disliking even peaceful antiwar spokesmen.

THE NIXON FOREIGN POLICIES

The new President appointed Henry Kissinger, a professor of international relations at Harvard, as his National Security Advisor. The two men privately formulated their own foreign policy, neglecting Congress and the State Department, and in some instances not even bothering to keep these two bodies informed. Kissinger believed such secrecy necessary in order to carry out plans quickly and effectively. Nixon agreed, for he cared relatively little about domestic affairs (once remarking that the nation did not need a President to handle internal matters), but deeply involved himself in foreign policies. He also harbored a strong desire to have a private, shielded presidency. Before some of his most momentous decisions, Nixon would isolate himself for long periods, talking with no one.

The President slowly changed the emphases of American foreign policy. He reduced the commitment in Vietnam (and showed less interest in newly emerging areas, such as Latin America and Africa), while opening new relationships with Russia and later China. Nixon responded to the new post-1956 world by de-emphasizing the Kennedy-Johnson policies in the more volatile southern half of the globe and working instead for a settlement with the two great Communist powers. Several factors forced this change. Perhaps most important, Nixon understood that the world contained not two great powers but, in his words, "five economic superpowers"—the United States, Russia, Japan, China, and the EEC. Since the first two balanced one another off militarily, these five powers "will determine the economic future, and because economic power will be the key to other kinds of power," they will determine "the future of the world in other ways in the last third of this century." Russia and China, moreover, were enemies. As Kissinger noted, "The deepest international conflict in the world today is not between us and the Soviet Union but between the Soviet Union and Communist China."

All this was not new. It had been apparent since 1960, but Nixon was the first President to act upon it, for he understood that this five-power world opened a marvelous opportunity for the United States to play off the other four powers against one another. He could, for example, cooperate with both the Chinese and Soviets to control the threatening economic expansion of Japan and Europe. Nixon could use American technology (such as computers) and agricultural products, which both Communist nations badly needed, to strengthen political ties and gain access for American business executives to the vast Chinese and Russian markets. Finally, if such ties were made, the United States could trade its products for Russian and Chinese help in stopping the Vietnam War so that American troops could be withdrawn on honorable terms. In all, Nixon's plans were imaginative and sweeping.

He understood, above all, that the United States had overreached itself during the 1960s with commitments that had already led to violence, inflation, and the political demise of Johnson. Thus he began by announcing a "Nixon Doctrine" in 1969, that pledged continued economic aid to allies in Asia and elsewhere but added that these allies should no longer count on the presence of American troops. He also announced that he would end the draft within two years, and that American troop strength would be systematically reduced in Vietnam while the South Vietnamese received more military equipment so that they could fight their own wars. This policy became tagged as "Vietnamization."

THE NIXON FAILURES, 1970–1971

Vietnamization, however, was failing by early 1970. As American troops left, the South Vietnamese proved incapable of driving out Communist forces. Using bases in neighboring Cambodia, a supposedly neutral state, the North Vietnamese and NLF threatened to bring down the Saigon government. Nixon responded with heavy bombing of the Cambodian bases but kept the raids secret from everyone except a few top officials in Washington and, of course, the Cambodians and Vietnamese. On April 30, 1970, after a conservative, pro-U.S. government suddenly came to power in Cambodia, the President announced that American and South Vietnamese troops were temporarily invading Cambodia to destroy the Communist bases. Having promised to end the war, Nixon was now actually expanding it into neighboring areas. Worse, the American troops did not succeed in destroying the bases, for after they retreated, the Communists simply moved back in and then threatened to overthrow the Cambodian government itself.

The effect on the American people was electric. Colleges, including many that had remained quiet during the 1960s, erupted into antiwar violence. The nation was shaken when four students were shot to death by Ohio National Guard forces during the antiwar demonstration at Kent State University. Polls showed that half the American people disbelieved Nixon's announcement that the invasion would shorten the war. A lack of confidence in the President's foreign policy seemed to be developing, a rare event in recent American history. Henry Kissinger privately shuddered at the possible consequences, for he believed that the antiwar demonstrations were not just against Vietnam policies, but

against authority of any kind, not just the authority of this President, but the authority of any President. . . . If confidence in him and in all institutions is systematically destroyed, we will turn into a group that has nothing left but a physical test of strength and the only outcome of this is Caesarism. . . .

The very people who shout "Power to the People" are not going to be the people who will take over this country if it turns into a test of strength. Upper middle-class college kids will not take this country over. Some more primitive and elemental forces will do that.

But demonstrations continued, and an angry Senate finally repealed the Gulf of Tonkin Resolution. The President, however, claimed that he could continue to fight in Southeast Asia, regardless of what Congress did, in order to protect American troops already in Vietnam.

Announcing that the Cambodian invasion had been successful in removing one threat to American troops, the President further widened the war in February 1971 by invading Communist bases in Laos. This time, however, South Vietnamese rather than American troops went in; it was to be a test of Vietnamization. South Vietnam flunked the test. Meeting tough resistance, its troops scattered and ran. The Communists retained their hold on strategic areas despite an intensification of American bombing that had been carried out secretly since 1964. By mid-1971 the Communists controlled more of Laos than ever before.

The failure of Vietnamization was one of two crises to confront Nixon. The other was a baffling economy—baffling in that, on the one hand, it was by far the world's greatest, having passed in 1970 the trillion-dollar level in annual gross national product (that is, the total product of all goods and services produced in the nation). On the other hand, it also suffered from inflation that made American goods more expensive and hence less competitive on the international market. United States products lost ground to such cheaply produced Japanese and German products as the Datsun and Volkswagen automobiles.

In 1971, and for the first time since 1893, the United States suffered an overall deficit trade balance. It paid out more money to satisfy its international debts ($45.5 billion) than it received from exports and other services abroad ($42.8 billion). The world's greatest economy was sick. In August 1971 President Nixon attempted to supply a remedy by devaluing the dollar, that is, reducing each dollar's worth in gold, which is the leading international exchange standard. This act cheapened the dollar and so made American goods cheaper and easier to purchase internationally. By early 1973 the inflation and deficits continued, so the President again devalued the dollar. American exports picked up, but inflation was not halted. Some economists advised that government controls be placed on prices and wages to keep them in hand. In mid-1970 Nixon firmly rejected such advice: "I will not take the nation down the road of wage and price controls, however politically expedient they may seem." A little more than a year later, he imposed such controls. They were removed before the 1972 election, and a rapid price rise occurred throughout 1973–74. The price of food, clothing, and other essential items skyrocketed. In mid-1973 the controls were reimposed. They reminded older Americans of government action during World Wars I and II. During the world wars, however, the controls had been largely effective. In the early 1970s they failed to stop a roaring, destructive rise of prices.

THE NIXON
SUCCESSES: 1971–1972

A year before the 1972 presidential election, Nixon's misfortunes in Vietnam and with the economy hurt his chances for reelection. Any President, however, can use his control of foreign policy to make dramatic headlines and some political gains if he has made adequate preparation and has a sense of timing. No one knew this better than Nixon.

In August 1971 he announced that he would become the first President to travel to China. Chairman Mao Tse-tung in Peking had happily cooperated, for he hoped to use his new friendship with the United States as a weapon against his major enemy, Russia, which was massing troops along the Sino-Russian border. In an instant, twenty-two years of Sino-American enmity began to dissolve, although it would take many decades before the two nations could ever become friends. Americans who had vocally disliked Red China for years could say little, for Richard Nixon had long been the most vocal. Nor was there an outcry when, over United States objections, the People's Republic of China replaced Chiang Kai-shek's Taiwan government as the representative of China in the United Nations. In February 1972 Nixon dominated the television screens as he

Kissinger, Nixon, and Chou En-Lai, Peking 1972.

exchanged toasts and praises with Chinese leaders. Americans over-whelmingly applauded his effort to ease tensions.

But he parlayed the journey into an even greater gain, for by pitting the two enemies, Russia and China, against one another for American favors, and by sending badly needed American wheat to both, he freed his hand to deal with North Vietnam without fear that the two great Communist powers might intervene. Since 1969 he had searched for an agreement with the North Vietnamese and hoped to reach one before the 1972 election, but none had been concluded. In April 1972 the North Vietnamese launched an offensive against the weakened American–South Vietnamese forces. The President responded with the heaviest bombing of the war on Hanoi, then mined North Vietnamese harbors. The mining endangered Russian ships using the harbors and was such a threatening move that Lyndon Johnson had flatly refused to do it. But now the Russians and Chinese made no active response.

Indeed, as the mines were being sown, the Russians welcomed Nixon in Moscow as the first American President to make that journey. United States and Soviet leaders signed an important pact limiting the number of defensive missiles each nation could possess. Both promised that the agreement was only the first of several that would reduce the number of nuclear weapons. The treaties would come none too soon, for the nuclear stockpile in the world amounted to the equivalent of 15 tons of TNT for every man, woman, and child on earth, and it was growing steadily.

In early 1972 a majority of Americans had disliked Nixon's Vietnam policies. After he mined and bombed North Vietnam, however, and then flew to Peking and Russia, the nation approved his policies by a ratio of two to one. He held this margin against the Democratic presidential nominee, Senator George McGovern of South Dakota, throughout the election campaign. McGovern had long been an outspoken opponent of the war. Nixon whipsawed him by claiming that the administration had steadily worked for peace in Peking and Moscow but had also showed how tough it could be in the mining and bombing operations. A week before the election, Henry Kissinger announced that he and the North Vietnamese would soon agree on a ceasefire. That announcement proved premature, for the war continued for 2½ years, but Nixon used it to pull in more votes as he and Vice-President Agnew defeated McGovern in every state but Massachusetts and the District of Columbia.

The President had used foreign policy much as a director uses music to build emotions to a pitch during a movie. "A lot of things are coming together at a point," said Nixon's right-hand man John Ehrlichman with a smile just before the election. "And it is a point, frankly, which we selected as a target time as a matter of enlightened self-interest."

It was the peak of the President's popularity and power. Beginning in mid-1973 the slide downhill for Nixon, Agnew, and even Ehrlichman would be swift. For they too finally fell victims to bloated presidential power and political corruption that had recent roots in the 1960s. Americans would long be haunted not only by the foreign-policy disasters of that decade, but by its domestic politics and social upheavals as well.

Suggested Reading

A critical, readable overview is Godfrey Hodgson, *America in Our Time; From World War II to Nixon* (1976). There is no comprehensive treatment of Johnson's foreign policies, but the following are useful: Doris Kearns, *Lyndon Johnson and the American Dream* (1976); Philip L. Geyelin, *Lyndon B. Johnson and the World* (1966); Richard J. Barnet, *Intervention and Revolution; U.S. and the Third World* (1968); W. W. Rostow's important *Diffusion of Power, 1958–1972* (1972); and Johnson's own *Vantage Point* (1971). On Vietnam start with Frances Fitzgerald, *Fire in the Lake* (1972); George Kahin and John W. Lewis, *U.S. in Vietnam* (1969); Guenter Lewy's controversial *America in Vietnam* (1978); Dave Richard Palmer, *Summons of the Trumpet: U.S.–Vietnam in Perspective* (1978); and the best source, *The Pentagon Papers*, available in 12-volume and 4-volume editions, and most handily in the Neil Sheehan, et al. edition published in paperback by *The New York Times* (1971). Some of the public opinion can be gleaned from Ralph B. Levering, *The Public and American Foreign Policy, 1918–1978* (1978); and Richard Scammon and Ben Wattenberg, *The Real Majority* (1970). The best survey is Irwin Unger, *The Movement: A History of the American New Left, 1959–1972* (1974); also see Charles Chatfield, ed., *Peace Movements in America* (1973). For more critical views, see Robert W. Tucker, *The Radical Left and American Foreign Policy* (1971); and Peter Clecak, *Radical Paradoxes: Dilemmas of the American Left, 1945–1970* (1973).

The best background for the Nixon years is Garry Wills, *Nixon Agonistes* (1970); Henry Kissinger's pre-1969 essays in *American Foreign Policy. Expanded Edi-*

tion (1974); and David Landau, *Kissinger* (1972). For the policies after 1969 see John G. Stoessinger's survey, *Henry Kissinger: The Anguish of Power* (1976); Lloyd Gardner, ed., *The Great Nixon Turnaround* (1973); Roger Morris, *Uncertain Greatness* (1977), especially for 1969–1971; Tad Szulc's detailed overview, *The Illusion of Peace* (1977); and Jonathan Schell's superb *The Time of Illusion* (1976), which links domestic and foreign policies. John Newhouse, *Cold Dawn* (1973) covers the first SALT agreement. Edward S. Mason traces economic policy in *The World Bank Since Bretton Woods* (1973). Nixon gives his side in *RN: The Memoirs of Richard Nixon* (1978).

On football in American life, a fine introduction is David Riesman and Reuel Denney, "Football in America," *American Quarterly* (1951), pp. 309–25.

Martin Luther King, September, 1967.

CHAPTER FIFTEEN

1963–1972

Consensus
and Confrontation

WE SHALL OVERCOME

New words and music arrangement by Zilphia Horton, Frank
Hamilton, Guy Carawan, & Pete Seeger

We shall overcome,
We shall overcome,
We shall overcome, someday
Oh, deep in my heart, I do believe,
We shall overcome someday.

We are not afraid,
We are not afraid,
We are not afraid today,
Oh, deep in my heart, I do believe,
We shall overcome someday.

We are not alone,
We are not alone,
We are not alone today,
Oh, deep in my heart, I do believe,
We shall overcome someday.

The truth will make us free,
The truth will make us free,
The truth will make us free today,
Oh, deep in my heart, I do believe,
We shall overcome someday.

We'll walk hand in hand,
We'll walk hand in hand,

We'll walk hand in hand today,
Oh, deep in my heart, I do believe,
We shall overcome someday.

The Lord will see us through,
The Lord will see us through,
The Lord will see us through today,
Oh, deep in my heart, I do believe,
We shall overcome someday.

Black and white together,
Black and white together,
Black and white together now,
Oh, deep in my heart, I do believe,
We shall overcome someday.

We shall all be free,
We shall all be free,
We shall all be free someday,
Oh, deep in my heart, I do believe,
We shall overcome someday.

Under the rubric of the Great Society, Lyndon Johnson achieved most of the domestic reforms that liberals had wanted ever since the end of World War II. Where the President and Congress did not act, the Supreme Court did, handing down landmark decisions in the sensitive areas of censorship, church-state relations, reapportionment, and criminal justice. Yet his presidency, shrouded always by the war in Vietnam, brought not the consensus that Johnson so anxiously sought but instead a dangerous level of divisiveness. The 1960s witnessed explosive riots in black ghettoes and a widespread rejection of the integrationist ethic. The decade was also marked by the growth of a radical right and a radical left, both of which, for different reasons and in different ways, repudiated liberal values. By 1968 all this had resulted in a highly unstable political situation. The Democratic party buckled under the strain. Richard Nixon, claiming to speak for the great majority of "silent" Americans, won the presidential election by pledging to restore tranquility. In order to buttress his political position, however, Nixon had to adopt some of the same programs that he had spent a lifetime denouncing.

LYNDON JOHNSON AND THE GREAT SOCIETY

Lyndon Johnson had greater success than any President since Franklin Roosevelt in putting across his legislative program. At first, Johnson benefited from the desire following John F. Kennedy's assassination to enact certain measures as a testament to the slain President. More important, after his sweeping triumph in 1964, Johnson could work with comfortable Democratic majorities in Congress. The Democrats—with majorities of 294–140 in the House, and 68–32 in the Senate—enjoyed their largest margin of control since 1937, the year Johnson had first entered Congress. The 71 freshman Democrats in the House, many of whom owed their election to the Johnson landslide, vied with one another in their willingness to cooperate with the White House. Then too, Johnson was a shrewd legislative tactician with a remarkable talent for discovering an individual's weakness and then exploiting it to the full. As one visitor remarked: "Lyndon got me by the lapels and put his face on top of mine and he talked and talked and talked. I figured it was either getting drowned or joining."

Johnson's Southern background and reputation as a moderate alienated many liberals who had admired the Kennedy style. Yet these same traits allowed Johnson to enact far-reaching programs without losing his broad popular constituency. Those programs often broke sharply with prevailing practice. The Revenue Act (1964) cut taxes by a whopping $11.5 billion even while the government was operating at a deficit. Advocates of an expansionary fiscal policy predicted correctly that the resulting boost in purchasing power would spur economic growth. The Housing Act (1965) provided rent supplements for low-income families displaced by urban renewal or otherwise unable to find suitable public housing. The government would subsidize that portion of their rent which exceeded 25 percent of their income. In 1965, too, Congress renovated the immigration laws, removing quotas based on race or national origin that had existed in some form for more than 50 years. The Great Society, however, channeled most of its energies into four other areas: the war on poverty, aid to education, medical care, and civil rights.

Publication of Michael Harrington's *The Other America* (1962) had done much to focus public attention on the problem of poverty. Harrington documented the existence of an "economic underworld" of some 40-50 million Americans, inhabited "by those driven from the land and bewildered by the city, by old people . . . and by minorities facing a wall of prejudice." He also explained how that world—which was off the beaten track of interstate turnpikes, insulated from the view of suburban commuters, and politically impotent—had become "socially invisible." Harrington believed that existing social welfare legislation bypassed the poor. Asserting that the welfare state was "not built for the desperate, but for those who are already capable of helping themselves," Harrington called for a comprehensive federal assault on poverty. This would require the extension of welfare benefits to the poor by expanding social security and minimum wage laws, providing medical care and new housing, and eliminating racial prejudice.

In January 1964 Lyndon Johnson called for an "unconditional war on poverty," and later that year Congress approved the Economic Opportunity Act as the chief weapon in that war. The measure created an Office of Economic Opportunity (OEO), which sought to provide education, vocational training, and job experience for impoverished youths. The OEO also sponsored community action programs with a view toward improving employment opportunities, health care, housing, and education in poor neighborhoods. These programs were supposed to elicit "the maximum feasible participation of residents of the areas and members of the groups served." The OEO, which spent $750 million in 1965 and $1.5 billion in 1966, succeeded in reducing poverty but not in eliminating it. Government statistics indicated that 15.4 percent of the American people lived in poverty in 1966, compared with 22.1 percent in 1959. Funds for OEO were always inadequate, and powerful local interests, anxious to get their hands on antipoverty money and patronage, often gained control of the community programs and used them for their own advancement.

The war on poverty was closely linked with federal aid to education. In the past such legislation had gotten snarled over the issue of assisting religious schools, but in 1965 the Johnson administration discovered that the antipoverty impulse provided an excellent rationale for school aid programs. The Elementary and Secondary Education Act (1965), which Congress passed in much the same form as Johnson requested, provided funds to local school districts according to a formula involving the number of children from low-income families in the county. The act also appropriated funds for the purchase of textbooks and other instructional materials that could be used by private as well as by public schools. Under this legislation, U.S. Office of Education expenditures soared from under $50 million in 1960 to $5.6 billion in 1973. Congress also followed Johnson's recommendation in approving the Higher Education Act (1965), which provided college scholarships for needy students, subsidized interest costs on loans to college students, and helped fund classroom construction.

In the case of health insurance, as in that of federal aid to education, Johnson enacted a program first proposed by Harry Truman twenty years earlier. To appease those who saw the specter of socialized medicine in any national plan, the administration tied health care to the existing social security system and allowed participating physicians to charge their "usual and customary fees" if these were reasonable. Moreover, it limited coverage to the poor and elderly, who were least able to afford medical care and least likely to be protected by private insurance plans. Medicare provided benefits covering approximately 80 percent of hospital expenses for all persons over age 65. Medicaid provided assistance in meeting doctors' bills for poor people, regardless of age, who qualified for public assistance. By July 1967, at the end of its first year of operation, 17.7 million of 19 million elderly Americans had enrolled in Medicare, one in five had entered a hospital under the law, and 12 million had used it to defray medical expenses.

Civil rights legislation rounded out the Great Society agenda. Early in 1964 the Senate passed a civil rights bill already approved by the House. The act, which grew out of John F. Kennedy's recommendations, barred discrimination on the basis of race in all public accommodations. These included restaurants, gas stations, places of entertainment, and hotels (except for the legendary "Mrs. Murphy's boardinghouse"—that is, a private residence renting fewer than five rooms for overnight lodging). Almost all such enterprises were held to affect interstate commerce—a gas station, for example, if its customers drove across state lines. The act also authorized the Justice Department to bring suit against state facilities, such as parks and auditoriums, that remained segregated. Finally, the act included an equal opportunity clause making it unlawful for firms with more than 25 employees to discriminate in hiring on the grounds of race, religion, sex, or national origin.

The measure also included provisions to safeguard the right to vote, but these were soon superseded by the Voting Rights Act (1965), which the President urged Congress to enact after violence erupted in Alabama. Early in 1965 Dr. Martin Luther King led a demonstration in the town of Selma, in a county where more than 15,000 blacks were eligible to vote but only 335 had been able to register. When state troopers attacked King's followers and extremists murdered a civil rights worker, Congress responded with a drastic measure. It affected counties that prescribed literacy or other tests for voting and contained a substantial nonwhite population, but in which relatively few Negroes actually cast ballots. In those counties, located primarily but not exclusively in South Carolina, Georgia,

Mississippi, Alabama, and Louisiana, the right to vote would no longer depend on literacy or character fitness. The only valid criteria would be age, residence, and citizenship. The Attorney General could appoint federal examiners to register voters, and the states, if they wished to protest, would have to appeal to a federal court in Washington, D.C.

Lyndon Johnson never passed up a chance to point out the historical significance of his legislation. To sign the education bill he traveled to the one-room schoolhouse he had attended as a child and asked his former teacher, 72-year-old "Miss Katie," to sit beside him. He journeyed to Independence, Missouri, to present the pen used to sign the Medicare bill to Harry Truman. He signed the voting rights act in the same room that Lincoln had used more than 100 years before to free the slaves conscripted into the Confederate army. Similarly, Johnson used grandiose terms in defining his objectives. He proclaimed that the Great Society "rests on abundance and liberty for all. It demands an end to poverty and racial injustice." Despite its impressive accomplishments, few would claim that the Great Society achieved that much. Michael Harrington, whose book had prefigured much of the antipoverty program, applauded Johnson's initiative but concluded sadly: "What was supposed to be a social war turned out to be a skirmish and, in any case, poverty won."

THE WARREN COURT: JUDICIAL ACTIVISM

In applying new remedies for the nation's problems, the President and Congress were joined by the third branch of government. Far from upholding the status quo, as it had often done in the past, the Supreme Court acted as a catalyst for social change. Of the justices most closely identified with the new activism, two—Hugo Black and William O. Douglas—had been appointed by Roosevelt; two others—Earl Warren and William Brennan—had been named by Eisenhower. The appointment of Arthur Goldberg in 1962 further tipped the scales toward judicial activism. Goldberg replaced Felix Frankfurter, who had long been the most articulate spokesman for the theory of judicial restraint. Frankfurter believed that judges must guard against the temptation to write their own biases into law and that society must not expect the Supreme Court to solve all its problems. After his retirement the Court moved boldly into areas it had once avoided.

In several important decisions, the Court curbed the erosion of civil liberties that had been under way since the 1950s. It found that membership in the Communist party did not alone constitute proof that an individual knew that the organization advocated the forcible overthrow of the government. Unless the government could demonstrate that a party member had such knowledge, conviction under the Smith Act was impossible. In 1965 the Court declared that the government could not require an individual to register as a member of a subversive organization, for to do so violated the constitutional prohibition against self-incrimination.

The Supreme Court, 1965: (standing, left to right) Justices Byron
R. White, William J. Brennan, Jr., Potter Stewart, and Abe Fortas;
(seated, left to right) Justices Tom C. Clark, Hugo L. Black, Chief Justice Earl Warren, William O. Douglas, and John M. Harlan.

The power of the House Un-American Activities Committee to force a witness, under threat of contempt citation, to answer questions about his acquaintances was sharply curtailed. Finally, the Court affirmed the right of
a Communist party member to obtain a passport for foreign travel. These
civil liberties rulings were, ironically, among the Court's least controversial.

Adhering to the path that it had charted in the school desegregation
decision of 1954, the Court threw its full weight behind the civil rights
movement. In 1963 the Court was forced to rule on cases stemming from
a refusal to seat blacks at lunch counters. It found that local ordinances
upholding segregation in private business establishments were unconstitutional, for they involved state action within the meaning of the Fourteenth
Amendment. Even if no such ordinances existed, public statements
upholding de facto segregation by city officials were held to constitute
such action and were therefore enough to invalidate Jim Crow practices.
In *Cox v. Louisiana* (1964) the Court reversed the conviction of Negro
demonstrators in Baton Rouge who had refused to disperse when so ordered by the police. The justices decided that breach-of-the-peace laws
could not serve as a pretext for preventing peaceable speech and assembly. The Court quickly sanctioned the civil rights acts of 1964 and
1965. It also ruled that delays in school desegregation were "no longer
tolerable," and in *Loving* v. *Virginia* (1967) it struck down a state law barring marriage between persons of different races.

Religious dissenters, no less than civil rights workers, received new forms of legal protection. In the early 1960s, 12 states required Bible-reading in public schools, and 30 others encouraged such exercises. Children in New York State recited a nonsectarian prayer: "Almighty God, we acknowledge our dependence upon Thee, and we beg Thy blessings upon us, our parents, our teachers and our country." A state court saw no objection to this. Although recitation might cause discomfort to nonbelievers, there was no need to "subordinate the spiritual needs of believers to the psychological needs of nonbelievers." But the Supreme Court, in *Engel* v. *Vitale* (1962), ruled the New York prayer unconstitutional on the grounds that it was a religious activity which placed an "indirect coercive pressure upon religious minorities." Then in 1963, the Court took up the case of Edward Schempp, a Unitarian, whose children attended a school in which biblical passages were read over the loudspeaker and students recited the Lord's Prayer. Those who did not wish to participate could wait outside the classroom. Schempp argued that this arrangement would penalize his children and make them feel like "oddballs." The Supreme Court agreed: "Through the mechanism of the State, all of the people are being required to finance a religious exercise that only some of the people want and that violates the sensibilities of others." The justices ruled that public schools could not show the slightest preference for any form of religion.

Nowhere did the Court break more decisively with the past than in the area of obscenity. In the mid-1950s, explicit sexual references in books, magazines, and motion pictures were illegal. A film was even banned which included the word "virgin," and such classics as D. H. Lawrence's *Lady Chatterley's Lover* were similarly proscribed. The Supreme Court began to change all this in *Roth* v. *United States* (1957). Although ruling that obscenity did not deserve constitutional protection, the Court nevertheless felt it necessary to propose a test of obscenity, which became "whether to the average person applying contemporary community standards, the dominant theme of the material taken as a whole appeals to prurient interest." Thus began years of controversy over the meaning of such terms as "prurience." In 1961 the Court decided that a magazine could indeed appeal to prurient interest so long as it did not reveal "patent offensiveness." The justices went a step further in *Jacobellis* v. *Ohio* (1963), asserting that "material dealing with sex in a manner that advocates ideas . . . or has literary or scientific or artistic value or any other forms of social importance may not be branded as obscenity and denied the constitutional protection." In 1966 the Court extended such protection to *Fanny Hill,* an eighteenth-century novel usually considered pornographic. A book could not be banned unless "it is found to be utterly without redeeming social value." Under that standard, nearly all restrictions on the right of an adult to obtain pornographic material vanished.

This expansion of individual freedoms also characterized other areas of Court action. Three classic decisions revolutionized criminal justice procedures. In *Gideon* v. *Wainwright* (1963) the Court decided that an indigent person charged with a felony—in this instance, entering a pool hall and committing theft—was entitled to representation by a state-appointed attorney, although Florida law provided legal aid only for capital offenses. In *Escobedo* v. *Illinois* (1964) the Court ruled in favor of a man who, when interrogated on a murder charge, was not informed of his right to remain silent or permitted to see an attorney. Five justices believed that when the police centered their investigation on a single suspect and sought to extract a confession, they must allow him to see a lawyer. Four members of the Court dissented: "Supported by no stronger authority than its own rhetoric, the Court today converts a routine police investigation of an unsolved murder into a distorted analogue of a judicial trial." A similarly close and bitter division prevailed in *Miranda* v. *Arizona* (1966), which involved a man who, after a two-hour interrogation, had confessed to charges of kidnapping and rape. The majority held that a confession could not be introduced as evidence unless the defendant had been informed at the outset of the interrogative process that he could see an attorney or remain silent, and that any information he provided would be used against him. The burden of proof was placed on the prosecution to show that a defendant knowingly waived the privilege against self-incrimination and the right to counsel. Four dissenting judges gravely warned that the ruling "will return a killer, a rapist or other criminal to the streets . . . to repeat his crime whenever it pleases him."

Judicial activism reached a culmination in the matter of legislative reapportionment. The Court in the past had skirted this issue, reasoning that if district lines were drawn unfairly, citizens should seek political, not judicial, redress. But in *Baker* v. *Carr* (1962) the Court entered the "political thicket." The case involved a resident of Memphis, Tennessee, who complained that because of malapportionment his vote for a member of the state legislature was worth less than the vote of a rural resident. The Supreme Court agreed that reapportionment was a proper question for judicial determination. Federal district judges were to set guidelines, and in 1963 the Supreme Court provided a clue as to what those guidelines should do when it overturned the county-unit voting system in Georgia, under which the candidate winning a majority in a county received all its votes. Justice William O. Douglas explained that political equality "can mean only one thing, one person, one vote." The Court applied this doctrine in *Reynolds* v. *Sims* (1964). Earl Warren, speaking for the majority, said that just as a state could not give a citizen two votes, so it could not permit any person's vote to count twice as much as anyone else's. Both houses of state legislatures had to be apportioned on the basis of population. Substantial equality, if not mathematical precision, was needed in determining the size of districts. Within a few years, the great majority of states had reapportioned their legislatures to conform with these rulings.

Most of the Warren Court's decisions sparked bitter controversy. One member of Congress called the justices an "unpredictable group of uncontrolled despots," and efforts were made to overturn certain rulings, particularly those concerning reapportionment and school prayer. In 1964 the House of Representatives passed a bill denying federal courts jurisdiction over apportionment, but the Senate refused to concur. A constitutional amendment that would have permitted the states to apportion one house of their legislatures on some basis other than population (if approved by voters in a referendum) passed the Senate in 1965 and 1966, but each time fell short of obtaining the required two-thirds majority. Similarly, in 1966 the Senate approved an amendment allowing voluntary participation in prayer in the public schools, but again by less than a two-thirds vote. Critics complained that the Supreme Court had become "a general haven for reform movements." There was, however, no minimizing the social and political impact of its rulings.

BLACK POWER AND URBAN RIOTS

Whatever differences may have existed within the civil rights movement at the outset of Lyndon Johnson's presidency, two points commanded nearly universal approval: the goal should be integration, that is, the creation of an essentially colorblind society; and the means, whether involving lawful action or extralegal protest, should be nonviolent. In the next few years civil rights workers, backed by the administration and the Supreme Court, achieved many of their goals. The legal basis of segregation was toppled, the obstacles to voting slowly removed, and federal assistance to the poor extended. To take one example: by 1970, 62 percent of voting-age Negroes in the 11 Southern states were registered, compared with 29 percent in 1960. In Mississippi, seven of ten blacks, rather than one of twenty, were registered. Despite these gains, the years 1964 to 1968 saw the emergence of many black leaders who, in one degree or another, repudiated integration and nonviolence in favor of separatism and self-defense. The result was a fragmentation of the protest movement.

The "Black Power" slogan was coined by Stokely Carmichael, who had for several years worked with the Student Nonviolent Coordinating Committee (SNCC). This organization had helped organize the sit-ins and freedom rides. At first it endorsed Martin Luther King's approach, but in the mid-1960s many in SNCC grew disenchanted with the existing civil rights program. They felt betrayed in 1964 when the Democratic convention refused to provide adequate representation for the Freedom Democratic party, which they had founded in Mississippi as an alternative to the lily-white state organization. SNCC workers also lost faith in nonviolence, for the act of turning the other cheek often created deep feelings of rage and hostility. Consequently, they became more receptive to the arguments of those, like Black Muslim leader Malcolm X, who advised: "If someone puts a hand on you, send him to the cemetery." An influx of white college students into the South to assist the civil rights movement also led some in SNCC to believe that such participation reinforced feelings of inferiority in Southern blacks. In June 1966, during a demonstration in Mississippi,

Carmichael shouted: "Black Power! It's time we stand up and take over! Take over! Move on over, or we'll move on over you!"

In the following months Carmichael elaborated his theory. Instead of seeking alliances with white liberals, who, he asserted, wished to perpetuate paternalistic control, blacks should do things for themselves. Instead of adopting nonviolent methods, "black people should and must fight back." Instead of demanding integration, which Carmichael considered "a subterfuge for the maintenance of white supremacy," blacks should develop their own cultural identity, purge their communities of outside control, and thereby achieve self-determination. Black Power looked toward the welding of Negroes into a cohesive voting bloc capable of controlling political organizations inside the ghetto or of creating autonomous parties in the South. It meant establishing self-sufficient business and consumer cooperatives, and taking over public schools in black communities. "We don't need white liberals," Carmichael told a sympathetic convention of the Congress of Racial Equality (CORE). "We have to make integration irrelevant."

Not surprisingly, the sharpest critics of this doctrine were themselves veterans of the civil rights crusade. Roy Wilkins of the NAACP branded Black Power "the father of hatred and the mother of violence." Bayard Rustin, an associate of Martin Luther King, pointed out that Negroes, as a minority, could not hope to achieve anything of substance without allies, particularly in the labor movement, among ethnic groups, and among poor whites. The organizations that endorsed Black Power—such as SNCC and CORE—were primarily composed of young people who disliked compromise, distrusted the establishment, and wanted fast results. Those that supported integration—such as the NAACP—believed that compromise was necessary, hoped to convert the establishment, and did not expect overnight triumphs. When Black Power advocates excluded NAACP field secretary Charles Evers from a rally in Jackson, Mississippi, he replied: "I'll be here when they're all gone."

Black Power spokesmen rejected nonviolence as well as integration. This justification of self-defense frightened many whites, but what frightened them even more were a series of explosions that rocked black ghettoes across the land. From 1964 to 1968 the United States experienced the most protracted period of domestic unrest since the Civil War. In 1964 Negroes rioted in the Harlem and Bedford Stuyvesant sections of New York City. A year later the Watts district in Los Angeles came to resemble a disaster area after a week-long riot left 34 dead, more than a thousand injured, and hundreds of buildings in ashes. To restore order, 15,000 national guardsmen were sent to the city. In 1966 more than two dozen major riots occurred, most of them marked by looting, firebombs, and sniper fire. A study group concluded that the year's events "made it appear that domestic turmoil had become part of the American scene." Dozens of riots flared in black ghettoes in 1967. In Newark, police and guardsmen fired 13,326 rounds of ammunition in three days. In Detroit, 43 people were killed, 7200 arrested, and the city thrown into chaos. The

Ghetto riots: Washington, D.C., 1968.

assassination of Martin Luther King in April 1968 led to the very thing the martyred civil rights leader most abhorred: race riots broke out in Chicago, Washington, and other cities.

These disturbances did not resemble the riots in Chicago in 1919 or Detroit in 1943, in which pitched battles between the races had taken place. Although violent clashes between whites and blacks sometimes erupted, riots in the 1960s primarily involved looting, burning, and physical assaults within the ghetto's boundaries. The target might be a store owned by a white merchant, or it might be a white policeman, but the black communities themselves bore the heaviest cost. The riots did not usually occur along the points of intersection between black and white neighborhoods not did they result from white resentment at Negro economic or residential advancement. In fact, recent population shifts had done much to create two separate societies. From 1950 to 1966, 98 percent of the total Negro population growth took place in metropolitan areas, mainly in the central cities. In the same period, 78 percent of white population growth occurred in suburban areas. From 1960 to 1966, 1.3 million whites actually moved away from the central cities. The National Advisory Commission on Civil Disorders, which was appointed by the President in 1967, found that the country was increasingly divided "into two societies; one, largely Negro and poor, located in the central cities; the other, predominantly white and affluent, located in the suburbs and in outlying areas."

It was this very division that the Commission, in its February 1968 report, blamed for the outbreaks. The Commission viewed the riots as a protest against conditions in the ghetto, and the ghetto as a product of white racism. The Commission pointed out that 16 to 20 percent of black city dwellers lived in "squalor and deprivation" and that 40 percent of the nation's nonwhite residents had incomes below the poverty line ($3335 for an urban family of four). It further noted that a black man was two times as likely to be unemployed as a white man, and three times as likely to be working in a low-paid or unskilled job. Chronic poverty bred disorder: "Prostitution, dope addiction, and crime create an environmental 'jungle' characterized by personal insecurity and tension. Children growing up under such conditions are likely participants in civil disorder." The Commission concluded that further strife could be prevented only by massive government programs to create jobs, improve schools, expand welfare benefits, and transform housing conditions in Negro communities.

Not everyone agreed with these findings. Black Power enthusiasts attacked the Commission's integrationist bias and its failure to find any analogy to the colonial rebellions in Asia and Africa. Some conservatives thought that the riots illustrated nothing more than a willingness on the part of young hoodlums to go on a rampage if encouraged to do so by television camera crews and racial demagogues. President Johnson simply ignored the Commission's report. By the spring of 1968 the civil rights movement had begun to lose its impetus, and this was amply demonstrated by Johnson's new legislative proposals. The Civil Rights Act of 1968 contained two parts, one designed to bar discrimination in the sale or rental of 80 percent of the nation's housing, the other designed to punish anyone who "incites or organizes a riot after having traveled in interstate commerce with the intention of doing so." Some congressmen supported the measure's open housing provisions, others its antiriot features. The President signed it in April. The final civil rights achievement of the Johnson years had to pay homage to an emerging white backlash.

THE RADICAL RIGHT

The swift pace of social change in the 1960s troubled a great many Americans. The enactment of Great Society welfare programs angered those who prized traditional values of individual initiative, thrift, and hard work. Supreme Court decisions infuriated many people who feared that law, order, and morality were breaking down. The advance of the civil rights movement angered those who believed in maintaining racial distinctions. Urban violence seemed, to many, to be the last straw. To some people it appeared that the sinister hand of the Communist conspiracy must have been responsible for all these developments. Others did not respond quite so irrationally but used political means to express their displeasure with what was happening.

Exploiting these fears and frustrations, dozens of right-wing organizations, some of which had quietly existed for years, attracted large followings during the 1960s. Often they preached a mixture of anticommunism and religious fundamentalism. Dr. Frederick Schwarz, for example, led the Christian Anti-Communist Crusade. He traveled around the country, establishing schools to teach the horrors of communism and depicting vividly what his listeners might expect when the Communists "come for you . . . on a dark night, in a dank cellar, and they take a wide bore revolver with a soft nose bullet, and they place it at the nape of your neck. . . ." Similarly, Reverend Billy James Hargis led a Christian Crusade that gained wide support. Hargis netted millions of dollars with fund appeals addressed to "Dear Fellow Country savers." Others on the right assumed a militaristic posture. Robert Bolivar de Pugh organized the Minutemen, who, equipped with rifles and gas masks, practiced nighttime maneuvers in the countryside to prepare for eventual guerrilla warfare against Communist invaders. Major General Edwin A. Walker emerged as a right-wing hero when he resigned his commission after the government foiled his attempt to indoctrinate the men under his command with true-blue American ideals. In 1963 Hargis and Walker undertook "Operation Midnight Ride," alerting people in 27 cities to the perils that they thought confronted the nation.

The most important of these groups was undoubtedly the John Birch Society. It was organized by Robert Welch, who had acquired considerable wealth in the family candy business (once even being chosen Candy Man of the Year) but then retired to devote himself to more important matters. In 1958 he created an organization that he named after an American intelligence officer who reportedly was killed in 1945 by Chinese Communists and whom Welch therefore considered the first casualty in the war against communism. "The truth I bring you is simple, incontrovertible," Welch told his followers: an insidious Communist conspiracy was creeping over the United States. In Welch's view, even such figures as Dwight Eisenhower and John Foster Dulles were, somehow, implicated in this conspiracy. Given the terrible nature of the threat, Welch decided that "for us to be *too civilized* is unquestionably to be defeated." The Birch

Society, therefore, was secret, hierarchical, and rigidly disciplined. It did not tolerate internal dissent.

Birchers had their greatest success in cities in Southern California and Texas, but the movement was by no means confined to those areas. It seems to have appealed primarily to the middle classes: professionals, white-collar workers, and those who owned small businesses. According to one estimate, it eventually acquired 60,000 members, its appeal lying not only in its doctrine but also in the gratifying sense of personal participation that it provided. Birchers filled out "Member's Monthly Memos" to report their accomplishments. These might include obtaining right-wing speakers for local groups, insisting that libraries purchase books favoring the conservative viewpoint, harassing "comsymp" or "comrat" speakers at forums, and pressuring local merchants into boycotting products made in Communist-bloc nations. The Birch society even devised an "Impeach Earl Warren" essay contest for high-school students. The winner, who added Justices Douglas, Black, and Brennan to the list of those who should be ousted, received a $1000 prize.

Welch distrusted most politicians, but he considered Senator Barry Goldwater of Arizona "absolutely sound in his Americanism." Goldwater reciprocated by commenting that Birchers seemed to be impeccably fine citizens. This alliance haunted Goldwater during the 1964 presidential campaign. He obtained the Republican nomination that year partly because few other serious contenders stepped forward at a time when almost everyone believed that the Democrats were unbeatable. Then too, Goldwater had spent years cultivating local party officials. But his choice also reflected a persistent belief in the existence of a "hidden vote," that is, a truly conservative vote that the Republican party could never obtain so long as it nominated liberal candidates. Goldwater made few concessions to Republican liberals, but he made an explicit overture to those on the right when, in accepting the nomination, he declared: "Extremism in the defense of liberty is no vice; moderation in the pursuit of justice is no virtue."

The themes that Goldwater sounded during the campaign were music to the ears of American conservatives. "The moral fiber of the American people is beset by rot and decay," Goldwater asserted. He traced this largely to the "political daddyism" of Lyndon Johnson and other politicians whose only concern was "the morality of get, the morality of grab." Goldwater noted ominously: "You will search in vain for *any reference* to God or religion in the Democratic platform." The Republican candidate promised to apply a carving knife to welfare state programs, attacked the busing of children to achieve school integration, and denounced Supreme Court rulings on school prayer, legislative reapportionment, and obscenity. The Democrats had an easy time portraying Goldwater as an extremist on domestic issues, just as they had in arguing that he would involve the nation in all-out war. Goldwater received 27 million votes to Johnson's 43 million, carrying only Arizona and five states of the deep South. One of every five people who had voted Republican in

1960 switched to the Democrats in 1964. When asked why, many said of Goldwater, "He's too radical for me."

One politician for whom Goldwater was not at all too extreme was Governor George C. Wallace of Alabama. Formerly a Democrat, Wallace broke with the party in 1968 to run for President on the American Independent ticket. Although Wallace was less an orthodox economic conservative than Goldwater, he too received the support of John Birch Society members and others on the far right. There were good reasons for this. Both men took a hard-line anti-Communist foreign policy. Wallace's choice of former General Curtis LeMay as his running mate exposed him to charges of warmongering (particularly when LeMay calmly asserted, "I don't believe the world would end if we exploded a nuclear weapon.") Like Goldwater, Wallace condemned federal antipoverty programs, blasted the Supreme Court, and called for the maintenance of law and order. Both believed that government and the courts had gone too far in enforcing desegregation. Both attacked liberal intellectuals, although Wallace was more pithy, as in his reference to "pointy head" "intellectual morons."

There was a good deal of truth in the remark that Wallace was a poor man's Goldwater, for the two appealed to different constituencies. Wallace received the bulk of his support in rural areas and small towns; Goldwater had done somewhat better in the large cities. Wallace exhibited surprising strength among union members and their families; Goldwater had tapped traditional sources of Republican strength among the professional classes. The typical Wallace supporter was likely to be less well educated than the Goldwater voter and also likely to be younger, for the Alabaman did quite well among voters in their twenties. Wallace was also more of a regional candidate, with half his popular votes coming from the South. He drew most of his support from people who normally considered themselves Democrats, whereas Goldwater had relied entirely on dyed-in-the-wool Republicans. In receiving 9.9 million votes, or 13.5 percent of the total, Wallace made the best third-party showing since 1924.

The right-wing impulse was, therefore, capable of assuming different forms. But victories were few and far between. One occurred when, in June 1968, President Johnson sought to name Justice Abe Fortas to replace Earl Warren who was retiring as Chief Justice. Opponents claimed that Johnson should have permitted his successor to select the new Chief Justice. What was at issue, though, was the future role of the Supreme Court. Conservatives recognized in Fortas a symbol of judicial activism. One congressman, denouncing Fortas's rulings on obscenity, sneered, "Good ole Abe—just exactly the kind of man the stripteasers have been looking for." Seizing on evidence of an apparent conflict of interests— clients of Fortas's former law firm had set up a fund that was once used to pay the justice's fee for lecturing at a law school—conservatives blocked the appointment. Late in 1968 Fortas asked that his name be withdrawn. In 1969 additional disclosures of a similar nature touched off a move for impeachment, and Fortas resigned from the Court.

THE RADICAL LEFT

If right-wing groups thought that the Johnson administration was dangerously radical, those on the left considered it viciously reactionary. American radicals never attracted a broad popular following during the mid-1960s, but they exerted greater influence than at any time since the 1930s. The war in Vietnam was primarily responsible for this, since it convinced millions of people that the government was engaged in an unjust, barbaric conflict and would do anything to continue on its immoral course. Just as the war provided an issue, so the university offered a constituency. In past wars, draft calls had always caused college enrollments to decline; this war saw them increase. In 1964, 40.3 percent of those aged 18 to 21 were enrolled in college. Four years later, the figure had risen to 46.6 percent. By 1968, therefore, 6,350,000 Americans were attending college. Only a tiny number ever joined a radical organization, and only a minority marched in protest demonstrations. But given the size of the student population—and given, too, its mobility, leisure time, and sense of generational cohesion—even a small percentage could provide the basis for a radical movement.

Radical groups in the 1960s held disparate views and were often torn by bitter factional discord. Yet certain beliefs characterized many, if not all, left-wing spokesmen. Many asserted that college students, or young intellectuals, would serve as the driving engine of social change. Students, in this view, were not a privileged lot but rather an "abused, processed, exploited" class. If students joined with their natural allies among blacks, the poor, and other disaffected groups, they could lead in creating a new order. Radicals in the 1960s, unlike those in the 1930s, muted the traditional Marxist reliance on the working class. Labor unions were proving themselves reluctant to admit workers from minority groups, and, even worse, often endorsed escalation of the war in Vietnam. In 1967 New York City construction workers demonstrated in support of the President's war policy. One carried a banner inscribed, "God Bless the Establishment."

Child-Care: Dr. Spock and the Peace Movement

Benjamin Spock was born in 1903. He attended Yale University, cast his first vote for Calvin Coolidge in 1924 ("my father said he was the greatest president we've ever had"), attended Columbia medical school, and in 1929 began practicing pediatrics in New York City. At the time, the most popular child-raising manual was John Watson's *The Psychological Care of Infant and Child* (1928). Watson believed that all human behavior could be described in terms of stimulus and response, that a person was "an organic machine that takes in food and lets out waste products." The chief danger facing the child was that he would be smothered by parental love and, consequently, become dependent rather than self-reliant. Warning against the "dangers lurking in the mother's kiss," Watson asserted that cuddling and fondling a child would lead to "invalidism," the inability to cope with the harsh realities of life. Children should be treated as though they were young adults. "If you must, kiss them once on the forehead when they say good night. Shake hands with them in the morning." Watson left a professorship at Johns Hopkins to become

Dr. Spock with nursery-age children.

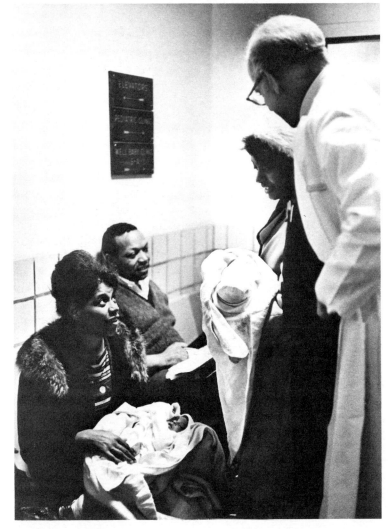

Dr. Spock conferring with parents.

vice-president of an advertising agency, where he applied his theory to the task of finding the right stimuli to induce consumers to respond to his clients' products.

In the 1930s and 1940s the study of child development was revolutionized by Dr. Arnold Gesell, who attempted to establish scientific norms for each stage of mental and physical growth. But it was Dr. Spock who popularized the new approach. His *Pocket Book of Baby and Child Care* (1946), written while he was serving in the U.S. Naval Reserve, completely contradicted Watson. Spock advised parents to relax, use their common sense, trust their own judgment, and "be flexible and adjust to the baby's needs and happiness." "Don't be afraid to love him and enjoy him. Every baby needs to be smiled at, talked to, played with, fondled—gently and lovingly—just as much as he needs vitamins and calories. That's what will make him a person who loves people and enjoys life." Spock, however, did not advocate total permissiveness. "Parents can't feel right toward their children in the long run unless they can make them behave reasonably, and children can't be happy unless they are behaving reasonably."

By 1957 Spock's book had gone through 58 printings; in the next six years, a new edition went through 60 additional printings. The book sold about a million copies a year, becoming the biggest seller (next to the Bible) in American history. During this period, Spock's career took him to the Mayo Clinic in Minnesota, the medical school at the University of Pittsburgh, and Western Reserve University in Cleveland. Gradually, he began to take a public interest in politics. In 1960 he supported John F. Kennedy, and in 1962, when the President resumed nuclear testing in response to Russian tests, Spock joined the peace movement. In 1964 he campaigned for Lyndon Johnson, but then became a sharp critic of the war in Vietnam. In 1967 Spock, and 28,000 other people, signed "A Call to Resist Illegitimate Authority" that branded the war in Vietnam illegal and unconstitutional, supported those who opposed the draft, and called on others to join in "this confrontation with immoral authority." Early in 1968 Spock

Dr. Spock at antiwar rally, 1967.

and four others were indicted for conspiring to counsel violation of the Selective Service Act.

The trial, which took place in Boston before an 85-year-old judge, lasted nearly a month. Spock took the witness stand to explain why he opposed the war in Vietnam. "I believed that we were destroying a country that had never intended us any harm. . . . What is the use of physicians like myself trying to help parents to bring up children, healthy and happy, to have them killed in such numbers for a cause that is ignoble?" Four of the defendants, including Spock, were found guilty, fined, and sentenced to two-year prison terms. But in July 1969 a U.S. Court of Appeals reversed the convictions on the grounds that the judge's instructions to the jury were improper. The charges against Dr. Spock were dropped. He responded, "I shall redouble my efforts to free the hundreds of young men who are now serving time for resisting the war."

Teargas used against demonstrators at the Pentagon, October, 1967.

Emphasizing the key role of students, radicals often focused much of their attention on the governance and curriculum of universities. They criticized the impersonal quality of education in a "multiversity," the imposition of restraints on political activity, the retention of outmoded academic requirements, the absence of courses "relevant" to an understanding of immediate social problems, and the maintenance of parietal rules that no one (except for deans and administrators) any longer took seriously. In addition, radicals attacked alleged university complicity in the conduct of foreign policy, centering their fire on research projects that helped develop new weapons systems or counterinsurgency plans, as well as on ROTC programs. Finally, radicals declared that universities were not engaged in a detached, objective search for the truth but were instead molding students to fit appropriate slots in the world of business, politics, and the military; scholarly objectivity was a myth. Since existing scholarship was committed to preserving the status quo, radicals called for a new scholarship frankly committed to changing things for the better.

This last argument was derived, in part, from the writings of Herbert Marcuse. In an essay entitled "Repressive Tolerance" (1965), Marcuse declared that society should not tolerate the expression of ideas that were "radically evil." Pure tolerance, by permitting evil ideas to obtain the same hearing as good ones, worked against the possibility of human liberation. The free marketplace would not work any better in the realm of ideas than in that of economics, Marcuse suggested, because most people lacked a sound basis for distinguishing truth from error. Marcuse therefore favored "the withdrawal of toleration of speech and assembly from groups and movements which promote aggressive policies, armament, chauvinism, discrimination on the grounds of race and religion, or which oppose the extension of public services, social security, medical care, etc." Tolerance should be subordinate to achieving a good society, and Marcuse was quite sure that "rational criteria" existed for determining the difference between what was liberating and what was repressive.

The critique of the liberal position on free speech and scholarship was part of a broader indictment of American liberalism. Radicals believed that domestic reforms served mainly to prop up a fundamentally immoral social system by siphoning off discontent. Tom Hayden, a founder of Students for a Democratic Society (SDS), found "little evidence to justify the view that the social reforms of the past thirty years actually improved the quality of American life in a lasting way." Many reforms were "illusory or token, serving chiefly to sharpen the capacity of the system for manipulation and oppression." Radicals also argued that liberals like John Kennedy and Lyndon Johnson were primarily responsible for American involvement in Vietnam. That involvement, said Hayden, "stems from the same framework of thought that determines domestic welfarism." Liberals had proclaimed an end to ideology only because they no longer believed passionately in any cause. "When they portray the end of ideology," said an SDS member, "it's like an old man proclaiming the end of sex. Because he doesn't feel it any more, he thinks it has disappeared."

It was easier to denounce the existing system than to formulate concrete alternatives to it. Aside from the demand for immediate American withdrawal from Vietnam, radical groups found it nearly impossible to agree on any specific program, or to discover issues with broad popular appeal. Critics of the left were quick to point out that its ultimate goals remained fuzzy and its agenda imprecise. Partly in response, many radicals repudiated a formal, rational approach to social problems and defended the virtue of spontaneity and intuition. "No amount of reason alone will tell us what is happening, or where we are headed," said one. "We don't have a road map because there are no road maps. There are no roads until we make them." In the existential act of revolt or resistance, it was hoped, meaning would be revealed.

In this the left reflected the ethos of what was loosely termed the "counter culture" of the 1960s. The counter culture, which often intersected with radical politics, implied a rejection of technocratic society. It took a variety of forms: absorption in rock music, adoption of certain clothing and hair styles, acceptance of a looser code of sexual behavior, extensive use of hallucinogenic drugs, and interest in mystical experiences. Theodore Roszak, whose *The Making of a Counter Culture* (1968) was both a chronicle and a defense, held that it was necessary to replace an older "cerebral mode of consciousness" with "non-intellective consciousness." Roszak denied that reality consisted only of what objective consciousness could describe. He favored "a naïve openness to experience" and a recognition that the warmly visionary could reveal as much as the coldly rational. Where radicals had once welcomed science and technological progress, now, Roszak said, they were beginning to recognize the dangers implicit in all large-scale, impersonal processes.

Radicals in the 1960s did not succeed in reversing American policy in Vietnam or in winning over large segments of the public. As their frustration mounted, some turned to violence. Bombs were planted in university buildings, banks, and other fortresses of the establishment, and several people were killed or maimed. The career of SDS illustrated this transformation. At its founding in 1962 SDS asserted: "We find violence to be abhorrent because it requires generally the transformation of the target, be it a human being or a community of people, into a depersonalized object of hate." But by 1969 members of an SDS faction known as the "Weathermen" had concluded that they could best assist the struggle of oppressed peoples by disrupting American society. A few hundred young people went to Chicago to "tear pig city apart." Dressed in "full street-fighting gear," chanting "pick up, pick up, pick up the gun," they stormed through the city smashing windows. "We were really out to fight," one recalled. "Each one of us felt the soldier in us."

Only a few engaged in such activities or justified them. More often the left favored nonviolent civil disobedience. In the case of peaceful demonstrations, violence was sometimes provoked by strong-arm police

Anti-war protest, 1968.

tactics. But whoever was at fault, much of the public came to associate radicalism with social disorder. In the end, the most telling critique of the left came from those who held that social gains required a willingness to compromise and the support of a popular majority, that nothing would alienate people more quickly than a casual acceptance of violence, and that means and ends were intimately related. Then in 1969, the left suddenly discovered that it no longer had to contend with liberal Democrats but rather with conservative Republicans.

RICHARD NIXON AND
THE NEW MAJORITY

Shortly after the 1968 election Kevin Phillips, a Nixon campaign aide, published *The Emerging Republican Majority*. The book attempted to explain why Nixon had won and how he might consolidate his position. Phillips believed that the Democrats' electoral base was shriveling while the Republicans' was steadily expanding. The GOP had a magnificent opportunity to make further inroads among ethnic voters (particularly Irish, Polish, and Italian Catholics), the working classes, and Southern whites. George Wallace's supporters were central to this effort, for Phillips thought that they were mainly conservative Democrats in the process of abandoning their traditional allegiances and preparing to support the Republicans. They represented large numbers of people who were fed up with judicial activism, moral permissiveness, forced integration, and massive welfare spending. Phillips suggested that the Republicans could safely ignore urban blacks, youthful dissenters, and liberal intellectuals. "From space-center Florida across the booming Texas plains to the Los Angeles–San Diego suburban corridor, the nation's fastest-growing areas are strongly Republican and conservative."

Phillips disclaimed any intention of setting forth the President's future plans. Yet Nixon's first administration, in many respects, faithfully adhered to Phillips's blueprint. Nixon recognized that the 1968 election left him in a most precarious political position. He received 43.4 percent of the vote, the smallest winning share since 1912. For the first time since Zachary Taylor's election in 1848, a first-term President failed to carry a majority in either house of Congress. The Democrats retained an edge of 58–42 in the Senate and 243–192 in the House. To ensure his reelection, Nixon, without alienating the Republican faithful, had to do several things: reassure blue-collar workers that Republicans would not dismantle the welfare state or create economic hardship; exploit social issues that could appeal to ethnic voters; and demonstrate to whites, in the South and in the suburbs, that he opposed forced integration.

In the realm of economics, the search for a new majority required considerable ideological flexibility. Nixon, an economic conservative who had always advocated a balanced budget, soon approached the problem of unemployment in a manner reminiscent of a liberal Democrat. Unemployment stood at 3.5 percent in December 1969, but it rose sharply to 6.2 percent in the next year. That represented the highest level of joblessness in a decade. To deal with it, the President resorted to planned budget deficits, which, he hoped, would create new jobs by pumping money into the economy. Early in 1971 he presented a "full-employment budget," one that would be balanced if the economy were operating at full tilt but that under existing circumstances would produce a $23 billion deficit. In January Nixon asserted: "I am now a Keynesian in economics." This, one observer noted, was "a little like a Christian crusader saying, 'All things considered, I think Mohammed was right.'"

Similarly, Nixon moved to an acceptance of economic controls to curb inflation. In 1969, recalling the World War II experience, he remarked: "Controls, Oh my God, no! . . . They mean rationing, black markets, inequitable administration. We'll never go for controls." But by 1971, as the rate of inflation spiraled to 5 percent, the nation experienced

Spiro Agnew, Billy Graham, and Richard Nixon at the Republican
Convention, 1968.

a trade deficit, and the stock market tumbled, Nixon reversed fields. In
August he imposed a 90-day freeze on wages, prices, and rents. In November he established a Price Commission and Cost of Living Council to
restrain both wage boosts and rent increases. The President later experimented with mandatory wage and price controls but then abandoned
them in favor of voluntary compliance. Nixon always approached controls
hesitantly, emphasizing the need for cooperation from business and labor.
But the controls, however cautious, helped restrain inflation during 1972
and largely defused it as a political issue. (In 1973 the annual rate of inflation would soar to 8.3 percent and have disastrous political consequences.)

Nixon campaigned in 1968 against the Great Society's "welfare mess," claiming that it was "time to quit pouring billions of dollars into programs that have failed." Yet his own welfare proposals looked toward reform of the system. The Family Assistance Plan, which he proposed in 1969, would have provided a minimum income of $1600 a year for a family of four, which, together with food stamps, would have meant an income of $2460. This was more than welfare systems provided in twenty states. The plan also offered income supplements for the working poor in order to reduce welfare rolls by making it more profitable to hold a job than to receive public assistance. To qualify, however, heads of households (except for the infirm and mothers with small children) would have to register for job training and accept "suitable jobs." This, Nixon said, would restore the incentive to work and identify welfare chiselers. He further claimed that his objective was not only to lift people out of poverty but "to erase the stigma of welfare and illegitimacy and apartness—to restore pride and dignity and self-respect." Most conservatives found the program entirely too ambitious. Most liberals thought it did not go nearly far enough and feared that it would force poor people to take jobs at substandard wages. The House enacted a version of the measure, but it died in the Senate Finance Committee.

THE SOCIAL ISSUE AND THE SUPREME COURT

Nixon's economic policies were not entirely successful in checking inflation or reducing unemployment, but they preserved a level of prosperity through 1972 that enabled him to attract working-class support. Beyond this, however, the administration brilliantly exploited the "social issue"— fears that stemmed from a rising crime rate, widespread use of drugs, increasingly permissive attitudes toward sex, and growing disdain for patriotic values. The President played on these fears, which cut across usual party lines, in everything from wearing an American flag in his lapel to denouncing the "Spock-marked" generation. Vice-President Spiro Agnew did the same in his attack on student protesters (an "impudent corps of snobs") and their "effete . . . hand-wringing, sniveling" apologists.

Three issues particularly aided Nixon among working-class Catholics. The President firmly endorsed federal aid to parochial schools, informing a Catholic audience that new ways should be discovered to provide direct assistance to nonpublic schools. Nixon also entered an explosive controversy over liberalization of the New York State abortion law, which the Catholic Church bitterly opposed. He told Terence Cardinal Cooke in May 1972, "I would personally like to associate myself with the convictions you deeply feel and eloquently express." In 1970 a Commission on Obscenity and Pornography, all but one of whose members had been appointed by Lyndon Johnson, recommended that all laws "prohibiting the sale, exhibition, or distribution of sexual materials to consenting adults should be repealed." The President repudiated the Commission, and

Agnew thundered, "As long as Richard Nixon is President, Main Street is
not going to turn into Smut Alley."

The social issue also embraced fears deriving from racial tension.
The President, who had received no more than 5 percent of the black
vote in 1968, had a mixed civil rights record. The administration supported the "Philadelphia plan" to eliminate discrimination on federal construction projects by establishing a quota system under which trade
unions had to accept a certain number of Negro youths as apprentices
and guarantee them union membership at the end of a training period.
The plan was upheld in the courts, but implementing school desegregation was a different story. The Justice Department favored the postponement of desegregation plans in communities where strong local opposition existed. In October 1969, however, the Supreme Court upset the
administration's strategy. In *Alexander* v. *Holmes County Board of Education*
the Court declared unanimously that "deliberate speed" no longer sufficed; school desegregation must begin "at once."

Given existing patterns of residential segregation, this decision
merely raised a more difficult question: should children be bussed to
achieve racial balance in the schools? There was no more highly charged
issue in the early 1970s. Public opinion polls indicated that 78 percent of
the people opposed the idea of busing. In some places, attempts to introduce such plans led to violence, disorder, and school boycotts. Maintenance of the "neighborhood school" became a central concern, particularly in the South, in the suburbs, and in ethnic enclaves in the large cities.
Many people had moved to the suburbs to live in better school districts.
Now they faced the prospect of sending their children back into the inner
cities every morning. Yet busing plans met with the approval of the Supreme Court in April 1971. In *Swann* v. *Charlotte-Mecklenburg Board of Education* the justices found that busing, even if awkward or inconvenient,
was an acceptable means of integrating "schools that are substantially
disproportionate in their racial composition."

The issue was tailor-made for a President intent on currying favor
with Southern whites, suburbanites, and uneasy ethnic groups. Nixon at
the same time reflected the nation's mood and contributed to its intran-
sigence. In March 1970 he called for an "open society" that "does not
have to be homogeneous, or even fully integrated. There is room in it for
communities. . . . It is natural and right that we have Italian or Negro or
Norwegian neighborhoods." He disagreed with those who said that "the
only way to bring about social justice is to integrate all schools now, everywhere, no matter what the cost in the disruption of education." The President reiterated this stand during the next two years. In January 1972 a
federal district judge in Richmond, Virginia ordered school boards to
employ busing to eradicate racial distinctions between schools. In March,
with Congress considering a constitutional amendment to forbid busing,
Nixon urged the legislators to impose a moratorium on the issuance of
busing orders by federal courts while a measure could be devised looking

toward a permanent solution. Congress then barred the implementation of such orders until all legal appeals had been exhausted. Although the bill did not go far enough to suit him, the President signed it in the summer of 1972.

Nixon also sought to use Supreme Court appointments as part of a broader political strategy. Having pledged in 1968 to appoint strict constructionists as a way of reversing the Court's activism, Nixon had the unusual opportunity of choosing four members in his first term. Late in 1969 he nominated Clement Haynsworth of South Carolina. Many considered this a way of paying a debt to Senator J. Strom Thurmond, a staunch conservative from South Carolina. Opposition to Haynsworth quickly developed when the Senate discovered that he had once acted as a judge in a case that could possibly have served his own interests. The Senate rejected the nomination by a vote of 55 to 45, with 17 Republicans deserting the President. Nixon next sent up the name of G. Harrold Carswell of Florida. A new storm arose, primarily because an extraordinarily high number of Carswell's decisions had been reversed by higher courts. He appeared to lack any intellectual distinction, as even a supporter, Senator Roman Hruska of Nebraska, conceded: "Even if he were mediocre, there are lots of mediocre judges and people and lawyers. They are entitled to a little representation aren't they? . . . We can't have all Brandeises and Frankfurters and Cardozos and stuff like that there." The legal profession, regarding the appointment as an insult, lobbied against it, and in April 1970 the Senate turned it down. Seeking to extract the last ounce of political advantage from the situation, Nixon said that the issue involved "the Constitutional responsibility of the President to appoint members of the Court." Carswell's rejection, he asserted, was an act of "regional discrimination" against the South.

Ultimately Nixon appointed Harry Blackmun of Minnesota to the vacancy. The three other appointees were Lewis F. Powell, William Rehnquist, and Chief Justice Warren E. Burger. In many respects the Court veered in a more conservative direction. It ruled more frequently on behalf of the prosecution in criminal trials, declaring that a defendant who disrupted a trial by disorderly behavior could, after a warning, be removed from the courtroom or even bound and gagged. It also held that a confession extracted by unconstitutional means did not automatically invalidate a conviction where other evidence of guilt existed. The Court also made it easier for prosecutors to establish the admissibility of contested confessions. With respect to obscenity, the Court held that laws against pornography, if they reflected community standards, were constitutional. With respect to reapportionment, the Court softened the one-person, one-vote rule to widen somewhat the permissible disparity between voting district populations. In 1973 the Court found that schools could be financed by property taxes even though disparities resulted, for, as Justice Powell said, "at least where wealth is involved, the equal protection clause does not require absolute equality or precisely equal advantages."

Yet the Court by no means pursued a course entirely to the Presi-

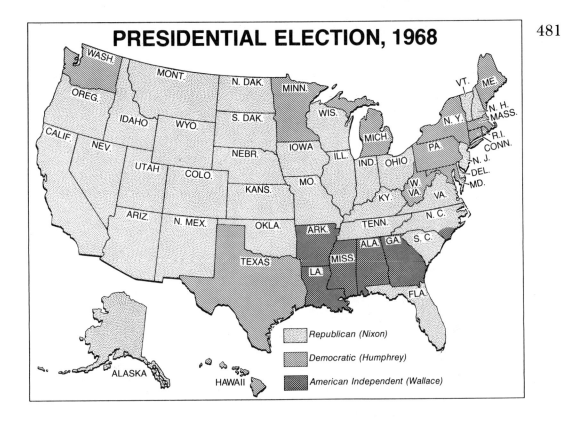

PRESIDENTIAL ELECTION, 1968

WASH.
MONT.
N. DAK.
MINN.
VT. ME.
OREG.
S. DAK.
WIS.
N. Y. N. H. MASS.
IDAHO
WYO.
MICH.
PA.
R.I. CONN.
CALIF.
NEV.
NEBR.
IOWA
ILL.
IND. OHIO
N. J.
UTAH
COLO.
DEL. MD.
KANS.
MO.
W. VA.
KY. VA.
ARIZ.
N. MEX.
OKLA.
ARK.
TENN.
N. C.
ALA. GA. S. C.
TEXAS
MISS.
LA.
FLA.
ALASKA
HAWAII

Republican (Nixon)

Democratic (Humphrey)

American Independent (Wallace)

dent's liking. In the cases involving school desegregation and busing, even some of Nixon's appointees disappointed him. In *Furman* v. *Georgia* (1972) the Court held, by a vote of 5 to 4, that the death penalty as then prescribed was imposed unfairly. It fell more heavily on the poor and violated the constitutional injunction against cruel and unusual punishment. Many states then attempted to make the death penalty mandatory for certain offenses, but the Court had greatly aided opponents of capital punishment. In *Roe* v. *Wade* (1973) the Court, in a 7 to 2 decision, asserted that states could not, except for reasons of health, prevent a woman from having an abortion during the first three months of pregnancy. Finally, the Court upheld civil liberties in two landmark decisions. In 1971 it ruled that the government could not prevent the publication of the *Pentagon Papers*. On June 19, 1972, the Court rejected the Attorney General's claim that the government had the right to use wiretapping against alleged subversives or domestic radicals without first obtaining a court order. Justice Powell said: "The price of lawful public dissent must not be a dread of subjection to an unchecked surveillance power." The decision, ironically, was handed down two days after burglars working for the President's reelection were arrested in Democratic national headquarters.

THE ELECTION OF 1972

By 1972 the President had taken great strides toward constructing what he called a "new majority." His task was further simplified when the Democrats nominated George McGovern of South Dakota. After the upheaval at the 1968 Chicago convention, the Democrats had thoroughly revised their procedures of delegate selection. In an attempt to open the party to groups that had been excluded, those procedures were democratized and rules were adopted requiring that delegations "reasonably" reflect the proportion of women, blacks, and other minorities in the population. The result was a convention unlike any seen before. Those groups with ample time, energy, and ideological fervor—such as upper middle-class activists in the antiwar, women's liberation, and civil rights movements—enjoyed greater representation than ever before. By contrast, the traditional power brokers—trade-union leaders, big-city mayors, and Southern bosses—enjoyed less. Labor leader George Meany voiced the resentment of these forces when, observing the representatives from New York, he exclaimed, "What kind of delegation is this? They've got six open fags and only three AFL/CIO people on that delegation!"

McGovern's difficulties were compounded when it was learned that his running-mate, Thomas Eagleton of Missouri, had a past history of mental illness. After days of hesitation, which apparently convinced some voters that he lacked a decisive temperament, McGovern replaced Eagleton with Sargent Shriver, who had formerly headed the war on poverty. But McGovern's chief problem was that the Republicans succeeded in centering attention on the social issue while calling him a radical who favored "the far-out goals of the far left." The code words in 1972 were amnesty, acid, and abortion, and it made little difference that McGovern favored only the first. Condemning American involvement in the Vietnam War as wicked and immoral, he urged amnesty when the war ended for those who had fled the country to avoid the draft. McGovern did not favor legalized abortion or the use of drugs, but many Americans believed that he did or that, in any event, his supporters did. Fairly or not, the McGovern candidacy came to symbolize a counter-culture lifestyle. McGovern did not help his cause by stating, "Quite frankly, I am not a 'centrist' candidate." One Democratic campaign worker sighed, "I felt like the recreation director on the *Titanic*."

Nixon never doubted the outcome. "The election was decided the day McGovern was nominated," he said. "McGovern did to his party what Goldwater did." Yet even Nixon was surprised by his margin of victory: 47 million votes (to McGovern's 29 million), 61.3 percent of the total vote, and a 520–17 electoral college majority. This mandate would dissolve sooner than anyone imagined. Nixon had once commented, "I've always thought this country could run itself domestically without a President; all you need is a competent Cabinet to run the country at home." Even in 1973 he continued to believe that domestic issues failed to excite people as much as foreign policy ("Unless it touches them directly—like busing—they don't give a damn"), tended to divide rather than unite the country, and allowed the President the least room for maneuvering. Above all, he thought that the economy was so strong that "it would take a genius to wreck it." As his second term unfolded, Nixon would find himself trapped in domestic problems of his own making, with his freedom of action increasingly limited, the nation united only in its criticism of his policies, and the economy in serious trouble. Indeed, the nation would soon ponder whether running itself "domestically without a President" did not better translate into running itself without Nixon.

Suggested Reading

For social and intellectual developments in the 1960s, consult William O'Neill, *Coming Apart* (1971); Ronald Berman, *America in the Sixties* (1968); and Morris Dickstein, *Gates of Eden: American Culture in the Sixties* (1977). For political developments, see Arthur M. Schlesinger, Jr., *Robert Kennedy and His Times* (1978). Lyndon Johnson defends his policies in *Vantage Point: Perspectives on the Presidency* (1971). Eric Goldman, who served as a presidential advisor, offers an appraisal in *The Tragedy of Lyndon Johnson* (1968); Doris Kearns takes a psycho-biographical approach in *Lyndon Johnson and the American Dream* (1976). Great Society welfare programs are examined in Sar A. Levitan and Robert Taggart, *The Promise of Greatness* (1976); Sar A. Levitan, *The Great Society's Poor Law* (1969); Peter Marris and Martin Rein, *Dilemmas of Social Reform* (1973); and Daniel P. Moynihan, *Maximum Feasible Misunderstanding* (1970).

Appraisals of the Supreme Court are provided in Alexander Bickel, *Politics and the Warren Court* (1965); Philip Kurland, *Politics, the Constitution, and the Warren Court* (1970); and Alexander Bickel, *The Supreme Court and the Idea of Progress* (1970). In *Hugo Black and the Judicial Revolution* (1977), Gerald T. Dunne examines the career of one of the most important twentieth-century jurists. Legislative reapportionment is discussed in Richard Cortner, *The Apportionment Cases* (1970). Rulings in another controversial area are treated in Harry Clor, *Obscenity and Public Morality* (1969); and Charles Rembar, *The End of Obscenity* (1968). Frank Sorauf, *The Wall of Separation* (1976), discusses Court rulings in the area of church and state.

For the relationship of Black Power to other protest strategies, see Benjamin Muse, *The American Negro Revolution* (1969); Stokely Carmichael and Charles Hamilton, *Black Power* (1967); Archie Epps, *Malcolm X and the American Negro Revolution* (1969); and Peter Goldman, *The Death and Life of Malcolm X* (1973). The causes and consequences of race riots are assessed, from varying perspectives, in the *Report of the National Advisory Commission on Civil Disorders* (1968); Robert Fogelson, *Violence as Protest* (1971); Edward Banfield, *The Unheavenly City* (1970); and Joe R. Feagin and Harlan Hahn, *Ghetto Revolts: The Politics of Violence in American Cities* (1973).

For discussions of the radical right, consult Alan Westin, "The John Birch Society," in Daniel Bell, ed., *The Radical Right* (1963); Richard Hofstadter, "Goldwater and Pseudo-Conservative Politics" in *The Paranoid Style in American Politics* (1967); and Marshall Frady, *Wallace* (1970). The controversy surrounding Justice Fortas is analyzed in Robert Shogan, *A Question of Judgment* (1972); the defeat of the Carswell nomination in Richard Harris, *Decision* (1971). Contrasting explanations of youthful dissent are provided in Kenneth Keniston, *Young Radicals* (1968); Lewis Feuer, *The Conflict of Generations* (1969); and J. Kirkpatrick Sale, *SDS* (1973). The impact of the war in Vietnam on American youth is analyzed in Lawrence M.

Baskir and William A. Strauss, *Chance and Circumstance: The Draft, the War and the Vietnam Generation* (1978).

An excellent account of the 1968 election may be found in Lewis Chester, Godfrey Hodgson, and Bruce Page, *An American Melodrama* (1970); a critique of the Democrats' strategy in 1972 is offered in Richard Krickus, *Pursuing the American Dream: White Ethnics and the New Populism* (1976). For Richard Nixon's political motivations see Garry Wills, *Nixon Agonistes* (1970); and Jonathan Schell, *The Time of Illusion* (1975). Leonard W. Levy, *Against the Law* (1974), is a scathing attack on the Burger Court's approach to criminal justice.

Both Jessica Mitford, *The Trial of Dr. Spock* (1969), and Lynn Z. Bloom, *Doctor Spock: Biography of a Conservative Radical* (1972), are informative.

Saudi Arabian Oil Minister Ahmed Zaki Yamani (middle of first row), at OPEC Conference, December 1978. The Conference decided on a 14.5 percent price increase in 1979.

CHAPTER SIXTEEN

The 1970s
The "New Realities"

THE CRUDE OIL BLUES
Written by Jerry Reed

Now listen people, let me tell you some news,
I sing a song called the Crude Oil Blues,
We're low on heat and we're low on gas,
And I'm so cold I'm about to freeze my—self.
We've got the Crude Oil Blues.

Gone to wintertime, sure gettin' cold to the
* bottom of my shoes.*
Well, my hands are shakin' and my knees
* are weak,*
But it ain't because of love, it's from the lack
* of heat.*
I got the Crude Oil Blues.

I'm goin' to tell you a story about this drunk
* I knew,*
He kept his basement full of home-made
* brew.*
But the winter got so bad it screwed up the
* boy's thinkin',*

He got so cold he had to burn all his
* drinkin'.*
He's got the Crude Oil Blues.

He said the wintertime can sure get cold to
* the bottom of his shoes,*
He said burnin' his booze just destroyed my
* soul,*
But there's one thing about it honey, when
* you're cold, you're cold.*
I got the Crude Oil Blues.

I read a sign on the pump in my favorite
* gas station yesterday that said,*
"He who expected nothin'
Ain't going to be deceived."

Shortly after his reelection in 1972, Richard Nixon stood at the peak of his career. Boasting that he had forged a "new majority," Nixon enjoyed immense authority in both foreign and domestic affairs. But in 12 months it all changed dramatically. By 1974 his administration was in shambles, and the President, facing impeachment, resigned. The crisis, however, went beyond White House corruption. Blacks, women, Native Americans, Hispanic-Americans and other groups demanded justice at a time when the economy was plagued by unemployment and inflation. One public opinion poll showed that more people than ever before believed "there is something deeply wrong with America." Jimmy Carter, elected President in 1976 on the promise to set things right, discovered the problems at home and abroad to be more intractable than he had imagined. In its quest for the American Century, the United States was running up against what the Carter administration called the "new realities" of the 1970s.

THE ECONOMY IN CRISIS

Perhaps the most important of those new realities was the economic system. That system resembled a patient whose ruddy cheeks hid a serious disease. Between 1945 and 1970 the value of all goods and services produced by Americans (the Gross National Product) doubled to an incredible one trillion dollars. Within just the next eight years, the GNP again doubled. The nation continued to be the globe's greatest producer with twice the GNP of such economic giants as Russia and Japan. American agriculture was so dominant that Chinese, Russians, Japanese, and other peoples often depended on it for their meals. The cheeks appeared rosy.

Illness nevertheless spread. Two-thirds of the trillion dollars in GNP that appeared between 1970 and 1978 was a mirage. It represented not an actual increase in goods, but, as one economist said, "inflation, inflation, inflation." A simple but useful definition is that inflation occurs in part because too much money chases too few goods. This was precisely one cause of the problem: in the 1970s the rate of U.S. productivity dropped dramatically until, in real, noninflationary dollars, it actually approached zero increase in 1976–77. The United States Government meanwhile churned out more and more dollars to chase relatively fewer goods.

In just ten years (1968–78), U.S. prices doubled. An inflation rate of 2 percent annually in the 1960s shot up to 9 percent in 1978. The average cost of a new house reached $54,000. Worse, food prices rose at an even faster annual rate of 10 percent.

Americans tried to beat inflation in one or more ways. First, they demanded higher salaries and stock or bank dividends (which, since productivity did not rise in proportion, only helped produce more inflation). Second, both spouses searched out jobs, thus forcing an already stumbling economy to absorb more wage-earners. Third, they used small plastic bank

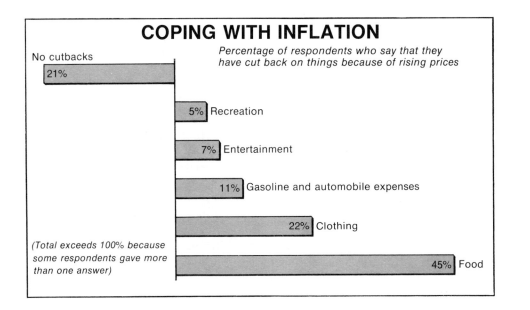

COPING WITH INFLATION

Percentage of respondents who say that they have cut back on things because of rising prices

No cutbacks — 21%

5% Recreation

7% Entertainment

11% Gasoline and automobile expenses

22% Clothing

45% Food

(Total exceeds 100% because some respondents gave more than one answer)

cards, that had multiplied in the 1960s like crazed fruit flies, to obtain installment credit. By 1979 economists warned that individual credit was stretched dangerously close to the breaking point. Fourth, as Figure 1 shows, they simply reduced consumption. That solution forced the poor and elderly to lower an already low standard of living.

The dollar was worth less abroad as well as at home. The reason was simple: in 1960, foreigners held $20 billion, but in 1979 they were swamped with $600 billion. The more dollars they held the fewer they wanted. Tourists discovered that some European taxi drivers and hotel clerks would no longer accept U.S. currency. The dollars had gone abroad partly to pay for military expenditures. Acting as guardian of the "free world," Americans learned, could be expensive. Most dollars, however, went overseas to make up massive deficits in the U.S. balance of payments in the 1970s. At home, the dollar's value fell, in part because Americans spent more than they produced. Overseas it fell because they bought much more than they sold. In 1978 the deficit balance of U.S. trade amounted to an amazing $30 billion.

The social costs of such an economic decline were steep. The system was in trouble at the very moment women, minorities, the elderly, and environmentalists demanded the most from it, and just as those born in the "baby boom" of the 1950s began to enter the job market in large numbers.

POPEYE IN A "STATE OF DISSOLUTION"

Beset by a new phenomenon of "stagflation"—that is, stagnation in production and inflation in prices—the economy endured its greatest trial since the 1930s. Americans tended to blame their woes on three causes. The five-fold rise of oil prices from $3.00 a barrel in 1972 to over $14.00 in 1979 attracted most attention. The rapid rise was triggered in October 1973 during the Egyptian–Israeli conflict when the United States and some Western European nations supplied Israel. The enraged Arab oil producing bloc sharply cut back shipments of petroleum to the United States and other pro-Israeli nations.

The Nixon administration refused to respond by imposing new controls or rationing, so home fuel oil tripled and gasoline doubled in price. Again, middle- and lower-income Americans, especially those depending on autos for their livelihood, and older citizens who had fixed incomes especially suffered. The profits of the multinational oil companies in 1973–74 meanwhile leaped as much as 800 percent higher than the year before.

The Nixon, Ford, and Carter administrations promised an effective energy program, but none appeared. Told they had to cut back their use of imported oil, Americans did just the opposite. Comprising only 6 percent of the world's population, they consumed one-third of its energy. Importing 1.5 million barrels a day in 1970, Americans bought 8.4 million barrels of the much more expensive product eight years later. This amounted to about half the oil they consumed. The nation thus depended more heavily than ever before on Arab producers—and the unpredictable politics of such producers as Iran and Nigeria. Oil and gas reserves in the United States steadily declined. As former Secretary of Commerce Peter Peterson said, "The era of low-cost energy is almost dead. Popeye is running out of spinach."

To blame Arabs entirely for the economic downturn, however, was not accurate. They had priced their oil in dollars, and as the dollar's value steeply declined after the mid-1960s, the Arabs watched their greatest asset sink with it. As early as 1970 they raised oil prices to make up for the dollar's decline and obtain capital for their own badly needed development. The 1973 war only accelerated this trend. The producers, moreover, returned billions of dollars to Western nations, and especially the United States, to purchase industrial goods, and expensive weapons.

Nevertheless, the net flow of dollars out of the United States worsened the economic problems. The federal government tried to help, but, according to some experts, only made matters worse. This was a second cause of the crisis: the government attempted to buoy the economy by pumping in more dollars than it took out in taxes. This policy reached a peak in 1976–77 when the Federal Budget deficit hit a peacetime record of $60 billion.

The policy accelerated inflation by providing billions more dollars, but not an equal number of goods. In 1979 President Carter became

frightened by the near-collapse of the dollar abroad and an uncontrollable inflation at home. He tried to counter by severely cutting the federal
budget deficit to under $30 billion and thus reduce the dollars flowing
into the economic bloodstream.

A third cause of the economic downturn was fundamental: Americans would not—or could not—sufficiently increase their productivity
(that is, the average output of goods per hour of labor). Between 1967
and 1977 Japan's productivity jumped 107 percent, and even Italy's (the
supposed "sick man" of Europe) increased 62 percent, but the United
States' rate of increase was only 27 percent, or half the rate of 1958–68.

No one could pinpoint a single cause of the decline, but economists
noted that after 1971 the number of patents issued to American inventors
steadily decreased. In 1978, foreigners obtained one-third of the patents
issued in the United States, an unheard-of figure in a land that prided itself on such products of "Yankee ingenuity" as Model-T cars and zippers.
Corporations worsened the trend by cutting back drastically on basic research. Worried by inflation, business executives settled for quick profits.
Government also reduced its support of basic research.

Some hoped productivity could be increased by allowing more competition. When, for example, the federal government decided to "deregu-
late" airplane travel in 1977–78, competition among airlines increased,
ticket prices dropped, more Americans traveled than ever before, and the
airlines profited. The possibility of similarly deregulating other industries,
however, was limited. Moreover, some large corporations actually reduced competition by merging with one another at the fastest rate in U.S.
history. In 1978 there were no less than 80 corporate mergers involving
$100 million or more. There had been only sixteen such mergers in 1975.

The *Washington Post* was one of many voices that believed the problem of productivity was deeply rooted: "A good many Americans' ideas
about work, incomes and economic growth changed around 1968," and
the results "may now be showing up in the nation's economic performance." Alfred Kahn, President Carter's chief inflation fighter, put it
more bluntly: "Inflation is a symptom and a reflection of a society that is,
in some degree, in a state of dissolution." Kahn's fear was supported by
one striking statistic. The greatest drain on U.S. resources in 1978 was
overseas oil payments of about $15 billion, but the second largest expen-
diture abroad was the amount sent secretly and illegally to Colombia and
elsewhere by Americans who used cocaine.

THE NATION'S NEW MAKEUP

The American economy faced a crisis at the same moment population
changes made ever greater demands on that economy. The most dramatic
demographic change in the 1970s, a precipitous decline in the birth rate,
was also the least expected. During the 1950s, the nation's population
grew by 29 million (from 152 to 181 million), and during the 1960s by 24
million. But from 1970 to 1979 the population increased by only 16 mil-

lion (to 221 million). As fertility rates fell to their lowest levels in the nation's history, and to about half the levels of the fecund 1950s, the United States approached a rate of zero population growth.

Whatever the causes of this historic reversal—whether improved methods of contraception, legalization of abortion, the impact of economic concerns, or the emergence of new cultural norms regarding family size—the long-range effect was predictable: the gradual aging, over several decades, of the American population. In 1950 only 8 percent of Americans were 65 years of age or older; by 1970 the figure was somewhat more than 10 percent. By 2000, demographers forecast, nearly 12 percent of the population would be elderly, and the median age of Americans would have risen from 29 to 35 years.

A geographical shift in population accompanied the demographic change and was, in part, a product of it. Since World War II, the South and West had experienced rapid growth, but as late as 1970 those regions still had 3 million fewer inhabitants than the 21 states of the Northeast and Midwest. In 1976, for the first time in the nation's history, the population of the South and West (the "sunbelt") surpassed that of the "snowbelt" states. This migratory stream had two major tributaries: retired persons attracted to Florida, California, and Arizona by warm weather; and workers lured by the aerospace, defense, electronics, aluminum, natural gas, oil, and tourist industries. The boom-town mentality of the "southern rim" was nicely captured by the Missouri real-estate promoter who declared: "If the devil came here and brought business and money to the town, I wouldn't complain."

Not only were Americans, as a people, having fewer children in the 1970s, and not only were they moving to different areas, but they were earning and spending more than ever before. Real personal income, after adjustments to take account of inflation, doubled from the 1940s to the 1970s. The pie, therefore, had gotten considerably larger, but it was not being divided much more evenly than at the end of World War II. The wealthiest fifth of American families received about 40 percent of all personal income, while the poorest fifth received about 5 percent. By the late 1970s the "poverty line" for an urban family of four was set at $6000. Nearly 26 million Americans, 12 percent of the population, fell below that standard.

Only massive government assistance enabled millions of other Americans to keep their heads above water. By 1976 social welfare expenditures under public programs at the city, state, and federal levels had rocketed to $331 billion. Even when adjusted for inflation and population growth, this figure represented an increase of 327 percent since 1950. Much of the increase could be attributed to extraordinary demands on the social security system. By 1976, 33 million retired workers and their dependents, disabled workers and their dependents, aged widows and widowers, and survivor children—that is, one out of every seven Americans—received social security checks. With cash reserves dwindling, Congress grudgingly agreed to a drastic increase in social security taxes to keep the system solvent. In addition, the federal government spent billions each year to provide the poor with food stamps, housing subsidies, and medical care.

Such programs particularly helped black Americans who continued to suffer disproportionately from poverty and unemployment. Of the nation's 25 million blacks, 7.5 million had incomes that placed them below the poverty line. Three of every ten, compared to one of every ten whites, lived in poverty. The unemployment rate among blacks, 13 to 14 percent, was twice that among whites, while the rate among black teenagers, 40 percent, was an explosive two and one-half times that among white teenagers. One in every 25 white households purchased food stamps, but one in five black families did. Commenting on the general quiet in black ghettoes during the late 1970s, one expert feared it might be only "the calm before the storm."

The black middle class, however, grew larger and more affluent. By 1976, 7 percent of black families earned more than $25,000 and 21 percent earned $15,000 to $25,000. One-third of all Negro workers held professional, managerial, clerical, and other white-collar jobs. The number of blacks enrolled in colleges increased steadily. So did the number who lived in suburbs. At the end of the decade, two black families in every ten (compared to four white families in ten) resided in suburban communities.

The ethnic composition of the American population also changed. The Immigration Reform Act of 1965, which had abolished national origins quotas, provided for the admission of 170,000 immigrants from Europe, Asia, and Africa (with a maximum of 20,000 from any one nation), and 120,000 immigrants from the Western Hemisphere (on a first-come, first-served basis). In addition, about 100,000 relatives of American citizens entered the United States each year without regard to these limitations.

The 1965 act had a dramatic effect in the 1970s, for Asia replaced Europe as the chief source of immigration. Indeed, in 1976 two immigrants arrived from Asia for every one who came from Europe. Meanwhile, millions of illegal aliens, most of them from Mexico and South America, also entered the country. In 1977 the government apprehended one million illegal aliens, but estimated that two or three escaped detection for every one who did not. Asian and Latin immigrants often settled near their ports of entry, contributing still further to the growth of such states as California, Texas, and Florida. As the South and West outstripped the Northeast and Midwest in population and political power, so they were also becoming the most ethnically diverse regions in the nation.

NATIVE AMERICANS AND WOUNDED KNEE II

Economic growth has long allowed Americans to climb the ladder of opportunity without pushing down everyone below them. But with growth and productivity rates declining, equality of opportunity was also endangered. Throughout the 1970s, women and minority groups nevertheless demanded more equality of opportunity. Some, such as Hispanic-Americans, did climb upward. Others, especially American Indians, continued to suffer great hardships.

Since the nineteenth century the American Indian had received even less economically than had blacks. After the Indian wars ended in the 1890s, the government tried to force the tribes to farm reserved tracts of land. Without experience in this type of agriculture, many Native Americans were unable to pay taxes or mortgages. Thousands of acres therefore passed at cut-rate prices into white hands. The Bureau of Indian Affairs (BIA), in the Department of Interior, meanwhile administered policy aimed at "acculturation," that is, destroying the Indian culture and forcing tribes to enter white society. Older Sioux in South Dakota recalled in the 1970s that as youngsters they had been beaten in school for wearing Indian clothes, and forced to chew pieces of soap if they spoke the Sioux language.

In 1934 the New Deal tried another approach with the Indian Reorganization Act. Tribal Councils were organized so that—in theory at least—Indians could govern themselves, spend governmental monies for their own purposes, and develop what remained of their culture. In practice, however, whites dominated policymaking. Some tribes in the Southwest held considerable wealth because they had happened to be given desolate lands that rested on huge oil reserves, but other tribes survived only by receiving large federal subsidies. Indeed, the Eisenhower administration considered the costs too high, so in the 1950s Indians were told once again to move toward acculturation.

Of all American minorities, Indians suffered most during the 1960s and 1970s. Their population grew at four times the national rate, reaching 792,000 in 1970, but life expectancy was only 46 years (compared with the national average of 69), infant mortality rates were the nation's highest, and the suicide rate was double the country's average. Reservations lacked industry and good schools. Unemployment rates above 50 percent were not uncommon. A startling 50 percent of Native Americans on reservations, and even 20 percent of those in cities, lived below the poverty level in the late 1970s.

When Indian leaders tried to deal with this tragedy, they divided sharply between young and old, between those living in urban and reservation areas, and between tribes. The Kennedy, Johnson, and Nixon administrations attempted to return policy to Indian officials. This, however, did little to dampen the anger of many Native Americans who joined militant youth groups (patterned on the black organizations of the 1960s), and, in 1968, formed the urban-based American Indian Movement (AIM). Few whites seemed to care.

Then came the second episode of Wounded Knee (for the first, see Chapter 1). Wounded Knee was a town in the Sioux Reservation of South Dakota. The reservation, twice the size of Delaware, contained 3 million

Native Americans standing guard near a church in Wounded Knee,
South Dakota, 1973.

acres of which one-third was owned by whites, one-third leased by Indians
to white cattlemen, and one-third used by the Sioux themselves. Seventy
percent of the teachers on the reservation were white. Pine Ridge, the
capital, was "a motley collection of shacks and houses of varying degrees
of decrepitude," according to one reporter, with "a fine, tan, gritty dust
. . . coating everything and getting into mouths and lungs, contributing
to the hacking cough that people seem to develop rapidly here."

The reservation contained some of the nation's worst poverty: half
the families were on welfare and a moccasin factory served as the main industry. Most of the employed were mixbloods (Indians having both Indian and white blood), who controlled the reservation and worked in patronage jobs handed out by Washington officials. Full-blooded Indians
lived in rural shacks where they tried to save themselves and their culture.
The school dropout rate was 81 percent. Alcoholism was rampant among
adult males. Considerable tension divided whites and Indians. When Raymond Yellow Thunder visited nearby Gordon, Nebraska, in 1972, he was
beaten and murdered. Two white attackers were released without bail and
charged only with second-degree manslaughter. Not wanting to cause further problems with the whites, neither BIA officials nor the Sioux half-
bloods controlling the reservation pushed for an investigation of the murder.

But led by women, an angry group of Sioux repudiated their leaders, whom they considered corrupt, and asked for help from AIM. In February 1973 two hundred AIM members and their supporters occupied Wounded Knee. They demanded that the government honor some 371 treaties it had broken and also insisted that the reservation's regime be radically changed. United States forces encircled the area, partly to keep the two Indian factions from attacking each other, but also to block the entry of food into the town. When AIM tried to move in reinforcements, government gunfire killed one Indian and wounded another. AIM and the Washington officials finally agreed to lift the seige and reexamine treaty obligations. The government, however, finally did little except bring suit against AIM leaders and sympathizers.

"Wounded Knee II" symbolized, but did little to help, the tragedy of the American Indian. Indeed, a white backlash erupted in the late 1970s. The backlash was notable in Congress, which had obtained almost dictatorial power over Indian affairs. White congressmen, many from Western states, proposed bills based on a ruthless policy of "termination"—that is, ending federal protection, revoking treaties, and opening Indian lands to the highest bidders. One embittered Native American spokesman believed "it all has to do with natural resources," for Congress wanted to "open up Indian lands to energy development interests, ranchers, and commercial fishermen." President Carter did little to help Indians. Despite Native American activism and a growing awareness among whites of the suffering on reservations, the supposed "reforms" of the 1960s and 1970s produced only more suffering and more hatred between Indians and whites, and among Indians themselves.

HISPANIC-AMERICANS AND THE NEW STEW

Hispanic-Americans, on the other hand, seized considerable political and economic power during the 1970s. Their success was partly due to their numbers. Natives of Puerto Rico, Cuba, and Mexico were the fastest growing minority in the United States. Numbering only 3.1 million in 1960, they accounted for 19 million two decades later. As many as 7 million, however, were Mexicans who entered the United States illegally to settle in such diverse spots as the desert Southwest and Chicago slums.

Hispanic-Americans organized until they helped shape the politics of Los Angeles (where they overtook blacks as the largest minority and gained rapidly on whites), New York City, and Miami. The six to eight million Mexicans in five Southwestern States were labeled "MexAmerica" since they virtually constituted a nation within a nation. Many Hispanic-American communities were staunchly devoted to the Roman Catholic Church and the role of the family unit. With these as cores for their organizations, they often succeeded in realizing their own version of the American Dream. Exiles from Castro's Cuba became a dominant economic force in Miami. Nationally, Hispanic-Americans built their own small congressional bloc in Washington.

Mural, East Los Angeles Housing Project.

Not everything went well. Gang wars (69 killings in Los Angeles alone in 1977), and unrelieved poverty (parts of New York City's Hispanic-American tenements were described as a burned-out wasteland), afflicted some of the new communities. The nation's economic downturn actually reversed a long trend: during the 1970s more Puerto Ricans returned home than settled in the United States. Relations with blacks became volatile when Hispanic-Americans moved to claim power in Los Angeles and New York. But overall, the Hispanic-American experience was the reverse of the Native American. Indians divided over whether to become assimilated into, or isolate themselves from, American society. Hispanic-Americans, however, did both: they profited economically by working within the society, but built political blocs to protect themselves. They demonstrated that American society is not so much a "melting pot"—for some ethnic groups have never melted totally into the mainstream—as it is a bubbling stew.

FEMINISM AND THE EQUAL RIGHTS AMENDMENT

American women also organized political blocs to obtain new rights. In 1963 Betty Friedan published the book that launched this feminist movement. According to Friedan's *The Feminine Mystique,* women had been taught ever since World War II that "their role was to seek fulfillment as wives and mothers" rather than develop their own potential to the fullest.

Instilled in the first instance by women's magazines, which published articles with such titles as "Have Babies While You're Young," "How to Snare a Male," and "Cooking to Me Is Poetry," the feminine mystique was further reinforced by educators who dissuaded college women from seeking careers. Visiting Smith College, Friedan spoke to a senior who explained matter-of-factly: "I guess everybody wants to graduate with a diamond ring on her finger. That's the important thing." Although women had accepted the feminine mystique because it seemed to promise a safe, secure existence, Friedan argued, it actually produced identity crises, feelings of emptiness, and a consequent guilt. To escape from "the comfortable concentration camp," the suburban housewife—and indeed all women—would have to reject stereotypical roles, strike out on their own, and develop "goals that will permit them to find their own identity."

In practical terms, that usually meant finding a job. In 1964 the federal government, more by chance than design, passed legislation that eventually transformed the position of women in the labor force. In debating Title VII of the Civil Rights Act, which barred discrimination in employment on the grounds of race, Congress added a provision also prohibiting such discrimination on the grounds of sex. The change was proposed by southern Democrats who hoped to make the bill's supporters look foolish, but who—to their own surprise—succeeded only in making the measure more comprehensive. For a time the new provision remained a dead letter, primarily because officials in the Equal Employment Opportunity Commission (EEOC), who were to enforce it, did not take it seriously. But by the 1970s Title VII became a major weapon in the drive to obtain equal employment opportunities for women. The EEOC not only claimed the cause as its own, but the agency's enforcement powers were enlarged and its jurisdiction reached into educational and governmental institutions.

The formation of the National Organization for Women (NOW) in 1966 provided an organizational focus for the feminist movement. The only surprising thing about NOW's original demands, in retrospect, was that they should have provoked such controversy. The group devoted most of its energy to lobbying, demonstrating, and filing class action suits to end discrimination in hiring and promotion. In addition, NOW insisted that women should be permitted to take maternity leaves without sacrificing their job seniority or retirement benefits, that working parents should be able to declare child-care expenses as tax deductions, that the government should fund day-care centers for children, and that newspapers should not publish separate want-ads for males and females. The organization also supported passage of the Equal Rights Amendment and repeal of laws limiting a woman's right to have an abortion. While proposing a new relationship between men and women, NOW stopped short of an attack on the institutions of marriage and the family: "We believe that a true partnership between the sexes demands a different concept of marriage, an equitable sharing of the responsibilities of home and children and of the economic burdens of their support."

Rally in Washington, D.C.

Too radical for some, NOW proved too conservative for others. The more militant advocates of women's liberation actually held views that conflicted sharply with those of Friedan and NOW. Radical feminists believed that women constituted "an oppressed class. Our oppression is total, affecting every facet of our lives. . . . We identify the agents of our oppression as men." Furthermore, "the institution of marriage is the chief vehicle for the perpetuation of the oppression of women; it is through the role of wife that the subjugation of women is maintained." These beliefs led, naturally enough, to an attack on the nuclear family. In *The Dialectic of Sex* (1970), Shulamith Firestone portrayed a brave new world of the future: adults who wished to live in "reproductive social structures" would apply for a license, good for seven to ten years, which would entitle them to live as a household and raise children. But childbearing would be "so diffused as to be practically eliminated." Anyone, of any age, would be free to form a friendship, sexual or otherwise, with whomever he or she wished, whenever he or she wanted, for as long as he or she liked. Fortunately for all concerned, in Firestone's opinion, "the incest taboo would have lost its function."

While radicals spent much of their time in such speculation, moderates spent theirs in political action. By the mid-1970s the feminist movement fought an intense battle to ratify the Equal Rights Amendment. The Amendment, which stated that "equality of rights under the law shall not be denied or abridged by the United States or by any State on account of sex," gave Congress the power to pass laws enforcing that provision. The

House approved the amendment in October 1971 and the Senate followed suit in March 1972. But Congress also stipulated that the amendment would have to be approved by the necessary 38 states within 7 years.

Although 28 states ratified it within a year, opponents thereafter dug in their heels. Late in 1978, as the deadline approached, only 35 states had ratified the ERA. In the meantime, 4 states had rescinded their ratifications. Feminists therefore called for an extension of the deadline. Many Senators who supported the ERA opposed this on procedural grounds, but in October 1978 the Senate, by a vote of 60–36, approved a three year-three month extension. This made ratification more likely, although the legality of the extension and the constitutionality of the state rescissions awaited resolution in the courts.

Whatever ERA's status, the new feminism was indelibly linked with crucial changes in women's role in American society. The number of working women, for example, increased dramatically. In 1960 women had made up 33 percent of the labor force; by 1978 they made up 43 percent of it. In the past, young women had typically entered the labor force for a few years, left while raising their children, then sought reentry—at a competitive disadvantage—when their children were grown. By the late 1970s the pattern was quite different: young women remained at work or left only briefly for the purpose of raising their children. More than half of all the mothers of pre-school and school-age children either were working or seeking employment. Women were also marrying at a later age. In 1960, 7 of every 10 women had married by the age of 24; the comparable statistic for 1977 was 5 of every 10. Finally, as the divorce rate rose to a record level, so did the number of families headed by women: from 2.9 million in 1970 to 5.2 million in 1978. Whether all of this meant that women were, as Betty Friedan had hoped, "finally free to become themselves," remained questionable. What could not be doubted was that the old feminine mystique had lost its force.

VIETNAM AND CIVIL LIBERTIES

In the mid-1970s the American people learned that the federal government had, for more than a decade, systematically violated their constitutional rights. First exposed by the *New York Times* in 1974, and then confirmed over the next two years in the reports of a House committee chaired by Otis Pike (Dem.-N.Y.), a Senate committee headed by Frank Church (Dem.-Idaho), and a special committee under Nelson Rockefeller, those violations had begun even before the Unites States entered the war in Vietnam. But that war, and especially the turmoil and dissent accompanying it, led the Central Intelligence Agency, the Federal Bureau of Investigation, and other agencies to mount their most aggressive campaigns against civil liberties. To a greater extent than any other war fought in this century, the war in Vietnam subverted the Bill of Rights.

The assault on civil liberties during the Vietnam era differed not only in degree but also in kind. During the First and Second World Wars, the Cold War, and the Korean conflict, federal officials who supported restrictions on speech and assembly believed their actions were legal—that they were justified, that is, by the existence of a national emergency. On just those grounds the Supreme Court upheld the constitutionality of the Espionage Act in 1919, the relocation of Japanese Americans in 1944, and the Smith Act in 1951. Moreover, the government usually, although not always, acted in an open, public fashion: laws were passed, executive orders issued, dissenters placed on trial. During the Vietnam war, however, all this changed. The Executive branch committed acts it knew were illegal and could not withstand the scrutiny of the Supreme Court. Consequently, the government did all it could to conceal its actions from Congress, the courts, and the people.

Nothing better illustrated the government's behavior than the CIA program known as "Operation CHAOS." Although the CIA was prohibited by law from spying on American citizens, the agency had begun to do so in the 1950s. In the summer of 1967, with antiwar demonstrations reaching a crescendo and with President Johnson convinced that the demonstrators were being funded by foreign powers, the CIA stepped up its activities. Although it discovered no foreign involvement, the agency nevertheless accelerated its campaign at President Nixon's behest in 1969. By 1974 the CIA had compiled dossiers on 7200 American citizens, stored the names of 300,000 individuals and groups in a computerized index file, opened 215,000 first-class letters, placed wiretaps on telephones, installed bugging devices in people's homes, and burglarized the offices of dissident groups. Speaking of the mail-opening program, one CIA official admitted, "This thing is illegal as hell." Even so, the program did not end until 1974 when its existence was disclosed.

Not to be outdone by the CIA, the FBI remodeled its own counterintelligence program. In the 1960s COINTELPRO began to shift its attention from socialist and communist organizations to black militants, the New Left, and the antiwar movement. The FBI did more than infiltrate organizations and place activists under surveillance, however. Undercover agents endeavored both to discredit antiwar groups by encouraging the use of violent tactics and to disrupt such groups by sending poison pen letters. When a high school student wrote to the Socialist Workers Party to obtain information for a term paper, an FBI agent alerted the principal of her high school and the local chief of police to the supposed menace. The ensuing harassment of the student, a House committee noted, had a "chilling effect" on free speech. The committee also summarized some of the other results of the FBI program: "Careers were ruined, friendships severed, reputations sullied, businesses bankrupted and, in some cases, lives endangered."

Two actions demonstrated Richard Nixon's cavalier disregard for civil liberties. In May 1969, furious that news of the "secret" bombing of Cambodia had leaked to the press, the Nixon administration placed wiretaps on a number of government officials and newspaper reporters. For

nearly two years the Justice Department monitored their phone calls although, as the President later conceded privately, the transcripts produced no evidence of subversion, but "just gobs and gobs of material: gos-
sip and bullshitting." In July 1970 Tom C. Huston, a presidential aide,
concocted a plan designed at once to expand and centralize the government's counter-intelligence operations. Proposing that surreptitious entry
be used to obtain information, Huston admitted: "Use of this technique is
clearly illegal: it amounts to burglary." But he explained further: "It is
also the most fruitful tool and can produce the type of intelligence which
cannot be obtained in any other fashion." The President approved these
recommendations, but when FBI Director J. Edgar Hoover objected (primarily, it seems, because he feared their implementation would reduce
the FBI's role), Nixon rescinded his approval.

The administration's contempt for civil liberties again reared its head
a year later. In June 1971 Dr. Daniel Ellsberg, a former Pentagon expert
on Vietnam, made public the secret "Pentagon Papers," which revealed
American policy in Indochina between 1945 and 1968. The administration first attempted to block their publication in newspapers, but the Supreme Court ruled against prior restraint by a 6–3 vote. A majority of the
Justices found that the government had failed to prove that release of the
documents would "inevitably, directly and immediately" injure the nation.
Indeed, Nixon never believed that the documents jeopardized the nation's security, although he did fear their release might set a dangerous
precedent. Ellsberg was then indicted for stealing government property.

At the same time the White House created a "plumbers" group of
intelligence experts to "stop security leaks and to investigate other sensitive security matters." One of the group's first tasks was to discredit Ellsberg, and this, in turn, seemed to require a covert operation. The
plumbers believed that damning evidence might be found in the office
files of a Los Angeles psychiatrist whom Ellsberg had been consulting.
The President's chief domestic advisor, John Ehrlichman, approved a
burglary of the office as long as "it is not traceable." In September 1971
the plumbers broke into the psychiatrist's office, but failed to turn up evidence that would, in their words, "nail the guy cold."

Daniel Ellsberg's trial for espionage and the theft of government
property was held in 1973. The government's behavior during the trial
was consistent with its behavior beforehand. First, even while the trial was
in progress, John Ehrlichman offered the directorship of the FBI to the
presiding judge, William Matthew Byrne, Jr. The offer, if not actually improper, was surely irregular. Second, the administration only grudgingly
confessed that it had masterminded a burglary of Ellsberg's psychiatrist's
office, and then urged Judge Byrne—unsuccessfully—not to make the information public. Third, the government did not reveal, until ordered to
do so by the judge, that the wiretaps it had installed in 1969 had inadver-
tently picked up some of Ellsberg's conversations. Furious at this behavior, Judge Byrne declared a mistrial and dismissed the charges against
Ellsberg. He noted that the circumstances in the case offended "a sense of

justice." That judgment was equally applicable to CHAOS, COIN-
TELPRO, wiretapping, the Huston plan, and, as the Watergate investiga-
tion had already begun to reveal, to a much broader range of White
House activities.

THE PRESIDENCY:
KING RICHARD

Since the era of Franklin Roosevelt, Americans had looked to the President for leadership in solving the nation's social and economic problems.
When Americans were asked in the 1970s which famous people, living or
dead, they would like as visitors to their homes, Lincoln was named first,
four other Presidents followed, and Jesus Christ came in eleventh, just
behind Harry Truman.

Such presidential popularity occurred in part because an increasingly
complex society seemed to require centralized direction. More important,
presidential authority was pumped up by 30 years of international crises.
Throughout the Cold War, Presidents exercised powers once reserved for
use in full-scale war, for many believed the executive needed a free hand
to respond quickly and energetically to foreign threats. Richard Nixon
carried the strong presidency to its furthest point in peacetime. After his
reelection triumph in 1972, cartoons appeared with the purple-robed figure of "King Richard."

Senate Democratic leader Mike Mansfield admitted that because of
the Cold War, Congress had handed much of its foreign policy power to
the President "on a silver platter." Too late, Americans were learning a
lesson taught more than 140 years earlier by Alexis de Tocqueville, a perceptive French visitor, in *Democracy in America:*

No protracted war can fail to endanger the freedom of a democratic country. . . .
War does not always give over democratic communities to military government,
but it must invariably and immeasurably increase the powers of civil government;
it must almost compulsorily concentrate the direction of all men and the management of all things in the hands of the administration. If it leads not to despotism by
sudden violence, it prepares men for it more gently by their habits. All those who
seek to destroy the liberties of a democratic nation ought to know that war is the
surest and shortest means to accomplish it.

Tocqueville emphasized a point that Americans often failed to understand: foreign and domestic policies intertwine and shape one another.

The President and the nation learned this the hard way. In June
1972 the White House "plumbers" were caught trying to burglarize Democratic party headquarters in Washington's Watergate Apartment.
Dismissing the break-in as a "bizarre incident," the President insisted that
the White House was not involved. But in May 1973 a Senate investigation into Watergate uncovered a cesspool of illegal administration activities. Key White House aides were implicated in an attempt to cover up the
burglary, and several admitted their guilt. Other revelations indicated
that Nixon's campaign staff (the Committee to Re-elect the President, or

CREEP as it was known), had illegally accepted large donations from corporations and individuals. In some instances the administration had apparently given the contributors political favors in return. In October 1973, with evidence accumulating that he had accepted payoffs from building contractors, Spiro Agnew resigned as Vice-President. The Justice Department permitted him to plead guilty to a charge of tax evasion. He was fined and sentenced to three years of unsupervised probation.

Nixon desperately tried to halt the rising tide of criticism, but his efforts were complicated by the discovery that an intricate recording system had for years been tape-recording almost all his White House conversations. Nixon refused to surrender these tapes, claiming that to do so would cripple the President's authority and violate the constitutional principle of separation of powers. When the courts ruled against him, he released a few tapes. But investigators found that several contained gaps at crucial points, gaps that could not, as the President claimed, have been caused by accident. To prove that he was, in his words, "not a crook," Nixon authorized publication of his personal tax returns. These showed that in 1970 and 1971, claiming deductions of dubious legality, he had paid a federal tax of about $800 annually on a salary of $200,000. Nixon had, moreover, paid no state income taxes since 1969 although he was a legal resident of California.

Charges were also levelled that expensive improvements on the President's oceanside residences at San Clemente, California, and Key Biscayne, Florida, had been made at the taxpayers' expense without justification. In one instance, the Secret Service claimed it had installed a $621 ice-making machine "to insure that the President was not using poisoned ice." The White House mess chief put it more directly: "The President does not like ice cubes with holes in them." An audit of his tax returns by a congressional committee added to Nixon's difficulties. The committee found that the President had improperly taken a $428,000 charitable deduction for donating his vice-presidential papers to the National Archives, had failed to report a capital gain on the sale of property, had incorrectly written off business expenses, and had failed to declare $92,298 worth of improvements made at San Clemente and Key Biscayne that were "undertaken primarily for the President's personal benefit." In April 1974, Nixon agreed to pay $444,000 in back taxes and $32,000 in interest.

WATERGATE AND THE PRESIDENCY

The effect of these disclosures on the presidency was stunning. By early 1973 Congress had endured continued insults from the administration. When some members of Congress protested the continued bombing of Cambodia and North Vietnam, for example, a State Department official cynically told them that the "justification" was "the reelection of President Nixon." One newspaper observed that "By that theory he could level Boston." But the Nixon administration's arrogance, Watergate coverup, and other illegal activities soon proved fatal. The Senate and House began to strike back.

They passed a landmark measure that limited presidential power to make war without Congress's assent. The War Powers Act of 1973 provided that (1) "in every possible instance" the President must consult with Congress before ordering U.S. troops into any hostilities overseas; (2) whenever the President dispatched troops to foreign lands he must, within 48 hours, send a full explanation to Congress; (3) he must withdraw the troops within 60 days unless Congress gave him specific authority to maintain them abroad.

To no one's surprise, Nixon vetoed the act. He argued that such a bill would have, for example, dangerously tied the President's hands during the Berlin confrontation of 1961 and the Cuban Missile crisis of 1962. Others opposed the bill for opposite reasons. They claimed it gave the President power to wage war on his own for 60 days without having to obtain congressional approval. Congress, however, believed it had found a useful middle ground, and that the measure would at least prevent future Vietnam-type interventions. The necessary two-thirds of the House and Senate voted to override Nixon's veto. That vote marked an important reversal in the 30-year enlargement of presidential power.

Watergate not only weakened Nixon's standing with Congress, but destroyed his ability to lead the Republican party. By 1974 even those who had stood by Nixon were shocked by each fresh disclosure. One Senator said that it was like waiting for the other shoe to drop, except "I don't know how many shoes there are to fall. I feel like I've been dealing with a centipede this past year." One poll found that only 24 percent of the voters classified themselves as Republicans, the smallest percentage identified with any major party in the twentieth century. The Democrats virtually swept the 1974 congressional elections, including such traditional Republican seats as one in Michigan that they had not held since 1932.

Watergate altered the American political landscape, as well as undermined many presidential powers. In the late 1960s a majority of Americans had identified the groups dangerous to society as: atheists, black militants, student demonstrators, prostitutes, and homosexuals. In 1968 and 1972, Nixon, by running on the social issue, had successfully exploited those fears. But by late 1973, pollster Louis Harris reported, none of these groups was considered harmful by a majority of people. Instead, the groups considered dangerous were: people who hired political spies, generals who conducted secret bombing raids, politicians who engaged in wiretapping, businessmen who made illegal campaign contributions, and politicians who attempted to use federal investigatory agencies for partisan purposes.

IMPEACHMENT: THE PRESIDENCY FROM NIXON TO FORD

To many Americans, the crises produced by inflation, the energy shortage, and mistrust in government were overwhelming, perhaps so overwhelming that they signaled the end of the American Century. By mid-1974, it even seemed possible that for the first time the President of the United States would be impeached by the House and convicted by the Senate for committing what the Constitution calls "Bribery, or other high crimes and misdemeanors." After—perhaps because of—30 years of Cold War, Americans suddenly faced their gravest political crisis in a century.

In late 1973 the House of Representatives ordered its Judiciary Committee to determine whether Nixon had committed impeachable offenses. During nine months of study, the Committee wavered in its view of whether the President should be impeached. Nixon's headline-making trips abroad, Americans' veneration of their President (whoever it might be), and the memory of Nixon's triumph in the 1972 elections raised dangerous political problems for Congress. The dilemma was especially acute in a year when the whole of the House and one-third of the Senate were standing for reelection. By July 1974, however, the Judiciary Committee had produced massive volumes of evidence that seemed damning to the President's case. Nor did Nixon help his cause by rejecting the committee's request for vital evidence. He withheld more than 100 tapes of private conversations on the grounds of "Executive privilege," asserting that they must remain secret or otherwise the President's ability to protect the national interest would be endangered.

Three weeks in the summer of 1974 marked a turning-point in American history. On July 24 the Supreme Court unanimously ordered the President to surrender 64 tapes to John Sirica, judge of the District Court in the District of Columbia where the Watergate trial was held. After listening to the tapes, Sirica could give all relevant portions to Special Watergate Prosecutor Leon Jaworski, who could then turn them over to Congress. The President thus had to retreat from his claim of Executive privilege for all his documents. For the first time, however, the Supreme Court also ruled that the President had the right of withholding information on the grounds of Executive privilege when the information concerned military or diplomatic matters. Since the tapes in dispute did not cover such national security issues, Nixon had to surrender them so that the courts could base their decisions on all possible evidence.

One week later, John Ehrlichman, who as the President's chief domestic affairs advisor had held great power, was found guilty of directing the break-in at the office of Daniel Ellsberg's psychiatrist. Ehrlichman was also found guilty of lying to investigators about his role in the crime. He received a sentence of 20 months to 5 years in prison. Four of Nixon's Cabinet officials, his two top White House assistants, and former Vice-President Agnew had now been named in criminal cases. In all, 38 officials associated with the Nixon administration had either pleaded guilty or been indicted for crimes. American history offered no parallel.

On July 30 the House Judiciary Committee completed six epochal days of public debate by recommending that the full House of Representatives should pass three Articles of Impeachment. The first Article accused the President of lying about, and trying to conceal, the role of his White House staff in the Watergate break-in. The second Article alleged that Nixon had ignored his oath of office, in which he had vowed to protect the constitutional rights of citizens. He had instead violated these rights by placing unlawful wiretaps on telephones and by using the FBI, CIA, and Internal Revenue Service to harass his political opponents. The third Article declared the President had refused to comply with congressional subpoenas for documents and taped conversations. Two other articles, one condemning Nixon's secret bombing of Cambodia in 1969–70 and another accusing him of income tax evasion and of using government monies for private gain, were rejected by the committee as inadequate reasons for impeachment.

The Judiciary Committee reached its decision after long, bitter debate and intense soul-searching. Republicans and Southern Democrats were especially uncomfortable as evidence against the President accumulated. But as a leading conservative from Alabama commented: "And . . . what if we fail to impeach? Do we ingrain forever in the very fabric of our Constitution a standard of conduct in our highest office that at the least is deplorable and at the worst is impeachable?" In the end, as many as 7 Republicans and all 21 Democrats voted for at least one of the Articles. The Committee's debate, which attracted a huge television and radio audience, had an immense political impact. Members could now "argue the case with their constituents" directly. This further diminished the President's power. Congressmen effectively used a medium that, until 1974, had been so manipulated by the White House that it had been called "Presidential television."

No one any longer doubted that the House would vote to impeach the President by a wide margin. Nixon's last hope lay in the Senate, but that hope quickly died. On August 5 he released the transcripts of three conversations he had held with his chief White House assistant, H. R. Haldeman, a few days after the June 1972 Watergate break-in. These tapes, Nixon admitted, showed that he had ordered the FBI to halt its investigation of the burglary. "Don't go any further into this case period!" he had directed. The President also conceded that he had kept this information from his own lawyers and from the impeachment inquiry. Granting that he had committed a "serious act of omission," and that impeachment in the House was "virtually a foregone conclusion," Nixon insisted that his behavior did not warrant a conviction in the Senate.

But the disclosure that he had obstructed justice and withheld the truth provided the "smoking pistol" for which many congressmen were searching. And the fingerprints were unmistakably clear. Support for the

August 9, 1974: Nixon leaving Washington, D.C.

President evaporated overnight. Republicans began a stampede for resignation or impeachment. The situation in the White House became tense. According to investigative reporters, Nixon began to roam the mansion at night, communing with the pictures of past Presidents, and at one point summoning Henry Kissinger to kneel with him in prayer. White House aides feared that if they pressured him to quit, Nixon might respond irrationally. All orders from the President to the military were carefully monitored by top civilian officials in the Pentagon.

Finally, on the night of August 7, Nixon met with Republican Senator Barry Goldwater of Arizona and Representative John Rhodes (Rep.-Ariz.), the House Minority Leader. They reported that the Senate would surely vote to impeach him. Even the 10 Republican members of the Judiciary Committee who had defended the President a few days earlier quickly reversed their positions. One member reportedly asked if the committee could reconvene so he could change his vote, but he was informed "that the train had left the station." Its destination became known on August 9, 1974, when for the first time in history an American President was forced to resign his office. Vice-President Gerald Ford, whom Nixon had appointed to replace Agnew, became Chief Executive.

The presidency, which had increasingly dominated foreign and domestic policies in the American Century, had finally been curbed by Congress and the Supreme Court. Yet Nixon's resignation occurred primarily because he had tape-recorded incriminating conversations, and then refused advice from close friends to burn the tapes. A disturbing question remained: whether the unconstitutional acts described in the Articles of Impeachment could have been uncovered if Nixon had not made the recordings, or if he had destroyed them before Congress learned of their existence.

Gerald Ford, moreover, unilaterally used his new power to protect Nixon from criminal prosecution. On September 8, 1974, the President announced that he was pardoning Nixon for all federal crimes the former President "committed or may have committed" during his years in the White House. Ford's announcement set off a storm of protest since it precluded a trial and thereby undercut proper legal processes. Two years later, the pardon returned to haunt Ford. It was an important reason why many Americans preferred Jimmy Carter instead of Ford in the presidential election. The political ghost of Richard Nixon continued to stalk the corridors of American history.

THE NIXON TAPES

On April 30, 1974, President Nixon made public more than 1300 pages of edited transcripts of White House conversations. On August 5 the President released the transcripts of three conversations he had held with H. R. Haldeman on June 23, 1972. In the following excerpts, *P* stands for the President, *D* for John Dean (former counsel to the President), and *H* for Haldeman.

[*June 23, 1972*]

H—Now on the investigation, you know the Democratic break-in thing, we're back in the problem area because the F.B.I. is not under control, . . . their investigation is now leading into some productive areas—because they've been able to trace the money. . . . And, and it goes in some directions we don't want it to go.

P—When you get in—when you get in [unintelligible] people say, "Look the problem is that this will open the whole, the whole Bay of Pigs thing, and the President just feels that ah, without going into the details—don't, don't lie to them to the extent to say no involvement, but just say that this is a comedy of errors, without getting into it, the President believes that it is going to open the whole Bay of Pigs thing up again. And, ah, because these people are plugging for [unintelligible] and that they should call the F.B.I. in and [unintelligible] don't go any further into this case period!

[*Sept. 15, 1972*]

P—We are all in it together. This is a war. We take a few shots and it will be over. We will give them a few shots and it will be over. Don't worry. I wouldn't want to be on the other side right now. Would you?

D—Along that line, one of the things I've tried to do, I have begun to keep notes on a lot of people who are emerging as less than our friends because this will be over some day and we shouldn't forget the way some of them have treated us.

P—I want the most comprehensive notes on all those who tried to do us in. They didn't have to do it. If we had had a very close election and they were playing the other side I would understand this. No—they were doing this quite deliberately and they are asking for it and they are going to get it. We have not used the power in this first four years as you know. We have never used it. We have not used the Bureau and we have not used the Justice Department but things are going to change now. And they are either going to do it right or go.

D—What an exciting prospect.

P—Thanks. It has to be done. We have been (adjective deleted) fools for us to come into this election campaign and not do anything with regard to the Democratic Senators who are running, et cetera. And who the hell are they after? They are after us. It is absolutely ridiculous. It is not going to be that way any more.

[*March 13, 1973*]

P—How much of a crisis? It will be—I am thinking in terms of—the point is, everything is a crisis. (expletive deleted) it is a terrible lousy thing—it will remain a crisis among the upper intellectual types, the soft heads, our own, too—Republicans—and the Democrats and the rest. Average people won't think it is much of a crisis unless it affects them. (unintelligible)

D—I think it will pass. I think after the Ervin hearings, they are going to find so much—there will be some new revelations. I don't think that the thing will get out of hand. I have no reason to believe it will.

P—As a matter of fact, it is just a bunch of (characterization deleted). We don't object to such damn things anyway. On, and on and on. No, I tell you this it is the last gasp of our hardest opponents. They've just got to have something to squeal about it.

D—It is the only thing they have to squeal—

P—(Unintelligible) They are going to lie around and squeal. They are having a hard time now. They got the hell kicked out of them in the election. There is not a Watergate around in this town, not so much our opponents, even the media, but the basic thing is the establishment. The establishment is dying, and so they've got to show that despite the successes we have had in foreign policy and in the election, they've got to show that it is, just wrong just because of this. They are trying to use this as the whole thing.

[*March 20, 1973*]

P—. . . See what I am getting at is that, if apart from a statement to the Committee or anything else, if you could just make a statement to me that we can use. You know, for internal purposes and to answer questions, etc.

D—As we did when you, back in August, made the statement that—

P—That's right.

D—And all the things—

P—You've got to have something where it doesn't appear that I am doing this in, you know, just in a—saying to hell with the Congress and to hell with the people, we are not going to tell you anything because of Executive Privilege. That, they don't understand. But if you say, "No, we are willing to cooperate," and you've made a complete statement, but make it very incomplete. See, that is what I mean. I don't want a, too much in chapter and verse as you did in your letter, I just want just a general—

D—An all around statement.

P—That's right. Try just something general. Like "I have checked into this matter: I can categorically, based on my investigation, say the following: Haldeman is not involved in this, that and the other thing. Mr. Colson did not do this; Mr. so and so did not do this. Mr. Blank did not do this." Right down the line, taking the most glaring things. If there are any further questions, please let me know. See?

D—Uh, huh. I think we can do that.

[*March 21, 1973*]

D—. . . So that is it. That is the extent of the knowledge. So where are the soft spots on this? Well, first of all, there is the prob-

Senator Sam Ervin swears in John Dean at the Watergate hearings.

lem of the continued blackmail which will not only go on now, but it will go on while these people are in prison, and it will compound the obstruction of justice situation. It will cost money. It is dangerous. People around here are not pros at this sort of thing. This is the sort of thing Mafia people can do: washing money, getting clean money, and things like that. We just don't know about those things, because we are not criminals and not used to dealing in that business.

P—That's right.

D—It is a tough thing to know how to do.

P—Maybe it takes a gang to do that.

D—That's right. There is a real problem as to whether we could even do it. Plus there is a real problem in raising money. Mitchell has been working on raising some money. He is one of the ones with the most to lose. But there is no denying the fact that the White House, in Ehrlichman, Haldeman and Dean are involved in some of the early money decisions.

P—How much money do you need?

D—I would say these people are going to cost a million dollars over the next two years.

P—We could get that. On the money, if you need the money you could get that. You could get a million dollars. You could get it in cash. I know where it could be gotten. It is not easy, but it could be done. But the question is who the hell would handle it? Any ideas on that?

D—That's right. Well, I think that is something that Mitchell ought to be charged with.

P—I would think so too.

[*March 21, 1973*]

P—. . . It has to do with the Ellsberg case. I don't know what the hell the—(unintelligible) . . .

P—What is the answer on this? How you keep it out, I don't know. You can't keep it out if Hunt talks. You see the point is irrelevant. It has gotten to this point—

D—You might put it on a national security grounds basis.

H—It absolutely was.

D—And say that this was—

H—(unintelligible)—CIA—

D—Ah—

H—Seriously.

P—National Security. We had to get information for national security grounds.

D—Then the question is, why didn't the CIA do it or why didn't the FBI do it?

P—Because we had to do it on a confidential basis.

H—Because we were checking them.

P—Neither could be trusted.

H—It has basically never been proven. There was reason to question their position.

P—With the bombing thing coming out and everything coming out, the whole thing was national security.

D—I think we could get by on that.

JIMMY CARTER AND THE "NEW REALITIES"

In 1971, when he became Governor of Georgia, Jimmy Carter regarded the presidency with "reverence." Then he had an opportunity to meet the men—Nixon and McGovern, Humphrey and Muskie, Reagan and Rockefeller—who had been contesting for the office over the years and, as Carter recalled, "I lost my feeling of awe about presidents." In early 1973, undaunted by the label applied to him by journalists—"Jimmy Who?"—Carter set out to win the Democratic nomination. By 1976, with his only political experience one term in the Georgia Senate and one term as the state's Governor, Carter recognized that the Watergate backlash might do wonders for his candidacy.

He portrayed himself as an "outsider" who never had been involved in corrupt Washington politics. To voters fed up with deception in high places, he promised "I will never lie to you." Gambling that his status as a Southerner, his image as an unknown newcomer without Washington connections, and his emphasis on personal integrity would strike responsive chords in the electorate, Carter collected Democratic delegates as a gambler gathers chips. "We figured the odds as best we could," he explained, "and then we rolled the dice."

In his speech accepting the Democratic nomination in June 1976, Carter placed himself squarely within the party's reform tradition. Calling for "an end to discrimination because of race and sex," he said: "Too many have had to suffer at the hands of a political and economic elite who have shaped decisions and never had to account for mistakes or suffer from injustice." Pledging support for a revamping of the income-tax structure, Carter lashed out at "unholy, self-perpetuating alliances . . . between money and politics." Urging enactment of new welfare programs, including a "nationwide comprehensive health program for all our people," Carter stated: "The poor, the weak, the aged, the afflicted must be treated with respect and compassion and with love." Although Carter also warned that government could not solve every problem, most of his listeners detected strong populist overtones in the speech.

Many things helped Carter in the campaign, not least President Ford's reputation as a bumbler. Ford tripped down steps on a state occasion, cut himself diving into the White House swimming pool, and bumped his head boarding a helicopter. Newsmen adapted Lyndon Johnson's cutting remark, that Ford had played too much football without a helmet, and made it crueller still: "He can't even play President without a helmet." Nor did Ford's choice of Senator Robert Dole of Kansas as his running mate help the Republicans. In a televised debate with his Democratic counterpart, Senator Walter Mondale of Minnesota, Dole charged that World War I, World War II, and Korea were "all Democrat wars." Such remarks angered Democratic moderates whom the Republicans badly needed on election day. Finally, Ford's own statement during a debate with Carter that, partly due to Republican policies, "There is no Soviet domination of Eastern Europe," cost the President crucial support from Poles, Czechs, and other Americans of Eastern European origin.

Yet the electorate, or at least the 54 percent that bothered to vote, responded to more than mishaps, mudslinging, and miscues. Ford did best among the affluent and the comfortable, Carter among the poor and disadvantaged. The vote, pollsters found, "fractured to a marked degree along the fault line separating the haves and the have-nots." Carter won about 55 percent of the Catholic and Jewish vote, but more than 90 percent of the black vote. The Georgian carried 10 of the 11 southern states (all except Virginia); in 7 of the 10 black voters provided his margin of victory. With a total of 40.8 million votes to Ford's 39.1 million, Carter emerged with a 297–241 victory in the electoral college.

Expectations that Jimmy Carter would preside over a new era of reform were short-lived. Within 100 days of his taking office, many people thought that Carter had begun "shifting to the right." Within a year, disgruntled liberals believed that Carter was the most conservative Democratic President since Grover Cleveland. Within 18 months, critics charged that Carter "is a Democrat who often talks and thinks like a Republican." And within two years, they sneered that Carter, "a counterfeit populist," was in truth "as Republican as Gerald Ford."

Liberals centered their fire on three aspects of the President's legislative program. They claimed that his energy bill, enacted in 1978 after a fierce congressional struggle, benefited the oil companies by deregulating natural gas prices; that his tax reform measure, approved in 1977, failed to close loopholes enjoyed by the wealthy and offered little relief to middle-income individuals; and that his medical-care proposals fell far short of the comprehensive health programs supported by Senator Edward Kennedy (Dem.-Mass.) By 1978 Kennedy had begun to complain that the administration was sacrificing the needs of "the poor, the black, the sick, the young, the cities and the unemployed."

Carter's policies undoubtedly reflected his own managerial outlook, his tendency to convert social problems into engineering problems and to seek technical solutions for them. Moreover, Carter found it necessary to placate members of Congress, especially chairmen of powerful committees. Demanding modifications in the energy and tax proposals, these Democratic leaders forced Carter to retreat or even surrender. The President could no longer invoke party discipline against Democrats who increasingly divided along geographical ("sun-belt" versus "snow-belt") and ideological lines. As the party system fragmented, congressional defiance of the White House became more common. In the late 1970s power shifted dramatically up Pennsylvania Avenue to Capitol Hill.

As presidential influence over—and party discipline in—Congress declined, pressure groups rushed to fill the vacuum. Carter had promised to attack the "unholy" alliance "between money and politics," but these groups, representing virtually every important economic interest in the country, nevertheless gained tremendous influence in Congress. They multiplied "like rabbits," Senator Edward Kennedy warned, "and are doing their best to buy every senator, every representative, and every issue in sight." The groups included trade associations (as the American Medical Association and National Educational Association), corporations, labor, and single-issues interests (anti-abortion or anti-gun control advocates, for example). They cemented their power by giving lavishly to congressional campaigns. Not surprisingly, Congress passed laws encouraging such gifts. Labor unions had long been allowed to contribute to campaigns, but corporations had not—until, that is, new laws in the 1970s permitted them to set up political action committees (PACs) to support sympathetic politicians. The PACs transformed political fund-raising, especially since the unions' political power seemed to be fading. By 1978 a top advisor to Carter mourned, "We have a fragmented, Balkanized society," with each special economic group "interested in only one domestic program"—its own.

Carter's policies were also influenced by his assessment of political realities: there seemed to be more votes to be had in 1980 on the right than the left. As one aide told him as early as December 1976: "We have an opportunity to coopt many of [the Republicans'] issue positions and take away large chunks of their normal presidential coalition." Carter, and most other politicians, sensed the shift in public opinion symbolized by the passage of Proposition 13 by California voters in mid-1978. Widely viewed as the opening salvo in a "taxpayers' revolt," Proposition 13 imposed stringent limitations on state spending for social purposes. Governor Edmund G. Brown, Jr., prescribed a similar dose of belt-tightening for the nation. He endorsed a proposed constitutional amendment that would prohibit federal budget deficits except in the event of war or national emergency.

Sharp divisions over the issue of affirmative action added to Carter's problems. Advocates of affirmative action, who viewed it as a long-overdue remedy for past societal discrimination, and opponents, who regarded the program as reverse discrimination against white males, awaited a definitive constitutional ruling from the Supreme Court. But the ruling, handed down in June 1978, proved anything but definitive.

The case involved Allan Bakke, who had twice been denied admission to the medical school of the University of California at Davis. Since the school reserved 16 of 100 places in its entering class for "disadvantaged students"—blacks, Chicanos, American Indians, and Asian Americans— and since Bakke had a better academic record than some admitted under this minority quota, he claimed he had been denied the equal protection of the law. By a 5–4 margin the Supreme Court ruled in his favor: the use of an "explicit racial classification," in situations where no former discriminatory behavior had been demonstrated, violated the Fourteenth Amendment. At the same time, however, the Court approved, by another 5–4 vote, programs that used race as "simply one element" in the admissions process. Justifying such "race-conscious programs," Justice Harry A. Blackmun said: "In order to get beyond racism, we must first take account of race."

The Bakke decision left the issue of affirmative action unresolved. Like a time-bomb, it threatened to blow up at any time. Any one of several cases could trigger the explosion, for the Supreme Court still had to rule on employment and promotion rights, issues that cut much more deeply than one concerning medical-school admissions. A worker for Kaiser Aluminum, for example, challenged an agreement between the company and the United Steelworkers that sought to upgrade minority workers according to a fixed formula: one minority worker was to be admitted to a training program for each white worker in the program, until the percentage of minority workers in skilled jobs was equivalent to their proportion of the population in the surrounding communities. Lower courts, however, found that this arrangement discriminated against white workers. Another case involved the American Telephone and Telegraph Company, which in 1973 had agreed to balance the racial and sexual composition of its work force in all departments. Timetables were established for the preferential hiring, promotion, and transfer of women and minority workers. The Communications Workers of America, however, challenged the settlement, claiming that it undermined the hard-won seniority rights of white males. Where the 1960s had seen a liberal-labor consensus on civil rights, the 1970s saw that consensus fracture over affirmative action programs.

More than anything else, however, the nagging problem of inflation limited Carter's freedom of action. To fight inflation, he believed, it was essential to reduce the federal budget deficit. But since the President also wanted to increase spending for national defense, he recommended a reduction in social welfare expenditures. Carter's proposed budget for 1980, therefore, elicited anger from liberals and cautious approval from conservatives. The Black Congressional Caucus termed the budget "immoral and unjust," while a Bank of America spokesman thought "it catches the right mood."

In January 1979 Carter's chief domestic policy advisor, Stuart E. Eizenstat, explained that the President's scaled-down domestic agenda was due to the "new realities" of the late 1970s. Those "unhappier realities" included "high inflation coupled with high unemployment, and widespread public cynicism toward the government." Such realities—combined with Carter's own managerial disposition, the erosion of presidential power, the enactment of Proposition 13, the rise of interest groups, and divisions over affirmative action—constituted the legacy of the 1970s. That legacy would undoubtedly help shape national priorities in the 1980s.

FOREIGN POLICY FROM KISSINGER TO CARTER

Americans not only faced a more fragmented society at home, but a fragmented global situation. Washington confronted complex problems in the Middle East, Africa, Asia, and Latin America that had little to do with Soviet Communism. Dealing with them became frustrating to Americans who prefer their foreign relations to resemble a football or baseball game—that is, of short duration with clearly identified opponents and a definite winner. Foreign policy refused to be so simple, and Washington officials therefore were easy targets for criticism.

One official, however, emerged with an enhanced reputation. In 1973, after having served as the President's National Security Advisor, Henry Kissinger became Secretary of State. That same year he finally succeeded in negotiating a Vietnam ceasefire with his North Vietnamese counterpart, Le Duc Tho. The two men were rewarded with the 1973 Nobel Peace Prize. Tho refused his share, correctly asserting that war between North and South Vietnam continued. The American troops left, however, and Kissinger accepted his share of the prize. "Half a prize for half a peace seems just about right," one journalist observed.

Jimmy Carter and the Born-Again Evangelicals

The United States has been the only Western country to undergo a major religious revival since World War II. The Evangelical sects have been in the vanguard, and their growth since 1945 has been spectacular, historically significant, and—until the 1970s—little noticed.

By 1976 it could no longer be ignored. According to polls taken that year, three of the four "most widely known" Americans were "born-again" Evangelicals: Reverend Billy Graham, their best-known spokesman; Gerald Ford, the first practicing Evangelical to become President and the only Chief Executive to have a son studying in seminary; and Jimmy Carter, whose "born-again" experience was shaped by his sister Ruth, a well-known and wealthy faith-healer.

A 1977 survey revealed that as many as one-third of all Americans, or about 70 million, called themselves "born-again" Christians. Ten million claimed to be converts since 1975. Recording stars Pat Boone and Johnny Cash, Senator Mark Hatfield (Rep.-Oregon), convicted Watergate figures Jeb Magruder and Charles Colson (whose best-selling autobiography was made into a movie starring "born-again" Dean Jones), and football quarterback Roger Staubach of the Dallas Cowboys were only a few of the better-known members.

The rewards were not only spiritual. Evangelicals accounted for $200 million of the $1 billion grossed annually by

Charles Colson at Southern Baptist Convention, 1975.

518 sales of religious books. Billy Graham's *How to be Born Again* had an initial printing of 800,000 copies in 1977, the largest for any hardcover book ever published, and another half-million soon followed. The Christian Broadcast Network, based in Virginia, made nearly $60 million annually from round-the-clock television shows over its own four stations and 130 affiliates. It began building a $50 million complex that included a satellite transmitter, law school, and hotel. A competitor, the PTL (or Praise the Lord) Club of South Carolina, gained $25 million from its daily, nationwide television shows in 1976. Bill Bright's "Campus Crusade for Christ," the fastest-growing evangelical group by the 1970s, planned a $50 million university and television structure in California. Oral Roberts, who founded his own university in Oklahoma, used lavishly produced television spectaculars to attract a worldwide audience of 60 million. While speaking to four continents in 70 languages through a space satellite system, Evangelicals also looked forward to "saturating the [United States] with the Gospel through secular TV." "Consider the impact of a Jesus spot at the end of the Super Bowl," an Atlanta organization speculated. "Millions of fans whooping it up and all of a sudden, whammo, the Lord appears."

Indeed, the Evangelicals' influence on professional sports was already noticeable. The Fellowship of Christian Athletes included celebrities who

Dallas Cowboy quarterback Roger Staubach, on the left, confers with Coach Tom Landry, on the right, during a critical moment in a 1979 game.

Jimmy Carter with a gift from the American Bible Society, 1977.

520 worked with church and civic groups while witnessing their faith publicly and often. When a member of baseball's San Francisco Giants (one of the most devout teams in professional sports) hit his first home run in four years, he announced that "God picked that ball up and carried it over the fence."

Many theologians were not assured. Martin Marty of the University of Chicago, a distinguished historian of re-

ligion, did not oppose evangelicalism in sports ("It has made a lot of really cruddy characters become more admirable"), but feared that born-again athletes too easily ignored the world "of materialism, idolatry of sports, spectatoritis, and violence by saying, 'Jesus legitimized my being here.'"

Evangelicals separated themselves from other churchgoers by following a strictly literal reading of the Bible (espe-

Singer Johnny Cash "witnessing" at a Stockholm, Sweden Pentecostal Church.

cially the Creation story in Genesis and Jesus' role in the Gospels). They also emphasized the responsibility of each person, instead of clerical or church authority. Evangelicals therefore tended toward individualism in politics, unfettered capitalism in economics, and a belief in the basic sinfulness of human nature in their theology. Most important, they believed an individual could be redeemed only by being "born again"— that is, confessing one's sin, accepting a resurrected Jesus as a "personal savior," and leading a new life. Being "born again" was often accompanied, if not caused, by such old-time revival techniques as emotional prayers, fervent singing, and shouted sermons.

In this and in other respects the Evangelicals had a long history. Evangelicalism first appeared during the Great Religious Awakening of 1730 to 1760 that whipped up fervor that lasted until—and shaped—the American Revolution. It reappeared between 1800 and 1840 as a strong territorial expansionist, reform movement that helped pave the way to the Civil War. A third wave between 1880 and 1920 spurred Prohibition. The fourth "great awakening" began in the 1940s and accelerated during the cultural and political upheaval of the 1960s. Billy Graham became the unofficial White House chaplain, especially during the Nixon administration. When other church officials asked him to protest Nixon's massive bombing of North Vietnam in 1973, Graham refused by saying he was responsible only for proclaiming "the message of God's love," not for political action.

Evangelicalism has been rooted in the Midwest-South "Bible Belt," and has grown most notably when national or personal crises caused individuals to search for new guideposts. Jimmy Carter exemplified both characteristics. After suffering his first major political defeat when he lost Georgia's gubernatorial race in 1966, his sister's faith lifted him out of a deep depression. He was "born again" after hearing a sermon entitled, "If You Were Arrested for Being a Christian, Would There be Any Evidence to Convict You?" Carter served as a missionary in Philadelphia and Boston, then became a leader in the 13-million member Southern Baptist Church. His open concern for racial justice, lessening poverty, and resolving international problems set him apart from Graham. The President exemplified a new political consciousness that appeared among some Evangelicals.

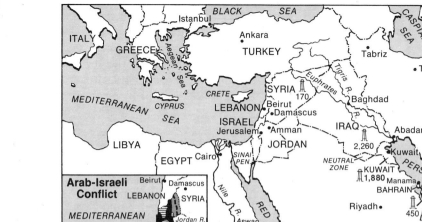

The Middle East.

Arab-Israeli Conflict.

UN partition of Palestine, 1947 (Jewish State)
Added to Israel after War of 1948–1949
Area controlled by Israel after Six Day War, 1967
Israeli-occupied area after October War, 1973
Israeli withdrawal after negotiations, 1975

Oil production (1000 barrels produced per day)

Kissinger followed with equally successful (from his and Nixon's view), if less publicized diplomacy in Chile. Since 1970 President Salvador Allende had turned Chile toward a more nationalist, independent course, and attempted to gain his nation's economic independence—and distribute its wealth more equitably—by seizing property owned by North American corporations and wealthy Chileans. Kissinger and Nixon secretly moved to undermine the new regime. By 1973 Allende's government suffered severely not only from its own economic errors but a cutoff of the U.S. aid on which Chile had long depended. Kissinger meanwhile strengthened Washington's ties with the Chilean army. In September 1973 the army struck. It overthrew and killed Allende, ended all attempts at reform, established a military regime, and then tortured and murdered thousands of political prisoners. Americans both North and South were saddened by Chile's new course, but Kissinger and Nixon were pleased that they had played a major part in overthrowing a government they had always mistrusted and feared. They believed the United States had proved that it could still guide the fortunes of third-world nations, at least those in Latin America.

Turning from Chile with satisfaction—and from Vietnam with obvious relief—Kissinger pledged his full attention to renewing frayed ties

with Western Europe. This important relationship had deteriorated politically and economically. The Nixon administration placed first priority on
détente with Russia and China. The policy worked well (Soviet Premier
Brezhnev was so pleased that he embarrassed Kissinger by kissing him
full on the mouth when they met), but relations with the Atlantic partners
suffered, for they feared the superpowers might be making deals that did
not consider Europeans' interests.

Before Kissinger could move to repair the Atlantic alliance, however,
war in the Middle East wrecked his plans. The roots of the conflict went
back to 1967 when the Egyptians blockaded several ports that were crucial
for Israel's security. On June 5, 1967, the Israelis suddenly retaliated. In
the "Six-Day War," they humiliated the Egyptians and their Arab allies by
seizing the prized city of Jerusalem (the world home of three great religious faiths—Islam, Judaism, and Christianity), sweeping across the
Sinai Desert to the Suez Canal, and wiping out large portions of the Egyptian and Syrian armies. The Arabs refused to discuss peace until Israel returned the conquered areas. The Israelis rejected this demand, claiming
that the new boundaries were necessary for their security.

Re-equipped with massive Soviet aid, the Egyptians and Syrians suddenly attacked Israel in October 1973. The Egyptian army redeemed itself. Israel staved off a major setback only with a brilliant crossing of the
Suez that enveloped large numbers of Egyptian troops and placed Israeli
forces in Egypt itself. Kissinger flew to the Middle East five times in six
months, and with cooperation from the Soviets (who feared a prolonged
war would result in Egyptian defeat), brought about direct Egyptian–
Israeli talks, the first since Israel was founded in 1948. A temporary settlement provided for mutual troop withdrawal and creation of a buffer
zone in the Sinai Peninsula. In early 1979, President Carter helped construct an Egyptian-Israeli peace treaty, but key territorial problems remained unresolved. After six years of intense U.S. diplomacy, the Middle
East remained a tinderbox.

The Egyptian–Israeli disengagement marked Kissinger's last major
success. A drum-beat of events between 1974 and 1976 put the United
States on the defensive, especially since they occurred in areas rich in raw
materials and sources of energy that Americans had coveted since the
1973 gasoline shortages.

Southeast Asia was the first crisis area. After pulling out its combat
troops, the United States cut aid to the Saigon government in 1974. During the spring of 1975, the North Vietnamese Communists launched an
all-out offensive. The beleaguered Saigon regime, shot through with corruption and deserted slowly by Washington, asked desperately for American help. Investigation revealed that two years before, Nixon had secretly
assured the South Vietnamese that in such a situation the United States
would use its great power to protect the South: "You can count on us," he
had told them. But in April 1975, Nixon was in disgrace at San Clemente, California. Across the Pacific television cameras recorded the sordid details of U.S. officials shoving aside former Vietnamese allies so the

Americans could escape by helicopter moments before the Communists seized Saigon. The long United States war in Southeast Asia was finally over.

Attention switched to Africa, where the Portuguese colony of Angola was enduring a revolution. Since 1970 Kissinger and Nixon had sided solidly with the dictatorial Portuguese regime. After the rebels finally forced Portugal to leave Angola in 1974, the American CIA entered to provide secret support for the more conservative of the black factions that reached for power. The Soviets, in turn, helped the other major faction—headed by Agostino Nehto—and flew in Cuban troops to help Nehto. The Americans were astounded. Kissinger warned the Russians they were escalating the conflict into a big-power confrontation. He and President Ford rushed to ask Congress for large amounts of aid to assist the U.S.-supported faction.

But this was no longer the Congress of the 1960s. The Senate believed that the United States had few interests in, and less power over, Angola. It told Kissinger to keep hands off. The situation quieted. Cuban troops, at Nehto's request, even protected the American-owned Gulf Oil Company, whose wells produced much of the nation's wealth. By 1979 Nehto himself was moving closer to the United States. Congress, meanwhile, had barely blocked a possible Vietnam-type involvement in Africa.

Jimmy Carter's foreign policy was no more successful than Kissinger's in shaping the newly emerging world to American desires. Warfare broke out in several African areas during 1977–79. It became especially violent around Angola and also between the white minority government in Rhodesia and black revolutionaries. Carter's National Security Advisor, Zbigniew Brzezinski, pushed for U.S. involvement. Using Kissinger's old argument, Brzezinski believed that the Soviets and their Cuban front-men (or "the Cubes," as he called them), were challenging the United States to a duel.

But Congress again opposed United States retaliation, and this time the legislators were aided by Andrew Young. A well-known black leader, Young had marched with Martin Luther King and served in Congress before his close friend, and fellow Georgian, Jimmy Carter named him U.S. Ambassador to the United Nations. Young successfully argued that Africa should be left to Africans, for neither of the two superpowers had the understanding or power to control affairs on the continent. Nor, he believed, could the United States single-handedly save the repressive minority white regimes in Rhodesia and South Africa.

Instead of resorting to military intervention, the deeply religious Carter hoped to take the lead in world affairs by championing human rights. "Our human rights policy," the President announced, "is not a decoration," but "the soul of our foreign policy." He consequently became a hero to political prisoners and others victimized by repressive regimes. To his embarrassment, however, the President could not always practice what he preached. For example, he publicly supported Russians who were imprisoned or exiled for criticizing the Soviet government. Moscow re-

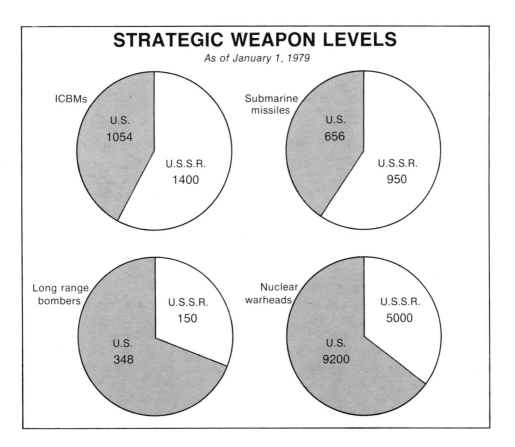

STRATEGIC WEAPON LEVELS

As of January 1, 1979

ICBMs — U.S. 1054 — U.S.S.R. 1400

Submarine missiles — U.S. 656 — U.S.S.R. 950

Long range bombers — U.S.S.R. 150 — U.S. 348

Nuclear warheads — U.S.S.R. 5000 — U.S. 9200

sponded by attacking Carter and hardening its position on many issues, including the Strategic Arms Limitation Talks (SALT) that aimed at bringing the runaway arms race under some control. Faced with having to choose between his human rights policy and the chance to control weapons that could wipe out civilization, Carter quickly quieted his rights program.

In Iran, the staunchly pro-American Shah was driven from power in 1979 by street mobs. Critics blamed Carter for having pushed the Shah to introduce political freedoms before it was safe to do so. The criticism was off the mark. The Shah had made a number of errors trying to modernize his country too rapidly. Outraged, conservative Moslem leaders finally rose up to challenge him. As in Africa, the U.S. influence in Iran was sharply limited, and the nation's problems were too complex to be blamed on Carter's human rights policy—especially since the policy had largely become muted anyway.

Carter did score two major diplomatic triumphs. In the first he again received critical help from a revitalized Congress. During March and April, 1978, the United States Senate, by the paper thin margin of a single vote, approved two historic treaties giving the Panama Canal to

Panama in the year 2000. The Panamanians had often rioted against the U.S.-built and controlled canal areas that had split their country in half since 1903. American military officials, moreover, concluded the waterway could not be effectively defended against the Panamanians.

The Senate debate on the treaties was bitter. "This," proclaimed a conservative opponent, "is the culmination . . . of surrender and appeasement that has cost us so much all over the world." In the end, the Senate leaders, Robert Byrd (Dem.-W. Va.) and Howard Baker (Rep.-Tenn.) saved the pact and Carter's prestige. They attached conditions giving the United States the right of unilateral military intervention to keep the canal open both before and after 2000, and provided that U.S. ships must have priority in passing through the waterway during future crises (such as another Cuban missile showdown). With these guarantees the Senate and Carter defused the Panamanian problem, improved relations throughout Latin America, and—in reality—neatly protected U.S. interests in the canal area.

Carter's second diplomatic victory occurred later in 1978 when, after 30 years of war and hatred, the United States and the People's Republic of China (the PRC) opened formal diplomatic relations. Most Americans welcomed the move, especially business executives who fervently prayed that the China market of 950 million potential buyers would be a welcome relief to the "stagflation" in the United States. For its own reasons, a new Chinese leadership cooperated. Threatened by the hated Soviet armed forces along their long common border, the Chinese rushed to modernize their economy, and particularly their military, with American technology. Spurred on by their common fear of Russia and the mutual need for economic ties, the two nations signed treaties in which China even agreed to import Coca-Cola, long a symbol of "American imperialism."

Carter played his "China card" partly to pressure the Russians to sign the SALT II agreement. In SALT II the two superpowers promised to freeze nuclear stockpiles and delivery systems at roughly their current levels (see Figure 2). These levels gave the United States an edge, but the value of supposed superiority was questionable since any war fought with these weapons would produce only victims, not victors. If the Soviets did not cooperate in the talks, Carter could threaten to establish closer links with China, perhaps even begin military ties.

Relations with the two Communist giants provided only one example of the kind of problems Americans would confront in the 1980s as they approached the two hundredth anniversary of their Constitution—a document that built one nation out of 13 separate states. Just as the Carter administration faced "new realities" at home, so it faced a fragmented world. Africans, Latin Americans, and Asians were more determined than before to obtain political influence and economic power. It remained to be seen how Americans, long used to the idea that this was to be the American Century, would respond to the aspirations of peoples who were now demanding what Americans had long cherished.

Suggested Reading

The historical context and excellent bibliographies on economic developments are in W. Elliott Brownlee, *Dynamics of Ascent* (1979); Joan Edelman Spero, *The Politics of International Economic Relations* (1977); and, for the specific crisis, J. C. Hurewitz, ed., *Oil, The Arab-Israeli Dispute, and the Industrial World* (1976). For demographic developments, see U.S. Department of Commerce, *Social Indicators, 1976* (1977); and Kirkpatrick Sale, *Power Shift* (1974). Recent developments in the black community are explained in William Julius Wilson, *The Declining Significance of Race* (1978); and Dorothy K. Newman, et al., *Protest, Politics, and Prosperity: Black Americans and White Institutions, 1940–1975* (1978). "American Indians Today" in *Annals of the American Academy of Political and Social Science,* March 1978; and Vine Deloria, Jr., *Behind the Trail of Broken Treaties* (1974) and good starting points. A key source is U.S. Department of Housing and Urban Development, *Hispanic-Americans in the United States: a Selective Bibliography, 1963–1974* (1974). Useful studies of the feminist movement include Jo Freeman, *The Politics of Women's Liberation* (1975); and Gayle Graham Yates, *What Women Want: The Ideas of the Movement* (1975). The erosion of civil liberties is detailed in Athan Theoharis, *Spying on Americans* (1979); Morton H. Halperin, et al., *The Lawless State* (1976); and David Wise, *The American Police State* (1976).

An excellent starting point on the presidency is Philip C. Dolce and George H. Skau, *Power and the Presidency* (1976). Richard Nixon gives his view in *RN: The Memoirs of Richard Nixon* (1978). Jimmy Carter's rise to power and the context of U.S. politics can be found in Jules Witcover, *Marathon: The Pursuit of the Presidency, 1972–1976* (1977); and James Wooten, *Dasher* (1978). Foreign policy in the 1970s is detailed in John C. Stoessinger, *Henry Kissinger* (1976); Tad Szulc, *The Illusion of Peace; Foreign Policy in the Nixon Years* (1977); John Stockwell, *In Search of Enemies* (1977) exposing the CIA's role, especially in Angola; Elizabeth Drew's fine essay on Carter's policymakers in *New Yorker,* May 1, 1978; and two key areas are examined in Jennifer S. Whitaker, ed., *Africa and the United States* (1978); and Michel Oksenberg and Robert B. Oxnam, eds., *Dragon and Eagle; U.S.–China Relations* (1978). The background for the Evangelicals can be found in Cushing Strout, *The New Heavens and New Earth* (1974); David F. Wells and John D. Woodbridge, *The Evangelicals* (1975); Barbara Grizzuti Harrison, "The God Band" in *More,* March 1978; and Denis Collins, "Nearer My God to the Goal Line," *Washington Post Magazine,* November 19, 1978.

Photo Credits

Chapter 1: **Opener** Culver Pictures   **5** Courtesy New-York Historical Society, New York City   **11** Brown Brothers   **15** Howard DeWald/Photo Trends   **16** Wayne Andrews   **17** Ezra Stoller   **24** Library of Congress   **28** National Archives

Chapter 2: **Opener** Culver Pictures   **42** Museum of the City of New York   **45** Brown Brothers   **47** Bettman Archives   **48** Freelance Photographers Guild   **49** Freelance Photographers Guild   **50** Wide World   **54** U.S.D.A., Forest Service   **61** Culver Pictures

Chapter 3: **Opener** Theodore Roosevelt Collection, Harvard College Library   **71** U.P.I.   **79** Museum of the City of New York   **80** Philadelphia Museum of Art, The Louise and Walter Arensberg Collection   **81** Addison Gallery of American Art, Philips Academy, Andover   **82** (top) Collection Corcoran Gallery of Art, Gift of Mr. and Mrs. John Sloan. (bottom) Courtesy Museum of Fine Arts, Boston, Charles Henry Hayden Fund   **84** National Archives   **87** Smithers Collection, Humanities Research Center, University of Texas at Austin   **93** U.P.I.

Chapter 4: **Opener** Culver Pictures   **107** New York Public Library   **113** U.P.I.   **114** Library of Congress   **115** Culver Pictures   **116** Freelance Photographers Guild   **120** U.P.I.   **123** National Archives   **127** U.P.I.

Chapter 5: **Opener** Wide World   **134** U.P.I.   **137** Freelance Photographers Guild   **139** Columbia Records   **140** Courtesy Chris Albertson   **141** Culver Pictures   **142** Courtesy of the Estate of Carl Van Vechten   **149** Brown Brothers   **161** U.P.I.   **164** Wide World

Chapter 6: **Opener** Culver Pictures   **175** Wide World   **178** Freelance Photographers Guild   **185** Culver Pictures   **186** Culver Pictures   **187** Freelance Photographers Guild   **187** Wide World   **191** Paul Dorsey/ Black Star   **192** Freelance Photographers Guild

Chapter 7: **Opener** Library of Congress   **201** Wide World   **204** Acme Photos   **209** U.P.I.   **210** Theatre Collection, the New York Public Library at Lincoln Center, Astor, Lenox and Tilden Foundation   **211** Theatre Collection, the New York Public Library at Lincoln Center, Astor, Lenox and Tilden Foundation   **212** Theatre Collection, the New York Public Library at Lincoln Center, Astor, Lenox and Tilden Foundation   **214** U.P.I.   **223** Wide World

Chapter 8: **Opener** National Archives   **234** Wide World   **238** Wide World   **241** U.P.I.   **242** U.P.I.   **243** National Archives   **244** Brown Brothers   **248** Freelance Photographers Guild

Chapter 9: **Opener** Library of Congress   **261** Bettmann Archives   **272** National Archives   **275** Dance Collection, the New York Public Library at Lincoln Center; Astor, Lenox and Tilden Foundations   **276** Barbara Morgan   **277** Dance Collection, the New York Public Library at Lincoln Center; Astor, Lenox and Tilden Foundations   **278** Dance Collection, the New York Public Library at Lincoln Center; the Astor, Lenox and Tilden Foundations   **281** Wide World

Chapter 10:   **Opener** U.P.I.   **297** U.P.I.   **298** Dwight D. Eisenhower Library   **305** Margaret Bourke-White, Life Magazine © 1943 Time Inc.   **306** Margaret Bourke-White, Life Magazine © 1940 Time, Inc.   **307** Margaret Bourke-White, Life Magazine © 1941 Time Inc.   **308** Margaret Bourke-White, Life Magazine © 1945 Time Inc.   **312** Culver Pictures   **319** George C. Marshall Research Foundation Photo

Chapter 11:   **Opener** Library of Congress   **327** Wide World   **330** Wide World   **335** Wallace Kirkland, Life Magazine © 1948 Time Inc.   **336** Credit with Caption   **337** Leonard McCombe, Life Magazine © 1970 Time Inc.   **338** M. Graham   **340** Wide World   **342** Wide World   **355** U.P.I.

Chapter 12:   **Opener** Joe Scherschel, Life Magazine © 1958 Time Inc.   **370** H. Cartier-Bresson/Magnum   **375** Burt Glinn/Magnum   **377** Burt Glinn/Magnum   **378** U.P.I.   **379** Joerns Gerots, Life Magazine © 1959 Time Inc.   **380** Peter Siion/Stock, Boston   **382** Dwight D. Eisenhower Library

Chapter 13:   **Opener** Library of Congress   **397** U.P.I.   **408** Charles Moore/Black Star   **411** Dan Budnik/Woodfin Camp   **412** Dan Budnik/Woodfin Camp   **413** Estate of David Smith, Courtesy of M. Knoedler and Company, New York   **414** Dan Budkin/Woodfin Camp   **415** Bruno Barbey/MAGNUM   **421** U.P.I.

Chapter 14:   **Opener** Philip Jones-Griffiths/Magnum   **430** Wide World   **435** Library of Congress   **436** Culver Pictures   **437** (top) Culver Pictures. (bottom) Myron Davis, Life Magazine © 1961 Time Inc.   **438** Jerry Liebman/deWys   **444** Wide World   **449** Wide World

Chapter 15:   **Opener** Benedict J. Fernandez   **458** Fred Ward/Black Star   **463** Burt Glinn/Magnum   **469** H. Hammid/Photo Researchers   **470** H. Hammid/Photo Researchers   **471** Henry Wilhelm/Black Star   **472** Leonard Freed/Magnum   **475** Rogert Malloch/Magnum   **477** Ken Regan/Camera 5

Chapter 16:   **Opener** © 1979 SIPA Press/Black Star   **495** U.P.I.   **497** Craig Aurness/Woodfin Camp   **499** Martin A. Levick/Black Star   **508** U.P.I.   **511** U.P.I.   **517** Wide World   **518** Wide World   **519** U.P.I.   **520** Photoreporters

Index